في ذكرى

مارك لينز

ALAA AL ASWANY

Democracy is the Answer
Egypt's Years of Revolution

Translated by Russell Harris, Aran Byrne
and Paul Naylor

GINGKO
LIBRARY

First published in Great Britain in 2014 by

Gingko Library
70 Cadogan Place
London SW1X 9AH

www.thegingkolibrary.com

The translator of each column is identified by their initials.

ISBN 978 1 909942 71 4
eISBN 978 1 909942 72 1

Typeset in Optima by Sarah Cleave
Additional work by Harry Boteler and Stephen Chumbley

A CIP catalogue record for this book is available from the British Library.

Printed and bound in Spain by Liberdúplex.

Contents

Introduction

I woke up on 25 January 2011 like it was any other day. I got out of bed and wrote until midday. I had heard about the demonstration that had been organised, but I was not optimistic that anything would come of it. I had taken part in many demonstrations against Hosni Mubarak before and they had all been more or less the same: a few hundred demonstrators would be encircled by thousands of police officers who would close in on the demonstrators, beat them and make arrests.

When I did go down to Tahrir Square in the afternoon I was met with an astonishing scene: Egypt had awoken from its sleep. Hundreds of thousands of Egyptians had poured out onto the streets, all chanting one slogan: "The people want the fall of the regime!" For the next 18 days I lived in Tahrir Square and these were, without doubt, the most wonderful days of my life. I learned a lot from the revolution and began to truly understand the meaning of "the people". There were two million of us living in Tahrir Square, and the number would double in the evenings. We all felt as though we were members of one family: we ate and drank together, we chanted slogans and sang songs together, and we also faced the deadly bullets shot by snipers together. We didn't show fear and we didn't retreat. We carried those who fell, and with each adversity we grew even more determined to bring down Mubarak no matter what the cost.

I'll never forget the moment when Mubarak's resignation was announced on television. Millions of Egyptians embraced each other and wept, overwhelmed by a joy they had never before experienced. The next day, millions of young people came out and swept away the rubbish from all the streets of Egypt; it was a sign that their country had been returned to them and that from now on, they would strive to keep it clean. But what went wrong after this?

Historians will face a difficult job uncovering the underlying causes behind the events that followed the fall of Mubarak. Contrary to their expectations, Egyptians found themselves facing deteriorating conditions – conditions that were worse than anything that they had suffered during the era of Mubarak. The prisons were opened up and tens of thousands of criminals were let out onto the streets to cause havoc and terrorise ordinary Egyptians. Law and order broke down and the living conditions of most Egyptian citizens deteriorated drastically. Then the Muslim Brothers took over: first, they gained control of the parliament by buying the votes of poor people, and then their candidate, Mohamed Morsi, took the presidency through dubious elections. On 22 November 2012, Morsi gave his presidential decrees immunity from legal challenge, thereby placing himself above the constitution and the rule of law. When this happened, millions of Egyptians took to the streets to demand that Morsi step down, insofar as he was now acting more like a despotic Turkish sultan than the president of a democratic country. In the absence of a parliament that could have held a vote of no confidence against Morsi and, thereby, forced him to resign, the Tamorod campaign[1] was started. Its aim was to collect signatures in order to show that the people had withdrawn their support for Morsi's presidency. I took part in this campaign myself, collecting the signatures of passersby in the streets of Alexandria.

In the end, 22 million people signed the petition and, on 30 June 2013, more than 30 million Egyptians took to the streets to demand that Morsi step down and that early presidential elections be held. In opposition to this, tens of thousands of Islamists came together for sit-ins in Rabaa Al-Adawiya Square and Al-Nahda Square. Their leaders incited them to fight the enemies of Islam, that is to say, those Egyptians who rejected God's rule, as represented by Mohamed Morsi. Egypt was on the verge of civil war until the army intervened to remove Morsi from power. It was at this point that a new star arose: General Abdel Fattah el-Sisi, the former head of Egypt's armed forces. The huge popularity he gained for his role in Morsi's ouster later enabled him to take the presidency of Egypt with ease.[2]

In the pages of this book you will find these successive events dealt with in more detail. In this sense, the book is a record of Egypt's experiences since the outbreak of the revolution. The articles collected here were originally weekly newspaper columns that were published in the Egyptian newspaper *Al-Masry Al-Youm* and the Lebanese newspaper *As-Safir*, over the course of three years. The articles were later translated and published around the world by various international newspapers and journals. For that reason, I was always conscious that I was writing for both an Egyptian audience and a wider international one.

I should point out that I am neither a historian nor a political analyst. I am a novelist, and as such I used fictional writing in my articles to portray how Egyptians felt during the often troubling and painful events they have lived through. I firmly believe that, as a writer, I had a duty to write these articles to convey the political message of those who took part in the revolution. In my

1 Tamarod was a grassroots protest movement in Egypt that was behind the nationwide demonstrations against President Mohamed Morsi a year after he took office. Tamarod, which means "rebel" in Arabic, was founded in April 2013 by members of the Kefaya movement – a prominent Mubarak-era protest group.

2 General Abdel Fattah el-Sisi was sworn in as Egypt's president on Sunday 8 June 2013, after winning 96.6 per cent of the presidential vote, beating the only other contender, Hamdeen Sabahi, who won 3.09 per cent.

mind, writers should not keep themselves locked away behind closed doors; they should live amongst the people, listen to their stories and try to give them a voice. In this sense, writing should be used to promote and defend human values. It represents an effective means of communication with the wider society. I tried to use what was happening in Egypt to convey a human message to my readership because I believe that when you write about human experiences, everyone can understand and identify.

As a writer, I never saw it as my role to impose my own views on those who read my work. Rather, I saw it as my responsibility to go out and listen to the people in order to better understand the situations they faced and then find a way to best express their thoughts, feelings and aspirations. I do not see myself as being separate from the people; however, from the beginning of the revolution, I understood that, as a novelist, I had a particular role to play in it, that I had a duty to defend the people and to defend human rights through my writing, as well as by directly participating in the events of the revolution. There are, of course, risks associated with both forms of protest; I have been attacked in Egypt, as well as abroad, because of things I have said and written. Many of my friends and fellow Egyptians, however, have paid a much greater price for protesting; they have been arrested, beaten, tortured, blinded by rubber bullets and killed in the streets. As an Egyptian, and as a writer, you have to be prepared for anything; the only other option is to surrender to tyranny.

At the time of writing, the mood in Egypt has changed and popular support for the revolution has declined significantly. Egyptians had high expectations after the fall of Mubarak, but they have suffered a lot over the last three years and, for many of them, life seems more difficult now. The military council and the Muslim Brotherhood bear political responsibility for the difficult economic climate and deteriorating living conditions in Egypt because they were in power during this period. The forces of counter-revolution sought to exhaust the Egyptian people by creating artificial crises, for which they then tried to blame the revolution. At the same time, they deliberately set out to smear the revolutionaries and crush them by carrying out a series of massacres. Under Mubarak, licenses for private-owned television stations were reserved for rich businessmen with close connections to the Mubarak regime. These channels continue to censor dissident voices and to tarnish the reputation of the revolutionary forces. They accuse them of treason and of being foreign agents, intent on toppling the state. Television is by far the most important medium in Egypt and these accusations have had a considerable impact on public opinion and attitudes towards the revolution. On top of this, in recent months there have been a number of terrorist attacks in Egypt that have forced it to declare a state of emergency. These attacks constitute a serious threat to the Egyptian state, and many believe that it is unhelpful to talk about the need for freedom of expression and democracy at the present time. The Egyptian people have been shaken by these attacks and are reluctant to say anything against the state institutions, including the army, the police and the judiciary, in case it undermines security. In my opinion, however, the best way to serve those in power is to criticise them, not to agree with everything that they do for the sake of showing a united front. It is our duty as citizens of Egypt to enter a dialogue with those in power and to hold them to account for their actions, especially if the Egyptian people suffer as a result of their decisions. This was one of the key demands of the Egyptian revolution.

But is the Egyptian revolution over? The simple answer would be to say 'yes', but it would not be accurate, because revolution does not simply involve political change, it requires fundamental change at the level of the individual – changes in individuals that, collectively, can completely alter society as a whole. When a revolution takes place, people suddenly behave in ways that are completely different from how they would normally act. People who have lived in fear of the governments' oppression all of their lives can, in the blink of an eye, overcome their fear and stand firm in the face of death for the sake of freedom. This amazing transformation can be seen in all the revolutions that have taken place throughout history. It is difficult to fully explain how and why such a transformation takes place, but one thing that is certain is that once such a change happens, it is irreversible. Once a citizen has conquered his fear of an oppressive government he will never fear it in the same way again. Revolutions might be impeded, they might stumble and the achievement of their aims can take longer than expected, but once the people have overcome their fear, there is no returning to the status quo.

As long as the spirit of the revolution lives within the few, it will eventually spread to everyone in the whole of society. It is inconceivable that the Egyptians – who revolted and brought down two presidents in the space of three years – will ever submit to despotic rule again. The future belongs to the revolution and despotism belongs to Egypt's past. That the revolution will ultimately prevail is inevitable, because no one can stop the future.

Alaa Al Aswany
October 2014

Translated from the Arabic by Aran Byrne

Chronology

25 January 2011: Tens of thousands of Egyptians take to the streets in unprecedented protests to demand the removal of President Hosni Mubarak.

28 January 2011: Dubbed the "Friday of Rage", Egyptians march in great numbers after Friday prayers in towns and cities across Egypt. The police forces clamp down on demonstrators; hundreds are killed and thousands are wounded.

2 February 2011: Pro-Mubarak supporters on horses and camels charge through Tahrir Square and attack demonstrators. The army does not intervene, even when thugs attack the square with rocks and Molotov cocktails.

11 February 2011: Vice President Omar Suleiman announces Mubarak's resignation and assigns power to the military council, who dissolve parliament and suspend the constitution, meeting two key demands of the revolution.

3 March 2011: Prime Minister Ahmed Shafik hands in his resignation and is replaced by Essam Sharaf, the former minister of transportation.

9 March 2011: The Tahrir sit-in is dispersed violently by army personnel and men in plainclothes. Numerous activists are beaten and tortured in the Egyptian Museum, while the army performs virginity checks on 19 female demonstrators.

19 March 2011: In the first post-Mubarak vote, Egyptians cast ballots in favour of the constitutional amendments sponsored by the military council.

8 April 2011: Mass demonstrations take place in Tahrir demanding the full dismantling of the old regime. Some army officers join the protests in uniform. The military violently disperses the protests and arrests the army officers.

7 May 2011: Churches are attacked in Imbaba as Salafists demand custody of a woman who allegedly converted to Islam but is reportedly held by the Church.

8 July 2011: Protesters stage one of their trademark million-man marches in Tahrir Square to pressure the army into speeding up trials of former regime figures and police officers accused of killing demonstrators in January.

23 July 2011: Thousands of demonstrators march from Tahrir Square to the Ministry of Defence to decry the unmet demands of the 8 July sit-in. Attacks on the demonstrators result in the death of activist Mohamed Mohsen.

3 August 2011: The trial of Mubarak begins. The former president, wheeled into a courtroom cage on a bed, pleads not guilty.

9 September 2011: Demonstrators storm the Israeli embassy building in Giza after the killing of several Egyptian army officers on the Egyptian-Israeli border.

9 October 2011: At least 25 Coptic Christians are killed following clashes with the army in front of the Maspero building in Cairo. The Copts had gathered in protest against the attack on the Mar Girgis Church in Merinab village by Muslim extremists.

19 November 2011: Hundreds are injured as the army bombards a small group of demonstrators with tear gas. Violence escalates over the next few days in Mohamed Mahmoud Street, one of the streets leading to Tahrir Square, leaving more than 40 dead.

21 November 2011: The cabinet submits its resignation and Field Marshal Tantawi, Egypt's de facto ruler, announces a date for parliamentary elections.

25 November 2011: Kamal el-Ganzouri, who served as prime minister under Mubarak from 1996 to 1999, is named as the new interim premier following the departure of Essam Sharaf.

28 November 2011: Egypt holds weeks-long parliamentary elections. Islamist parties secure a majority of seats in the lower house of parliament.

16 December 2011: An army crackdown on demonstrators who were staging a sit-in in front of the Council of Ministers near Qasr El-Aini Street, Downtown Cairo, sparks fresh violence that leaves 17 dead.

14 January 2012: Nobel Prize winner Mohamed ElBaradei abruptly announces his withdrawal from the upcoming presidential elections.

25 January 2012: Hundreds of thousands take to the streets of Egypt to mark the first anniversary of the January 25 Revolution, chanting against the ruling military council to demand "justice for the revolution's martyrs."

1 February 2012: Seventy Ultras Ahlawy members (supporters of Al Alhy Football Club) are killed in clashes in Port Said Stadium.

23, 24 May 2012: The first round of voting in presidential elections presents 13 candidates. Morsi and Ahmed Shafik, the last prime minister under Mubarak, emerge as the top two finishers, to face each other in a run-off.

30 June 2012: Morsi is officially sworn in as president.

8 July 2012: Morsi issues his first presidential decree demanding the reinstatement of the dissolved People's Assembly, parliament's lower house. The move provokes mass protests by revolutionary forces who denounce the decree.

5 August 2012: Sixteen Egyptian border guards are killed by unknown assailants on the Egypt-Israel border. The attack is the first in a series of assaults targeting security personnel in Egypt's restive Sinai Peninsula.

12 August 2012: President Morsi carries out a reshuffle that leads to the resignation of Field Marshal Hussein Tantawi and Chief of Staff Sami Enan.

11 September 2012: Mass protests erupt across the Muslim world following the appearance of a US-made film mocking Islam and the Prophet Muhammad. More than 70 are killed, including the US ambassador to Libya.

22 November 2012: Morsi unilaterally decrees greater powers for himself, giving his decisions immunity from judicial review and barring the courts from dissolving the Constituent Assembly and the upper house of parliament.

30 November 2012: More than 100,000 demonstrators march on the presidential palace, demanding the cancellation of a constitutional referendum.

4 December 2012: Mass protests continue to demand the cancellation of Morsi's decree. For the first time, hundreds of thousands march on Cairo's presidential palace to demand the postponement of the constitutional referendum.

11 December 2012: Egypt is divided between mass protests in support of Morsi's constitutional declaration in front of Cairo's Rabaa Al-Adawiya Mosque and a counter-rally demanding the decree's cancellation outside the presidential palace.

15, 22 December 2012: In the two-round referendum, Egyptians approve the constitution, with 63.8 per cent voting in favour. Turnout is low.

25 December 2012: Egypt formally approves the new constitution.

25 January 2013: Hundreds of thousands hold protests against Morsi on the two-year anniversary of the start of the revolt against Mubarak.

7 April 2013: Muslim extremists attack a Coptic cathedral during the funeral of four Christians killed in sectarian violence the day before.

30 June 2013: Millions of Egyptians demonstrate, calling for Morsi to step down. Eight people are killed in clashes outside the Muslim Brotherhood's Cairo headquarters.

1 July 2013: Large-scale demonstrations continue and Egypt's military gives the two sides 48 hours to resolve their disputes, or it will impose its own solution: replacing Morsi with an interim administration, cancelling the Islamist-based constitution and calling elections in a year.

3 July 2013: Military ousts Morsi and announces that he has been replaced by Adly Mansour, chief justice of the Supreme Constitutional Court, until new presidential elections. Muslim Brotherhood leaders are arrested and tens of thousands of Morsi supporters protest in Cairo's streets.

5 July 2013: Adly Mansour dissolves the Islamist-dominated upper house of parliament as Morsi's supporters stage mass protests demanding his return. Clashes between pro- and anti-Morsi groups in Cairo and Alexandria, and violence elsewhere, leave at least 36 dead. The Muslim Brotherhood deputy leader, Khairat el-Shater, is arrested.

8 July 2013: Egyptian soldiers open fire on pro-Morsi demonstrators in front of a military base in Cairo, killing more than 50.

24 July 2013: General el-Sisi calls on Egyptians to march in support of the new government's battle against "terrorism". Two days later, vast numbers of Egyptians march in demonstrations comparable in size to those during January 2011.

14 August 2013: Riot police clear two sprawling encampments of Morsi supporters at Rabaa Al-Adawiya and Al-Nahda Square, sparking clashes that kill at least 638 people. Vice President Mohamed ElBaradei resigns in protest.

16 August 2013: Heavy gunfire rings out throughout Cairo as tens of thousands of Muslim Brotherhood supporters clash with armed vigilantes. The clashes kill 173 people nationwide, including police officers.

20 August 2013: Mohamed Badie, the leader of the Muslim Brotherhood, is arrested – one of thousands detained in the largest crackdown against the group since the 1950s.

21 August 2013: An Egyptian court orders the release of former president Hosni Mubarak.

16 September 2013: Police reimpose order in Delga, a southern Egyptian town that had been overrun since 14 August by Islamist hardliners, who had ransacked the town's churches.

23 September 2013: A court bans the activities of the Brotherhood and freezes its assets. Already decimated, the move formally returns the group to the underground status it held during successive dictatorships since the 1950s.

6 October 2013: Policemen kill at least 57 pro-Morsi supporters as they march through west Cairo, in the fifth mass killing since his overthrow.

4 November 2013: Mohamed Morsi attends the first hearing of his trial for incitement to murder demonstrators in December 2012. Morsi refuses to recognise the court, sparking pandemonium among the lawyers present.

24 November 2013: Interim president Adly Mansour signs off a new law that essentially bans street protest.

27 November 2013: Prosecutors issue arrest warrants for two of Egypt's highest-profile secular activists, Alaa Abd el-Fatah and Ahmed Maher.

1 December 2013: A 50-strong committee finishes redrafting Egypt's constitution, ahead of a January referendum.

18 December 2013: Prosecutors announce new charges against Morsi, accusing him of masterminding an elaborate seven-year plot involving Palestine's Hamas and the Iranian Revolutionary Guards.

14, 15 January 2014: Over 98 per cent of participants vote for the new constitution, but turnout is only 38.6 per cent, amid suppression of the constitution's critics.

24 February 2014: Egypt's interim government resigns en masse in a surprise move. The announcement was made by interim prime minister, Hazem el-Beblawi, who gave no clear reason for the decision.

3 June 2014: General Abdel Fattah el-Sisi is officially confirmed as Egypt's, president after the country's electoral commission announced that he had won 96.1 per cent of the vote.

The President Has Fallen but the Regime Still Stands

1 March 2011

In his television appearances, Ahmed Shafik[1] comes across as a tactful and mild-mannered man, and the state information service also speaks highly of his administrative efficiency, but with all due respect to Ahmed Shafik, he is not suitable to be the post-revolution prime minister. There is a great difference between partial suitability and the revolution. The revolution aims to bring about radical change, to destroy the old regime completely and to set up a new structure in its place which accords with its principles and aims.

This is how revolutions have been throughout human history. The Egyptian revolution erupted on 25 January to put an end to the corrupt and unjust regime of Hosni Mubarak and to establish true democracy. To this end, the Egyptian people have paid a crippling price: hundreds of people have been killed, hundreds more have been blinded by rubber bullets and no one knows if the thousands who have disappeared are dead or alive.

The success of the revolution is testament to the strength and bravery of the Egyptian people. After the removal of Mubarak, it seemed natural to expect that Egypt would go through a transitional period and achieve democracy by taking a defined number of steps that can be listed as follows:

1. The dissolution of the People's Assembly,[2] the Shura Council[3] and local governments that were fraudulently formed by the previous regime.

2. The dismissal of all politicians connected to the former regime.

1 Former commander of the Egyptian Air Force and long-serving minister in Hosni Mubarak's government. Shafik was appointed prime minister in the final days of Mubarak's rule. *See* Glossary.

2 The People's Assembly is the lower house of a two-tier Egyptian parliament. It has been the key organ in the country's vision of democratic parliamentary life, though since its modern inception in 1924, it has been hamstrung by flawed elections, limited powers and the tenacious persistence of an overwhelming executive authority.

3 Established by Anwar Sadat, the Shura Council was the upper house of then Egyptian parliament. One third of Shura Council members were directly appointed by the president. The remainder were elected. The body had a consultative legislative role, and was also responsible for appointing the heads of Egypt's state-owned media organisations.

3. The separation of the judiciary from the Ministry of Justice in order to achieve judicial independence.

4. The formation of committees of independent judges to investigate claims of corruption. The committees will present their findings to the attorney general.

5. The scrapping of the old constitution and a general declaration of constitutional principles followed by the election of a committee to formulate a new and permanent constitution.

6. The formation of a nationally unified government made up of approved representatives that are not connected to the previous regime. They will be in charge of carrying out the country's affairs during the transitional period and must forego the right to stand as candidates in the forthcoming elections.

7. The rescinding of Emergency Law[1] and the special courts, and the granting of general freedoms including those of forming political parties, free association, peaceful demonstration and the press. Parliamentary elections should take place in two years' time so that Egyptians have the chance to express their political thoughts and to ensure that an elected parliament truly expresses the will of the people.

8. The release of all political prisoners and the prevention of arrest and torture, the abolition of the state security service[2] and the fair trial of all officers who have violated the dignity and humanity of the Egyptian people.

9. The appointment of the first ever democratically elected parliament.

These are not some quickly thought-up and cobbled-together steps, but are recognised worldwide to be the *sine qua non* for any state transitioning from dictatorship to democracy. After Mubarak stepped down, the Egyptian people expected a peaceful transitional period. They did not expect to find members of the former regime, including Ahmed Shafik, still in power. Shafik swore an oath to Hosni Mubarak and his politics and philosophy belong exclusively to the former regime. He bears political responsibility for the slaughter of demonstrators at the hands of the police and the regime's thugs, and has broken his promise to investigate these killings. Shafik has been against the

1 Emergency Law was established in Egypt in 1958 and has remained in effect since 1967. When activated, the law allows security forces to detain people without warrants, circumvents traditional criminal courts, permits interceptions of communication and restricts gatherings such as demonstrations.

2 Also known as the State Security Investigations Service (SSI). It was the highest national internal security authority in Egypt and was the main security and intelligence apparatus under Mubarak.

revolution since the beginning as he did not believe that Mubarak would be forced from power. He openly mocked the revolution, comparing Tahrir Square to London's Hyde Park, sneering at the people occupying the streets and promising the mourners "sweets and chocolate".

Mubarak's resignation and the success of the revolution came as a violent political crisis for Shafik as he had been a loyal supporter of the regime for many decades and considered Mubarak to be his leader, teacher and commander. It is unthinkable that he might be entrusted with implementing the demands of the revolution which toppled his leader. Under Shafik, the corrupt local councils were still in existence, fraudulent trade unions continued to provide henchmen to attack demonstrators, and the headquarters of the National Democratic Party (NDP)[1] remained open with Muslim Brotherhood members enlisting there and being brought out in preparation for the upcoming elections. Under Shafik, the state security service continued operating at full force with the aim of suppressing the revolution. There was no investigation into the police officers that opened fire on Egyptians. Instead, his minister of the interior, Mahmoud Wagdy,[2] went on television to praise the police force for successfully carrying out their duty, that is by using snipers to kill Egyptians, blinding them with rubber bullets and running them over with armoured cars. The minister of the interior considers these horrible crimes to be laudable police activity. And even more oddly, he stated in his television appearance that it was a small minority of the demonstrators that were hell-bent on committing acts of violence and that foreign snipers were amongst the demonstrators.

The minister of the interior continued to accuse the demonstrators of being agents, intent on causing trouble and of serving foreign agendas, the same old logic used by the regime of Hosni Mubarak. The most provocative statements issued by the minister of the interior were those in which he confirmed that the state security service would not be dissolved and that he would not investigate any of its officers. In fact, he went to great lengths to praise the role played by the state security service.

All that is to say that the minister of the interior considers it praiseworthy and within the national interest to arrest demonstrators without legal justification, to beat them up, to torture them viciously and subject them to electric shocks, to abuse their wives and daughters in front of them, to sabotage the Egyptian nationalist movement, to subvert the state media, and to go so far as to drag the whole country into ruination by appointing corrupt and often inept individuals to positions of leadership. These are all tried and tested methods

1 The National Democratic Party (NDP), Egypt's former ruling party, was established by President Anwar Sadat in 1976, and remained the country's dominant party until the overthrow of Hosni Mubarak. *See* Glossary.

2 Mahmoud Wagdy is former head of the prisons department at the ministry of the interior. He was appointed by Hosni Mubarak on 31 January 2011, replacing Habib el-Adly.

used by the state security service for many a long year.

In any case, we must thank the minister of the interior for his frankness in expressing the attitude of Ahmed Shafik's government, which is essentially the same as that of the Mubarak regime. The head of security for the province of Buhaira expressed it most clearly in a filmed speech he gave to his officers in which he stated that the police officers were the masters of Egypt and that anyone laying a hand on them would find it cut off. Those who agree with this statement must also believe that no Egyptian, regardless of position or profession, is anything more than a servant of the police and that any servant who tries to get above himself should be given a deterrent sentence. There is nothing new in all of that. This was the thinking of the Mubarak regime for decades: to have a sense of superiority over ordinary Egyptians, to degrade them, to deprive them of their human rights and to commit crimes against the innocent in order to hang onto power. It is strange and regrettable that those officials kept their jobs even after Egyptians rose up against Mubarak and toppled him. Hosni Mubarak may have been toppled, but his regime did not fall.

The political scene in Egypt bears witness to the fact that there are clearly two contradictory desires amongst those in power: a positive desire to stand shoulder to shoulder with the Egyptian people and to bring about the demands of the revolution. This is reflected in the wishes of the armed forces that have guarded the revolution from the very first day. It was the armed forces that protected Egyptians when the Mubarak regime schemed against them by withdrawing the police, setting prisoners loose in the streets and ordering them to terrorise innocent people and cause chaos. The government, under the control of Ahmed Shafik, has worked hard to impede any real change and abort any democratic transformation by scapegoating a few former officials.

The Egyptian people ask themselves how officers have evaded trial for the killing of demonstrators with live ammunition. They also want to know why Habib el-Adly[1] is being tried for money laundering rather than on charges of killing demonstrators. Why have members of the police force disappeared from sight and why have the armed forces been tasked with security duties? Is the intention to wear out the army so that they turn against the revolution or to punish Egyptians by providing them with so little security that they start to be nostalgic for the Mubarak era? If the reason for the disappearance is the tense state of relations between the police and the people, then it is only natural that this tension will remain until those officers who killed innocent people are given a fair trial. So why has the state security service not been disbanded and why is it still being relied upon and its role praised?

Why have there been no trials for the pillars of the former regime, i.e., the cronies of Mubarak and his sons, such as Safwat el-Sherif, Fathi Sorour

1 Habib el-Aldy was the longest-serving minister of the interior under Hosni Mubarak. *See* Glossary.

and Zakariya Azmi.[1] Why have the tens of thousands of political detainees not been released, most of whom have spent long years in detention with no legal representation? Why the great hurry to carry out parliamentary elections in two months' time when we know that during a period of transition there should be sufficient time given to the general freedoms necessary before elections so that their results can be considered an expression of the people's will? What is the use of tinkering with the old constitution rather than calling for a new constitution that will bring about true democracy?

There are many questions but only one answer. Ahmed Shafik does not express the will of the Egyptian people. After his failure to put down the revolution, he is now trying to obfuscate and reverse its gains. Shafik's government is a real obstacle to change because it is simply granting the remnants of the former regime time to regroup and gather strength. Under Shafik, the former unjust and corrupt regime has managed to stay in power with only a few cosmetic changes.

We must all work to bring down the government of Shafik so that the revolution can achieve its aims and Egypt can head towards the future it deserves and for which hundreds of people have paid with their lives.

Democracy is the answer.

RH

The Sickness of Dictatorship

3 March 2011

Straight after graduating, I worked as a resident doctor in the oral surgery department of the college of medicine at Cairo University. They were the worst days of my life. The whole department of oral surgery was riddled with corruption. Favouritism and favour-paying enabled the sons and daughters of the rich to get what they did not deserve. It was an open secret that examination results were tampered with and there was no end to financial and administrative irregularities. The patients, forced to seek free healthcare, were treated so badly and with such contempt that it was criminal. However, what I suffered from most was the systematic bullying and the arrogant, overbearing and humiliating treatment meted out by the senior members of the department. One of the professors supervising the master's thesis of a teaching assistant used to call him "ass" in public. When this professor walked into the

1 Mubarak's longest-serving officials: Safwat el-Sherif, minister of information for 22 years and chairman of the Upper House for seven; Fathi Sorour, the parliament speaker for 20 years; and Zakaria Azmi, the president's chief of staff for 22 years.

department he would ask anyone there: "Where's the ass? I want to see him."

The teaching assistant would step forward with an obsequious smile on his face and say: "Here I am, sir."

I recall upbraiding the teaching assistant for allowing his dignity to be sullied, but he replied: "The professor is like a father to me."

"But your father should respect you and not humiliate you like that with everyone watching."

The teaching assistant let out a sigh: "Which scenario is better? That the professor treats me with respect and I fail my exam, or that he calls me whatever he likes and I get my degree sooner?"

That was the prevailing logic in the department: abandon your dignity if you want to get on professionally. Put up with the humiliation and if it gets too much, take it out on the nurses and interns who are further down the scale from you.

One day the head of our department called me to his office. Peremptorily he asked me to go to the main railway station in Cairo to buy him a train ticket to Alexandria. There were some people in his office with him and I did not want to show him up in front of them so I went to the clinic next door and telephoned his office.

"I am sorry, sir, but I cannot go and buy the ticket for you," I said.

"Why not?" he replied.

"Because I am a dentist, and not an office boy or your assistant."

The head of the department laughed contemptuously and replied: "You seem to be off your head. Pass the receiver to someone who has worked here a long time."

I called one of the teachers over, handed him the telephone and heard him saying: "Yes, sir. At your service, sir."

The teacher, who had a doctorate in surgery, went off to buy the ticket in a state of happiness because the head of department had singled him out for this praiseworthy task. I resigned from that dreadful place and travelled to the United States where I studied for my masters degree at Illinois University. I had to attend lectures with the second year students, and during a seminar on histology, an American student raised her hand and told the professor: "I haven't understood. Could you go over the explanation again?"

The professor wiped out what he had written on the blackboard and then went over the explanation again. But the student still did not understand so asked the professor to explain it one more time. As the professor turned to wipe the blackboard for the second time, he raised his hands in the air in a sign of exasperation, at which point the student shouted: "Why are you exasperated by my stupidity? I am not stupid. If I was, I wouldn't have got the grades to get me here."

There was total silence and I, coming from Cairo University, expected all hell to break loose. Instead I was surprised to see the professor smile gently and tell the student: "Please accept my apologies; I did not mean to belittle you. I shall now try as hard as I can to give you a clearer explanation."

This brought home to me two contradictory attitudes: at Cairo University, bullying and humiliation were part and parcel of showing respect to your superiors. At Illinois University, however, students were treated with respect and were rewarded for their efforts. The gap between these two approaches has nothing to do with any gulf between East and West, but that between dictatorship and democracy. Dictatorship spreads like cancer from the presidential palace through society. The individuals subjected to this treatment turn into petty dictators who mete out punishment and bully the weak. A democratic ruler works in the service of the people who have chosen them through free elections, whereas a dictator has no respect for their people, believing them to be lesser beings. Hosni Mubarak used to address members of the intelligentsia, artists and university professors by their first name, belittling them while at the same time expecting them to respond with obsequiousness. There was even one incident when Hosni Mubarak patted a well-known journalist on the belly and made foul comments about him in front of his colleagues. That senior journalist took it as an honour and proudly regaled people with the story: "Just imagine. The president called me by name ... He always treats me like an old friend!"

This vile and degrading way of treating people is in stark contrast to the behaviour found in a democratic society, where a street-sweeper and head of state have equal rights, and it follows that a cat may look at a king. In a democratic country, public officials are subjected to greater scrutiny than ordinary people as it is in the interest of the general public.

The sickness of dictatorship always spreads from the political to the moral sphere. In a democratic society each individual knows his or her place, but in a dictatorship this is often changeable and subject to the whim of the dictator. There is the example of the law professor who hoists their legal flag in the service of the regime, tailoring the law to suit the dictator's whim and eating away at the rights of the ordinary people. Then, if the dictator no longer needs their services, the great jurist joins the opposition and demands that the regime be changed. But the moment the ruler summons the law professor, they come running to offer their services once again. There is also the television screenwriter who actively condemns corruption but creates programmes that pay homage to Hosni Mubarak and depicts the state security service in a rosy hue. The officers are portrayed as national heroes rather than corrupt criminals who have tortured and abused the Egyptian people.

This moral deformity is one of the ramifications of dictatorship. In a democratic society, people do not need to be in the pocket of a corrupt official to achieve professional success. The very foundation of democracy is justice and people should prosper according to their talent and hard work.

Perhaps my dear readers will understand what I am driving at behind these notions. Many of you will have seen the televised debate between Ahmed Shafik and me while he was still in office.[1] I had planned to confront Shafik in a controlled and measured way about his role in the killing of hundreds of demonstrators and the disappearance of thousands of Egyptians whose families have no idea whether they have been arrested or shot dead. However, the exchange escalated quickly and Shafik went on the offensive, showering me with insults and threats that amounted to defamation of character.

In a democratic system, the head of state is the servant of the people and they treat him with respect. In Egypt, after the revolution, no citizen will kowtow to the president, and no citizen will boast that the president has insulted them or patted them on their belly. Henceforth, the president must understand that Egypt has changed, that a street-sweeper is an Egyptian citizen and it is his right to make the president of the republic accountable for their actions.

After my encounter with Ahmed Shafik I was sent hundreds of tweets of support from Egyptians at home and abroad. I am proud of every word that those dear people wrote, but the greatest mark of honour I received came from the father of the late Mohamed Ramadan, the youngest person killed in Alexandria, who was shot in the head at close range by a police officer. His father wrote to say: "I must thank you. When I saw you on the television I felt that the blood of my late son Mohamed was in good hands."

Democracy is the answer.

RH

Five Attitudes Towards the Revolution

15 March 2011

It was two o'clock in the morning and I found myself walking through Tahrir Square. Feeling stressed, I lit a cigarette and threw the empty packet onto the ground. A lady in her seventies came over to me, greeted me warmly and told me she loved my writing. I thanked her but she suddenly looked at me and said: "Please pick up your empty cigarette packet."

I felt embarrassed. I bent over quickly and picked up the discarded packet.

"You can put it in the rubbish bin over there," she said.

I did as she told me and walked back over to her, shamefaced. She smiled

1 Baladna bel Masry, OnTV (Cairo, 2 March 2011). The author says special thanks to Naguib Sawiris, Yusri Fawda, Reem Maged, Albert Shafik and Hamdi Qindil for making this interview possible. *See* https://www.youtube.com/watch?v=xePLkYq7EuY

at me: "We're building a new and different Egypt now. We have to keep it tidy."

This is just one of many memorable incidents which I experienced during the revolution. Another time, I was standing with a group of demonstrators when one young man got overexcited and started shouting obscene slogans against Suzanne Mubarak, wife of Hosni Mubarak. The other demonstrators berated him, saying: "We are here to demand our rights, not to shout insults." Over a period of three weeks, millions of Egyptians gathered together in towns and squares in the name of revolution. There was not one report of sexual harassment or petty theft during this entire time and the demonstrators made sure to clean up all public spaces after their sit-ins.

The Egyptian demonstrators acted with dignity and respect during the revolution. In fact, revolution per se is a great human achievement as it brings out the best in people and moves them to a place beyond their moral shortcomings. When people rise up in revolt, they immediately become more thoughtful because they are forced to face arrest and death, and sacrifice their own freedoms.

It has been asked whether all Egyptians took part in the revolution, and the answer is no. There has never been a revolution in history in which every single person took part. In my opinion there are now five different attitudes towards the revolution:

First: The revolutionaries. These noble Egyptians rose up in the name of freedom and paid a crushing price for the sake of their country. According to the Ministry of Health, more than 800 Egyptians have been killed, 1,200 have been blinded by rubber bullets and thousands of people are still missing. These enormous sacrifices have made the revolutionaries even more determined to realise the goals of the revolution and they are no longer afraid of the regime.

Second: The observers. These Egyptians suffered under the corrupt and unjust regime of Hosni Mubarak but were not prepared to make any sacrifice in order to achieve their rights. They are people exhausted by the struggle for sustenance who focus on their day-to-day concerns. They mumble the occasional complaint but then leave the rest to God. The observers were surprised by the revolution and watched the events unfold on television rather than taking part. They tend to oscillate between supporting the revolution and opposing it. At the start, many of them believed the propaganda disseminated by the state media and thought that the revolutionaries were paid agents. Then they saw how people were being killed in the streets and they felt for them, but when they heard Hosni Mubarak stating how he wanted to die in his country, the observers were moved to tears. Then, the day after, when the massacre of demonstrators happened, they went back to supporting the revolution. The people who observe the revolution want change but at no cost to themselves.

They want to see democracy achieved without any personal losses or disruptions. They are stuck, body and mind, in the pre-revolutionary stage.

Third: The enemies of the revolution. This group are against the revolution because they risk being put on trial or imprisoned. They come from various social and professional strata: ministers, businessmen, leading figures in the NDP, state security officers, corrupt journalists, people involved in petty corruption and fixers. They felt safe as long as Ahmed Shafik remained in power as he was a close associate of Hosni Mubarak and had not put a single officer on trial for the killing of demonstrators. On the contrary, the minister of the interior under Shafik had praised the officers of the state security service for carrying out their national duty. When the military council selected Essam Sharaf[1] as a replacement for Prime Minister Ahmed Shafik, the enemies of the revolution panicked and started shredding documents and destroying evidence of their wrong-doing. State security officers disappeared from their offices and started causing chaos in the service of two aims: firstly the creation of a wedge between the army and the revolutionaries in order to make the army withdraw its support for the revolution, and secondly by putting pressure on the observers in an attempt to turn them against the revolution.

Fourth: The Muslim Brotherhood. Like many Egyptians, the Muslim Brotherhood took part bravely in the revolution, showing true heroism in protecting demonstrators from attacks by the police and the regime's thugs. However, the inherent problem with the Muslim Brotherhood is the distance between their moral rectitude as individuals and their political tractability as an organisation. Most of the Brothers are good and devoted people but their leadership has put the interests of the association first, hence their historical support of all autocratic rulers in Egypt without exception, from King Farouk and Isma'il Sidqi, the strongman of the Sha'ab Party, through to Gamal Abdel Nasser and Anwar Sadat. The Muslim Brotherhood bucked the national consensus and participated in the last elections held by Mubarak, and then did the same again by sitting down to negotiate with Omar Suleiman[2] who wanted to whitewash the former regime by having his photograph taken with the government's opponents. The Brotherhood is again repeating the same old mistake by standing side by side with the NDP and supporting the constitutional changes they know to be unsound. This will only serve to get in the way of democracy and undermine the revolution's achievements. The Brotherhood passed a resolution in support of these constitutional changes in order to secure a large number of seats in the People's Assembly.

Fifth: The armed forces. The revolution would not have succeeded

1 Essam Sharaf served as minister of transportation from 2004 to 2005. During the revoltuion, he earned a reputation for his opposition to corruption and concern for workers' rights. *See* Glossary.

2 Omar Suleiman (1936–2012) was Egypt's former vice-president and long-time spy chief to Hosni Mubarak. *See* Glossary.

without the protection of the armed forces. From the very first day, they played an essential role in the revolution and saved the Egyptian people from the corrupt regime. However, the Egyptian people would like them to answer the following questions:

1. What is the legal status of the deposed president, Hosni Mubarak? Is he retired, in custody or under house arrest? Does he still have the right to use the presidential aircraft and palaces? When will he be put on trial for the crimes he committed against the Egyptian people and when will arrest warrants be issued for his most important cronies such as Safwat el-Sherif, Zakariya Azmi and Fathi Sorour?

2. The armed forces are fully aware of the criminal role played by state security officers over decades, from abusing, torturing and blackmailing citizens to sabotaging the whole country by putting agents and journalists in positions of leadership regardless of their abilities. Some high-ranking men and state security officers have been sent for trial, but most are still at large and doing their utmost to spread disorder and stir up unrest. They have the resources and expertise to create havoc in the media and amongst the political parties. The destruction of documents, sectarian strife and demonstrations by the Copts or the Salafists are just a foretaste of what the state security service can achieve. Why do the armed forces not use the emergency regulations to arrest the state security officers and put them on trial?

3. After the fall of Hosni Mubarak there were factional demands all over Egypt because a number of ministers and university departments were in cahoots with the Mubarak regime. Why did the armed forces not create an independent oversight committee to investigate corruption allegations and to forward suspect findings to the attorney general. The only way of putting an end to the factional demonstrations would be to reassure the people that justice would be done at some time or other.

4. Why do the armed forces want to bring the transitional period to a close? It is claimed that they want to finish this difficult job in the shortest time possible and return to their primary function of protecting the state. That sounds reasonable and feasible, but would it not be better to take up the suggestion made by the professors of law and appoint an acting military-civilian presidential council to remove leadership responsibility from the armed forces during the transitional period? That would provide sufficient time for the parties to organise themselves and the resultant elections would then express the will of the Egyptian people.

5. It goes without saying that a constitution falls when the regime that represents it falls. So why this insistence on tinkering with the old constitution? Not only did all nationalist forces (except for the Muslim Brotherhood and the NDP) reject the amendments, but Judge Zakariya Abdel Aziz[1] considered them as irrelevant to the Egyptian people. How can a referendum on the constitution be held in this deteriorating security situation? Why do we not follow the advice of the professors of constitutional law and publish a document showing the principals of the constitution, then hold elections for a constituent assembly to draw up a new constitution that expresses the will of the people? If the response is that the security situation does not allow the holding of elections, we shall point out that as a referendum on the constitutional amendments was going to be held in this deteriorating security situation, we can doubtless also manage to hold elections for a constituent assembly.

Naturally, these legitimate questions in no way detract from our admiration for the great national role played by the armed forces. However, Egypt is at a critical point and we must all speak honestly and openly so that the country can embark on the future it deserves.

Democracy is the answer.

RH

Before the Revolution Becomes a Wasted Opportunity

22 March 2011

After the success of the 1919 revolution when the British yielded to the will of the Egyptians, King Fuad[2] appointed a committee to draw up a constitution. The nationalist leader, Saad Zaghloul[3], objected to this and demanded the election of a constitutional assembly to draft a democratic constitution that would express the will of the people. However, King Fuad would not budge. A committee was convened to draft the 1923 Constitution, which granted the

1 Judge Zakariya Abdel Aziz is a prominent Egyptian judge and former head of the Cassation Court. He is known for his leading role in the movement demanding the independence of the judiciary in 2005-2006 under ousted president Hosni Mubarak. Abdel Aziz was also involved in the Judges for Egypt movement which was accused of having links to the Brotherhood.

2 King Fuad I (1868–1936) was the first king of Egypt following its independence from Great Britain.

3 Saad Zaghloul (1859–1927) was an Egyptian revolutionary, and leader of Egypt's nationalist Wafd Party.

king the right to dissolve parliament at any time.

This serious constitutional flaw led to the corrupting of political life, which turned parliament into a plaything of the king. Over a period of 30 years, the Wafd Party, which enjoyed a crushing majority, only held power for six. The irony is that, despite its shortcomings, Saad Zaghloul accepted the 1923 Constitution even though democratic change was within reach. As undisputed leader of the nation, Zaghloul could have mobilised the Egyptian people in order to finish the revolution and to claim their right to a just and democratic constitution. But it was a lost opportunity and the Egyptian people did not get the freedom they had fought for.

After the 1952 revolution, Egypt wasted another opportunity for democratisation. The anti-democratic trend amongst the Free Officers[1] won out and, on 16 January 1953, they issued an edict dissolving all political parties, expropriating their funds and headquarters. The Wafd Party was at that time in the majority and should have called upon the Egyptian people to make a stand against the Free Officers in order to preserve the democratic system. However the Wafd Party made no objections and the country then fell into the grip of dictatorship for sixty consecutive years.

Egyptian history is replete with lost opportunities for achieving democracy and we are now faced with yet another hurdle. The great revolution of 25 January forced Hosni Mubarak to step down and hundreds of Egyptians lost their lives for the sake of freedom. From the outset, the revolution has been beset by an aggressive counter-revolution both inside and outside Egypt. A few days ago the Kuwaiti *Al-Dar* newspaper wrote that the Egyptian authorities have come under great pressure from Arab rulers, headed by the king of Saudi Arabia and the ruler of the Emirates, not to put Mubarak on trial. The newspaper reported that these Arab states are threatening to end all relations with Cairo, stop all financial aid and withdraw investment from Egypt should Mubarak be prosecuted. They even threatened to dismiss the five million Egyptians working in their countries if their demands were not met.

Israel has also continued to defend Hosni Mubarak on the grounds that he is their closest ally in the region. The Israeli media has not hidden its concerns about real democratic change in Egypt and the US administration has the same fears, of course. The reason that government officials in the both United States and Israel are worried is because they understand Egypt's position and its capabilities: they know that if Egypt transitions to a democracy it will become a powerful force in the Arab world. The great American intellectual, Noam Chomsky, wrote in the *Guardian* newspaper that the US supports the dictatorship in Egypt not out of fear of extreme Islam, as has been claimed, but out of fear that an independent

1 A group of nationalist officers in the armed forces of Egypt and Sudan that instigated the Egyptian revolution of 1952. Originally established in 1945 as a cell within the Muslim Brotherhood under Abdel Moneim Abdel Raouf.

Egypt will break free of America's patronage.[1] Chomsky adds that the American administration will do all it can to make sure that the next Egyptian president does not stray from the path mapped out for them.

There are many internal and external forces waiting to ambush the revolution. Inside Egypt, the real cornerstones of the Mubarak regime are still hale and hearty. The NDP continues to have support throughout the country and is filling its headquarters with hundreds and thousands of party members who will do anything to regain power under a new name, as well as hundreds of state security officers who abandoned their posts after the revolution in order to stir up trouble in the streets. There are also tens of thousands of local council members, heads of governorates and universities, deans appointed by the security service, press and media bigwigs, leading businessmen and heads of the fraudulent trade unions, and thousands upon thousands of members of the former regime, who are all plotting against the revolution.

So, what are the aims of the counter-revolution? Here we need to look back at the declarations made by Mubarak to the world media before he stepped down: "I would like to step down, but I am fearful of chaos in Egypt. I am afraid that Egypt will fall to the Muslim Brotherhood." The counter-revolution is now trying to make all Mubarak's fears come true in order to show the whole world that he was right all along.

The counter-revolution is creating as much chaos as possible so that Egyptians no longer feel safe and will therefore start to resent the revolution and accept any compromise in return for stability. They deliberately kept the police off the streets throughout Egypt and released tens of thousands of criminals from prison, who were given arms and instructed to attack civilians. This scheme continued throughout the government of Ahmed Shafik, and then, when Essam Sharaf became prime minister, incidences of vandalism and sectarian strife intensified in order to discredit the revolutionary government despite the best efforts of the new minister of the interior, Mansour el-Essawy,[2] to restore order in the absence of the police. Preventing the police from defending the nation was an act of sabotage and treachery, and the order must have come from an authority that has greater sway over the officers than the minister of the interior himself. The emergence of groups of thugs throughout Egypt is also not a matter of serendipity but a carefully planned operation. The guard outside the polling station in Muqattam stood by as Mohamad ElBaradei[3]

1 Noam Chomsky, "It's not radical Islam that worries the US – it's independence", *Guardian*, 4 February 2011. *See* http://www.theguardian.com/commentisfree/cifamerica/2011/feb/04/radical-islam-united-states-independence

2 Mansour el-Essawy is a former head of security for Giza, which is in greater Cairo, and is a former governor of Minya in Upper Egypt. He was appointed interior minister to the interim government led by Essam Sharaf on 5 March 2011, replacing Mahmoud Wagdy. *See* Glossary.

3 Mohamed ElBaradei, a former head of the UN nuclear watchdog and a Nobel peace laureate, ran in the 2011 presidential elections and acted as vice president following Mohamed Morsi's ouster in 2013. *See* Glossary.

came under brutal attack as members of the NDP pelted him with stones. And in the Shubra district [of Cairo], particularly over the last two days, these thugs have been allowed to shut off streets, intimidate people and shoot at random, leading to the deaths of citizens. Not a single policeman or soldier intervened to offer protection. Is this somehow connected to the fact that Shubra is home to Copts who announced that they rejected the constitutional amendments? Was the aim to intimidate the Copts into accepting the amendments, or was the aim simply to punish them for having believed that Egyptians deserve a new constitution?

Furthermore, the state media only covers certain trials as they still receive instructions from the state security service. The press rushed to film Ahmed Ezz, Zuhair Garana and Ahmed el-Maghrabi[1] being interrogated in prison uniform. This violates all professional and humanitarian standards. The aim was to appease angry Egyptians and to make them feel that justice was taking its course. With all due respect to the person and position of the attorney general, there are still many unanswered questions. Why has there been no investigation into Hosni Mubarak and members of his family? Why have Zakariya Azmi, Fathi Sorour and Safwat el-Sherif not been put on trial? Why did the attorney general not investigate the 24 complaints filed by workers in the civil aviation sector against Ahmed Shafik for the misuse of state funds?

During Ahmed Shafik's tenure as prime minister, why did he not order the attorney general to investigate a single officer for the killing of civilians? And after the resignation of Shafik, why did the state prosecution service order the release of those officers accused of carrying out killings as part of their job? Does their release not enable them to destroy any incriminating evidence? What is the point of putting the guilty on trial if justice is carried out selectively, allowing people to try others according to incomprehensible standards?

Instead of electing a constituent assembly to issue a new constitution that expresses the will of the people and transitions Egypt to democracy, we have been surprised to see Hosni Mubarak's suggestion to make a limited constitutional amendment carried out by a committee selected according to some arcane criteria. This was followed by a hasty referendum whose subject matter people were not empowered to understand and which was organised in such a manner that citizens could only vote for or against all the amendments, with the NDP making an alliance for the first time with the Muslim Brotherhood to support the amendments.

The Brotherhood has shown again that they are ready to change their political stance according to their interests, and after they collected thousands

1 Three leading associates of Hosni Mubarak put on trial on charges of abusing their positions and stealing public money. Zuhair Garana was the former tourism minister; Ahmed el-Maghrabi held both the tourism and housing portfolios at different times; and Ahmed Ezz was a businessman who was a leading member of the National Democratic Party (NDP).

of signatures in support of ElBaradei[1] they turned against him and formed an alliance with the NDP instead. It would seem that the principles of Islam, as far as the Brotherhood is concerned, were completely set aside during the elections. In order to achieve power, the Brotherhood is prepared to do anything, from accusing their opponents of being foreign agents and infidels to buying votes by handing out free sugar and oil. The Brotherhood's strong showing, while not representing their true size in Egypt, does the counter-revolution a great service. On the one hand it leads to a greater polarisation of Egyptians against a religious backdrop, and it destroys the national unity created by the revolution, and on the other hand it confirms to those who sympathise with the revolution in the West that Hosni Mubarak was the last bulwark against extremists.

Those like me who are disturbed by the warmth displayed by the media towards Aboud al-Zamar[2] – who is, after all, a murderer – must understand that the image of Aboud al-Zamar is of ultimate value to the counter-revolution. When he sits behind the cameras with his bushy beard, reminiscent of Osama bin Laden, and states that it is legitimate to shed blood in the name of religion, millions of foreigners, who have sympathised with our revolution, will be moved to abort the revoltuion in order to protect Egypt from extremists.

The results of the referendum have been declared in favour of the amendments to the constitution. Despite my joy at the high turnout of voters, and despite my full respect for the choice of the electorate, I must also state that the manner and the speed of this process of transition goes against the interests of the revolution and Egypt itself. If the organisers truly want to be of service to democratic change then they must change the plurality voting system which leads to the division of seats between members of the NDP and the Muslim Brotherhood. It is unacceptable that these two parties be solely responsible for drafting the constitution, when it was the Egyptian people that shed so much blood for the revolution.

We must listen to the professors of law, the majority of whom have stated that drafting a constitution by means of a parliament elected in this manner does not represent the will of the Egyptian people. The great Egyptian revolution will not turn into another wasted opportunity, even if decisions continue to be forced upon us in this way. No one, no matter how powerful, can prevent the Egyptian people – who were able to bring down Hosni Mubarak – from achieving their freedom.

Democracy is the answer.

RH

1 The Muslim Brotherhood backed ElBaradei's campaign for political change in Egypt and helped him to gather signatures and support.

2 Aboud al-Zamar is an Islamic fundamentalist and former military intelligence colonel in the Egyptian army. He was sentenced to life imprisonment in Cairo after being captured by the Egyptian government for being implicated in the assassination of President Anwar Sadat on 6 October 1981. He was released in March 2011.

What Did the Monkey Say to the Lion?

29 March 2011

It was a beautiful forest, vast and lush. The animals lived together happily and peacefully until the elephant and the lion took control. The elephant proclaimed himself king of the forest, and the lion its loyal guard. The lion carried out his duties faithfully and competently; all night long he would roam the areas just beyond the forest in search of intruders. If he came across any unwelcome predators, he would bravely pounce on them before they could reach the animals of the forest and do them harm. For this reason, the animals living in the forest held the lion in great esteem and respected him.

On the other hand, however, the elephant was corrupt and oppressive. He gathered two groups of followers around himself: the pigs and the wolves. The pigs stole food from the other animals, and they were so filthy that nowhere in the forest was free from their foul smell. Then there were the wolves; they terrorised the other animals and abused those that asked for fair treatment. How many animals were killed in cold blood by the wolves, simply for objecting to the actions of King Elephant!

The animals endured the oppression of the king for many long years until they could take no more. One day they rose up against the elephant and a great battle took place – the like of which had never been seen in the forest. The wolves fought fiercely in defence of their king, but with astonishing bravery, the other animals rushed into the battle, wave after wave. They fought with desperation in order to liberate the forest from oppression. The wolves killed dozens of the animals but this only increased their determination to triumph. After two days of bitter fighting the wolves became exhausted and fled, with the pigs following close behind. The animal revolutionaries surrounded the elephant king who now spoke with a voice that trembled with fear: "What do you intend to do with me?"

The giraffe answered him defiantly: "Justice demands that we put you to death for the brutal crimes that you have committed. However, we do not want to stain the purity of our revolution with your blood. We want you to leave the forest and never return."

The elephant answered: "But without me the forest will descend into chaos."

"No, it is you who brought disorder to the forest through your oppression and iniquity," said the giraffe. Then he ordered the elephant into exile, shouting: "Leave! Leave!"

From every direction, the angry voices of all the other animals chimed in and chanted: "Leave! Leave!"

Realising that the game was up, the old elephant asked the animals to let him have an hour's respite to put his affairs in order before leaving. The animals agreed to this but they kept a close eye on him throughout because they knew that he was treacherous by nature. At one point, however, the elephant and the lion went behind a tree, far away from the animals. When they returned the elephant lifted up his trunk and proclaimed: "From now on the lion shall be responsible for ruling the forest in my place."

At this, the animals cheered with joy, because they loved the lion and had faith in his courage and integrity. The lion, however, roared and said: "I thank you, but I cannot rule the forest and continue to be its loyal guard at the same time. I will take over as its ruler for the period of a week or two until you find a new king."

The animals were happy with this and cheered in agreement, then they turned again to the elephant and renewed their chanting: "Leave! Leave!"

The elephant acquiesced. He flapped his large ears, lowered his trunk, turned and left the forest that he had plundered and oppressed. The animals followed him until he reached the land beyond the river. Once out of sight, they returned to the forest and celebrated their freedom. Each species of animal expressed its joy in its own particular way: the deer leaped around with beautiful grace, the monkeys shouted as they swung from tree to tree, the zebras brayed harshly and exuberantly, and the wild rabbits did somersaults.

A state of bliss prevailed for several days, during which the animals felt as though they were breathing clean air for the first time. The future seemed bright and the animals felt optimistic that they could face any problems they might now encounter. However, the animals could not decide who should be the new king of the forest. Should it be the old fox, renowned for his shrewdness and life experience? Should it be the brave and gentle giraffe that led them in the revolution? Although the debate was heated, all of the animals felt proud that they were taking part in choosing the new king. After a week had passed, however, something happened that spoiled the good mood: the foul smell of the pigs returned to the forest. The animals were greatly troubled by this and rushed to the lion to ask for his help: "O great lion, we can smell the foul stench of the pigs; they must have returned to the forest to steal our food."

The lion gave them a blank look and said: "Don't worry, I will do what needs to be done."

The animals took leave of the lion, certain that he would do his upmost to protect them from the pigs. However, the stench of the pigs grew stronger each day and the animals were worried that they had entered the forest in even greater numbers. As they were trying to get to grips with this unsettling development, they discovered that the wolves had also returned to the forest during the night and wreaked havoc. They had devoured a large number of the wild rabbits and killed a zebra that had tried to fight them off. They had also savaged a beautiful, young gazelle that later died from her wounds. The animals rushed back to the lion to again ask him for his help. He gave them the same blank look and said: "Go back and I will do what needs to be done."

The giraffe responded to this gently and politely, saying: "But this is what you said to us before, O great lion. Why do you not stop the wolves from entering the forest? Why do you not protect us when we are sleeping like you always did before?"

The lion roared in annoyance and then raising his voice threateningly he said: "Did you not understand what I said? I told you that I will do what needs to be done. Now go!"

The animals felt distressed as they left him. With his hoarse voice the zebra said: "What was the point of our revolution? The foul smell of the pigs has returned and the wolves continue to attack and kill us – everything is just as it was before we deposed the elephant."

The voice of the giraffe stammered with emotion as he answered, saying: "I don't understand: the lion could easily do away with the pigs and the wolves. Why does he let them come into the forest?"

The fox forced a smile and said bitterly: "Listen everyone, it seems as though we have been duped; we were naive to believe that the lion would take a stand with us against the despotic elephant."

An old monkey answered him, saying: "Don't be so hasty. Remember that the lion stood by our side and helped us to get rid of the elephant."

The giraffe stretched his neck and said: "Yes, the lion has a strong code of honour. He is on the side of good."

The fox smiled again, and with a faltering voice, he said: "There is no doubt that the lion is honourable; however, he is also a close friend of the deposed elephant." A heavy silence prevailed after these words were spoken. The fox continued: "Listen everyone, I have an idea that will help us get to the bottom of all this." The animals all looked at him expectantly. "If the lion does indeed still fraternise with the elephant then he must go and meet him during the night. One of us can follow him in order to find out what is going on."

Hearing this, the animals cheered with approval. A young monkey said excitedly: "Fox, I wish to be entrusted this task. I will observe the lion during the night."

The fox regarded him cautiously and said: "Monkey, you are well suited to carry out this task because of your cleverness and your ability to move quickly. However, in all honesty, I fear your recklessness; you often act without thinking about the consequences."

The monkey screeched and twice jumped into the air, then he said: "Fox, give me a chance to do this and I promise that I will act wisely."

That evening, the monkey crouched on the branch of a high tree at the edge of the forest. He watched as the lion carried out his usual patrol of the area. Suddenly, the pigs and the wolves appeared. His heart felt heavy as he watched the lion allow them to enter the forest; the lion remained motionless, simply looking on as they went in. From the top of his tree, the monkey continued to observe the lion as he started to move out of view. With great skill the monkey swung from one tree to another so as to keep the lion in his sight. After some time, he saw the lion greeting the deposed elephant – a meeting that appeared to have been pre-arranged. The monkey paid close attention and listened attentively to the conversation between the two.

The next day the animals went again to complain to the lion that the stench of the pigs had become unbearable and that the wolves had been getting into the forest. The lion yawned and said calmly: "I will handle this matter."

At this moment the monkey hastened to speak: "Honoured lion, I know that you have no intention of doing anything to keep the pigs and the wolves out of the forest."

The lion looked closely at the monkey, then he let out a terrifying roar, and bellowed: "How dare you speak to me in this manner!"

A heavy silence fell over the animals, but then the monkey jumped in the air – as was his custom when agitated – and said: "Lion, I saw you meet with the deposed elephant and I heard what you said to each other."

The lion was visibly shocked by the monkey's revelations. He said: "Have you become so insolent that you now spy on me?"

"Lion, forgive me, I overheard you by chance," said the monkey.

The lion roared and said: "Tell me what it is that you all want then."

The monkey responded: "Can I ask you why you continue to meet with the elephant in spite of all the crimes that he committed against us?"

"The elephant is my friend and mentor; I hold him in great esteem," said the lion.

Calmly the fox asked: "Are you with the elephant or with us?"

"I am with you, of course – but also with the elephant."

"You cannot be on the side of the oppressor and the oppressed at the same time," answered the fox.

The other animals began to despair, and all were too afraid to speak until the monkey plucked up the courage and said: "Lion, we animals love and respect you, and we know that you are upright and honourable. If keeping ties with the deposed elephant means doing what is wrong, then you must change your loyalties and stand for what is right – this is what we expect of you. We do not want to suffer the elephant's wickedness; all we want is to live our lives freely. Dozens of our friends sacrificed their lives for the revolution, in order to put an end to oppression. O great lion, we know how much you love the forest and how you fight to protect it. All we want is for you to do what is right. We will not leave from here until you pledge to protect us from the pigs and wolves."

The animals cheered when the monkey had finished his speech. The lion, however, was quiet and looked to be in deep thought. Then he roared loudly, and pronounced his final decision:

Democracy is the answer.

AB

Masters of Egypt

5 April 2011

Some days ago, scores of police officers in Alexandria staged a sit-in to protest the trial of three of their colleagues for the killing of demonstrators. The same thing took place in a number of governorates across Egypt with 48 police officers in Suez tendering their resignations.

Since the start of the revolution, more than 820 Egyptians have been killed and 1,200 have been blinded by rubber bullets, not to mention the thousands who have disappeared and whose families have no idea whether they are dead or in unknown places of detention. These disastrous human losses did not happen during a war against foreign enemies but were acts committed by Egyptian police officers against the persons of Egyptian citizens like them. One police officer, by the name of Wael al-Koumy from Alexandria, has been accused of personally killing 37 people.

Why then are the police officers angry at the trial of their colleagues for killing demonstrators? How would these officers feel if their own sons and daughters had been beaten or killed? And why are they so dismissive of the relatives' demands for justice? The answer to these questions requires an understanding of the culture in which the police officers of the Mubarak regime were educated.

In a video that went viral on the internet, the former director of security of the Buhaira Governorate tells his officers: "We are the chosen few who protect the Egyptian people. We are their masters. If anyone stretches out their hand against their master, what will their reward be?"

"We'll cut off their hand!" the officers reply as one.

This sad exchange illustrates the attitude of the police in the Mubarak era. A police officer felt superior to ordinary citizens, no matter their social standing or education. They considered themselves above the law and able to do whatever they wanted to the Egyptian people. They could beat them, arrest them and torture them to death without the threat of serious repercussions.

To generalise would be misleading and wrong, because there are thousands of police officers that carry out their duty devotedly under difficult conditions and for what is hardly a living wage. However, many officers from the criminal investigation and the security branches of the police carried out horrendous crimes against the Egyptian people, some of which have been documented in local and international reports. We must then ask ourselves how a police officer can change from being a guardian of the law to being outside of it? What makes a motivated and intelligent individual turn into a corrupt and arrogant police officer that beats and tortures people? Psychological studies suggest that any individual, no matter how decent and kind, can turn into a killer after going through a repressive security-training institution as a result of the following:

1. They find that blind obedience to orders represents the prevailing system in the police station and quickly become compliant and ready to carry out any order no matter how savage.
2. They find themselves in a group of colleagues who practice brutality as a matter of course and they fall in with their behaviour through fear of ridicule or rejection.
3. They persuade themselves that the victims are enemies of the state, saboteurs or agents of foreign powers. They view their crimes as part of their duty to protect the nation.

This justification of brutality can help us to understand the psychological crises experienced by many police officers after the revolution. The absence of the police and the failure of its officers to maintain security may be a result of a plot by elements of the old regime in order to foment chaos, but it also reflects the attitude of many police officers post-revolution that have refused to go back to work. Many officers do not want to work because they feel demeaned, betrayed and wronged. The revolution has turned their world upside down as it challenges everything that they have been taught. For example, torture will no longer be regarded as necessary for the protection of the state as the revolution considers it to be a shameful crime whose perpetrators should be brought to justice. This crisis of confidence is not in the interest of Egypt or of the revolution. Some officers have arrested and tortured people they believed to be saboteurs and [foreign] agents, but those very saboteurs are winning and bringing down the regime of Hosni Mubarak.

Some days ago Habib el-Adly was in court facing charges of corruption, and there was unprecedented security precautions taken to protect him. Not only were there armoured cars, guards and central security soldiers, but also inside the building itself police officers formed a human wall to prevent journalists getting any pictures of el-Adly in the courtroom cage. The safety of the murderous Habib el-Adly was clearly more important to those officers than justice for their own country.

On the same day, at a football match between Zamalek and the Tunisian Club Africain, according to eyewitnesses, the police failed to secure the ground and allowed scores of hooligans to enter armed with sticks and knives. The police officers then opened the gates so that the crowds could storm the pitch and attack the players. A video recording of the incident shows that the police officers on the pitch did absolutely nothing to deter the hooligans.

The contrast between the behaviour of the police officers in those two situations is telling. Some police officers still hold Habib el-Adly in high esteem regardless of the crimes he has committed against the Egyptian people. They refused to allow journalists to take pictures of el-Adly in the courtroom cage because they consider any stain on his image to be a blow to their own self-esteem. At the same time, many police officers are determined to bring down the revolution by neglecting their duty and creating chaos in the streets so that Egyptians hanker for the days of Mubarak.

The legacy of Hosni Mubarak and his regime is a country beset by problems, including the soured relationship between the Egyptian people and the police. In order to reconcile this relationship there must be immediate and fair trials of the police officers, regardless of rank and status, that were involved in the torture and killing of demonstrators. Only then will the Egyptian people know that those officers left in their jobs are decent and honest people.

The state security service must be dissolved, as it has done nothing over the past decades except torture, abuse and spy on Egyptians in an attempt to destroy the Egyptian national movement. With all due respect to the minister of the interior, Mansour el-Essawy, and my confidence in his integrity and ability, I do not agree with his decision to dissolve the current state security apparatus and simply rebrand it as Homeland Security. This service employs officers of the former regime, many of whom have been involved in the torture and killing of revolutionaries. Will they suddenly sign up to, and respect, concepts of human rights? Revolutionary Egypt does not need a state security apparatus because it does not need to abuse or torture its citizens. Oppressive security services can only be found under authoritarian regimes. In democratic countries there are agencies that collect data in a legal manner and if it finds sufficient evidence against a citizen it will then forward it to the investigatory authorities, i.e., the attorney general.

Permanently disbanding the secret police will restore Egyptians' complete confidence in the regular police.

It is also necessary to encourage a complete transformation of police culture. Despite most police officers being decent people, their professional environment did not cultivate a regard for human rights, and investigations were generally carried out with a heavy hand. At a recent seminar organised by the *al-Ahram* newspaper on reconciling the people and the police, one officer stated: "The sacking of the state security police is regrettable because they are the cream of the police force and most of them are highly skilled public servants."

I do not know what skills the esteemed officer was talking about unless he meant their gift for beating people, treating them like animals, and applying electricity to their squishy bits. His words are oddly reminiscent of the Mubarak regime and their attempts at self-preservation. A few days ago, a state security officer in the town of Bagour went to arrest a man who had been sentenced to three years in prison. When he did not find the man at home, he arrested his wife instead and when the accused's father objected, the officer shot him dead. In fact the officer was arrested and sentenced to prison, but his behaviour reflects the old-style brutality of the secret police that Egypt must rid itself of post-revoltuion.

After the police force has been thoroughly purged, we will have to come up with a popular mass initiative to get the people on better terms with the police by organising friendly visits to police stations to rebuilt trust in them. Volunteers will be able to help renovate the burned-out police stations and police officers will visit the families of those who died in the revolution in order to reinforce the notion that police officers are decent Egyptians who work to keep the nation safe.

Then police officers will be able to go to work, not as the masters of Egyptians, but as citizens with the same rights and duties who will participate with us in building a new Egypt, a country of freedom and justice.

Democracy is the answer.

RH

How to Fight Counter-revolution

12 April 2011

The French proverb states: a debt paid is a friend kept (*les bons comptes font les bons amis*), meaning true friends should respect and trust each other in order to safeguard their friendship. This proverb can be applied to the relationship between the Egyptian people and the armed forces. From the very first day, the armed forces stood shoulder to shoulder with the revolutionaries to make a stand against tyranny. They continued to protect the Egyptian people and willingly took on the onerous role of guiding Egypt through the transitional period. However, the Egyptian people have a number of reservations and questions that the armed forces must answer if the relationship is to survive post-revolution.

The mass demonstrations organised by revolutionaries across Egypt played an important role in bringing down the regime of Hosni Mubarak. Every Friday, hundreds of thousands of Egyptians would gather together to hold discussions and voice their demands. Last Friday, in Midan al-Tahrir, the demonstrators were joined by a number of uniformed officers who held up banners and slogans against their leadership. These officers had a sort of emotional effect on the civilian demonstrators, asking them to protect them against the military police. In truth, no army in the world would allow its military to behave in this way and the rebellious officers were quickly arrested and taken away for questioning. The arrest was violently carried out by the state security service who used live ammunition to break up the demonstration, which led to the injuring of scores of civilians and the death of at least one demonstrator.

This just goes to show that the police force, which abandoned Egypt to armed thugs for two months, are prepared to take action when their role is one of brutalising Egyptians. It also became evident that the state security service, which tortured exploited Egyptians for decades, has not been dissolved, but still carries out its work in coordination with the army. As Egyptians watch their compatriots being shot at with live ammunition and wounded, they cannot help but feel that the Mubarak regime has come back with all its ugly practises. The following day, the military council convened a press conference in which they stated that the army did not fire live bullets at the demonstrators, and that those using live ammunition were people belonging to the old regime led by Ibrahim Kamel against whom an arrest warrant had been issued. We are inclined to believe the military council but do not understand the frequent incidences of military police aggression against civilians.

In another incident, individuals from the military police attacked students at Cairo University with clubs and cattle prods in order to break up a sit-in organised by students of the Faculty of Mass Communications. They arrested a number of professors but failed to open an investigation into this lamentable act of aggression. A third incident involved two young men and a young woman who were arrested for demonstrating in Tahrir Square. Amnesty International issued a detailed statement confirming that they had all been subjected to hideous torture at the hands of the military police. There accounts were supported by the affidavits of other female demonstrators who had also been subjected to utterly demeaning strip searches and virginity tests. Army officials fervently denied these accusations and announced an investigation into the incident but no findings have been published. Thus we have multiple instances of assault against citizens by individuals from the army but no justice has been served.

When the armed forces arrest demonstrators, they do not differentiate between vandals and ordinary citizens, sending them all for trial by the military courts. It could be said that it is a military principle to issue swift, deterrent sentences but unfortunately we do not see the same principle applied to the corrupt officials of the former regime. After ten weeks of the revolution, officials such as Fathi Sorour and Mufid Shehab are still at large. This week Safwat el-Sherif was summoned to testify about his role in the attack on demonstrators, the so-called Battle of the Camel[1], which took place two months ago. There is also the case of Zakariya Azmi[2] who managed to keep his job in the presidential palace until his arrest a few days ago. The military council includes some law experts who certainly knew that suspending the accused from his job and putting him in preventative custody would have been necessary in order for justice to be done. In the time before his arrest he was able to use his position to destroy incriminating evidence and to influence the witnesses.

Leaving Mubarak's cronies at large leads to the destruction of incriminating evidence. Does it make sense to try Zakariya Azmi for owning four apartments and four villas when every child in Egypt knows that that is only the tip of the iceberg? Is it permissible for Ibrahim Kamel to be implicated in plotting against demonstrators and yet we leave him at large for two months and only arrest him when he carries out another conspiracy? People in Egypt are left asking who will be the first to face a speedy trial; they suspect it will be the unfortunate demonstrator who has violated the curfew or Mubarak's corrupt cronies.

The revolution takes its legitimacy solely from the Egyptian people who rose up on 25 January against the regime. The people took over the authority of the armed forces in order to see through the aims of the revolution. The most important demand of the Egyptian people, since the start of the revolution, is that of putting Hosni Mubarak on trial for the heinous crimes he has committed against Egyptians. So why has he not been put on trial yet?

The army has stated that Mubarak is under house arrest, but law professors have confirmed that for him to be staying in his village in Sharm el-Sheikh does

---

1 The Battle of the Camel took place in Tahrir Square on 11 February 2011 when supporters of then president Hosni Mubarak charged demonstrators on horseback and camels. It became one of the most notorious incidents of the anti-Mubarak uprising and left nearly a dozen people dead. Safwat el-Sherif was accused of contacting MPs, members of the NDP and financiers of the party, inciting them to disperse the demonstrators in Tahrir Square by force and violence.

2 Zakaria Azmi was the National Democratic Party's (NDP) deputy for El-Zeitoun district in eastern Cairo and chief of the presidential staff. He was tried in a criminal court on charges of corruption and misuse of power.

not fulfil the conditions of house arrest. He has also made use of this period of freedom to hide the money which he and his family members have pillaged from the Egyptian people. He even appeared recently on the Arabiyya television channel to deny the accusations that he has accounts and assets abroad.

The US secretary of state, Hillary Clinton, has already confirmed to Hasan Nafi'a, a professor of political science, that Mubarak's funds in the United States amount to millions of dollars. The *Guardian* has estimated his fortune to be somewhere between 40 and 70 million dollars. The delay in putting Hosni Mubarak on trial has afforded him the opportunity to hide his ill-gotten gains. Who will be responsible to history and the nation if Hosni Mubarak gets off scot-free?

Another question: the speaker of the military council has given warnings about a counter-revolution. A counter-revolution is a long series of plots planned and carried out by cronies of the old regime which most often succeeds in bringing an end to a revolution and restoring the old regime, as happened in Iran in 1953 when the counter-revolution managed, under the leadership of the US and UK secret services, to remove the legitimate government of Mohammed Mossadegh.

This was repeated in 1973 in Chile when the counter-revolution, under the leadership of the US secret service, removed Salvador Allende, the legally elected president. Thus counter-revolution is a grave danger that lurks behind any revolution. We must take definitive steps to protect the Egyptian Revolution:

1. The dissolution of the regional assemblies that include 50 thousand members of the National Democratic Party (NDP) who all gained their seats by fraud and graft. They have the necessary funds to enlist people to plot against the revolution.

2. The dissolution of the NDP on grounds of political corruption in Egypt. It has also established itself as the official headquarters of the counter-revolution.

3. The dismantling of the state security service who are working in the interest of the Mubarak regime in order to spread chaos and sectarian tension and who, regrettably, possess all the necessary tools for sabotage, such as intelligence information, arms, expertise, agents and money.

4. The precautionary arrest of senior officials from the corrupt Mubarak regime in order to process them for trial. How is it that Gamal Mubarak can roam freely between Cairo and Sharm el-Sheikh to hold working meetings with his aides? What do we expect the purpose of

these meetings to be? Nothing but plotting against the revolutionary government and the armed forces in order to avenge his father who was deposed by the revolution.

5. The dismissal of all those officials who belong politically to the corrupt Mubarak regime, such as university and college deans and provincial governors, and their replacement by independent, clean and honest people.

6. The restoration of security in Egypt by working to get the police to take up their duties again. This can be achieved by a campaign of purging and appreciation, i.e., purging the police of their corrupt elements and putting on trial the criminal officers who have killed Egyptians with live ammunition, and at the same time showing our appreciation for the honest officers who have carried out their duties under difficult circumstances and whom the Mubarak regime wronged as it did the rest of the Egyptian population. Many ideas have been put forward to solve the police issue, including making use of law graduates and reassigning the military patrols for police work.

These demands have been made time and again to the military council but it has taken no steps to implement them. Supporters of the old regime are now plotting faster than ever and they will not hold back from setting all of Egypt aflame in order to restore their former power and to avoid prosecution. With my full appreciation and respect for the military council, we hope that it will not put off taking steps to protect the revolution. Protecting the revolution is a national duty that the armed forces must not hesitate to carry out.

Democracy is the answer.

RH

The Writing on the Wall

19 April 2011

The moment the former president Hosni Mubarak felt a twinge in his chest, he was rushed to the military wing of the Sharm el-Sheikh International Hospital, where all the necessary x-rays and tests were carried out. The results showed a slight heart arrhythmia, which the doctors were able to treat and regulate. At around seven o'clock in the evening, the director of the hospital carried out another examination on the former president. As he removed his stethoscope, the director turned to him and said: "Sir, your health is perfect, thank God. You just need a few days' peace and quiet."

Mubarak nodded and thanked the director.

"I'll leave you alone now, sir, so that you can get some rest. I will be back in the morning, but there are two nurses here for you. If you want anything, sir, just ring the bell."

Mubarak was stretched out on the bed, wearing blue silk pyjamas. His hair was dyed the usual pitch-black colour. He looked around him. The room was clean and airy and equipped with every mod con: a fridge, a huge flat-screen television and a laptop computer. There was also a sofa and comfortable seats for the visitors, and shade-giving plants grew in pots against the wall facing his bed. The lighting in the room was dim. The former president could control the strength of the light with a dial on the wall next to him, but he felt more comfortable in the gloom. Mubarak felt at ease there and thought that the doctors and nurses in the hospital were treating him with love and respect.

He said to himself: "They represent the majority of Egyptians who still love me and appreciate all that I have done for this country; unlike those shady elements that took part in the demonstrations on 25 January. Those demonstrators are all agents of foreign security agencies set on destroying Egypt. They have been spreading chaos throughout Egypt in the name of their so-called 'revolution'. Now they want to put me on trial. Well, they're welcome to try! Let's see if they are clever enough to find the accounts and assets in my name."

The former president snuggled down in his bed. He folded his hands across his chest and gazed up at the ceiling. He was just drifting off to sleep when he became aware of some strange blue lights that started flashing around the room like searchlights. Mubarak jolted upright in bed and stared in astonishment at the moving lights. Suddenly, an unknown voice called to him: "You can only hear me, you cannot see me."

Mubarak shuddered. He reached out to ring the bell for the nurse, but it did not work.

"There is no point trying to summon help. No one can save you," warned the voice.

Fear spread quickly across Mubarak's face. He looked up and in a hoarse voice asked: "Who are you and what do you want?"

"Who I am is not important. I have come to speak to you about the trial which you will face," said the voice.

"I am ready to go on trial. I have full faith that the judiciary will find me innocent."

"You are obviously feeling reassured now that your American lawyer has removed your name from any foreign bank accounts. I do not forgive you."

At this Mubarak started to yell in anger, but the voice said: "Calm yourself and keep your voice down. You are not being put on trial just for the money that you stole. You were not a bank manager but the president of Egypt for thirty years during which you ran the country into the ground."

Mubarak looked shocked and offered nervously: "The whole world has seen the good that I have done for Egypt."

There was the sound of laughter in the room, and then the voice said: "I have come today to share with you some of these great achievements. I have put together a special presentation. Look over there, look."

All of a sudden, the faces of boys and girls, children no older than ten, flashed upon the wall. The faces stared fixedly into the distance as if they could see something others could not. Their faces were extremely pale and many of them had lost their hair and were bald. The sight of them was unnerving. The voice said sorrowfully: "These are just some of the thousands of children afflicted by cancer while you were in office as a result of the carcinogenic pesticides and substandard food which your cronies imported and sold to the Egyptian people."[1]

"I was not responsible for that," Mubarak stuttered.

"So you are still stubborn? Do you deny knowing who imported the carcinogenic pesticides and who protected them from punishment?"

Mubarak flashed an angry look, as if to say that he would not reply to this. The voice continued: "Now look again, the picture has changed."

Instead of the faces of sick children, there were now men and woman with swollen bodies and blue faces whose eyes looked as cold as those of the dead.

"These are some of the people who died in the sinking of *MS al-Salam Boccaccio 98*.[2] Do you recall them?"

"I had nothing to do with their deaths," said Mubarak.

"But you are the cause of all their woes. It was due to the injustice they faced in Egypt that they travelled to the Gulf in search of work. They were treated badly and were humiliated by their bosses when they got there, and then were drowned on their way back by your regime. I believe you know who owned the ferry, who their partners were and where they are now. When the families of the victims held a demonstration demanding the corpses to be brought up from the wreck, they were harshly attacked and beaten up by the state security forces.

"That was regrettable," said the former president.

"What is regrettable is that you did not acknowledge the depth of the catastrophe and instead of going to meet the victims' families to show your respect, you went to watch the national football team practice. A video has

1 Youssef Wali, the former deputy prime minister and minister of agriculture and land reclamation, was accused of importing substandard food products and accepting bribes to import carcinogenic French pesticides into Egypt.

2 A passenger ferry that sank on 3 February 2006 in the Red Sea en route from Saudi Arabia to Egypt, carrying Egyptian workers and pilgrims returning from Mecca. The owners were eventually put on trial on charges of corruption and negligence.

also emerged of you making light of the ferry of death catastrophe, laughing heartily as if those who died were not human beings."

Hosni Mubarak said nothing for a moment or two and then asked: "Please can you leave me now, I would like to sleep."

"No. You have not seen all that I came here to show you. Look."

Now the image on the wall changed to naked men's bodies, with visible signs of beating, strung up by the feet like animals in a slaughterhouse.

"This is just a sample of the tens of thousands who were hideously tortured by the state security service," said the voice.

Mubarak looked and saw a group of soldiers trying to rip the clothes off a woman. The woman was struggling and screaming.

Hosni Mubarak gulped. The voice continued: "This is what the state security service was doing in your era. They abused women in front of their husbands in order to break them and make them confess to what they wanted."

Mubarak was silent, as if he was aware that there was no point in objecting. The voice carried on: "Look now. This is your last great achievement."

The images of the torture victims disappeared and were replaced by the face of scores of young men and women, their heads and torsos pierced by bullets. They all had the same calm expression on their faces, as if they were at ease and were now resting. The voice said: "You are the first president of Egypt to have killed Egyptians with live ammunition and the first president to use snipers against his people. These are all your victims during the revolution – many hundreds of Egyptians lost their sight to rubber bullets and the number of dead is in the thousands. Then there are the thousands who have disappeared and who, we will discover, have been killed. That is your achievement."

Mubarak said nothing, but the voice went on: "I want you to put yourself in the shoes of one of the mothers of Egypt who has lost their child. Just think how hard they worked to raise their children and how proud they would have been when they finished school. But you shattered their dreams and killed them in order to stay in power and hand it over to your son."

"Shut up. Please leave me alone," yelled Mubarak.

"I only speak the truth," replied the voice.

Clearly ruffled by the accusations, Mubarak shouted: "Even if I did make mistakes, I was fighting to defend Egypt."

"You did your duty in the armed forces, no more and no less, but that will not make us forgive the crimes you committed against Egypt over the past thirty years. You were not fighting alone, but were joined by thousands of officers and soldiers, many of whom fought better than you. Do you remember General Saad el-Shazly?"[1]

1 General Saad el-Shazly was a military commander and Egypt's chief of staff during the October War. Following his public criticism of the Camp David Accords, he was dismissed from his post as ambassador to Britain and Portugal, then sent into exile in Algeria.

"No comment"

"El-Shazly was a national hero. He was the chief of staff credited with the 'High Minarets' operation that led to the army's victory in the 1973 war.[1] What did you do to el-Shazly? You prevented him from being honoured and even forbad mention of his name. You put him in prison with no regard whatsoever for his honourable military record."

Mubarak put his hands over his ears and started shouting at the top of his voice: "I told you, I don't want to listen."

Suddenly the lights came on in the room and the two nurses appeared with the hospital director behind them. They seemed alarmed. The director rushed over to Mubarak and said: "I hope you are alright, sir."

Mubarak sighed and mumbled: "There are moving images on that wall which I don't wish to see, doctor. Please help me."

The doctor looked at the wall but saw nothing. He gave Mubarak a knowing look and whispered something to one of the nurses who swiftly took out a syringe from one of the drawers and handed it to the doctor, who said: "If you don't mind, sir, I'm going to give you something to calm you down and help you to sleep."

"I don't want to see those pictures again."

The doctor smiled and said: "I can reassure you, sir, that you will not see them again."

The director stepped closer to Mubarak and slowly gave him the injection. He stood by his side waiting for it to take effect. After just a few minutes Hosni Mubarak's body gradually started to go limp, his eyes closed and he fell into a deep sleep.

Democracy is the answer.

RH

Walk Like an Egyptian, Roar Like a Lion

26 April 2011

Professor Denis Weber was regarded as one of the most important histology specialists in the world. During the 1980s and 1990s there was hardly a histology journal that did not include a paper written by him.

It was my happy fortune to have studied under this great man at Illinois University in the United States, and to have him supervise my Master's thesis. During one of his seminars, he asked our small group of advanced

1 Part of the Egyptian military operation to cross the Suez Canal and seize the Bar-Lev Line of Israeli fortifications on 6 October 1973.

medical students to read certain papers and to give a précis of them to our colleagues. He would discuss the papers with us and then evaluate our performance himself. Two weeks after the start of term, Professor Weber asked us to share our opinions on his course. I was astonished by his request as I could not find fault with any of his teachings. The other students, however, took it in turns to honestly evaluate the seminars, criticising the amount of papers they were asked to read which they considered to be off-topic. A female student added that she would like more explanation from Professor Weber because he often rushed over some of the points assuming that we had understood them.

Comments about Professor Weber's teaching methods came forth thick and fast, with him listening carefully and noting them all down. Finally he responded to some of the comments and promised to remedy his mistakes, adding that some of our requests could not be granted for various reasons. At the end of the class he smiled and told us: "I thank you all for your comments. They have been most useful for me."

I left the class with questions ringing in my head. Why would a great professor take the trouble to listen to criticism from first-year students who were of little consequence when compared to his lofty position in academia? Why did Professor Weber consider the students' critique of his teaching methods to be of use rather than deeming them uppity or arrogant?

Professor Weber, like most great intellectuals, was a polite and humble man, but there was an objective reason for his behaviour: he grew up in a democratic society where authority is linked to responsibility and respect for others. In an authoritarian society, however, authority is measured by the amount of power it wields.

A democratic official has respect for people's dignity and listens with interest to their opinions, always trying to respond to their requests. They are not afraid to overturn a decision that they have made in error. An authoritarian official imposes his decisions on people by force, rejecting all criticism of his behaviour. They will not acknowledge any mistakes, especially if they feel it will damage their reputation.

This disparity in attitudes towards power is evident in the behaviour of the rulers themselves. An elected democratic ruler understands that their subjects have granted the power and that they have been appointed to serve the people and fulfil their needs. An authoritarian ruler takes power and hangs onto it through force. It follows that the people's needs are of little interest to him compared to his need to control the oppressive organs of state as the sole guarantor of his rule.

That was Hosni Mubarak's concept of rule. He never paid any respect to the will or the dignity of the Egyptians and never missed a chance to sneer at them or belittle them. Mubarak cared only for himself and his prestige consisted of his ability to impose what he wanted on Egyptians even if it was against their wishes or interest.

Mubarak treated his subjects as if they were minors, incapable of knowing what was good for them. He openly stated that the only alternative to his rule was anarchy because the Egyptian people were incapable of governing themselves in a democratic system. During his thirty-year dictatorship, Hosni Mubarak effectively brought the country to its knees through poor leadership and bad decisions. When the revolution broke out, millions of Egyptians took to the streets to demand change, chanting: "Change! Freedom! Social Justice!"

Egyptians have paid a crushing price for the revolution: hundreds of people have been killed and injured, and thousands are still missing. The armed forces agreed to protect the revolution during the transitional period to democracy and the Egyptian people feel a sense of gratitude towards them and the great role they have played. However, the announcement of the new provincial governors last week dealt a considerable blow to the revolution, making it feel as if Hosni Mubarak was still ruling Egypt.

Most of the new governors are people from the corrupt Mubarak regime, including some who are guilty of falsifying election results and financial corruption. Others used the security service to arrest student political activists within the sacrosanct compounds of mosques, or are themselves former offices of the state security service that have tortured and abused fellow Egyptians. Ayman Nour, head of the Tomorrow Party,[1] has accused the governor of Qena, Emad Shehata Michael, of having personally supervised his beating and torture in 2007. Instead of being put on trial for their horrendous crimes, the state security officers are being rewarded and appointed as governors.

Egyptians expected the revolutionary government to make the position of provincial governor directly electable, as is the case in all countries where democracy is respected. Elections are the best way of showing whether someone is competent and of respecting the will of the citizens. Some might argue that present conditions do not allow for the election of provincial governors, but it would still have been possible, at the very least, to choose new candidates with a clean background who have not participated in corruption, repression or vote rigging. I cannot understand the reasons behind appointing these governors and cannot help but ask who chose them.

Was it the military council or the government? Does the individual who drew up this list live in such isolation that they have not heard of the revolution? Or is it a reminder that even though the revolution toppled Mubarak, it

1 The Tomorrow Party, also known as Al-Ghad, was established in 2004 by Ayman Nour, a former New Wafd parliamentarian. The party was sidelined from the political scene during Mubarak's last years in office due to internal splits and legal battles. It reemerged again as a licensed political party on 9 October 2011 under the name Ghad Al-Thawra Party (*Revolution's Tomorrow Party*).

will not be able to change the way jobs are handed out as rewards for loyalty rather than ability?

It was natural that violent demonstrations would break out in numerous governorates over the appointment of these governors. The demonstrations in Qena in particular reached a worrying level as the decision to appoint a governor lacked sensitivity and an understanding of the region. The power of the great tribes in Qena has put paid to any concept of independent civil society. Everything that takes place in Qena is decided by the tribal leaders and carried out by their tribe members. In addition to that, like all the other governorates in Upper Egypt, it experienced an obscene level of injustice in the Mubarak era. The levels of unemployment and poverty in the region confirm that the state is neither interested in the population of Upper Egypt nor does it care about their suffering. All these factors have led to mass demonstrations in Qena, but the Egyptian government is dealing with the crisis in the old manner: it is acting as if nothing has happened. When the demonstrations started becoming serious the government tried to diffuse the anger by setting up discussion committees, which will inevitably lead to nothing. Discussions with the authorities, unless they are binding, are like whistling in the wind. As the demonstrations increased in Qena, Yehia el-Gamal[1] came out in defence of the decision, and declared: "The new governor of Qena is staying in his job. He has not, and will not, tender his resignation."

El-Gamal was sending a clear message to the people of Qena: "Your opinion is worthless and will have no effect. I make the decisions, and whether you like it or not, you will accept everything I decree."

This is the dictatorial logic prevalent before the revolution, which is now redundant after the fall of Mubarak. The moment Yehia el-Gamal's statement was broadcast, demonstrations in Qena quickly spread to new areas across Upper Egypt. The state security service and remnants of the NDP took advantage of the crisis and steered the demonstrations in a violent and dangerous direction by instructing their supporters to shut down the railways and motorways. Then some extremist agents of the state security service were paid to give the problem a sectarian hue by posing as demonstrators and declaring that they were rejecting the new governor because he was a disbelieving Copt. Then, in an unprecedented act, the extremists held up the flag of the Kingdom of Saudi Arabia instead of the flag of Egypt, their own country. The wrong choice of governors, the government's hesitation and el-Gamal's provocative statements have all provided a golden opportunity for people to conspire against the revolution by creating anarchy and inflaming sectarian strife. We ask the much admired prime minister, Essam Sharaf, to take a clear position on this crisis. As prime minister of the revolution, does

1 Yehia el-Gamal is an Egyptian lawyer and politician who served as the deputy prime minister under both Ahmed Shafik and Essam Sharaf.

he agree with the appointment of governors accused of torture, murder and corruption? And why was the list of appointees not rescinded the moment problems arose?

Egypt has entered a new era, one where there is no fear, no servility and no humiliation. Anyone who tries to ignore this truth will find it thrust upon them by the Egyptian people. In revolutionary Egypt it will no longer be possible to impose wrongful and corrupt decisions on the people using force. Henceforth no power will be able to impose what they do not wish on the millions of Egyptians who stood and faced death on the streets for the sake of freedom.

Tenaciously clinging to an unjust and mistaken decision by claiming to be safeguarding the state's prestige is an erroneous and out-dated concept. Respectable countries gain prestige by respecting the will of their citizens and not by authoritarianism. Even the simplest citizen, be he a street-sweeper, will have the right to criticise the head of state and hold them to account for their policies and decisions. When the people decide that they do not want some official or other, no matter what his position, that person should not stay in their job a single day longer. Power belongs to the Egyptian people alone, and the will of the people supersedes all other authority. When we speak, you have to listen.

Democracy is the answer.

RH

How Did the Revolution Reach Montreal?

3 May 2011

The affair started with three Canadian authors: Linda Leith, Ann Charney and Mary Soderstrom. Years ago they met and decided to set up a Canadian literary festival called Metropolis Blue whose aim was to allow the public to meet authors from all over the world and to hold public readings and discussions. In April 1999 the first Metropolis Blue literary festival was held in the city of Montreal. The festival was a success and year after year it garnered international recognition and became one of the most important literary festivals in the world. Every year the festival awards international prizes for works written in Western languages. In 2007 the festival decided to dedicate an important annual award to Arabic literature, with the support of the Abu Dhabi Authority for Culture and Heritage and named in honour of the Emirati poet al-Majidi ibn Dhaher who lived at the end of the seventeenth century. The principal criterion for the prize is literary excellence, associated with the quality of a body of work, publication history, and the international reception of the work. In recent years the highly regarded prize has been won by great literary figures such as the Lebanese novelist Elias Khoury,[1] the Syrian author Zakariya Tamer[2] and the Iraqi poet Saadi Yousef.[3] This year the jury chose me, thank God, as the first Egyptian author to win the Metropolis Blue Arab Literary Prize. I travelled to Montreal and accepted the prize in a wonderful ceremony organised by the festival committee. A Canadian actress was chosen to read out excerpts from my work in French and English. The audience were a mixture of foreigners and Arabs, including the Egyptian ambassador to Canada, Wael Abu al-Magd, who is much loved and respected in Canada. I gave a speech thanking the audience and the jury for awarding the prize to me. I also had the opportunity to speak with the ambassador about literature and the revolution in Egypt.

The Canadian writers I met were in awe of the Egyptian revolution. One author approached me and said: "You have made history in Egypt. For the first time after the success of the revolution, we saw revolutionaries cleaning the streets. You should be proud to be Egyptian because we are all very proud of you."

Canada is considered an example of a democratic state whose citizens include immigrants of all creeds and colours, but they are all equal before the law. They have a unified law on the role of religion that applies to everyone without discrimination. A Muslim has the right to build a mosque according to the same regulations that apply to churches or synagogues. There is a long-established Jewish community in Canada. Since the 1970s, steady streams of Jewish immigrants have settled in the country, mostly from eastern Europe. A number of the Jewish practices and customs, particularly those of the ultra-Orthodox Jews, have set the Jewish community apart from other Canadians. After sunset on Fridays, they do not use electricity, cars or anything that works with a motor. Despite the unusual nature of these customs, the state respects the Jews' right to practice religion as they so wish. However, there is an ongoing conflict between these ultra-Orthodox Jews and the Canadian government that demonstrates the limits of the civil state when trying to interfere with the lives of its citizens.

These Jews leave their cars on the Sabbath in places where parking is prohibited and as a result they have to pay parking fines. The Jewish community have tried many times to be absolved from these fines on the basis that their religion does not allow them to drive their cars on the Sabbath. However, the

1 Elias Khoury is a Lebanese novelist, playwright, critic and a prominent public intellectual. He has published ten novels, which have been translated into several foreign languages, as well as several works of literary criticism.

2 Zakariya Tamer is one of the most widely read and translated short story writers in the Arab world, as well as being the foremost author of children's stories in Arabic.

3 Saadi Yousef is an Iraqi author, poet, journalist, publisher, and political activist. He has published thirty volumes of poetry and seven books of prose.

Canadian government has insisted upon collecting these fines because the law has to be applied to everyone without discrimination. Another incident: the Jewish community has received government support to build a hospital. Most of the people who work in the hospital are Jewish and observe the tenets of their religion. On one occassion, a Christian patient came to the hospital for treatment and his family gave him pork sandwiches (which is restricted in Jewish dietary laws). There was an argument between the hospital administration and the patient who insisted upon eating his pork sandwiches, and he was promptly transferred to another hospital.

At this point the Canadian government intervened and demanded that the Jewish hospital either change its policy towards non-Jewish patients or risk losing all of their government funding. The hospital administration complied with government instructions and stopped interfering in the choices of the non-Jewish patients. The concept here is that the civil state (which we are demanding in Egypt) is not a state that positions itself for or against religion. The civil state is a neutral entity in which religion and politics are separate form each other, and which gives all citizens equal rights, regardless of religion, colour or sex. If a state has a confessional tinge, or is biased towards one particular religion, it would not be able to apply the law with impartiality. My Canadian friends told me that the Muslim community in Canada does not cause any problems, respects the law and is looked upon favorably by Canadian society.

The day after I received the award, I was invited to a meeting organised by the Egyptian Association of the Egyptian Students' Union in Montreal. The meeting took place in a large hall that was full to the gunnels with scores of Egyptians from the whole gamut of Egyptian life abroad: young and old people, women in veils and uncovered, Copts and Muslims. The hall was brimming with enthusiasm for the revolution. An Egyptian woman in a hijab stood at the front of the crowd and led the chanting of revolutionary slogans. Then we all sang "Biladi, biladi" [the Egyptian national anthem], and stood for a moment of silence in memory of those who gave their lives for the revolution. The Egyptians in Montreal are fine examples of Egyptians. They have been living in Canada for a long time and many of them are well-educated and work in high profile jobs. The revolution has had a great effect on them, bringing them all together for the first time. When the events of 25 January took place, they all spontaneously went to a pro-revolution demonstration in front of the consulate. It was here that the Egyptian Association in Montreal was formed. They now meet once a week, come rain or shine, to swap news and discuss the latest events in Egypt. The people at the meeting had followed the events in Egypt as closely as if they lived there, and had many questions about the future of the revolution. I quoted to them the wonderful statement made by Pope Shenouda III: "Egypt is not a country we live in but a country which lives in us."

The Egyptians in Canada are happy that, for the first time, they can practise their right to vote in the parliamentary and presidential elections, but all of them, and particularly the Copts, are worried about the sudden prominence of the Muslim Brotherhood and the fundamentalist Islamic associations. I told them that we have to differentiate between the Muslim Brotherhood and the fundamentalist Wahhabis. The Brotherhood, in spite of my differences with some of their philosophy and political positions, believe in the rules of democracy and are not extremists, having given up violence in the 1960s. Thus it is their right to form their political parties, which can be compared in some ways to the right-wing Christian parties in the West.

Of course the fundamentalist Wahhabi associations have the right to express their thoughts, but those thoughts are often reactionary and not suitable for modern times. I would ask all those who accuse me of being unreasonable to read the religious edicts of Sheikh ibn Baz and other imams who consider democracy an un-Islamic principle. They do not condone demonstrating or strikes and dictate obedience to a Muslim ruler even if they are unjust. They would ban males and females from mixing together in school or at work, and consider music and other artistic expressions, such as sculpture, theatre and cinema, un-Islamic. In addition, the Wahhabi associations (except for the death by torture of Sayyid Bilal[1]) worked in complete collaboration with the state security service for a long time. I firmly believe that the sudden appearance of the extremist Wahhabis is not serendipitous, but has been deliberately orchestrated by the regime. In a recent interview with an American television channel, Hosni Mubarak stated: "I want to leave power but I fear the chaos, the extremists and the anti-Coptic animosity which will be set loose in Egypt."

Back in Canada, the discussion moved onto to the subject of Kamilia Shehata[2] and the Christian women who were rumoured to have converted to Islam and whom the church was trying to bring back to its fold. I told them that most of the sectarian problems were brought about by the former regime in an attempt to justify its dictatorial rule, and I stated that in a democratic state freedom of belief is enshrined in the law and that it is not up to the church, Al-Azhar[3] or any other body to try to win back someone who has changed their religion. One of the people present stood up and said: "I am a Copt and I think that the Egyptian church made a mistake in deciding to detain the women

1 Sayed Bilal was a Salafist from Alexandria. He was taken into police custody on 5 January 2011 as a suspect in the bombing of All Saints Church on 1 January 2011. One day later, his body was handed over to his family showing signs of torture. Bilal's murder came less than 20 days before the onset of the 2011 Revolution.

2 Kamilia Shehata's disappearance in July 2010 sparked protests across Egypt. It was believed that she had been held by the Coptic Church after converting to Islam. However, Shehata was discovered on 23 July at the home of a friend in Cairo and denied being kidnapped. The incident inflamed sectarian tensions between Egypt's Muslim majority and Coptic Christian minority.

3 The prestigious university mosque of Al-Azhar, situated in Cairo, is the foremost centre of religious learning in the Muslim world and plays a significant religious, intellectual and political role in Egypt.

who were rumoured to have embraced Islam. Kamilia Shehata should stand in front of everyone and declare her belief. If she is a Muslim then no one has the right to detain or punish her. If she is a Christian then those people who accused the church of abducting her should be put on trial."

Those present applauded heartily and I felt myself transported back to Tahrir Square when the Copts all held hands to form a human chain to defend the Muslims who had gathered to say their prayers en masse, or when the Copts said Mass before Friday prayers. At the end of the meeting, people crowded around me, asking me what they could do to help the revolution. They all wanted to do something for Egypt. I told them that with the will of God they would be the strength that Egypt needs to move to the future. I told them that Egypt will not go backwards, will not be defeated or broken so long as there are devoted and wonderful Egyptians like them.

Democracy is the answer.

RH

Who Is Pushing Egypt Towards Chaos?

10 May 2011

Last month I had dinner near Al-Hussein Mosque in the old city. I chatted with the waiting staff at the restaurant and was surprised when one of them said to me: "If you go to Al-Hussein Square, be on your guard. These days it's full of thugs and criminals."

When I asked him why the police didn't arrest them, he replied: "I asked the chief of the local police the same thing. He told me that he knows each and every one of these individuals but that he has received orders not to arrest them no matter what they do."

A similar thing happened to the well-known Egyptian writer Medhat El Adl when he was in Sharm el-Sheikh. He saw thugs sexually harassing some female tourists and went to report the incident at the local police station. The officer in charge said to him: "Before the revolution, we used to arrest such people and make them leave the city, but now we aren't allowed to take them on."

This is difficult to believe because there is nothing preventing the police from enforcing the law; they simply do not want to carry out their duties. There are robberies and assaults against Egyptians every day, yet the police are doing nothing to prevent these crimes. The thugs are attacking everything in Egypt: police stations, courthouses, even churches and hospitals. When armed thugs stormed Al-Matariyyah Hospital and terrorised doctors and patients for four hours, the police looked on impassively and did not act. The thugs opened fire at the hospital and killed one patient and left one of the doctors with a deep wound to his foot. The bottom line is that the police force in Egypt is broken: they neither want to protect the people, nor to perform their duties.

There is a culture of disdain for ordinary people in the police force and many police officers believe that security can only be achieved through violence, oppression and torture. As such, many officers in the police force view the success of the revolution as a victory against them and a direct blow to their self-esteem. They consider themselves above the law and, not knowing how to treat citizens respectfully, their response has been to refrain from giving protection to the Egyptian people. The police are punishing Egyptians for rising up in revolution and are offering them a stark choice between being repressed and abused by them, or being terrorised by thugs and criminals.

Furthermore, many police officers were involved in corrupt practices under the old regime. They were getting large sums of money through illegal means until the revolution put an end to this. They had grown accustomed to having these extra sources of income, but now must make do with their basic salaries and this has made them resent carrying out their work.

The police force has been badly managed. The minister of the interior, Mansour el-Essawy, is a decent man, who does not have blood on his hands, but he has failed to clean up the police force and get it functioning normally again. Most of el-Essawy's current assistants are the very same ones that worked for the former minister of the interior, who is currently on trial charged with corruption and the killing of demonstrators. A number of senior police officials who have been accused of the killing of demonstrators have not been suspended from their posts. One such individual is Farouk Lashin, who is the former director of security for Al Sharqia Governorate. He was referred for trial on the charge of killing demonstrators, but instead of suspending him from his position, he was promoted to the post of director of security for Giza Governorate. Such practices are indefensible and they reveal much about the situation in Egypt right now. What confidence can we have in a police official who is charged with killings but who, nevertheless, remains in his job? Does it not seem likely that he might use his position to destroy any evidence that might otherwise be used to convict him? Similarly, it is also extraordinary that many officers of the state security service, who tortured people for years, are still in their jobs as though the slate has been wiped clean – perhaps this is because the organisation changed its name to Homeland Security. What can we expect from such officers whose entire expertise consists of beating up citizens, hanging them by their feet and torturing them? Is it possible that such officers can change overnight from being torturers to upstanding investigators that respect the rule of law and human rights? Of course, there are many police officers who are not corrupt, who do not torture people, nor kill demonstrators. Some of these upstanding officers formed the Police Officers Coalition[1]. They met with el-Essawy to present a number of proposals designed to rid the force of corrupt officers; the minister, however, did not make use of these proposals and, unfortunately, nothing was implemented.

Not all of the bad things we see happening now in Egypt can be blamed on the inaction of the police, of course; a wider conspiracy is being implemented that seeks to drag Egypt into a state of complete disorder. The enemies of the revolution desire such conditions as a prelude for achieving what they ultimately want. Both domestic and foreign elements are involved in this conspiracy. The principal characters of the old regime are currently in prison pending their trials, but their supporters are abroad and ready to spend millions of dollars in order to sabotage the revolution. There is no doubt that they are in collusion with elements from state security that have all the necessary means to bring ruin to Egypt. These elements have detailed intelligence about every institution in Egypt and they have expertise, weapons and agents planted everywhere. As for the foreign elements that are plotting against the revolution, the first amongst these is Israel, a country that supported Hosni Mubarak till the bitter end. Israel has made clear that it is unhappy about the changes in Egyptian foreign policy since the revolution. For the first time in decades, Egypt is now pursuing its own national interests without consenting to Israel's demands. Egypt is negotiating the sale of gas to Israel at a fair price, has decided to reopen the Rafah border crossing in order to break the siege against the Palestinians in Gaza and is making efforts to repair its severed relations with Iran. It would be naive to imagine that Israel, which has one of the most powerful intelligence agencies in the world, will look on idly as Egypt rises and becomes a powerful democratic state that can threaten Israeli interests.

There are also the ruling families in the Gulf States who have defended Hosni Mubarak and made every effort to waylay his trial. These regimes in the Gulf are against the Egyptian revolution and have come to the aid of Hosni Mubarak, not just because he was their friend and lucrative business partner, but because they fear that the revolution is setting an example for the rest of the Arab world. They find it troubling that Egypt could overthrow a corrupt and oppressive president, give him a fair trial and convict him. They do not want a revolutionary movement to reach the oil-rich Gulf countries, which are still organised along tribal lines. The ruler of the state is the patriarch and elder of the tribe. The people are not allowed to go against them or criticise

1 A group of disenchanted police officers that lobbied for official recognition as a police union with an elected leadership. Their initiatives icluded: cleansing the police force of corrupt generals; improving work conditions; training; and increasing salaries and pensions.

their policies no matter how unsound or oppressive they are. For decades, the Salafist groups in Egypt have had close ties with both Egypt's security services as well as the Saudi regime; this might help explain why these groups are now playing a significant role in recent acts of destruction.

One important consideration remains: the Egyptian armed forces undertook to protect the revolution and pledged to fulfil all of its demands. Egyptians will never forget the great role played by the armed forces, but their handling of the riots has been dangerously inconsistent from one incident to the next. The military police were heavy-handed when they broke up the student sit-in at the Faculty of Mass Communications at Cairo University, using stun batons to remove the students. Similarly, on 9 March of this year, the military police arrested demonstrators in Tahrir Square and handed them over to military courts that subsequently sentenced them to prison terms ranging from one to three years. On the other hand, however, the army did not resort to this kind of excessive force when they encountered other, more serious incidents. In Qena Governorate, for example, where citizens obstructed the train line and blocked off the highways, the military police did not intervene or make any arrests. Some of the Salafists in Qena carried out an attack against a Coptic citizen and cut off his ear, yet the perpetrator was not even arrested. The only consequence was a reconciliation session in which the Copt waived his rights.

When a church was being destroyed in the city of Atfih, the military police did not intervene to prevent it, nor did they arrest any of the perpetrators. While it is true that the armed forces rebuilt the church at their own expense, which was a good thing to do, nevertheless, justice is not done unless the law is properly enforced. The Salafists have burned down holy shrines in numerous governorates and not one of them has been arrested. This has only encouraged some of the Salafists to up the ante: they besieged a cathedral and threatened to storm it in order to free Kamilia Shetata, the Christian woman whom they claim converted to Islam and was being held prisoner by the Coptic Church. Forcing your way into houses of worship and terrorising peaceful people that are simply engaged in prayer is a crime that should be punished under the law. Again, the military police has not arrested a single person in connection with these attacks on churches, but have imposed a ban which stops them from entering.

It soon became clear that the Salafist claims about Kamilia Shetata were false when she appeared on a Coptic television channel denying that she had ever converted to Islam and stating that she would continue to be a Christian. The very next day, however, a new rumour was spread about another Christian woman who had converted to Islam and was then forcibly held by the Coptic Church. In response to this rumour, a video recording taken from a Paltalk chat room was then circulated on a number of websites which showed an individual imploring fellow Muslims to attack Saint Mina Church in the district of Imbaba. He assures them that the Muslim woman is being held in a house next to the church and calls on Muslims to search the house in order to locate her. He gives the audience directions to the church and says: "Raid the house. Remove every Christian you find inside and question them. There are 300 of you out there so it should be easy."

Groups of armed men in masks attacked Saint Mina Church and set fire to it. They pulled back when gunfire started to be exchanged, and when the battle ended after several hours 11 people were dead – both Muslims and Christians.

This raises some questions: if the Egyptian police are inoperative and cannot be relied upon, then why did the military police not step in to stop the thugs from attacking the church? Why did they not use the stun batons to suppress them like they did at the Faculty of Mass Communications? Which is more serious: a peaceful sit-in by students, or attacking a church and torching it? Our armed forces have long protected Egypt and have embraced the revolution. Now, however, we need them to carry out another important task for the nation: to enforce the law, immediately and decisively, against anyone who breaks it. Right now, Egypt is faced with only two options: either establishing the rule of law or sliding into chaos.

Democracy is the answer.

AB

Who Killed General al-Batran?

17 May 2011

The late police general, Mohamed al-Batran, was head of the prisons department at the Ministry of the Interior, a senior security position that made him responsible for all Egyptian prisons. He was known for his diligence, integrity and competence, and his death in the early days of the revolution was considered both tragic and mysterious.

After the revolution broke out on 25 January, the Ministry of the Interior, under the leadership of Habib el-Adly, committed horrendous crimes in an attempt to quell the uprising, even using professional snipers to kill unarmed demonstrators; raising the death toll to 1,000 people, not to mention the swathes of people who lost their sight to rubber bullets. On top of this, thousands of people remain missing; they are believed to be detained in secret facilities, or else dead and buried in unmarked graves.

On 27 January, the Mubarak regime carried out a shocking, criminal act intended to put an end to the Egyptian revolution: el-Adly and his subordinates opened the prisons and allowed the inmates to escape in an attempt to punish the Egyptian people and deter them from demonstrating. The prison officers would provoke the prisoners into rioting, then open fire on them before opening the prison gates; in that way, the officers received protection, for they could say under questioning that they resisted the prisoners, but in the end could not stop them escaping.

According to a report in the newspaper *Al Shorouk*, el-Adly insisted the plan to free the prisoners be carried out and asked his senior officers to send any officers who failed to carry out orders to court martial, or to kill them if necessary. Since General al-Batran was in charge of the prisons in Egypt, it would have been impossible to release the prisoners unless he either agreed or was removed. The general's sister, Manal al-Batran, asserts that her brother knew of el-Adly's plan to release prisoners and refused to carry it out.

On the evening of 27 January, General al-Batran heard that a riot had broken out in Al-Fayoum prison, so he headed there at once to get the situation under control. He did not leave until he was certain that all of the prisoners were back in their cells under lock and key. General al-Batran had foiled el-Adly's plan, and no prisons were emptied over the following two days thanks to his vigilance and dedication to duty. At this point, el-Adly and his aides realised that al-Batran would prevent them carrying out their plan and must therefore be taken care of.

On the morning of 28 January, General al-Batran called his sister and told her: "Habib el-Adly wants to set the entire country ablaze." At six o'clock in the evening, the general was told that another riot had broken out, this time in Al-Qata prison in Qalyoubia Governorate, so he headed there at once. While he was en route, a senior official in the Ministry of the Interior advised him to go home, saying the situation was now under control. Al-Batran, knowing that in his absence the prisoners would be allowed to escape, hastened towards the prison to carry out his duty. He arrived to find the prisoners in a state of uproar because one of the prison officers had opened fire and killed a prisoner. General al-Batran was furious and shouted at the officer: "How could you kill an unarmed prisoner? I'll have you court-martialled and I'll prosecute you myself!"

Al-Batran gave strict orders to the officers in all the guard towers around the prison not to open fire under any circumstances, then he bravely went in unarmed to meet with the prisoners. He managed to calm them down and persuaded the prisoners to return to their cells. When el-Adly's followers realised that their plan was about to fail a second time, the officer who had killed the prisoner gave the order to one of his colleagues to open fire. The shooter fired two rounds which killed General al-Batran on the spot. By assassinating al-Batran, the biggest obstacle to el-Adly's plan was removed;

the prisons of Egypt were thrown open and 24,000 convicts were allowed to escape.

Manal al-Batran, has since accused two officers working at the Al-Qata prison of killing her brother. She has identified them by name in several reports submitted to the attorney general and has supported her allegations with the recorded testimonies of numerous prisoners. I myself have seen the video recordings in her possession that were also submitted to the attorney general. Thus, while the case itself is clear, the circumstances surrounding the investigation are strange and inscrutable.

In an official statement, the Ministry of the Interior announced that General Mohamed al-Batran was the head of Al-Fayoum prison and that he had been killed by prisoners during their escape. This is blatantly false: he was in fact the head of the prisons department and was killed in Al-Qata prison, not in Al-Fayoum. This erroneous explanation misled public opinion and helped to divert attention away from the actual scene of the crime giving the suspects time to hide incriminating evidence.

Three months after the murder of al-Batran, the Ministry of the Interior has yet to open an investigation into the killing. It is inconceivable that any interior ministry in the world would, when a senior official is killed on duty, would not open an inquiry to discover the truth. This raises the question: has the current minister of the interior, Mansour el-Essawy, even heard about the killing of General al-Batran and, if so, why hasn't he opened an investigation into the crime?

There has also been a distinct lack of cooperation between the attorney general and the Ministry of the Interior over the killing of al-Batran. The general's family asked the attorney general's office to visit Al-Qata prison in order to examine the crime scene and listen to the testimony of its prisoners, but the attorney general's office refused on the grounds that the Ministry of the Interior says the security situation in Al-Qata prison makes an investigation impossible. In light of this we have to ask ourselves: how can prosecutors investigate a complicated murder, like that of General al-Batran, without examining the crime scene? And furthermore: if the security situation in the prison is so bad, why can't military police be brought in to protect the investigators so that they can carry out their work?

The general's family submitted a report to the attorney general's office in which they named two officers from the prisons department as being involved in the murder of al-Batran. Instead of indicting these officers, the attorney general's office merely summoned them to give testimony about the incident. This is strange and inexplicable behavior on the part of the prosecution.

The attorney general's office asked for the police reports about the crime from the very department where the two accused officers work. It is truly incomprehensible that the prosecutor did not realise that the two accused officers would use their influence to distort the report. Did they really believe that the two accused officers would submit any findings that might lead to them being convicted of al-Batran's murder?

The prosecution asked the Ministry of the Interior to listen to the testimony of the prisoners who appear on the video recordings and state that General al-Batran was killed by the two officers named. The ministry, however, responded by sending a letter to the prosecution stating that the testimonies were considered invalid as the prisoners names were not given in full. A few days later, unidentified persons torched the offices of the prisons department, completely destroying the testimonies.

General al-Batran's family subsequently submitted a new statement in which they ask for the Ministry of the Interior to be excluded from the gathering of evidence, since the suspects themselves work for the ministry, and this only serves to compromise its impartiality. The general's family requested that the military police carry out the investigation, but before the attorney general could respond to these requests, the Ministry of the Interior announced – on the very same day – that riots had broken out in Al-Qata prison and the prisoners had been reassigned to a number of other prisons. For this reason, the evidence needed to convict the killers would be scattered and the chance to get justice for al-Batran's family would be lost.

One does not need great intelligence to grasp that there are people working inside the Ministry of the Interior to protect those suspected of killing al-Batran. At this point, we should remind ourselves that most of Habib el-Adly's aides and those loyal to him are still in their jobs; we cannot expect them to cooperate in incriminating themselves. As much as it offers us an inspiring example of a great man carrying out his duty to the end and sacrificing his life for his country's security, the murder of General al-Batran also highlights the problems facing Egypt.

After the revolution overthrew the president, his family and his top aides, for reasons which are not clear the foundations of the regime have remained intact. The heads of the universities and other state institutions, who cooperated with the state security service and who had previously extolled Mubarak and his wife, are still there. Members of the NDP that got their seats on local councils through crooked means have kept their positions. Most of the big players in the media who worked with the state security service, misled the Egyptian people, and who called for the killing of those taking part in the revolution, are also still there. Furthermore, many of the officers of the state security service – who for decades abused Egyptians, tortured and raped them – simply kept their jobs when the state security service was dissolved and rebranded as Homeland Security. Senior officials in the security services who are facing charges of killing demonstrators are, likewise, still in their positions, and some of them have even been promoted. What can we expect from those who support the old regime when they have been allowed to remain in their jobs? Can we expect them to implement the aims of the revolution and bring about changes that would lead to their dismissal and imprisonment?

The logical explanation for what is happening right now is that those who let 24,000 prisoners escape are in contact with these criminals and are instructing them to carry out the acts of destruction we are now witnessing on a daily basis. The security forces look on as Egyptian blood is shed and then, after each massacre, Minister of the Interior el-Essawy comes out to assure us that security will be restored, but it will just take a few months. Meanwhile supporters of the old regime are conspiring to destroy the revolution; they seek to push Egypt further and further towards chaos so that they can escape being brought to justice. The revolution cannot achieve its goals unless all of the corrupt elements that remain loyal to the old regime are rigorously purged from the country's institutions.

We call on the armed forces, which protected the revolution and took the side of the people, to carry out an impartial investigation into the killing of General Mohamed al-Batran. I am certain that the findings of such an investigation would be startling, because those responsible for his killing, and those who are protecting the killer from being brought to justice, are the very same people who are plotting against the country, spreading chaos and trying to bring ruin on it in order to prevent change. But Egypt's future remains bright; no one shall be able to return the country to the old days of oppression.

Democracy is the answer.

AB

Tyranny Begets Tyranny

24 May 2011

This is the story of Ahmed Agiza, one-time leader of the Islamic extremist group known as the Vanguards of Conquest that carried out a number of terrorist attacks both in Egypt and abroad. In 1999 Agiza fled Egypt to seek political asylum in Sweden, but while the Swedish authorities were assessing his application, the Egyptian government issued a notice for his extradition. Human rights organisations in Sweden rallied public opinion against his extradition on account of Egypt's horrendous human rights record. Demonstrators in Sweden demanded that Agiza not be handed over to the Egyptian government because he would be tortured, as was the case with tens of thousands of other Egyptian detainees. The Swedish government was caught between Swedish public opinion and the pressure being exerted by the US government, which insisted Agiza be sent back to Egypt. The Swedish government found a compromise: it obtained a diplomatic assurance from the Egyptian government stating that Agiza would not be tortured, and in 2001, it handed him over.

The Ministry of the Interior in Egypt did not keep its promise and Agiza was brutally tortured on his return. When news of his torture reached Sweden, the demonstrators took to the streets once again to accuse the Swedish government of facilitating the torture of Agiza. The government was forced to apologise and admit that it had made a grave error in handing Agiza over to the Egyptian regime. Subsequently, Ahmed Agiza filed a lawsuit against the Swedish government for aiding his torture and a Swedish judge awarded him the sum of 300,000 euros in damages.[1]

While reading the details of the case, I found myself wondering why were the Swedish people angry with their government for its role in the torture of Ahmed Agiza. The victim was not a Swedish citizen. He wasn't European. He was neither Christian nor Jewish. He had not even been granted political asylum and was really facing terrorism-related charges in Egypt. The answer is that the Swedish demonstrators were not defending Agiza as an individual; they were defending the value of human life itself. A responsible government cannot extradite an individual if they are at risk of torture and degrading treatment. It is a basic human right to be treated equally with respect and dignity. In my opinion, this principle represents the pinnacle of human progress: to defend the right to humane treatment regardless of nationality, religion or political ideology. When will the Egyptian people understand that the value of human life is more important than the opinions an individual may hold? When will we learn that everyone, however different they may be from us, has the same human rights as we do? Does religion not teach us this concept and bring us closer to our own humanity?

The reality is that a true understanding of religion must be firmly rooted in the idea that we are part of a wider humanity. The most important aspect and the essence of religion is the protection of the values of humanity, namely truth, justice and freedom. The problem is that religion is often misunderstood, and instead of promoting progressive human values, it becomes a source of hatred and violent prejudice. How is that seemingly tolerant and religious people can become fanatical? We must remember that religious belief cultivates a degree of exclusiveness. A person of faith often holds the conviction that their religion is the one, true religion. Muslims believe that Jews and Christians have distorted their own holy book; Christians deny the prophethood of

1 *See* Amnesty International, [Sweden:] The case of Mohammed El Zari and Ahmed Agiza violations of fundamental human rights by Sweden confirmed, AI Index: EUR 42/001/2006, 27 November 2006.

Muhammad, and Jews reject both Christianity and Islam, believing that the true messiah is yet to come. There are also hundreds of millions of people throughout the world who believe in Buddhism, Hinduism or the thousands of other religions. This belief, that you alone possess the truth, can translate into prejudice and feelings of superiority as it assumes other religions are "other" or lesser religions. It can lead to the dehumanisation of others, since you no longer view them as being your fellow humans, but as something other, whether they be Copt, Muslim or Jew. At this point you feel that it is permissible to violate the rights of others because they are not like you. Only you are right, and all others are wrong, and therefore, they should not enjoy the same rights as you.

There are countless examples of how religion has lost its essential humanity and become intolerant. However, there are also many examples of the exact opposite. When Caliph Umar ibn Al-Khattab[1] entered Jerusalem, the Patriarch of Jerusalem, Sophronius, invited him to visit the Church of the Holy Sepulchre. As he walked around the church, the Muslim call for prayer was heard. Sophronius invited the caliph to pray inside the church, but the caliph declined through fear that his followers would later demolish the church and build a mosque in its place. Instead, Umar left the church and prayed nearby on the ground where the Mosque of Umar was later built. Umar ibn Al-Khattab valued the rights of both Muslims and non-Muslims and believed in equality. This attitude is sadly missing amongst the religious fanatics now in Egypt.

Some Islamists are up in arms about the French government's ban on face coverings in public places, but conversely they see nothing wrong in preventing Coptic churches being built in their own neighbourhoods. As a matter of fact, they view the building of a Christian church in the neighbourhoods where they live as an insult to Islam. Some of these Islamists defend the right of Muslims to hold citizenship in Europe but then state publicly that an Egyptian Copt can never have the right to be president of Egypt. There is fanaticism on both sides, of course. Some Copts call for the implementation of civil society but then turn round and welcome the transformation of the church into a political party that speaks in the name of all Copts. Then there are other Copts who defend freedom of belief only when a Muslim converts to Christianity. If it happens the other way round, however, they see nothing wrong with the Coptic Church detaining a Christian woman who has converted to Islam until she reverts to Christianity.

A true understanding of religion will make us more humane, but when our understanding is misconceived we are driven to feel hostility and hatred towards others. Religion can become a divisive force, particularly

1 The second rightly-guided caliph and companion of the Prophet Muhammad. He oversaw major expansion of the Islamic empire and allowed conquered peoples to continue to practice their own religions, rather than insisting they convert to Islam, provided they paid a poll tax.

when it is exploited for political ends. There are two ways for politicians to win votes from the electorate: either by appealing to voters with their policies, or by manipulating their religious sentiments. The run-up to the free elections in Egypt can be seen as evidence to support this. Only last week the supreme guide of the Muslim Brotherhood accused intellectuals who do not agree with him of being enemies of religion. Furthermore, Mohamed Salim al-Awa, the legal scholar and renowned Islamic thinker, held a press conference and called for all parliamentary candidates to begin their speeches by invoking God. He then went on to accuse those calling for the elections to be postponed of being infidels. Then there is Sobhi Saleh, a leading member of the Brotherhood, who said that the Muslim Brothers do not recognise Muslims with either leftist or liberal tendencies as true Muslims. By this he means that there are two kinds of Muslim: the superior kind, who are members of the Brotherhood, and the lesser kind of Muslims: those that disagree with them. In this way religion can lead to feelings of contempt between those who hold different ideas.

The only way to eradicate bigotry is to create a civil society in which religion does not dictate the political rights of the people. The law must recognise the rights of all citizens regardless of their religion, gender or ethnicity. A civil society does not necessarily mean that the state is either atheistic or anti-religious; rather, it is a society where the different religions of all its citizens are accorded equal respect and none are discriminated against. The concept of a civil society is not alien to the people of Egypt. When Muhammad Ali ruled Egypt from 1805–48, he laid the foundations for a civil society and built a modern Egypt based upon educating Egyptians to a professional standard, regardless of their religious faith. The notion of a civil society took root during the Egyptian revolution of 1919, when the idea of Egyptian citizenship took hold for the first time. Under the leadership of the Wafd Party, the most important and popular political party, Egyptians fought a long struggle to achieve two goals: independence from British occupation and the establishment of a democratic state based on the values of civil society and the separation of religion and politics. In 1937, King Farouk wanted his coronation to take place in Cairo Citadel, to create the impression of him as being the Muslim caliph. The prime minister, however, Mustafa el-Nahhas,[1] who was also the leader of the Wafd Party, protested that the Egyptian state was based upon the values of civil society and he insisted that the ceremony took place in the parliament building and, thereby, emphasise the democratic nature of the country. There is another well-known story involving el-Nahhas and a young politician who had handed him his political manifesto.

1 Mustafa el-Nahhas (1879–1965) was a judge, cabinet minister, prime minister and leader of the nationalist Wafd party, and was a dominant figure in Egyptian politics until the revolution of 1952.

El-Nahhas looked over it before quickly handed it back to its owner, saying: "Why do you talk about God in a political manifesto? As soon as you do so you become a charlatan that is attempting to manipulate people's religious sentiments." This is not to say that el-Nahhas was against religion, in fact, we know that he was devout and that he took his religious obligations as a Muslim seriously. Nevertheless, he knew the dangers of exploiting religion in order to gain political power.

In order for Egypt to advance it must transition to a healthy democracy, and this can only happen by adopting the values of a civil society. Countries such as Saudi Arabia, Irán and Sudan offer us examples of political systems that are based upon religion, and they clearly reveal how this leads to bigotry, sectarianism, tyranny and oppression. Islamists in Egypt have the right to express their political opinions, just as other citizens, but they cannot monopolise religious discourse and accuse their opponents of being infidels or enemies of religion. I have the right to object to the ideas of the Muslim Brotherhood without anyone accusing me of being opposed to Islam itself. The Egyptian people rose up in revolution on 25 January and many sacrificed their lives to free the country from Mubarak's corrupt and oppressive regime, and to establish a democratic, civil society in Egypt. Let's not vanquish political despotism only to fall into the clutches of religious despotism.

Democracy is the answer.

AB

Are We Tilting at Windmills?

31 May 2011

> The greatest era of Islam – when Muslims ruled the world and created a great civilisation – took place when we lived under the protection of a caliphate that governed according to the Islamic law. In the modern age, the foreign imperialists put an end to the caliphate and corrupted the minds of Muslims with Western ideas. When this happened the Islamic world went into decline; it became weak and backward. The only way to bring about an Islamic renaissance is to restore the caliphate.

I have often heard this speech from preachers in mosques and from members of various Islamist groups. Many people in Egypt and the wider Arab world agree with these sentiments. It is true that Islam was once considered one of the greatest civilisations in the world. For centuries, Muslims were at the forefront of every field of human learning, distinguishing themselves in art, philosophy, chemistry, algebra and geometry. Many years ago, I studied Spanish literature in Madrid and attended a lecture on the history of Al-Andalus.[1] At the start of the lecture, the professor turned to the three Arabs in the class and said: "You should be proud of the civilisation your forebears created in the Iberian Peninsula." I do not dispute the greatness of the early Islamic civilisations and the contributions they made to the wider world, but the call to restore the caliphate in the Islamic world is problematic. Islamic history suggests that the ways in which successive Islamic dynasties came to and held on to power is fundamentally incompatible with the principles of Islam.

The Islamic world was governed justly and in accordance with the principles of religion for a short period of 31 years following the death of the Prophet Muhammad, almost fourteen centuries ago. This period comprises the successive reigns of the "rightly-guided caliphs"[2] – Abu Bakr, Umar ibn Al-Khattab, Uthman ibn Affan, and Ali ibn Abi-Talib – who, taken collectively, ruled for a period of 29 years (632–61 CE). The remaining two years are made up by the brief reign of one of their later successors: Umar ibn Abd al-Aziz[3], a caliph of the Umayyad dynasty who ruled in the early eighth century (717–21 CE). As for the rest of Islamic history, no other ruler has governed in accordance with the principles of religion. Even during the aforementioned 31 years of good governance, a number of transgressions were committed by the ruling caliphs. Caliph Uthman was nepotistic and bestowed gifts and important positions on his own relatives, which inevitably led to an uprising and his eventual murder. After this came the First Islamic Civil War[4] which divided Muslims into three camps – the Sunnis, the Shias, and the Kharijites – and ended with the murder of Caliph Ali ibn Abi-Talib[5], a close companion of the Prophet, and one of the greatest and most learned

1 Al-Andalus is the name used to refer to the Iberian peninsula territories that were ruled by Islamic regimes between 711 CE and 1492 CE. The territorial limits of Al-Andalus varied over time, although they diminished steadily from the eleventh century onwards.

2 The first four caliphs make up what is regarded by Muslims as the Rashidun, or the caliphate of the rightly-guided (632–61 CE). These caliphs were all early converts and close companions of the Prophet Muhammad. For the most part, they continued to model the ideals of Islamic government: upholding proper religious practice and social justice.

3 Umar ibn Abd al-Aziz (717–20 CE), also known as Umar II, was an Umayyad caliph who introduced measures to create a uniform judicial system. Shifted the emphasis of the empire from Arab to Muslim, recognising all Muslims as equal.

4 The First Islamic Civil War (656–61 CE), or fitna, gave rise to the earliest heresies in Islam. It produced temporary political unity, but it introduced permanent religious division in the Muslim community.

5 Ali ibn Abi Talib (597–661 CE), cousin and son-in-law of Muhammad, was the fourth caliph of the Sunni Muslim community, and first imam of the Shia.

of all Muslims. Soon after, Muawiyah ibn Sufyan[1] of the Umayyad clan established a brutal and despotic regime that became dynastic in nature. He forced the people to pledge their allegiance to his son and heir, Yazid, who assumed power after his father's death. This precedent essentially put an end to the right of Muslims to select their own rulers and transformed the nature of governance from something designed to ensure justice, into something to be seized and maintained by force.

The Umayyads were particularly brutal and were ready to commit the most horrific crimes in order to maintain their rule. After their victory at the Battle of Harrah, the Umayyads sacked the holy city of Medina and killed many of its inhabitants. Later, the Umayyad caliph, Abd al-Malek ibn Marwan, sent an army under the command of Al-Hajjaj ibn Yusuf to subjugate Abd Allah ibn al-Zubayr, who had rebelled against Umayyad rule and who was taking his stand at the Grand Mosque in Mecca. Al-Hajjaj besieged Mecca with his army and even damaged the holy Ka'aba after bombarding the Grand Mosque with catapults. He then stormed the mosque and Abd Allah ibn al-Zubayr was slain inside. Thus, everything was considered permissible when it came to holding onto power, even attacking the Ka'aba, the most sacred point within the most sacred mosque in Islam.

After the Umayyads, the caliphate of the Abbasids opened up a new chapter of slaughter, which they too used as both a means to take power as well as maintain it. The Abbasids hunted the Umayyads down and killed them mercilessly. They dug up the graves of the Umayyad caliphs and desecrated their bodies as an act of vengeance. The second Abbasid caliph, Abu Ja'far al-Mansur, killed his own uncle, Abdallah ibn Ali, believing him to be a threat to his rule. He then turned his attentions to arranging the assassination of Abu Muslim Khorasani, the general who led the Abbasid revolution. The first Abbasid caliph was Abul-Abbas as-Saffah; allegedly given the name as-Saffah ("shedder of blood") because he killed so many people. According to a well-known story he had the remaining Umayyad princes brought before him and slaughtered as he watched. It is believed that he had their bodies covered with a carpet, whereupon he ate and drank while the princes still writhed in their death throes underneath. When he had finished he said: "By God, never before have I enjoyed such a pleasant meal."

As for abiding by the morals of religion, with the exception of a few rulers who were renowned for their piety, most of the Umayyads and Abbasids openly drank alcohol with their companions every night. Governance had very little to do with religion; it consisted of ruthless and bloody struggles for influence, wealth and power, in which every kind of act was permissible, even attacking the Ka'aba and damaging it. The great era of a caliphate that

1 Muawiyah ibn Sufyan (602–80 CE) was the first Umayyad caliph and nephew of the third Sunni caliph, Uthman. The caliphate became an absolute monarchy under his rule .

governed in accordance with Islamic law is a myth. Except for the brief period of 31 years, such a thing did not exist in the last fourteen centuries. The question then is this: how does true Islamic governance, which lasted for so brief a time, differ from the long history of despotism under the name of Islam? The difference between them is the difference between justice and injustice, between democracy and despotism.

The Islamic world practiced modern democracy many centuries before the West adopted it. Before his death, the Prophet Muhammad did not choose a successor to act as ruler of the Muslims, but instead appointed Abu Bakr to lead the believers in prayer. By doing so, he showed a preference for Abu Bakr as a successor, while at the same time granting the believers the right to select their own ruler. When the prophet died, the leaders of the Muslim community gathered in Medina to select a caliph, not dissimilar to a modern-day parliamentary meeting. Muslim representatives took turns to discuss the matter at hand before choosing Abu Bakr to assume leadership of the community. After these events, Abu Bakr delivered a speech to the Muslims in which he said: "O People, I have been chosen to lead you, though I am not the best amongst you. Obey me as long as I obey God and His prophet, but if I disobey them, then you shall not owe me obedience." These words represent a constitution of sorts, defining the relationship between the leader and the citizens. It is notable that Abu Bakr did not say that he was God's successor, nor did he talk about having a divine right to rule. He humbly stated that he is one of the people and not even the best amongst them. This democratic concept, which is the true essence of Islam, would last only for a brief period before being replaced by a different, undemocratic one: the idea that the ruler is the shadow of God on earth. As Muawiyah put it: "The earth is God's and I am God's deputy. What I take is mine, and what I leave for the people is a favour to them from me."

Abu Ja'far al-Mansur, the Abassid caliph said: "O People, we are now your leaders and your protectors. We shall govern you in the name of God, who invested us with His authority. I am God's deputy on His earth and the guard of His wealth." When Caliph Abd al-Malik ibn Marwan gave a sermon from the pulpit that Prophet Muhammad used to speak from, he said: "By God, if anyone commands me to be pious after speaking from here then I shall chop off his head."

Democracy was replaced by a divine right to govern. Those who opposed this rule were considered infidels and apostates who should be killed. For the sake of fairness, we should state two facts at this point. Firstly, those caliphs who came to power by means of plots and killings often turned out to be competent rulers who governed well and expanded their territories, creating a vast Islamic empire. Nevertheless, under no circumstances can the ways in which they took power be considered as being in accord with the principles of

Islam. Secondly, bloody struggles for power were not limited to Muslim rulers in those times. The same bloodshed occurred in Europe, where the nobility fought to capture thrones and fought to keep them.

The difference here is that while people in the West now view these struggles for power as a brutal phase of their history that had to be undergone in order to arrive at democracy, there are still some Arabs and Muslims calling for a restoration of the Islamic caliphate who actually claim that it was a just institution that followed the law of God. The dreadful history of political struggle in Islamic countries is well known; the events of this history could not be further from the true law of Islam. In light of this, I am somewhat bemused by this strange desire to see the caliphate restored. Those calling for the restoration of the caliphate belong to one of two distinct groups: the first are Muslims who have never read Islamic history, or, having read it, will not accept the truth when it contradicts their religious sentiments. Their reverence for Islam causes them to revere Islamic history itself, thus, they tend to idealise history in ways that are not compatible with fact. The second group are members of Islamist groups who exploit the religious feelings of simple people in order to further their own power. They usually offer you one of two choices: either you accept their idealised image of the caliphate, or they accuse you of being a secularist and an enemy of Islam; either you help them come to power by propagating lies about history or else they will call you an infidel and threaten to chop off your head.

The essence of Islam is justice, freedom and equality. This essence was realised for a short period of time when the principles of democracy were adopted. As for the remaining history of Islamic rule, however, you will not find such noble principles, just a long and brutal struggle for power in which everything was permitted. Whether we like it or not, this is the truth. Therefore, the attempt to portray an idealised version of the history of the Islamic caliphate will not result, unfortunately, in anything other than the construction of a delusional fantasy. Such endeavours are reminiscent of delusional fantasies described by the great Spanish writer Miguel de Cervantes in his famous novel *Don Quixote*. The ageing protagonist of the tale becomes so absorbed with reading ancient books of chivalry that he becomes possessed by the desire to be a knight – the age of chivalry has, by this time, passed, however. Nevertheless, he dons a suit of armour, draws his sword, and subsequently, imagining that windmills are monstrous giants, he attacks them.

The only way to bring about a renaissance is to apply the true principles of Islam. These are freedom, justice, and equality. This can only be achieved by establishing a civil society, where all citizens are equal before the law, regardless of religion, gender or ethnicity.

Democracy is the answer.

AB

Who Will Protect Egypt From the Police?

7 June 2011

Recently in Alexandria, a young man and his fiancée went to Borg El Arab Airport to pick up two women relatives who were returning from their pilgrimage in Mecca. They were driving back to their home when two cars full of armed thugs came up behind them. The young man, who was driving the car, tried to outrun them but the thugs gave chase and drove the car off the road. The car flipped and plunged into a canal, killing all four passengers. When the relatives of these innocent victims went to the police station, they were shocked to find that the incident had been registered as a simple traffic accident. They demanded to speak to the chief of police in Alexandria, who said to them: "There is nothing we can do about the thugs because they are armed. If we try to go against them, we will be accused of beating up young revolutionary activists." This incident, which was written about by Hamdi Rizq in *Al-Masry Al-Youm*, sums up the prevailing attitude of Egyptian police officers. The thugs and criminals that escaped from Egypt's prisons are attacking ordinary citizens while the police stand idly by. The message to the Egyptian people is clear: we will not protect those who rose up against us.

There are countless instances of neglect of duty on the part of the police. When thugs attacked Al-Matariyya Hospital they terrorised the patients and doctors for four hours, killing one patient in front of his family. Although police officers were on duty at the hospital, they did not intervene to stop the attack. This was not an isolated event; the same thing has happened at El Sahel Hospital, Kasr El Aini Hospital, Arish Hospital and elsewhere. In the West there is a term for this type of action: a "sit-down strike" – when the strikers go to work but refuse to carry out their jobs. Some police officers have gone further and are now directly involved in exacerbating the breakdown in law and order in Egypt. *Rose al-Yousef* magazine recently published an interview with one of the thugs responsible for setting fire to a Coptic church in Cairo's Imbaba neighbourhood. He told the magazine that the head officer of Imbaba police station had paid him 2,000 Egyptian pounds to torch the church and that two ex-members of the now dissolved National Democratic Party (NDP) were also present when the agreement was made. The thug even identified these agents provocateurs by name. If this had taken place anywhere else in the world there would have been an immediate investigation into the claims. The Egyptian authorities, however, have not questioned the accused or taken action.

The Egyptian police force acted as the repressive arm of Mubarak's regime for decades. In police stations and the offices of the state security service,

Egyptians were degraded, tortured and raped. It is not only the police that are responsible for this brutal treatment. The attorney general's office is also to blame for neglect of duty as it failed to conduct inspections in Egypt's police stations and prisons.

When the revolution errupted on 25 January, the police force rounded off its crimes against Egypt by killing nearly 1,000 demonstrators, blinding 1,400 and wounding 5,000. Almost 1,000 people are still missing, the majority of whom are presumed to to be dead and buried in unmarked graves. When the police force was put to flight by the revolution, it decided to withdraw its officers entirely allowing Egypt to descend into lawlessness. The security vacuum created by this withdrawal was exacerbated by the opening of prisons and the escape of almost 24,000 convicts. This was an act tantamount to high treason.

There has been no concerted effort to bring the perpetrators of these heinous crimes to justice. The Ministry of the Interior knows the identity of the snipers that killed dozens of demonstrators, but has yet put them on trial. Furthermore, the senior officials who gave the order to open fire on the demonstrators remain in their jobs, even though they have trials pending. None of the state security officers that worked as torturers, electrocuting detainees and hanging them up like animals to be slaughtered, have been prosecuted for their crimes; some have been transferred to other departments, the majority, however, have ended up in Egypt's new security agency Homeland Security.

Mohamed al-Batran, the late police general and former head of the prisons department, was murdered because of his refusal to allow the prisoners to escape, according to the testimony of his sister Manal al-Batran. She has also named the two officers responsible for the killing of her brother, but the attorney general's office has summoned them as witnesses to the crime rather than interrogating them as suspects. The Egyptian people cannot possibly regain confidence in the police force as long as those who have shed the blood of innocent people are not brought to justice.

The media has twisted events to suggest that it is in fact the police that have been wronged. There has been a malicious attempt to obfuscate justice by insisting that the officers who killed demonstrators were acting in self-defence. But no one has asked what drove people to attack the police stations in the first place, and why this did not happen in the first days of the revolution? The truth is that attacking the police stations was a result of officers firing at demonstrators from inside the buildings. I can personally vouch for this myself. On Friday 28 January, I was at a demonstration in front of the American University of Cairo when snipers started shooting at us. The dead began falling to the ground all around us and, in retaliation, the demonstrators tried to climb into the buildings where the snipers were posted to restrain them. It was the Egyptian people who were lawfully defending themselves, not the murderous police officers who gunned down Egypt's youth to please Hosni Mubarak and

Habib el-Adly. If the officers were defending the police stations, why did they aim their guns at the heads and chests of the demonstrators rather than at their feet, as the law stipulates? And who established the case for self-defence? Should this not be decided by a judge in a court of law rather than the police officers themselves.

A culture of corruption and arrogance was prevalent in the police force during the era of Mubarak. Police officers were able to gain respect through high-handedness and violence, and considered themselves above the law and exempt from prosecution. It is astonishing that some police officers are up in arms about their colleagues being tried for killing demonstrators. They seem to treat Egyptian citizens as though they were lowly animals; rabbits or chickens that can be killed with impunity. Police officers that have absorbed this culture, who have learned to abuse Egyptians, cannot change overnight into upstanding officers that will treat the people with respect and protect their rights.

The police force has apparently been purged of corrupt elements, but Habib el-Adly's aides are still in their jobs, as are the senior officers on trial for killing demonstrators, and other high-ranking officials charged with corruption. What are we to expect from a chief of police who is on trial for killing demonstrators but who still remains in charge of security? Are we to believe that he will concern himself with maintaining law and order while he is facing charges that may lead to life imprisonment? Or, rather, would he instead do his utmost to cause as much disorder as possible so as to escape punishment?

Despite all of these criminal factions within the police force, there are also a number of officers who have served with honour and integrity. Many of these upstanding officers were mistreated under the Mubarak regime and have since formed the groups such as the Coalition of Police Officers, and Officers But Honest Ones. They tried hard to persuade the minister of the interior to carry out real reforms in order to purge the police force of corrupt leaders that colluded with the Mubarak regime. Instead of listening to them, however, the minister put pressure on them until they were forced to announce the dissolution of their coalition.

When any revolution takes place, society splits into three different blocs. There is the revolutionary bloc: this is made up of those citizens who carried out the revolution and who are ready to make sacrifices in order to achieve its aims. There is the counter-revolutionary bloc: this is made up of those who benefited from the old regime and fear the loss of their privileges, or those who fear being brought to justice for their crimes and who fight fiercely to counteract the revolution. Lastly, there is the silent bloc composed of the observers. This bloc is made up of those citizens that suffered under the old regime but who were not prepared to make the sacrifices necessary to get rid of it. These are people who did not join the revolution but watched it take place on their televisions. It comprises of people who oscillate between supporting the revolution and attacking it. It is this last bloc, the silent bloc, that is the focus of counter-revolutionary plots. The counter-revolutionaries continuously put pressure on this bloc in order to make them turn against the revolution and to make them long for the return of the old regime. This is precisely the role that the Egyptian police force is now playing. Their refusal to carry out their duties is an attempt to terrorise Egyptians into surrender and to prevent the Egyptian economy from improving. How can we bring back tourism and investment when there is no rule of law and thugs are roaming the country?

In order to put an end to this crisis, the minister of the interior, Mansour el-Essawy, must be dismissed. He is an honest and decent man but he has not been successful in this position. A new minister of the interior should be appointed from the armed forces, because cleaning up the police force can only be achieved by an outside agent. There must also be a systematic purge of all senior officers connected to the old regime, and the immediate suspension of those currently on trial for killing demonstrators. Upstanding officers should be used to purge the force, restore its effectiveness and promote a better culture amongst new graduates so that the next generation of police officers will respect human rights. Lastly, the salaries of police officers must be increased to a level that allows them to lead a respectable life.

The police force's neglect of duty in protecting Egyptians is a scandalous conspiracy. It is my hope that the military council will intervene immediately to put an end to it and restore security. God willing, law and order will be restored and then Egypt will go forward.

Democracy is the answer.

AB

Would a Civil State Allow Sharia Law?

14 June 2011

If you are an Egyptian who cares about the future of your country, then you are now faced with two choices: either you support the Muslim Brotherhood and the Salafists, and help them come to power in Egypt, or you disagree with them and risk being denounced as secular or an enemy of Islam. Sobhi Saleh, a leading member of the Brotherhood, has previously stated: "There is no such thing as a liberal Muslim or a leftist Muslim; there are only Muslims and infidels." He believes that the Muslim Brotherhood is the only party that truly represents Islam and that its opponents are non-believers and infidels. Similarly, Sheikh al-Mahallawi[1] is known to have said: "Those who call for a civil state in Egypt are infidels and heathens." Accusing someone of being an infidel is a very serious matter in Islam that can have serious consequences. If there are a hundred reasons for considering a Muslim to be an infidel and only one reason that they should be considered a believer, then Muslims should consider that person a believer and withhold the accusation. Prophet Muhammad warned against false accusations when he said: "If anyone calls another Muslim an infidel, then the accusation will hold true for one of them. If the accusation is true, then it is the accused. But if it is untrue, then it is the accuser who is the infidel, for wrongly accusing him."

Nevertheless, not a week passes without news of the Salafists or the Muslim Brothers denouncing one of their opponents as an infidel. It is not just political-Islamist leaders that are making these accusations; preachers in the mosques are doing the same thing. I have received numerous letters from readers in which they tell me how the sermons of preachers in the mosque focus on attacking those who call for a civil state, accusing them of secularism and atheism.

In Egypt, a number of political groups are deliberately exploiting people's religious sentiments in order to gain power. They are prepared to go to great lengths to defeat their opponents, even accusing them of being infidels. Such behaviour was evident during the recent referendum on the amendments to the constitution. These amendments excluded changes to Article 2, which stipulates that Islam is the religion of the state. Some Islamists distributed leaflets calling on Muslims to vote in favour of the amendments in order to preserve Egypt's Islamic identity. A rejection of them could lead to a ban on the call to prayer and the wearing of the hijab, and the legalisation of gay marriage. Whether done deliberately or out of sheer ignorance, this woeful campaign to mislead the public and vilify those in favour of a civil state misrepresents two different political concepts.

A democratic civil state is one in which sovereignty belongs to the people and the nation. It has a legal system that views all citizens as equal regardless of their religion or faith. A religious state, on the other hand, is a state in which the ruler assumes power in the name of religion, not in the name of the people. There are two kinds of religious state: the theocratic state whose ruler considers themself to be God's representative on earth; they rule according to the notion of divine right and cannot be deposed. The second kind of religious state is one in which the ruler forms an alliance with the clergy in order to rule in the name of religion. Anyone who opposes the ruler is considered a heretic.

It is difficult to find an example of a religious state that has been fairly governed. They are synonymous with injustice and tyranny. We need only

1 Imam of Mosque of Qaid Ibrahim in Alexandria.

to compare any contemporary democratic state with countries such as Saudi Arabia, Iran and Sudan to see the danger posed by a religious state and negative outcome it has on personal freedoms.

Secularism is based on the idea that there should be greater concern for worldly matters rather than religious ones. It gives precedence to the world we live in rather than where we will go after we die; it gives priority to known realities rather than unknown ones. For this reason, secularism is antagonistic towards all religions. As for liberalism, this is a doctrine that derives its name from the Latin word *liber*, which means "free". Liberalism is a movement promoting social and political awareness that aims to free people from the bonds that limit their freedom and their potential. It is based upon the idea that the autonomy of the individual should be upheld, as well as political and civil rights. The freedom granted by liberalism, however, is not absolute. It is restricted by laws, which can vary according to a given country's particular moral code and values. Economic liberalism is predicated on the idea of a free market economy which opposes state intervention in economic activities, leaving the market to regulate itself. Some intellectuals speak about social liberalism, which advocates state intervention in the economy and tries to find a middle ground between unrestrained capitalism and socialism, freedom and equality. It is concerned with social services, such as health care and education, and is keen to get people into work. Atheism is the rejection of religion in its entirety. It considers religious texts purely human creations that are not sacred, nor do they convey absolute truth.

If we look at these definitions and their various meanings we can see how incoherent the political battle raging in Egypt is, as the cards are stacked to exploit the religious feelings of ordinary citizens so that the Islamists will obtain power. The division of people into two camps – Islamists and secularists – represents a completely false and unfair dichotomy. Those who disagree with the ideas of the Islamists do not necessarily oppose Islam itself, and those who are calling for a civil state are not necessarily secularists or atheists. They may, in fact, be devout Muslims who simply refuse to allow religion to be used as a cover for authoritarian rule, which is by definition oppressive and unjust. The truth is, since the beginning of the twentieth century, the struggle of the Egyptian people has always been for a democratic civil state. If we put aside the Brotherhood's agenda for Islamisation, no other political body has called for the establishment of a religious state, that is until the 1970s when Wahhabism was exported from the oil-rich Gulf States.

If we are to agree with Sheikh al-Mahallawi that those who advocate a civil state are to be denounced as infidels, then this means that Saad Zaghloul, Mustafa el-Nahhas, Gamal Abdel Nasser, Anwar Sadat, and other Egyptian leaders were also infidels, because each and every one of them called for the separation of religion and state. The truth is that a democratic civil state is neither secular nor atheistic; it stands at an equal distance from all religions and treats all citizens the same. The Muslim Brotherhood has coined a new idea: they are now calling for a civil state that has an "Islamic point of reference". If they are referring to Islamic principles such as justice, freedom, and equality, then these are already the bases for a civic state, thus no additional "reference points" are needed. If it means setting out sacred principles that cannot be discussed and imposing them on people in the name of religion, then we would be dealing with a despotic religious state merely masked by a different name.

The question is: can sharia law be implemented in a democratic civic state? The answer is yes, certainly, as long as this is something that the people have chosen freely. If an Islamist party believes that Egyptian law does not comply with the principles of the sharia, then it has the right to try and change the law. However, to do this, the party must produce a political programme that clearly explains to the electorate those laws that it seeks to change in light of the sharia. Then, if the party wins a majority of votes in free elections, it will have the right to implement its political programme. On the other hand, however, if the Islamic party were to come to power and subsequently consider that it has a duty to impose its version of religion without consulting the people, then, again, we would be dealing with an oppressive government that uses religion as a cover for despotism. You might answer that the result would be the same in both cases, but there is a distinct and important difference in method: when you appeal to the will of the people, changing the law is legitimate, because the people expressed their will by voting in favour of change. It is when you impose beliefs on the people that you violate their right to choose which laws and principles they want.

Furthermore, ideas about imposing the rule of religion vary according to the different views of those who advocate it. To enlightened thinkers, such as Tarek el-Bishry[1] and Ahmed Kamal Aboul Magd, the concept of imposing the sharia is viewed very differently from the way it is viewed by Salafist scholars. Sheikh Abu Ishaq al-Heweny, for example, believes that studying at a non-Islamic law faculty goes against Islam, and that all females that study at Egyptian universities are sinners because they study alongside their male counterparts in the same lecture halls. He asserts that only men should study Islamic law, because in the opinion of the sheikh, no matter how learned a woman may be, she will always be inferior to a man.

As for the economic problems in Egypt, Sheikh al-Heweny has proposed an excellent solution. He suggests that Egypt invite a foreign, non-Muslim state (Sweden, for example) to convert to Islam. Then, if the Swedish government

1 Tarek el-Bishry is an Egyptian thinker and judge, considered one of Egypt's top legal minds. On 15 February 2011, el-Bishry was appointed by the military council to head the committee set up to propose constitutional changes in the aftermath of the revolution.

rejects Islam, Egypt should declare a jihad. When Egypt invades Sweden, defeats and occupies the country, the Swedes would be given the choice of either embracing Islam or paying the *jizya* tax required of non-Muslim subjects. Imposing the *jizya* on the Swedes would provide income that would help revive Egypt's economy. However, if the Swedish enemy refused to either convert or pay the *jizya* tax, then it would be our right, as Muslims, to enslave them. The Swedish males taken as slaves could be made to work in exchange for food and clothing. As for the women taken as slaves – and Swedish women are renowned for their beauty – their Egyptian masters would have the right to take them as concubines. An Egyptian man could have sex with his Swedish concubine without the need for a marriage contract, because according to Islam she would be his lawful property. If an Egyptian had more concubines than he needed, or if he grew tired of one, then he could simply sell her at the slave market and earn some money. Sheikh Al Heweny was videotaped expounding these incredible ideas. So what are we to do if a man who has this kind of mentality comes to power in Egypt and then imposes his vision of religion upon us?

The Egyptian revolution took place in order to liberate Egyptians from despotism and oppression. The Egyptian people will never allow religious tyranny to replace the political tyranny they fought to get rid of. If the Islamists want to carry out their political programme, they must first put it to the Egyptian people, who hold the ultimate authority in a democratic system. If the electorate votes in favour of the Islamists' programme, then no one has the right to object, because the will of the people would be clear. However, if the people reject it, then no one has the right to impose it on them under any circumstances.

Democracy is the answer.

AB

What to Expect from the Military Council

21 June 2011

Imagine that you have a great job and you earn the kind of salary that most people can only dream of, but your boss is arrogant and spends the whole day putting you down. You have two choices: either you refuse to be humiliated in this way and quit, or you can try putting up with the abuse, in which case you get to keep your salary and enjoy the financial comforts. The first option – putting your dignity first and refusing to accept abuse, regardless of the consequences – is the choice that a true revolutionary would make. Revolution means forfeiting personal advantage in favour of an ideal, and rejecting that which degrades your humanity. Such choices were made during the Egyptian revolution: the millions of Egyptians who took to the streets, knowing that they were risking their lives, did so for the sake of dignity and freedom. Every single one of them was prepared to die so that they, and their children after them, could live with dignity and respect.

Given the high price paid by the Egyptian people during the revolution, they are now deserving of the changes they fought for. If the revolution is to be successful, there can be no compromise or reform. Reform would merely mend some of the old system's weaknesses while keeping it intact. Revolution, however, aims at fundamentally doing away with the old corrupt system and building a new and better one in its place. The Egyptian revolution has been extraordinary for several reasons. Firstly, it was able to bring down one of the most repressive regimes in the world through peaceful protest. Secondly, those who carried out the revolution cleaned up the streets themselves; this is evidence of highly civilised behaviour. Thirdly, although the revolution was a triumph, the revolutionaries did not take power, but instead asked the military council to step in and guide the revolution through the transitional period. And although we may not always agree with the actions of the military council, their presence at the start of the revolution helped to protect the revolutionaries and restore order. The military council refused to open fire on the demonstrators and they took the side of the revolution before Hosni Mubarak announced his resignation. The military council showed courage in siding with the revolutionaries as the outcome was uncertain. They would have paid a high price if Mubarak stayed in power. Nevertheless, the Egyptian people are feeling anxious and apprehensive about the future; they ask the military council to take action so that the aims of the revolution can be realised.

Armed forces throughout the world are disciplined organisations that are often conservative in nature. They are reactionary organisations based upon conformity, obedience and carrying out orders. With the armed forces now acting as head of state during the transitional period, the decisions issued by the military council resemble military commands and are often carried out without recourse to the Egyptian people. On several occasions, action has preceded dialogue, indicating that decision makers do not take the outcomes of the dialogue seriously.

The criticisms levelled against the military council regarding their performance have not been well received. Recently, the military council has summoned a number of its critics for trial in military courts, including talk show host Reem Maged, and the journalists Rasha Azab, Nabil Sharaf El Din and Adel Hammouda. Even the celebrated intellectual, Mohamed

Hassanein Heikal,[1] was not spared after allegedly downplaying the role of the Egyptian Air Force during the October War.[2] His opinion offended the pilots who had taken part in the war and they filed a complaint with the attorney general's office. In a democratic society, all citizens are entitled to file complaints, but it is unusual that the pilot's complaints about Heikal were passed on to the military prosecutor's office directly. The message here is clear: those who criticise the military council will risk being court-martialled. Referring thinkers and intellectuals to the military prosecutor's office, just like referring civilians to the military courts, infringes on freedom of expression and is a human rights violation. It is an unacceptable and unjustifiable act that the military council must abandon immediately if they are to be respected by the Egyptian people.

After the revolution, legal scholars agreed unanimously that the old constitution was no longer valid as Mubarak had stepped down. They called for the election of a constituent assembly that would draft a new constitution for the Egyptian people. The military council rejected this demand and decided to make changes to the old constitution, as suggested by Mubarak. The military council then proceeded to put together a committee of legal scholars, many of whom belonged to the Muslim Brotherhood and had no expertise in constitutional law. A referendum was subsequently held on the constitutional amendments and huge numbers of Egyptians came out to vote, reflecting their enthusiasm for democracy. Although the referendum was democratic and fair, certain improper practices did take place during the run-up that undoubtedly affected the result. Places of worship – both mosques and churches – disseminated propaganda about the referendum, which would constitute a serious infringement of electoral law in any democratic country. Some Islamists portrayed voting in favour of the amendments as a religious duty, and deceived people by saying that the referendum was critical for maintaining Egypt's Islamic identity. They distributed tens of thousands of leaflets far and wide, deliberately targeting uneducated people in rural areas. In the end, a large majority voted in the referendum in favour of the constitutional amendments.

After the vote, however, something very surprising happened: the military council undermined the result of the referendum by announcing a 63-article interim constitution even though the referendum had proposed amending nine articles only. This divided the Egyptian people into two groups. One group held that declaring an interim constitution annulled the results of the referendum and they demanded that the elections be postponed until after a new constitution is written. They feared that the Muslim Brotherhood, the Salafists and those with ties to the now dissolved National Democratic Party

1 Mohamed Hassanein Heikal was editor-in-chief of the Cairo newspaper *Al-Ahram* and has been a commentator on Arab affairs for more than 50 years.

2 October War (1973), also known as the Yom Kippur War, was fought by the coalition of Arab states, led by Egypt and Syria, to regain lands occupied by Israel since 1967.

will win a majority in the next parliament, and that this majority will then produce a biased constitution that will not reflect the will of all sections of Egyptian society. The second group wanted the elections to go ahead as planned and believed that the results of the referendum should be respected no matter what. As a matter of fact, I opposed the constitutional amendments in the referendum, but do not agree with annulling the results on the grounds that 14 million Egyptians came out to vote in favour of the amendments and we cannot ignore the will of the people.

It should be said, however, that there are risks involved in appointing a constituent assembly to draft the constitution prior to the elections. It is difficult to guarantee that the constitution will reflect the will of the Egyptian people. The solution to this problem, as I see it, is to hold the parliamentary elections according to the current schedule and then to appoint one hundred members of the parliament to draft a new constitution. This should then be passed on to another committee of individuals from outside parliament. This would ensure wider participation whilst also respecting the result of the referendum and ensuring that the new constitution reflects the wishes of the Egyptian people as a whole. The military council must take care to ensure all groups are given a voice in the drafting of the constitution.

Although the revolution succeeded in forcing Mubarak to step down, the military council has kept many of his officials in their jobs including the presidents of universities appointed by the state security service, corrupt media personnel who were in the pocket of Mubarak, and most of the senior officials in the Ministry of the Interior who served the old regime. The newly appointed governors of Egypt's governorates all have ties with the old regime and could have been selected by Hosni Mubarak himself. Some of them are even former members of the now dissolved secret security service who should have been put on trial rather than honoured with governorships. Furthermore, many senior members of the local councils and the labour unions, who got their positions through rigged elections and who were complicit in the crimes of the old regime, have been left untouched by the military council, nor have the bodies that they belong to been dissolved.

The situation in Egypt is far from clear and many are struggling to see the benefits of a revolution that has left Mubarak's associates still in power. The old regime is conspiring against the revolution from within and preventing any real change from taking place. It is incumbent upon the military council to immediately take steps to purge state institutions of remnants of the old regime and to create positions for the young activists that were instrumental to the success of the revolution. If it were not for their vision and courage then nothing would have changed in Egypt.

Egypt is at a crossroads; what happens next will determine the country's future for generations to come. In my opinion, the current battle is not between Islamists and secularists, but between the forces of democracy and the forces of fascism. The fascists believe that society cannot be trusted to govern itself and that the state should have full power to impose its ideals on the people by force. The democratic camp, however, includes enlightened Islamists, leftists, liberals and the thousands of Egyptians that rose up in revolution so that sovereignty would belong to the people. The fascist camp includes supporters of the old regime, who think the people are not qualified to exercise democracy, and who are therefore unable to grasp the logic of the revolution or sympathise with its legitimate demands, and religious extremists who do not recognise the people's right to govern themselves in the first place and who consider themselves representatives of God Almighty, free to enforce their understanding of His rules as they wish. These people give themselves the right to set fire to churches, demolish the tombs of holy men, destroy statues, and denounce anyone who disagrees with them as hostile to Islam and as infidels. They can never understand or respect democracy. We expect the military council to take the side of the democratic forces and take the necessary measures to protect the civil state for which the revolution was made. Only then will the future begin in Egypt.

Democracy is the answer.

AB

An Egyptian Mother to Field Marshal Tantawi[1]

28 June 2011

She still remembers all the little details. She remembers when she found out that she was pregnant, and how her newborn son seemed so small and almost doll-like in her arms. She still remembers the delight she found in his laughter. She remembers his first words and his tiny little fingers, and how he clumsily swayed back and forth when he took his first steps. She remembers how she used to worry when he had bouts of diarrhoea and when he had a fever, and how he would cry every morning as she washed his face, carefully combed his hair and then put on his uniform and took him to school before she went to work. She remembers how naughty he was as a child and how rebellious he became when he hit puberty and his voice broke. She remembers how desperately she struggled to get him through secondary school, how she borrowed money from her relatives to pay for private tuition. She still remembers

1 Mohamed Hussein Tantawi is an Egyptian field marshal and former statesman. He is former chairman of the military council acting as the de facto head of state after the ouster of Hosni Mubarak. *See* Glossary.

how happy she felt when he got good grades and was accepted to study engineering at Cairo University. She remembers how proud she felt watching him going off to college each day, carrying a large ruler in his hand, and how she would comfort herself by reciting prayers for his protection.

She already had a son and a daughter when this one was born. He had been an "accident", as she would sometimes whisper to her female friends. But he was also her favourite, and the most comely of the three. Her husband had been dead for two years now, and the older son and daughter had both moved away when they married. Her favourite son, however, was always with her, and his very being brought her endless joy and happiness.

On this particular Friday, she did not wake him; she deliberately let him sleep so that he would not go out to the demonstrations. She feared for his safety, but at the same time she knew that she couldn't stop him from going out. When he woke up late, he jumped out of bed and scolded her for not waking him earlier. She lied and said she had forgotten but he quickly washed and got dressed.

How surreal these events seem now. Why was he in such a hurry to go out and why did she stand in his way, shouting: "Where are you going? The Friday prayers have finished!" He wasn't angry. He just smiled at her warmly and embraced her tightly. Why did she give in and let him go? Why did she hold on to him so tightly, kissing him until he gently pushed her away and kissed her hand before turning to leave? She can still hear the sound of the door closing behind him as she walked into the kitchen. There she stood, preparing his favourite meal. She rolled pieces of marinated chicken in breadcrumbs before dropping them into hot oil. She was cheerful as she cooked this meal; she was imagining how he would devour the pieces of chicken when he returned home. She heard a noise and remembered that she had left her mobile phone in the living room. She took the pieces of chicken out of the oil, turned off the heat, quickly dried her hands and rushed to answer it. The number of the caller was unknown. When she answered she heard the voice of a young man who said that he was a friend of her son. He assured her that her son was fine but he had fainted and had been taken to Kasr El Aini Hospital. The last thing she remembers is the coloured pattern of the chair's fabric that she had been staring at.

She got dressed and went out into the street to wave down a taxi. She remembers that the driver said something about Hosni Mubarak, but she cannot recollect what it was exactly, or how she replied. All of the details of her journey to the hospital are blurry or have been forgotten entirely. She will never forget, however, the face of the receptionist at the hospital. She told him the full name of her son and said: "I'm his mother. A friend of his called me to say that he had fainted and had been brought here."

The receptionist went through the register, then he slowly raised his head and said: "I"m sorry to inform you that your son has passed away."

She didn't scream. She looked at the receptionist as though she hadn't understood what he had said. She simply could not believe it. She was sure that there must have been a mistake. It was not possible that this could have happened. He had gone out and he would be coming home; she had cooked chicken for him just the way he liked it. They must have made a mistake; Kasr El Aini, like all the other public hospitals, was completely incompetent.

It was at this point she yelled: "Check his name again!" The receptionist looked at her with sadness in his eyes, then he showed her the register so she could see for herself. Her son's name was recorded on a hastily written page headed: "List of the Deceased". She let out a scream and struck her face in despair. The hospital workers and visitors gathered around her. Women she did not know took her in their arms and tried to comfort her; they too were crying.

Some minutes later she was in the hospital's morgue. A hospital worker whispered his condolences in her ear before leading her to the cold chambers. He opened one of the units and slid out the long tray on which lay the body of her son. The man pulled back the cover to reveal her son's face. He looked as if he was sleeping. He was just as he was when she had seen him last. He wore the same clothes that he had bought for the Eid holiday: denim jeans, a white shirt and a navy blue jumper. His face looked calm and had the trace of a smile. The only difference was the hole; a strange black hole that looked as though someone had carefully drawn it right between his eyebrows.

Later she heard what had happened. Her son had been at a demonstration when police officers opened fire on the demonstrators with live ammunition. Some of the demonstrators were hit and fell to the ground around her son. He had tried to drag the injured demonstrators to a nearby car to take them to hospital, but was deliberately shot down by a sniper. The bullet had pierced his skull and killed him instantly; one bullet for an entire life. All of her memories and dreams had been crushed with the single squeeze of a trigger. The man who killed her son was not part of an invading army; he was an Egyptian citizen who had been trained for years to kill with accuracy and professionalism.

The bullet hole in her son's face was real, but everything else was like scattered dust whirling before her eyes: the death certificate, the burial permit, the funeral, the tranquillisers she took every night after his death, the ceremonies to honour the mothers of martyrs and all the sophisticated speakers with their evocative words, certificates expressing esteem for her son and glass ornaments engraved with his name and the title "Martyr of the Revolution". All these events are just echoes, shadows. The only true reality is that her son is no longer here. He won't come home in the evening, whistling as he unlocks the door to the apartment. He'll never again sit down at his desk to go over his lessons. He won't sleep in his bed again and she won't wake him up in the morning to go to university. She'll never hear his voice or see him again. At night she lies in bed and wonders: "Is there no way he could have lived? Could he not have been spared somehow? If only he had been late for the demonstration for some reason, if only he had not been in the sight of the sniper, if only he had moved aside suddenly and the bullet had missed him. Why did the sniper choose to kill him? Why couldn't he have lived for just a few more years, or just one year, or even just a few months? If only I could see him one more time, talk to him a little and place my hand on his head, hug him and kiss him. Then he could return to death."

She asked God's forgiveness for having such thoughts. For five whole months she did everything she could to get justice for her son. She hired lawyers and tried to file charges. She went to different offices and filed more charges. She answered all their questions and summoned witnesses who all confirmed the same details. She attended the trials of police officers that were accused of killing demonstrators to try and find the sniper who had killed her son. After five months, she had got nowhere and could not accept that her son's killer was still free and going about his daily life life as normal: eating, drinking, sleeping and spending time with his family.

The martyr's mother longed to meet Field Marshal Tantawi, the head of the military council. She would promise not to waste his time, but wanted to ask him: "Field marshal, where are the snipers who killed our children? The Ministry of the Interior knows who they are, so why have none of them been arrested and put on trial? Not one sniper has been prosecuted. Is this justice, field marshal? My son is a martyr and, God willing, he is in heaven, but his killer must be put on trial. Egyptian law punishes those who steal chickens or who poison livestock; is the life of my son worth less than the life of an animal? Field marshal, how is it that the police officers that are on trial for killing demonstrators are still in their jobs? Why have they not been suspended from work so as to prevent them from interfering with witnesses and influencing the outcome of their trials?

"Why did the criminal court in Alexandria allow the police officers facing charges to remain at large for four months pending the date of their trial? What are we to expect from the senior officials inside the Ministry of the Interior who have remained in their jobs despite being accused of killing demonstrators? Will they devote their energies to maintaining law and order or to finding a way to avoid conviction? Why is the former minister of the interior, Habib el-Adly, being prosecuted by a judge who many people believe should himself be under investigation for corruption? Why is Habib el-Adly being protected by the state security service and when will they actually put an end to the general state of lawlessness in Egypt?

"Why does the current minister of the interior, Mansour el-Essawy, continue to exonerate officers accused of killing demonstrators, insisting that they were acting in legitimate self-defence? Is it appropriate for a minister to pass judgment before a trial reaches its verdict, and thereby, impede justice in this way? In any case, did the demonstrators start attacking police stations spontaneously, or were the attacks a result of the police officers first opening fire on the demonstrators in an attempt to disperse them? Were the snipers acting in self-defence? Were the police vehicles that ran over demonstrators acting in self-defence? Why is it that everyone who demands justice for the martyrs is accused of slandering the police? There are, of course, many upstanding officers in the police force, but those who committed murder must be tried and sentenced accordingly. In this revolution Egypt sacrificed the finest of its young for the sake of freedom. They died so that we might live in dignity. Isn't it the most basic justice that we should punish those who killed them?"

The mothers of the martyrs and all Egyptians await the field marshal's response.

Democracy is the answer.

AB

What is Holding the Military Council Back?

5 July 2011

Several weeks ago I received an invitation to meet with some members of the military council to exchange views about the situation in Egypt. I spent a few hours with three of the council's generals and came away from the meeting with a very good impression. I learned that they had a thorough understanding of domestic and foreign affairs, as well as genuine commitment to the revolution and the nation. Nevertheless, I also sensed that these generals were not the ones making the final decisions, but that their role was to simply convey the different viewpoints to a higher authority. At that time, I still believed that the military council would introduce the changes demanded by the revolution, as it had promised to do in its initial statements. However, six whole months have passed since the start of the revolution and not one of our demands has been met. On the contrary, it often appears as though the military council is pushing things in the opposite direction. So, on Friday 8 July the Egyptian people sent a strong message to those in power: millions took to the streets all over the country to demand that the military council implement the goals of the revolution.

Why has the military council been so hesitant to implement these changes? We know that there are regional and international forces that are hostile towards the Egyptian revolution. Some of the ruling families in the Gulf have continued to defend Hosni Mubarak and they are now putting pressure on the military council to prevent Mubarak from being put on trial. Perhaps they are motivated by some kind of loyalty towards their old friend Mubarak, or perhaps it is because his sons, Gamal and Alaa, were partners with some of the Gulf emirs in business ventures worth millions of dollars. The most likely reason, however, in my opinion, is that the Egyptian revolution will change the notion of governance throughout the entire Arab world. Henceforth, a country's ruler will no longer be the symbol of the nation, nor the elder of the tribe, as is the case in the Gulf; rather, they will be public servants employed by the people, and if they err, they will be brought to account and prosecuted. If this democratic notion of a leader's role were to be transferred from Egypt to the Gulf, it would create serious problems for the region's ruling families. Israel, backed by the United States, is also working hard to bring down the revolution. This is because it fears that democratic transformation in Egypt will make the country a strong regional player that will take a leading role in the Arab world. However strong these foreign pressures may be, they do not fully account for the military council's reluctance to introduce the changes demanded by the revolution. After all, although we may criticise the military council's political performance, it should not be forgotten that it is ultimately part of the wider Egyptian military, which has always strongly guarded the nation's autonomy and been highly vigilant against foreign interference in Egyptian decision-making.

So what then is holding the military council back and preventing it from introducing the changes demanded by the revolution? Here we should remember that Hosni Mubarak was not simply a despot who plundered Egypt, subjugated it and caused it to decline in every field of activity. Mubarak is also responsible for creating a despotic regime based upon a particular political vision. It consists of an absolute monopoly of power. In 1986, he appointed the late General Zaki Badr[1] to the position of minister of the interior. He was renowned, not only for his brilliant talent in crushing opponents, but also for his great fondness for shouting obscenities and scandalously insulting everyone around him. Zaki Badr managed to offend Egyptians from all walks of life, but Mubarak continued to stand by his side. That is, however, until he gave a fateful speech in Banha in January 1990 in which he insulted everyone in a manner that could not be tolerated. *Al Shaab* newspaper published the text of the offending speech and Mubarak had the minister dismissed. The

1 General Zaki Badr (1926–97), former minister of the interior, began a crackdown on Muslim militants opposed to the Egyptian government. He was accused by human rights groups of sanctioning torture in prisons.

editor of *Al Shaab*, the late intellectual Adel Hussein, told me that he later met with Hosni Mubarak, who took him aside and said: "Adel, don't imagine for a moment that Zaki Badr was dismissed because of what you published in *Al Shaab*. No, I decided to dismiss him for my own reasons." So, from this we can infer that Mubarak viewed any kind of responsiveness to public opinion as a form of weakness that lessened his prestige as a ruler.

Hosni Mubarak consistently monopolised decision-making and maintained an exclusive right to appoint and dismiss ministers without justifying his motives. Furthermore, none of his ministers had the authority to make decisions or act independently of Mubarak. It is clear that the military council is operating on the same notion of power as Mubarak. After Mubarak stepped down, all of the legal scholars specialising in constitutional law agreed that the existing constitution was no longer valid and that a new one should be drafted by an elected constituent assembly. The military council, however, decreed that a committee should be formed to amend the existing constitution and then they held a referendum on the amendments. The results of the referendum were then overruled by the military council, which then announced a separate interim constitution. Time and again, the military council has unilaterally taken decisions that do not correspond with public opinion or with the ideas of the revolution. At least half of the ministers in the government set up by the military council formerly belonged to the Mubarak regime, as well as the majority of the newly appointed governors. Some of them were officers from the state security service and therefore guilty of abusing Egyptians and treating them like animals. Instead of putting them on trial, the military council rewarded them by appointing them as governors. Furthermore, the military council kept Yehia el-Gamal in office as deputy prime minister despite public dissatisfaction with his performance. Not to mention the military council's appointment of Mohamed al-Urabi[1] as minister of foreign affairs – a man who was always singing Mubarak's praises, describing him as the greatest leader in the history of Egypt.

The military council has consistently ignored dozens of calls for the institutions of the state to be purged of people with links to the Mubarak regime. This prevarication has given the counter-revolutionary forces time to gather strength and they are now carrying out acts of destruction with the aim of creating a state of disorder in order to put pressure on the Egyptian people. It seems that the military council has adopted Mubarak's well-known formula: "Say what you like and write what you like; he who rules will do as he likes regardless." Like Mubarak, the military council has distanced themselves from the Egyptian people and are slow to respond to their demands. When millions

1 Mohamed al-Urabi served as as minister of foreign affairs in Essam Sharaf's cabinet. He resigned after just one month in office "out of respect for the revolution", making him one of the shortest serving foreign ministers in Egypt's modern history.

of Egyptians took to the streets to demand change, the military council took almost a day and a half to issue a statement through Prime Minister Essam Sharaf. His response ignored most of the revolution's basic demands, and was reminiscent of he rhetoric used by the now dissolved National Democratic Party.

Mubarak's political vision also gave state institutions ostensible independence only. He insisted that Egypt was a state comprised of institutions and that he would never interfere with the independence of the judiciary. In truth, Mubarak controlled everything that happened in Egypt. He was the supreme head of each institution and he controlled the judiciary by means of the Judicial Inspection Department – a department that was subordinate to the minister of justice, who was personally appointed by the president himself. Mubarak exerted so much pressure on the judges that they became like instruments of his rule. Most of the judges rejected being used in this way but some judges acquiesced and oversaw the rigging of elections. Furthermore, documents have emerged which prove that some judges colluded with the state security service by delivering predetermined rulings in some cases. Despite repeated requests from senior judges to purge the judiciary, six months have passed since the revolution and the military council has taken no decision to do so, nor has it made any efforts to bring about judicial independence. Indeed, the military council spared the office of the attorney general and the attorney general himself, who was well-known during the time of Mubarak for his special relationships with certain politicians. His close links to powerful people compromised his position and often prevented him from taking the necessary ruling in a number of cases relating to police corruption and violence. He also failed to conduct inspections of premises belonging to the state security service, as well as police stations, where abuses against Egyptians were rampant, and because of this failure, these practices were allowed to continue unabated.

Mubarak strived to extol democracy while crushing his opponents. Under Mubarak, the state security service abused and tortured tens of thousands of Egyptians in police stations and buildings belonging to the state security service. Even as this was going on, Mubarak never missed an opportunity to laud the democratic transformation Egypt had witnessed under him. Today we see a similar thing: the military council extols the revolution in its statements and asserts its commitment to the rule of law, while at the same time referring thousands of Egyptian civilians to the military courts for trial. Egyptian citizens risk being arrested or court-martialled for taking part in a demonstration or a sit-in. Conversely, those who plundered, abused and killed Egyptians are being tried in the civilian courts.

In the end, the military council is being held back and prevented from meeting the demands of the revolution because it is adhering to the same political principles as Mubarak. While there's no doubt that the military council is sincere and committed to the success of the revolution, they cannot create a new system using the same methods that were employed by Mubarak when he was in power. The military council's governance has been reactionary and threatens to bring the country to a standstill, or worse, a dangerous confrontation. The millions of Egyptians who made one of the greatest revolutions in history consented to entrust their revolution to the military council, but six months have passed and nothing has changed. The revolution's demands are straightforward and legitimate: the Egyptian people want justice, the purging of state institutions and democratic reform. We have the right to know where Hosni Mubarak is being kept, what the state of his health really is, and why he is being treated better than any other normal prisoner. We have a right to know where Gamal and Alaa Mubarak are, and to have a representative sent to confirm that they really are in prison. All state institutions must be thoroughly purged of Hosni Mubarak's allies, and the police force must be purged of corrupt officers. They must all be justly tried, beginning with Hosni Mubarak and his former minister of the interior, Habib el-Adly. The issue of social justice must be addressed by establishing a minimum wage that will ensure that the poor have a decent standard of living, and higher wages should be capped to prevent a drain on public funds. These are the revolution's demands and they will not be abandoned, no matter what sacrifices have to be made. The military council should listen to the voice of the Egyptian people before it is too late. Hundreds of Egyptians have already sacrificed their lives, and thousands have suffered injury, all for the sake of the revolution. But the Egyptian people are fully prepared to sacrifice more blood and lives to gain freedom.

Democracy is the answer.

AB

Has the Revolution Gone Awry?

5 July 2011

The American comedian George Carlin was known for his dark humour and acerbic wit. During one of his shows, he was asked what he would do if he found himself on a flight that was about to crash. Carlin's response was that he would, of course, save himself by shoving and pushing past the "women and children, midgets and dwarves, cripples, war widows, paralysed veterans, people with broken legs … [and] the emotionally disturbed." This humorous image illustrates how some people will do anything to save themselves and their own selfish interests. Whenever I see our new minister of foreign affairs, Mohamed al-Urabi, I am reminded of Carlin's words. Mohamed al-Urabi was one of Mubarak's most loyal and closest associates and he often spoke fondly of the former president and his family. He considered Mubarak an exceptional leader, the like of which Egypt had never seen before, nor will ever see again. According to an article published in *Al-Wafd* newspaper, al-Urabi once said: "God loves Egypt because He has favoured it with a peerless gift whose name is Gamal Mubarak."

Mohamed al-Urabi is now minister of foreign affairs in the post-revolution government – a revoltuion that has ousted his exceptional leader and thrown the "peerless gift" Gamal Mubarak in prison.

This is not an unusual happenstance in post-revolution Egypt: many of the senior officials now charged with making governmental decisions were amongst Mubarak's biggest supporters. Samir Radwan, the current minister of finance, was a member of the policy committee under the old regime and a close associate of Gamal Mubarak. Gamal recommended him to Youssef Boutros Ghali, then minister of finance, who appointed him as one of his advisers in 2005. Furthermore, Hosni Mubarak personally made Radwan a member of the People's Assembly by presidential appointment. As minister, Radwan played an important role in formulating Mubarak's economic policy, but now he claims to be a supporter of the revolution, again bringing to mind George Carlin's escape plan from the plummeting airplane.

The problem here is not so much the duality of the ministers, but that the revolution has ousted Mubarak but not his regime. The senior officials in the Ministry of the Interior, who aided Habib el-Adly in abusing, torturing and killing Egyptians, are still in their jobs. Bigwigs in the media, who for so long misled public opinion by pandering to the former president, are still in their positions. The judges who oversaw rigged elections are still practicing law. The state security officers who committed horrific crimes against the Egyptian people have not lost there jobs, and some have even been appointed as governors in recognition of their services to the regime. What are we now to expect from all of these officials? They did not call for the revolution, nor are they sympathetic with its goals. They are trying to conspire against the revolution by impeding change and fostering conflict. The conspiracy against the Egyptian revolution has become obvious and its main characteristics can be summaried as follows:

First: The trials of senior officials from the old regime are deliberately conducted at a slow pace, so that the anger of people dissipates and they eventually forget all about it and get back to busying themselves with their daily affairs. Why, even now, has Mubarak not been tried? Where is the truth amongst all these conflicting reports about his health?[1] Why has he not been treated like a normal prisoner? Where are his sons, Alaa and Gamal Mubarak, and why don't we see pictures of them in their prison cells? Why are the senior officials being held in Tarra prison given special treatment? Who let Hussein Salem[2] flee the country, and why was Interpol not notified from the outset? Why were Zakariya Azmi, Fathi Sorour, and Safwat el-Sherif only arrested two months after the revolution – a period long enough for them to sort their affairs, hide incriminating evidence and smuggle their ill-gotten assets abroad? Why did the state take six months to offer support to those wounded in the revolution or the families of those who had been killed? Why did the late activist Mahmoud Qutb not receive proper medical attention for his wounds in Nasser Hospital while Sharm el-Sheikh hospital was evacuated for Suzanne Mubarak to receive dental care? Why did the Egyptian government intervene to bring in a German doctor to check the precious health of Hosni Mubarak?

Second: The continuous state of lawlessness and the failure of the police to carry out their duty. The withdrawal of the police was a deliberate attempt to terrorise Egyptians, disrupt tourism and prevent foreign investment. The military council want to blame the revolution for the country's ruin and to portray the revolutionaries as thugs and foreign agents, while at the same time praising the police officers as heroes. Police officers who stand accused of murder remain in their jobs and many of the trials have been delayed for months, enabling these police officers to pressure the families of the victims into altering their statements.

Third: Attempts to polarise the revolutionary forces and foster conflict between the liberals and the Islamists by creating the impression that, as a result of the revolution, Egypt has irrevocably fallen into the hands of extremists. It is worth recalling how the newspaper *Al-Ahram* printed a picture of a man whose ear had been cut off under the headline: "Salafists cut off the ear of a Copt." Let's not forget how the media celebrated Aboud al-Zumar as though he were a national hero. Perhaps this will help us understand why churches and Copts are attacked almost on a weekly basis without any police intervention. In effect it continuously discredits the Islamists and ruins the image of the Egyptian revolution both in Egypt and abroad.

Fourth: The scale of the economic crisis has been exaggerated with repeated statements about how Egypt is on the verge of bankruptcy because of the revolution. The argument, however, is deceptive as it was Mubarak who left the country in dire economic straits with 40 per cent of people living

1 The state news agency, amid high tension over the election of a new president, quoted medical sources as saying the former head of state was "clinically dead". Other sources claimed that he was on life support after suffering a stroke. Mubarak showed up to his trial on a hospital stretcher.

2 Hussein Salem is a fugitive businessman wanted on charges of corruption for attempting to monopolise gas sales to Israel.

below the poverty line, and unprecedented levels of unemployment – with one in every three residents of Cairo living in slums. The revolution has not yet governed. If there are post-revolution crises, then they are the responsibility of the military council that has taken over the president's responsibilities and the government that it has formed.

The events in Tahrir Square last week have multiple implications. Thugs were let loose to incite riots and attack the Ministry of the Interior in order to give the police a pretext for attacking demonstrators. This reveals the level of hostility felt by high-ranking police officers towards the revolution. For what else compels a police officer to drive around in a vehicle insulting the mothers of demonstrators over a loudspeaker? What caused a senior security officer in Agouza to insult the mother of Ahmed Zein el-Abidin, who lost his life in the revolution, to kick her in the stomach and assault her son, Mohamed, before arresting him so that he faces a military tribunal. These shameful attacks by police on the families of the revolution's martyrs have been accompanied by a smear campaign created by a group of journalists, broadcasters, and producers who still take their orders from the state security service, re-branded as Homeland Security. As for Mansour el-Essawy, I believe that the conspirators against the revolution could not hope for a better minister of interior, for he believes that he should defend his officers no matter what they do. What happened in Tahrir Square last week was the dress rehearsal for a major conspiracy to completely abort the revolution.

The question now is this: has the Egyptian revolution gone awry? On 11 February when Mubarak was forced to step down, millions of Egyptians went out into the streets to celebrate. After the victory, however, they returned to their homes instead of continuing in Tahrir Square and selecting spokespeople to negotiate with the military council until their demands were fulfilled. The second mistake was that the revolutionaries became divided before the demands of the revolution had been met. Instead of abolishing Mubarak's constitution and calling for a new one to be drafted, the military council preferred to take up Mubarak's own proposal to simply amend some of the articles of the existing constitution. A referendum was held and the people voted in favour of the amendments, but the military council bypassed the results to put in place their own 63-article interim constitution. The referendum divided the revolutionaries into two factions: the liberals and the Islamists. A fierce rivalry has broken out amongst them, with the liberals calling for a new constitution to be drafted before the next elections, and the Islamists calling for elections to be held first. Both factions have been so busy attacking each other that they have forgotten that the regime that the revolution sought to overthrow has not gone away. What good would new elections do if they are supervised by a Ministry of the Interior staffed by Habib el-Adly's aides and supporters, and by judges who have previously overseen the rigging of elections but have not been dismissed from their positions? What can we expect from a constitution drafted by legal scholars who previously worked to serve the interests of the dictatorship?

The Egyptian revolution has entered a critical phase, and stands at a crossroads. So what now is to be done? We have to remember that Hosni Mubarak enjoyed the enormous support of Israel and from most Western states and Arab states. No one could imagine that he could be ousted. Yet the Egyptian people did it. Only those who made the revolution can protect it. This is why the demonstrations taking place next Friday are important; their aim is to put the revolution back on track. We must put aside our ideological differences and return to how we were during the revolution: Copts, Salafis, and Muslim Brothers together, with veiled next to non-veiled women. We shall demand neither a constitution nor elections; rather, we will demand that state institutions be purged of those with links to the old regime. We will demand that those accused of killing demonstrators be fully and justly tried. We will demand an unequivocal end to the prosecution of civilians in military courts. We will take to the streets on Friday, God willing, prepared to pay the price for freedom. And we will be, just as we were during the days of the revolution, ready to die at any moment – for our lives are not more precious than the hundreds who willingly sacrificed theirs for the sake of Egypt's future and the dignity of its people.

Democracy is the answer.

AB

The Story of Abu Shama

19 July 2011

There was once a street, whose residents were like those of any other street – some were difficult to like but most of them were decent people who worked hard to provide for their children. Their lives could have gone on as normal, but fate had other plans for them. One night, shortly before dawn, the neighbourhood was woken by the sound of screaming and gunfire. The residents went out on their balconies to see what was happening. The noise was coming from the apartment at the end of the street that belonged to Hassan and his beautiful new bride. The noise died down and when morning came they found Hassan's body lying in the street with a piece of paper pinned to his chest that read: "This is what happens to anyone who defies Abu Shama."[1]

The news of what had happened spread quickly: masked gunmen had tried

1 Shama means "mole", i.e., this is a nickname for "the one with the mole".

to rape Hassan's wife, and when he tried to protect her they turned on him and killed him. Their leader, the infamous Abu Shama, then found Hassan's wife and raped her. Panic took hold of the residents of the street and they rushed to the nearby police station to report the incident to the senior police officer. He was a good-natured man in his late forties; the people trusted him and believed him to be both brave and honest. He assured the residents that he would arrest Abu Shama that very day, or the following day at the very latest. The next day, however, another attack took place at the home of Farag the barber. Abu Shama and his gang bound and gagged Farag's three children and then Abu Shama violently violated his wife. When Farag put up a fight they killed him and dumped his body in the street bearing the same message: "This is what happens to anyone who defies Abu Shama."

Time and again the same thing would happen to the residents of the street: a husband would put up a fight and be killed, then his wife would be raped. Abu Shama kept on killing husbands and raping their wives, and each time the residents buried one of the husbands they would go to the same police officer and plead with him to do something. The senior police officer was honest with them and said: "This kind of crime is very difficult to prevent. I cannot predict who the next victim will be, and I don't have enough officers to protect every wife in the neighbourhood. They are armed and not from around here so they will be difficult to find." The residents despaired when they realised that the police could not protect them. Some of them decided to move away, but most of the residents had no choice but to stay put; they could not afford to buy a new apartment and move their whole family.

Abu Shama continued to assault and rape the women of the street, but now none of the husbands were killed. All of the husbands had ceased trying to defend their wives. Some offered some token resistance in order to save face but then gave in and let Abu Shama have his way with their wives. At first, the husbands went around with their heads bowed in shame, not daring to speak with anyone or even look at them. Little by little, however, they started to get used to the fact that their wives had been raped and didn't feel as bad, perhaps because they weren't alone in their suffering. Many men came to see it as part of life and were even openly thankful that Abu Shama raped only their wives and not their virgin daughters, which would have spoiled their chances of marrying. In whispers, the wives would secretly discuss Abu Shama's extraordinary sexual potency, such that none of them had come across before. The women never saw Abu Shama's face because he never removed his mask, but they all described the large black mole that he had at the base of his neck.

In his Friday sermon, the imam of the local mosque, Sheikh Abdel Baset – whose own wife had been raped a number of times – said that because they were coerced, the men who allowed Abu Shama to rape their wives were blameless under Islamic law, insofar as putting up resistance would mean certain death for them. Even though Sheikh Abdel Baset was lenient on this subject, he was extremely strict when it came to observing the more superficial aspects of religion. He refused to shake hands with women, or to speak with any woman who was not wearing the hijab.

Ahmed Abdel Qader, the well-known leftist intellectual, came up with a theory after his own wife had been raped by Abu Shama several times. He would stand in the coffee shop and say: "The sense of shame that a man feels when his wife sleeps with someone else is based solely on the reactionary idea, inherited from decadent bourgeois culture, that he owns her body." If anyone objected to this, Abdel Qader would cut the discussion short by saying: "Listen my boy, I'm not going to waste my time on you. Have you read Descartes or Nietzsche? Have you heard of Hegel or Spengler?" In this way he cowed his listeners and silenced them. Then the great intellectual would continue: "Read these philosophers and you will understand that when Abu Shama rapes your wife, it is, in essence, a mere act of impingement: just one piece of flesh penetrating another, no more and no less."

The position taken by Sheikh Abdel Baset and Abdel Qader was nothing compared to the attitude of some of the husbands who would ask Abu Shama for money or favours after he had raped their wives. Abu Shama would give them what they wanted, but would take pleasure in humiliating them by mentioning intimate details about their wives. The morals of the people in the street changed and they became selfish, hypocritical, resentful and wary of others. They hated to see others prosper and rejoiced in their misfortunes. Some of them even turned to drugs and alcohol perhaps to mask the sense of humiliation, while others turned to extremist interpretations of religion. Wearing the hijab or the niqab, and having a beard became the beginning and end of religion. These extremists disagreed over superficial matters and they exchanged slanderous insults and accused each other of being sinful infidels. None of them cared to admit that they were doing nothing to prevent their wives from being raped on a regular basis.

For two and a half years the neighbourhood lived through this nightmare. One day, however, a resident of the street named Karim married a local woman called Maha. Karim was the son of Haji Musaylahi, whose wife had been raped by Abu Shama, just like all the others. On Karim's return from his honeymoon, he went to perform the Friday prayer at the mosque, but when Sheikh Abdel Baset began to justify inaction in the face of coercion, Karim stood up and said: "Sheikh, religion does not teach us to stand by idly and let our honour be destroyed." The congregation turned on him but Karim did not back down. "Your wives are raped because you gave in. But so long as I'm alive, I will not permit it to happen to my wife. You shall see." Some people in the street ridiculed him but many others agreed with him and joined his cause as if they had been waiting for someone to give them the courage to resist.

The news about Karim and his supporters reached Abu Shama, and the very next day he descended on Karim's apartment in order to rape his wife. A terrible battle ensued; the sounds of which rang out through the entire street. It lasted for almost an hour, and afterwards, the dead bodies of three of Karim's supporters were brought out. Then Karim himself appeared, dragging the body of Abu Shama along the ground. They took off his mask, revealing his ugly face, and the people arrested the members of his gang. Everyone cheered and shouted "God is great!" and the police chief turned up and embraced Karim and his companions one by one. He said to them: "By your courage you have restored the honour of us all." The people were euphoric as they could now put the past behind them. The husbands forgot about what had happened to their wives and the street was filled with optimism.

Not long after, however, a string of thefts took place, thefts of every kind: the shoes of people praying in the mosque were stolen, handbags and jewellery were snatched from women in the street, and people were mugged late at night. The people in the neighbourhood began to lose hope and some of them started saying that Abu Shama, although a criminal, did at least protect the street from thieves.

One night a thief threatened Hamdi, a local shop owner, with a knife and emptied the cash desk before escaping on a motorbike. Hamdi called out for help and wailed like a woman, but when Karim and his friends appeared he yelled at them: "God damn you, you have ruined this street! We're being robbed every day in broad daylight. This never happened under Abu Shama."

Karim could not endure this and shouted back: "So you'd rather watch your wife being raped in front of your own eyes than be robbed of a few Egyptian pounds?" Had some more level-headed onlookers not intervened a fight would have broken out between them. Karim came to realise that what Hamdi said reflected the feelings of some people in the street – the ones who had gotten used to their wives being raped by Abu Shama and were content to put up with it so long as they received some recompense for the loss of their honour. Karim and his supporters went to the senior police officer and said to him: "Do your job and protect the people."

An expression of anger appeared on the policeman's face, but he kept his composure and said: "Security will be restored soon."

"You have been saying that for a long time, yet you haven't done anything."

"I'm making every effort," said the police officer.

"You know very well that the people committing these thefts are members of Abu Shama's old gang; they are terrorising the people in revenge for his killing," said Karim.

"There's no evidence to support what you say."

"I don't need any evidence."

"What is it that you want, Karim?" said the police officer.

"Are you with us or against us?"

"Have you forgotten that I was the first to congratulate you on your victory?" said the officer.

"You talk but you don't do anything."

"Careful what you say."

"I have faced death and my friends have been killed before my own eyes. Your threats don't frighten me," replied Karim.

After an angry silence, Karim suddenly had a thought and marched right up to the officer and shouted, "Open your shirt!"

The officer became agitated. He attempted to stand up but Karim anticipated this and seized his neck with his hand; he squeezed it and prevented him from moving. With his other hand he undid the policeman's collar and opened his shirt. At the base of his neck Karim saw a large black mole.

Democracy is the answer.

AB

Do you Support the Revolution?

26 July 2011

Like all Egyptians, I am proud of the Egyptian army, but feel it is my duty to direct some criticism towards the policies of the military council, which is currently acting as head of state in Egypt. A few days ago, thousands of revolutionaries marched to the Ministry of Defence to submit their demands to the military council, in a peaceful and civilised manner. In response, the military police cornered the demonstrators and allowed hundreds of thugs to attack them with Molotov cocktails, swords and tear gas canisters. This horrific assault on peaceful demonstrators left hundreds injured, as the police had been given orders not to intervene. The military police did nothing to protect the demonstrators, leaving them open to attacks by groups of thugs hired by the old regime. Such behaviour is unacceptable and the military council must explain why they have so far ignored the demands put forward by the revolution. Six months have passed since Mubarak stepped down and nothing has changed. The demands are outlined below:

First: The majority of Egyptian judges are upstanding citizens and act in good conscience when carrying out their rulings. The judicial system in Egypt, however, is not independent as the judges are answerable to the Judicial Inspection Department, which is subordinate to the minister of justice, who in turn is appointed by the president. The judges have repeatedly called for the Judicial Inspection Department to be transferred from the jurisdiction of the Ministry of Justice and placed under the authority of the Supreme Judicial Council. The military council, however, have not answered their request.

There are also judges that are incentivised to work as legal advisors for various state bodies in return for lucrative returns. This can compromise their impartiality as they often work on cases against those bodies for which they worked as legal advisors. The April 6 Youth Movement[1] recently published a document that angered the military council as it highlighted this conflict of interests The document shows that Judge Mustafa Suleiman Abul Yusr, who took over the investigation of Hosni Mubarak, works as an advisor for EgyptAir; a company that is under the jurisdiction of the Ministry of Civil Aviation. It is easy to imagine how potentially embarrassing it could be if this judge was commissioned to investigate the claims that the former minister of civil aviation, Ahmed Shafik, is guilty of wasting public funds. In this case, the judge would be required to investigate the very minister who paid him his monthly salary. Getting rid of this practice of allowing judges to work as legal advisors for state bodies is a prerequisite for creating an independent judiciary. The military council has again ignored this demand. Rulings arrived at by the Court of Cassation have shown that there are judges who have knowingly overseen rigged elections. Senior judges have repeatedly called upon the military council to dismiss these corrupt judges, but no action has been taken. It is a basic demand of the revolution that the judiciary system is purged to ensure its independence and to reassure the public that trials are fair.

Second: Despite my respect for Attorney General Abdel Meguid Mahmoud and the office he holds, we should, nevertheless, point out that he allowed political considerations to interfere with the requirements of his position after being appointed by Hosni Mubarak. Under his leadership, the office of the attorney general failed to carry out inspections of the detention centres in which thousands of Egyptians were brutally tortured. These premises belonged to the state security service, as well as the police, yet the attorney general did not order prosecutors to investigate any of the officers involved. Furthermore, since Ahmed Shafik resigned as prime minister, 24 claims have been made against him and he stands accused of wasting public funds. Three whole months have passed since the claims were submitted, but the attorney general has not ordered an investigation into them. It is clear that we need

1 The April 6 Youth Movement is an Egyptian activist group established in 2008 by Ahmed Maher and Ahmed Salah in order to mobilise support for the workers in El-Mahalla El-Kubra, who were planning to strike on 6 April. See Glossary.

a new attorney general to be appointed, preferably one that is sympathetic towards the spirit of the revolution. Some names have been put forward, such as Zakariya Abdel Aziz and Hesham el-Bastawisi, who are both considered outstanding judges whom Egypt could be proud of. Therefore, the dismissal of Attorney General Abdel Meguid Mahmoud[1] is a basic demand of the revolution.

Third: The military council continues to turn tens of thousands of civilian demonstrators over to the military courts while those who are charged with corruption and the killing of demonstrators enjoy preferential treatment by being tried in regular civilian courts. The military council has so far refused to dissolve the local councils and the National Democratic Party, stating that they will not take any extraordinary measures. We had to wait a long time before the NDP and the local councils were dissolved by the courts. We are glad that members of the military council respect the law, but trying civilians in the military courts is a flagrant violation of legal principles as well as international treaties to which Egypt is a signatory. Furthermore, the administrative court in Qena recently issued a ruling that prohibited the trying of civilians in military courts. The court also ordered that all those in the custody of the military justice system be released and retried in regular civilian courts. Why then does the military council not abide by the law and carry out this ruling? The enforcement of the prohibition on trying civilians in military courts is a basic demand of the revolution.

Fourth: During the revolution, 1,000 Egyptians lost their lives and almost 5,000 were injured at the hands of the authorities. It is believed that 1,000 Egyptians are still missing, but are most likely dead and buried in unmarked graves. Six whole months have passed since these horrific crimes were committed and only one police officer has been convicted on charges of killing demonstrators. This exception, however, was the trial of a police sergeant who was convicted in absentia and who remains a fugitive. The revolution has called upon Minister of the Interior Mansour el-Essawy to suspend those officers who are accused of killing demonstrators to prevent them from putting pressure on the victim's families to alter their testimonies. The minister of the interior, however, seems intent upon protecting the killers and has helped foster the conditions that will enable them to escape punishment. He has not suspended them from their jobs, and in fact, some of these officers who have been accused of killing demonstrators, such as Wael el-Koumy in Alexandria, have even been promoted and transferred to more prestigious departments where they now receive salaries that are three times higher than the ones they used to get. The suspension of all officers

1 Abdel Meguid Mahmoud was removed from office by Mohamed Morsi on 22 November 2012 after the constitutional declaration was announced. On 2 July 2013 the Egyptian Court of Cassation deemed his removal illegal and reinstated him again as attorney general.

accused of killing demonstrators pending the conclusion of their trials is a basic demand of the revolution.

Fifth: Egyptians witnessed groups of snipers occupying the roofs of houses and killing dozens of demonstrators in cold blood. As a matter of fact, there is video footage that clearly shows a group of snipers on the roof of the Ministry of the Interior building in Cairo, with their commanding officer directing them to kill the demonstrators. Where are these snipers and why have they not been arrested? The minister of the interior said that the snipers were not operating under the jurisdiction of the police force, but then documents emerged that confirmed the opposite is true. This leaves us with two possible explanations: either the minister does not know what is going on in his own ministry or he is lying. Both explanations are adequate grounds for his dismissal from office. Exposing the identities of the snipers and putting them on trial is a basic demand of the revolution.

Sixth: Since the beginning of the revolution, we have called on the military council to purge state institutions of those with links the old, corrupt regime. We warned them that leaving them in their positions would enable them to conspire against the revolution. The military council, regrettably, did not respond to our demands and left the old regime in place, and we are now paying the price for this decision. Most of the assaults and acts of destruction have been orchestrated by those loyal to the old regime. A few days ago the demonstrators at the sit-in in Alexandria seized a state security officer who was trying to infiltrate the demonstration and confiscated his identity card. The officer's mission was to act as an agent provocateur: he was to join the demonstration and throw stones at the armed forces so that they would open fire on the demonstrators. A few days prior to this event, a group of thugs confessed to public prosecutors that a former, prominent member of the now dissolved NDP had paid them large sums of money to break up a sit-in taking place in Saad Zaghloul Park in Alexandria in honour of those killed during the revolution. Even Dr El Sebai, the famous forensic pathologist who fabricated reports for police officers, was merely disqualified for a period of two months before returning to his normal medical practice. It seems as though the authorities foresee that they will have a continuing need for his spurious reports. Purging state institutions of those with ties to the old regime is a basic demand of the revolution.

Seventh: The state media has not been purged and has now fully resumed its old tactics of misleading the public in its attempt to discredit the revolution. One of the lies propagated by the media is that the revolution is responsible for the economic crisis in Egypt. This is completely false. Firstly, it is the Mubarak regime that is to blame for creating the severe economic crisis. Indeed the crisis was itself a primary cause for the revolution. Secondly, the Egyptian revolution cannot be blamed for the crisis because the revolutionaries did not actually take power. Consequently, the military council bear sole responsibility for all of the problems that have arisen since Mubarak stepped down as it has been the acting head of state. If the tourist industry and investment in Egypt have been negatively impacted, then the reason behind that has been the deterioration of the security situation. The Egyptian police have neglected their duties for six months, so we have the right to ask: what has the military council done to restore law and order, so as to assist the recovery of the economy? Why did the military police in Qena do nothing when demonstrators blocked the railway line to Upper Egypt for an entire week?[1] Why did the military police not intervene when the church in Atfih was destroyed, or when the churches in Imbaba were set ablaze? The restoration of law and order is a basic demand of the revolution. For this reason we call for the dismissal of the present minister of the interior and the restructuring of the police force.

Eighth: Why is Hosni Mubarak still in Sharm el-Sheikh? Is it proper that a civilian defendant should be allowed to choose the city in which he stands trial? Is there any truth to the rumour that Hosni Mubarak has travelled to Saudi Arabia and back more than once? Why have we not yet seen a single picture of him? And what is the truth behind all these contradictory reports about his health? Why has he not been transferred to the hospital in Tora prison and why is he not treated like any other normal prisoner? Why can he not be visited like an ordinary defendant, and why were the members of the special committee that went to visit Gamal and Alaa Mubarak not given access to them at the prison? Do Egyptians not have the right to know the truth? The trial for Hosni Mubarak and his family, in accordance with justice, is a basic demand of the revolution.

These are the demands of the revolution that demonstrators everywhere have been calling for. All of these demands are just and legitimate, and it is in the power of the military council to fulfil each and every one of them, yet it does not respond. The current crisis afflicting Egypt is the logical outcome of the military council's policies, which have been slow-moving, blundering and completely ignorant with regard to what the Egyptian people want. Egypt's future lies in the fulfilling of the revolution's demands – in no way can this be postponed or evaded.

Members of the military council, are you with the revolution or against it?

Democracy is the answer.

AB

1 Thousands of mostly Muslim demonstrators swelled through the streets of Qena to demonstrate against the recent appointment of a new Coptic Christian governor, Emad Mikhail, who had served in the police force of deposed President Hosni Mubarak.

How to Abort the Revolution in Six Steps

2 August 2011

Dear general, if the revolution took you by surprise, don't panic. Don't let the sight of millions of angry demonstrators frighten you. Stay calm. Take a deep breath and pull yourself together. You should know that a revolution is something extraordinary; it is a rare event in which people demonstrate great courage and confront their own death for the sake of freedom and dignity. Revolutions are the exception; generally, people will put up with injustice because they fear being punished for standing up for themselves, or because they do not wish to jeopardise their own petty interests. The evidence for this lies in the fact that there have been relatively few revolutions in human history. Circumstances have placed you at the summit of power in the aftermath of the revolution, so don't be frightened by the roar of the angry crowds in the streets. They are like animals – strong and full of rage, but highly irrational. You are the skilled animal tamer who, with deft lashes from your whip, will be able to tame them and put them back in their cages. To succeed in this, simply take the following six steps:

First: Glorify the revolution and denounce the deposed dictator. You must openly condemn the former era with complete conviction. Of course, you feel sympathetic towards the former dictator; he was, after all, your colleague and friend for decades. However, you must publicly curse his name and shout: "Long Live the Revolution!" The people will be taken in straight away: no one will remember your relationship with the ousted dictator for 40 years, or how you never once objected to the crimes he committed. People will believe you because they want to believe that you support the revolution, and people often tend to believe something simply because they want it to be true. Don't go overboard in cursing the old dictator, however, because this might arouse suspicions. Curse him once or twice, but no more than that. But you must constantly glorify the revolution. The citizenry must wake up in the morning to songs that glorify the revolution and then go to sleep to them at night. In this way, even though none of the revolution's aims have been fulfilled, nevertheless, people will feel as though it has been a success. Furthermore, this routine will make the Egyptian people believe that all happenings are a result of the revolution, exclusively.

Second: Keep the old regime intact. Never give in to the demands of the revolutionaries and don't change anything about the old regime – this would be a huge mistake. In the beginning they'll put you under severe pressure to make changes. Wait patiently until the pressure reaches its peak, and then make some small, superficial changes that don't fundamentally impact the structure of the old regime. What does the captain do when the ship is being pulled under the water? He must throw anything heavy overboard until the ship regains its buoyancy. This is precisely what you must do. Select some politicians who are unpopular with the people, then have them arrested and put on trial. Their trials have to be slow and complicated so that, in the end, people lose interest and forget what the trials were about in the first place. Meet with these unpopular politicians and explain to them that you'll never abandon them. Tell them that they will not be harmed, that the trials are just a political show to appease the people, nothing more. Make sure that, when they are in prison, they continue to enjoy the comforts that they are accustomed to; it should be as though they are still living in their luxurious mansions. Be careful never to abandon members of the old regime; these people are your loyal soldiers. If you neglect them, you won't be able to replace them, and then you'll find yourself alone and with no one to support you against the angry masses. The corrupt judge who will tailor their rulings according to how you instruct him by telephone, the prosecutor who will tamper with the evidence at your request, the well-known media personality who daily receives instructions from the security forces before they go on the air and the brutal police officer who'll torture and kill dozens of people in defence of the regime. These are all valuable assets that you must use to the fullest. Meet them in secret and assure them that the old system remains as it was and that it will not change in the future. Be generous towards them so that they will wholeheartedly identify themselves with your cause.

Third: Let the country slide into steep decline. You have to understand why the revolution happened. Society was divided into three groups: those who benefited from the regime, the revolutionaries, and ordinary people. The revolutionaries were few in number and made little impact because the regime continually suppressed them. The largest section of the population was made up of ordinary people; the regime worked against them but they didn't have the courage to object. The revolution erupted when the revolutionaries were able to persuade ordinary people to join with them. This is the revolution's weak spot; it is here that you should direct your blows. You must put pressure on the ordinary people so that they go back to being passive onlookers. To this end you need to aggravate crises throughout the country. Cut off the water that peasant farmers require and make sure that they cannot source the fertilisers they need, this way their crops will fail and the land will lie fallow. Have workers thrown out on the street because the factories shut down. Ensure that civil servants receive their salaries late and that any bonuses which they were promised are denied them. The police must completely vanish from the streets so that theft, violence and thuggery can flourish. Employ agent provocateurs to infiltrate groups of demonstrators, then have them attack public buildings and block off the railway lines. At the same time use your agents in the media to sow fear amongst the people; their role should be to amplify the crises and make every problem appear to be caused by the revolution. In this way, it will take root in the minds of the people that the country is on the verge of famine and anarchy because of the revolution and for no other reason.

Fourth: Strike at the revolutionaries unity and divide them amongst themselves. Never forget that the revolutionaries' are your real enemies. They don't trust you and they will grasp the extent of your plotting from the outset. You need to sow division amongst them. Make use of security reports to gain insight into their ideological and political attitudes. Although they were united by the revolution, in order to effect a regime change, you'll find that there are significant differences amongst them. Make up some issue, and then hold elections or a referendum so that the revolutionaries split into two opposing camps. When this is accomplished, form a secret alliance with one of the two camps against the other. It's always best to team up with religious fascists against the forces that advocate democracy. Fascists make excellent allies because they don't believe in democracy; they cynically exploit it as a means to gain power for themselves. They believe that they alone possess the truth and, consequently, they despise anyone who disagrees with them and have no respect for the rights of others.

The fascists are like a disciplined army that will put itself fully under your command. They will crush everyone who opposes you and support everything you say or do – all you have to do is promise them power. These fascists speak in the name of religion and zealously perform their prayers, but you'll be astonished by their capacity to lie and dissemble. They will break their oaths and betray the revolution with as much ease as lighting a cigarette. Tell the fascists to organise mass demonstrations as a show of strength. When the people see their military formations, their grim faces and hear their aggressive shouting, they'll panic, and many of them will ask themselves if the revolution that removed the dictator was a good idea in the first place. At this moment, various demonstrations need to spring up – these will be made up of groups set up for this purpose by the security agencies. Those who got rich under the old regime will provide funding and the media will provide the publicity. These new demonstrators will sing chants in praise of the ousted dictator; they will extol him as a great hero, and weep in front of the cameras as they recount the humiliations he suffered. In this way the revolution will split into two groups with opposing viewpoints. If you successfully execute these steps, then the revolutionaries will be besieged on every front. The fascists will threaten and attack them; ordinary people will come to believe that their demonstrations are the reason for the economic crisis and the breakdown in law and order. When this happens, the number of revolutionaries will die down and things will go back to being how they were before the revolution happened. That is to say, there will be a small group of committed activists whom the majority of people do not sympathise with.

Fifth: Contain the revolutionaries and discredit them. When ordinary people have abandoned the revolution and the fascists have turned against it, you must put in motion a large-scale, smear campaign to discredit the revolutionaries. This is easily accomplished; you have supporters in the media, the police and the judiciary. All you have to do is fabricate some documents and pictures that show that the revolutionaries are traitors and agents working for foreign powers, which instructed them to foment revolution. You need to put out dozens of television programmes and hold dozens of seminars to discuss this serious matter. Was the revolution truly indigenous, or was it orchestrated by foreign elements? Was it a case of the imperialist nations taking revenge against the now ousted dictator because he had always defended the independence of his country? You know very well that the dictator was, in fact, a traitor who cooperated with many foreign intelligence agencies, but necessity is its own justification. When the time is right, your spokesperson should announce that you have ordered an investigation to uncover the extent of the role played by foreign states in planning the revolution. Were there foreigners who instructed certain people about what they should do during the outset of the revolution? The fascists will fully support you and they will tell lies to discredit the revolutionaries because, ultimately, they want to take power for themselves. Ordinary people will become agitated and many of them will come to believe that the revolutionaries are nothing but traitorous fifth columnists. You'll laugh heartily when you see how the young revolutionaries, who only a few weeks earlier were looked upon as national heroes, are now hounded by disapproving looks and accusations of treason.

Sixth: Strike the fatal blow. Encourage the decline of economic conditions and the security situation. This shift will destroy the morale of ordinary people and they will start to despise the revolution as a result. Then, when things are at an all-time low, explain to the people that the crisis is acute and that things will likely get worse. Next, using this explanation as a pretext, ask the demonstrators to stop their protests and sit-ins so that conditions can stabilise and production resume. The revolutionaries, of course, won't agree to stop demonstrating. They will immediately feel as though you have tricked them and stolen the revolution. They'll realise that you were only pretending to protect the revolution, and have, in effect, contained it and obstructed its objectives. Small numbers of revolutionaries will come out and demonstrate again, calling for you to stand down – but this will be their own downfall. The fascists will attack them fiercely because of their own ambitions to get into power, while ordinary people, feeling disappointment and frustration, will denounce them and curse the revolution. The revolutionaries will try to explain their point of view but they will be wasting their breath: no one will listen to them. The fascists will accuse them of treason and of acting in service of foreign agendas, and ordinary people will blame them for the prevailing poverty, unemployment and anarchy. Send someone to photograph what's happening in the public squares; when you see that the ordinary people – who were once ready to die for the revolution – are now cursing the revolution, striking the revolutionaries and driving them out of the squares, then, and only then, will you have successfully accomplished your task. Then, take a vacation, you'll have earned it. Celebrate and be proud of what you've achieved: you will have succeeded in aborting the revolution.

P.S. I got the idea for this article when I was reading about the revolutions that occurred in the Comoros Islands.[1] The article has no connection with what's now taking place in Egypt, of course.

Democracy is the answer.

AB

How to Save the Revolution

9 August 2011

On 11 February, I was walking down Kasr El Aini Street on my way to Tahrir Square when a group of demonstrators gathered around me and asked how I thought the revolution would play out. As I was talking with them, I suddenly heard a loud scream that stopped me in my tracks. I became anxious because it reminded me of the screams I heard in the early days of the revolution when the snipers started shooting and demonstrators began dropping to the ground from gunshot wounds. This time, however, the scream was different. It came from a woman wearing a hijab who rushed out from a juice shop and shouted: "Mubarak has stepped down!"

I don't remember in detail what happened next because I, along with millions of others, rushed to Tahrir Square to celebrate the revolution's triumph. We were caught up in feelings of joy and pride that Egypt had not experienced since the October War in 1973. I could see grown men weeping, overcome by emotion. I stayed in Tahrir Square celebrating with the demonstrators until the early hours of the morning. When the demonstrators began to disperse a small number of people spoke up to say that we should not leave the square until all of the revolution's demands had been met. Their appeal, however,

1 The Comoros Islands underwent a political crisis that started off in 1997 with the separatism on Anjouan. The political authorities on the island had turned the population of the island against the central government, advocating at first reunification with France, and later a greater autonomy bordering on independence.

fell on deaf ears. Most of the people believed that the revolution had been won and that matters should be handed over to the military council who would work to introduce the changes sought by the revolution. We trusted the military council as they had supported the revolution and refused to open fire on the demonstrators. However, I now believe that the biggest mistake of the revolution was for demonstrators to leave the squares across Egypt when Mubarak stepped down from power. We should have formed a body to represent the interests of the revolution, whose members would meet the military council in order to oversee the implementation of our demands. A number of truths have come to light since that time.

Although Mubarak resigned, the regime was not overthrown. To appreciate this fact we only have to consider how the Egyptian government preserved the state security service or how Mansour el-Essawy continues to protect the police officers and snipers who killed demonstrators. Actually, it is enough to simply look at the list of newly appointed governors to appreciate that it is only Mubarak who has gone. His regime, however, continues to govern the country.

We should, in all fairness, pay tribute to the military council for protecting the revolution, but we should also remind ourselves that they never really subscribed to the vision of the revolution. The military council has not implemented any of the revolution's demands except when it has been put under intense popular pressure to do so. This may be due to the military culture that prevails amongst members of the military council, a culture based upon respecting authority and carrying out orders without question. The military council's motive was always different from the will of the revolution. The revolutionaries believed that ousting Mubarak was the first step towards removing the old regime entirely before creating a new revolutionary system. It seems, however, that the military council wanted to preserve the regime by sacrificing Mubarak. The disparity between the demands of the revolution and the actions of the military council is the root cause of the problems now facing Egypt. If the military council had implemented the revolution's demands from the start, then Egypt would now be making a real transition towards democracy. It should be emphasised here that my criticism regarding the policies of the military council in no way detracts from my genuine respect for the Egyptian army as a whole. However, the military council is currently the acting head of state, and for this reason, the Egyptian people have a right and indeed a duty to critique its policies.

After Mubarak stepped down, a number of intellectuals and scholars submitted studies to the military council that detailed how to remove the old regime from the state's institutions and, thereby, pave the way for a truly democratic system. The military council, however, was unresponsive and delayed taking the steps required to protect the revolution, giving those with links to the old regime the perfect opportunity to conspire against the revolution. These conspiracies have been backed by foreign countries, including Arab ones that oppose Egypt's transition towards democracy because it would make Egypt a powerful, regional state that would lead the whole Arab world. For six months there has been a succession of conspiracies against the revolution, as if to punish the Egyptian people for rising up in the name of freedom and dignity. Egyptians are living in fear because police officers loyal to Mubarak are ignoring their duties and failing to protect the people from rampaging thugs, most of whom have links with senior figures in the old regime. On top of this, the state media, which is still controlled by members of the old regime, has continued to blame the revolution for the current economic crisis in Egypt. This portrayal is completely untrue; the revolutionaries did not come to power and can therefore not be held responsible for the dire financial situation. The revolution handed power over to the military council, who must bear the primary responsibility for everything that has happened in Egypt since Mubarak stepped down.

Demonstrations and sit-ins have continued across Egypt to put pressure on the military council to respond to the revolution's demands. After many months, the military council has finally bowed to pressure for the public trial of Hosni Mubarak. Although the sight of Mubarak in the dock was a great success for the revolution, a number of things that happened during the trial are cause for concern. The families of those killed in the revolution were prohibited from entering the court, thugs who support Mubarak were allowed to turn up armed with bricks, which they threw at the families of those killed, and the security services intervened to exclude specifically named journalists and lawyers from attending the trial. Furthermore, at the end of the court session, the television cameras captured scenes of Gamal and Alaa Mubarak, and former minister of the interior, Habib el-Adly, as they left the court – they looked so at ease that it was as though they were simply coming out of the cinema. They were laughing together, and their hands were not tied as the law requires. In fact, the head of the military police and the senior police officers that were present greeted the former minister so warmly that one would think he was still in office. At the same time, the military police were attacking demonstrators at a sit-in being held in Tahrir Square by the families of those killed in the revolution. I myself heard reports from young women and girls who had been verbally abused and severely beaten by the military police. Even though it was Ramadan, the military policemen had no qualms about entering Umar Makram Mosque, without removing their shoes, to arrest peaceful demonstrators. The day after, some young revolutionaries went to Tahrir Square in the evening to break their fast and and were again attacked by military police, who insulted and abused them exactly as if Mubarak were still ruling Egypt. Since then, Tahrir Square has been shut down completely;

it is now occupied by dozens of soldiers, as though the military council were trying to tell us: "You've seen Mubarak in the dock. From now on we shall not allow you to demonstrate or even to object."

The Egyptian revolution has now entered a critical phase and we must act to save it from becoming a military coup. Revolution implies comprehensive change, whereas a coup merely involves limited change at the top. If we do not act quickly, Mubarak will simply be replaced by a new ruler who will govern within the same system, with the same mentality and employing the same practices. The successive conspiracies against the revolution have exhausted the millions of Egyptians that had hoped that their lives would improve after the success of the revolution. We need only compare the state of optimism that prevailed in Egypt after Mubarak stepped down and the state of anxiety and restlessness that has now seized the Egyptian people. The crisis has been compounded by certain Islamists who believed that acquiescing to the military council was the surest way to gain power for themselves. They have become virtual spokesmen for the military council in the media. They laud the council night and day, approve of everything it does, and say nothing about its mistakes, however grave they might be. The current malaise amongst the revolutionaries represents an opportunity for its enemies to attack it. The heroic youth of Egypt who, through their courage and their sacrifices, altered the destiny of the country and the wider region, have faced a barrage of unfounded accusations about being foreign agents. The incidents in Cairo's Abbasiya district[1] were contrived to justify an attack on demonstrators: hundreds were injured and one young man, Mohamed Mohsen, lost his life. The repression and abuse of demonstrators has continued throughout this period, as if the regime is taking revenge on them for the overthrow and subsequent detention of Mubarak. So what is to be done now? I believe that there are three steps that must be taken to save the revolution:

1. All the forces that support the revolution must unite now and without delay. A group that represents the revolution must be formed in order to submit its demands to the military council and, at the same time, to control the demonstrators so that there is no indiscipline that can be used to attack the revolution.

2. We need to agree on what changes are required to ensure free and fair elections, then we must put pressure on the military council to implement these changes. I want to emphasise here that putting pressure on the military council is not a call for its dissolution, as they remain the nation's last line of defence despite their recent transgressions. The demands are: putting a stop to the prosecution of civilians in military

1 On 23 July 2011, thousands of demonstrators tried to march from Tahrir Square to the Ministry of Defense to decry the unmet demands of the 8 July sit-in.

courts, the release of those detained in military prisons, the dismissal of the current attorney general and the appointment of a new one from amongst the leading figures involved in the movement for an independent judiciary. Furthermore, the judiciary must be purged of those judges who oversaw rigged elections or who are guilty of collaborating with the state security service. The police force must be purged of crooked and corrupt officers, and those accused of killing demonstrators must be suspended from duty until their trials have been concluded. Lastly, the election law must be amended to meet the demands of the various political forces. These demands are necessary to ensure that elections reflect the will of Egyptians, and to compromise on these demands would simply mean that the next elections will be rigged.

3. If we can achieve these demands and guarantee free and fair elections, then we must subsequently call for elections to be held as soon as possible so that power can be transferred to an elected, civilian government. It is not in our interests to engage in lengthy discussions about the constitution and its governing principles. All such debates will delay a transfer of power to the people and add to the divisions between political groups, and in the end will not take us anywhere.

If we want to save the revolution, we must take these steps immediately. The 1,000 Egyptians who were killed, the 1,400 who were blinded, the 5,000 who were injured and the 1,000 who have disappeared – most likely killed in the early days of the revolution – are heroes who made sacrifices for the sake of achieving comprehensive change in Egypt, not for partial reform. They made sacrifices for a real and thorough revolution, not simply for a coup that would see one tyrant replaced by another within the same old system. Fulfilling the demands of the revolution is the only way that Egypt can go forward.

Democracy is the answer.

AB

The Interrogation of Asmaa Mahfouz

16 August 2011

Before the revolution, only Egyptians using the internet knew the name of activist and blogger, Asmaa Mahfouz. She uploaded videos calling on Egyptians to come out and demonstrate in order to get rid of Mubarak. She was an attractive dark-skinned Egyptian girl who wore the hijab, and her messages were incredibly moving and from the heart. She reminded us of our own daughters and sisters, but she also had a certain nobility that distinguished her. Although young, Asmaa was concerned with the fate of the country and decided to dedicate herself to the revolution and to achieving freedom. After the success of the revolution, she continued to express her point of view with candour and she openly criticised the performance of the military council on more than one occasion. She also recorded what she saw at the Abbasiya demonstration, and documented the savage attacks on demonstrators by thugs with swords and Molotov cocktails while military policemen simply looked on and did nothing to prevent the carnage.

Two days ago, Asmaa received a summons from the military prosecutor's office to come in for questioning. The next morning Asma went to the prosecutor's office with her lawyer and found a large group of young people gathered outside in solidarity with her. She greeted them warmly and thanked them for coming out to support her even though it was a hot day and they were fasting for Ramadan. After a short while a military police officer appeared and barked at her: "Are you Asmaa Mahfouz?"

"Yes," she answered.

"So you're the great leader? Come with me for your interrogation."

Asmaa and her lawyer followed him to the door of the interrogation room, then the officer stopped, turned around and said to her: "You must go in alone." The lawyer objected and insisted on accompanying her inside, but the officer stated firmly: "The interrogator wants to speak to her alone."

The lawyer realised there was no point in arguing and stood aside as the officer knocked on the door and waited for permission to enter. The officer greeted the military interrogator who was sitting behind a desk, then he turned and left the room. Asmaa's head was bowed; she was fatigued by the heat and from fasting. The interrogator said to her: "Come in, come in."

His voice was familiar; she had heard it many times before. She looked up and was so startled that she thought she might have been dreaming. Sitting behind the desk was Hosni Mubarak. He was wearing his military uniform with medals pinned to his breast. He leaned back in his chair, smiled and said: "Take a seat, Asmaa."

In a state of panic, she shouted: "You're Hosni Mubarak!" The interrogator smiled as she continued: "You have deceived us! How did you escape from prison?"

Mubarak laughed and said: "I've been here for many years."

"How can you be here and there at the same time?" she asked.

"It's complicated and would take too long to explain."

"If you are here, then who is it that appears in the dock during your trial?"

"Listen, I'm not here to answer your questions, I'm here to question you."

"I need to know how you escaped," demanded Asmaa.

Raising his voice Mubarak cautioned her, saying: "If you don't stop disrupting these proceedings, I'll have you thrown into a military prison on the charge of not complying with the interrogator."

There was silence now as Asmaa re-examined his face. There was no doubt about it; it was Hosni Mubarak. He appeared to be relaxed, calm and in good health. She thought about rushing out of the building to tell the demonstrators gathered outside. As though he could read her mind, Mubarak said: "Be reasonable and behave sensibly. Don't do anything you might later regret. Understand that your fate is in my hands. Now, I'll begin the interrogation."

"You don't have the right to refer civilians to military courts," Asmaa said.

"I may not have the right, but it is within my power, nevertheless." Asmaa was silent and Mubarak now took an official tone: "Why do you speak ill of the armed forces?"

"Like all Egyptians, I am proud of the Egyptian army," she answered.

Mubarak looked through the papers in front of him and said: "But on Facebook you made unseemly comments about the military council."

"I was criticising its policies," she replied.

"That is surely an offence against the army."

"No, the offence is to stay silent about its mistakes. The military council is the acting head of state during the transitional period and I have a right to criticise its performance."

"Who are you to criticise the military council?" asked Mubarak.

"I am an Egyptian citizen."

"You're nothing but a deluded child that needs to be taught some manners."

"Is this how you conduct a legal inquiry?" asked Asmaa.

Mubarak returned to looking through the papers. "You made a comment on Twitter with the intention of inciting Egyptians to carry out assassinations."

"That's a ridiculous and false accusation. All I said was that if the killers are not punished, then the families of those who were killed in the revolution will take the law into their own hands."

There was another silence, then Asmaa suddenly exclaimed: "You know, this interrogation is illegal. Firstly, because it's being conducted without a lawyer and, secondly, because you are facing criminal charges. You do not have the right to question me."

Mubarak became visibly angry: the muscles of his face contracted and he struck the desk with his hand. "I told you I have been here for years! Do you understand?"

"You can say what you like but I won't answer your questions," said Asmaa, defiantly.

"It will only be to your detriment if you don't."

"No matter what you do, I will never accept that you have the right to question me," she said.

"I'll have you detained. I'll make an example of you," he said.

"Fine, detain me then."

Mubarak began to laugh and said: "Aren't you a brave girl. No, I won't detain you. Let's forget about the interrogation and just talk together, shall we?"

"What do you want?" asked Asmaa.

Mubarak got up and walked to the refrigerator and took out a soft drink that made a popping sound when he opened it. "Are you breaking your fast so early?" asked Asmaa.

"I'm ill, so I'm exempt from fasting during Ramadan," he answered.

Mubarak took a gulp and then belched. "Look, Asmaa," he said, "I just want you and your friends to mind your own business and think about your futures because the subject is now closed."

"What subject?" asked Asmaa.

"The uprising is finished, thanks be to God."

"But, we made a great revolution."

"You have ruined the country," said Mubarak.

"No, you are the one who has ruined and plundered Egypt, you are the one who has abused and killed Egyptians."

"The Egyptian people still love me. I've seen demonstrations in support of me in Mustafa Mahmoud Square and Roxy Square."

"Those demonstrators were either hired or they were beneficiaries of your corrupt regime," replied Asmaa.

Mubarak smiled and then sighed, as though humouring a naive child. "Okay, Asmaa," he said, "You called for my resignation and my trial, but what have you actually gained?"

"We have gained freedom," she answered.

At this, Mubarak laughed loudly. "Did you get freedom or anarchy?"

"So long as we are rid of injustice, everything else pales in comparison."

"I'm still here. It's true you see me standing in the dock, but I exist everywhere. Everything that happens in Egypt is still done according to my wishes; as a matter of fact I'm more powerful now than ever before. My supporters are everywhere."

"We'll purge Egypt of all your followers." said Asmaa.

"You don't have the right. Wasn't it your crowd who denounced the rigging of elections? Well, the upcoming elections will be free and fair, and they'll bring my people to power. My supporters will win the majority and it is they who will form the next government."

"What do you mean?" asked Asmaa.

"Some day you will realise that I'm not merely a person. I represent a way of thinking, a particular outlook on life, a comprehensive and integrated worldview." Mubarak paused for a moment then he smiled and continued: "Some of those who were previously my enemies are today my allies, and when the elections are held, they will vote how I want them to."

"We will continue to apply pressure until there is complete change," said Asmaa.

"That's simply no longer possible."

"In the same way we ousted you, we will also oust your regime."

"Egyptians have begun to despise the revolution," replied Mubarak.

"That isn't true," said Asmaa. "All you have to do is go outside and you will see dozens of young activists standing in solidarity with me."

"Egyptians have an inherent dislike for revolution. They prefer to submit to a strong leader, even if he oppresses them. I offered to remain in office as president until September but you rejected it, and what has been the outcome? Tourism has ceased, investment has dried up, the Egyptian people are exhausted and frustrated, and they fear for their children's safety because of these thugs roaming the streets. There are shootings and killings taking place throughout the country."

"You are the cause of this," said Asmaa. "It was your supporters who unleashed the thugs, your people are the ones who conspire to impoverish and terrorise the Egyptian people so that they will come to regret that the revolution ever happened."

"In war, everything is permitted," retorted Mubarak.

"We will prevail, you shall see."

"This is fantasy, nothing more. The people have already turned against the revolution. As a matter of fact, many now consider you traitors."

"You're insufferable," said Asmaa.

Mubarak smiled, but he was clearly annoyed. "Is it proper to speak in this manner to someone who is as old as your grandfather?"

"I'm speaking to a tyrant who caused the deaths of thousands of Egyptians."

"While you and your fellow activists stand accused of being agents in the pay of foreign countries," said Mubarak.

"You propagate lies to discredit the revolution. These accusations that were made by General Hassan al-Ruwaini[1] are baseless and we have filed a complaint against him with the military prosecutor."

Mubarak smiled and said, "You filed a complaint against al-Ruwaini?"

1 General Hassan al-Ruwaini, a member of the military council, told Egyptian media that the April 6 Youth Movement was being funded by foreign entities. Al-Ruwaini also accused the Kefaya Movement of being sponsored by foreign organisations with political agendas in Egypt. The allegations were refuted by Kefaya spokesman Abdel Halim Qandil, who later filed a report calling for al-Ruwaini to be interrogated over his comments.

"Yes," answered Asmaa.

"Then I am the one who will investigate it," said Mubarak.

"If you investigate the complaint against General al-Ruwaini, then I can already guess what the result will be."

Silence returned and Mubarak looked at her with contempt. Asmaa stood up and said: "I'm leaving."

"I'm warning you."

"Do what you please," she answered.

"Fine, then wait outside for the prosecutor's decision," said Mubarak.

Asmaa picked up her bag and turned to leave. As though provoked by her defiance, Mubarak said: "You do realise that the charges against you could land you in military prison for ten years?"

Asmaa regarded him and said calmly: "During the revolution I left home every day knowing that I might die at any moment. The snipers under your command killed other activists right in front of me. We no longer fear death. Do whatever you like; Egypt will defeat you and your supporters."

Asmaa walked out and slammed the door behind her. Her lawyer and dozens of supporters were standing outside waiting for her. They gathered around her to ask what had happened in the interrogation. She hesitated for a moment, then sighed indignantly and said: "Do you know who interrogated me?" They looked at her expectantly, "Hosni Mubarak," she said. They didn't appear to be surprised by this answer.

Then one of them spoke up and said: "No matter what they do, the revolution will be victorious!" Everyone agreed with him.

Democracy is the answer.

AB

How Should We Respond to Israeli Aggression?

23 August 2011

On 17 November 2004, three military police officers were on guard duty in the Egyptian town of Rafah. At three o'clock in the morning they spotted an Israeli Merkava tank moving towards them. The tank stopped at a distance of 20 metres and opened fire on the officers. Two of them, Ali Sobhi el-Naggar and Mohamed Abdel Fattah, were killed on the spot while the remaining officer, Amer Abu Bakr Amer, was seriously injured and later died from his wounds in hospital. This is one of many instances in which Israel has attacked Egyptian soldiers and police officers stationed at the border. Yet, on every occasion, the crime has invariably gone unpunished. The Israeli government issues a public apology and promises to investigate the attack, but then the matter goes no further. Following one such attack, Hosni Mubarak met with his dear friend Benjamin Netanyahu.[1] After the meeting, a foreign journalist approached Mubarak and asked if he had spoken with Netanyahu about the Egyptians that Israel had killed. Mubarak answered him disdainfully, saying: "What do you want Netanyahu to do? He has apologised and that's the end of the matter."

Hosni Mubarak did everything in his power to please Israel, so much so that one Israeli leader even described him as a strategic asset to the Jewish state. Mubarak agreed to release the Israeli spy Azzam Azzam[2] from prison and did not demand that Israel pay any compensation for the Egyptian prisoners of war it had killed during its wars with Egypt. He sent the Egyptian ambassador back to Tel Aviv where agreements were signed to sell gas to Israel at prices below market value, and put intense pressure on Hamas to satisfy Israel. Mubarak's aim in pleasing Israel was to gain the support of the Zionist lobby in the United States so that he could install his son Gamal Mubarak as the ruler of Egypt after him. To this end, Mubarak was willing to overlook the death of countless Egyptians. But in a rare exception, the families of the three military police killed in 2004 filed legal claims for compensation and each was awarded 10 million dollars by the Egyptian courts. The court's logic was that the international courts had fixed the same amount as compensation for each victim of the Lockerbie bombings, when a passenger plane exploded while flying over Scotland. The Egyptian courts asserted that compensation regarding the victims of killing should not vary, insofar as the value of a human life is the same whether the victim is an Arab or a Westerner. This historic ruling – which even now has not been put into effect – was issued by the fourth circuit of the Court of Appeal in Cairo, which was presided over by Judge Ahmed al-Bardisi, with fellow judges Hamdi Ghanem and Ahmed Suleiman, and with Said Zoheir as clerk of the court.

In my opinion, outrage at Israeli aggression is both justified and commendable. Egypt has changed since the revolution, and the humiliating treatment meted out by Israel under the Mubarak regime must now end. Israel must understand that its ally, Mubarak, is being tried on criminal charges and the Egyptian people will not allow those who are guilty of killing innocent people to escape justice. The question then is this: why have Israeli forces once again crossed into Egyptian territory and attacked its military personnel?

1 Benjamin Netanyahu is an Israeli politician, and the current prime minister of Israel. After the revolution, Netanyahu stated that he expected any new Egyptian government to adhere to the peace treaty with Israel.

2 Azzam Azzam is an Israeli Druze who was convicted in Egypt of spying for Israel, and jailed for eight years. He maintained his innocence throughout the ordeal, and since, no credible evidence was presented at his trial, and no additional evidence was ever released.

To answer this we need to consider Israel's position with regard to the Egyptian revolution. Noam Chomsky has written against the argument that the United States and its allies were working to counteract democracy in Egypt due to a fear of the Islamists coming to power.[1] Instead, Chomsky argued that the United States do not actually consider the Islamists a real threat and have, in fact, allied itself with the most hard-line Islamists in order to further its own interests. For decades the US has been allied with Saudi Arabia, the home of extremist Wahhabi ideology, and has also supported Muhamed Zia-ul-Haq of Pakistan,[2] an infamous dictator whose regime strictly imposed the sharia using Saudi money. According to Chomsky, the threat to the US does not come from the Islamists but rather Egypt becoming a truly independent state. Chomsky argued that the US accepted the removal of Mubarak, but would make every effort to ensure that the next president of Egypt does not deviate from the path that has been determined for him – just consider the desperate attempts to get Omar Suleiman and Ahmed Shafik in the presidency.

Chomsky's article leads us to understand that Israel, backed by the United States, is in a state of panic on account of the changes taking place in Egypt. Israel knows very well that Egypt has an enormous potential not possessed by any other state in the region; a democratic Egypt would constitute a great, modern power that would lead the entire Arab world and direct events throughout the wider region. It is logical, therefore, to assume that Israel will do everything in its power to disrupt Egypt's transition towards democracy. In the last six months, since Mubarak's resignation, Israel felt no need to intervene because the situation in Egypt has been unpredictable and utterly disorganised. The constitution was amended, then it was repealed by a constitutional decree, law and order broke down and then the economy went into steep decline because both tourism and investment dried up. Perhaps the most critical issue, however, is the division amongst the supporters of the revolution: a bitter conflict broke out between the Islamist groups and those who advocate a civil state. Everyone became preoccupied with the lengthy argument about what should happen next, whether a new constitution should be drafted prior to holding elections, or whether elections should be held first. On top of this, the actions taken by the military council did not serve to protect the revolution; rather, they aided senior figures from the old regime to launch a counterattack against the revolution. There was also the unfortunate confrontation between the revolutionary activists and the military council, which descended into mutual accusations, campaigns of

1 Noam Chomsky, "It's not radical Islam that worries the United States – it's independence", *Guardian*, 4 February 2011. *See* http://www.theguardian.com/commentisfree/cifamerica/2011/feb/04/radical-islam-united-states-independence

2 General Zia-ul-Haq was the sixth president of Pakistan, after having seized power in a bloodless coup on 5 July 1977. As president, he suspended political parties, imposed strict censorship on the press, and declared martial law in the country (nominally lifted in 1985).

arrests, and military trials. No doubt Israel was monitoring the situation in Egypt, confident that the revolution would tear itself apart.

Then suddenly, on the initiative of the military council, Al-Azhar resumed its historical role and prepared a document for national consensus, defining the outlines of the future Egyptian state. All of the various political factions approved of Al-Azhar's document[1], even the most hard-line Salafists who only voiced concern regarding superficial aspects in the document. This put a stop to the arguing over the constitution; the revolutionary forces united once again and Egypt took a big step towards democracy. The next obstacle was to persuade the military council to hold free and fair elections that would bring an elected government to power. It was at this point that Israel decided to intervene forcefully to sabotage the revolution. It began with the sudden appearance of heavily-armed groups that attacked police stations in Sinai in order to undermine state control in the region. The aim was to provide evidence of a security breakdown in Sinai, which would justify the Israeli aggression that soon followed. Israeli forces then entered Egyptian territory and killed several Egyptian officers, leaving several more wounded. The objectives of the Israeli attack are several: to test the new rulers of Egypt and to throw them off balance, to give the impression that they cannot protect the country and to thwart democratic transition. The aim could also be to draw Egypt into a reckless military confrontation that would undo the revolution completely (as Gamal Abdel Nasser was drawn into conflict in 1967). So what now is to be done? Egypt must respond to acts of aggression in such a way that will make Israel understand that the days of Hosni Mubarak, who cared nothing for the rights and the dignity of Egyptians, are gone forever. There are some urgent and effective steps that must be taken:

1. The Israeli ambassador must be expelled from Cairo and the Egyptian ambassador should be recalled from Israel. Egypt should immediately begin international legal proceedings against Israel in order to compel it to pay out substantial compensation for all Egyptians that it has wrongfully and unjustly killed over the years. The historic ruling issued by Judge Ahmed al-Bardisi and his colleagues should serve as the international standard for damages in cases of compensation. In this way, Israel will have to pay out millions of dollars as punishment for its horrendous crimes.

2. All existing agreements between Egypt and Israel should be either reviewed or annulled, from the Qualifying Industrial Zone (QIZ)[2] protocol to the agreements regarding the sale of gas and the export of cement.

---

1 "Al-Azhar Document on the Future of Egypt," June 2011. The document expressed support for a democratic state based on a constitution approved by the citizenry. *See* http://www.sis.gov.eg

2 Iniative that allows Egypt and Jordan to export products to the United States duty-free, as long as these products contain inputs from Israel.

3. The peace treaty must be amended to permit Egyptian troops to be deployed throughout the region. The treaty contains a clause to allow its modification provided that both parties agree to this. If Israel refuses to approve the necessary amendment then we have the right, according to the treaty itself, to submit the matter to international arbitration and we have experts in international law who can wrest our rights from international courts, as they did in the case of Taba.[1]

4. It is our duty to support our armed forces in their confrontation with Israel and also to press the military council to take the necessary steps that will bring about Egypt's first democratic elections in 60 years. Our demands have been articulated and are well-known: the speedy execution of the plan to create an independent judiciary; the disqualification of those judges who oversaw rigged elections during the Mubarak era; the purging of crooked and corrupt officers from the police force; the dismissal of the current attorney general, whose political accommodations during the Mubarak era led him to compromise the duties of his office; the appointment of a new attorney general who is sympathetic to the aims of the revolution, such as Judge Zakariya Abdel Aziz, Judge Ashraf el-Baroudi, Judge Hesham el-Bastawisi, or other such leading figures who are noted for their advocacy of an independent judiciary; the immediate end to the trial of civilians in military courts; the release of the thousands of people who have been detained in military prisons and their retrial in civilian courts; the enactment of a ban on political propaganda inside mosques and churches; the granting of Egyptians living abroad their right to vote in the elections; and lastly, international monitoring must be allowed during the elections to demonstrate to the world that the elections are free and fair.

5. After taking steps to ensure that elections will be free and fair, the elections must be held at the nearest possible opportunity. Egyptian politicians must rise to the occasion by acting responsibly and putting the wider national interest before their own narrow concerns. That the elections are conducted in a fair and proper manner is much more important than the actual results themselves. If we are to be truly democratic then we must respect the right of the people to vote for whomever they want, even if we disagree with their choices.

The mass demonstrations, the sit-ins, the loud cheers, and the removal and burning of Israel's flag from the balcony of the Israeli embassy – all of these are

1 Taba is a strip of beach on the Red Sea near Eilat claimed by both Israel and Egypt. After a long dispute, the issue was submitted to an international commission composed of one Israeli, one Egyptian, and three outsiders. In 1988, the commission ruled in Egypt's favour, and Israel returned Taba to Egypt in 1989.

honest and spontaneous acts that reflect a righteous, popular anger. However, in my opinion, they fall far short of how we should effectively respond to Israel's aggression. The best way to respond is to ensure that Israel does not achieve its aims, and the only way we can do this is through the transfer of power to an elected government, so that the Egyptian armed forces can devote themselves to the task of fighting, and so that Egypt can advance towards the future it deserves.

Democracy is the answer.

AB

God Bless Your Hands, Ali Farzat

30 August 2011

Dear reader, if you are not yet familiar with the art of Ali Farzat you are doing yourself a great disservice. Farzat is an internationally acclaimed Syrian artist and one of the most important political cartoonists in the Arab world. As an Arab, I felt proud when I saw Farzat's work appear in major international newspapers such as the *Guardian* and *Le Monde*. He was born in the city of Hama in 1951 and his exceptional talent was apparent from an early age: when he was only twelve years old he sent a cartoon to the Syrian newspaper *Al-Ayyam* and was surprised to find his drawing published on the front page a week later. He received a letter from the newspaper's editor who expressed his gratitude and admiration, and who never imagined for a moment that the cartoon was the work of such a young boy. Through his dedication to art and hard work, Ali Farzat has been able to develop his talent over the years and claim his rightful place amongst the great cartoonists of the Arab world such as Salah Jahin, Ahmed Hegazy, Naji al-Ali, Mustafa Hussein, Ahmed Toughan and others.

Farzat believes that a cartoonist must have a flair for satire, and that skill in drawing is secondary. The cartoonist's art seeks to expose the contradiction between how something really is and how others would have us believe it to be. Because Farzat is so discerning when it comes to the real truth of something, his drawings are always succinct, economical, honest, straightforward, stark, and unambiguous. With surprising simplicity, Farzat's drawings are able to encapsulate the world in such a way that makes us experience, and think about, the ugliness all around us as well as make us strive for the beauty of truth and justice. Farzat's drawings convey meaning directly. It is as though his pen is a gun; when he takes aim and squeezes the trigger his images hit their mark with perfect precision. His drawings confront us with the naked truth, no more and no less. For Ali Farzat, cartoons are not an art form merely intended to give enjoyment – his aim is never to simply entertain or to make people laugh. Rather, he uses the art of the cartoon as a highly sophisticated and effective weapon in the struggle for humanity. Ali Farzat fights for freedom, he defends human rights and human dignity at all costs no matter what the consequences.

An artist with Ali Farzat's international appeal could quite easily have gone to live in Paris or London where he would have been welcomed and respected. He could have gained renown as an activist living in safety abroad, like so many others have done. Instead, however, he insisted on remaining in the country of his birth, simply stating that he did not think he would be able to draw people if he lived so far removed from them. Had Ali Farzat wanted, he could have taken office as Syria's minister of culture. He would not have had to pander entirely to the authorities, he would simply have had to stay within the limits of what would have been allowed and remain silent about injustice and oppression. This would have meant, however, that he would have had to think carefully about what he drew and make compromises so that his cartoons only dealt with approved subjects, in other words, he would not be able to present the complete truth. Farzat rejects such constraints, however, believing that truth must be presented without compromise and that to do otherwise would be fraudulent.

Strangely, at one time there was genuine friendship between Ali Farzat and Bashar al-Assad. It came about during the time when Bashar was studying ophthalmology in London and his father was still the president of Syria. At this time Bashar took an interest in the arts; he began visiting Farzat's exhibitions and admired his work. In this way a friendship developed between them, so much so, that Bashar even visited Farzat at his home. Perhaps Bashar was, at one time, genuinely eager to introduce real democratic reforms in Syria and maybe this is why the Syrian regime, in the early days of Bashar's presidency, permitted Farzat to publish his famous magazine *Al-Domari*,[1] the first independent magazine to be published in Syria since the 1960s.

The magazine was a unique phenomenon: firstly, because of the biting satire in its articles and cartoons which resembled that found in the famous French newspaper *Le Canard enchaîné*; secondly, because its style was blunt rather than vague, and it openly criticised despotism and corruption; and thirdly, because despite the modest funds behind it, it still managed to gain an enormous following and a level of circulation never known by the state newspapers, on which Syria's ruling Baath Party had spent millions but which no one read because they were full of ridiculous propaganda and lies. Due

1 During Ottoman times a "domari" was the person who lit the street lamps in Syria prior to the introduction of electricity.

largely to the success of *Al-Domari*, Farzat had to endure every kind of harassment and persecution by the authorities, but he continued to publish his magazine without bowing to the pressure, compromising, or making deals with the regime. Little by little, however, *Al-Domari* became such a problem for the Syrian regime and its intelligence services that they saw no other option but to revoke its licence and close it down.

Ali Farzat has a determined character, however, and he didn't despair. When the Syrian regime closed down his magazine he began to explore the vast possibilities of the internet. He set up his own website and as soon as he had put his cartoons online they became the talk of Syria. Bashar al-Assad was furious with his former friend and once he even stated, "At one time I called Ali Farzat a friend, but he has stabbed me in the back." Thus, Bashar the ophthalmologist ultimately turned into Bashar the despot; he came to view Farzat's defence of truth as a personal affront. Such is the nature of this despotic ruler that he understands friendship to mean nothing more than absolute loyalty and submission to him. In fact, he considers himself to be the embodiment of the nation itself – whoever supports him and is in agreement with him is considered to be patriotic, while someone who defends freedom and human rights is considered to be a traitor and an agent of foreign powers. Not surprisingly, there is striking similarity, if not uniformity, amongst the worldviews of Bashar al-Assad, Hosni Mubarak, Ali Abdullah Saleh, Zine El Abidine Ben Ali, and all the other despots – in each case we find the same lies, the same criminality, and the same disregard for morals. All that matters to them is holding onto power by any means and at any cost.

When the Syrian revolution erupted, and the Syrian regime responded brutally against innocent, unarmed citizens, simply because they were demanding their human rights, Ali Farzat could not stand by idly looking on. He took up his own particular weapon and created drawings that I believe will live forever in the annals of Arab art. Amongst his cartoons we find the image of an armed soldier who represents the Syrian regime and stands ready to open fire on a blindfolded detainee; however, both stand at opposite ends of a wooden plank that is balanced on the summit of a mountain peak and both will fall to their death if either makes the slightest movement. When Bashar al-Assad announced that he would repeal emergency law, Farzat drew a cartoon of huge thug, again representing the regime, whose enormous shadow is cast against a wall. Bashar al-Assad is seen in the cartoon painting over the thug's shadow with whitewash in order to hide it. Even though the dark shadow is being blotted out by the whitewash, the thug remains as conspicuous as ever.

The Syrian regime's brutal crackdown on the revolution is still ongoing and so far has resulted in the deaths of more than 2,000 people, not to mention the thousands who have been injured or detained. Despite this, the regime of Bashar al-Assad continues to lie and hold conferences to ostensibly gain approval for spurious reforms, by which he seeks to deceive the people. Because of this, Farzat drew someone sitting on the toilet and pulling a toilet roll upon which are written the resolutions of these conferences. As Syrians continue to insist on freedom, and as the revolution spreads throughout Syria, the horrific crimes committed by members of the security services and thugs who support the regime have only increased. They have begun storming mosques and gunning down people who are praying. A popular singer emerged during the revolution whose name was Ibrahim Qashoush. He took part in the demonstrations and began making songs, the lyrics of which called for Bashar to step down. A few days ago, regime thugs abducted Qashoush, killed him, then brutally ripped out his vocal chords and threw his body in the middle of a road so that when people found him he would be a lesson to anyone who dares demand that Bashar al-Assad give up power.

The regime's brutality has had the opposite effect, however; it has only made Syrians even more determined in their support for the revolution. As for Ali Farzat, he has stood alongside them in the front line, with remarkable courage he has continued to take potshots at the regime's despotism. Because of this, the regime felt it necessary to silence him by any means necessary and to make an example of him. Last Thursday, Ali Farzat finished work and got into his car to drive home from his office. He was followed by a white car that cut in front of him and forced him to come to a halt. Four burly thugs got out of the white car and forced him out of his, then they brutally attacked him. They beat this innocent man until his blood soaked his clothes and spilled onto the ground. The focus of their assault was not just his head, but also his hands – they concussed him and they broke his fingers.

This nature of this barbaric attack is filled with significance. The Syrian regime is armed with every kind of weapon, yet, it seems that it prefers to use its weaponry to kill thousands of its own people rather than use them against Israel. It has not fired one shot at Israel for 40 years, but it is unable to tolerate a frail, gentle artist who has only his pen and his art. They struck his head and crushed his hands because they fear the truth that he presents in his exceptional drawings. This Eid al-Fitr, instead of being at home amongst his family and loved ones, Ali Farzat will be lying alone in a hospital bed, his body battered and his brilliant fingers – the fingers that for so long have produced drawings that will remain forever in our hearts and minds – broken. I write these words in the hope they reach Ali Farzat; I want him to know how much we Egyptians love him, how much we love Syria, and the extent to which we feel for the suffering of our fellow Arabs there. As for our own situation in Egypt, it is far from ideal: after we succeeded in deposing Hosni Mubarak, we were surprised to find that his regime did not fall with him but remains in power even now. Despite the troubles in Egypt, however, we have not forgotten our brothers and sisters in Syria for one moment.

Dear reader, I urge you to visit Ali Farzat's website[1] and view his wonderful drawings so that you will come to appreciate just what a world-class artist he is. I also want you to know how awful the crime that was committed against him is. Bashar al-Assad is the one who is ultimately responsible for this savage attack on one of the most important artists in the Arab world. Ali Farzat, you are just one man but you are an example for us all. You have paid the price for being courageous and honourable in a country ruled by a despotic and oppressive regime. They committed this crime against you because they fear you. They possess a colossal apparatus of repression while you have only your pen. Yet, you are stronger than them, because you represent truth while they represent only falsehood and corruption. You are the future, Ali Farzat, and they are the dark past. Your day will inevitably come, Ali, and they will be abandoned to the dustbin of history where they belong. Bashar al-Assad's regime is finished; all that it is has left is the rod of oppression, but this will soon be broken and Syria will gain its freedom. Ali Farzat, my friend, God bless your hands.

Democracy is the answer.

AB

Tomorrow You Will Stand Accused

6 September 2011

On 9 March, George Magdy Ata and four of his relatives were exiting from the metro station at Tahrir Square just as the military police were forcibly breaking up a sit-in protest. These five young men, all of whom have jobs in respectable companies, were arrested and court-martialled on charges of possessing Molotov cocktails and assaulting the military police. The military prosecutor presented only ten Molotov cocktails as evidence for the conviction of the 200 defendants who stood accused, meaning groups of 20 defendants each possessed one Molotov cocktail between them. Perhaps the strangest thing about this case was that one of the accused, a young man by the name of Roumani Kamel, is partially paralysed as a result of contracting polio, which would have made it practically impossible for him to have assaulted the military police. After only 24 hours, the five young men were found guilty and sentenced to three years in prison. It was only after they had spent several long weeks in a military prison, and after their families had wept in front

1 *See* http://www.ali-ferzat.com/

of the media and pleaded with the authorities to show clemency, that their punishments were reduced to one-year suspended sentences.

And there are other such cases involving Egyptian citizens. A taxi driver in Beheira Governorate by the name of Sayed Sobhi Abdelhamid had a son who had just obtained his diploma in commerce. He bought him a car so that he too could work as a taxi driver. Subsequently, however, when the son was driving the car from Rosetta to Alexandria, he was surprised to find the road closed. On account of this, an altercation broke out between him and the head of the Edku police station. He was arrested and referred for trial in the military courts on charges of thuggery and possessing a weapon. He was found guilty and sentenced to five years' imprisonment with hard labour, with five years probation upon his release. There is also the case of 25-year-old Ahmed Abdelrahim from Alexandria; one of his neighbours reported him to the police for adding an extra storey to his house without first obtaining a building permit. He was arrested, sent to the military courts and sentenced to five years in prison. When his family complained he was retried and given exactly the same sentence.

In the space of only seven months, 12,000 Egyptian civilians have been court-martialled. Referring civilians for trial in the military courts is a flagrant violation of the principles of justice, the rule of law and human rights. It contravenes international treaties to which Egypt is a signatory. Everyone has the right to be tried in the proper way; they have a right to be tried by a judge who operates completely independently of the ruler. A military judge does not have such independence because the military justice system is answerable to the Ministry of Defence, and although a military judge is well versed in the law, nevertheless, he is ultimately a military officer who is subject to orders, and the way he conducts his work can be influenced by his superiors who can either reward his behaviour or impose disciplinary action on him according to the circumstances.

The referring of Egyptian civilians to military trials is, therefore, clearly unjust and constitutes a violation of the civilians' rights. On top of this, the manner in which military trials are conducted fails to provide even the most basic legal safeguards. It is near impossible for the families of the accused to find out where their loved ones are being detained, and when they do, they are often not allowed to choose a lawyer to represent them. This is partly due to the fact that defendants are often tried together in batches of five or ten. The speed at which the trials are conducted cannot possibly ensure that justice is served. Is it just that someone be sentenced to five years in prison following a trial that has lasted no more than one or two days? Is it fair that an Egyptian civilian who stands accused of adding a storey to his house without having the necessary licence be tried in a military court while the former minister of the interior, Habib el-Adly, and his aides, who killed hundreds of Egyptians, are tried within the proper legal system where they enjoy full legal safeguards? The decision of the military council to refer civilians for military trial raises a number of questions:

First: Why do the military police deal so harshly with Egyptians? According to reports by human rights groups, both Egyptian and international, members of the military police have abused Egyptians and committed serious human rights violations against them. On 9 March something unprecedented happened: 17 women who were taking part in a demonstration were arrested by the military police and subsequently forced to endure virginity tests. The women pleaded with the officers to desist but it was to no avail; they were ordered to remove all of their clothes and lie down naked, not knowing whether the men were genuine doctors or simply there to watch the spectacle. They were photographed naked and their genitals were examined in front of the men who were standing around. The testimonies of these women, who are known by name, have been fully documented on video. This grievous incident constitutes an indecent assault against Egyptian women, whose honour the military police were supposed to protect, not violate.

Dozens of demonstrators' testimonies have been documented in which they state that they have been insulted, severely beaten and subjected to electric shocks after they have been arrested by the military police. To humiliate those in custody, the officers have ordered them to kneel, or forced them to lie down on their stomachs before walking on top of their backs. Here I will quote from a testimony that was documented by the El Nadim Centre for the Rehabilitation of Victims of Violence. The statement was made by an Egyptian woman called Zainab who was arrested on the second day of Ramadan in Tahrir Square, she states: "A number of officers seized me by both my arms. As they were escorting me, one of them lifted up my blouse and started striking me directly against my bared flesh. While he was doing this he insulted me in the most degrading ways imaginable. It was not the beating that caused me so much pain; much worse was the humiliation I felt from being insulted and having my body exposed. I still thank God, though; this happened in Tahrir Square – a spot where many of Egypt's bravest lost their lives." Zainab might be considered lucky because some of the military policemen took pity on her and spoke with their commander, who eventually had her released.

But why do the military police deal so harshly with demonstrators? In considering the contempt in which they seem to hold the demonstrators, I don't believe that they differ much from the now dissolved state security service. It seems that those who work within a repressive state apparatus have a psychological need to view their victims as spies, prostitutes or enemies of the state – they have to misrepresent their victims to themselves so that they can silence their own consciences and carry out acts of torture and oppression.

Second: Do military trials even help to eliminate thuggery? Clearly, they do not. For a start, military trials rarely even involve the prosecution of genuine thugs, and in any case, if thugs are to be prosecuted this could quite easily be done under the proper, civilian judicial system. Egypt is currently experiencing a disastrous break-down in law and order; the Mubarak regime released 24,000 convicted criminals from the country's prisons in order to terrorise Egyptians. Furthermore, even now, the police force has not been purged of senior officials with links to the former regime, who seem to be intent on withholding security in order to punish Egyptians for the revolution and make them regret that it happened in the first place.

The question here is this: what exactly have the military police done to restore security? The answer is that they have done almost nothing in this regard. Military trials have targeted journalists, people working in the media, revolutionary activists, demonstrators and ordinary citizens; only on rare occasions have they involved the prosecution of real thugs. It was thugs who cut off the ear of a Coptic citizen in Qena Governorate, but so far they have not been arrested. It also happened in Qena Governorate that such people shut down the railway line for ten days, yet they were not arrested by the military police. On top of this, a number of churches were torched in Atfih and Imbaba and the perpetrators were caught on video, but again, the military police made no arrests. As a matter of fact, a certain bearded man appears in the video recordings inciting people to set fire to the churches and the military police did not even approach him. Then there are the events that took place in Abbasiya in which thugs attacked and beat demonstrators. One demonstrator, Mohamed Mohsen, was even killed right in front of the military police who, as usual, looked on without intervening.

Third: Should Field Marshal Tantawi's decision to release some of the detainees be considered a good initiative? Although Field Marshal Tantawi's decision to pardon some of those who have been convicted is a good-natured gesture, nevertheless, it is clear evidence that the military justice system is not independent – if someone holds the power to grant amnesty, then, equally, they also possess the power to impose prison sentences. In a state that is based upon the rule of law, however, no one, not even the head of state, has the power to interfere with the rule of law. Such well-meaning interventions are not what is needed in Egypt. There must be an end to the trial of civilians in military courts. Civilians should be tried within the civilian judicial system.

Fourth: Why does the military council persist in trying civilians in military courts? The only explanation is that they want to retain an effective means of repression that enables it to manipulate public opinion and silence anyone who opposes its policies. During the revolution, Egyptians broke through the barrier of their fear, and with the police force demoralised, the military council had to face the revolutionaries alone. The real objective behind referring civilians for military trial is to return Egyptians to a state of obedience and submission. When the young men realise that taking part in a demonstration might cost them a few years in a military prison, and when young women understand that by joining a demonstration they are taking the risk that they might be stripped naked and forced to take a virginity test in front of strange men, then Egyptians will revert to a state of fear, pessimism and acquiescence to the military council – even if its decisions are wrong and unjust. So far the military trials have not fully achieved their objective; the flame of the revolution continues to burn and the Egyptians remain determined to gain their rights no matter what the cost.

Putting an end to the practice of referring civilians to military courts is our common cause. The National Association for Change[1] has called for a demonstration against the trying of civilians in military courts; it is to be held in Tahrir Square next Friday. I believe that all Egyptians have a duty to take part in this demonstration. Although we have disagreed about the role of religion in the state and other political matters, we must not allow ourselves to be divided concerning everyone's right to a fair trial. The lives of a 1,000 Egyptians were sacrificed in the revolution and another 1,000 are missing, presumed to have been killed and buried in unmarked graves. On top of this 1,400 lost eyes because of the rubber bullets and 5,000 more were injured. These sacrifices cannot have been in vain; we simply cannot allow the military police to step in as a replacement for the state security service. Any attempt to disgrace the dignity of the Egyptian people cannot be countenanced, under any circumstances. The dignity of the most humble of Egyptians is of greater importance than the highest authority in the country – this is what the revolution taught us.

Dear reader, if you stay silent and do not speak out against military trials today, then tomorrow it may be you who stands in the dock. You might just be innocently walking in the street at the wrong time and in the wrong place – when a sit-in or a demonstration is being broken up – and you'll find yourself arrested on trumped-up charges, such as, thuggish behaviour, using Molotov cocktails, assaulting the military police or insulting the armed forces. The prosecution of civilians in the military courts must end immediately.

Democracy is the answer.

AB

1 Founded by Mohammed ElBaradei, the National Association for Change ia a broad opposition coalition pushing for pro-democracy constitutional reforms.

The Revolution Must Continue

20 September 2011

On a recent trip to Italy I was approached by a young woman at the Festivaletteratura in Mantua, one of Italy's biggest literary festivals, who said to me: "You should be proud of what you have achieved. With courage, you were able to bring down one of the worst dictatorial regimes in the world. You have proved that ideas are stronger than repression, and truth is mightier than bullets." During my visit, I held seminars and press conferences in five Italian cities: Mantua, Arona, Rome, Napoli and Bari. In each city, I am proud to say that I felt the support of the Italian people for the Egyptian revolution. Then, in the middle of the tour, there was an attack on the Israeli embassy in Cairo.[1] The right-wing Italian media seized this opportunity to paint the revolution in a bad light, exaggerating the incident and intimating that Egypt had fallen into complete anarchy. I found myself being asked lots of questions about escalating violence in Egypt and the motives behind the embassy attack. I emphasised that the tension between Egypt and Israel stemmed from the unlawful killing of six Egyptian soldiers by Israeli forces at the border crossing. I also tried to reassure them that the security situation in Egypt had not broken down to such a degree as would lead to anarchy, and that the tourist areas in particular had been completely secured by the armed forces. In my opinion, the attack on the embassy was orchestrated by elements that wanted to sully the reputation of the revolution, both in Egypt and abroad.

The Egyptian ambassador to Rome did not make a statement to explain the situation to the Italian public, despite it being his job to clarify events and dispel rumours so as not to damage tourism to the region. In response to the ambassador's silence, the Egyptian youth in Italy released a statement that outlined the special relationship between the current ambassador and Ahmed Aboul Gheit,[2] the former Egyptian minister of foreign affairs. The ambassador was a close associate of Aboul Gheit, who was eager to appoint him in Italy before stepping down as minister. The Egytian ambassador to Rome therefore belongs to the old regime, hence his reluctance to speak out about the embassy attack and defend the revolution.

What is happening in Italy is only a reflection of what is happening in Egypt. Egyptians have undertaken one of the greatest revolutions in their history but ordinary citizens have seen little change to their daily lives. Even

1 On 9 September 2011, several thousand demonstrators forcibly entered the Israeli embassy in Giza, Greater Cairo, after breaking down a recently constructed wall built to protect the compound.

2 Ahmed Aboul Gheit is a retired Egyptian diplomat who served as minister of foreign affairs from 11 July 2004 to 6 March 2011.

though Mubarak has been deposed and his cronies put on trial, the past eight months have seen a rise in crime and food prices, as well as a break down in law and order. For many Egyptians, circumstances have worsened and the future is even more uncertain. The Egyptian revolution did not take power and is therefore not responsible for the current situation in Egypt. The only party responsible is the military council, which has taken on the role of head of state and people's assembly during the transitional period. The Egyptian people rose up against Hosni Mubarak in revolution and successfully removed him from power and when the army came down into the streets, the revolutionaries celebrated their victory and then returned to their homes convinced that the military council would fulfil the aims of the revolution. In hindsight, the revolution made a mistake by not differentiating between the great patriotic role of the armed forces and the political role of the military council. They did not support the revolution, neither did the military council ever oppose the Mubarak regime for the simple reason that it was a part of it.

The revolution considered the ousting of Mubarak as the first step in ridding Egypt of the regime, while the military council saw it as a necessary sacrifice in their bid to preserve it. The military council stood side by side with the Egyptian people at the start of the revolution, but have not adopted any real measures to protect it and seem unable to particpate in the destruction of the old regime. Despite its eloquent diplomatic expressions, it is clear that the military council does not agree with the revolution and does not share its vision for change. The trial of Mubarak and other senior officials came about after the military council had come under intense pressure from the revolutionaries. They have so far refused to meet the demands of the revolution, and have even resorted to repressing Egyptians using the military police and military courts.

The military police are guilty of the following crimes: indecently assaulting female demonstrators and submitting them to virginity tests, torturing male demonstrators and disregarding their humanity, and illegally trying 12,000 Egyptians before military courts. All of these misdemeanours prove that the attitude of the military council is at odds with their earlier assertions in support of the revolution. Certain members of the military council has also accused the brave revolutionaries of being foreign agents, but have so far been unable to provide any evidence to support their claims.

The military council's attachment to the old regime is the root cause of the problems now facing Egypt. Instead of writing a new constitution, the military council proposed to amend some articles of the old constitution and then hold a referendum on the amendments. It was not long before it overturned the result of the referendum and announced an interim constitution of 63 articles. In this way, the shape of the future political system of Egypt was decided without the consent of the Egyptian people. This constitutional chaos led to fragmentation and divisions amongst the political parties, which could have been prevented had the military council listened to the demands of the revolution. The military council kept all elements of the Mubarak regime intact: from the judges who oversaw rigged elections, to the attorney general who made political concessions in the Mubarak era, to the leaders of the police force who committed crimes against the Egyptian people, and to the snipers who killed hundreds of Egyptians. Even the state security service, whose main duty was to torture and humiliate Egyptians, this terrible institution that the revolution demanded to be got rid of and its members brought to trial for its crimes, the military council is set on keeping, after changing its name to Homeland Security (as if our problem with state security was down to its name).

By resisting all change, the military council has allowed the enemies of the revolution to conspire against it. Very quickly, a wide and effective network of enemies of the revolution was created: journalists, government officials, wealthy businessmen, police officers and members of the sham People's Assembly. These are the ones who organised and implemented all the crises we suffered after the revolution, from shortages of food, petrol and diesel, to sectarian strife and the burning of churches under the very eyes of the military police and police officers, to acts of vandalism, the perpetrators of which have never been traced. All of this is one conspiracy that seeks to spread chaos and destruction all over our country with the aim of thwarting the revolution at any price, because democratic change will bring an end to the careers of the remnants of the Mubarak regime and may result in them being prosecuted and thrown in prison.

What happened on 9 September expresses the depth of the crisis we are going through. The revolutionary parties called for a million-strong march with the title "Correcting the Path," demanding an end to civilians being brought before military courts and a timetable for the transfer of power from the military council to an elected civilian government. Numerous political parties made an alliance to derail Correcting the Path and some Islamist organisations refused to participate in the demonstration because it was keen to please the military council and guarantee for itself the greatest number of seats in government. A huge media campaign was launched to undermine Correcting the Path using the same old means: a fake programme, hypocritical guests and false opinion polls. Furthermore, the Ministry of Agriculture paid five million Egyptian pounds to bring thousands of farmers to Cairo International Stadium for the celebration of Farmers' Day, in an attempt to divert attention from the demonstrations.

After all this, once again the Egyptian people have proven that they still hold the embers of the revolution and in numerous provinces millions of Egyptians went out in mass demonstrations. Even the farmers who were brought from their villages left the farcical celebration in the stadium and joined the demonstration in Tahrir Square. The success of Correcting the Path was singular and complete and had many implications. First, the Islamist organisations which the military council rely upon to direct the revolution were unable to control a major revolution that the Egyptian people wrote with their blood. Second, however much the military council redoubles its repressive practices, it will not be able to thwart the revolution, because it is facing Egyptians who are completely different from the ones Mubarak ruled for thirty years. At the end of the day, it was inevitable that incidents and attacks would be orchestrated to distract attention from the success of the million-man march and these actions would be justified by Emergency Law.

I do not want to waste the reader's time in proving that the attack on the Ministry of the Interior and the Israeli embassy were nothing but a conspiracy orchestrated against the revolution. I will just ask this: why did the police forces withdraw before the attack and why didn't the military police move a finger for hours and left the attackers to do what they wanted in the Ministry of the Interior and the Israeli embassy?

The current crisis in Egypt involves two sides: a great revolution that wants to destroy the old regime to build a new country, and a military council that is resisting change with all its might. What are we to do? The solution is for the revolutionary parties to unite and demand that the military council revoke the Emergency Law, bring to an end the trying of civilians before military courts and any kind of special court, and applying the Treason Law[1] to prevent the remnants of the old regime from corrupting the next People's Assembly. After that, the military council must quickly hold elections so that power is transferred to a civilian government. If the military council refuses to implement these legitimate demands, the Egyptian people will go back out on to the streets to demonstrate and it will be victorious, as it was victorious before.

Democracy is the answer.

PN

What Does Egypt Lack?

27 September 2011

Two years before the revolution took place, I received a call from the French theatre director, Jean-Louis Martinelli, who was interested in adapting my novel *Chicago*. I thought it a wonderful idea and he came to visit me several times in Cairo to discuss his plans for the play. Jean-Louis Martinelli is one

1 The Treason Law, approved in August 2011, bars anyone found guilty of corrupting political life, as well as former regime figures, from holding political office.

of the most important stage directors in France; he has managed a number of important French theatres and currently manages the famous Théâtre des Amandiers in Nanterre, just outside Paris.[1] Martinelli is well-known for his cultural sophistication, his liberal ideas, his commitment to humanitarian causes and his defence of human rights even when this goes against an official position taken by the French government. He has achieved distinction due to the creative ideas and constant innovation he has brought to the field of theatre. His work is concerned with the human experience and offers refreshing theatrical experiences that are accessible to everyone.

Martinelli is about 60 years of age, but is highly active and full of energy, as though he were still in the prime of his youth. At our first meeting, he explained to me that he feels that it is his duty as a French artist to present theatrical productions that affirm our shared humanity, beyond what our ethnic or religious differences may be – in the end, as human beings, we all experience the same thoughts and feelings.

I thanked him for deciding to adapt my novel and for involving me in the process, but insisted that he take artistic ownership of the piece and do as he so wished. I would not interfere with his adaptation of it for the stage because I was of the opinion that this was his sphere, and I put my trust in him entirely. Despite this conviction, however, Martinelli insisted on showing me how the piece had developed and sent me the script so that I could read it. He had dropped the title of my novel, instead naming the play: *J'aurais voulu être égyptien* ("I would have liked to be Egyptian").

The Théâtre des Amandiers is located half an hour's drive from the centre of Paris and was founded by the great French writer and intellectual, André Malraux, when he was minister of culture under Charles de Gaulle. I was invited to go to France and see the play for myself and I experienced the same joy and wonder I had felt when I saw the film adaptation of my novel *The Yacoubian Building* for the first time in New York. These characters from my novel that I had created and nurtured suddenly appeared right in front of me, just as I had imagined them. Apart from experiencing these wonderful feelings, I also thought about something of greater importance: a writer from Egypt was now able to have his work performed in one of the most important theatres in France. This is the kind of international recognition that Egypt fully deserves.

I took my seat in the auditorium which was packed with French theatre-goers; they had come to see how the esteemed Martinelli would present, for the first time, a play based upon an Egyptian novel. As the lights went down, a group of men and women burst into the auditorium, shouting in the most startling manner. Some members of the audience openly objected to this disturbance, but it quickly became apparent that these intruders were, in fact,

1 Jean-Louis Martinelli left the Théâtre Nanterre-Amandiers in December 2013 to start is own company Allers/Retours.

the actors themselves. The great Martinelli had employed a *coup de théâtre*: the actors would enter through the stalls rather than from behind the stage. The whole concept of the play's performance was innovative. A group of actors sat at a long table to read their parts in the play; at any given moment an actor would move into position to perform his or her part, then, once done, withdraw to a corner or return to the table, at which time, another actor would stand and do the same. In this way, the drama unfolded while all of the actors were present on the stage. Indeed, Martinelli used them as a background for the play itself: when a dialogue was taking place between actors, other actors in the background provided a visual element which complemented the principal performance of the scene.

I was hugely impressed by Martinelli's ability to exercise complete control over the actors and events. Even though the play lasted for three full hours, the rhythm of the performance meant that the audience was never bored, but eagerly watched the events of the drama unfold. Another thing that I found astonishing and original was the way in which Martinelli cast his actors: the actor's appearance did not seem to inform his choice. In my novel there is a character called Ahmed Danana; he is an Egyptian who has been sent to Chicago to complete a doctorate, however, he is also working as an agent for the state security service. In the play, Martinelli cast a French actor, named Eric Caruso, to play the role of Danana. Part of the actor's costume was to wear a fake paunch so that he would resemble the character as I had described him in the novel. But why did Martinelli not cast an Arab actor for the role of Danana? In answer to this, he told me that he had wanted to emphasise the universality of the character because he believes that we all share in the basic experience of being human, and that the same basic characters recur throughout the history of the world's literature. In light of this idea, he decided to defy the conventional expectations of the audience and cast a French actor to play the part of an Egyptian who comes from the depths of the countryside, and in fact, after only a few minutes, the actor succeeds in convincing you that he really is Ahmed Danana.

When the play ended the audience applauded rapturously for a quarter of an hour. The actors came out from backstage and bowed for the audience four times as the applause continued. At the invitation of the director, I went up on stage and shook hands with all of the actors. I met them again afterwards and when I spoke with them I gained a true and profound understanding of the value of the work that they do. It is their belief that the need for art is now greater than ever. They are all professional actors but they consider themselves to be exponents of art and life, not merely people who are just paid to act, as one of them said to me.

I should mention here that the Théâtre des Amandiers, like most major theaters in France, receives government subsidies. There is an established principle in France that the state must support the theatre financially because without such support they would seek profits at any price and this would have two negative outcomes: firstly, artistic merit would be sacrificed in favour of simple entertainment, and perhaps, sexual titillation; secondly, there would be a rise in the price of tickets which would mean that theatre would become the preserve of the rich, with the poorer sections of society being deprived of seeing artistically valuable productions. The price of a ticket at the Théâtre des Amandiers, as with most French theaters, does not cost more than a meal in a cheap restaurant. That the people have a basic right to experience culture is an established principle in France – one which right-wing governments have not been able to overturn. Most of the major stage directors in France, including Marinelli, are leftist and have publicly opposed the policies of President Sarkozy. Despite this, they continue to receive subsidies from the French government so that they can continue to serve the public through their art. The reason for this is that no one in France sees the president as the "father of the nation" or any other of those false and empty notions that were for so long used to justify despotism in Egypt.

When I had come out from the performance I could not help but think about this question: what does Egypt lack that would enable it to achieve this kind of artistic advancement? The truth is that the artistic resources possessed by Egypt are no fewer than those in France. We have talented writers and directors and we have our own artistic tradition that we should be proud of. One need only consider the histories of the cinema in France and in Egypt: the first screening of a motion picture took place in Paris in December 1895, while the first screening of a motion picture in Egypt occurred in Alexandria in November 1896. In other words, cinema reached Egypt only 11 months after its beginnings in France, which means that Egyptians knew of it before many European countries did. Egypt has every potential for an artistic renaissance, but years of despotism and extremism have stifled its potential. Despotism puts people in jobs that they do not deserve and makes officials loyal to the ruler rather than to the people. This has led to corruption and the decline of culture as we witnessed when Farouk Hosny, Mubarak's minister of culture, tried to buy support of Egypt's intellectuals and artists. His only concern was pandering to Mubarak and his wife by organising cultural events devoid of any real content. I remember how, when Martinelli met me after attending the Alexandria Film Festival in Mubarak's time and I asked him his impression, he told me: "I felt they had invited me to take some commemorative photographs and after that they didn't know what to do with me."

The second danger threatening Egyptian culture is the proliferation of the Wahhabi concept of Islam, backed by oil money. Wahhabism is hostile to all art. Art employs the imagination to portray reality with all its flaws, whereas the extremist mentality is, by nature, closed to any kind of imagination. The extremists in Egypt exist outside of the notion of true civilisation. They attacked the great Egyptian writer Naguib Mahfouz[1] because he depicted people who frequent bars. Nor do they understand the value of Egypt's great antiquities; they want to cover up the faces appearing in ancient Egyptian art because they fear that Egyptians will worship the images as idols. Their attitudes need to change so that they can join civilisation. When the audience watched Martinelli's wonderful play they were seized by powerful human emotions; however, if an extremist had of been present, he probably would have felt nothing more than unease because an actress was not wearing a hijab, or because one of her fellow actors held her arm as part of the performance. There is a fundamental incompatibility between extremism and art: it is impossible for an extremist to appreciate art, just as it is impossible for someone who does appreciate art be an extremist.

Despite this, however, I am more optimistic than ever about the future of art in Egypt. The great Egyptian revolution broke out and deposed Mubarak who is now being tried for his many heinous crimes against Egyptians. The battle is not over, however; in fact, it has only just begun. Right now an attempt is being made to reanimate Mubarak's regime, and the counter-revolutionary plots to prevent change and put pressure on Egyptians to abandon the goals of the revolution continue unabated. But the flame of the revolution still burns and, God willing, it will triumph. My advice to anyone who thinks that they can prevent change or deceive and oppress the Egyptian people is to consider the fate of Hosni Mubarak and his sons as they stand in the dock of a criminal court. The bright future of Egypt has begun and we will never go back to how things were before.

Democracy is the answer.

AB

Muslim, Christian or Human Being?

27 September 2011

In the first instance, do you consider yourself a Muslim, a Christian, or a human being? Is your first allegiance to your religion, or is being part of a wider humanity more important? The way in which you answer these questions will inform your view of the world and also how you treat other people. If you view yourself as a human being, first and foremost, then it follows that you

1 Naguib Mahfouz (1911–2006) was an Egyptian writer who won the 1988 Nobel Prize for Literature. He was regarded as the Arab world's most prominent literary figure and his work has been translated into over 40 languages.

will respect the rights of others regardless of their religious beliefs. If you have a correct understanding of religion, you will also value and respect others because religion, in its essence, stands for the defence of human values, such as justice, freedom and equality. However, if your identification with a religion takes precedence over your humanity, then you have started down a dangerous path that often leads to intolerance and violence.

Religion is not simply a point of view; it is a system of belief that rejects the full validity of other, different religions. The road to bigotry begins when an individual believes that his or her religion is the one true religion. This attitude towards other religions inevitably leads to resentment and conflict as it assumes that followers of other religions are misguided. By looking down on others in this way, you will gradually start to dehumanise them. No longer will you view people of other religions as individuals, you will view them all as being one and the same. If you are a Muslim, you will not look on your Coptic neighbour as a human being with his own personality but as a Copt whose behaviour and temperament is distinctively Coptic. At this point you will take another step towards sectarian hatred. You will say things such as: "I don't like these Copts; they're horrible and bigoted."

Soon you might reach the stage where you view people of other religions disgusting and unclean because they have not been made pure by the one true religion. When you have reached this stage, dear reader, you have become a bigoted religious extremist. It is now very likely that you will commit criminal acts against others and violate their rights because you have misunderstood religion and this has led you to hate and despise others.

The question here is this: how did Egyptians practice their religion in the past? The truth is that Egyptians are a very religious people, with a history of understanding and tolerance. Egypt has welcomed immigrants of all religious faiths and ethnic groups: from Armenians and Italians, to Greeks, Jews and Baha'is. Egyptians have always enjoyed the right to religious freedom, and can, for the most part, live their lives as they see fit. Each citizen was personally responsible for their own actions before God and the law.

In 1889, the great Egyptian imam, Muhammad Abduh,[1] proposed a more tolerant interpretation of Islam that sought to prove that Islam was compatible with modernity. This tolerant, home-grown understanding of Islam endured in Egypt until the October War broke out in 1973, in which thousands of Syrian and Egyptian people died. At this time, the price of oil rose severalfold, giving the oil-producing states in the Gulf unprecedented economic power. And because the Saudi regime has long depended on its alliance with Wahhabi clergy for its stability, millions of dollars were spent

1 Muhammad Abduh (1849-1905) was a religious scholar, jurist, and liberal reformer, who led a late nineteenth century movement in Egypt and other Muslim countries to revitalise Islamic teachings and institutions in the modern world. He served as grand mufti (supreme legal authority), and as rector at Al-Azhar University.

propagating the Wahhabi doctrine of Islam throughout the world.

The economic crisis forced millions of Egyptians to emigrate to Saudi Arabia for work, but when they returned, many came back steeped in Wahhabi ideology. The Wahhabi interpretation of Islam, quite unlike the Egyptian concept, is dogmatic and bigoted; hostile to democracy and unfair to women. Wahhabism generally reduces religion to rituals and practice, taking an interest in the form of religion at the expense of the substance. Egyptian men living in the land of Wahhabism quickly learn that if their wives' hair is exposed in public, the *mutaween* – Saudi Arabia's 'religious police', who impose morals by force – will intervene immediately. At the same time, however, Egyptians living in Saudi Arabia become aware that such laws do not apply to Americans, Europeans, princes, and other powerful people; they are strictly enforced only when it comes to Egyptians and other less-esteemed nationalities. In Saudi Arabia, Egyptians are taught that failure to perform the daily prayers is one of the gravest sins. At the same time, however, it is acceptable for a Saudi employer to abuse Egyptian staff, deny them proper payment for their work and have them thrown in prison if they stand up for their rights. Such injustices are outside the sphere of religion according to the Wahhabi way of thinking.

Over the last decades, Wahhabi ideology has spread in Egypt; the most dangerous seed that it has sown is a contempt and hatred for Copts. An article by Professor Essam Abdel Gawad, recently published in *Rose al-Yousef* magazine, gathered together a number of statements made by Wahhabi scholars. According to Sheikh Said Abdel-Azim: "There can be no affection for Christians and no friendship with them. It is not permissible to associate with them or celebrate with them on their religious festivals, because their unbelief only increases on their holy days." Then there is Sheikh Abu Islam who says: "Christians need to come to their senses; everything they believe in is contrary to truth and reason." Sheikh Yesser Borhami asserts that: "Muslims are not permitted to participate in Coptic rituals because Copts are idolaters." As for Sheikh Ahmed Farid, he states that: "Muslims must not offer condolences to Copts when one of their loved ones dies, nor should they hold out any hope for them regarding the afterlife because all Copts shall burn in hell." These are just some examples of speeches made by Wahhabi sheikhs in mosques and on Saudi satellite-television channels. In any decent country such statements would be considered criminal incitements of sectarian hatred. Unfortunately, these Wahhabi sheikhs are allowed to poison the minds of Egyptians and fill their hearts with hatred and bigotry – neither the law nor basic morality is preventing them.

What can we hope to expect from people who think in this bigoted way? The events that took place a few days ago in the village of Al-Marinab in Aswan Governorate would seem to provide a clear answer to this question.

In the village of Al-Marinab, Copts have been praying in St George's church since 1940. The walls of the church had fallen into disrepair so an official permit was obtained from the authorities to restore them. At this point, a group of Wahhabi Salafists came forward and objected to the restoration of the church. Instead of the authorities enforcing the law and protecting the church, officials from the police and the army convened an informal meeting with the parties involved. At this meeting, the Salafists dictated conditions for allowing the repairs to go ahead, stipulating that the church should have no loudspeakers, no domes, and no crosses. The officials from the police and the army did not object to the Salafists' conditions and the church was forced to accept them. Even though the church accepted these unfair conditions, it was unable to protect itself against the Salafists. On the Friday following their agreement, a Wahhabi preacher of the local mosque incited the congregation against the church. As soon as the prayers had ended, these fanatics headed straight for the church and surrounded it, set fire to it, and burned it down to the ground. Neither the police nor the army intervened to protect this house of God. As for the governor of Aswan Governorate, who happens to be a notable from the ranks of the old Mubarak regime, he denied that there had ever been a church in the village, suggesting that everything that had happened was merely all some sort of fantasy in the minds of the Copts.

The growing number of criminal attacks on churches since the revolution is highly alarming and suspicious. There have been similar attacks elsewhere in Egypt: in Fayoum, in Ismailia, Imbaba, Ain Shams and Atfih. This raises some questions.

Firstly, the military council has assumed the powers of both head of state and of parliament during the transitional period, and is, therefore, responsible for the running of the country. Now, in light of this, why is it that officers in the military police deal so harshly with demonstrators – beating them, torturing them and dehumanising them – while they simply look on idly while Salafists torch churches and shrines, cut off the ear of a Coptic citizen and block the train lines for a period of ten days, as happened in Qena? Why do the military police use an iron fist to deal with demonstrators but tread lightly when dealing with the Salafists? Why do representatives from the police and the army sit down and negotiate with Salafists, and submit to their demands as though they were the representatives of a foreign state more powerful than Egypt? What special legal status do the Salafists have that gives them the right to inspect churches, dictate the conditions under which they can be repaired, prevent them from being built, demolish them and even burn them down to the ground? Do the Salafists enjoy a special political relationship with the military council, or is it merely that all this lawlessness and sectarian violence serve the political interests of the military council, since they can use the situation to justify staying in power on the pretext of maintaining law and order, and protecting the Copts from attacks by extremists?

Since the nineteenth century, the Egyptian people have struggled and thousands of them have given their lives for two objectives: independence and a constitution. It was the hope of all of Egypt's leaders to build a modern democratic state, from Saad Zaghloul to Gamal Abdel Nasser. Contrary to the repeated claims made by Wahhabis, none of Egypt's leaders were secularists who were hostile to Islam. Rather, they stood for culture and civilisation; they understood that a civil state where citizens are treated as equals regardless of their religion is the only way that a country can achieve progress.

Any attempt to undermine the civil structure of the state will lead to real disaster in Egypt. If the Salafists cannot tolerate the existence of a church, then what will they do to us – Muslims and Copts – if they were to come to power in Egypt? When Islam is understood correctly it makes us more humane, more tolerant and more respectful to others. Showing contempt towards the Copts and attacking them is a woeful criminal act that has no basis in true religion.

Democracy is the answer.

AB

Religious Fascism in Egypt

11 October 2011

What is your opinion on Saad Zaghloul, Mustafa el-Nahhas and Gamal Abdel Nasser? Were they not our great leaders who fought long and hard for Egypt's independence and freedom? Why did they all demand a civil state rather than a religious state? Were they considered infidels or enemies of Islam? No, on the contrary, they were dedicated Muslims and Mustafa el-Nahhas is often held up as an example of religiosity. Another question: were Egyptians less Islamic before the 1980s than they are today? Again, the answer is no – the majority were decent God-fearing Muslims that carried out their religious obligations dutifully. So, Egyptians were Muslim before Wahhabism reached Egypt. What is the difference between the moderate Islam of Egyptians and the Islam of the Wahhabi sheikhs? Egyptians believe that the essence of Islam can be found in the great human values of justice, freedom and equality. They never thought of using Islam as a political manifesto to get into power. Again, we are reminded of the conversation between Mustafa el-Nahhas and a young politician called Ahmad Hussein. As soon as el-Nahhas read the word "God" in Hussein's political manifesto, he got angry. "The word of the Almighty is too superior and too great to be written in a political manifesto," he said. "Talking about God in a political manifesto will make you a charlatan."

All Egyptians (with the exception of the Muslim Brotherhood) used to treat Islam as a great religion and not a political manifesto. Then, after the 1973 war, oil prices skyrocketed and by the end of the 1970s, political Islam had spread to Egypt funded by the super-abundance of oil money from the Gulf. Political Islam aims to get to power through three principal notions:

First: That there is a Western imperialist conspiracy against Islam that necessitates us to declare holy war on the West. I disagree with this idea. Western governments may be imperialist but Western peoples are not necessarily so. We have seen how millions of Westerners organised demonstrations against the war in Iraq and how they supported the Arab revolutions. Most Westerners, on an individual level, are not enemies of Islam. Likewise, the official Western establishment does not oppose Islam itself, but opposes all that compromises its own interests. Therefore, if Islamic governments accord with the imperialist interests of the West, it will do everything in its power to support them such as it did with the government of Saudi Arabia, General Zia-ul-Haq in Pakistan and the Taliban movement before the West turned against it. If you are Muslim, Western imperialism will only be against you if Islam makes you start a revolution or demand your rights that have been taken away. But if you collaborate with imperialism and fulfil its interests, it will support you in spite of your beard and *jellabiya*,[1] and your religious zeal.

Second: That God's law has been displaced and we must re-establish it, lest we become infidels.I disagree with this idea because wherever justice and truth are in force, God's law is also being upheld. Here we must not mix up sharia (God's law) and *fiqh* (legal interpretation). God's law is divine and everlasting, whereas legal interpretation is human and changeable. Islamic legal scholars must work hard to make religion relevant to modern times so that it helps people instead of limiting their freedoms. For example, if the punishment for stealing is chopping off the hand and the ruler found that implementing this punishment would only cause bigger problems (as was the case in Sudan where it led to the country being divided), is it not the right of the ruler to decide to use chopping off the hand as the maximum penalty and imprisonment as a lesser punishment? Didn't Umar ibn Al-Khattab annul the punishment of chopping off the hand during the years of famine? If there is a law that does not contradict God's law and serves justice, surely it is also sharia? Isn't everything that does good in the world and gives people justice a fulfilment of God's law?

1 A full-length outer garment, native to the Nile Valley.

Third: That Islam has set down for us a defined form of government that we must follow. While Islam set the principles of government it did not define the form. Upon aceding to the Caliph, Abu Bakr gave the following speech:

> People, I have been given authority over you but I am not the best of you. Therefore, if I act well, help me and if I err, set me straight for honesty is faith and deceit is treachery. The weak man is strong with me for I will see he gets his due, but the strong man will be weak if he takes it away, God willing. When a nation ceases fighting for God's cause, God strikes them with degradation. Whenever abominations spread through a nation, God brings them misfortune. Obey me as long as I obey God and His Prophet. If I disobey God and His Prophet, then have no obedience to me.

This speech contains the principles of Islamic governance. A ruler is no better than their subjects and does not rule by divine power but by the will of the people, who have the right to hold the ruler to account. These principles of government in Islam are the same as the principles of democracy: freedom, equality, the rotation of power and the sovereignty of the people. These great principles were never fulfilled in Islamic history except for a very short period under the four rightly-guided caliphs and for two years during the rule of the Umayyad Caliph, Umar ibn Abd al-Aziz. After this, the Islamic caliphate turned into a rapacious kingship: the great principles set down by Abu Bakr were abandoned and a brutal and bloody struggle for power began.

This is a historical fact but it does not diminish the achievements of the Islamic state, because despotic rule was the prevalent characteristic of all states in that period and also because the Islamic state made vast contributions to civil society and was a pioneer in both the sciences and arts. But our pride in the achievements of the early Muslims must not lead us to reproduce the tyrannical regime that used to rule them.

Advocates of political Islam confuse history and religion and consider the Islamic caliphate (a human invention not prescribed by religion) as a religious obligation. This dangerous misunderstanding has occurred in every country where political Islam has risen to power, giving rise to despotic governments that compromise basic freedoms in the name of religion. It is democracy that is the true application of the principles of Islam. If we attempt to reproduce the political structure of the Umayyad or Abbasid dynasties, we will certainly descend into despotism however good our intentions. But even if we differ on an ideological level with political Islam, don't they have the right to seek power by democratic means? The answer is that yes, they certainly have the right. But here we must make a distinction between democratic Islamist organisations and organisations espousing religious fascism.

Many supporters of political Islam believe that they alone represent Islam and consider anyone who disagrees with them as enemies to Islam. As with other fascist movements throughout history, they are fully prepared to impose their ideas on others by force.

Some of these supporters have engaged in criminal activity in order to forward their cause. They have attacked churches and Christian shrines, burned down video shops and looted Coptic businesses. They are also responsible for the murders of innocent foreign tourists and countless Egyptian citizens. These fascists treat Copts and liberals with disdain and heap insults and accusations upon them. If they were to come to power in Egypt, there would be no music, theatre or cinema, and no political parties to oppose them. There would be no tourism and the artefacts of Ancient Egypt would be locked away and kept out of sight, lest the Egyptian people worship false idols. There would be no great literature, as they blame great writers like Naguib Mahfouz for the decadence of the Egyptian people. Religious fascists threaten to plunge Egypt into total darkness by manipulating Egyptians' religious sentiments to obtain power. Any normal candidate would try hard to convince voters of his political manifesto, but the religious fascists do not present a manifesto. They tell people: "If you are Muslims, we are Islam. If you don't vote for us, you are secularists and infidels."

The problem is that religious fascism is not strictly an Egyptian creation as it is funded by oil money from the gulf. In an article published by *Middle East Monitor*, Curtin Winsor[1] recalled that in 2003 during a US Senate hearing, it was announced that over a twenty-year period, Saudi Arabia had spent 87 billion dollars on spreading Wahhabism throughout the world. To this number we must add the millions of dollars pouring in from non-governmental Wahhabi organisations prevalent across the Gulf. In Egypt, Salafist and Wahhabi organisations are now spending unprecedented amounts in their bid to gain power, even distributing hundreds of tonnes of food products at nominal prices to voters. One Wahhabi party opened more than 30 offices over a matter of months in Alexandria alone. Don't we, as Egyptians, have the right to know who is funding these parties? Why haven't the military council investigated the funding of the Salafist parties?

The revolution now faces two dangers: first, the conspiracies by remnants of the former regime to cause chaos and impede change at any price. They plan to change the revolution into a mere coup d'état that removed the head of state but left the old system in place

The second danger is that the religious fascists will gain power in the elections. Since Salafist sheikhs declare that democracy is religiously

1 Curtin Winsor was an American diplomat and former special emissary to the Middle East.

prohibited and un-Islamic and since they railed against the revolution and said that it is against religion to remove one's ruler, we can only expect them to use the democratic system merely as a ladder to power which they will then kick away so that nobody else can use it after them.

The noble principles of Islam can only be applied through a real civic state open to all citizens regardless of their ideology or religion.

Democracy is the answer.

PN

The Moment of Truth has Arrived

17 October 2011

Imagine that you were an officer in the state security service and you were still in your job. Before the revolution, you tortured hundreds of Egyptians and you know that the forthcoming elections will produce a civilian government that will most certainly dismiss you and put you on trial. Would you maintain law and order, or would you do everything in your power to spread chaos in Egypt in order to save yourself? If you were the chairman of a bank, appointed by Gamal Mubarak, what would you do after the revolution? Would you help to revive the failing economy until a new government comes and dismisses you, or would you use your expertise to bring about an economic crisis in order to delay your certain fate? If you were a provincial governor appointed by Mubarak, would it not be in your interest to stir up sectarian tension in order to put off the change that will sweep you away?

In the aftermath of any revolution, if supporters of the former regime stay in their jobs, they will certainly plot to sabotage the country and delay change. All other successful revolutions throughout history have destroyed the former regime in order to realise their demands. In Egypt, however, twenty million Egyptians brought about a great revolution, in which many gave their lives, and succeeded in forcing Hosni Mubarak to step down. They then went back home and left the revolution in the charge of the military council. A real misunderstanding took place: the revolutionaries saw the overthrow of Mubarak as a first step towards overthrowing the old regime, while the military council thought that Mubarak's departure was an inevitable sacrifice in order to preserve the old regime. We must again differentiate between the armed forces as a national institution and the military council as a political authority with whom it is our right to disagree. The military council refused to open fire on demonstrators and this praiseworthy decision accords with the traditions of the great Egyptian army. However, at the same time the military council did not bring about the revolution; it neither expected the revolution nor understands it.

Until the revolution, the military council dutifully supported Mubarak, but the Egyptian revolution overthrew the dictatorship and the military council had to deal with the consequences. During the Battle of the Camel, thousands of armed thugs entered Tahrir Square with the aim of attacking and killing revolutionaries. The events took place in front of soldiers who neither opposed the thugs nor protected the revolutionaries from them. When asked, they replied: "our orders are to remain neutral". Remaining neutral between peaceful demonstrators and hired armed thugs simply means giving the Mubarak regime the upper hand. A video emerged, which showed General Hassan al-Ruwaini talking to revolutionaries after the Battle of the Camel, and asking them to disperse. When a revolutionary tells him that he is planning to remain in the square until Mubarak steps down, al-Ruwaini sneers at him: "Let's see who pays your first month's salary while you are on the street."

The military council held Hosni Mubarak out of sight in his palace in Sharm el-Sheikh for two whole months after the revolution. Eventually they had no choice but to give in to popular pressure and put Mubarak on trial. Everything that has happened in Egypt since the revolution can be summed up as the struggle between two wills: the will of the revolution that calls for real change and the will of the military council that clings to the old regime and is desperately resisting change. The current state officials and decision makers are the same people the revolution wanted to overthrow; it is as if we are asking the old regime to help overthrow itself. State security officers, the leadership of the police, provincial governors, most ministers and senior bankers, and the media – they are all dyed in wool cogs of the Mubarak regime and are fundamentally opposed to the revolution. The result has been a series of plots and conspiracies that have delayed democratic change. It has also worked to push the revolution in the opposite direction in an attempt to contain and neutralise it. The revolution wanted a new constitution but the military council listened to Mubarak's legal advisors and implemented referendum on limited constitutional amendments, then announced a temporary constitution that in practice undermined the results of the referendum and defined the Egyptian state in a way that reflected the wishes of the council, not the will of the people.

A few days ago the *Tahrir* newspaper published a document showing that 165,000 thugs are still working at the expense of the state security service. What do we expect from these thugs who are immune to arrest? They are doubtlessly working to spread such chaos that Egyptians will start to resent the revolution and regret having demanded freedom. *Tahrir* also published a document that EgyptAir sent to its employees on tourism in Japan, asking travel agencies not to send Japanese tourists to Egypt as the security situation did not permit it. There are countless other examples of corruption and sabotage, including the tragic Maspero massacre in which many citizens were crushed to death. We will not be able to understand what happened at the Maspero massacre if we do not acknowledge that the Mubarak regime is still ruling Egypt. The governor of Aswan deliberately stirred up sectarian tension, and the military council refused to remove him from his job even though this had been recommended by an independent committe. The military council is working in complete collaboration with the police whose leadership is still loyal to Mubarak, as well as with the state security apparatus (now rebranded as Homeland Security).

It was a peaceful march whose location and time was announced in advance and in which thousands of Copts participated along with many Muslims out of solidarity with their legitimate demands. Suddenly anonymous armed groups appeared and attacked buildings as well as members of the armed forces, providing them the excuse to mistreat the demonstrators, which was the purpose of this pathetic piece of theatre. In all previous incidents, without exception, from the burning of the church in the village of Sul to the events of Abbasiya, these thugs were filmed by demonstrators committing horrific crimes and have also admitted to the media that they were being paid by members of the National Democratic Party. So why did the military police not arrest and take them in for questioning? Why did the military police in Qena allow extremists to block the railway line to Upper Egypt for ten days? How can Mubarak's thugs, armed with knives and other such weapons, attack the families of those killed in the revolution without the military police detaining any of them?

Meanwhile the military police attack, torture, and kill only the revolutionaries. The key question in the Maspero disaster is: were Egyptian citizens run over by armoured cars? The answer, unfortunately, is yes they were. The horrendous crime was captured on video and most of the corpses in the morgue show signs of having been crushed by armoured cars. One day soon, when the dust has settled, and when there has been an end to the campaigns of defamation, incitement and lies led by the state media, Egyptians will find themselves looking back on a horrendous massacre committed against Egyptian citizens by individuals of the Egyptian army.

In 1906 five officers from the occupying British forces went on a pigeon-hunting trip in the Egyptian countryside. A series of misunderstandings led to an argument between the English officers and Egyptian peasants, which ended with the death of an Egyptian peasant and a British officer who succumbed to sunstroke as he was trying to escape. Lord Cromer, the British consul-general convened a show trial that sentenced four Egyptian peasants to death and others to various periods in prison. This affair became known to history as the Denshawai Incident. The martyrs were mourned by the whole of Egypt, from ordinary Egyptians to the great activist Mustafa Kemal[1] and poets such as Hafez Ibrahim and Ahmed Shawqi who composed wonderful odes inspired by the catastrophe. In Britain, many politicians and intellectuals came out against the Denshawai massacre, with the great English playwright, George Bernard Shaw writing:

> If her [England's] empire means ruling the world as Denshawai has been ruled in 1906 – and that, I am afraid, is what the Empire does mean to the main body of our aristocratic-military caste and to our Jingo plutocrats – then there can be no more sacred and urgent political duty on earth than the disruption, defeat, and suppression of the Empire ...[2]

Violent protests forced Lord Cromer to resign and the British government to repeal the sentences handed out to the peasants and release them. To this day Egyptian schoolchildren are taught about the massacre as conclusive evidence of the cruelty of the British occupation. And here we have to make a sad, but vital, comparison: the Denshawai massacre had five martyrs whereas the Maspero massacre had 24. Moreover the military council has not apologised for the killings and not a single soldier has been put on trial. However the military council has stated that the military court will carry out investigations, which positions it as both poacher and gamekeeper.

There is another big difference between Denshawai and Maspero. The British soldiers killed the Egyptians as residents of a British colony, but the members of the military police killed Egyptian citizens like themselves. The Egyptian people pay taxes for the armed forces to buy armoured cars, supposedly to protect the nation, except that they were used to crush and kill the very people who had paid for them. The Maspero massacre has simply crowned the series of horrendous crimes committed by individuals of the military police against Egyptians, from stripping women demonstrators and subjecting them to virginity tests, to torturing, electrocuting and abusing demonstrators. These crimes have been documented and allegedly investigated by the military courts but we have not seen, and will never see, the findings. The Maspero massacre has brought us face to face with the truth that the Mubarak regime is still ruling Egypt and is doing all it can to abort the revolution and prevent change. The military council must now choose whether to protect the criminals who killed peaceful demonstrators at Maspero Square or to comply with the military justice and traditions and transfer the case to a neutral legal committee for justice to be done and the criminals to get their just deserves.

1 Mustafa Kemal (1874–1908) was an Egyptian lawyer and journalist. He is remembered as a fervent Egyptian nationalist and an articulate advocate of Egyptian independence.

2 "Preface for Politicians", *John Bull's Other Island*, George Bernard Shaw (London: Penguin, 1907)

The Egyptian revolution is now standing completely alone, having been abandoned and plotted against both inside and outside Egypt. But the revolution, by the grace of God, and the people who have made it, will be victorious and carry Egypt on to the future it deserves.

Democracy is the answer.

RH

What the Military Council Didn't Hear

25 October 2011

My friend Yosri Fouda is the host of the Egyptian talk show, *The Last Word*. Last week he invited me to take part in his show and to comment on a rival programme that featured General el-Assar and General Hegazy of the military council. Despite my full respect for the generals, their appearance on the show was disappointing because they confined themselves to praising the decisions of the military council. The following day, Fouda called to inform me that the episode had been cancelled and asked me to meet him. When I asked him what had happened, he said: "I was put under pressure to cancel the episode, so I decided to suspend the whole program. In my work, I am ruled only by my conscience and will never be told what to do by any party whatsoever."[1]

I have met few people as courageous and principled as Yosri Fouda. His admirable stand against the military council sets an example for other honest journalists who refuse to compromise their principles for personal gain. The military council is unable to accept any criticism, however earnest or sincere, and have begun a wide-reaching brutal campaign against freedom of expression in Egypt. Before cancelling the episode of Yosri Fouda's show, the military police had carried out violent attacks on other television stations such as Alhurra, 25 January and Al-Jazeera Egypt Live, and removed scathing articles from certain newspapers. We respect the armed forces as a national institution, but during the transitional period the military council combines the powers of the head of state and the legislature, and so we have a right to criticise its political decisions publicly through the media.

During the revolution, the military council refused to open fire on the demonstrators; a wise and patriotic decision that won them the trust of the

1 In October 2011, Fouda suspended his show in protest of what he called the "efforts by the country's military rulers to stifle free expression". He said "This is my way of self-censorship, either to say the truth or to be silent." The show went off air for three weeks and was resumed on 13 November 2011.

revolutionaries. After Mubarak stood down from power, the demonstrators returned to their homes confident that the military council would safeguard the revolution and implement their demands. The military council has since gone against the wishes of the demonstrators and has instead imposed its own will upon the revolution. The outcome is that the Egyptian revolution has faltered and stalled.

Everything that has happened in the aftermath of the Egyptian revolution reflects the military council's desperate attempts to resist change and preserve the Mubarak regime. The revolutionaries wanted a new constitution, but the military council refused and held a referendum on limited amendments to the 1971 constitution. It then ignored the result of the referendum and declared that the new system of government would be presidential. In other words, the military council has dictated the shape of the future state without consulting the Egyptian people. The revolution asked for local councils to be dissolved and the National Democratic Party disbanded, but it was not until many months later that these steps were taken through court rulings. The military council has kep Mubarak-era officials in place in all state institutions. The revolution demanded that corrupt National Democratic Party members be disqualified from public office, but as yet the military council has done nothing to prevent this regression. As a result, remnants of the Mubarak regime have been able to stand as candidates in the coming parliamentary elections.

The revolution was started for the sake of dignity. It was our dream that all Egyptians would be treated with humanity and respect, and would be granted equal rights. The revolution demanded that the state security apparatus be disbanded, on account of its crimes against the Egyptian people, but the military council preserved this odious organisation after changing its name to Homeland Security. It does not take great intelligence to realise that the state security apparatus has been behind most of the crises facing Egypt, from sectarian strife to gang violence and the breakdown in law and order. State security officers belong to the Mubarak regime and are doing all in their power to prevent any change that would lead to their prosecution and imprisonment. They possess all the necessary resources to sabotage and cause chaos: precise intelligence, informants and infiltrators everywhere, and abundant sources of money obtained from the remnants of the Mubarak regime. The military council has not only saved the state security service but has also added a new tool of repression: the military police. In a few short months, military police personnel have committed savage crimes against Egyptians for which nobody has been brought to account: beating and torturing demonstrators, conducting virginity tests on Egyptian women and crushing demonstrators with a tank in the massacre of Maspero Square. In the aftermath of each of these crimes, the military council announced the opening of investigations but the results of these are unknown. The revolution demands an unbiased enquiry into the

Maspero Square massacre in which 27 Egyptian citizens died.

Since the start of the revolution, the military council has enjoyed a special relationship with the Islamist organisations. As expected, the Muslim Brotherhood has distanced itself from the revolutionaries by putting the interests of their party before the collective aims of the revolution. After calling for a new constitution, the Muslim Brotherhood then accepted the military council's amendments and threw themselves behind the military council, becoming in effect its political wing. A few days ago, *Al-Masry Al-Youm* published a story which intimated that the Muslim Brotherhood had tried to buy votes during the election campaign by distributing free meat and vegetables, all of which were subsidised by the military council.

These double standards extend to legal procedures. To date, 12,000 civilians have been tried before military courts and given prison sentences. Bringing civilians to trial before military courts is a violation of their human and legal rights, and of the international treaties Egypt has signed. The military council has been inconsistent in its approach to justice; demanding military trial for certain citizens and not others. The thugs that burned down churches and destroyed Christian shrines were not arrested by the military police or investigated by them, neither were the criminals that blocked a railway line for almost two weeks in Qena. At the same time, when a member of the April 6 Youth Movement was caught writing slogans on a wall about the forthcoming elections, he was swiftly arrested by the military police and referred to the military prosecution, which ordered that he be held in military prison. In another case, the lawyer Jamal Eid, along with some of his colleagues, brought a complaint before the attorney general against Osama Haikal, the minister of information under Mubarak. Haikal stands accused of inciting sectarian violence against Copts on state television during the Maspero Square massacre. Surprisingly, the attorney general immediately passed the case to the military courts. Thus it is the military council that decides whether civilians should be tried in military or civilian courts.

A further example of double standards was when the military council decided to monitor the foreign funding of civil society organisations. It is true that Egyptians have a right to know the funding sources for all organisations, parties and institutions in Egypt. However, we note that the military council is very particular about the organisations it monitors. The Muslim Brotherhood and members of Salafist parties spend millions of Egyptian pounds a day on election campaign material. Do the Egyptian people not have a right to know how the Brotherhood and the Salafists came to have all this money? Has the military council taken any measures to reveal the sources of funding for the Muslim Brotherhood and the Salafist parties?

Egypt now faces serval crises, from the breakdowns in security to the economic meltdown and slump in tourism; the majority of which have been implemented by government officials loyal to the old regime. The biggest problem is the breakdown in law and order, exasperated by the release of thousands of thugs and convicted prisoners by the Mubarak regime. The Egyptian police have abandoned their duty and refused to protect the Egyptian people upon the orders of senior police officers who are still loyal to Mubarak. The minister of the interior is struggling to control his ministry. He claimed that the snipers who killed demonstrators did not belong to the police force but then backtracked when evidence emerged to suggest the opposite was in fact true. Why didn't the military police dismiss the minister of the interior and restructure the police force in order to restore confidence and return stability to Egypt? Why didn't the military police intervene to save Egyptians from the attacks of thugs? The military police only intervenes forcefully in two situations: either to oppress demonstrators, or to rescue officials of the old regime that find themselves mobbed by demonstrators.

The policies of the military council have led to despondency amongst Egyptians, who have ben weakened by their sufferings. They have also given a golden opportunity to the remnants of the Mubarak regime to contain the revolution, strip it of its power and prevent it from fulfilling its aims. The revolution is now passing through a critical moment. The Mubarak regime – with the help of the military council – is trying to regain power and there are serious indications that members of the National Democratic Party will have the majority in the People's Assembly. We will never allow this farce. The Egyptian people have made grave sacrifices in the name of revolution and will never allow the remnants of the old regime to control the People's Assembly.

The blood of the revolutionaries has been entrusted to us and we must defend the revolution until its aims are fulfilled and Egypt begins a future far from the shadows of the past and the remnants of the corrupt regime.

Democracy is the answer.

PN

A Conversation Between Two Important Men

1 November 2011

First man: "You haven't been in touch for two days."

Second man: "I'm very sorry, sir. Only the most urgent and pressing matters could prevent me calling you. I am exhausted, I've been working day and night. I have the weight of the world on my shoulders."

First man: "May God assist you. I realise you are carrying a heavy burden, but you must stay in close contact with me at all times. I need to discuss many important things with you as and when they happen."

Second man: "I am your servant, sir. I will never forget everything you have done for me."

First man: "Thank you. Do you have any news? I heard that one of these kids died in Tora prison."

Second man: "Sir, the police officers are under a lot of pressure."

First man: "The police officers are fine, upright men. I'll never forget the stand they took in January when they defended the legitimate government. I can't believe that we are now putting them on trial for simply carrying out orders."

Second man: "Unfortunately, developments necessitated that they be tried in order to assuage the people's anger."

First man: "So what's the story behind this kid in Tora prison?"

Second man: "His name is Essam Atta.[1] The military court gave him a two-year prison sentence. It appears that he was caught smuggling a SIM card into the prison. When he spoke to the prison officer in a provocative manner, the officer decided to teach him a lesson. The kid couldn't take the punishment and died."

First man: "Be careful. It could turn into a bigger controversy – like what happened in the case of Khaled Saeed."[2]

Second man: "Rest assured, sir. We are taking every precaution. All relevant departments have provided conclusive evidence that he swallowed a package of drugs and died as a result of an overdose when the package opened in his stomach."

First man: "Good, but remember that the reports about Khaled Saeed presented a similar story, and the people were still up in arms."

Second man: "That was then. There will be no such reaction this time around. The people are tired and worn out; they are content with whatever we do."

First man: "If people are content, then why did they rise up and rebel against a legitimate government? Do you think I understand nothing of what happened last January?"

---

1 Essam Ali Atta served a two-year jail term in Cairo's high-security Tora prison following his conviction in a military tribunal for an apparently "common crime". He was tortured to death, provoking accusations that the increasingly unpopular junta is failing to dismantle Hosni Mubarak's brutal security apparatus.

2 Khaled Saeed was a young Egyptian man who died under disputed circumstances in the Sidi Gaber area of Alexandria on 6 June 2010, after being arrested by Egyptian police. Photos of his disfigured corpse spread throughout online communities and incited outrage over allegations that he was beaten to death by Egyptian security forces.

Second man: "Not at all, sir, but let me say this: the events of last January got out of hand because the security forces made a mistake. They let the people gather and they believed that they could then disperse them using force. The lesson here is that we shouldn't let them gather in the first place: force must be used pre-emptively and decisively before any gathering can develop into a mass demonstration."

First man: "We should have been much tougher from the start. We thought that Egyptians were good people. By my life, I never imagined they would act in such a way!"

Second man: "They are good natured people, sir. The problem is these kids; they use the internet and facebook to incite hate."

First man: "They are agents working for foreign countries. They are traitors and usurpers who want to ruin the country."

Second man: "We have held the country together, thank God, and the demonstrators in Tahrir Square are starting to lose popular support."

First man: "How did that come to be?"

Second man: "Because the situation in Egypt is unbearable: no rule of law, no tourist industry, and a spiralling economy – the whole country is in chaos. All the sects are at each other's throats. Every day there are strikes and sit-ins, thugs and killings, and bandits on the roads. People are frightened for themselves and their children."

First man: "Excellent. Let them see the consequences of their actions. The important thing is that the people realise that all of their suffering is because of the demonstrators in Tahrir Square."

Second man: "Of course people understand that now, and that's why they hate them. We exposed them in the media and exposed them as foreign agents. Now when they try to hold a demonstration or a sit-in, you find it's the upstanding citizens themselves who attack them and hand them over to the military police."

First man: "These are the true Egyptians."

Second man: "In any case, sir, I do hope you can forget the events of last January."

First man: "Can I tell you the truth? The events we witnessed last January were so shocking that I can never forget them."

Second man: "Sir, believe me, what happened in January is over and done with; such things will never happen again."

First man: "How can you be so sure?"

Second man: "It was a sudden outburst, but the situation has now changed. We dealt with it politically and put a stop to it. Most Egyptians have now come to regret what happened. They want to return to how things were before. The people are now saying: 'Things were better before. At least we had security.' As for the agitators who caused all this trouble back in January, they won't be given another chance to rise up ever again. They are divided amongst themselves and are at each others' throats: the Islamists attack the liberals, and the Salafists attack the Copts. The demonstrations in Tahrir Square are finished. We have learned our lesson, sir. As a matter of fact, the people working for state security are doing an excellent job. We know each group's Achilles heel and we know how to manipulate them. The troublemakers used to organise demonstrations after the Friday prayers that attracted millions, but now they are lucky to get more than a thousand people turning up."

First man: "God grant you every success."

Second man: "We have a detailed plan, sir. The kids that continue to make trouble are being arrested and thrown into prison. We'll keep hunting them down one by one until they're completely finished. Incidentally, did you see the papers today, sir?"

First man: "I get all of the papers brought to me every day, both Arabic and English. I don't have the inclination to read them, though. Between you and me, I sit watching satellite television all day."

Second man: "Ah, but there was a piece of news that's bound to please you. We have begun to prosecute all of those responsible for inciting the events of last January. We are bringing the first bunch to trial, and then we will prosecute the rest."

First man: "I hope you break them. Destroy them for destroying Egypt."

Second man: "We will, sir."

First man: "There are also some journalists and writers amongst them who want to act the hero by inciting the people to rise up."

Second man: "Don't worry sir, we know who each and every one of them are; the security services sent us detailed files on them. Furthermore, we have started to apply pressure on those who own the television channels and the owners of newspapers. We will deal with these would-be heroes when the time is right."

First man: "You know, sometimes I feel as though I am living through a nightmare. And on top of everything else we now have these ridiculous candidates running for president. Have you seen what these people are like? Who are these kids? It is as though the presidency of Egypt is some sort of joke, every

Tom, Dick and Harry wants to run the country!"

Second man: "Let them nominate themselves all they like, it won't matter, sir."

First man: "But what about ElBaradei? He is someone who worries me. Since his return to Egypt he has done nothing but cause trouble."

Second man: "The situation with ElBaradei is under control, sir. Only the other day he was prevented from speaking at Ain Shams University."

First man: "Good work."

Second man: "You'll be even more delighted when you see the results of the elections, God willing."

First man: "What do you plan to do?"

Second man: "Well sir, there are a number of considerations with regard to this, but if we play our hand well the results of the elections will be a foregone conclusion. Firstly, the constituencies are very large. Thanks to this, these scruffy kids down in Tahrir Square don't have the capability to get their message out to the voters. Secondly, although the National Democratic Party has been dissolved by a court ruling, its old members remain respected figures. They have served the country and no one can stop them from putting themselves forward as candidates. We now have eight parties that have emerged out of the old NDP and, God willing, they'll win the majority at the polls. It should be said though, that the elections are going to take place under difficult circumstances. The security situation is very bad and it will continue to deteriorate. The lawyers and judges are at each others' throats, and the courts have more or less shut down. Judges have been attacked by thugs and they fear for their own safety. For this reason they have refused to oversee the elections. Furthermore, the police and sections within the Ministry of the Interior are on strike – these strikes are not expected to end before the date of the elections."

First man: "You mean the elections might not go ahead?"

Second man: "We are prepared for every eventuality. If the elections don't go ahead as planned then so be it. But when they do take place, the results will be in our favour. We will control the next parliament, sir."

First man: "My friend, where have you been all this time? If we had done things your way from the beginning we could have spared the country all of these afflictions."

Second man: "It was decreed by God, sir. Whatsoever He wills, He causes to come about."

First man: "God is gracious."

Second man: "Tell me, Your Excellency, is everything well with you? And your children, have you heard from them?"

First man: "They are well, and they call me every day. I believe they had an issue concerning the food they were being served?"

Second man: "We took care of it, sir. They selected a personal chef and he is now cooking their meals for them."

First man: "Excellent, you take care of everything!"

Second man: "I try to do what I can, sir. I'm glad to hear your wife returned safely."

First man: "God bless you, she came to me straight from the airport."

Second man: "I trust she had a pleasant trip?"

First man: "She did, thanks. You know that she has to travel to London every ten days or so to meet with our lawyers and make arrangements."

Second man: "I'm aware of that, sir. Do you have any further orders for me, Your Excellency?"

First man: "Thank you, that is all for now."

Democracy is the answer.

AB

Anxiety for the Future

15 November 2011

Imagine that you are a student living with your friends in a furnished apartment, dividing the rent between you. Each housemate has their own habits and traits: one of you studies all night, while another wakes up early and goes to bed early, and a third studies while listening to loud music. But you learn to live together and compromise. There are shared duties that must be fairly distributed amongst you, namely cooking and cleaning, and making sure bills get paid on time. It is important to arrive at a fair system that balances your rights and your duties; one that you can all stick to. It wouldn't be a fair if one of you came up with a set of rules and imposed it on the other housemates, so you decide to sit down and discuss the best way to live together. This simple example illustrates the meaning and value of a national constitution.

As individual members of society, just like the students renting the apartment, we have to sit down together to write the constitution ourselves.

The word "constitution" in Arabic is derived from a Persian word meaning "basis". A constitution is a collection of legal rules that define the nature of the state. It decides on the composition and jurisdictions of the institutions within it, and sets the relationships they have to each other. It also decides the rights and duties of the individual. All around the world, when a people want to write a constitution, they sit down and discuss their needs, much like the students who live together. Each strata or group of society elects representatives who form a Constituent Assembly that suggests the articles that are to make up the constitution. These articles are debated in public then put to the people in a general referendum.

We cannot restrict the right to compose the constitution to the party who won in the elections, firstly because the Constituent Assembly has different specifications to the legitimate parliamentary body. Members of the Constituent Assembly are elected because they represent a certain sector of society, or because they have the necessary legal experience to write the constitution. However, this same person may not be a suitable member of parliament due to his advanced age, or his inability to communicate with the masses. When we entrust the writing of the constitution to parliament, we get into a situation of conflicting interests. Since it is the constitution that limits the powers of the People's Assembly, we cannot ask the members of the People's Assembly to set their own powers. As half of the People's Assembly currently has to consist of workers and farmers, we can hardly imagine that these workers and farmers would agree to a new constitution that abolished the condition that half of parliamentary members have to be workers and farmers. That being said, the political party that has gained the majority in the election does have the right to impose its political program on the minority. If the parliamentary majority were socialists, for example, it would be the right of the government they had formed to impose its socialist program. However, this same majority does not have the right to write a constitution according to its will and disregard the interests of the other parties because a constitution must speak for all classes of people, even those who have lost the elections or who never participated in them in the first place.

Egyptian society contains a great many diverse groups, amongst them professionals, workers, farmers, Sa'idis,[1] Nubians and Copts. The constitution must express the interests of all these people. If Egypt had four or five Hindu or Buddhist citizens, the constitution must respect their rights and needs. This is the established and conventional concept of a constitution, and after the Egyptian revolution succeeded in overthrowing Mubarak, experts in constitutional law agreed that the old constitution had lapsed with the fall of Mubarak. They advocated electing a constituent assembly, but the military council rejected the will of the revolution and decided to implement

1 Sa'idi is a generic term used in Egypt to refer to a person from Upper Egypt.

constitutional amendments that Mubarak announced in his last moments, even though the revolution had rejected them.

The military council took charge of setting up a committee for constitutional amendments that strangely contained only one scholar of constitutional law, Atef el-Banna. As for the rest of its members, with all due respect to them, they were all lawyers with little or no experience in constitutional law. Furthermore, the committee contained only two political creeds: half of its members were affiliated with the Mubarak regime and the other half were Brotherhood members or those who sympathised with them.

The amendments were made and a referendum was held under the watchful eye of the military council. At this point, the Muslim Brotherhood stepped in to help the military council even though – like all the revolutionaries – they had been demanding a new constitution. Nevertheless, they went back on their view and agreed to the amendments and did everything in their power to carry out the will of the military council. The Brotherhood resorted to morally reprehensible election tactics and spread the rumour amongst ordinary citizens that to refuse the amendments and ask for a new constitution would eliminate Article 2, which stipulates that Islam is the state religion, even though this article was not part of the amendments in the first place.

The people voted in favour of the amendments, and despite the transgressions of the religious current during the referendum, moral and national duty required that everyone respect the result. The surprising thing was that it was the military council that did not respect the result of the referendum and announced an interim constitution of 63 articles that had not been approved by the Egyptian people. The interim council decided on behalf of the Egyptian people to keep both the Shura council and the quota for workers and farmers in the People's Assembly. They even decided that Egypt would now be governed under a presidential system rather than a parliamentary one.

With the announcement of an interim constitution, the military council overturned the result of the referendum in both practical and legal terms and imposed a political system on the Egyptian people without seeking their approval. Meanwhile, the Brotherhood and the Salafists ignored the military council's transgressions and decided to back the military council regardless. The Muslim Brotherhood, in their dealings with the military council, is repeating the same mistakes it made with other rulers of Egypt before them: King Farouk, Isma'il Sidqi, Gamal Abdel Nasser and Anwar Sadat. Each time the Brotherhood participate in national movements, they will at some point break away from the national ranks and move closer to those in power, who inevitably use them to undermine the national opposition. Then, once they have fulfilled their purpose with the Brotherhood, they throw them aside, or turn against them and crack down on them.

So, the cart has been put before the horse and all of Egypt has been pushed in the wrong direction. The Brotherhood have transformed into what seems to be the political wing of the military council. They openly praise the military council and attack those who criticise its decisions. It has got to the point where the Salafists are chanting "Field Marshal, you are the Prince of Egypt", and one of the leading figures in the Brotherhood describes the members of the military council as "darlings" while branding the nationalists calling for a constitution before elections as "devils in the form of men". With extremists appearing ever more frequently and the rising attacks on Copts and their churches and shrines, Egyptians (both Muslims and Copts) are growing increasingly anxious about the major constitutional disorder the military council has put us in.

The constitution, which is supposed to represent all people, risks being written solely by extremists who think that music is religiously prohibited and that the breath-taking artefacts of Ancient Egypt are nothing but idols that should be hidden so that Egyptians are not tempted to worship them. At this point, the military council realised the danger of the situation and began to call for what it termed "the guiding principles of the constitution" to divert Egypt from the disaster of having a constitution that would have turned it into an Afghanistan or a Somalia. The Brotherhood and the Salafists were enraged and rejected the constitutional principles quite simply because they want to write the constitution by themselves, according to their ideas, and not in the interests of society.

The military council's latest attempt to remedy the constitutional predicament was the document presented by Ali al-Silmi, the deputy prime minister. This document, "On the Guiding Principles of the Constitution", guarantees the civilian nature of the Egyptian state, as well as stipulating for the first time the correct way of forming a constituent assembly, that is, by electing representatives from different sectors of society. But the document, nevertheless, is distorted and corrupted since it puts the method for the creation of the Constituent Assembly at the mercy of the military council, which has absolute power over the constitution and those who write it. The document also makes the armed forces a separate entity to the Egyptian state cannot be investigated or held to account by the Egyptian people.

Therefore, after taking us one step forward, al-Silmi's document takes us ten steps back. The document puts two choices before Egyptians, both of them unpleasant: either we keep the civilian state in exchange for making the army immune and unanswerable for its actions, or if we do not allow the army to be the trustees of the state, we must face the danger of Egypt falling into the hands of extremists. The choice is now a civilian state in the custody of the army, or freedom and the danger of extremists.

Al-Silmi's document deals another blow to the already struggling revolution. For nine months, the Egyptian people have been ground down by deliberate breakdowns in security, unrest, artificial crises, food shortages and rising prices. The mood of optimism and self-confidence that swept over Egyptians following the overthrow of Mubarak has turned into a sad state of frustration and anxiety for the future. How do we save the revolution?

1. The conflict between the Islamists and the liberals must come to an end and all the revolutionary parties must come together as one.

2. A body must be elected to represent the revolution encompassing all the governorates of Egypt and involving all parties. This body should be able to mobilise millions on the streets so as to be able to put pressure on the military council to implement the aims of the revolution.

3. The revolutionary parties must present an alternative to al-Silmi's document. I hope that we can all accept the document issued by Al-Azhar as the basis of a democratic state. At the same time, we must agree to a method of electing a Constituent Assembly that does not ignore members of parliament while guaranteeing also the complete representation of all sections of society.

4. We must return to the streets in our millions to prove to the military council that the revolution is still in the hearts of the millions of Egyptians who made it with their blood and who will never allow it to be thwarted.

Egypt is being pulled by two forces: the old regime that wants to return Egypt to the past, and the revolution that wishes to propel it towards the future. The revolution will certainly be victorious, God willing.

Democracy is the answer.

PN

The Emperor Has No Clothes

22 November 2011

Once upon a time, there was an emperor who was fooled by a crafty tailor. The tailor managed to convince the emperor that he could make him an amazing magical robe that only the wise could see.[1] The emperor was won over by the skill of the crafty tailor and went out to his ministers wearing no

1 "The Emperor's New Clothes" was first published with "The Little Mermaid" in 1837 as the third and final installment of Andersen's *Fairy Tales Told for Children*.

clothes, saying to them: "Behold! What do you think of this magical robe that only the wise can see?"

"It is a great robe, master," said some of the ministers who were scared of angering the emperor.

"My Lord, never in our lives have we seen a robe more beautiful and splendid than this," said another group of ministers who were after the emperor's rewards.

Also in the room was a small child. "Where is this robe you are all talking about?" he said innocently. "The emperor has no clothes."

The ministers tried to silence the child. They poked, pinched and threatened him but he kept on shouting: "The emperor has no clothes." They beat the small child and forced him from the room so that the.

The story of the emperor is well-known, and has many messages. The ministers who compliment the emperor on his imaginary coat are afraid of the brutality of the emperor or they are hungry for his rewards. As for the innocent child, he wants nothing and so speaks the truth, whatever the price.

This story of the emperor is currently being played out in Egypt. The Egyptian people succeeded in deposing Hosni Mubarak and delegated power to the military council in the transitional period. Through a raft of policies, the military council was able to grind down Egyptians and spread division amongst the revolutionary forces. It was able to gather round it politicians and political parties willing to please it so as to get into power. The only ones who have stayed faithful to the revolution are the young people that called for the revolution in the first place and paid the price of freedom with their blood. These true revolutionaries are like that brave child who confronted the naked emperor with the truth. The millions of Egyptians who went out onto the streets, faced death and offered up martyrs had no political ambitions and wanted nothing but to see their country free, strong and respected. These revolutionaries represent what is most noble in Egypt.

I am writing this article from France, where I held seminars in Paris, Lyon and Marseille. I have met many French people that were impressed by the great revolution taking place in Egypt. More than once, I have heard French people saying that the youth of the Egyptian revolution inspired the whole world, and even that the influence of Tahrir Square has spread to protest movements in all corners of the globe.

As much as I felt proud to be an Egyptian, I was saddened by the news of a new massacre that had taken place in Tahrir Square. What did the peaceful demonstrators do to be so savagely attacked? In what country in the world is it possible that demonstrators are killed and shot in the face with rubber bullets for expressing their opinion in a peaceful fashion? These are crimes against humanity that are punishable by international law and the criminals who committed them will never escape punishment.

The most recent massacre committed by the armed forces on the order of the military council brings home a number of truths about the military council and the role they are playing in this brutal farce. The military council was a vital part of the Mubarak regime and was thoroughly complicit with it. We never heard of Field Marshal Tantawi and his men opposing the tyranny of Mubarak or his crimes, or of them questioning his decisions. The military council did not participate in the revolution. In fact, in the Battle of the Camel it left bands of armed thugs to kill demonstrators and did not intervene to protect them. The military council refused to open fire on the demonstrators, and this was a national and moral position that certainly goes to their credit (even though Field Marshal Tantawi later backtracked and denied that he received orders from Mubarak to kill the demonstrators).

It must be made clear to everyone that it was the revolution that gave the military council legitimacy to govern during the transitional period. After the revolutionaries made Mubarak relinquish control, they consented to let the military council act on behalf of the revolution and work to fulfil its aims. But, with great regret, the military turned from the executor of the revolution to a tyrannical power. It imposed decisions and policies on Egypt that caused the revolution to break down and lose its way and allowed the old regime to sabotage the revolution.

The military council has absolute control over Egypt since it holds in its hands both the executive and legislative powers. Therefore, it is solely responsible for all that has happened in Egypt after the overthrow of Mubarak. The revolution is not responsible whatsoever for any of the crises that are going on now for the simple reason that the revolution never took any power for which to be held accountable. The breakdown in law and order, the spread of thuggery, the rising prices, the deterioration in the economy and the decline in tourism, all of these problems stem from the incorrect decisions that the military council has taken. It must now act with expediency to form a coalition government from the revolutionary forces and hand the running of matters over to this government until an elected, civilian power is voted in.

While the military council is adopting a violent, repressive policy against the revolutionaries, we find that at the same time it is showing the upmost warmth and affection to all the adherents of the Mubarak regime, the majority of whom are some of the biggest killers, criminals and thieves in Egypt. The officers who killed hundreds and wounded thousands of Egyptians during the revolution, the thuggish minister Habib el-Adly, even Hosni Mubarak himself, are enjoying fair trials before civilian judges and have the best forms of legal protection and medical care. Meanwhile, the military council is eagerly bringing the youth of the revolution before military courts on trumped-up charges and throwing them in prison.

Bringing civilians before military courts contravenes the simplest principles of justice, violates human rights and contradicts the international treaties that successive Egyptian governments have signed. However, the military council is intent on bringing civilians to military trial, as it represents a new tool of oppression to add to the state security apparatus, which still employs the same methods in its work despite changing its name to Homeland Security.

The military council does not see the difference between the regime and the state. Therefore, it considers that the fall of the old regime did damage to the Egyptian state. It is this muddled understanding that explains the military council's desperate defence of the Mubarak regime, which still sits at the head of authority in Egypt. The military council refused to purge the police of its corrupt leadership and refused to purge the judiciary of its corrupt judges. It refused to dissolve the local councils until after a judicial ruling had been passed and also refused to dissolve the National Democratic Party. Then, after a judicial ruling had been made to dissolve it, the military council allowed the members of the odious National Democratic Party to form new parties and enter parliament. Ten months after the revolution, most state officials still belong with heart and soul to the Mubarak regime. Their staying in power constitutes a grave danger to the revolution and to Egypt as a whole. The majority of the crises now occurring are artificial and orchestrated by the remnants of the Mubarak regime. They want to spread chaos and bring a halt to the change that will result in them losing their positions, and the majority of them being prosecuted and going to jail.

In its dealings with the political parties, the military council is neither neutral nor fair, since it applies the rules to some of them and not to others. The military council strictly monitors the funding sources of the Coalitions of the Youth of the Revolution[1] and some civil society organisations. Meanwhile, General Roweini, a member of the military council, made baseless accusations about members of the April 6 Youth Movement which he was unable to prove and refused to apologise for. At the same time, the millions of Egyptian pounds spent by the Brotherhood and the Salafists every day on election campaign materials goes unchecked by the military council who never stop to ask where this money came from. The Salafists and the Brotherhood, for some reason that will become clear with the passing of time, have a special understanding with the military council, who have agreed to turn a blind eye to their funding sources while being openly hostile to the youth of the revolution and trying to defame them in government media, which is still as misleading and sycophantic as it was in the Mubarak era. The only explanation there can be for the military council to ambush

1 The Coalitions of the Youth of the Revolution organised post-revolution events and met with the military council to negotiate the demands of the revolution.

the revolutionaries is that the revolutionaries are confronting it with the truth and are neither flattering it nor scared of it, and will not give up on the aims of the revolution whatever the cost.

The military council has disregarded the dignity of Egyptians and repressed, beaten, killed and humiliated them time and time again whether by way of the military police or the security forces. After all these crimes have been committed against the peaceful demonstrators, the military council starts to hold investigations in a military court, thus becoming both judge and jury at the same time, which undermines the legitimacy of the investigation and what is more, they are shelved and we never hear anything more about them. Who was it that killed the demonstrators? Who was it that sexually assaulted the female demonstrators by carrying out the despicable virginity tests? And what was the punishment enacted on these criminals? Not a thing. Therefore, Egyptians are within their rights to lose confidence completely in the justice of the military council.

What is happening in Egypt has become as clear as day. The military council is following policies that will lead to the preservation of the Mubarak regime but without Mubarak and his family. Instead of dismantling the old regime and building a new system that is respectable and fair, the military council is bringing back the old regime and want change to be limited to the resignation of Mubarak.

The thwarting of the Egyptian revolution and its transformation into a mere coup d'état was carried out in several stages, starting with amending the old constitution instead of writing a new one, then holding the referendum which led to the division of the revolutionary forces. After that, the reputation of the youth of the revolution was sullied and Egyptian citizens were pressurised through artificial crises until they became exhausted and turned against the revolution. The successive massacres were orchestrated to repress the revolutionaries and return them to how they were before the revolution started.

However, what the military council does not understand is that after the revolution, Egyptians are free of fear and will not accept injustice any longer. Our duty now is to unite to save the revolution. All political divisions must be left aside so that we can get back into one line and pressurise the military council into forming a respectable revolutionary coalition government to take power until there are elections for the civilian authority which will take over from the army. Egypt will not go backwards.

Democracy is the answer.

PN

Five Questions About the Crisis

29 November 2011

1. What is the basis of the military council's legitimacy in governing Egypt during the transitional period?

On 11 February, Omar Suleiman announced that Hosni Mubarak had stepped down from power and was now in the process of transferring his presidential powers to the military council. Here we see a strange contradiction, for a deposed president does not have the authority to give his powers to anyone. This would be like a dismissed company director continuing to appoint new employees for the company when he started a new job. In this case, these appointments would be illegal because the director who was dismissed no longer has the authority to appoint anyone. Following this example, the deposed Mubarak does not have the power to appoint the military council because he himself has lost legal authority and therefore is not able to give it to anyone else. From a legal point of view, the 1971 constitution does not allow the military council to govern Egypt since it stipulates that in the situation of the president of the republic being unable to carry out the duties of his position, the President of the Supreme Constitutional Court will assume power in his place.

Neither the constitution nor Mubarak, after his deposition, can be a valid source of legitimacy for the military council.

So where did they derive their legitimacy? The only legitimacy for the military council is the Egyptian revolution. On 11 February, there were 20 million revolutionary Egyptians in the streets celebrating the fall of Mubarak and if they had rejected the military council taking authority, they certainly would have got what they wanted. But it was the revolutionaries who trusted the military council, gave it legitimacy, and mandated the council to carry out the objectives of the revolution. The military council derived its legitimacy from the revolution, and when it lost the trust of the revolutionaries it lost with it the only support for its legitimacy. Now we understand why the military council asked for a referendum to stay in power: it is seeking a new legitimacy separate from the legitimacy of the revolution. It exploited Egyptians' trust in the army and continued to act as a political authority, which in effect hampered and obstructed the path of the revolution and brought us this crisis. This fallacy must be corrected: The revolutionaries, who want to see the military council step away from its political role, certainly do not want to get rid of the armed forces. On the contrary, they respect them and are proud of them, and want them to be free to carry out their national duties.

2. Has the military council been protecting the Egyptian revolution?

The military council refused to open fire on demonstrators, a stand that goes to their credit. But what happened after that? For the last nine months, the military council has not been protecting the revolution at all. In fact, the opposite is true. The military council believe that the removal of Mubarak would satisfy the revolutionaries and put an end to the demonstrations. Therefore, instead of the sweeping change for which the revolution was started, nothing has changed but the person of the president. The Mubarak regime still rules Egypt, from the state security service State Security Investigations Service which has resumed its criminal activity with full vigour, to the leadership of the police who are loyal followers of the Habib el-Adly and who continue to kill demonstrators and disregard their human rights, to the attorney general who was obliged to make limitless political concessions in the Mubarak era, to the judges who oversaw the rigging of the elections, to the heads of banks appointed by Gamal Mubarak, to the sycophantic journalists working for state security, and to the senior officials in every state institution.

The situation in Egypt is the first of its kind. A revolution was started to topple the Mubarak regime, but the military council stepped in to save the regime and kept it in power. The outcome has been unfortunate but predictable. The Mubarak regime has contained the revolution and thwarted any real change through carefully planned steps. eliberate breakdown in law and order, the release of thugs and violent convicts to terrorise people, the failure of the police, with the consent of the military council, to perform their duty, deliberate price increases and strikes by interest groups, which the authorities deliberately ignore so that the demonstrators turn to vandalism and blocking roads. Misleading media campaigns aim to convince people that the revolution is the reason for all these crises, as well as sectarian conflicts, in which State Security officials specialise, like setting fire to churches in full view of security forces and military police, who look on without intervening.

The final blow against the revolutionaries happened one week before the elections on 19 November. The savage assault on injured demonstrators in Tahrir Square was intended to lure the youth of the revolution into an unequal battle in which they would be crushed. Members of the security forces and military police assaulted the demonstrators who came to defend the injured. After clearing the demonstators from the square, the military police then opened it again so that the demonstrators would hurry back to the square to be crushed once more.

The events were carefully planned, as were the violent clashes that took place on Mohamed Mahmoud Street. The public were told that the demonstrators had tried to storm the Ministry of the Interior and that security forces were acting in self-defence when they opened fire on them, despite the fact that Mahmoud Street does not lead to the Ministry of the Interior. However, the youth of the revolution derailed the plan when they went out into all the squares in Egypt in support of the revolution. This surprise confounded the Mubarak regime, which became embroiled in ever more savage crimes against peaceful, unarmed demonstrators. Security forces personnel, under the auspices of the military police (as testified by forensics) killed demonstrators with live ammunition as well as aiming guns at their eyes before releasing toxic gases. When the regime realised that the revolutionaries were determined to protest whatever the sacrifices, they had no choice but to make minor concessions. The military council dismissed the Sharaf government but formed a new one under Kamal el-Ganzouri,[1] confirming that the military council disregards the will of the revolution and is determined to monopolise power and defend the Mubarak regime to the last.

3. Why don't we let the military council stay in power until the country is passed over to an elected president?

Because the military council is an extension of the Mubarak regime. Should we expect the Interior Ministry officials loyal to Mubarak to help us restore law and order so that we can dismiss them and put them on trial? Should we expect the bank chiefs appointed by Gamal Mubarak to contribute to stimulating the economy until an elected government comes and dismisses them and maybe puts them on trial on corruption charges? A video has emerged of a police officer firing rubber bullets at the faces of demonstrators and receiving praise from his colleagues for taking out the eye of an innocent person. This recorded incident goes to show that after the revolution the Mubarak regime treats Egyptians in the same way after the revolution as before. The attorney general called for the officer to be investigated but the Ministry of the Interior refused to hand him over and his colleagues all rose to his defence. Naturally, the officer in question cannot follow the orders of his superiors to blind the demonstrators then be prosecuted for following them.

The only way to save the revolution is to form a revolutionary consensus government with presidential powers, not subordinate to the military council, a government that can restore law and order and conduct fair trials for all those who have committed crimes against Egyptians.

The military council knows that the formation of an independent government would bring an end to the Mubarak regime so it is manoeuvring and negotiating with the political parties, and asking them to form advisory boards that no one will ever consult. The military council wants to buy time until the elections begin. While the people are distracted by the elections,

1 Kamal el-Ganzouri is an Egyptian economist who served as prime minister of Egypt from 7 December 2011 to 2 August 2012. *See* Glossary.

el-Ganzouri will be announced leader and his government will stamp out what remains of the revolution.

4. Why are the military council so keen to hold the elections despite the worsening of the security situation and the incompetence of the institutions responsible?

The revolution constitutes the only legitimacy for the military council and it is looking for the new legitimacy a cooperative parliament would provide. The military council has done all that it can to exclude the revolutionaries from the People's Assembly. It refused to disqualify members of the National Democratic Party and instead allowed them to form ten new parties so that they can use the money they stole from the people to buy votes and get into parliament. The elections have been planned around one clear aim: to form the next parliament from the remnants of the old regime as well as the Brotherhood, in whom the military council has found a firm, loyal partner that is prepared to do all it is asked of in exchange for government positions.

5. What are we to do?

Circumstances are such that the Egyptian revolution has to fight on two fronts: it must continue demonstrating and protesting until the military council complies with the will of the revolution, dismisses el-Ganzouri and forms an independent government headed by someone aligned with the revolution. We are not concerned with the political affiliation of this future prime minister; what is more important is how faithful he is to the principles of the revolution. Whether it is ElBaradei the liberal, Abdel Moneim Aboul Fotouh the Islamist,[1] or any other equally credible person. A revolutionary prime minister is the only person capable of protecting the revolution and correcting its path. This is the demand on which we must unite, and to achieve it we must press on with all our strength and we must take part in elections. If the elections go ahead with no fraud then a number of revolutionaries will get into parliament. If however the elections are rigged, the revolutionaries will be first-hand witnesses to this betrayal of trust and the rigged elections will be cancelled by will of the people. The will of a people who were able with their courage and their sacrifices to make Mubarak step down, cannot be defrauded by anybody. The Egyptian revolution is passing through a critical moment. The military council has kept the Mubarak regime that is regaining its strength and heaping blows on the revolution with the aim of thwarting it. But the people who made the revolution are the ones who will protect it until it becomes victorious, God willing.

Democracy is the answer.

PN

1 Abdul Moneim Aboul Fotouh was a prominent figure within Egypt's Muslim Brotherhood but was forced to leave after he declared his intention last year to stand for the presidency.

What Happened to the General?

13 December 2011

The general and the sheikh have a lot of things in common. They are both over seventy, but still in good health. They both go to bed in the early evening and get up early in the morning. They also both live in the same neighbourhood: El-Tagamu El Khamis – one of the finest districts in all of Cairo. Furthermore, the magnificent mansion where the sheikh resides is not far from that belonging to the general. In light of this, it was not difficult for them to meet whenever the need arose. After the new developments that took place last week, the sheikh decided to give the general a call and request a meeting with him. The following day, at eight o'clock in the morning, a black Mercedes pulled up outside the general's mansion. Two of the sheikh's bodyguards quickly jumped out of the vehicle; one of them went to open the sheikh's door to help him out, while the other glanced around him with a ready hand on his gun.

The general was sitting at a table in a large room off from the reception hall. When the sheikh was shown in, the general greeted him and the sheikh embraced him affectionately, then they sat down together. Breakfast was already on the table; the meal brought together French-style cuisine and traditional Egyptian dishes. The Nubian servant spoke clearly and in a refined manner as he served the meal, which included croissants, pâté, cheese, meat and spinach, as well as savoury Egyptian pastries and stewed beans. This was a working breakfast, as diplomats might say. The two men began to eat and the general started the conversation by saying: "My congratulations on your success in the elections, you grace."

"Praise God, our Lord granted me victory, and there is no victory without the His grace."

"Naturally I am delighted by your sweeping victory, but to be honest, I do have a bone to pick with you," said the general.

"Really, general?"

"My dear friend, whenever you disagree with a decision that I have taken, why not simply call me personally instead of criticizing me in public?"

"If you say so, general," said the sheikh before biting into a boiled egg which he was holding in his hand.

Suddenly, however, the general became agitated and exclaimed: "Incidentally, this isn't the first time. You always tell me one thing but then do the opposite."

The sheikh knitted his eyebrows; he seemed alarmed by the general's tone: "General, this is hardly worth a mention."

"Hardly worth a mention? Are you trying to advance your interests at my expense?"

"I've done nothing wrong. I merely expressed my opinion through the media. However, I won't do it again out of respect to you," said the sheikh.

"I don't need your deference."

"General, you know that I respect you, but you mustn't forget that I represent the people."

"It was me that wanted you to win at the polls, so you won. Had I wanted you to lose, you would have lost. Remember that."

"With all due respect, general, you're not the reason for my success. I won by the grace of God and by my own effort."

"Clearly you actually believe what you are saying."

"My dear general, please control your temper. You know that I respect you but I expect the same respect from you."

The general looked as though he was ready to strike the sheikh, but then whispered something to his servant, who left the room for a moment before returning with a small briefcase. The servant placed the briefcase on the chair beside the sheikh. There was brief silence, then the general said: "Please take the briefcase home with you. Open it and examine the contents well."

"What's in it?" said the sheikh.

"All of your misdeeds have been fully documented. We have a list of all the funds you have received."

"What funds are you talking about?"

"You know very well what I'm talking about: the money that poured in from abroad. You'll find copies of the cheques you took along with the amounts and the dates they were cashed."

"General, please!"

"Inside you will find evidence of your involvement in buying votes. We have video recordings which show how you exploited people's ignorance and poverty in order to get them vote for you."

"General, you really don't need to talk like this."

"I'm going to present all this as evidence when I press charges against you and then we can leave the whole matter to the judiciary."

"Sir, please don't do that."

"Have you got something against the law being enforced, your grace?"

"No sir, I merely fear your anger."

The general sighed, leaned back and sipped his cup of tea. "You need to listen to what I say to you then."

"Very well, general."

"Don't imagine for a moment that you are stronger than me or that I cannot put you back in your place."

"Sir, my religion commands me to obey you."

"Good. From now on, if you have any comments you must come to me first before going to the media. Do you understand?"

"Understood, sir," said the sheikh. Then, somewhat flustered: "It grieves me, sir, that even now you would doubt my loyalty."

"It's your deeds that matter, not your words," answered the general, calmly.

"Sir, I had been calling for a new constitution for Egypt from the very beginning. That was the position I took publicly. But when I learned that you wanted to amend the existing constitution, I completely changed my position and supported your policy, if you recall, sir." The general nodded his head and the sheikh continued: "I have not taken a single position that did not conform with your own, sir – and I have lost many friends on account of this. Even during the unfortunate, recent bloodshed I didn't utter a single word against you, sir." Silence prevailed for a moment before the sheikh again spoke up exclaiming: "Have I not done well, sir?"

"You do well when you do as you're told," replied the general.

"I am yours to command," answered the sheikh.

The sheikh and the general then moved on to discuss aspects of their future cooperation. When they had finished eating, the general suggested that they have coffee in his study. They walked down the long reception hall until they came to a door that led into the general's opulent and spacious study. The general sat down behind his large wooden desk, and invited the sheikh to sit on the easy chair opposite. The general had prepared some notes containing things that he wanted to discuss with the sheikh. The men talked for an hour and there was complete agreement between them. The meeting ended on a friendly note; the general walked the sheikh to his car and waved to him as the car drove off.

The general felt very satisfied that they had come to a mutual understanding. He returned to his office to make a start on the pile of reports that lay unfinished on his desk. His servant hastened to bring him a cup of coffee as he read though his papers and made a number of important calls. After working for an hour or so, the general leaned back in his chair and placed his hands behind his head, closing his eyes for a brief moment. When he opened them, the general saw something strange: there were ghostly shapes moving on the wall opposite him. The general began to panic; he stared harder at the shapes and discerned what appeared to be the faces of four or five young men in their twenties. All of the faces looked the same: they were cold and vacant with empty dark hollows where their eyes should be. The general tried to convince himself that he was tired and overworked, and that the images on the wall were just hallucinations. He closed his eyes briefly to rest, but when he opened them the faces were still there in front of him. More and more faces appeared on the wall; there were others now that bore gunshot wounds in their foreheads and necks. They all wore the same stern and frightening expression.

The general became disorientated. He leaned forward and slumped over his desk with his head in his hands. After two minutes or so he raised his head, but tried to avoid looking at the wall. He rose from his chair and turned off the lights, hoping that this would banish the ghostly faces. His heart was pounding as he turned his head towards the wall. There were now even more faces than before; crowded together and convulsing with pain, as if they were choking on tear gas. The general could see other faces in the crowd, faces that looked as if they had been crushed by the wheels of a car.

The faces were moving towards the general, with determination and intent. The general reached for his bell and rang it loudly several times. When his private secretary rushed in, the general tried to compose himself. They exchanged some casual words, but when the general noticed the secretary glance nonchalantly at the wall, he realised that it was only he who could see the terrifying faces. The general dismissed his secretary and then hastened from the study. Again, he tried to convince himself that the faces were nothing but the inventions of a tired mind and that there was no other possible explanation.

The general made every effort to gain control of himself. He carried on the day as normal and even took his wife and eldest daughter out for dinner in the late afternoon. When he came home, his wife went up to bed and left him alone in the large lounge located on the first floor of the mansion. He was still feeling anxious and was afraid to enter his study in case the ghostly faces appeared again. As the general turned to leave the room, he glanced at the large curtain in front of him and saw the very same faces: those with missing eyes, those choking on gas, those bearing gunshot wounds and those that had been crushed and mutilated by being run over by the wheels of vehicles. The general was terrified; he trembled and almost screamed. He lifted his hands so as not to see the faces of the dead, but before he could cover his eyes he noticed that his hands were completely covered with blood.

What has happened to the general?

Democracy is the answer.

AB

Defending Egypt's Revolution

20 December 2011

Can a person live without food and drink? Of course not. These are fundamental needs, and a person will die if they are denied them. But can a person live without dignity? The answer, unfortunately, is yes. A person who has lost their dignity can still live if they have food and drink. History has seen the phenomenon of slavery, where for centuries millions of human beings lived without dignity, and indeed many people have lived in humiliation and indignity under tyrannical rule.

For thirty years, millions of Egyptians lived without dignity under the rule of Hosni Mubarak. They put up with humiliations and kowtowed to those in power to gain their favour. For many, staying alive was far more important than maintaining their dignity. They grew accustomed to a lack of dignity and respect, because they either feared punishment or coveted material gains. They had put up with the brutality of police officers and called them "sir" or "pasha". They had become habituated to mistreatment at work and found themselves playing the hypocrite to win favour. They had got used to detention camps, torture and indecent assaults, which they ignored as long as they happened to others. They advised their children to keep their eyes to the floor and not to demonstrate against or oppose the ruler, however he had wronged them. Millions of Egyptians used to consider hypocrisy as tact, cowardice as wisdom, and silence as common sense. The Mubarak regime harboured a deep resentment for Egyptians, believing them to be lazy, unproductive, ignorant people, who had got used to chaos and did not deserve democracy. It was this disregard for the Egyptian people that made the Mubarak regime confidant that it was in full control, until the revolution stirred.

The Egyptian revolution was a miracle by any standard. A generation of Egyptians had emerged that were free of all the afflictions of tyranny and were ready and willing to stand up against injustice. These young Egyptians, who make up half the population, possess a loyalty and commitment to noble values that defies explanation. They grew up in a society afflicted by a corrupt and bias media and had no access to good education. Despite all this, the youth of the revolution appeared suddenly and brilliantly, as if Egypt was a giant and bountiful tree that is always able to produce fresh green leaves, however stricken it is with diseases. The first aim of the revolution was to give the Egyptian people back their dignity. This came as a great shock to Mubarak and his cronies as these same people had borne humiliation for many long years. What had happened to them? What had made them determined to get their dignity back?.

Twenty million Egyptians participated in the revolution, in addition to a further 40 million who sympathised with the revolution. On the other hand, there were several million remnants who benefited from the Mubarak regime and who were opposed to the revolution. This estimate suggests that there are sill around 20 million Egyptians who did not benefit from the Mubarak regime but neither participated in the revolution nor sympathised with it. This silent group are the submissive Egyptians, who suffered under the Mubarak regime but were not prepared to make any sacrifices for the revolution. They were made to feel both anxious and embarrassed by the revolution, which made them reconsider the presuppositions upon which they had built their entire lives. When the military council took power, the Egyptian people trusted that they were capable of implementing the aims of the revolution. However, the military council has resisted any meaningful change and succeeded in keeping the Mubarak regime in power. It refused to draw up a new constitution, but instead made amendments to the old constitution and asked the Egyptian people to vote in favour of these limited changes. It then bypassed the results of the referendum and declared an interim constitution of 63 articles, which outlined the political system without taking into account the wishes of Egyptians.

The military council allowed the security situation in Egypt to deteriorate. It did nothing to prevent the successive crises that turned the lives of ordinary citizens into a living hell and made a section of the population – the submissive Egyptians – turn against the revolution and regard it as the cause for all of their problems. After initially portraying the revolutionaries as national heroes, the state media launched a campaign to sully their reputation, accusing them of being foreign agents and anarchists that wanted to topple the state.

From the beginning, the military council tried to divide the revolutionary bloc into Islamists and liberals, and deliberately played on the fears of each. Sometimes they would cozy up to the Islamists and gesture to the liberals, who would come running, frightened of an Islamist constitution. Then, after having appeased the liberals, the council worked to win back the Islamists' favour. In this way, those who were once comrades in the revolution have moved into an endless cycle of infighting and accusations that have fragmented and weakened the forces of the revolution.

The military council organised the elections in a way that kept the youth of the revolution out of parliament and left the door wide open for the Islamists to gain a majority. To be fair, I admit that the Islamists enjoy a genuine and impressive popularity on the streets, and no doubt would have gained a large portion of the votes in any honest election. But what happened in the elections was very different. A supreme electoral commission was brought in to help, but rather did nothing to enforce the law and completely ignored electoral crimes committed by the Islamists. When it was clear to all that the Islamists would win most of the seats, the military council then exploited the fears of the liberals and formed an advisory council to cut the Islamists down to size. The conflict has raged on between the revolutionary factions in a way that will maintain the military council's place in power.

To the outside world, Egypt appeared to have fallen into complete anarchy. The major nations were concerned about what was happening in the biggest Arab state and took care to protect their interests in the region. When Israel attacked the Egyptian borders and killed five Egyptian officers on Egyptian soil, the military council did nothing to bring Israel to account for its crime. This was a message for the United States from the military council to the effect that the policies of Hosni Mubarak would be followed to the letter and after this the US State Department gave the military council its complete support. In fact, US statements lauding the military council contain the same phrases with which they used to heap praise on Hosni Mubarak.

In this way, the Egyptian revolution has been thwarted by the old regime and is now on its last legs. The revolutionaries have been blocked and excluded from parliament and their image has been sullied. It will not take much to for the military council to break the will of the revolutionaries forever. The Islamists don't want to anger the military council, greedy as they are for parliamentary seats. Meanwhile, senior liberal figures are at the military council's table, hungry for positions in the future cabinet. As for the submissive Egyptians, their anger at all these crises and conflicts has turned into a real hatred of the revolution. They pine for the days of Mubarak in which their lives were full of humiliation and degradation but at least they were stable and safe.

There have been several attacks against the demonstrators, all organised in the same manner. The security services pay thugs to burn and vandalise public property and Egyptians are seized with panic and believe that the revolutionaries are the culprits. This is followed by brutal attacks on demonstrators, not just to kill and blind them, but to frighten the Egyptian people into a state of submission they were in before the revolution.

All those who witnessed the shocking crimes committed by security personnel and the army will no doubt be asking themselves why the assaults demonstrators were carried out in public. What will the army gain by beating an elderly lady or exposing the genitalia of a female demonstrator and taking off her clothes in front of the cameras? The sole objective of this is to break the will of the Egyptian people and return them to servitude.

The battle currently raging in Egypt is between the revolution and the Mubarak regime. The steadfast determination of the demonstrators in the face of adversity and abuse comes from the feeling that they are the only remaining force of the revolution. They fight, not in retaliation for the martyrs killed at Mohamed Mahmoud Street, or the sit-in outside the Council of Ministers, but to defend the integrity of the revolution and to make sure that it achieves its aims. Each time the Mubarak regime gathers to vanquish the revolution, it is pushed back by the fierce resistance of the revolutionaries. As a result, the Mubarak regime continues to commit more and more barbaric crimes in order to break the will of the revolutionaries.

The revolution has not yet been broken; the more brutal the Mubarak regime grows, the more intense the resistance. Now it is our duty to rise above all differences and unite against the Mubarak regime. Despite the many flaws, I think we must accept the results of the elections and give our full support to the next People's Assembly, because in the end it is the only body elected by the Egyptian people. All efforts must be concerted in one direction: a transfer of power from the military council to a civilian government formed by the People's Assembly, today rather than tomorrow.

Democracy is the answer.

PN

See No Evil

27 December 2011

More than a month ago the European television channel Arte contacted me to make an hour-long program about my literary work. Arte is one of the most important cultural channels in France and its decision to devote a whole show to an Egyptian writer is no doubt good for me and also for Egyptian literature. The French journalists arrived at my office in Garden city in good time, but both looked anxious and ill at ease. They told me that they had spent the night at the Ismailia Hotel, overlooking the now infamous Tahrir Square. They were woken by the sound of gunfire and saw an armed officer opening fire on demonstrators, attacking them savagely and indecently assaulting the female demonstrators. They immediately took out their cameras and started filming the attacks on the demonstrators. After half an hour, they were interrupted by a group of thugs who broke down the door of the room and started hitting them with metal canes. They broke some of the cameras and made sure that they had destroyed all footage of the attack.

I asked the journalists what they planned to do now. They believed the authorities had organised the attack on them, so they saw no point in making a formal complaint to them. The journalists insisted on going ahead with the interview, and proposed we move to our second location: a boat on the Nile. As we were leaving my office, I was approached by some people waiting outside. One of them came up to me and said: "Don't speak to those Westerners; they are spies,."

"They are not spies," I said. "They are respectable French journalists and they have the necessary permits to film on the street." The stranger started shouting vile insults at me and – were it not for the brave intervention made by my neighbours – they certainly would have attacked us. It was clear that the attack had been planned. I went to the police station to give a formal account of the incident and then went with the French television crew to record the rest of the program.

Two days later, I was on my way home when a neighbour telephoned me to say that the same person, who had showered me with insults, was standing outside my house with a group of 20 people. They were shouting insults and threats in an attempt to terrify my family. Once again, my neighbours intervened and moved them off and I gave another formal account to the police.

Later that evening, a female demonstrator by the name of Hadir Makkawi appeared on television with talkshow host Wael el-Ebrashi and said that members of the military police had arrested her and threatened to beat her with electric cables unless she made a video accusing me, along with my friend the revolutionary filmmaker Khaled Youssef,[1] of inciting her and her associates to hold sit-ins and commit acts of vandalism. The woman did as they requested, but her conscience demanded that she contact the media to tell the truth. On the same night, a television presenter closely linked to the state security service said that after the poisoning incident – in which demonstrators were given poisoned *hawawshi* (spicy minced meat sandwiches) – I went to the sit-in at the Council of Ministers and encouraged the demonstrators to break the security cameras filming them.[2] This incident is nothing but a tissue of lies. Although I visited the sit-ins on various occasions to show my support, I did not return after the incident with the *hawawshi*. The presenter was lying and the state security officer who uttered these futile words had a poor imagination.

The next day, a daily national newspaper published a story about a plot to assassinate me along with a group of other revolutionaries. The newspaper claimed that the attack would be carried out by Syrian and Iranian agents, and that the source for this story was a White House official. It was difficult for me to believe that either the Iranian regime, entangled as it is with the West regarding its nuclear program, or the Syrian regime – that is killing its people and launching its last stand for survival – would find the time and effort to kill Egyptian citizens. Stranger still that a White House official would contact a

1 Khaled Youssef is an Egyptian director and screenwriter. His films are noted for their use of improvisation and a realistic cinéma vérité style. He has established a solid reputation as a filmmaker who does not shy away from controversial issues such as rape, political corruption and homosexuality.

2 Dozens of demonstrators outside the Council of Ministers abruptly fell ill after eating food provided by an unidentified passerby.

journalist at an Egyptian newspaper and hand him this scoop, rather than leaking the story to the international press. The following day, a national magazine published a picture of some friends with the caption: "the inciters".

The military council, with the support of the state security service and its followers in the media, has launched a ferocious war against those who dare to criticise the military council and their actions. The aim is to defame the critics of the military council's policies and terrify them into silence. They want us to turn a blind eye to the brutal attacks against demonstrators, but we will never forget Maspero Square, Mohamed Mahmoud Street, and the Council of Ministers. These massacres are all documented with video evidence, and the military council alone is responsible for them. We shall continue to speak the truth. The military council can do whatever it wants, but our lives can never be more valuable than the lives of the young Egyptian revolutionaries that Hosni Mubarak killed and that the military council has continued to kill.

But what the military council is doing is neither strange nor mysterious. It is carrying out a precise plan to contain and then undo the revolution, as if it never happened. This very same course of events happened in Romania. In 1989, the Romanian people rose up against the dictator Nicolae Ceausescu[1] and prevented the army from coming to his aid. He was put on trial and executed by the revolutionaries along with his wife, Elena. In the transitional period, authority passed to one of Ceausescu's aides, Ion Iliescu. In the beginning, Iliescu praised and welcomed the revolution, but soon there were dreadful breakdowns in security in Romania (afterwards found to be the work of Iliescu) as gangs of unknown thugs began to attack people's houses and vital public facilities. As the army moved in to confront them, Romania became a battleground that gave rise to a feeling of panic and insecurity amongst Romanian citizens. With the deliberate breakdown in law and order, prices rose and life became extremely difficult.

All the while, the regime-controlled media played a dual role. It spread panic and lies, and deliberately sullied the image of the revolutionaries, so much so that citizens, ground down and exhausted, accused them of being foreign agents. When the revolutionaries felt that Iliescu was trying to thwart the revolution, they organised a big demonstration and marched under a banner: "Don't steal the revolution". Iliescu made a televised appeal to the "noble citizens" of Romania asking them to combat the traitors. Meanwhile, in secret, Iliescu summoned thousands of mine workers to the capital and provided them with weapons. They attacked the revolutionaries and killed a great number of them. The Romanian revolution came to an end shortly after as Iliescu was perceived to have restored order, nominated himself for the

1 Nicolae Ceausescu (1918–89) was a Romanian Communist politician who was General Secretary of the Romanian Communist Party from 1965 to 1989, and as such was the country's second and last Communist leader.

presidency and was victorious in two successive rounds of rigged elections. This is how the Romanian revolution, having been a source of pride, turned into a subject for derision and ridicule.

The Romanians launched a violent revolution and many of them fell, but in the end instead of the dictator Ceausescu, his aide Iliescu took power. Please note what Ahmed Shafik (who plays the role of Iliescu in the Egyptian version) is doing now. This is a man against whom the Civil Aviation Authority has presented 36 complaints to the attorney general, accusing him of wasting public money and corruption. But the attorney general has not investigated these complaints, even though he received them in March. Meanwhile, Shafik is conducting a huge election campaign in order to assume power as the president of Egypt. The truth is as clear as day. No reasonable person, whatever their political inclinations, can watch women dragged along the ground and abused, and demonstrators shot dead, without condemning the military council.

Here I quote one of the most senior fighters in the armed forces, the retired General Hamdy el-Shorbagi, who sent a message to the military council on his personal Facebook page. El-Shorbagi said that the repression that was meted out on Egyptian demonstrators came from a few mentally ill officers and troops who may have possessed authority but possessed neither the honour of their profession nor a conscience. He said that he had witnessed for himself the capture of 28 Israeli soldiers during the October War of 1973 and saw how nobly the Egyptian army had treated them. As for killing Egyptians and indecently assaulting Egyptian women, General el-Shorbagi considers these actions have brought disgrace on the Egyptian army.

What to do now?

A committee must be formed to investigate the massacres committed by members of the police and the army against the demonstrators. However, this committee must be completely independent of the state institutions which are still loyal to the Mubarak regime. The committee must be headed by an independent judge well known for his integrity, such as Judge Zakaria Abdel-Aziz, Ashraf el-Baroudi or Mahmoud el-Khodeiri. Furthermore, the committee will have the right to investigate both military personnel and civilians. This committee will make sure justice is served and punish all those who have committed crimes against the Egyptian people.

Despite my reservations about the elections, the next People's Assembly is the only elected body representing the will of the people and must be given unrestricted powers to form a government instead of the government of Kamal el-Ganzouri that was foisted on the people.

The presidential elections must be brought forward because the situation in Egypt has worsened to such a degree that it cannot be remedied except by a transfer of power from the military council to an elected president.

These three steps are necessary to get out of the crisis. Those who want to thwart the revolution should know that the millions of Egyptians who revolted for the sake of freedom will not allow their revolution to be thwarted or stolen.

The revolution will be victorious – God willing – so that Egypt can begin the future it deserves.

Democracy is the answer.

PN

Five Types of Honourable Citizen

3 January 2012

Let us imagine that a man returns home one evening and suddenly, as he is going up the stairs to his apartment, he sees a criminal trying to assault and rape a woman. The woman is yelling and trying to escape while the attacker is ripping at her clothes. The man, who has inadvertently witnessed the incident, has four possible reactions:

1. He could rush to save the woman from the attacker even if it costs him his life. In this case, he is a brave, honourable and chivalrous man.

2. He could make haste to his flat and call the police. In this case, he is an ordinary man who does not possess exceptional bravery but at least feels a responsibility to stop the crime.

3. He could retreat to his flat and continue with his evening as normal, completely forgetting the incident and leaving the woman to her fate. He is a cowardly man without a conscience.

4. He could refuse to save the woman, and instead throw insults at her while she is being raped. Here the man makes an ugly specimen of human behaviour and in my opinion would need psychiatric help.

Unfortunately some Egyptians have recently adopted this fourth shameful way of thinking. Members of the police and army have committed savage crimes against demonstrators in Maspero Square, on Mohamed Mahmoud Street and at the Council of Ministers. They have been blinded by rubber bullets, killed with live ammunition, and women and girls have been indecently assaulted and dragged along the ground by soldiers. All of these crimes, which have been filmed and recorded by demonstrators, have angered the Egyptian people and turned a number of them against the military council.

However, there remains a group of Egyptians who deliberately downplay the seriousness of these crimes, and often put the blame on the victims. The military council lavishes praise upon these individuals and refers to them publicly as "honourable citizens". To the military council, honourable citizens are those who turn a blind eye to the brutal crimes carried out by their officers, and those that support its efforts to undo the revolution. How can we stand idly by while these supposedly honourable citizens blame the victims of abuse for crimes committed against them. How can we allow them to cover up divert our attention away from sexual abuse and harassment directed at our mothers and our sisters? How can we discuss the future with these honourable citizens when those that have killed and abused our children go unpunished?

These honourable citizens are a strange phenomenon in Egyptian societ and can be divided into five categories:

First: The loyal minister. Hosni Mubarak's concept of a minister was the same as that of the military council. The primary duty of any minister is to defend the decisions of the ruling authority and to justify their mistakes and crimes. So, after all of these heinous crimes were committed against Egyptians, not one minister came forward to tender their resignation or protest because they knew that their duty was to obey the orders of the military council. Prime Minister el-Ganzouri promised, in front of the world's media, to give complete protection to the demonstrators; he would not allow them to be abused (physically or verbally). However, soon after this announcent came the massacre of demonstrators in front of the Council of Ministers, and el-Ganzouri did not show the slightest degree of shame or regret because he considered himself to be acting on behalf of the military council.

Second: The opportunistic liberal. This type of honourable citizen is commonly found amongst university professors, intellectuals and professionals. The opportunistic liberals consider themselves more entitled to a life of comfort and ease than others. They are prepared to flatter, deceive and cooperate fully with the state security apparatus if it benefits them directly. They have no qualms about acting as informers, and will voluntarily name and shame colleagues who oppose the military council. They are prepared to do anything in order to obtain a ministerial post. They not only ignore the brutal crimes committed by the police and army against the demonstrators, but they are also prepared to offer political justifications for these infractions. The opportunistic liberals ally themselves with the military council because, whatever changes happen within government, the council will still be in a position to reward them favourably.

Third: The hateful extremist. This type of honourable citizen embraces an extremist interpretation of Islam that preaches hatred and violence as opposed to love and tolerance. The extremist's incorrect interpretation of Islam pushes them to attack anyone who dares to disagree with them, and considers them infidels, shameless degenerates or foreign agents plotting against Islam. The extremists hate everyone who do not share their extremism, and they rely on conspiracy theories to maintain their extremist views. They firmly believe that Islam is the victim of internal conspiracies, orchestrated by the secularists, liberals and leftists, as well as major foreign conspiracies by Western, crusader powers.

Nobody can convince the hateful extremist that the liberals and leftists are patriotic Egyptians who paid a high price in the revolution, in which there were no religious slogans. It is impossible to convince them that all the liberal or leftist leaders of Egypt, from Saad Zaghloul to Gamal Abdel Nasser, believed in a civil state but embraced Islam as a great religion, not as a political program to be used to obtain power.

It is not possible to convince the hateful extremist that the Western nations are concerned only with their own interests. The United States' closest ally, after Israel, is the Saudi regime, which is the source of Wahhabi ideology and teachings. Indeed, the Taliban was set up and supported by the CIA for years. General Zia-ul-Haq, former president of Pakistan, was working with the CIA while at the same time establishing a strict Islamic regime with Saudi backing. Furthermore, the United States only opposes Hezbollah and Hamas because they are resistance movements, not because they are Islamic. The hateful extremist will not listen to reason. They believe that anybody who disagrees with them politically are enemies of Islam and therefore deserving of punishment.

When millions of people around the world were horrified by the video of an innocent Egyptian woman being dragged through the streets and kicked by a group of soldiers, well-known salafist sheikhs appeared on a Wahhabi television programme to mock the victim and question her honour. The reason for this behaviour is that these sheikhs want to appease the military council in order to gain power. The incident would only warrant anger if the soldiers had attacked one of their followers. They see no reason to defend the honour of ordinary Egyptians that are, in their opinion, enemies of Islam. How can these sheikhs claim to speak in the name of Islam when they are incapable of understanding the basic principles of their own religion.

Fourth: The corrupt collaborator. This type of honourable citizen became common due to rampant corruption. Under Mubarak, Egyptians had three choices: move abroad, participate in corrupt activities to survive, or continue rejecting corruption and pay a heavy price. Thousands of Egyptians did not join the National Democratic Party but they practiced corruption daily in the workplace. They convinced themselves that Egypt was incapable of reform, and therefore accepted corruption as a means of survival. These are the bribe-taking officials, the teachers who formed private study groups and the doctors who sold illegal medication. The corrupt collaborators did not take part in, or support, the revolution because it reminded them that compliance was a choice, and because real democratic change would put an end to the corrupt earnings that they have become accustomed to. They support the repression and killing of demonstrators so that they can resume their corrupt activities.

Fifth: The terrified and submissive. These are the people that submitted to, accepted, and accommodated the Mubarak regime. The submissives are frightened of any real change because they value their security above all else. They refuse to sympathise with the demonstrators who are killed and harassed because to do so would lead them to criticise the military council; and they are psychologically incapable of thinking in isolation from an authority that protects them, even if it also represses them and violates their human rights. In the end, the brutal crimes that were committed against demonstrators have proven that most Egyptians are still faithful to the revolution despite the military council's attempts to break the will of the revolutionaries and reverse the revolution. But these crimes have also shown that the Mubarak regime affected Egyptians psychologically and they are unable to see the truth and to take moral responsibility for their own actions.

Achieving the objectives of the revolution is the only way to build a democratic state. It will also ensure that Egyptians recover their mental and intellectual health, so that they can become truly honorable citizens.

Democracy is the answer.

PN

A Conversation Between a Revolutionary and an Honourable Citizen

10 January 2012

An honourable citizen was sitting in a cafe after the evening prayer. He was happily smoking a water pipe and sipping a cup of mint tea. A young man in jeans and a Palestinian kefiyyeh approached the honourable citizen and handed him a piece of paper, smiling: "Sir, I invite you to the peaceful demonstration on 25 January so that the aims of the revolution can be fulfilled."

"Shame on you!" shouted the honourable citizen, throwing the paper on the table. "Isn't it enough that the country has been left in ruins? What do you lot want? Tourism has stopped and production has come to a halt. You've destroyed the country, may God destroy and curse you all!"

The youth smiled. It seemed that he was used to hearing these accusations. "Instead of insulting me, could we talk about this calmly?" he asked.

"Go ahead," said the honourable citizen, "but there's one thing I'd like to say. I will never allow you to insult the Egyptian army; they are the finest soldiers in the world."

"The Egyptian army belongs to the people," said the young man. "Every household in Egypt has a family member serving as an officer or a private. My uncle is an officer, and my cousin is too. I love and respect the army just as you do. But I oppose the decisions of the military council."

The honourable citizen shrugged his shoulders. "Are you playing games with me? The military council is the leadership of the army. If you oppose it, this means you are insulting the army."

"In no way am I opposing or insulting the army," replied the youth. "The military council is performing the role of the President of the Republic. That means I have the right to take issue with its political actions."

"This is just what you lot excel in," said the honourable citizen, "coming out with big words that nobody can understand."

"Please listen to me, sir," said the youth calmly, "let's suppose that you have a toothache and you go to the dentist to have it treated. This dentist is also an officer in the army. If this dentist breaks your tooth, do you not have the right to go to another doctor?"

"Of course you do."

"And if you insult this doctor, does that mean you're insulting the army?"

"Certainly not. What does the army have to do with my tooth?"

"Well this is the same logic we are following. We are opposing the military council's political role but not the army itself."

The honourable citizen puffed on his shisha. "What do you want exactly?" he said calmly. "Hasn't Hosni Mubarak been deposed and put on trial?"

"Mubarak being deposed won't make any change in itself. Mubarak could have died or been overthrown in a coup. More important than Mubarak's ouster is changing the regime itself. The aim of the revolution is for our country to become a respectable nation and for the Egyptian to have his rights and keep his dignity."

"And that still hasn't happened?"

"Not at all. The Mubarak regime is just as it was. Nothing has changed. The leadership of the police is the same. So far, not one of those who killed demonstrators has been properly prosecuted. The judges who rigged the elections in the Mubarak days are still in their positions, the state security apparatus is just as it was."

"Won't change come little by little?"

"We've had a year and no change has happened."

"But didn't we elect a People's Assembly to speak in our name?"

"The elections for the People's Assembly may not have been rigged but they were not fair."

"Why?"

"For many reasons. For one, article four of the constitutional declaration says that "No political activity shall be exercised nor political parties established on a religious basis." Now I ask you, sir, are the Brotherhood and the Salafists religious parties or not?"

"Of course they are religious parties. And why did we elect them? Because people are good and follow their religion."

"The military council went against their own constitutional declaration and allied with the Brotherhood and the Salafists. They gave them the opportunity to commit all kinds of infractions in the elections without doing anything to stop them."

"Don't you think the Brotherhood would have won whatever the circumstances?"

"The Brotherhood would have gotten a good result because they are popular, but the elections were constructed in such a way to guarantee the Brotherhood and the Salafists would get the majority."

"Wait a minute, I've really had it up to here with you. Nothing pleases you. I mean what are we supposed to do about the People's Assembly? Boycott that as well?"

"For the sake of Egypt, we must work with the future People's Assembly, because for all its faults, it is the only elected body we have."

The honourable citizen looked askance at the youth as if he didn't believe him. "OK, so why do you want to hold a demonstration on 25 January instead of letting the People's Assembly get on with its work?"

"Sir, the reliability of the People's Assembly cannot be guaranteed because it has been formed amidst agreements and deals. The People's Assembly may demand that the aims of the revolution be fulfilled or it may side with the military council against us. Because of this, millions of people must come out and demonstrate peacefully on 25 January to make sure it will definitely stick to fulfilling the aims of the revolution."

"I don't understand."

"OK, if you hire a lawyer to represent you at a trial and you don't have confidence in him, what would you do?"

"Withdraw the power of attorney."

"And if there were circumstances that prevented you doing this, what would you do then? Wouldn"t you go with him to the hearing to make sure he behaved well?"

"Of course."

"My point exactly. We must make sure that they are sticking to the aims of the revolution."

The honourable citizen smiled. "Excuse me young man, I forgot to ask you if you would like a drink."

The youth's face shone with gratitude and he asked for a cup of Arabic coffee.

"Don't presume that I am one of those with links to the old regime," said the honourable citizen. "In fact, I am for the revolution."

"So why don't you want to defend it?" asked the youth.

"I am scared that my country will be destroyed. I am scared that Egypt will become like Somalia. I mean, are you happy with the state the country is in now? Gang violence, anarchy, economic recession, everything has ground to a halt."

"Egypt in the days of Mubarak was the pits. You must remember that people were dying in queues for bread and cooking gas. The revolutionaries have not been in power for a single day; responsibility for the deterioration of the country must lie with the military council which is governing the country. If it had implemented the goals of the revolution and not those of the Mubarak regime, things would not have stayed this way."

"How's that?"

"Let's say you're a state security officer. For 20 years you've been torturing and degrading people. Or let's say you're a senior official who is a criminal. Would it be in your interests for change to take place, for a respectable government to come in who would bring you to justice for your crimes, or, rather, would it be in your interests to create chaos?"

"Of course not, it would be in my interests to mess up the country."

"There, you've said it yourself. The reason for all these problems is that the military council has protected the Mubarak regime."

The honourable citizen's face showed signs of confusion. "My God, one doesn't know where the truth lies anymore," he said a in quiet voice, as if talking to himself. "When I see what's on television I'm convinced that you are anarchists and criminals, but if I'm honest, what you are saying is logical. I have a slightly awkward question for you though."

"Go on."

"Is it true that you get funding from America?"

The youth laughed. "Sir, if we got funding would I look like this? I am a computer engineer by trade, but after the revolution the company I was working for shut down. Now my family are giving me money until I find another job. Thank God I'm not married and that my needs are modest."

"So what is all this about funding then?"

"There are some organisations that receive funding from abroad, but the funding is legal and the government knows about it."

"What does 'legal' mean? How can patriotic people take money from foreigners?"

"You're right. I am against funding on principle and I want to say that the young people who took part in the revolution refused funding and didn't take a penny."

"What you say is correct."

"Not only this. It's a citizen's right to know the sources of funding for any organisation operating in Egypt. The military council has the right to investigate funding and make it public."

"At last, you agree with something the military council has done!"

"Of course, the military council has the right to monitor the funding of domestic organisations, but unfortunately it never monitors the funding of the Brotherhood and the Salafists."

"How's that? The Brotherhood the Salafists, my God, they really have a lot of money. They came here distributing everything: cooking oil, sugar, gas canisters, cloth, meat."

"So isn't it our right to know where they are getting all this money from?"

"It's our right, but what is the solution now? That the country is split in two: you on one side, and the military council on the other!"

"We are determined to achieve the aims of the revolution and the first of these is prosecutions."

"The prosecution of whom?"

"Do you have children, sir?"

"I have a daughter, Sheema, who's in secondary school, and a son, Waleed, who's in primary school."

"Has anyone ever tried to molest Sheema?"

"It happened once. I came down and beat the culprit to a pulp."

"Why did you beat him?"

"If anyone comes near my children, I'll show them what for!"

The youth opened his bag and showed a few photographs to the honourable citizen who seemed deeply affected by what he saw.

"What is this? How appalling! How did this happen?"

"These are some photographs of the women who were dragged through the streets and assaulted by the police and army, aside from those who died or lost their eyes. Haven't you seen these images before?"

"To tell the truth, I never read the newspapers and these photos were never on television."

"Imagine if the families of those who were killed and injured demand that those who killed their children be prosecuted. Are they wrong to do that?"

"No, it's their right."

"OK, and if the people who killed their children belong to the military council, is it not proper that the investigation be led by an impartial body headed by an independent judge?"

"That would be proper justice."

"Does your daughter Sheema use a computer?"

"Of course, she's very clever."

"Take this CD and get her to show you it. Then you can find out why we are demanding the prosecution of those who killed young men and indecently assaulted women."

The old man took the CD and put it carefully in the pocket of his *jellabiya*.

"Thank you for the coffee, sir," said the youth as he rose to leave.

"It is I who must thank you," replied the old man.

"Will you come with us on 25 January?"

"God willing, I will come with you."

The youth embraced the honourable citizen, then warmly shook him by the hand and went on his way.

Democracy is the answer.

PN

What Does Mohamed ElBaradei Want?

16 January 2012

Dear reader, do you have a son or daughter in the sixth year of primary school? If you were to pick up their social studies textbook you would find much material detailing the so-called achievements of Hosni Mubarak over the past thirty years. The lesson uses the expression "President Mubarak" (not "the former", or "the deposed"), and after going through his deeds in the realm of foreign policy, the economy and social cohesion, the book refers to the Egyptian revolution in one sentence: "However, all these attempts by President Mubarak were insufficient to satisfy the people and they rose up in a revolution aimed at regime change."

That is what our children learn about Hosni Mubarak and the revolution – a complete presentation of his imaginary achievements and not a word about his awful crimes against Egyptians, and then right at the end a terse, obfuscating and distorted sentence about the revolution. What will a student think when they learn by heart these supposed achievements of Mubarak and then see his photograph during his trial, with him lying on a bed in the courtroom cage? The student will obviously think that Mubarak is a great man who has been wronged and then they will resent the revolution that toppled him. This is merely one example of the lies with which the Ministry of Education distorts the consciousness of Egyptian students. We have recently seen more than one subject in school examinations that accuses the revolutionaries of being corrupt, and which accused the nationalist movements, such as Kefaya and April 6 Youth, of being agents in the pay of foreign powers.

The lies do not reflect the personal opinion of the author of the textbooks, but are the general policy of the Ministry of Education which possesses venerable bureaucratic machinery for setting syllabuses and examinations. Its officials can only decide a political issue after consulting their superiors who toe the required political line. The pro-Mubarak, anti-revolution syllabus is just one of the many phenomenon demonstrating that Mubarak is still ruling Egypt. In a few days time, the Egyptian revolution will be one year old, but which of its aims have been realised?

In every country in the world, if a revolution succeeds in bringing down the regime, the constitution automatically falls with it. Then a constitutional council is elected to draft a new constitution that expresses the aims of the revolution. In Egypt, however, the military council refused to draft a new constitution, proposing instead limited amendments to the old constitution. A referendum was held on these amendents, but the military council annulled the results and implemented a temporary 63-clause constitution, which had not been voted on or approved by the Egyptian people. The military council has wasted Egypt's opportunity to draft a constitution peacefully following the revolution, and has therefore thwarted our attempts to achieve real democracy in Egypt.

The revolution came about in order to restore Egyptians' dignity, and it demanded the dissolution of the central security apparatus which had become a human slaughterhouse where thousands of Egyptians had been tortured and brutalised, but the military council insisted on keeping it, merely changing its name to the Homeland Security. The revolution demanded that the police force be purged of its leading figures who were loyal to Mubarak, and that serious trials be held for those who had killed demonstrators, but not only did the military council leave the police apparatus untouched, but even those police officers who killed demonstrators and whose trials are dragging on endlessly, have kept their jobs and many have been promoted.

In addition, the military council stood idly by as security broke down – a result of the refusal of the civil police to carry out their duties. It is no wonder that the military police, who abused demonstrators so horribly, did not lift a finger when they saw some Egyptians cutting the railway line and causing chaos in Upper Egypt. It is as if the military council is making life increasingly difficult for Egyptians in order to nurture resentment of the revolution.

The military council has left most of the high-ranking Mubarak regime officials untouched in word and deed, and we just see more of the same old behaviour and thinking. In cabinet meetings Kamal el-Ganzouri, the prime minister, vows to protect the demonstrators, but when they are killed and women are dragged along the ground and abused, el-Ganzouri feels no sense of embarrassment about his false promises. Then he speaks of a serious economic crisis threatening Egypt and in the same week we discover that the governor of the Central Bank has kept a sum of 55 billion pounds in the name of Hosni Mubarak out of the state budget. The same shenanigans that used to happen in Mubarak's days – as if the Egyptian revolution had not taken place.

Not only do most judges in Egypt act independently of their conscience, but the legal system is not independent for it is subject to the legal oversight directorate whose head is appointed by the Minister of Justice who is appointed by the president. The revolution demanded that the judicial system be purged of judges who facilitated vote-rigging, but the military council has kept the sham judges in power and obstructed the law on the independence of the judiciary. Now we see the consequences: in three consecutive massacres 86 demonstrators were killed, crushed by armoured vehicles, tear gas and live ammunition, not to mention the thousands who have been injured and the scores of Egyptian women dragged along the ground and abused. Until now, there has been no serious trial of the security or army individuals who committed these crimes. On the contrary, the young revolutionary, Ahmad Douma,[1] has been arrested and imprisoned, revolutionaries have been dragged into court on trumped-up charges, and the blogger, Nawara Negm,[2] has been accused of "deluding public opinion into believing that corruption still exists", an accusation which comes from I know not where, but has no basis at all in law. Travel restriction orders have been issued against a number of activists including Mamdouh Hamza and Ayman Nour, whereas Omar Suleiman, number two in the Mubarak regime, travels freely in a private aircraft and meets kings and heads of state.

The military council held an unfair election, through which it aimed to grant a majority of seats in parliament to the Islamist political association, allowing them to form religious parties in direct contravention of article four of the constitutional announcement which the Military Committee itself drafted. The Military Committee formed a supreme electoral council which turned a blind eye to all sorts of electoral and political abuses by the religious parties, starting from political propaganda in the mosques, to the buying of votes, trying to influence votes of committee members, and the millions of pounds spent by the Muslim Brotherhood and the Salafists. The military council has overlooked these financial irregularities presumably because it is too busy

1 Ahmed Douma, a prominent Egyptian activist and blogger, was famously arrested under each consecutive Egyptian government in recent years. He is a member of the Egyptian Popular Current.

2 Nawara Negm is an Egyptian journalist, blogger and human rights activist based in Cairo, Egypt. Her blog gained nationwide popularity during the revolution.

monitoring the activists who criticise its policies, such as the human rights associations and the April 6 Youth Movement, which was accused by the military council of receiving funds from abroad even though the allegations have not been substantiated. I am not against people who lean towards political Islam, they are Egyptians and nationalists, and although I give them my full respect the truth must be stated and a determination must be made as to whether these elections were fraudulent or not, taking into account the many reports of vote-rigging.

After a whole year, the only aim the Egyptian revolution has achieved is that of the rather dubious trial of Mubarak. The military council has successfully managed to change the revolution into a coup d'état. Instead of a thoroughgoing change paving the way for the establishment of a democratic state, the military council has made do with changing the person of the ruler. We are now discovering that we have exchanged one authoritarian government for another. Nothing in Egypt happens without the military council's approval, and if things carry on like this we will have a president elected according to the wishes of the military council who will control him behind the scenes. This is the scenario which made Mohamed ElBaradei announce that he was withdrawing from the presidential elections.

ElBaradei's stance has many dimensions, the most of important of which being that ElBaradei is a decent and trustworthy man and his devotion to the revolution is above and beyond any personal ambition. ElBaradei stuck to his guns and refused to compromise his principals or to horse-trade in order to get into power. He did not step over the bodies of dead demonstrators, as others did. ElBaradei refused to deceive us by playing the role of a presidential candidate in a sham democracy.

In the light of the current situation, would it even be possible for a candidate to win the presidential elections without the blessing of the military council? The answer is a resounding no. How can we expect fair elections when the state security service continues to intimidate and kill its opponents? How can we expect decent presidential elections in the shadow of a non-independent judiciary and a supreme electoral committee that does nothing to stop voting irregularities or to put an end to the misinformation from the corrupt media which follows orders from the state security and discredits opponents? How can we expect decent elections when the upper echelons of the police are in bed with Mubarak, and when the military police beat scores of judges during the last elections because they insisted on taking the ballot boxes away themselves?

The message that ElBaradei wants to send to the nation is quite clear: we cannot create real change with the same old tools. We cannot build a real democracy in the shadow of Mubarak, who is still ruling. We cannot construct a new state before we have removed all the corruption of the old regime. The Egyptian revolution succeeded in toppling Hosni Mubarak, but the military council set the revolution off course and left the Mubarak regime as it was. It is our common duty to attempt to realise the aims of the revolution.

As for the next parliament, despite our reservations about it, it remains the only body that has been elected by the Egyptian people, and it follows that the national interest, in my opinion, obliges us to accept this parliament. However, its legitimacy will be defined by its performance. If parliament realises the aims of the revolution it will be a legitimate parliament. If it starts horse-trading or forms alliances that damage the revolution and dilute the rights of Egyptians, it will be devoid of legitimacy.

That is why we must all go onto the streets on 25 January to demonstrate peacefully and show the military council that the revolution is continuing. I hope that millions of Egyptians in all the provinces will go out on the street and declare clearly that the revolution, created with their blood and for which they have paid with their lives, will never fail or stray from its aims. The revolution is the truth and everything against it is vain deceit. The revolution is the future and those who oppose it belong to the past. The revolution will win, thank God, so that Egypt can embark on its future.

Democracy is the answer.

RH

Why Should We Demonstrate Tomorrow?

24 January 2012

Imagine that you were leaving your office after work one evening and you were attacked by a group of strangers. What would you do if they hurled foul abuse you, pushed you to the ground and beat you? Your natural reaction would be to defend yourself. However, if you found the odds stacked against you, wisdom would dictate that you should run for your safety, or even for your life. This is exactly what happened to the revolutionary journalist Nawara Negm last week. As Nawara was leaving her office in the Television Building, she was set upon by a group of thugs who beat her up and insulted her. A video of the incident was later uploaded to YouTube and reveals a number of truths:

First: Those who attacked Nawara were an organised group under a leader who directed the attack and gave orders that are clearly audible in the video: "Hit her, hit her again, film her being beaten …"

Second: The attack on Nawara was carried out as revenge for her having criticised the policies of the military council. The leader of the thugs can be heard telling the passers by that they were beating Nawara because she had been "creating strife between the army and the people."

Third: The attackers made sure to beat Nawara in a manner that left no visible bruising. Their aim was not to injure her but to humiliate her. In filming the incident and putting the video on YouTube, their plan was, according to their way of thinking, to humiliate Nawara and break her spirit.

Fourth: Nawara showed courage which is both rare and deserving of respect. She stood there completely on her own in front of a group of thugs who could have killed her at any moment. Nawara faced her attackers and took the beating with true tenacity. She neither backed away, nor ran off; she neither cried nor did she appeal for help. The attackers wanted to film Nawara crying and pleading, or fleeing in terror, but she came out on top and anyone who looks at the video will be in awe of the courage Nawara displayed.

Attacks have been carried out continuously on Egypt's revolutionary women with the sole aim of humiliating them. During the sit-in outside the Council of Ministers, Ghada Kamal, a young pharmacist, was arrested and savagely beaten by soldiers who could be heard shouting: "We're going to gang-rape you, tonight." Again, the aim was to humiliate and shame Ghada Kamal, but exactly the opposite happened. Ghada Kamal came out of the incident stronger and having won the respect of people for her courage and tenacity.

Last March, the military police arrested a group of female demonstrators in Tahrir Square. After they had been savagely beaten and dragged along the ground, their clothing was ripped off and they were subjected to virginity tests. One of the victims was Samira Ibrahim, a brave woman from Upper Egypt who spoke out about the attack and demanded that the officers be arrested and put on trial. The attacks were not limited to young revolutionaries; officers were known to have beaten and abused older women as well in an attempt to bring shame on them and their families. These women have bore the attacks with dignity and have become more resolute and devoted to the revolution. The perpetrators want to humiliate the revolutionaries because all other methods have failed. The revolutionary youth are the rock upon which all attempts to abort the revolution flounder.

The military council has preserved Mubarak's form of government and will do anything to thwart the revolution through a carefully thought out plan which is being implemented in stages, starting with the creation of one crisis after another in order to make Egyptians' lives as hard as possible. We have witnessed the intentional break-down of law and order, price hikes, the scarcity of petrol and basic foodstuffs, groups of citizens being allowed to block roads and railways for days while the civil and military police look on and do nothing. The revolutionaries have been accused of being agents of foreign powers and put on trial facing trumped-up charges. And finally, we must mention the support being given to remnants of the former regime who are paid to appear on television and praise Mubarak in an effort to undermine the revolution and present it as just another opposing point of view instead of an objective reality that has changed the whole of Egypt. The aim of all this is to make Egyptians doubt the value of the revolution, resent it and perhaps even regret that it took place. The plan would have been successful had it not been for the young revolutionaries.

They were the first people to call for a revolution and the ones who paid the highest price by being prepared to face death for its sake. They can neither be intimidated nor bought off. They are not in it for personal gain; they do not want seats in parliament or jobs in the government. These are the young people who have guarded the revolution and have suffered as a result. It is for that reason that three massacres have been carried out against them: Maspero Square, Mohamed Mahmoud Street and Council of Ministers, in which 85 people were shot dead and gassed, with many losing their eyesight to rubber bullets, such as the heroic Malek Mustafa and Ahmed Harara (a dentist blinded in both eyes). However, the revolutionary youth have won out in the end having valiantly faced attacks from professional armed soldiers. The spirit of the revolution has not been broken and, rather than being weakened, it has emerged from each tragedy more tenacious and more determined to bring about a revolution.

Mass demonstrations took place in most of the governorates of Egypt in support of the revolution and in solidarity with the revolutionaries. The Mubarak regime knew that it could not abort the revolution as long as millions of young people were out defending it so vehemently. Time and again, the regime has tried to break the spirit of the revolutionaries and humiliate them. They did not take into account that the revolutionaries do not fear death, but present their chests to the bullets, and even if they lose an eye they keep on smiling. The regime hoped that if the revolutionaries were publicly humiliated they would lose their self-respect and their spirit would break. But even this last attempt failed completely and in the aftermath of every attack, the revolutionaries come back with increased pride and dignity and a greater determination to achieve the aims of the revolution.

Tomorrow, 25 January 2012, is the first anniversary of the Egyptian revolution. We have to ask ourselves which of the revolution's aims have been realised:

First: Have Egyptians regained their humanity and dignity? Unfortunately the organs of repression have been arresting innocent citizens, imprisoning, torturing and brutalising them. Moreover a new machinery of repression has been added to the old one, and alongside the state security service we now have the military police with their proven proficiency in torturing and abusing Egyptians.

Second: Have Egyptians regained a feeling of justice? The judiciary has remained the same as it was in Mubarak's days. The special military courts have been trying civilians, and the judiciary itself is not independent, with its investigative branch being subordinate to the minister of justice who in turn is appointed by the military council. Judges who oversaw the vote rigging in the election are still in their jobs and the perpetrators of the crimes of killing demonstrators and abusing women demonstrators have not been put on trial to date. On the contrary, citizens opposed to the policies of the military council have been sent for trial by kangaroo courts, just like in Mubarak's day, on the same mendacious and hollow charges such as disrupting the peace or sowing communal strife. And now they have started to charge revolutionaries with "inciting public opinion into believing that corruption is still happening."

Third: Have those who killed demonstrators got their comeuppance? The trials of officers accused of murder have proceeded at a slow pace and with month-long adjournments. After every hearing the officers accused of murder have been set free to go back to their offices, and they have all kept their jobs. Many of them have been promoted as some sort of reward for killing Egyptians.

Fourth: Has the minimum of social justice been achieved? The Egyptian state is still being run in the interest of the wealthy and is ignoring the rights of the poor. While el-Ganzouri is begging for international loans and aid from the Arab states in a manner demeaning to all Egyptians, he (with the backing of the military council) has done nothing about the 44 billion pounds in the name of Hosni Mubarak in the Central Bank, with no one daring to incorporate this in the state budget. They are also ignoring the 90 billion pounds set aside in private trusts, which is spent outside the state's oversight. The military council has so far turned a blind eye to the hundreds of ministerial advisors who receive monthly salaries of hundreds of thousands of pounds without so much as lifting a finger. This money comes from the people of Egypt, half of whom live in abject poverty and put up with inhuman conditions.

The Egyptian people have paid a crushing price for this revolution: 1,100 people have been killed, 1,800 Egyptians have been blinded and tens of thousands injured. So one year after the revolution we discover that the only aim of the revolution that has been achieved is the trial of Mubarak and some of his gang – a trial that many law professors deem a show trial devoid of any real value. Tomorrow we must all go down onto the street throughout all of Egypt and hold peaceful demonstrations to remind everyone of the revolution's aims.

We will go out into the street tomorrow not to celebrate, but to demonstrate our devotion to the goals and aims of the revolution. Tomorrow, 25 January 2012, will be a milestone in the history of Egypt and in the fate of the revolution. If only a small number of pro-revolution Egyptians go onto the street, that will mean, God forbid, that the plan to abort the revolution has achieved its aim (even if only temporarily), but if millions of Egyptians demonstrate in support of the revolution, it will send a clear message to all interested parties that the Egyptian revolution, despite all the plots against it, is still alive and kicking and will win out in the end, with the will of God.

Democracy is the answer.

RH

What Can We Expect from the Brotherhood and the Salafists?

31 January 2012

Tarek el-Bishry is an honourable judge and an accomplished historian. From his books, we have learned a great deal about the modern history of Egypt, but he belongs – intellectually at least – to the political Islamist school of thought. As both judge and historian, el-Bishry knows that whenever a revolution succeeds in toppling the regime in power, the constitution created by the defunct regime is no longer valid. It is then up to the revolution to form a new constitution in accordance with their demands. Yet in the aftermath of the revolution, el-Bishry decided to side with the military council and accepted an offer to chair the committee formed to introduce limited amendments to the 1971 constitution. The military council held a referendum on the amendments made by el-Bishry's committee, then went against its outcome and announced a temporary constitution of 63 articles without consulting the Egyptian people. As a result, Egypt has been deprived of a new constitution and the opportunity to bring about democratic change.

The question is this: how could a man of intellect, integrity and patriotism stand in the way of real change in Egypt? The answer is simple: el-Bishry decided to ally himself with the military council in order to guarantee the political dominance of the Muslim Brotherhood in Egypt.

Since the start of the revolution, soldiers and police officers have committed henious crimes against demonstrators. They are responsible for three successive massacres – Maspero Square, Mohamed Mahmoud Street and at the Council of Ministers – in which many innocent Egyptians died. Demonstrators have been killed by live ammunition, blinded by rubber bullets and assaulted in the streets for taking part in the revolution. The video of a young woman being dragged through the streets, stripped of her clothes and then kicked by soldiers drew condemnation from around the world. But despite the brutality of this act, a famous sheikh appeared on a Wahhabi television programme, alongside two Salafist sheikhs, and laughed about the incident. When ElBaradei issued a statement denouncing the assaults on the female demonstrators, the sheikh presenter sarcastically commented: "What a faithful boy! All of them [i.e., the liberals] are getting religious now!" And when the newspapers reported that a veiled woman was dragged and stomped upon by soldiers, the sheikh responded: "So who put the veil on this woman? Could this not be a conspiracy to foment strife between the Salafists and the army?"

The sheikh presenter is publicly outraged whenever the police prevent a woman from wearing the veil in a Western country (in accordance with the law there), but does not defend a veiled Egyptian woman when she is assaulted in her own country. The sheikh is unwilling to protect those that do not belong to the Muslim Brotherhood or the Salafists. The sheikh cannot imagine that virtue exists outside of his own group. In his opinion, you can't have a conscience and condemn indecent assaults unless you are pious, and you can't be pious unless you are a Muslim, belonging to the Muslim Brotherhood or the Salafists. Any injustice or assault on non-Muslims is of no interest to the sheikh. He considers everything that furthers the interests of the Muslim Brotherhood and the Salafists to be religiously acceptable; anything that hinders their reaching power is a conspiracy or plot carried out by enemies of religion.

In a spontaneous reaction to the indecent assaults on Egyptian women during the revolution, a group of female demonstrators came out to violently condemn the attacks carried out by the military police. At this point, the Muslim Brotherhood party official responsible for women's affairs, Manal Abu al-Hassan, accused the female demonstrators of being financed from abroad and having a foreign agenda (the same accusation Mubarak used to make against his opponents) and said that those who stage sit-ins in tents are "drowning in filth and impurity."

Manal Abu al-Hassan has proven that she does not care about the women being dragged through the streets and assaulted, because they are not members of the Muslim Brotherhood. She has no shame in accusing tens of thousands of demonstrators of treason because they are standing in the way of the Brotherhood reaching power.

Several months ago, I wrote an article that likened the principles of Islam to the principles of democracy: freedom, justice, and equality. But I also stressed that Islam did not specify a particular system of government. As soon as the article was published, I received dozens of messages full of slanderous insults, and one religious channel even devoted an entire programme to insulting me and questioning my religion and patriotism. Last month the fatwa committee of Al-Azhar issued an official report that supported my claim that Islam has never specified a particular system of government. The opinion of the fatwa committee passed without comment and nobody objected to, or insulted, the sheikhs of Al-Azhar. This is evidence that some Islamists judge the truth according to the speaker, instead of judging people by the truth.

The unfortunate truth is that many Muslim Brothers and Salafist suffer from double standards and often ignore the facts and take positions defending injustice. They do this either out of hatred towards those who disagree with them, or because they are desperate to gain power. Some have called this behaviour "opportunism", but in my opinion the term is not sufficient. The problem starts with how the Muslim Brotherhood and the Salafists view themselves as representatives of Islam, as opposed to another national faction presenting its political vision. They believe that they have been chosen to enforce the word of God on Earth, so it follows that their battles are never political ones, but resemble more closely a struggle between good and evil.

This concept of aggressive superiority explains why the Muslim Brotherhood has always violated the national consensus and allied with despotic rulers against the will of the people. Why else did the Brotherhood ally with Isma'il Sidqi, and support King Farouk? Why else did they support Gamal Abdel Nasser when he abolished the majority of political parties, and signalled the end of the line for democracy? And why else did the leader of the Muslim Brotherhood say in 2005 that he supported Hosni Mubarak and wished to meet him? The issue here is not just about opportunism; it is a natural result of practicing politics with religious sentiments. Those adherents of political Islam will never shy away from forming an alliance with any power, no matter how oppressive or unjust, if it enables them to establish what they believe is God's rule.

To be fair, we should emphasise that this behaviour does not apply to all members of the Muslim Brotherhood and the Salafists. There are high-ranking Islamists who recognise what is right and bravely defend it, regardless of their political interests or what the consequences may be. For example, Abdel Moneim Aboul Fotouh (the best candidate put forward by the Muslim Brotherhood in decades), Sheikh Hazem Abu Ismail[1] and Sheikh Wagdy Ghoneim[2] (even though I disagree with some of their hard line positions). But

1 Hazem Abu Ismail is an Egyptian lawyer and Salafi Islamist politician that enjoyed popular support and was well-known for his anti-American rhetoric. He was disqualified after it emerged his dead mother held an American passport.

2 Sheikh Wagdy Ghoneim is an Egyptian-Qatari Islamic preacher and writer.

these three individuals are independent and far from the those making the decisions.

Political Islam requires that you practice politics with religious sentiments and this leaves you with two options. The first is that you feel obligated through your correct understanding of religion to adhere to what is right and defend the rights of the oppressed, even if they are opposed to you in opinion or faith. The second is that you disregard the rights of your opponents and view them as nothing but atheists, degenerates and traitors.

After winning a majority in parliament, the Islamists must now decide which choice to make. The situation in Egypt needs no explanation. The military council, which was appointed by Hosni Mubarak, has worked hard to preserve the Mubarak regime and turn Egyptians against the revolution through manufactured crises. The military council wanted to abort the revolution, distort its image, and transform it into a mere coup d'état. However, things have not worked out in the way the military council desired.

On the revolution's first anniversary, millions of Egyptians came out in mass demonstrations to affirm that they are still loyal to the revolution. Taking this into account, the position that the Muslim Brotherhood and the Salafists take in parliament will be critical; they will have to choose whether or not to remain inflexible in their conviction that they alone represent Islam. In this case, they will replace the goals of the revolution with a moral agenda – as in Sudan, Afghanistan and Somalia – and rather than building a state based on justice, they will preoccupy themselves with trivial matters such as banning films and concerts, and punishing women who wear trousers and bathing suits. In such an intellectual vacuum they will become ensnared in alliances and deals that will at once appease the military council and destroy the aims of the revolution. In sum, this will result in the Muslim Brotherhood and the Salafists losing their legitimacy and credibility.

The other option is to develop their vision in a way that allows them to respect their opponents, and to realise that they offer an interpretation of religion, rather than religion itself. Those who disagree with them are not necessarily conspiring against Islam. Political Islam must embrace the goals of the revolution and work to fulfil them, however much this would earn them the ire of the military council.

If the right choice is made, the revolution will achieve its goals and the Brotherhood and the Salfists will go down in history as the founders of the modern Egyptian democratic state. I hope that the Muslim Brotherhood and the Salafists make the right choice, so that Egypt gets the future it deserves.

Democracy is the answer.

PN

Four Telephone Calls in a Deluxe Hospital

6 February 2012

There is an elderly patient, more than 80 years old, who is staying in the most luxurious hospital in Egypt. He has an entire floor of the hospital to himself that has been opened up to create what amounts to a "royal suite" fitted out with all the latest mod cons, as well as a grand bathroom with a jacuzzi. The patient doesn't like to read, so he divides his time instead between watching the gigantic television in the sitting room and speaking on the telephone to his friends and loved ones. Yesterday, the patient had four telephone calls that went as follows:

The First Call (with a man with a hoarse voice)

Man: "Good morning, did you hear about what happened at Port Said?[1]"
Patient: "I feel sorry for the young people who died."

Man: "They deserved it! Aren't they the ones always insulting the police and threatening to lynch the heroic officers that defended the police stations? To hell with them – they haven't seen anything yet! Now there are gangs robbing banks, kidnapping tourists and killing people in broad daylight. They will soon learn that the police officers are still their masters."

Patient: "You're right, this is what happens when people listen to troublemakers."
Man: "Now people spend all their time reminiscing about the good old days."

Patient: "Too little, too late. Anyway, what's your news? Are you well?"

Man: "You know the prison warden was once a colleague of mine. He served with me in the security forces when he was a junior officer. He is a decent man and never lets me go without."
Patient: "A very fine man, indeed."

Man: "Last week, out of the goodness of his heart, the prison warden let me set up a treadmill in my cell so that I can run every morning. You know how I always like to keep fit."

Patient: "Yes, indeed! You used to have three wives, did you not? What are you going to do now you're in prison?"
Man: "Things will sort themselves out, God willing" (*they both laugh*)

Patient: "I hope so, but what's this I hear about purging the police force?"

1 On 1 February 2012, over 70 people were killed and up to 1,000 injured, at a premier-league football match in Port Said, between Al-Ahly and home-team Al-Masry.

Man: "Empty words my friend. The police is a cohesive force. They should be purging the country of those traitorous rich kids who destroyed it in the first place. If the revolutionaries try to do anything to the police force, it will surely backfire. They are angry because all the senior officers are still loyal to the regime. But it is taking its toll, the police officers are fed up of being attacked by the media and they don't want to go to work. Fine, if they don't like the police, then let them fend for themselves."

Patient: "But I heard that some police officers are working with the revolutionaries and have formed a coalition calling for a purge."

Man: "Those officers only did it out of spite towards their more senior colleagues. The important thing is that all the top officers are with us."

Patient: "I'm proud of the leadership of the police force, may God protect them. And how are the officers in the security forces?"

Man: "They pass on their regards and wish you well."

Patient: "A man from the security forces is worth a hundred men."

Man: "I do have a favour to ask of you, sir. Today in prison we are making stuffed pigeon and we know how much you like stuffed pigeon."

Patient: "You son of a … how did you know?" (they both laugh)

Man: "That's my job, sir! We decided that we couldn't possibly eat pigeon without you. Would you allow me to send some over to you?

Patient: "Thank you, I really do like stuffed pigeon but the problem is that it will raise my blood pressure."

Man: "Don't worry, sir. The doctor will prescribe you some medicine for that. We'll send the pigeon with a driver now."

Patient: "Very well, you're too kind."

The Second Call (with a woman who speaks excitedly)

Patient: "Hello my love, how is Rome?"

Woman: "I can't talk for long. I must give my response to the Italian estate agent!"

Patient: "Good."

Woman: "I have put our palace in Rome up for sale, as we agreed, but unfortunately he's offering us 20 per cent below the market value. You know how crafty these Italians can be. When they found out that the palace was yours, they thought you must be in trouble and tried to take advantage."

Patient: "Tell them they've got it wrong. I am not in trouble and if the palace or any other property was bought in my name, nobody can do anything about it. Tell them I am selling it because I need liquidity for our companies."

Woman: "I explained all this to them, but the buyer wants a lower price. Should I sell or not?"

Patient: "Of course not."

Woman: "That's what I thought too. I'll reject his offer and insist on the asking price. I'll talk to him and call you back. OK?"

The Third Call (with a foreign man, who speaks English with a heavy accent)

Foreign Man: "Good evening, sir."

Patient: "Good evening, where have you been my dear friend?"

Foreign Man: "You are always in my thoughts, but I didn't want to bother you at this time."

Patient: "I am in your debt. You have proven yourselves to be faithful friends in the full sense of the word."

Foreign Man: "And you are also a loyal friend. We will not forget the many great things you have done in the service of our country. Together, we have fought terrorism and you also protected the lives of our young people. You are an eternal friend and I was upset to hear that your life was in danger."

Patient: "I fear for my life because the situation in Egypt is unstable. It is impossible to predict what will happen."

Foreign Man: "I have talked to our contacts in the US administration and they have told me that the agreements they made will remain valid. No harm will come to you. This assurance is from us and from the US administration."

Patient: "I cannot thank you enough.".

Foreign Man: "Through the US administration, we also have influence in the Gulf."

Patient: "How so?"

Foreign Man: "There were some governments in the Gulf that wanted to lend their support to the new Egyptian government, but we asked the US administration to pressure the Gulf monarchs to stop this support."

Patient: "Your actions are wise, as usual."

Foreign Man: "We cannot allow Egypt to have any support before we know her intentions towards us."

Patient: "Anybody who refuses your friendship is either an extremist or a fool."

Foreign Man: "If only they could learn from you, sir! Very well, once more I beg you not to worry. Get well soon."

Patient: "I thank you. Pass on my deepest gratitude to your colleagues."

The Fourth Call (with a man who seems from his voice to be old and overworked)

Old man: "Hello sir, how are you? I know I have not been a good friend of late and I am sorry."

Patient: "I am aware of your circumstances and the Lord is with you. Be brave."

Old man: "But sir, the situation is very difficult. It seems as if the Egyptian people have gone mad. They are agitated and will not listed to reason."

Patient: "I have been following these events and I am as surprised as you are. Are these people really Egyptians? I do not recognise them. They have been living amid chaos for almost one year and yet they will not see sense."

Old man: "Sir, on 25 January I had a shock. Millions of people, in all the provinces of Egypt, went out to support the revolution. A revolution? What rubbish! The country is ruined."

Patient: "Enough. They have chosen anarchy so let them do as they please. Don't pay heed to these anarchists or change anyone in the police or the judiciary or the media, or in any ministry. All these talents! They cannot be replaced, especially the attorney general. On no account change him! You'll never be able to find another like him."

Old man: "Sir, be assured that we'll allow them to talk about it, but nothing will be changed."

Patient: "What more do they want? They have got rid of their president and put him on trail. Did they not call for democracy and fair elections?

Old man: "Rest assured, sir, we have the situation under complete control."

Patient: "And what happened in the People's Assembly? I was worried by some of the things said by the representatives. Did you not make an agreement with the sheikh? It seems he has gone back on his word."

Old man: "No, sir. The sheikh will go through with our agreement, everything is well. But he explained to me that he has many members who don't know anything about our agreement. Also, he has a lot of enthusiastic young men and he must allow them to talk and put them at ease."

Patient: "The country's ruined. Every man and his dog has become a leader!"

Old man: "Rest assured sir, in the end the decision rests in our hands and what we say goes. Nothing will change."

Patient: "You're right. We must deal with these people harshly. Shoot whoever gets close to the Ministry of the Interior or the Ministry of Defence, but don't forget those who are provoking them, those writers and media figures trying to take my place as leader. Those who are inciting people. Do you know for sure who they are?"

Old man: "I know them, sir. They will soon pay dearly for what they have done."

Patient: "You must punish them and disgrace them, so that people know what they're really like. Tell the officers from the security forces to work on them. "

Old man: "Every step we take is in coordination with the security forces."

Patient: "May our Lord help you succeed."

Old man: "Anything else, sir?"

Patient: "Keep following my orders, and do not disappear."

Old man: "I am under your command, sir."

Democracy is the answer.

PN

When Will the Mubarak Regime Fall?

13 February 2012

Last Saturday, the famous broadcaster Dina Abdel Rahman went to present her daily show on Al-Tahrir TV network and was surprised to find that the management had cancelled her appearance and replaced her with another female anchor. Dina Abdel Rahman is one of Egypt's most successful broadcasters thanks to her courage and commitment to presenting the truth, free from political bias and prejudice. In her programs, Dina exposed several of the heinous crimes carried out by the state security forces during the revolution. Last summer, she resigned from her position at Dream TV after the owner of the channel pushed her to be less critical of the military council. It was because of this that she moved to the Al-Tahrir network, yet here she is, months later, being dismissed by the network's owner, Solaiman Amer. Amer is a businessman accused of illegally appropriating large tracts of land to build Solaimaneyah City.[1] According to *Al-Badil* website, Amer reached a special

1 Solaimaneyah City is a man-made complex north west of Cairo. The site is comprised of hotels, golf resorts and luxury spas.

agreement with the military council by which he cancels all broadcasts that criticise the military council, and in return they overlook the Solaimaneyah charges. Within weeks, all broadcasters that openly criticised the policies of the military council were removed, including Hamdi Qandil, Ibrahim Eissa, Doaa Sultan and now Dina Abdel Rahman.

Al-Tahrir claimed that the dispute with Dina Abdel Rahman was the result of a financial disagreement but these claims remain unproven. Needless to say, Dina's reputation has not been sullied by these events because she refused to compromise her principles. Even though she has lost her show, she has earned the respect of millions of Egyptians.

The same day, newspapers published a story that Mamdouh Hamza[1] would be investigated by the state security service on suspicion of sabotage and working to overthrow the state. Hamza is one of the most prominent construction engineers in the world, whose achievements are a source of pride for the Egyptian people. He also played a key role during the revolution, supporting the demonstrators and helping them to achieve their goals. The investigation being led by the security service is based on an audio recording in which Mamdouh Hamza – seemingly letting slip his hellish, diabolical scheme – pledges to "destroy Egypt and burn it to the ground". Any Egyptian child could tell you that the recording is false, and has been put together in a way that is both unprofessional and unintelligent. This is not the first time that Mamdouh Hamza has been punished for his criticism of the military council's policies. Along with other fellow revolutionaries, he was subject to investigation on a number of charges, amongst them "deceiving the public into thinking that corruption still exists". This is reminiscent of the trumped-up charges meted out by the Mubarak regime to punish its opponents, such as "disturbing social peace", "creating confusion amongst citizens" and "inciting hatred against the regime". Just like Dina Abdel Rahman, Mamdouh Hamza is above these trivial accusations. Nevertheless, it demonstrates the dirty tactics deployed by the military council to discredit those that disagree with their policies. This far-reaching campaign is not restricted to fabricated evidence and harassment at work either; the military council has orchestrated a number of attacks that have been carried out by paid thugs. The most recent attack was on government minister Mohamed Abu Hamed,[2] in retribution for his demand that power be immediately transferred from the military council to civilian control.

1 Mamdouh Hamza is a prominent Egyptian engineer and industrialist. He has supported various youth groups connected with the revolution, and has provided logistical support for people attending sit-in's in Tahrir Square, such as organizing the delivery of food, loudspeakers, blankets, tents, and waste collection trucks.

2 Mohamed Abu Hamed Shaheen, former vice chairman of the Free Egyptians Party, was an elected member of the post-revolutionary People's Assembly of Egypt, representing Kasr El Nil district in Cairo. He is the former head of the Free Egyptians Party's parliamentary bloc. He resigned from the party in early March 2012.

It is becoming increasingly difficult to differentiate between the rule of the military council and the Mubarak regime. Mubarak's aim was to stay in power for as long as possible and ensure that power was transferred to his son. Although the military council readily intervened to prevent this and declared itself protector of the revolution, it has done little to advance the cause of the revolution. It has stifled progress and turned the revolution into a coup d'état in which the ruling figure may have changed but the regime remains the same.

The military council allied itself with the Muslim Brotherhood to benefit from their popularity and their organisational capabilities. In return, it helped the Brotherhood achieve a parliamentary majority. The military council prepared the electoral lists in such a way as to make it easier for the Brotherhood to win the elections. A Supreme Presidential Electoral Commission (SPEC) was established, but it did nothing to prevent infractions such as vote-buying and fraud. The Muslim Brotherhood distributed sugar, oil and meat in order to obtain votes, and mosques continued to distribute and spread propoganda. In the end, the Brotherhood and the Salafists achieved the result the military council wanted for them.

These elections may not have been rigged, but they certainly were not fair. The Egyptian revolution was stuck between the military's hammer and the anvil of the Brotherhood. The military council seeks to abort the revolution and remain in power behind the scenes, while the Brotherhood seeks to attain power at any price. The Brotherhood has gained a parliamentary majority, so must now submit themselves to the demands of the military council.

Now the question is: will the current People's Assembly be capable of investigating General Hamdi Badeen, commander of Egypt's military police, for the crimes his troops committed, all of which were caught on tape? Will the People's Assembly withdraw its support for Prime Minister el-Ganzouri, or even from the interior minister following the Port Said massacre, maliciously orchestrated as revenge against young revolutionaries and members of the Egyptian Ultras network?[1] The People's Assembly has so far contented itself with sending a fact-finding committee, whose report blamed the security forces, the Football Association and the crowds, without mentioning the role of the military police in the disaster. All the evidence confirms – although I hope I will be proved wrong – that the People's Assembly is incapable of going against the military council. While there are certain ministers (both liberals and Islamists) who are working hard to ensure the correct positions are being adopted, the majority are on the side of the Muslim Brotherhood and have sworn obedience to their supreme guide, a man who is merely fulfilling the terms of his agreement with the military council.

1 Ultras, or hard-core fans of Egypt's Al-Ahly football team.

Meanwhile, the military council has kept all the officials from the Mubarak regime in their jobs; from the judges who oversaw electoral fraud, to the attorney general, the chairman of the Central Auditing Organisation,[1] the governor of the Central Bank and the commanders of the security forces that killed a multitude of Egyptians with no regard for human life.

It has been reported that former Interior Minister Mansour el-Essawy paid large sums of money to officers accused of killing demonstrators in an attempt to boost morale. Thus, while the martyrs' families were demanding justice, the interior minister was distributing monthly rewards to the killers. The military council is responsible for the lawlessness, chaos, armed gangs, increased prices and lack of foodstuffs because they were acting as head of state during the transitional period. The military council can not be excused on account of their political inexperience, because they rejected the formation of a civilian Presidential Council, insisting instead on monopolising power and treating ministers as mere secretarial staff.

The military police have stood idly by as roads have been blocked, trains stopped and churches burned down. They have only intervened to save a member of the Mubarak regime from aggressions, and to attack demonstrators that have come out against the military council. What is more, the military council did not allow Egyptians time to pick up the pieces after these trials. Instead, it continued to terrify citizens by insisting that there were grand conspiracies to topple the state, without once presenting the slightest shred of evidence to this effect.

It was expected that the Egyptian people, tired of crises and terrified of lawlessness, would in the end grow resentful of the revolution and accept all decisions made by the military council. But the massive demonstrations that spread throughout the Egyptian provinces on the first anniversary of the revolution prove that Egyptians are still committed to fulfilling the aims of their revolution. Meanwhile, the military council has launched a series of repressive campaigns against the youth of the revolution – the most noble and courageous of Egypt's children – which have turned into sad massacres aimed at breaking their resolve. Despite the dozens of martyrs and the thousands of injured who have fallen, the youth of the revolution emerged victorious, and their will unbroken. This is when the media began a wide-ranging organised campaign to sully the revolutionaries' image. The media, who once portrayed these same revolutionaries as national heroes, now accuses them of being traitorous agents funded by foreign entities. General Hassan al-Ruwaini has also accused the April 6 and Kefaya movements of being funded by outside sources, and did not apologise when he failed to substantiate his baseless accusations.

---

1 The Central Auditing Organisation is an independent auditing institution established in Egypt in 1942 as an instrument of public finance control.

The military council has also come out against certain civil society organisations, accusing them of acquiring funds through illegal means and aiming to split Egypt into three states. The campaign against these organisations raises many questions. Why did the military council remain silent about these organisations for a whole year, during which time they operated in full view? Why didn't the military council react this forcefully when Israeli troops violated our borders, killing six soldiers and officers? Did an undisclosed dispute erupt between the military council and the American administration and this campaign is their way of punishing the Americans? If the military council truly rejects foreign funding, and demands that all organisations and parties have transparent budgets, then naturally they would have our full support. The investigation of foreign funding extends only to civil organisations, not religious ones. Why hasn't the military council looked into the Brotherhood and the Salafists' funding and investigated the source of the millions of Egyptian pounds they spent during the elections? Could it be that the sources of the Brotherhood's funding are overlooked because it is the military council's ally, while the civil organisations – which played the important role of exposing the heinous crimes committed against demonstrators – are being punished?

If the military council remain in power, it will lead to the writing of a flawed constitution, and the election of a president whom the military council will control from behind the scenes, just as it controls the prime minister now. The time has come for the military council to surrender power to an elected civilian body, so that the army may return to its barracks and fulfil its primary mission of defending the country. The revolution will not be silenced.

Democracy is the answer.

PN

Are They Really Religious?

20 February 2012

Last summer, a friend of mine was driving his elderly mother from the Northern Coast of Egypt to Cairo. On the way, his mother, a diabetic, complained of a sudden fatigue so my friend went to find the nearest pharmacy. He asked the bearded pharmacist behind the counter to inject his mother with insulin, but the pharmacist shook his head and said to him: "Sorry, but I never perform injections on women because that is against God's law. Find your mother a female doctor to give her the injection." My friend tried hard to persuade the pharmacist, telling him that the area was remote and it would be difficult to find a female doctor at short notice, and that his elderly mother surely did not represent a sexual temptation to the pharmacist. Still, he refused to inject the insulin.

Similarly, *Al-Masry Al-Youm* recently published a report about hospitals during Ramadan. It revealed that certain members of staff working in intensive care units and accident and emergency would leave work after breaking the fast and not return for two hours so that they could perform night prayers in the mosque. During this time, the patients were left to their own devices, irrespective of the severity of their condition. Evidently, these religious individuals consider performing the night prayers much more important than caring for the innocent, sick person for whom they are responsible.

This week, this same strange logic appeared at the Ministry of the Interior. For thirty years, Hosni Mubarak used the police force as a tool to oppress and humiliate the Egyptian people. Police officers tortured hundreds of thousands of Egyptians and actively participated in the regime's wrongdoing, from rigging elections, to fabricating charges and recruiting false witnesses to testify against the regime's opponents. Throughout the revolution and after it, many police officers committed heinous crimes against the demonstrators, from indecent assaults, to killing them with live ammunition. The revolution called for the purging and restructuring of the police force, returning it to its fundamental role: protecting citizens and upholding their rights. However, the military council has preserved the structure of the police force with the same leaders, all of whom belong to the Mubarak regime.

Last week dozens of police officers came forward to announce that they planned to grow their beards following the practice of the Prophet. When the Ministry of the Interior informed them that shaving the beard has been an established rule of the police force ever since it was founded, they revolted and insisted upon their right to grow a beard. The most troubling thing about these developments is that these very same officers have been involved in police brutality. Didn't they witness how their colleagues killed demonstrators, how innocent people were tortured at police stations and security forces headquarters? We never heard any of these pious officers objecting to these crimes, but now they are announcing a sacred battle to grow their beards, as if religion is a matter of appearance.

In Egypt there are thousands of mosques that are always full of millions of worshippers, so many that often they lay carpets on the ground outside the mosque and lead prayers on the streets. But does this seemingly fervent devotion to performing religious obligations affect the way Egyptians behave towards one another? The simple answer is no. Many Egyptians cling to the outward manifestations of religion, making sure they perform all the required prayers, but are far from being honest and pious in their daily interactions with others.

If this discrepancy between religious belief and personal conduct occurred in only a few individuals, it would be enough to dismiss them as hypocrites. But when it afflicts such large sections of society, it constitutes a social phenomenon that must be examined. Those religious people that put form over substance are not necessarily hypocrites or bad people, they are quite simply practicing religion as they have understood it and learned it. The interpretation of religion currently in vogue in Egypt places far more importance on acts of worship than on conduct in general. This version of Islam is not quintessentially Egyptian in nature. Balanced, sincere, truthful Egyptian religiosity has been displaced by Wahhabi Islam, coming from Saudi Arabia and the countries of the Gulf.

For thirty years, the massive wealth generated by oil has been used to flood Egypt with Wahhabi ideology. The objective behind this support of the Wahhabi sect is primarily political, since the Saudi regime is based on an alliance between the royal family and Wahhabi sheikhs. It follows that the spread of the Wahhabi sect bolsters the political system of that country. At the same time, millions of Egyptians have migrated to the Gulf in search of livelihood and subsequently returned to Egypt full of Wahhabi ideas. In the Gulf, interaction between men and women is completely forbidden, but Saudi Arabia has one of the highest rates of sexual harassment and rape in the world. Alcohol is forbidden, but many Saudis get drunk in secret. The law does not apply to the princes, who can do whatever they like safe in the knowledge that they will escape punishment. There, an Egyptian learns that performing the prayers at their correct times is not voluntary, like in Egypt, but a compulsory duty and that missing prayers is a punishable offence. They learn that if a woman's hair is showing, despite her best efforts, the police have a duty to arrest her and beat her until she covers herself properly.

Yet despite this strictness in personal appearance and acts of worship, Egyptians often find that their Gulf sponsors act reprehensibly and steal from them. If an Egyptian brings a formal complaint to court, the judiciary will always favour locals over a migrant and they will rarely get their money back. Here we have the origin of this social phenomenon: the discrepancy between religious belief and personal conduct is a social disease that has travelled to us from the oil-rich countries and spread like the plague.

Unfortunately it has also spread to political Islamist groups. When the revolution began, most of those belonging to the political Islamic movement did not take part. The Muslim Brotherhood announced that they would not be involved in the demonstrations, but they did join the revolutionaries after the police withdrew (and to be fair, young men from the Brotherhood played an admirable role in defending the demonstrators during the Battle of the Camel). As for the Salafists (and they are more numerous than the Brotherhood), they took a very clear stand against the revolution. Their sheikhs in Egypt and Saudi Arabia issued religious decrees saying that the demonstrations were forbidden and that Muslims must obey a Muslim ruler (even if he is wicked). They stated that democracy was also forbidden, because it advocates government by the people, while they believe that God alone can rule. But when the revolution succeeded in deposing Hosni Mubarak, the Salafists suddenly changed their mind and started forming political parties and participating in the democracy that only a few days earlier had been forbidden. The Brotherhood and the Salafists promised to support the military council as long as it allowed them to win a majority in parliament. The military council successfully put in place regulations for the elections to the advantage of the Brotherhood and the Salafists while the Supreme Presidential Election Committee turned a blind eye to any vote rigging or foul play.

Again, these strict Muslims, who are angered by missed prayer and unveiled women, see no wrong in exploiting voters' poverty and buying their votes with cooking oil, sugar and meat. The Brotherhood and the Salafists got their majority in the People's Assembly through elections that – while they may not have been rigged – were certainly not fair. Despite reservations about the elections, the Egyptian people supported the parliament because it is the only elected body able to protect the revolution and uphold its aims. However, day after day we find that parliament is incapable of confronting the military council and demanding change. The representatives ignored the military council's participation in the numerous massacres in which hundreds of people lost their lives and many thousands were injured. It has so far done nothing to bring those responsible to account.

The People's Assembly has turned into a speaker's corner, a talking shop that does not lead to any useful or influential decisions. We have seen how representatives cause trouble and attack the minister of supply because they consider him an easy target. They are not prepared to say a word against the military council because it has the power to dismiss them. The discrepancy between outward religiosity and the essence of religious teaching is seen in parliament; its members have done nothing to defend justice and have preoccupied themselves with inconsequential matters. Some members refused to swear the constitutional oath unless the words "the law of God" were incorporated. Meanwhile, as the police were hunting down demonstrators in the streets and using live ammunition, a respected member of the People's Assembly made the call to prayer during a session of parliament, resulting in a lengthy debate about whether or not it was acceptable to do so under the dome of the parliament building. Another strange discussion arose when a representative, speaking metaphorically, said that: "this government are hardly angels." This provoked consternation amongst the representatives because in their opinion the word "angel" is not allowed to be used in any analogy.

The military council, after successfully forming an obedient, conciliatory parliament, is now ready to implement the next step in its plan to control the government. It is looking to the Brotherhood and the Salafists for a consensus president who would be under its complete control. To this end, the military coucil has issued by decree an election law that requires the formation of a supreme commission whose decisions cannot be revoked in any way. So, citizen, what if you saw electoral fraud with your own eyes in your area and you were able to take photographic evidence of it? If you presented this evidence to the SPEC and they said that there had been no electoral fraud, you would never be able to appeal because the commission's word is final, irreversible and cannot be contested. The strange legal immunity enjoyed by the SPEC removes Egyptians' basic, natural right to lodge a complaint or appeal against administrative decisions. Meanwhile, those religiously committed brothers from amongst the members of parliament do not find anything in all of this that merits protest. In fact, they have supported the military council in setting the stage for tightening its control over the government of Egypt.

True religion impels us to defend the humanitarian values of truth, justice and freedom. This is the essence of religion, and it is far more important than growing a beard or making the call to prayer under the dome of the parliament building.

Democracy is the answer.

PN

A Secret Report on a Consensus Candidate

27 February 2012

Top Secret (not to be opened except by the director of the organisation)

Dear General,

Following our meeting with the consensus presidential candidate, held in the presence of your Excellency and my fellow officers in the organisation – where you confirmed that Mr (...) will be the candidate whom we must support in the presidential elections – please find below a number of suggestions regarding this matter. I hope that they meet with your approval.

Before we begin to support the consensus candidate, we must be sure of his complete loyalty to us and that we will have total control over him now and in the future. General, Egypt is in a delicate situation and this means that we must be fully on our guard. This candidate whom we are now to make a president of Egypt must do all that we ask of him, especially in the key issues that will influence the nation's future. We must not allow the next president of Egypt to turn against us and surrender to troublemakers and anarchists. Before the election campaign gets underway, I suggest ensuring we have full control over the candidate by two means, both the political and the personal. In regards to the political, we must think of some legal means to invalidate the presidential elections which we would not make public now but which could be employed at any time we wanted to bring them to a stop. As for the personal side, you will find attached to this letter a detailed report on the candidate and a complete list of his relationships with women, his habits and the places he frequents. We have CDs, videos and pictures of his private life that would cause scandal and ruin his reputation at any moment. I await your instructions on this matter.

In order to achieve the desired result in the elections, we must continue to exert pressure on the Egyptian people. We will continue to employ the usual means – rising prices to exacerbate food crises, shortages of petrol, cooking gas and subsidised bread – but at the same time we will send convicts to attack the most vulnerable citizens living in poverty. We must spread chaos everywhere. Egyptians must understand that their so-called "revolution" is nothing but a catastrophe that breeds anarchy (just as His Excellency, President Mubarak, predicted in his last speech). We must send in our agents to escalate sectarian clashes and instigate workers' strikes in all state institutions. We must pay them to mobilise demonstrators to block the highways and stop the movement of trains. Last week, we paid groups of thugs to board West Delta Company buses, start arguments with the drivers and beat them up. The attacks on the drivers went on for a number of consecutive days until the drivers announced that they were going on strike, shutting down all their routes.

The security breakdowns must increase and become more widespread and more dangerous (here I commend the attack on two members of the despicable committee that recommended that His Excellency, President Mubarak, be transferred to a prison hospital). My officers will coordinate with businessmen to make funding arrangements and the activities of the thugs will increase over the coming period. Armed robberies and night-time shootings must continue and bank raids should be carried out during daylight hours to further exasperate the situation and convince citizens of the absence of security.

The bank robberies fulfil two important objectives: they scare citizens but also make them fear for their savings, leading them to withdraw their funds and thus contribute to the economic crisis. At the same time, the gangs of armed thugs must continue to attack citizens and seize their cars on the highways (such as the Cairo ring road and Wady Natrun Road). Convicts must be sent to attack schools and nurseries so that panic spreads amongst parents. The gangs of thugs must keep up their daily raids on hospitals and attack doctors and nurses. I suggest that the attacks be carefully calculated to spread panic without killing any patients if at all possible, because this may push citizens to fight back.

Meanwhile, media outlets must portray these crises in a way that exaggerates their connection with the events of 25 January. They must focus on how anarchy prevails and that Egypt is on the verge of bankruptcy so that citizens come to hate the January 25 revolution and blame it for all of their misfortunes. The aim here is to push the Egyptian people to their limits so that they are ready to accept anything that will restore order, and will consequently vote for the candidate we put forward. At the same time, they will overlook any irregularities in the electoral process because they want stability at any price.

As regards to state media, we have re-established control over the cooperative elements and have mobilised new journalists, presenters and producers. We have put pressure on privately owned channels and threatened to open cases into their financial irregularities unless they get rid of any troublemaking media figures. There was only one television channel that did not respond to our pressure but a gang of thugs was sent to attack them as a preliminary measure, until we arrive at a permanent solution and are able to have it shut down. A vast media campaign has been organised that will portray the presidential elections as a great historical and national triumph for the Egyptian people. Furthermore, anyone who raises doubts about the integrity of the elections will then seem like a traitor who has been hired to spoil the celebration for national democracy.

Those who incite disorder now are the same people who led the events of 25 January. They are known by name and belong to various political currents: liberals, Islamists, revolutionary socialists and independent public figures. These troublemakers must be subjected to a comprehensive campaign by all media outlets until it is rooted in people's minds that they are agents funded from abroad. At the same time, they must be worn down with constant complaints presented by respectable citizens to the attorney general accusing them of sedition, causing chaos, disturbing social harmony, provoking hatred of law and order and receiving funding from foreign organisations. These investigations must all receive heavy media coverage. Last week, we put together a video of a young female activist sipping beer, which successfully destroyed her credibility amongst family and peers. In another operation, some thugs were paid to attack one of the leaders of the troublemakers as he was addressing a popular conference in Imbaba.[1] The video was then distributed as proof that these people had risen up against him because he was an agent and a hired man.

As your Excellency knows, the Islamist movement is not one single body but is composed of different strands. It would therefore be impossible to control it. What is more, amongst the Islamists there are few who are being cooperative with us. In fact, the largest faction supports the "revolution" and have a close relationship with the anarchists from non-Islamist movements. Over the past year, Islamist youths have gone against the instructions of their sheikhs and joined in the demonstrations with the anarchists. Therefore, General, the announcement your Excellency made in the meeting that an agreement had been reached with a well-known Islamist group to support our candidate, made me most happy. They are very well organised, and their members swear loyalty to their president. They have vast experience, precise organisation and are using effective methods to win in the elections from distributing oil, sugar and meat to the poor for free, to influencing voters both inside and outside the polling stations. They have followers in every constituency that we would be able to appoint as supervisors of the polling stations, as we did in the elections for the People's Assembly. Through our alliance with this group, we will guarantee a large voting bloc for our candidate.

We must also put forward some obscure candidates that people have never heard of before. This will give the impression that the elections are a real competition and not a sham. As the number of obscure presidential candidates increases, people will cling ever more closely to our candidate. In the midst of anarchy, breakdowns in security and successive crises, the Egyptian people cannot possibly choose an unknown person to be president of the republic. Instead, they will certainly place their trust in our candidate, who has held senior government posts for many years.

Our candidate must use a strong religious message to strengthen his image as a committed Muslim (as you know, this couldn't be further from the truth). Our candidate must announce that he will enforce Islamic law as soon as he gets into power. He must also demand the immediate prohibition of alcohol, and the banning of women from wearing bathing suits and bikinis. This message will be useful, because it will draw in simple-minded voters, especially in the countryside and in the poorer areas. We have made good contacts with a large number of mosque preachers and we will give them clear instructions on how to support our candidate. In their Friday sermons, they must get the message across that our candidate is a statesman and the only one able to apply Islamic law and rid Egypt from the effects of secularism, liberalism and atheism.

1 This leader was Hamdeen Sabahi, leader of the Egyptian Popular Current and a co-leader of the National Salvation Front. The rally was to mobilise support for larger anti-Morsi protests planned for June 30, which called for early presidential elections.

The election publicity campaign will be based on a number of questions directed to people: "Are you a Muslim? Do you want to see Islam victorious over infidel secularism? Then you must vote for the consensus candidate." Meanwhile, a contrary image must be created for the rival candidates. We must portray them as agents of the Church who get their funding from the United States and whose aim is to strip Egypt of its Islamic component, turn it into a secular country and ban minarets, as happened in Switzerland. The simple-minded must think that the rival candidates want to spread decadence and allow gay marriage. As for the rival Islamist candidates, we must portray them as terrorists and extremists who are unable to take on the responsibility of the presidency. If they enjoy popularity, we must deal them a decisive blow (I note here that the operation to beat up candidate Abdel Moneim Aboul Fotouh was a model of careful planning and successful execution).

The traditional means to change the results of the elections can still be used if necessary. In the attachment to this report is a list of ways to change the results (either during the sorting or counting of the votes- the "round-robin voting form",[1] multiple national ID numbers for each voter, and so on). These methods, if they are discovered, will not lead to the elections being cancelled since the decisions of the Supreme Presidential Election Commission that monitors the elections are final, and cannot be revoked or even disputed.

General, these are the suggestions for the support of the consensus candidate. I await your instructions.

Yours Sincerely,

Lieutenant Colonel (...)

Democracy is the answer.

PN

When Will They Stop Insulting Us?

5 March 2012

A few weeks ago, the German president, Christian Wulff, was forced to resign after being caught up in a corruption scandal involving a dubious loan that

1 In Arabic simply "round card", this is a clever way to commit electoral fraud. A middleman for the candidate enters the polling station and instead of using his voting form he hides it in his clothes and passes it to the candidate's team. The candidate's team then marks their candidate's box on the voting form and gives it to someone they have bribed to sell their vote. This person then enters the polling booth, takes a new voting form but puts the old voting form given to them by the candidate's team in the ballot box. They then leave the polling station and give the new voting form back to the candidate's team, who mark it.

exposed his long-suspected improper ties to business executives. Similarly, the former secretary of state for energy and climate change in Britain, Chris Huhne, was caught speeding and later resigned after he was charged with attempting to pervert the course of justice by persuading his former wife to take his driving licence penalty points. The public considered Huhne's behaviour inacceptable and immoral, and he was forced to step down as a member of parliament.

Such incidents happen all the time in democratic countries, because state officials are expected to be honest and trustworthy; if an official is involved in any illegal activity, they are immediately removed from their position. I remembered these events as I was following the so-called foreign funding case, which is still pending before the Egyptian courts.[1] The military council accused a number of international civil society organisations of receiving illegal foreign funding. The military crackdown on charitable organisations was unusual because the two sides had worked together closely for more than a year before the accusations surfaced. Even stranger that these organisations all requested more than once to be legalised and the military council stalled in giving them licences.

I do not agree with foreign funding in principle, and I hope that legislation is passed to ban it outright. However, it is odd that the military council's anger should be directed solely at civil society organisations and not religious organisations and political parties that, according to government reports, have received hundreds of millions of dollars from Gulf countries. The military council is exhibiting its usual double standards by exempting the Brotherhood and the Salafists from any accountability, while launching a sweeping campaign against civil society organisations, accusing their staff of spreading chaos and planning to overthrow the state.

The trial turned into a big media show during which the military council tried to portray itself as a tough, national authority that would never succumb to Western pressure. Then the scandal broke: the court judges abandoned the trial in protest of the pressures exerted by Judge Abdul Moiz[2] (under instruction from the military council) to lift the travel ban on the foreign suspects. At this point, Abdul Moiz rushed to transfer the trial to another session, headed by a judge (an ex-state security officer) who agreed to lift the ban. Then, an American military aircraft actually landed at Cairo airport and took them away, in violation of the most basic legal principles.

The Egyptian people felt humiliated by this case; they saw their national sovereignty and the laws of their country openly flouted – the same humiliation

1 An Egyptian court sentenced several dozen workers from international civil society organisations to jail in a case that has infuriated the US government and democratic activists around the world. The workers were accused of accepting illegal foreign funding but denied any wrongdoing. The judge in the case also ordered the permanent closure of all the organisations involved.

2 The head of the Cairo Appeals Court.

they felt when they saw Egyptian women dragged through the streets and indecently assaulted, when they saw young men crushed by tanks, blinded and killed by Egyptian soldiers. The comparison between the US government, which is determined to defend its citizens even when they are facing trial, and the military council that disregards the dignity of Egyptians again and again, begs the following question: why do Western governments uphold the rights of their citizens, whereas the authorities in Egypt care nothing for theirs? The answer to this, in my opinion, is down to three factors:

First: The nature of government. The way a ruler comes to power defines their behaviour while they are in office. A president who comes to power in free elections will always be subject to the will of the people and their scrutiny. They cannot rule tyrannically or disregard people's rights. The military council rules Egypt in the same way as Mubarak: it holds power only because it possesses the strength necessary to maintain it. Therefore, it is only natural that the military council does not acknowledge the rights of ordinary citizens, because the Egyptian people neither chose the military council nor do they have the power to get rid of it if they wanted to. The military council, like any tyrant, is not accountable to the people. This disregard and contempt for the people usually spreads from the tyrant to their ministers because they know that no one will hold them accountable or force them to resign. Instead, they flatter and kowtow to the ruler because they know that they are untouchable as long as the ruler is satisfied with them.

Second: The extent to which the judiciary is independent. In democratic countries, the judiciary is completely independent and nobody, not even the head of state, can interfere in its decisions. The most senior official knows that any minor representative from the attorney general's office can bring a charge against them. Legal prosecution is feared by officials and they take care to respect the law. In contrast, the judicial system in Egypt is not independent, and its work is subject to the authority of the head of state because the Judicial Inspection Department, which oversees judges' rewards and penalties, is subordinate to the minister of justice, who is in turn appointed by the president of the republic (or the military council).

In the end, the minister of justice fully controls the judges' fate. In addition, the president of the republic appoints the attorney general, who holds the power to launch investigations and make charges. Then there's the system of "internal secondments", whereby certain judges are permitted to work as consultants in specific ministries for huge bonuses, at the same time as they are judging cases, which fundamentally undermines the principle of judicial neutrality. Even though the judicial system is far from being independent, the majority of Egyptian judges are free to exercise their conscience. However, by doing so they often pay a high price in terms of income and peace of mind.

The momentous stand against the military council made by the Cairo Criminal Court, headed by Judge Mohamed Mahmoud Shukri, is just one noble example of what thousands of judges have been doing throughout Egypt. In 2005, more than two thirds of Egyptian judges fought a momentous battle to secure the independence of the judiciary. History will remember that these noble judges refused to be false witnesses to rigged elections. They are still struggling, not for distinction or rewards but in defence of justice. Nevertheless, a small number of judges were involved in cooperating with the despotic regime as has been proven by the Court of Cassation.

In the wake of the revolution, many people called for the judiciary to be purged of the judges who supervised the rigged elections, but the military council retained them because it needs their services. In fact, the Supreme Judicial Council prepared a law integrating the realisation of complete judicial independence, but the military council suspended this law because it would deprive them of control of the judiciary. We cannot give Egypt back its dignity and its rights without an independent judiciary.

Third: The prevalent understanding of religion. In democratic countries, officials do not discuss their religion or their religious practices because the only criterion for judging people is by their morals. It is your right to embrace any religion, whether it be Christian, Muslim or Jewish. Freedom of belief and religious practice is guaranteed for all citizens. Your religion is your own private affair whereas your performance at work and how you treat others, are the true criteria for which you are judged by other people and before the law. If the head of state is caught lying, they will be stripped of their position because they no longer deserve the trust of the people. In a democratic country, morals are the way to gauge religiosity and showing outward signs that you are religious is not an indication of good morals. The same concept forms the essence of true Islam.

Justice, freedom and equality are the fundamental principles of Islam and everything else is considered secondary. However, many people's understanding of Islam has become nominal and limited, particularly in parliament. We see now that the concept of religiosity amongst many members of parliament is superficial as there is a disconnect between religious faith and personal conduct. Certain individuals are trying to pass a resolution requiring schools to suspend lessons to hold the noon prayer, yet they do nothing to avenge the deaths of dozens of young Egyptians who died at the hands of the military council. These individuals are cowards; they are too scared to utter a bad word about the military council. They have long beards and prayer marks on their foreheads, but they do not hesitate to adopt hypocritical policies to satisfy the military council. When Representative

Ziad el-Eleimy[1] slipped up and said something that insulted Field Marshal Tantawi, these pious representatives rose up to punish el-Eleimy even though he made this remark outside parliament. However, when a representative inside parliament directs outrageous accusations against senior national figures such as Mohamed ElBaradei, they refuse to reprimand them and instead applaud and congratulate them.

They applaud someone who accuses ElBaradei of treason, even though the Brotherhood gathered 600,000 signatures in support of his programme of democratic reform in Egypt. That happened before the revolution, when the Brotherhood needed ElBaradei's backing. Now they need the backing of the military council. Their positions always change according to their interests and this political changeability is immoral. This political inconsistency is incompatible with morality, and everything that is incompatible with morality is of necessity incompatible with religion. History teaches us that if we limit religion to its outer form and practices, we may go on to commit immoral actions with a completely clear conscience. Egypt will not change unless our understanding of religion changes first.

As much as it was an insult to our national dignity, the scandal over the sudden departure of the defendants in the foreign funding case made us face up to an important fact: Hosni Mubarak has fallen but the system he set up is still governing Egypt. The military council is a continuation of Mubarak in both its mentality and its actions; it insults Egyptians just as Mubarak used to insult them. It will not stop insulting us unless we fulfil the goals of the revolution and found a just and free nation.

Democracy is the answer.

PN

Awaiting Military Trial

12 March 2012

If you have a daughter, presumably you love her and worry for her safety, and could not bear to see any harm come to her. You would not allow anybody to touch her inappropriately or attack her, and you would be prepared to defend her with your life. Your daughter is a part of you and you live to protect her. How would you feel if your young daughter took part in a peaceful

1 Ziad el-Eleimy was a founding member of the Egyptian Social Democratic Party. El-Eleimy's statements about the military council caused a row among MPs after he referenced a famous Egyptian proverb in which Tantawi was allegedly characterised as a donkey, which is considered an insult in Egypt.

demonstration and was taken away by soldiers who beat her and subjected her to a barrage of vile abuse? How would you feel if your young daughter was completely stripped of her clothes and made to stand naked in front of a group of soldiers, who became aroused as they stared at her body? How would you feel if you found out that the female jailer in the military prison had said to your daughter: "Lie down on the bed, so that this gentleman can check whether or not you are still a virgin." How would you feel if your daughter was forced to lie down and be examined by a so-called doctor who left the doors and windows open so that everybody could watch.

British soldiers committed no such crimes against Egyptian women during the decades of occupation, neither did Egyptian soldiers do the same to Israel women they captured during the war. These crimes, I am sorry to say, were committed by Egyptians against fellow Egyptians. On 9 March 2011, dozens of demonstrators were arrested in Tahrir Square by military police and then brutally tortured. Afterwards, 17 Egyptian women were sent to a military prison, where they were beaten and given electric shocks. They were stripped of all their clothes in front of the soldiers and then forced to undergo virginity tests, which constitute an indecent assault and an obscene violation of the most basic humanitarian principles, as well as legal and military practices. Those soldiers who indecently assaulted our daughters and sisters were supposed to be protecting and keeping them safe.

The real aim of the virginity tests was to break the spirit of the demonstrators and humiliate them. After the crime had been committed, the women were threatened by the security service to keep silent and unfortunately all of them were too frightened to speak out, except for one brave woman called Samira Ibrahim, who decided to take on the criminals who had indecently assaulted her. When news spread and the virginity tests turned into a huge public scandal, the military council at first denied their involvement. They later issued a statement to acknowledge the tests, but continued to threaten and put pressure on Samira Ibrahim to retract her testimony. Ibrahim became more determined to demand justice and even managed to persuade other victims to come forward.

The problem is that the military council has the same tools as Mubarak at its disposal and has complete control over state institutions. The virginity test case was heard before a military court, which is not considered independent because the military judge must answer to his superiors and Field Marshal Tantawi has the right to reject the verdict of any case as he so wishes. This week, the military court acquitted the officer charged with indecently assaulting Egyptian women in the virginity tests case. This verdict means that injustice still reigns in our country. The Mubarak regime is still in control and the law is still applied according to who you are, your social class and your political opinions.

When Samira Ibrahim entered the military prison, she was shocked to find a large picture of the deposed President Mubarak hanging on the wall. Samira asked the officer: "Why do you keep a picture of Mubarak?"

The officer let out a stream of curses, then said: "Hosni Mubarak is still our president and we love him."

The military council is a product of the Mubarak regime in word and deed, and has succeeded in turning the revolution into a coup d'état. The revolution considered the removal of Mubarak the first step towards overthrowing his regime and building a new system of government. The military council, on the other hand, considered the removal of Mubarak an unavoidable step to save his regime. The military council is responsible for all the artificial crises that have turned ordinary Egyptians against the revolution. It is the driving force behind the breakdowns in security, the rising prices, the economic crisis and all the massacres that were committed against Egyptians at Maspero Square, Mohamed Mahmoud Street, the Council of Ministers and Port Said. It is also primarily responsible for the virginity tests, for those demonstrators who were blinded, shot, poisoned with gas or crushed with tanks, and for the daughters of Egypt who were indecently assaulted and dragged through the streets. This is the truth and we can never be silent until all those who killed Egyptians and dishonoured women are brought to justice, and the criminals receive their just reward.

Whenever we criticise the military council, we must make it clear that our criticism is not levelled at the armed forces as a national institution, of which we can all be proud. The Egyptian army does not belong to the military council, but to the people of Egypt. During the transitional period, the military council assumed the function of head of state and, as this is a political power, it is natural that we should scrutinise its performance. It is our right, nay our duty to correct its faults and express our opinions however harsh they may be as long as our aims are in the national interest.

The military council is much like its deposed high commander, Hosni Mubarak, and cannot bear criticism. It ignores those who speak the truth, preferring instead to listen to the sycophants and flatterers, and it considers itself beyond reproach. According to the military council, justice is shooting Egyptian citizens with live ammunition and indecently assaulting women without being held to account. If we say that the military council is politically responsible for all these crimes, its leaders get angry and accuse us of being provocateurs intent on toppling the state. This is the same logic as Mubarak, who considered any criticism of his policies to be an attack on Egypt as a whole and that his opponents were nothing but a small band of reviled hirelings.

The military council has done everything it can to abort any real change in Egypt. It wants to control the government even if it is not in charge of it directly. In Egypt we now have an elected House of Representatives, a prime minister, and many government ministers, but none of them have any real power. All they can do is talk, hold meetings and issue statements but it is the military council that have the final say.

In continuation of this same policy, the military council set up the Supreme Presidential Electoral Commission (SPEC), all of whose decisions have been made irrevocable and cannot be overturned or disputed. According to a statement issued by the campaign team for the presidential candidate Abdel Moneim Aboul Fotouh, there have already been signs of fraud in the elections for the presidency. Employees of the registry office have been writing recommendations forms for a certain candidate and failing to write them for the other candidates. When people went to register an official report of these irregularities, the police officer refused and told them to go to the SPEC.

In recent days, a number of fabricated cases have been rolled out against the opponents of the military council including: Mamdouh Hamza, Abu Al-Izz al-Hariri, Ziad al-Eleimy, Wael Ghoneim, Nawar Nigm, Asmaa Mahfouz, George Isaac, Buthaina Kamel, Yosri Fouda, Reem Maged and Sameh Naguib, as well as myelf.

I am honoured to be amongst these names because they represent the most noble and most honourable public figures in Egypt. This trial was clearly fabricated in order to imtimidate and provoke the revolutionary forces. According to the military council, 700 "decent citizens" presented complaints to the attorney general against me and my co-defendants. Of course, they made exactly the same accusations as Hosni Mubarak used for so long to get rid of his opponents: making confusion, disturbing social order, defaming the leadership of the armed forces, working to bring down the state, causing instability, and so on. All of these are fake, baseless charges with no legal basis.

The attorney general announced in a statement that the complaints had been referred to the military courts because this matter came under their jurisdiction. Is it permissible to accept complaints from persons who have nothing to do with the subject of the complaint? Could I submit a complaint in which I accuse one person of insulting another person when I know neither of them? And how could 700 citizens bring forward complaints to the attorney general at the same time? Did the attorney general's office listen to the statements of 700 people, and if so how much time did this take? And if it was not the attorney general who had listened to them, is it permissible to accept their complaints without first making sure of their identities and listening to their statements?

The attorney general is endorsing a strange practice that is against the law and makes it easy for anyone to send in a frivolous complaint by mail and have it accepted. Furthermore, why did the attorney general quickly refer these complaints to the military courts before listening to our statements? We are not soldiers so why are we being judged before a military court? Where is the military aspect in this bizarre trial?

We may have criticised the military council as a political power, but we never talked about military matters. The trial is void from beginning to end, but the military council wants to punish us because we dared to criticise its policies. The head of the military courts announced that he was in the process of studying the complaints brought against us to see what steps he would take. This statement is a clear threat. The head of the military courts is trying to tell us: "If you stop criticising the military council we will leave you in peace. Otherwise, I will bring you to military trial and you could end up in military prison." We reject this threat. We are not afraid of a trial because we are in the right and the military council is in the wrong. If stating one's opinion is now a crime in the eyes of the military council, then we insist on committing this crime. We will continue to speak the truth forever more.

The military council as a political power is responsible for mistakes and shortcomings that have claimed the lives of more than 300 people and left thousands wounded, not to mention the women who were dragged through the streets and indecently assaulted. The military council must understand that as a political power it is neither infallible nor above accountability. We await an official summons from the military courts. We are not scared and we will never refrain from speaking the truth whatever price we pay.

Democracy is the answer.

PN

Who Will Welcome Pope Shenouda?

19 March 2012

This place is impossible to describe because it is not like any other and defies imagination. Roughly speaking, it is a vast garden filled with large fruit-laden trees and beautiful flowers that sway in a light, refreshing breeze. The garden has a circular door adorned with roses and in front of it stands a handsome bearded man, wearing a cloak of pure white, whose face radiates a curious light. All around the garden, thousands of people are gathered displaying signs of happiness and joy. From time to time, the man goes to the door to welcome the new arrivals. Yesterday, the man rose to welcome Pope Shenouda[1], who approached him with brisk, upright steps. The wrinkles had disappeared completely from the pope's face, his back had become straight, he was free from aches and pains and his hair was completely black as if he was in his twenties again. The man bowed and said: "Welcome, Your Holiness. We are honoured."

The pope looked at him in amazement and said: "Hello, my son. What is your name?"

"I am the guardian angel."

"How did you know I was coming?"

"I know everything about my guests, because I am charged with welcoming them. Follow me, if you please."

The guardian angel went ahead, followed by Pope Shenouda. They walked down a vista of trees, flanked by rows of colourful flowers. At the end of the vista, the pope was surprised to see four people standing, smiling and waving as if they had been expecting his arrival. He noticed that one of the people standing was a turbaned sheikh wearing a kaftan. The pope waved to them warmly. The movement of his hand had become stronger, and he felt as if he had regained his old vigour. The guardian angel stood between the pope and the well-wishers and said in a cheerful voice: "All our Egyptian guests wanted to have the honour of welcoming you, but we have chosen these four friends as representatives for them."

The sheikh stepped forward and shook hands with the pope, saying: "Peace be upon you, Your Holiness. I am the martyr Emad Effat, a sheikh of Al-Azhar. They shot me dead during a sit-in at the Council of Ministers." The smile of the pope grew wider as he enthusiastically shook his hand.

Next, a young man came forward and said: "We are honoured, Your Holiness. I am the martyr Alaa Abdel-Hady, a medical student at Ain Shams University. They shot and killed me at the Council of Ministers a few days before I was due to graduate."

Alaa took two steps back and the third young man came forward, bowed and kissed the hand of the pope then said: "I am the martyr Mina Daniel. They killed me in the Maspero Square massacre."

The pope made the sign of the cross, then the fourth young man presented himself saying: "Your Grace, I was crushed by a tank in Maspero Square. My name is Michael Mosad."

Once again, the pope made the sign of the cross and his face showed signs of anguish and despair. "I am happy to be in your company. You have learned that martyrs stay with their Lord and never die."

---

1 Pope Shenouda III was the 117th Pope of Alexandria and Patriarch of the See of St. Mark. His episcopate lasted 40 years, four months, and 4 days from 14 November 1971 until his death on 17 March 2012.

The guardian angel made a sign to the martyrs, who sat down on a sofa while the pope sat next to the guardian angel on a sofa opposite. Sheikh Emad smiled and said: "We Muslims believe that martyrs do not die, but are alive with their Lord."

The guardian angel smiled and said: "Here, the martyrs live in tranquillity, praise be to God. But I often ask myself why such a large number of Egyptian martyrs are coming up to us, despite the fact that Egypt has not gone to war for 40 years."

"You should direct this question to Hosni Mubarak and the military council", said Michael Mosad.

The whole party laughed, then Sheikh Emad said: "Do you know, Your Holiness, that all Egyptians, whether Muslim or Coptic, grieved when you died. I saw Saint Mark's Cathedral this evening and it was a truly moving scene."

"Do you watch television here?" replied the pope, visibly surprised.

The guardian angel laughed and said: "Our guests here have no need for television. They have only to think of any one thing and their minds will visualise it clearly. If you think of the cathedral now, you will see it in your mind."

The pope closed his eyes and thought of the cathedral. He saw tens of thousands of Egyptians who had come to take one last look at his body. Smiling, he opened his eyes and said: "May God bless them all. Egypt has always been one country and one people."

"Your Holiness", said Alaa enthusiastically, "we offer many praises to God for the tranquillity in which we live, but we follow what is happening in Egypt and feel sad that the revolution for which we gave our lives has been aborted."

Sheikh Emad nodded his head in agreement, sighed and said: "Almost two months have passed since the elections for the People's Assembly. It's clear that its members are incapable of doing anything without the approval of the military council. If this situation continues, the People's Assembly will be like Mubarak's parliament, a mere talking shop, a means to anesthetise public opinion and a tool in the hands of a tyrannical power."

"What do you expect from the People's Assembly, when the speaker moves around in an armoured BMW while half the population live under the poverty line in slums?" said Alaa sarcastically.

Pope Shenouda continued to listen to them but did not speak.

"If you allow me, Your Grace," said Mina Daniel, cutting in, "from your actions we have learned honesty and bravery. Would you allow one of your sons to ask you a difficult question?"

Sheikh Emad and Alaa got up to leave but the pope urged them to stay, saying: "You are both Muslims, but I am your father as I am their father. I have nothing to hide from you. Speak, Mina, I am listening."

"I have died, and many young men died with me and were injured in the Maspero massacre." said Mina. "Afterwards, I was shocked to see members of the military council – the ones responsible for the massacre – coming to the church to offer their condolences. Your Grace, why did you welcome them?"

"Mina, my child," said Pope Shenouda, "the church is open to everyone, because it is the house of our Lord. Also, didn't the Messiah teach us love and tolerance?"

"But Your Grace," said Mina, "the military council bears primary political responsibility for happenings during the transitional period. More than 300 people have died in successive massacres: Maspero, Mohamed Mahmoud Street, Council of Ministers and Port Said. Why doesn't the Church take a clear stand and demand that the military council bring the ones responsible for these massacres to trial?"

The pope remained silent, as if choosing his words carefully, then said slowly: "Mina, my child, when I was your age I was as passionate as you, if not more so. But as I got older, I learned the danger of making any decision when one is angry. Do you think I did not grieve for my children who died in all these massacres? Do you suppose I wasn't angry when I saw Egypt's daughters dragged through the streets by Egyptian soldiers? I swear by the Messiah that the scene of the woman being beaten and abused by soldiers is still vivid in my mind."

"But Your Grace, you did not speak out demanding the punishment of those responsible for these crimes."

"Sometimes, silence speaks louder than words."

"Promise you will not be angry with me, Your Grace."

"Speak, Mina."

"Your Grace, why were you always praising and speaking well of the deposed Mubarak when he was unjust and corrupt? Why did you always exalt his son, Gamal Mubarak, who wanted to inherit Egypt as if it was his father's estate?"

The tension mounted, and the guardian angel smiled and said, "I think it would be best to leave His Holiness to rest."

The pope raised his hand in protest. "I am not tired. Listen, Mina. You are responsible only for yourself. You chose the revolution and paid for it with your life to become a martyr, but my decisions do not concern only myself. Every position I adopt will affect millions of Copts and Muslims, and all of Egypt. Often I am obliged to adopt positions that you might not like, but it is necessary and there is no escaping it."

"Your Grace, am I to understand from this that you support the revolution?" interrupted Mina.

"Of course, my child. When the people demand freedom and justice, the

Church must support them."

The group became silent. Then the pope laughed and said: "Speak, Mina. I can see another question burning inside you. You want to ask me why I did not announce my support of the revolution from the beginning. The answer is as I told you before, I must consider every word I say with care. Do you think I am oblivious to the fact that thousands of Copts participated in the revolution? Do you think I did not know about the dozens of priests who joined the revolution and held mass in all the squares of Egypt? I knew and I was praying for you all."

"Permit me, Your Holiness," said Dr Alaa, "the Brotherhood allied itself with the military council and created a false, impotent People's Assembly. Now, in violation of the constitutional declaration, they control half of the Constituent Assembly and will make a constitution to suit the Brotherhood and the military council. After this, they will install a president who obeys the military council. I was hoping Your Holiness could speak honestly about all of this."

"It's too late." said Pope Shenouda, laughing. "If I spoke now, nobody down there would hear me."

They all laughed. "I was hoping," said the pope, more seriously, "that the revolution would give Egyptians back their dignity and keep their lives safe. But I found that just as many martyrs were falling after the revolution as they fell before it. I urge you to be optimistic, and do not submit to defeat. Those who died did not die in vain. The revolution will be victorious and will hold the ones responsible for all these crimes to account. History teaches us that revolutions are never defeated. They may be hindered, they may lose the way, but they will certainly be victorious in the end."

The group fell silent, then Mina said, with some embarrassment: "Forgive us, Your Grace, if we overstepped the mark."

The pope smiled and said quietly: "I could never be angry with you. God knows how much I love all of you. I thank our Lord that I will remain here with you. Someday, I shall remind you of this debate. Soon, from up here we will see Egypt begin the great future it deserves."

The four martyrs rose to greet the pope once more. Alaa and Sheikh Emad shook his hand, while Mina and Michael bowed and kissed his hand.

"Your Holiness, your words have put our minds at rest. Many thanks," said Sheikh Emad.

The martyrs turned to leave but Pope Shenouda remained behind, following them with his eyes, a contented look upon his face.

Democracy is the answer.

PN

You Can Have Your Constitution; We Will Have the Revolution

29 March 2012

Imagine that you want to build a house. You have the necessary finances, but you do not have the skills required to build the house yourself so you hire a builder to do the work on your behalf. As building a house is a specialist operation, it must be carried out in compliance with safe construction practices and requires building materials with strict specifications. You must also contract a building surveyor to supervise and approve the work of the builder. The surveyor manages the building project and is the one who sets out the specifications for the building materials and makes sure the builder follows safe construction practices.

This is the correct way to build a house. But what if the builder told you that he didn't need a building inspector and that he would select all the building materials himself? What if the builder said to you: "What's the difference between me and the building surveyor? We are both builders. I will carry out the construction and supervise myself."

Of course, you would have to refuse this proposal because of the conflict of interest; it is in the builder's interest to use the cheapest materials and ignore faults in construction. The surveyor, on the other hand, is impartial and their job is to set the specifications and ensure that the construction process meets these same specifications.

A similar conflict of interest has arisen in Egypt regarding the writing of the constitution. The committee charged with this task is like the building surveyor, and the People's Assembly is like the builder. The builder cannot do the work of the surveyor and also supervise himself, just as the People's Assembly cannot write a constitution to suit its own interests. The constitution is the origin of all the laws that define the relationship between the state authorities, so it is completely unacceptable for one of these powers to interfere in the writing of it. The constitution establishes the powers of the People's Assembly, so it is inadmissible that the People's Assembly decide these powers for itself. This constitutional principle was agreed upon by the most senior scholars of constitutional law in Egypt. On 17 December 1994, the Supreme Constitutional Court of Egypt, headed by Judge Awad el-Murr, ruled that:

> The constitution creates the state institutions, namely the State Council[1] and the government, and dictates their responsibilities and the laws by

1 The State Council (Majlis al-Dawla) is a judicial body that gives legal advice to the government, drafts legislation, and exercises jurisdiction over administrative cases.

which they govern. Therefore, it is not permissible for a power that was created by the constitution to create a constitution.

So, it is not permissible for the People's Assembly – which was one of the bodies created by the constitution – to write a constitution. In order to circumvent the above logic, the Brotherhood and Salafist members of parliament have called for a specially selected committee to write the constitution for them. However, half of this committee belong to the People's Assembly and the Shura Council – and that means the Brotherhood and the Salafists – and the other half is comprised of people who belong to political Islam. For moderation, they added a few independents to act as extras or false witnesses to the crime of hijacking the Egyptian constitution. Will this biased, hand-tied committee be able to control or limit the powers of parliament when members of parliament hold an absolute majority within it? Could this committee revoke the rule that 50 per cent of People's Assembly members must be workers or farmers[1] when there are workers and farmers amongst its members? Could this committee dissolve the Shura Council when it has members who belong to the Shura Council? Could we imagine that the members of the People's Assembly would ever revoke their privileges and place limits on themselves while they are writing a constitution over whose writing committee they have complete control?

The Brotherhood and the Salafists say that they are elected by the people, so it is their right to write the constitution on the people's behalf. This is a great fallacy, because the duties of the People's Assembly are completely different from those of the Constituent Assembly. We elect a person to the Constituent Assembly either because they possess a wide knowledge of the law and constitutions, or because they belong to a religious minority or group whose opinion must be expressed in the constitution. But this same person may not be a suitable representative of the people. Conversely, we elect a representative to the People's Assembly based on their ability to communicate with the masses and also their political experience. But this same representative may not have what it takes to write the constitution. Whichever party holds the majority in the People's Assembly has the right to form a government and implement their policies. It never has the right to monopolise the writing of the constitution according to its own interests. It must be ensured that all Egyptians are involved in the constitution through representatives from every social group and every minority.

In fact, representing minorities in the constitution is far more important than representing the majority. If Egypt had one single Buddhist or Hindu citizen, it would be necessary to take him or her into consideration during the

1 The 50 per cent quota for workers and farmers in Egypt's Parliament was introduced by President Gamal Abdel Nasser in 1964.

writing of the constitution in order to guarantee that their rights as a citizen would be protected. The Brotherhood and the Salafists must refrain from tampering with the constitution and allow the Egyptian nation to represent itself in all its diversity so that we have a constitution able to found the modern democratic state for which hundreds of people sacrificed their lives during the revolution.

Here we must ask ourselves why the Brotherhood and the Salafists are ignoring the obvious truth, and cold-heartedly uprooting the principles of constitutional law. Have the Brotherhood and the Salafists suddenly all become cheats and liars? The answer is of course no. Like all political movements, political Islam – despite our idealogical disagreement with it – contains cherished national figures and some renowned individuals. So why do they ignore and distort the truth? The simple answer is because their motives are religious and not political or ideological. Their desire for power is driven by religious faith.

Here it is necessary to make the distinction between the religion of Islam and political Islam. Every Muslim is, by necessity, Islamic. If you are Muslim, you want to apply the teachings of Islam to all aspects of your life, as the religion of Islam requires. As for political Islam, it is a political project that uses Islam not as a religion but as a political strategy through which to gain power then to install a caliph to rule the whole Islamic world.

The idea of political Islam is out of place with modern Egyptian history because all Egyptian leaders, since Mohammed Ali in the nineteenth century to the present day, have been Muslims and have derived their great humanitarian principles from their faith. From Islam they learned truth, justice and freedom but never considered religion to be a political strategy. Mustafa el-Nahhas, leader of the Waft Party, was a strict Muslim who zealously carried out his religious duty. However, he drew a strict line between religion and politics to the extent that he once refused to read a party manifesto because it contained the word "God", saying to the party leader: "Whenever you write the word 'God' in party propaganda, you immediately turn into a fraud."

The followers of political Islam have a right to exercise their political freedom, but it is our duty to explain that using religion for political purposes will undoubtedly lead to bad practice.

Religion is an exclusivist belief, meaning that the followers of any religion believe that their religion is the only true religion. The Muslim considers that the religion of God is Islam, and that all other religions are spurious. Religion is not a point of view that can be discussed, but constitutes a doctrine that its followers are willing to defend with their lives. However well-educated and open-minded a person may be, as soon as someone questions their religion they will react violently and behave viciously in defence of their faith. This is the nature of religious belief and it is completely different to having a political opinion which is ultimately recognised as a human judgement that can always be criticised or changed.

Practicing politics with religious sentiments usually leads to intolerance and attempts to obtain power by any means without considering the needs or rights of others. It is difficult for the followers of political Islam to acknowledge the rights of their political opponents because they believe them to be opposed to religion itself, and therefore infidels, sinners or agents of the West and Zionism or – in the best case scenario – a sexual degenerate trying to spread obscenity amongst the faithful. They believe that if you are against the Brotherhood and the Salafists, you are against Islam itself. As a result, they do not respect those who disagree with them because they consider them enemies of God and his Messenger.

Advocates of political Islam – as one of their leaders once exclaimed – treat the elections as a battle, a war between Muslims and the enemies of Islam. It would be completely inconceivable to stop fighting and listen to the opinions of the enemies of religion, and acknowledge their rights if you were able to take them away for your benefit. The Brotherhood and the Salafists do not view the constitution as a social contract that must express the will of all the people. They consider the writing of the constitution to be an opportunity to change Egypt from a civil state to a religious state monopolised by sheikhs with unfettered powers based on their interpretation of religion, however foreign and incorrect this interpretation may be.

Forming a constitution writing committee in this biased, flawed manner will lead to the writing of a constitution that will never represent Egyptians. The writing of a constitution and the presidential elections are the final scenes in a drama that the Brotherhood and the military have scripted together. A political deal under which the Brotherhood agreed to form the political wing of the military, agreeing with all its policies, guaranteeing its privileges in the constitution and supporting the presidential candidate whom it favours. In exchange, the military council will help them gain a majority in parliament through unfair and undemocratic elections. So, we have a restricted People's Assembly that does not dare to go against the orders of the military council, and we have a military council that stands by as the Brotherhood and the Salafists violate the right of the Egyptian people to have a constitution that speaks for all Egyptians and would make Egypt a modern nation.

Write your constitution as you wish, but it will remain your constitution only. You will not be able to impose it on the people. The revolution will continue until Egypt is free of tyranny and power is returned to the people, and has nothing to do with the deals of the Brotherhood and the military.

Democracy is the answer.

PN

Do They Represent Islam?

2 April 2012

What would you do if a person you trusted turned out to be a liar? If they went back on their promises and obscured the truth? Eventually you would lose confidence in this person. But what if this liar wore a white robe, had a long beard and presented himself as an Islamic cleric striving to implement God's law. This would complicate matters because the crime committed by this individual would be twofold: he has lied, but has also set a bad example as a Muslim. What is happening in Egypt is different in that those who speak in the name of Islam, however much they lie or break promises, always find people to defend them and make excuses for them.

Those who rush to their defence are not stupid or simple-minded: they consider those who speak in the name of Islam to be a part of Islam and to represent its values. Therefore, any talk of their mistakes or their wrongdoing constitutes an attack on Islam. The Brotherhood and the Salafists have broken all of their promises. They pledged to compete for only a quarter of the seats in the People's Assembly, and then ran for all of them. During the elections they committed all kinds of electoral offences, from vote buying to defaming their competitors with malicious rumours and questioning their religious faith. They pledged to write the constitution with the participation of all the other political parties but then monopolised the constitution writing committee themselves. Time and again they swore that they would not put forward a presidential candidate, but they unsurprisingly went back on their word and presented Khairat el-Shater[1] as their candidate. There is video footage of Salafist sheikhs taking a stand against the revolution and calling for the demonstrators to return to their homes. They even decreed that the ousting of Hosni Mubarak was un-Islamic, with some of them saying that democracy, elections and the alternation of power were also forbidden and un-Islamic. But after the revolution succeeded, they backtracked and changed their opinions, formed political parties and fought in the elections.

This reversal of position – that has no convincing basis in Islamic law – exposes the hypocrisy of their position. Either they lied when they declared democracy to be un-Islamic, or they lied when they endorsed it in order to gain power. If any other political group had committed these moral shortcomings their reputation would have suffered considerably, but many Muslims refuse to condemn the Brotherhood and the Salafists because they

1 Khairat el-Shater was the Brotherhood's original candidate, but in April 2012 the military council barred el-Shater from the presidential race because he was only released from prison in March 2011, in violation of election rules stating that a candidate has to be released from prison for 6 years before he can become a candidate

think that they represent Islam.

This bogus veneration of individuals has nothing to do with Islam, and is in fact the opposite of the Islamic injunction that all individuals, however exalted their status, should be held to account for their mistakes. Abu Bakr and Umar ibn Al-Khattab were some of the Prophet's closest companions and both held the position of caliph. They were criticised harshly by the Muslim community, but received people's criticism with an open mind and tried hard to defend their decisions and admit to any wrongdoing. Perhaps the difference between the culture that allows criticism of the caliph and the culture that bans disobedience of the ruler, and treats sheikhs as sacred and immune from criticism, is the same as the difference between periods of renaissance and periods of decline in Islamic history; the difference between a true understanding of religion and a false one that comes close to revering individuals as infallible.

Taking advantage of the religious sentiments of ordinary people has always been a weapon in the hands of tyranny. In 1882, when Ahmed Urabi[1] mobilised the Egyptian army to defend Egypt from the British invasion, the English instructed the Ottoman Sultan, under his title of Caliph of the Muslims, to issue a religious decree declaring the actions of Urabi had violated the tenets of Islam, and unfortunately this influenced ordinary Egyptians and was one of the reasons why the Urabi revolution failed. In 1798, the French army, under the command of Napoleon Bonaparte, came to occupy Egypt. Bonaparte was an atheist, but he wanted to exploit the religious sentiments of the Egyptian people to his advantage. He spread the rumour that he had converted to Islam, wore eastern dress and led the Friday prayers at the mosque. As soon as he arrived in Cairo, he delivered an extraordinary speech, beginning with "In the Name of God ..." and other religious formulas. "Inhabitants of Egypt!" it said, "the French are true Muslims. They marched to Rome, and overthrew the Throne of the Pope, who excited the Christians against the professors of Islamism."

In this way the religious sentiments of ordinary people have been manipulated time and again throughout our history to serve the interests of unjust, tyrannical powers. A true understanding of religion does not permit the veneration of people, no matter what their status. Instead, it lays down great humanitarian principles of freedom, justice and equality. History teaches us that whenever men of religion are venerated and raised above the rest of humanity, religion becomes a regressive tool leading to despotism in the name of religion.

Perhaps that is what Omar Suleiman, vice president to the deposed Mubarak, had in mind when he set out his plan to thwart the Egyptian

1 Ahmed Urabi was an Egyptian nationalist who led a social-political movement that expressed the discontent of the Egyptian educated classes, army officials, and peasantry with foreign control.

revolution; a plan later adopted by the military council. Suleiman allied himself early with the Muslim Brotherhood, because he was confident that they would always be able to manipulate people's religious sentiments and mobilise them to fulfil their political aims. On 4 February 2011, before Mubarak had stepped down, Omar Suleiman held a meeting with the Muslim Brotherhood. Afterwards, Saad el-Katatni,[1] now speaker of the People's Assembly, came out and said that Suleiman had spoken objectively of a conspiracy to set the country on fire and that the Brotherhood had a duty to help Mubarak's vice president tackle the conspiracy. El-Katatni also said that he had agreed with the deputy of the deposed leader to lift the emergency measures, hold consultations with the demonstrators to clear the squares, make constitutional amendments and hold trade union elections.[2] In other words, when they were confident that they had fulfilled their interests, the Brotherhood supported Omar Suleiman and disregarded the demand of the revolution for a new constitution and set about convincing demonstrators to leave the squares.

From the very beginning, the Muslim Brotherhood has put its political interests above the aims of the revolution. If any other Egyptian politician had done the same, they would be denounced as a traitor of the revolution. But the Brotherhood has found people to protect them and defend them from criticism. The Brotherhood and the Salafists worked with the military council to convince people that agreeing to the constitutional amendments was a religious duty for every Muslim. They claimed that rejecting the amendments amounted to a conspiracy against Islam led by the Copts, secularists and communists.

In this way, the referendum turned into a religious battle between the believers and the infidels and Egypt lost a historical opportunity to write a new constitution that would have ensured a democratic state built on sound foundations. But the military council rejected the new constitution because it would have led to the downfall of the Mubarak regime, which they are determined to defend. Unfortunately, after the revolution the Brotherhood and the Salafists have become the political wing of the military council. Many Egyptians approved the constitutional changes without knowing what they meant, as indicated by Article 28, which gives the SPEC immunity from appeal and which will no doubt be used to rig the elections. Many Egyptians who voted in favour of the constitutional amendments now oppose this article and did not realise that it was included in the amendments. They were led to believe that a vote in favour of the amendments protect Islam.

On the day of the referendum, I went to vote and, as I was waiting in the

1 Saad el-Katatni is an Egyptian Islamist politician who has been the chairman of the Freedom and Justice Party (FJP) since October 2012. Prior to this, he served as the first secretary-general of the FJP and was a member of the Guidance Office of the Muslim Brotherhood.

2 Trade unions or "professional syndicates" are powerful civil society organisations in Egypt.

long queue, I got talking to the man standing in front of me.

"Do you agree with the amendments?" he asked me.

"I will reject them," I said, "because after the revolution we must write a new constitution."

"I will agree to them because Sheikh Mohammed Hassan told us all to support the amendments."

"If you'll permit me to say this," I said, becoming annoyed, "you should make up your own mind."

"Sheikh Hassan knows one hundred times better than I do," said the man, smiling. "Who am I to go against the opinion of Sheikh Hassan?"

I am certain that there are thousands of Egyptians that behave in this manner. They completely close their minds (going against what Islam commands of us) and submit to whatever their favourite sheikh says. They side with their sheikh so obstinately that they reject the opinions of senior Islamic scholars such as Imam Muhammad Abduh and Imam al-Ghazali if their views are at odds with that of the sheikhs. They viciously attack anyone who criticises their sheikh. Just try, dear reader, to go on the internet and criticise one of the salafist or Brotherhood sheikhs. The sheikh's followers will quickly heap vile threats and curses on you. The people attacking you are devoted Muslims and may well be cultivated people in their daily lives, but they see you as simply an enemy of religion because you dare to criticise their sheikh, who in their opinion represents religion itself. In his sermons, Sheikh Mahlawi of Alexandria always insists that liberals and leftists are all enemies of Islam. When one of the worshippers took objection to what the sheikh was saying, he threw him out of the mosque (which is the house of God) saying: "Whoever hates me, hates the Islam I want to follow."

This erroneous concept of religion that leads to the veneration of sheikhs was the reason behind the Brotherhood's deal with the military council. Whether the thing at stake is constitutional amendments, a presidential candidate or something else, the Brotherhood and the Salafists will immediately turn the issue into a religious vote. There will be the sheikhs' opinion, which of course they will see as the opinion of Islam as a whole, and the opinion of those who oppose them, who are all enemies of religion.

So we see how the political debate has turned into a religious struggle under a concentrated bombardment of lies and deceptions and the military council can now guarantee the results it wants without resorting to rigging the ballot boxes as Mubarak used to do. However, nobody can deceive the people forever. The military council's collusion with the Brotherhood and the Salafists, who have abandoned the aims of the revolution in exchange for getting to power, appears clearer and more unpleasant than ever before. Egyptians have started to realise that the Brotherhood and the Salafists do not represent Islam, but they represent only themselves.

Islam says that: "the truth is not known through men, but men are known through the truth." The Egyptian revolution, after those who betrayed it had betrayed, and those who conspired against it had conspired, to be sure it stumbled and fell. But it is still strong and alive. The revolution is ongoing and will succeed, God willing, in bringing Egypt the future it deserves.

Democracy is the answer.

PN

How to Become an Extra

9 April 2012

A religious Jew went to see his rabbi and told him: "O rabbi, I cannot bear my life. I earn very little and my house is overcrowded, what with my wife and four children. Can the Lord provide a solution for my misery?"

The rabbi asked him to grant him 24 hours to think it over and the next day when the religious Jew went back to see the rabbi he saw him sitting with a pig next to him, but before he could ask anything, the rabbi interjected: "The Lord wants you to take this pig and live with it in your house with your wife and children."

It was a strange notion, but the religious Jew trusted the rabbi and so he took the pig home with him. A week later he came back to complain to the rabbi: "The pig stinks to high heaven and it goes around the house defecating everywhere. Please, rabbi, let me get rid of it."

The rabbi smiled and said: "You have to keep the pig until the Lord allows you to get rid of it."

The next week the religious Jew turned up looked completely harassed. The moment the rabbi spoke to him, he burst out crying: "Have pity on me, rabbi. The pig is driving me out of my mind. Our house is full of pig shit, the furniture is ruined and we cannot sleep. Please rescue me."

The rabbi looked at him and smiled: "Alright. Go home and put the pig outside the house."

A week later, when the rabbi asked the man how things were going, he laughed and said: "Thank God, rabbi. It's true that we don't have two pennies to rub together and that we all live crammed into a tiny house, but we're so happy that we could get rid of the accursed pig."

This old joke carries an important notion. When someone complains about his unfortunate lot and is forced to live in an even worse situation, in the end it will wear down his resistance and oblige him to put up with injustice.

That is the method the military council has used on us. After Mubarak was deposed, the military council took over the reins of government and promised to prepare the state for the democratic process, but we have now seen clearly what the military council intends for us. It has preserved the Mubarak system of government at the same time as creating a series of crises, such as the breakdown in law and order, total anarchy, shortages of staple food commodities and fuel. All of these artificial crises were intended to prepare Egyptians for what is happening now. After the suffering of Egyptians reached its apogee, the Mubarak regime re-established itself anew, in the form of the candidacy of Omar Suleiman, a former leading intelligence officer of Mubarak. The military council expects Egyptians to behave like the religious Jew in the anecdote – that they should be delighted with Omar Suleiman because he is the only one capable of solving the crises created by the military council itself. Order will be restored and then Egyptians will forget that they revolted against the Mubarak regime and will sheepishly obey Omar Suleiman and the military council. Omar Suleiman is being pushed into power through undemocratic and unfair elections that have been discredited due to the following reasons:

First: A lack of transparency. In any true democracy, a presidential candidate must declare the sources of his electoral campaign funding, but the military council has completely ignored this regulation. There are candidates who are spending millions of pounds each month and who are never questioned as to the source of these copious funds. Who is paying for the hundreds of air-conditioned buses which ferry around the candidates' supporters? A small election hoarding costs around 10,000 pounds a month, with a large one in a choice location costing up to 200,000? Some of the candidates have plastered thousands of hoardings all over Egypt, and Egyptians have the right to know who is funding these candidates. Also, what is the truth behind the rumours that some Arab states have been providing financial support to candidates? Can a foreign country (even if an Arab one) determine who the president of the republic of Egypt will be? Omar Suleiman is a close friend of Israel, and Israeli officials have been publicly expressing their hope that Suleiman will govern Egypt as the successor of Mubarak, "a devoted friend of Israel", and at the same time Suleiman is supported by the king of Saudi Arabia who sent him his private jet and hosted him for negotiations even though he does not have any formal position.

Second: The selective application of the law. The law has been applied to some of the presidential candidates, whereas others have been absolved of any legal ramifications whatever they do. The Egyptian Foreign Ministry made an enormous effort to get hold of the US passport held by the mother of one of the candidates, Hazem Abu Ismail, and as a result he was disqualified. At the same time, no one in Egypt dares, as it seems, to challenge Ahmed Shafik, who, according to the 35 charges issued against him, has been accused of corruption and wasting public funds. The charges laid against Shafik are a legal precedent in Egypt. These charges were passed on to the attorney general a year ago, but so far Shafik has not been investigated. The strange thing is that the office of the attorney general has confirmed that the charges against Shafik have been passed on to the military court but the head of the military court has stated that he has not received any charges against Shafik. That must mean that the charges against Shafik have gone missing between the attorney general's office and the military court building.

Omar Suleiman has committed many crimes against the Egyptian people, including having full responsibility for exporting gas to Israel at knock-down prices and losing Egypt billions of dollars. He is the person most responsible for the siege of Gaza, over which scores of Palestinians have been killed, and he is also responsible for the torture of detainees who, according to the international press, were renditioned to Egypt to be tortured and have confessions extracted from them before being flown back to the United States. It is Omar Suleiman who attempted to abort the Egyptian revolution and almost broke out in tears as he announced that his mentor, Mubarak, was leaving power. It was he who stated that in his opinion Egyptians are too backward for democracy. Omar Suleiman should be on trial for treason. He should be politically isolated but the military council has continued to protect him in order, at the right moment, to thrust him into power so that he can restore the Mubarak regime and bring an end to the revolution.

Third: State intervention on the side of the military council's candidate. During the registration of presidential candidates, civil servants in a number of government institutions rushed to register Ahmed Shafik and Omar Suleiman. Some employees of the electoral rolls, following instructions, facilitated the registration of Ahmed Shafik while putting obstacles in the way of revolutionary candidates. The corrupt Egyptian state apparatus, kept in place by the military council, will intervene with all its might to ensure Omar Suleiman wins, using the old methods such as mass voting by civil servants and vote buying in rural and poor districts. We just have to look at the scene of Omar Suleiman presenting his candidature documents surrounded by a group of senior civil and military police officers for his protection. These officers, who allowed the whole of Egypt to descend into chaos, and the police and military officers who killed demonstrators, dragged Egyptian women along the ground and abused them, these are the same officers who today offer their complete protection to Omar Suleiman, Mubarak's deputy, out of respect and deference to Mubarak.

Fourth: The use of religion in political discourse. In contravention of the law, most preachers in mosques throughout Egypt have taken to speaking of politics in their sermons. This took place during the referendum on constitutional amendments, and it took place during elections for the upper and lower houses, and it will certainly take place during the presidential elections. If we add to that the fact that the Mubarak regime still exists in its old form which kept most of the preachers subservient to state security officers, then the mosques will not be used this time for the benefit of the candidates of political Islam but for that of Omar Suleiman for whose success the military council will use all means at its disposal.

Fifth: The supreme electoral committee's decisions are above the law. Following the method of Hosni Mubarak, a supreme electoral committee has been put together to supervise the elections, but its decisions are not subject to appeal. Any incident of vote rigging, large or small, or documented, if not recognised by the supreme electoral committee will be set aside. Not only does Article 28 of the constitutional declaration, which gives immunity to the decisions of the supreme electoral committee, go against logic and the law, but it contravenes the constitutional declaration itself which confirms that under Article 21 all administrative decisions are subject to legal appeal. This article was carried over from the old constitution according to the wishes of the military council and with the agreement of the Brotherhood in order to enable the military council to make Omar Suleiman president.

These appalling legal defects show most clearly that the presidential elections are neither free nor fair. They are a farce prepared by the military council and the Brotherhood to ensure the result they wish. It is like any dramatic farce in which there are leading actors and extras. The brigadiers of the military council and the Muslim Brothers are the stars of the show because they are secretly hand in glove with each other in schemes about which we, the spectators, know nothing. The extras are the independent candidates, whether they be from the Islamist trend, liberals or rightists, and are great nationalists who back the revolution. Most of them are presidential material, but so far they have ignored the fact that they are playing subsidiary roles in a drama whose outcome is a foregone conclusion. Unfortunately they are more akin to the extras that play bit parts, lighting the main character's cigarette, before disappearing forever from the stage. The candidates of the revolution should know that they are not taking part in elections but in a vicious campaign which the military council is waging to try and restore Hosni Mubarak to power in the form of his deputy Omar Suleiman. I hope that the revolutionary candidates will unite behind one name, someone we can all stand behind as we go into a battle which, I believe, will definitively, please God, bring about the second wave of the revolution which will free Egypt of the Mubarak regime and allow it to embark on its future.

Democracy is the answer.

RH

How to Save the Revolution in Four Steps

16 April 2012

Imagine that you live in an apartment and across the hall lives a person that you do not like. You have had countless problems with this neighbour; he is selfish and only thinks of himself. This neighbour talks about principles, but often ignores them if they can further his own interests. Over the years, your relationship has deteriorated and you no longer speak to each other. Then, one night a tremendous fire breaks out and the neighbour rushes out and asks for your help to extinguish the fire. What would you do then? Would you tell him: "I will not help you, even if the whole building goes up in flames and all our children along with it"? Or would you take the danger of the situation into account and help your neighbour to extinguish the fire, saving the building and its occupants? The answer is obvious.

This analogy sums up the current situation in Egypt. The neighbour who has repeatedly let you down is the Muslim Brotherhood, the building is Egypt, and this period of Egypt's history is no less dangerous than the horrible fire. The Muslim Brotherhood, along with the military council, is responsible for the dark days currently facing Egypt. The Brotherhood allied itself with the military council to devise the shameful constitutional amendments that they now complain about. They encouraged the Egyptian people to vote in favour of amendments they did not really understand, and turned the constitutional referendum into a battle between believers and infidels. The Brotherhood abandoned the revolutionaries in the massacres in Maspero Square, Mohamed Mahmoud Street and at the Council of Ministers, and it was reluctant to condemn the military council for their involvement. The Brotherhood blamed the revolutionaries and accused them of thuggery and of serving foreign interests. The Brotherhood who appropriated the Constituent Assembly, monopolised the writing of the Egyptian constitution, and tailored it according to their wishes. They also attempted to gain control of the Central Auditing Organisation through a draft bill, which would have given the speaker of the People's Assembly the power to appoint the head of this organisation.

All of these were grave mistakes committed by the Muslim Brotherhood in order to serve its narrow interests. In the end, it was the revolution that paid the price for the Brotherhood's transgressions. The revolution has failed to achieve the goals for which hundreds of martyrs have died, not to mention the thousands of Egyptians that have been injured and the daughters of Egypt who were abandoned by the Brotherhood while soldiers abused them in the streets. The Muslim Brotherhood has since realised that all their political gains were for naught, because the military council only wants to use them as puppets to serve their own interests. Only then did the Brotherhood clash with the military council and rejoin the revolution to present the draft Political Isolation Law, which the revolution had long demanded. And so, the Brotherhood returned to the Square to shout for the fall of the military council alongside the revolutionaries.

So what should the revolution do about the Brotherhood? Should we join hands with them, restore unity and once again become a solid revolutionary force, as we were during the first days of the revolution? Or will any cooperation with the Brotherhood end in its usual fashion, with them abandoning their principles to fulfil their political goals? This question cannot be answered without understanding what is currently happening in Egypt.

For 14 months after the ousting of Mubarak, the military council succeeded in hindering the revolution's demand for democratic change. The Egyptian people have fallen victim to an organised scheme aimed at emptying the revolution of its substance, stamping it out, sullying its image and pressuring Egyptians through fabricated crises such as breakdowns in law and order, lack of food and a debilitating economic crash. When the Egyptian people had hit rock bottom, the name of Omar Suleiman was put forward as a presidential candidate, as if he were the Egyptian's saviour from the catastrophe they were living through.

Whether Suleiman's candidacy is excluded or not, the significance of his nomination remains pertinent, as it reflects the intentions of the military council to restore the regime of Hosni Mubarak. The actions of the SPEC confirms its decisions are based more on politics than the law, because every decision it has made suits the will of the military council. How was Omar Suleiman's nomination accepted before the numerous complaints brought against him had been investigated? How did Suleiman obtain 50,000 recommendation forms in two days? Why was he suddenly excluded from running on an innocent and unconvincing technicality?[1] How could a director of the General Intelligence Directorate[2] miscount the number of recommendation forms that he submitted with his nomination?

Why won't the SPEC show evidence to support the claim that Sheikh Hazem Abu Ismail's mother was an American citizen? The reluctance of the commission to provide evidence suggests that it either has no proof or that it is deliberately obfuscating the issue to provoke thousands of Sheikh Hazem's

1 Suleiman was reportedly excluded on the basis of the geographical distribution of his signatures of support. A candidate must have 1,000 signatures from 15 separate governorates to qualify.

2 General Intelligence Directorate is an Egyptian intelligence agency responsible for providing national security intelligence, both domestically and transnationally, with a counter-terrorism focus.

supporters into causing chaos on the streets, thus preventing the elections from taking place. How can the SPEC accept the nomination of Ahmed Shafik before the 35 complaints against him for squandering public funds are investigated? These complaints were communicated to the attorney general a full year ago but no investigation has taken place. The attorney general's office gave their assurance that they sent the complaints against Shafik to the military court but the head of the military court has stated that he has not received any charges against Shafik.

There are two possible outcomes. Either the presidency is won by a candidate, supported by the military council, that will restore the old regime and facilitate the military council's control of the reins of government from behind the scenes. Or, if it is not possible to impose their candidate, the military council will cause problems and total chaos that will prevent the presidential elections from taking place, leaving the military council in power indefinitely.

The Egyptian revolution is passing through the most difficult phase of its history. The danger that threatens it resembles a great fire engulfing a densely populated building. It is our patriotic duty to do our utmost to save the revolution. This goal cannot be achieved unless the following steps are implemented:

First: The Muslim Brotherhood must sincerely apologise for allowing the revolution to fall into disrepute. It must then present proof of its goodwill by forming a genuine consensus in the Constituent Assembly that would satisfy all factions and parties and give the constitution real legitimacy. In return, the civilian revolutionary forces must accept the Brotherhood's apology and unite with it so that we may restore the revolutionary unity that will help to save the revolution.

Second: We must all learn to coexist with those whom we disagree with, and respect their rights. The liberals and leftists must learn that the Muslim Brotherhood and the Salafists are not a bunch of reactionary fascists, but in fact are patriotic citizens who took part in the revolution and sacrificed martyrs. They also happen to possess an Islamic political agenda, which we should respect even if we disagree with it. We must protect their right to formulate their agenda and put it before the Egyptian people. In return, the Brotherhood and the Salafists must realise that they alone cannot assume responsibility for Egypt, even if they represent the majority. They must learn that they can never change Egypt's identity to become an Afghanistan or a Saudi Arabia. They must be aware that the liberals are neither enemies of Islam, nor immoral, degenerate agents of the West. In fact, many of them are no less religious than the Islamists themselves; it is simply the case that they are not convinced by the idea of political Islam. After all, it was the fierce battle between the two wings of the revolution – the Islamists and the liberals – that was one of the main factors that helped the military council to impede change in Egypt.

Third: All the signs indicate that the presidential elections will be neither honest nor fair. Once unity is restored amongst the revolutionaries, pressure must be exerted on the military council to give real assurances of the election's integrity. Article 28 of the constitution – which makes the decisions of the SPEC irrevocable – must be repealed because it is an aberration that goes against logic and justice, while also contradicting Article 21 of the constitutional declaration, forbidding any form of irrevocability concerning administrative decisions. The electoral budgets of all presidential candidates must be subject to oversight by the Central Auditing Organisation, and the funding sources of each candidate must be made public. There must be real guarantees to make state institutions free of political interference so that employees are not ordered to vote en masse for the military council's candidate, as was the case with the recommendation forms submitted in favour of Ahmed Shafik and Omar Suleiman. Candidates belonging to Mubarak's regime must be excluded in accordance with the Law of Political Isolation, which was ratified by the People's Assembly. Immediate investigations must also be opened to review the complaints submitted against Ahmed Shafik and Omar Suleiman.

Without fair rules that guarantee transparency, equal opportunity and the rule of law, the presidential elections will descend into political farce. Holding fair elections may be a tough ask, but it is possible if we all unite behind this purpose. Experience has proven that the military council does not move in the right direction except under popular pressure. It was the mass demonstrations organised by the revolutionaries that forced the military council to put Mubarak on trial and disqualify Omar Suleiman from standing as candidate, albeit temporarily.

Fourth: State institutions are completely in the pocket of the military council, from the police and state security service to the military police, who dragged Egyptian women through the streets and murdered the revolutionary youth. In other words, the military council is still employing all of Mubarak's tactics to control the course of events. However, if the revolutionary forces were to unite, they would possess two tools for change: the Square and the parliament. The Square is the public assembly for the Egyptian people has always been a place in which the revolutionaries can express their demands. Parliament will become an important tool to protect the revolution and to achieve its goals. After all, we saw how much the Mubarak regime was shaken when the People's Assembly approved the Law on Political Isolation which targeted remnants of the former regime. The unity of the revolutionaries will gain hinder the military council's plan to bring the revolution to an end.

The revolution faces a real threat which forces us to choose: either we remain fragmented, hurling accusations and insults at each other and so enabling Mubarak's regime to put a decisive end to the revolution, or we overcome our differences and immediately unite in order that the aims of the revolution, for which thousands of Egyptians have paid the price with their blood, are fulfilled. The revolution will continue until Egypt is free from tyranny and it will succeed.

Democracy is the answer.

PN

Who Pays the Price for Dignity?

30 April 2012

Imagine that you're working in a company and one of your colleagues verbally abuses you. Under normal circumstances, you would defend yourself and demand to be treated with respect. But what happens if the colleague is actually the director of the company? This complicates matters and leaves you with two choices: to respond with dignity and suffer the consequences or to swallow your pride in order to keep your job.

This introduction is necessary to understand what is happening to Egyptian workers in Saudi Arabia today. It is important not to generalise or speak ill of the Saudi people, who are generally valued and cherished in Egypt. However, we cannot ignore the thousands of documented acts of injustice that have afflicted Egyptian people living in the Gulf for decades. First and foremost is the horrendous sponsorship system (*kafala*), which is considered a form of slavery by the United Nations.[1]

Under the sponsorship system, an Egyptian worker – be they a doctor or construction worker – is required to pay a share of their salary to their Saudi sponsor. The worker is at the mercy of the sponsor or employer, and is not even allowed to travel abroad without their consent. A simple complaint from the sponsor could result in your dismissal from work, or even imprisonment.

A cursory glance at the reports of human rights organisations, or the files of the Egyptian Ministry of Foreign Affairs, shows thousands of instances where Egyptians have beem robbed, dismissed from work and arrested without charge. The clear injustices faced by many Egyptians in Saudi Arabia have continued for three decades for the following reasons:

First: The high levels of poverty and unemployment in Egypt have forced many to look for work abroad. Those who leave Egypt for Saudi Arabia have lost their livelihoods and are often willing to endure anything to provide food for their children. The sponsor is aware that the Egyptian workers will endure

1 Migrant workers constitute more than half the national workforce in Saudi Arabia; they fill manual, clerical, and service jobs, Many suffer multiple abuses and labour exploitation, sometimes rising to slavery-like conditions.

unjust conditions because they have no other choice. They buy the hard work and commitment of these desperate Egyptians and will take full advantage, exchanging their workers like human commodities.

A few years ago, two Egyptian doctors working in Saudi Arabia were arrested and tried under mysterious circumstances. They were sentenced to imprisonment and flogging. At the time, I wrote an article defending their right to a fair trial and was inundated with dozens of letters from readers who told me many sad stories about the unjust and degrading treatment Egyptian workers were subjected to in Saudi Arabia. But the strange thing was that some readers wrote to me requesting that I stop defending the doctors who had been treated so unjustly; they were scared that the Saudi authorities would retaliate and dismiss other Egyptian workers from their jobs as a result.

Second: The Mubarak regime cared little about its citizens, torturing them and violating their rights. Therefore, this made it somehow illogical and unacceptable for it to protest about their dignity being compromised abroad. Because the military council is an extension of the Mubarak regime in thought and deed, it now finds itself in this same predicament. How can the military council defend human rights abroad when it is the first to compromise them on home soil. They have arrested thousands of Egyptians and allowed them to be killed in continual massacres, while their officers drag Egyptian women through the streets and assault them in public.

Third: The law in Saudi Arabia does not meet the standards of international justice: people are not equal before the law, but instead are ranked according to their nationality and social standing. For example, the laws that apply to Egyptians in Saudi Arabia could never be applied to Americans or Europeans residing in the region. The Saudi princes are also considered above the law and can behave as they see fit. This concept of the law, which belongs in the Middle Ages, deprives Egyptian workers of their basic legal rights, namely the right to a fair trial.

Fourth: Following the October War in 1973, the price of oil dramatically increased making Saudi Arabia a major regional power. This economic stimulation was the result of a war fought by Egyptian soldiers, who paid the price of victory with their lives. This pushed the late president Anwar Sadat to officially request the Gulf Cooperation Council (GCC) to allocate a fixed proportion of oil revenue to Egypt and Syria, since the oil boom came through God's grace and the sacrifices of the Egyptian and Syrian soldiers. Sadat's request was dismissed, but an abundance of oil money flowed into Egypt for other reasons. Firstly, for political reasons, millions of dollars were poured in to support the extremist Wahhabi movement, as the Saudi regime is in effect an alliance between the Wahhabi sheikhs and the Al-Saud family. The spread of Wahhabism in Egypt and throughout the world helps to maintain the stability of the Saudi regime.

Saudi oil money is also used to establish a network of people throughout Egypt with close ties to Saudi Arabia. Wherever you go in Egypt, you will find Egyptians with strong ties with Saudi Arabia, from those working in Saudi media outlets, to Salafist sheikhs who work for Saudi religious television channels for huge salaries, to sheikhs from Al Azhar who teach at Saudi universities, and Egyptian businessmen working with Saudi clients. Even amongst the presidential candidates, the majority are hesitant to direct criticism towards the Saudi regime in defence of Egyptian rights.

This has always been the situation in Egypt during Mubarak's rule. The Egyptian people were subjected to injustices at home and abroad without the slightest investigation or accountability. When the revolution began, the Saudi regime took a clear stand against it and exerted unprecedented pressure on US president, Barack Obama, first to save the regime, then to prevent Mubarak's trial. The enmity of the Saudi regime towards the revolution is natural because the establishment of a real democracy in Egypt would act as a model for the entire Arab world, and would therefore threaten the autocratic Saudi regime that still resists any real political reform.

The Saudi regime failed to realise the extent to which the revolution had changed the Egyptian people. This was obvious in the case of Ahmed al-Gizawi, a brave lawyer and revolutionary who defended many of the demonstrators before military courts. He moved on to defending Egyptian workers detained without trial in Saudi Arabia, thus finding himself in litigation with the Saudi king himself. When al-Gizawi went to perform Umrah with his wife, he was confident that the Saudi regime would not be able to punish him for his political position, as Islam considers all those who go on pilgrimage guests of the Almighty and none are permitted to do them harm.

Unfortunately, as soon as he landed in Saudi Arabia, al-Gizawi was arrested. Those who asked about him were told that he would be flogged and imprisoned for insulting the king of Saudi Arabia. A few days later, Saudi authorities announced that al-Gizawi had been found to be in the possession of more than 21,000 Xanax anti-anxiety pills, which are banned in the country.

This silly accusation merits no discussion. Al-Gizawi is a brave fighter who has been arrested several times in defence of his principles. What made him suddenly turn into a drug dealer? Is he stupid enough to travel with such a huge amount of drugs that would have made leaving Cairo airport – where all baggage is searched by x-ray – impossible? Moreover, that amount of tablets would weigh more than 60 kilograms and the baggage allowance for al-Gizawi's flight was only 30 kilograms. Cairo airport records confirm that the weight of al-Gizawi and his wife's bags did not exceed this limit. Also, why didn't the Saudi authorities announce these charges from the beginning? Where is the video footage of the inspection of the bag in the presence of al-Gizawi, as stipulated under international law? Why did the Saudi authorities leave al-Gizawi's wife to go free when the bag of alleged drugs belonged to them both?

What happened to al-Gizawi has occured many times before to Egyptian citizens in Saudi Arabia; they have been unfairly arrested and dismissed from their jobs, and nothing was done about it. So perhaps the Saudi authorities did not expect any serious reaction from the Egyptian people. However, the revolution returned a sense of dignity to the Egyptians and mass demonstrations broke out in front of the Saudi embassy denouncing the injustice and calling for a fair trial for al-Gizawi.

Throughout the world, demonstrations are a legitimate means of protest that are usually directed at government officials. Had these demonstrations taken place outside the Saudi embassy in London or Washington, the Saudi regime would not have had the nerve to object. But as for Egyptians daring to claim their rights, this is something the Saudi regime is not accustomed to, and did not tolerate. Saudi Arabia withdrew its ambassador for consultations and closed its embassy. Consequently, the military council was greatly confused and Egyptian Prime Minister Kamal el-Ganzouri issued an apology, as did the foreign minister, whose consul in Saudi Arabia rushed to condemn al-Gizawi before the investigation even got underway. The sheikhs of Al-Azhar also apologised, although no one knows why.

The military council is behaving in the same way as the Mubarak regime. The entire Egyptian state has apologised simply because Egyptians dared to demand a fair trial for an Egyptian citizen. As for the Muslim Brotherhood, who refused to apologise for their deal with the military coucnil, or for surrendering the principles of the revolution for their own interests, they rushed to apologise to Saudi Arabia through el-Katatni, the president of the People's Assembly. Evidently, having close ties to the Saudi regime is more important to the Brotherhood than the dignity of the Egyptian people.

Those abandoning al-Gizawi are the same ones who abandoned the Egyptian revolution, namely the military council, the government of el-Ganzouri and the Muslim Brotherhood. The revolutionaries are the only remaining party that are prepared to stand up for dignity and to demand a fair trial for al-Gizawi.

By closing the Saudi embassy and ceasing the issuance of visas to Egyptians, the Saudi regime seeks to assert that it has the right to deal with Egyptians as it pleases, without being held accountable. This message has been rejected, and the Saudi government should realise that the time of freely disregarding the dignity of Egyptians has passed, never to return again.

We will continue to support al-Gizawi's right to a fair trial and we demand the release of all Egyptians detained in Saudi prisons. We demand that they and their families be compensated for the injustices they suffered.

The Egyptian people, who offered hundreds of martyrs and thousands of injured to obtain their freedom, will not allow anybody – whether inside or outside Egypt – to attack Egyptian dignity.

Democracy is the answer.

PN

A Conversation Between a Presidential Candidate and an Important Person

7 May 2012

Presidential candidate: "Good morning, sir. I'm sorry for not being in touch; I have been incredibly busy with the election campaign. Every day I visit a different province and hold an election rally. I'm exhausted from it all."

Important person: "Keep it up! Nothing comes easily."

Presidential candidate: "I am your loyal disciple, sir. You have shown us how to work hard and to give it our all."

Important person: "Is there anything you need?"

Presidential candidate: "Not at all, sir, God bless you. I am just calling to congratulate you on the Abbasiya operation. It was truly magnificent sir, you taught those young anarchists an important lesson."

Important person: "God be praised that the operation carried out with such precision. The state security officers did some truly fine work."

Presidential candidate: "They are patriotic men, indeed, and they know exactly what they are doing. We could never do without them. To keep the state security apparatus was a very wise decision."

Important person: "Of course. If we had listened to those young anarchists in Tahrir Square and disbanded the security forces, all hell would have broken loose. No power in Egypt can do without the state security officers. They're the only ones who can fix the country."

Presidential candidate: "The best thing about the Abbasiya operation was that those who taught the anarchists a lesson were not the army or the police. Ordinary Egyptians, tired of anarchy, they were the ones who came down and beat those holding the sit-in to death. Truly honourable citizens."

Important person (laughing): "They were honourable citizens to be sure, but they also made a lot of money!"

Presidential candidate: "Sir, it was no great loss. After what happened, nobody will dare to hold sit-ins and demonstrate now. The country is stabilising and calming down; production has started again. We can't have them opposing and demonstrating against every decision the state takes."

Important person: "No, all that belongs to the past. From now on, we will deal firmly with troublemakers, even those prisoners' families at the military courts. As soon as they started shouting, the police and the army descended on them, gave them a sound beating and taught them a lesson."

Presidential candidate: "God bless you, sir. You know, if we had dealt firmly with these troublemakers from the beginning, President Mubarak would still be cherished and respected."

Important person: "It's Habib el-Adly's fault. He underestimated the situation. In the end, everything comes down to fate."

Presidential candidate: "I feel sorry for President Mubarak. You know today is his birthday."

Important person: "Of course I know. I called him to wish him happy birthday. May God be with him."

Presidential candidate: "You are always such a gentleman. If you don't mind, sir, I have a number of important things I wish to discuss with you."

Important person: "Well?"

Presidential candidate: "Sir, I'm sure you are aware that a number of my men sit all day surfing the internet and follow what's going on. They found a video of a group of thugs getting out of army cars and beating up the demonstrators. Then there is this old lady who appeared on Dream TV and said she saw with her own eyes the thugs carrying weapons from the El Waily police station."

Important person: "And what else?"

Presidential candidate: "Sheikh Hafez Salama keeps saying that the military police stormed the Al-Nour mosque, fired rounds and arrested some of the worshippers in the mosque."

Important person: "Anything else?"

Presidential candidate: "My point is that the state security should put pressure on the media not to let these stories get out and influence public opinion."

Important person (*becoming somewhat animated*): "Obviously, the state security gave clear instructions to national journalists and writers to work together to calm people down. But listen, I have something I want to say to you. A video, witnesses, Sheikh so and so said whatever; all of these things used to matter to us. Now they don't. Whoever wants to film can film. This is who we are and this is what we do when there is a riot. If someone chooses to demonstrate, they must understand the risks. We must clean up this country of all these troublemaking kids. Today I came across some statements made by Sheikh Jalil from the Centre for Islamic Research. Know what he said?"

Presidential candidate: "What did he say, sir?"

Important person: "The esteemed sheikh said that the ruler of any Muslim country has the right to kill a third of his people for the sake of the other two thirds. This is the view of Islam and thanks be to God we are Muslims!"

Presidential candidate: "Wow, sir, he really said that?"

Important person: "So keep on letting whoever wants to film, film. We are in control and from now on if anyone causes a riot we will break their necks."

Presidential candidate: "Sir, I am truly astounded by you. You always have a vision of the future, you always allow me to see things more clearly and guide my thoughts. God bless you, sir, and keep you safe for Egypt's sake."

Important person: "However, I must add that by teaching these troublemakers a lesson we should never break the law."

Presidential candidate: "Absolutely not, sir. It was you who taught us to respect the law."

Important person: "Exactly, Egypt is a country of institutions. Whoever has evidence can present it to the attorney general safe in the knowledge that he will take the necessary steps right away."

Presidential candidate: "Of course. The attorney general is an excellent man."

Important person: "Truly, the attorney general has a rare and perhaps unequalled legal experience."

Presidential candidate: "Before, sir, you know that I took on some difficult responsibilities and devoted all of my time to my work. Of course, any person who works in Egypt must have enemies ... and success certainly leads to envy and spite. They love to raise doubts about any respectable person and make false accusations about him."

Important person: "Enough beating around the bush. Get to the point!"

Presidential candidate: "Sir, you know after Mubarak stepped down, those hateful people brought complaints against me. God knows all of them spurious. This happened more than a year ago. Last week, all of a sudden they summoned me for investigation. Are you happy about all of this, sir?"

Important person: "What do you want me to do about it?"

Presidential candidate: "Sir, I have served Egypt with the utmost degree of honesty and integrity. I learnt from you all about self-denial and sacrifice for the love of Egypt. And at the end of it all, they are putting me under investigation!"

Important person: "If you are clean, why are you scared of the investigation?"

Presidential candidate: "No, sir. I am not scared. But what concerns me is that you are pleased with me. If you are pleased with me, sir, I will go into the investigation confidently."

Important person: "I certainly could not interfere with the investigation."

Presidential candidate: "Cut out my tongue, sir, before I asked you to interfere with the investigation! I learnt the respect of the law from you, sir. All I want to know before I go in for questioning is if you are pleased with me or not. I am worried that I have done something to make you angry, sir, without meaning to."

Important person: "My God, you are really persistent."

Presidential candidate: "Please, sir, put me at ease. Are you pleased with me?"

Important person: "I am pleased with you, my friend. Do you feel better now?"

Presidential candidate (*sighing*): "Thank God. As long as you are happy with me, sir, I will go into the investigation confidently."

Important person: "OK that's enough, let me get back to my work."

Presidential candidate: "Sir, I am too greedy of your generosity but I have one last very important thing."

Important person: "Can't it wait? I have much to do."

Presidential candidate: "No sir, please, this matter cannot wait. I learnt from you all about democracy and respecting the will of the people. But sir, the country is passing through a very delicate moment. Everything hangs in the balance. The presidential elections are approaching and the opinion polls are very worrying. The president of Egypt must be a wise, sensible, established figure who knows how to lead the country to safety. How can we hand Egypt over to a religious fanatic like Abdel Moneim Aboul Fotouh or a Nasserist like Hamdeen Sabahi or that communist youth Khaled Ali?[1] They are all talk and have never had any responsibility in their whole lives. If any one of these people won the elections, it would be a disaster."

Important person: "The Egyptian people can distinguish good from bad."

Presidential candidate: "Completely correct, sir."

Important person: "I make it clear to you that the presidential elections are fair."

Presidential candidate: "Extremely fair, sir."

1 Khaled Ali is a prominent Egyptian lawyer and activist. He is known for advocating for the reform of government and private sector corruption and for promoting social justice and labour rights.

Important person: "After the voting is over, the result will be announced by the Supreme Presidential Elections Commission. The decisions of the commission cannot be contested. Anybody that raises doubts about the result of the elections or tries to pull one over on us, we know how to stop their tongue."

Presidential candidate: "OK, sir. All of this is well and good. I know the people are great and know exactly what they are doing and I am sure the elections will be fair. But sir, under your guidance we were accustomed to express our true feelings and I am anxious, sir. Being president of Egypt is a dangerous position to hold, and if one of these three people, if Aboul Fotouh, Hamdeen Sabahi or Khaled Ali win the elections and become president, it will be a disaster. None of them are stable. If any one of them were to govern Egypt for a week, God knows where the country would end up."

Important person: "Do not worry."

Presidential candidate: "I wish I didn't, sir. Tell me something to put me at ease."

Important person: "I told you not to worry."

Presidential candidate: "What does this mean, sir?"

Important person: "Do you not understand Arabic or what? I said don't worry, which means 'don't worry.'"

Presidential candidate: "OK, I understand. God bless you sir, and keep you safe for Egypt's sake."

Democracy is the answer.

PN

How to Carry Out a Massacre

14 May 2012

A successful massacre needs time and planning, as well as expertise and organised action. A massacre has similarities to a surgical operation; the success depends upon the skill of the surgeon, his diagnostic precision, and his dexterity. The following are the steps necessary to create a successful massacre:

First: Understand the meaning of massacre. What is the difference between controlling demonstrations and committing a massacre? In the first situation, you use your powers to control the demonstrations and do so clearly in full view of everyone, whereas a massacre is a specialised task; an unambiguous message directed at one group of people. A massacre targets a specific group such as football fans, Islamists or socialists. The targeted group itself will be massacred out of sight of other people, and the massacre will be planned so that public opinion does not side with the victims. Following a massacre, opinion will be divided, with some doubting that it happened at all, and others admitting that some excesses may have taken place but that the victims brought it upon themselves. A massacre is like the following situation:

You meet your opponent in a crowded place and smile straight at them like an old friend. Then you go over to him and surreptitiously whisper some foul curses in their ear. Your opponent is riled by your comments and tries to attack you. Those watching will intervene to defend you because, in their opinion, you have done nothing to provoke the attack.

Second: Focus on your aim. The aim of any massacre can be summed up in one phrase: will-breaking. You have to make the rebels understand that there is a crushing price to pay for their rebellion so that they cower and desist. At certain moments, good planning is necessary. When a popular revolution breaks out, millions of people are involved and it is difficult to stifle the will of a large group. At that point, you must divide the rebels into groups and then carry out a number of massacres against each group so that, in the end, the people's will is broken. Another example: before carrying out vote rigging, it is useful to carry out a massacre against political activists – the people who will go out onto the streets to demonstrate and hold sit-ins in protest over the rigged election results. They must be intimidated, terrorised and killed in good time so that others will be to afraid to object to the rigging of the elections. You will be amazed at the result, because a successful massacre has a magical effect. The most tenacious and brave of the rebels, if subjected to abuse and humiliation, if they see their colleagues struck down in front of their eyes, may see their courage desert them as they turn into a cowardly, submissive citizen.

Third: Carry it out carefully. Your soldiers must not wear military uniform when carrying out a massacre, as that will lead to a number of problems. There is nothing worse than the image of a soldier in uniform killing or beating his compatriots. The people who carry out the massacre must wear plain clothes and avoid being filmed. Whether they are your soldiers or mercenaries, the result is the same. There will be hundreds of unknown people who attack demonstrators, beat them, drag them along the ground and kill them or abuse the women. After that, who would dare accuse you of having organised the massacre? The matter will appear too be a clash between unknown groups. Your soldiers should appear in front of the cameras as if they are trying to quell the clashes and save the victims.

Fourth: Prepare public opinion for the massacre. It is important to weaken the people by creating crises to precede the massacre. A complete breakdown in security and a lack of fuel and basic foodstuffs and steep price hikes will make people's lives impossible. The exhausted and frightened citizen will be more receptive to the massacre, more than a satisfied citizen who may perceive the truth of the events. You must control public opinion by reaching out to journalists and broadcasters, as well as operatives of the security forces, who will follow orders in return for money and jobs. They have various means at their disposal, from eye witness testimonies and fictitious letters to newspapers, to false news stories and invented incidents. They also have access to strategy experts who will be willing to repeat the lies with complete authoritativeness. These media personalities are resourceful and often cunning, and will be able to come up with lies to justify the massacre.

Fifth: Use a moral cover. The media cannot help you to cover up the massacre unless you have used a moral cover for it. The demonstrators have to be lured to an area that represents the state in some way, one of the ministries, such as the Ministry of the Interior. The easiest way is to infiltrate the demonstrators and urge them to head towards a ministry building. At the same time, your forces must keep the road clear so that the demonstrators can get as close as possible to the building. You know well that any building in the world can be protected against peaceful demonstrators with essentially simple means: two sets of tall barriers topped with barbed wire at a distance of 300 metres can prevent any demonstrator from attacking or even getting close to it. Do not protect the building in this way. You must encourage the demonstartors to approach the building, and if you do use barbed wire, it must be flimsy and at such a low level that even a child could jump over it. At the same time, start your media campaign in the newspapers and on the television channels, and encourage officials to voice their fears about an impending attack by the demonstrators. People must read and hear that there is a plot to overthrow the state by those treacherous demonstrators, who have received funding from abroad to attack the Ministry of the Interior. This campaign will lead to a state of exasperation amongst the demonstrators, which you must exploit by broadcasting an urgent statement confirming that public buildings are the property of the people and those attacking them must be traitors to their country and agents of foreign interests. End the statement by calling upon the demonstrators to protect the property of the people and to return whence they came, warning them that you will not countenance any attack on public installations.

The statement should be made in a tone that is paternalistic and shows patience over the mistakes of your children with whom you may, at any moment, have to deal with severely. The public will stand by you to protect the state.

Sixth: Set the zero hour. Do not start by beating the demonstrators. You must get your agents to mingle with the demonstrators and then to start moving towards the ministry, while ordering your forces to fall back and let them through. Your agents should be filmed throwing Molotov cocktails at the ministry. This image should be published on the front pages and broadcast on the television news under the headline: "This morning, demonstrators threw Molotov cocktails at the Ministry of the Interior." At the right moment, give the starting signal and allow your plain clothes officers to attack the demonstrators, as the members of your armed forces close off all means of escape. Your men must be armed with knives and sticks as well as with live firearms. It is important to get your officers riled up by making slanderous comments about the demonstrators, making it clear that the violence is justified and indeed honourable. The women must be subjected to sexual abuse because this is the most effective way of breaking their will. A woman can defend herself against beatings, but if you take off her clothes and humiliate her in front of jeering men, then her resistance will be broken down and she will not participate in another demonstration or protest. The men arrested must serve as an example. They must be kept standing, completely naked, as they are subjected to violent beatings. They must be abused and electrocuted in front of their colleagues so that they lose their dignity and standing.

During the massacre the media will keep saying that unknown people have clashed with the demonstrators and that both sides are armed, that your forces have been trying to quell the clash and to protect state installations. This will persuade people to accept the abuse and killing of demonstrators as a necessary sacrifice that they brought upon themselves by attacking the Ministry of the Interior. They will ask why they went there in the first place, and why those women who complain about being abused joined in the demonstration when they should have stayed respectably at home.

Seventh: Create an additional catastrophe. This is a tried and tested method. During the massacre, have some of your men go off and set fire to a nearby museum or historic building. The media will rush to photograph the historic building being devoured by flames and fire engines will certainly be prevented from reaching it. At this point the press will do much shouting and screaming and gnashing of the teeth about the great cultural patrimony that is being burned down. People's great sadness over the destruction of their country's landmarks will soon turn to far-reaching anger against the demonstrators who have caused such damage, and the media will be overflowing with letters from decent citizens calling upon you to put these saboteurs down with an iron fist.

Now that you have carried out the massacre and managed to break the will of those who oppose you, you have to regain your composure and never allow what you have done to be seen to be your doing. Convene a press conference to declare your deep regret over the death of the victims because they are all children of Egypt and their blood is the blood of the Egyptian people. State that you will open far-reaching investigations into the painful incident and call upon anyone who has information to hand it over to the investigative authorities immediately so that they can take the necessary steps. Finally, say a few moving words about the prestige of the state and the protection of public installations. Then call upon the devoted children of the homeland not to allow infiltrators to destroy our beloved country, and ask them to desist from holding demonstrations at this sensitive stage in the country's history but to keep the country's productivity moving along and to preserve stability.

This article has no connection whatsoever to the military council.

Democracy is the answer.

RH

Are These Elections Fair?

21 May 2012

Tomorrow will mark a new chapter in the history of Egypt; for the first time, the Egyptian people will participate in presidential elections without knowing the outcome in advance. This is one of the greatest achievements of the revolution to date and we are grateful to the 20 million Egyptians who went out onto the streets and faced death and arrest so that Egyptians could decide the fate of their own country. There is no doubt that we are witnessing a great historical moment, but the question remains: are these elections truly fair?

Unfortunately, the oversees vote has been mired by signs of possible electoral fraud. *Al Watan* newspaper published two photographs of Egyptian voters in Saudi Arabia tampering with the ballot boxes. In fact, the secretary general of the Supreme Presidential Electoral Commission (SPEC) himself, Hatem Bagato, announced that more than 60 Egyptian citizens living abroad went to cast their ballots only to find that their names had already been used to vote.

Meanwhile, many citizens living in Egypt have discovered that the names of their deceased relatives are still on the electoral register, perhaps the most famous case being Zahra Saeed, who discovered that the name of her brother, Khaled Saeed – the famous martyr of Alexandria and symbol of the revolution – was still recorded on the electoral register. Strangely, nobody has opened an investigation into any of these cases.

The act of voting is only one step in the electorial process. Thus, while the elections may not be fraudulent, they can at the same time be unfair and undemocratic. There are established rules throughout the world for democratic elections, and the military council and the SPEC have committed serious violations of those rules:

First: a lack of transparency. One of the most basic principles of democracy is that voters should know about the wealth of the presidential candidates and how they have financed their election campaigns. However, the two candidates representing the Mubarak regime – Ahmed Shafik and Amr Moussa[1] – have refused point blank to reveal the size of their assets. This refusal should have guaranteed their disqualification from the presidential race, because the law places a cap on spending in election campaigns and makes it an obligation for candidates to reveal their funding sources. But the SPEC did not enforce this law and the streets of Egypt are filled with election advertising that has cost millions of pounds, without Egyptians knowing where the money has come from. The large billboards across Egypt bearing the picture of Ahmed Shafik cost 100,000 Egyptian pounds a month to rent. Who gave Shafik millions of pounds to spend on advertising? And if Shafik paid for them with his own money, how did he come to possess such vast wealth on a government salary?

The same question could be asked of the Muslim Brotherhood candidate Mohamed Morsi, who also spent millions of pounds on advertising during his election campaign. The funding sources of the Muslim Brotherhood are unknown and it is not subject to any auditing whatsoever. This dubious refusal to disclose the cansidates' election finances and personal wealth violates the basic principles of democracy and makes these elections non-transparent and unfair.

Second: The non-enforcement of the law. After Mubarak was deposed, the military council formed a committee to carry out amendments to the 1971 Constitution under the leadership of Tarek el-Bishry, a member of the Muslim Brotherhood. The committee did what was asked of it and put Egypt in a major predicament by retaining Article 28 in the amended constitution. This article makes the decisions of the SPEC non-appealable and was described by the Administrative Court itself as odious and one of the relics of tyranny. During the referendum, the Brotherhood and the Salafists tried to encourage ordinary citizens to vote in favour of the amendments – to satisfy the military council – and made the vote into a religious battle between Muslims and infidels, which ended in the approval of the article. The extraordinary immunity that the Supreme Election Commission enjoys is contrary to custom and law, and indeed to the constitutional declaration itself, which bans immunity for administrative decisions.

The SPEC has so far ignored the 35 complaints levelled against Ahmed Shafik for squandering public funds, despite the fact they were logged almost

1 Amr Moussa is an Egyptian politician and diplomat who was the secretary general of the Arab League, a 22-member forum representing Arab states

one year ago. The attorney general alleges that the complaints were passed on to the military courts but this was later denied by the military courts. When Essam Sultan mentioned Shafik's wrongdoing in parliament, the complaint was passed on to the illegal gains department, where it was then conveniently lost. In a democratic country, would it be possible for a presidential candidate's legal standing not to be effected by documented complaints of corruption and of squandering public funds?

The SPEC did something even stranger when the People's Assembly passed the legislature for the Political Isolation Law. Instead of applying the law, as it was duty-bound to do, and disqualifying Ahmed Shafik from the race, the SPEC transformed from an administrative committee into a legal committee and refused to apply the law, bringing the matter before the Supreme Constitutional Court. So whereas thousands of civilians were brought before military courts and the youth of the revolution were sentenced to prison on fabricated charges, the dozens of complaints against Shafik were waived because he enjoys the favour of the military council. Similarly, the law that forbids using places of worship to spread political propaganda has not been enforced. Preachers in the mosque continue to use their sermons to urge the congregation to vote for the Brotherhood candidate. Then there is the law against buying votes, which has been ignored by the Brotherhood who have been out on the streets distributing oil and sugar to the poor in order to obtain their votes, and no one enforces the law against them. In the absence of the rule of law the elections are unfair before they start.

Third: Preferential treatment. The principle of equal opportunities between candidates has been completely disregarded. The relationship a candidate has with the military council will determine how they are viewed by the state. It follows that the system in place does not treat Ahmed Shafik in the same way as it treats a candidate of the revolution. Furthermore, it does not treat the supporters of Shafik in the same way as his opponents. During his election campaign, Ahmed Shafik was often set upon by revolutionaries in Upper Egypt because of his affiliations with Mubarak. The demonstrators considered his candidacy as a violation of the law and a betrayal of the blood of the martyrs. Each time the demonstrators mobbed Shafik, the security forces descended upon them immediately so that Shafik could safely get away, because he was a student of Mubarak and a friend of the colonels in the military council. When employees at the Civil Aviation Authority held a press conference at the Egyptian Journalist Syndicate (EJS) to reveal the serious financial transgressions committed by Ahmed Shafik during his period in office at the ministry, a group of thugs loyal to Shafik appeared and raided the Syndicate, beat up all the participants and broke up the conference by force. This barbaric attack on the Journalists Syndicate took place within sight of the civilian and military police who did not intervene to stop the attack because it was in Shafik's interest. Despite the high-sounding rhetoric spouted by the military council about justice and democracy, the way they have treated the presidential candidates has varied according to their relationship with the military council, which negates the principle of equal opportunities and makes the elections undemocratic.

Fourth: The prevention of Egyptians living abroad from voting. There are approximately nine million Egyptians living abroad who fought a bitter struggle to obtain their constitutional right to vote in the elections of their country. The Mubarak regime did not want to give them the right to vote because of their large number, and because they lived outside the control of the regime, both of which would make them an influential factor in the result of the elections. After the fall of Mubarak, the military council continued to prevent those Egyptians living abroad from voting until a final verdict was issued giving them the right to vote. At this point the military council's advisors – the same advisors as were under Mubarak – resorted to a bureaucratic trick to empty the judicial ruling of its meaning; they restricted the right to vote only to Egyptians who were in the possession of a national ID number, despite the fact that having an Egyptian passport was enough to prove the identity of the voter, as is the case all over the world. This condition prevented the majority of Egyptians living abroad from exercising their right, and in these elections only 600,000 expatriates are registered to vote. The elections cannot reflect the will of the people if more than eight million citizens are deprived of their right to vote, because this huge portion of the electorate is enough to change the result of any election.

The presidential election, which begins tomorrow, is as far as can be from a fair election, for the military council has set the rules to achieve the result it wants. These are not democratic elections, but a decisive battle between the Egyptian revolution and the Mubarak regime; a regime which the military council supports and protects, fabricating numerous crises from breakdowns in security, to fires, to lack of food and fuel. All of this is to intimidate and frighten Egyptians in preparation for a certain moment where Mubarak's candidate will be propelled onto the scene and be called a hero, who will bring back security and find solutions for all the crises. The Mubarak regime is fighting desperately to put Ahmed Shafik in the presidential seat so that its parasites and thieves can return to their privileged positions once more. Shafik will abort the revolution and persecute the revolutionaries just as he said he would. In contrast, the revolution wants to see a revolutionary president implement the real change the military council has been obstructing for more than a year. This is a battle between the future and the past. The revolution must fight this battle with all its strength to prevent fraud and make a candidate who supports the revolution successful.

I support the candidature of Hamdeen Sabahi, and I consider him the one most capable of achieving the goals of the revolution. However, the battle must never be between one revolutionary candidate and another, but between a candidate who is for the revolution and a candidate of Mubarak, between the revolution that wants Egypt to embrace democracy and return the Egyptian his rights and dignity, and the Mubarak regime which wants Egypt to go backwards and return to producing corruption and tyranny and repression. The revolution is still ongoing and it will triumph and give Egypt the future it deserves.

Democracy is the answer.

PN

Before You Cast Your Vote

4 June 2012

Imagine that you are playing playing in a football team and during the match you found that the referee was blatantly biased in favour of the other team? What would you do if you saw the referee disallow perfectly legitimate goals scored by your team and allowed the other team to win unfairly? Would you play on, knowing that the referee would never allow you to win, or would you withdraw from the match to show your protest against the unfair referee? This is the choice facing the Egyptian revolution today.

The revolution placed its trust in the military council to manage the country during the transitional period to fulfil the aims of the revolution and prepare the country for true democracy. However, the military council preserved the Mubarak regime and supported its efforts to bring the revolution to an end. The military council implemented a detailed plan to thwart the revolution and return Mubarak's cronies to power. They began by defaming the revolutionaries and accusing them of being foreign agents. Then they targeted the Egyptian youth in brutal massacres in which hundreds of civilians were killed and blinded with rubber bullets and in which Egyptian women were indecently assaulted. They created artificial breakdowns in security and fabricated crises pressuring citizens to turn against the revolution. The climax of this was their support of Ahmed Shafik for the presidency; an attempt to return everything to what it was before the revolution. Furthermore, Judge Ahmed Rifaat dismissed the case against Gamal and Alaa Mubarak and declared the innocence of all the individuals from el-Adly's Ministry of the Interior who were responsible for the killing and wounding of thousands of Egyptians. Now that the plan has been carefully carried out, we face a choice in the second round of presidential elections between Ahmed Shafik, Mubarak's loyal follower, and Mohamed Morsi, the Muslim Brotherhood candidate. Faced with all this uncertainty, before you cast your vote, we must remember certain facts:

First: Article 28 gives the Supreme Presidential Elections Commission (SPEC) immunity, taking away the right of the citizen to make a legal challenge or to oppose its decisions. This article is, as described by the Administrative Judiciary Court, "from the remnants of tyranny" and it also contradicts both logic and law. In fact, it contradicts the constitutional declaration issued by the military council that prohibits immunity of any administrative decision from appeal. The pliant legislators who work in the service of the military council say that a referendum was held on Article 28 therefore it cannot be revoked except by referendum. But the response to this is that when Egyptians voted in the famous referendum on nine amendments to the constitution, the military council disregarded the result and made a constitutional declaration containing 63 articles that it foisted on the Egyptian people without consulting them. It also extended the state of emergency without holding a referendum, contrary to what is written in the constitutional amendments.

Now the military council is preparing to announce the Complimentary Constitutional Declaration that it will impose on Egyptians. Time and again it has broken the law so that it can implement what it wants. If it wanted to revoke Article 28 it would have done so, but it wishes this article to stay so that it can propel Ahmed Shafik into the presidency.

Second: According to the announcement of Judge Zakaria Abdel-Aziz, vice president of the Court of Cassation, the SPEC committed a gross legal mistake when it allowed Ahmed Shafik to run for the presidency. It should have applied the political isolation law passed by parliament that excludes Mubarak-era politicians. Instead, they passed the matter on to the Constitutional Court to decide upon, while at the same time allowing Shafik to remain in the running for the presidency. Here we find legal faults surround the SPEC on every side. Despite the fact it is formed of judges, the SPEC is an administrative body and therefore under no circumstances does it have the right to refer laws to the Constitutional Court. If we were to presume – for argument's sake – that the SPEC was a judicial committee, it would have committed a different gross legal fault for it should have put the elections on hold until the Constitutional Court had come to a decision on the political isolation law. However, it allowed Shafik to remain in the running when the legality of his candidature was under threat pending the decision of the court. This fault puts the position of president of the republic in jeopardy because if Shafik gained the presidency and the Constitutional Court were to apply the political isolation law, this would necessitate stripping Shafik of his position and holding the elections again. If Shafik lost in the run-off, and if the political isolation law was applied, it would be Mohamed Morsi who would be deprived of the presidency and the elections would have to be held again because the votes gained by Shafik during his campaign would now be illegal as they could have gone to his competitors. For this reason, Judge Zakaria Abdel-Aziz demanded that the entire election be cancelled because in any eventuality their result would be illegal and unconstitutional.

Third: For the first time in Egyptian history, a citizen has run for the position of president of the republic chased by more than 35 charges of corruption which no one has investigated and have been vacillating between the Attorney General's office and the military courts for a year and a half. In the end, they were ignored to protect Shafik at the insistence of the military council who want to propel him to the presidency. In any democratic country, just one charge of corruption would be enough to bring down the president, whereas in Egypt 35 accusations of corruption have been buried to fulfil the desire of the military council to install Ahmed Shafik as president of Egypt. Now the question is: what will happen if Shafik wins the presidency and is then found guilty of the corruption charges and is sentenced to prison? Will he practice his duties as president from his prison cell, or will we wait until his term in office finishes and see him leave the presidential palace and go straight to prison? This level of farce is enough to remove the legitimacy of any elections in any country.

Fourth: The first round of the elections was marred by gross violations and obscene instances of fraud. What is more, we should not rely too much on the international observers because many of them are working in the interests of the major nations. A few days before the elections, former American President Jimmy Carter invited me along with a group of intellectuals including Galal Amin,[1] Ragia Omran[2] and Khaled Fahmy[3] for a meeting. Together, we discussed the activity of the Carter Center and the ways in which they will monitor the elections. During this meeting, I got the impression that Jimmy Carter had come to Egypt not to monitor the elections but to attest to their integrity. I recall mentioning to him that some presidential candidates were buying the votes of the poor with money, oil and sugar, and that instances of vote-buying could be proven by video recordings available on the internet. At this point, he smiled and said: "I consider this a way to help the poor and it happens in many countries." After these words, I do not consider Carter's testimony on the Egyptian elections convincing, nor would I ever rely on it.

The presidential elections have been marred by many instances of fraud, all of which have been documented and proven. The names of the deceased

1 Galal Amin is an Egyptian economist and commentator, and professor of economics at the American University in Cairo.
2 Ragia Omran is a leading Egyptian human rights lawyer and women's rights activist.
3 Khaled Fahmy is professor of history at the American University in Cairo

have been used to vote and army personnel voted for Shafik in violation of the law that prevents them from voting. Ballet boxes were left for a whole night unsupervised and representatives of the candidates were prevented from guarding them. Some ballot boxes containing the votes of Egyptians living abroad were left in consulates without guard or supervision for an entire week. I call to mind here the testimony of Judge Waleed Sharabi, member of the organisation Judges for Egypt, who claimed that the number of eligible voters had been scandalously manipulated to facilitate electoral fraud. In the space of only 14 months, between the referendum in March 2011 and the presidential elections, the number of eligible Egyptian voters increased by 5,874,525. This cannot be explained by any natural means as the citizens who reached the legal voting age (18) this year numbered less than one million. This proves that this large number of voters was accrued in the context of deliberate electoral fraud. Given this fact, Judge Waleed Sharabi called for Egyptians to boycott the presidential elections because they were void and fraudulent and demanded that they be completely cancelled and repeated only after the members of the SPEC had been changed.

The biggest mistake Egyptians could make is to consider the runoff election between the Brotherhood candidate Mohamed Morsi and the military's candidate Ahmed Shafik a true contest. The runoff, if it ever happens amidst all these flaws, will undoubtedly put Shafik into the presidency. If the Brotherhood wanted to rise to a level of national responsibility, they themselves should have demanded that the elections be cancelled and repeated after Shafik was disqualified and brought to trial. Unfortunately, the Brotherhood repeated exactly the same mistakes. As soon as a chance to gain power is waved in front of them, they are blind to any other consideration no matter how important.

The second round of the elections is illegal and will be rigged just like the first round so that Shafik can assume the presidency. If Egyptians question this fraudulent result after Shafik has assumed the presidency, they will be harshly repressed. This is what the military council promised on its Facebook page when it wrote: "Whoever opposes the result of the second round wants to spoil the celebration of democracy and will be clamped down upon." This same threat was repeated by Ahmed Shafik when he met members of the American Chamber of Commerce, details of which appeared in an article in the New York Times in which he said: "If I gain the presidency, I will bring back security within one month and I will use brute force and executions to do so." This is perhaps the first time in history that a presidential candidate threatens his citizens with execution and asks them to elect him at the same time.

Dear reader, if you go to cast your vote in the second round, you are giving Shafik the presidency of Egypt. The runoff has no legality until the political isolation law is applied to Shafik and he is brought to trial for corruption charges, until there has been an investigation into instances of electoral fraud and until Article 28 is removed. Then the elections can be started again.

If these legitimate demands are not met, I will not participate in this charade of a second round. On election day, I shall go and spoil my vote. If a large number of voters spoil their votes, this will send out a powerful message confirming the illegality of the elections. What is the legitimacy of a president who came to his position by all these gross violations? What is the legitimacy of a president when the number of spoiled votes is more than the number of votes supporting him? The revolution is ongoing so that we can put pressure on the military council to hold the proper, fair elections Egypt deserves after the revolution.

Democracy is the answer.

PN

The Phenomenon of the Tame Citizen

12 June 2012

Twenty years ago I was working as a dentist for a governmental department, and one morning I was treating a member of staff. He was lying in the dentist's chair with his mouth open and a metal clamp fitted around one of his molars so that I could put in a filling. While I was occupied with my work, the door of the surgery burst open and the department's head of security walked in and unexpectedly said: "Please finish with your patient straight away. The head of the department is coming to have his teeth looked at."

"I still have half an hour of work to do until I can release the patient," I told him.

"I'm not sure if you understood me. You must finish him off right now because the director is on his way to the surgery," said the head of security in an authoritative and provocative tone.

"I cannot let the patient leave my surgery with a tooth exposed," I protested. "The director should have contacted me first through the secretary to make an appointment."

The head of security smiled sarcastically and said: "The head of the department does not make appointments. Whenever he wants his teeth looked at, you must be ready."

"I do not work for the head of the department, but for a governmental department of which he is the head," I said.

"For the last time, get rid of this patient because the director is on his way," said the head of security unequivocally.

"I will not release this patient before I have finished his treatment," I yelled.

The patient had his mouth open and was unable to speak but I noticed that he was making some noises and signalling to me. I removed the metal frame from his mouth and to my utter astonishment, the patient leaped from his chair and apologised the the head of security: "Tell the head of the department to come at once. I am happy to wait and finish my treatment later."

The patient then left the room with the head of security to personally welcome the head of the department and escort him to the surgery.

I was disappointed by the patient's attitude. I had tried to defend his honour but he had let me down by welcoming the degrading treatment meted out by the head of the department. I had done the right thing and acted in the patient's best interests but he was accustomed to abuse and humiliation. In his view, pleasing the head of department was more important that preserving your dignity. Fawning over his superior could yield rewards and privileges whereas defending what was right could cost him dearly.

I recall this incident now as I am trying to understand what is happening in Egypt. The Egyptian people carried out a monumental revolution that many historians and political scientists consider one of the greatest revolutions in history. Millions of Egyptians went out into the streets in the name of revolution and were beaten, killed, and blinded by rubber bullets. Thousands of them were killed or injured in order to restore freedom and dignity to the Egyptian people. In the end, the revolutionary forces triumphed and forced the tyrant to give up power. But how, after this great revolution, can it be possible that Ahmed Shafik, a supporter and loyal disciple of Mubarak, has been allowed to run as a presidential candidate?

The answer is that the military council has resisted change and preserved the Mubarak regime, which in turn has carried out a well-executed plan to undo the gains of the Egyptian revolution. It deliberately tarnished the reputation of the revolutionaries and tried to crush them through a series of artifical crises. It then put Ahmed Shafik forward as a presidential candidate, thus disregarding the polical isolation law which disqualified politicians assosciated with the former regime. The military council also ignored the 35 charges of corruption pending against Ahmed Shafik and did all they could to ensure his victory in the first round of the elections. The results were rigged in his favour, as the run-off elections will be too.

The military council is determined to propel Ahmed Shafik to the presidency in order to protect their own interests and restore the old regime to power. The military council bears primarily responsibility for for obstructing change and thwarting the revolution. All this is true but it is not enough to explain what is happening. Why have all the problems – the breakdown in law and order, the artificial crises and the rising prices – driven some Egyptians to turn against the revolution while, at the same time, they have not broken the will or shaken the faith of the revolutionaries, who have faced a succession of massacres at the hands of the police and the army? Why does one Egyptian curse the revolution because he can't find petrol for his car, while Ahmed Harara, who lost both his eyes during the revolution, is still smiling and is more determined than ever to achieve the goals of the revolution because of his sacrifice?

It seems certain Egyptians are more involved with the revolution than others. The Egyptian revolution, like all revolutions, did not involve the whole Egyptian people, and after the revolution, the people split into three groups:

First: The revolutionaries, who were determined to see the revolution through whatever sacrifices they had to make.

Second: The remnants of the fallen regime (*fuloul*) who will fight passionately to bring back the old regime in order to protect their own interests and to avoid prosecution.

Third: the tame citizens (like the patient whose teeth I was treating), who were able to put up with the corrupt regime and who were not prepared to pay the price for change. The vast majority of Egyptians still support the revolution, but we must acknowledge the phenomenon of the tame citizens who were taken surprise by the revolution and who watched the events unfold on their televisions without actively taking part. When they were certain Mubarak had been deposed, the tame citizens took their children out into the squares to take souvenir photographs. They are the ones who have been most affected by the propaganda against the revolution and the ones who have been most angered by the succession of artificial crises. Now they are openly cursing the revolution, even though the revolutionaries have not been in power during the transitional period. Why don't they direct their anger at the military council, which has performed the functions of the head of state and has had primary responsibility since Mubarak was deposed? The tame citizens may lack political awareness, but I believe that they were against the revolution from the start.

They had adapted to the old regime and reconciled their life to corruption. Their ideas about the world became distorted as a result – courage was equated with stupidity and sycophancy was a form of shrewdness. Tame citizens were not necessarily connected to the interests of the Mubarak regime directly, but they made their own networks of corruption which enabled them to obtain money through methods that were illegal or at least immoral: the petty officials who took bribes in all government departments, the doctors in government hospitals who forced poverty-stricken patients to go to private clinics, the teachers who blackmail their students into taking private lessons, the journalists who colluded with the state security service, misled public opinion and propagated lies in order to defend the regime.

How could we ever expect such people to support the revolution? It would be natural for them to hate the revolution because it brought them face to face with themselves. They strayed from the straight and narrow when they convinced themselves that change was impossible and that they could not fix the world's problems. Therefore, they had to abandon their principles and accept injustice and humiliation in order to make a living and bring up their children. Then, suddenly, they discovered that other Egyptians, who had suffered the same hardships, were rising up and demanding freedom and dignity.

Tame citizens, insomuch as they were affected by the moral corruption prevalent under Mubarak, now constitute the bulk of the supporters of the counter-revolution. They are ready to overlook the facts if it means overturning the revolution and returning everything to the way it was. These same people saw with their own eyes Egyptian women being dragged through the streets and indecently assaulted by army personnel. There only response to this tragedy was to question the reasons why the women had attented the demonstrations in the first place. These are the people who saw army tanks crush demonstrators in Maspero Square but refused to believe their eyes and accused the Copts of attacking the army. And now these very same people are ignoring the fact that Ahmed Shafik's candidature goes against law and logic, and that he was responsible for the killing of demonstrators in the Battle of the Camel and smuggling the money of Mubarak and his sons abroad. These tame citizens support Shafik and say that he will bring back security, and by this they mean the security of the old regime that corrupted them and which they now long for.

The Egyptian revolution held up a mirror to Egyptian society and showed it the scars left behind by the Mubarak regime. At the same time, the determination of the military council to propel Shafik to the presidency served as the final revelatory scene in a play, in which everybody takes of their masks. While millions of revolutionary Egyptians took to the streets to reject the return of the Mubarak regime under Shafik, the tame citizens have shown the extent of their opportunism and their hatred of the revolution. As soon as it became clear that Shafik would be the next president of Egypt – by fraudulent means – many well-known intellectuals changed their stance from supporting the revolution to supporting Shafik, in the hope of obtaining positions they have long dreamed of. Some journalists who up to this point had supported the revolution, began to promote Ahmed Shafik in the form of televised debates that were effectively blatant advertisements, though we do not know who has paid for them. Even the private television channels that sided with the revolution have now turned to promoting Shafik and suppressing any criticism directed towards him, because the owners of these channels are businessmen who know that satisfying the future president will yield them gold.

This is the moment of truth. While revolutionary Egyptians have set an example of bravery to the whole world and sacrificed everything for freedom and dignity, the tame citizens did not understand the revolution, did not need it, and in reality do not deserve it. They are submissive and corrupt individuals that work only for their paltry gains and small-minded interests. The struggle now is between the revolution and the Mubarak regime that absorbed the first shock and has reorganised its ranks to launch a vicious attack to regain power through Shafik.

This being said, we should not become pessimistic. Revolution means profound change and once it starts it inevitably reaches all aspects of society. Revolutions might falter but they are never defeated. A revolution is a unique human phenomenon and once it comes about, it is bound to continue. Revolution means that at a certain moment people put their principles ahead of their interests. They break the barrier of fear and accept death for the sake of freedom. Revolution is a rebirth by which people purge themselves of contamination and of their mistakes to start a life that is clean, just and free. The spirit that revolution revives in a nation never dies, however many conspiracies are hatched and massacres take place. The revolution will continue, God willing, and will achieve its objectives.

Democracy is the answer.

PN

Why Did Mohamed Morsi Win?

25 June 2012

How many times have you said, or heard someone else say, that Egyptians are not ready for democracy? How many times have you said, or heard someone else say, that Egyptians need someone to educate them and teach them how to exercise their political rights?

I have heard people state these opinions scores of times inside and outside Egypt, and I always explain to them that the history of modern Egypt shows that the Egyptian people have always behaved with real political awareness. I continue by telling them that they are talking about the Egyptian people as if they were a hypothetical concept or expression, rather than real people. The Egyptian nation is made up of millions of people who may differ in their social background or education, but at a certain moment a common national feeling and outlook makes them take a unified and often correct stance. It is the Egyptian nation that has made all the Egyptian revolutions.

On 25 January, thousands of demonstrators came from Imbaba to join those in Tahrir Square. Those simple and poor people were the ones who protected the demonstrators against attacks by the state security service. Had it not been for them, the revolution would not have succeeded. It is the Egyptian people who are the true heroes of what happened last Sunday, 24 January, a landmark date in the history of Egypt and the whole Arab world. Over the course of 16 months, the military council has been carrying out a carefully planned scheme to abort the Egyptian revolution. A breakdown in law and order, sectarian incidents, the terrorisation of the population, and manufactured shortages of essential commodities, in addition to systematic campaigns to defame the revolution, and massacre after massacre of revolutionaries in which many men have been killed and women abused at the hands of individuals from the police force and the army. The design was to put so much pressure on Egyptian citizens that they would cling to anyone who could restore order. That is why Ahmed Shafik was supported and protected from 35 documented cases of corruption against him and from the Political Isolation Law.

When the [election] results showed that Shafik and Morsi would have to enter a run-off, all indications pointed to a Shafik victory. The Brotherhood lost the sympathy of most revolutionaries, as a result of their having hijacked the victory of the revolution for their own interests. Moreover, a large sector of the Copts are terrified of the Brotherhood and decided to vote for Shafik, in addition to the remnants of the old regime who have been supporting Shafik's campaign financially, because it is their last chance to get back in power. Add to that the whole apparatus of the state, which has supported Shafik with all its strength, starting from the senior figures in the Ministry of the Interior and the state security service, and including the ministries, institutions and state media which has gone back to its old lying ways, and the private media owned by businessmen most of whom, for the sake of their own enormous business interests, have thrown their support behind Shafik.

Many people, myself included, have decided to boycott the elections in protest at Shafik being a candidate as opposed to being disqualified and put on trial. Due to all these aforementioned circumstances, it was inevitable that Shafik would win, but something most surprising occurred – the Brotherhood could not gain more than five million votes for Morsi in the first round, but when it came to the run off, eight million Egyptians decided to vote for Morsi, not because they belonged to the Muslim Brotherhood but because they knew that if the old regime were to get back into power the Egyptian revolution would be over.

That millions voted for the Brotherhood candidate was the surprise blow of a nation aware enough to upset all predictions and frustrate the scheme of aborting the revolution. The military council fell into a dilemma and a few hours before announcing the election results they issued a constitutional declaration restricting the powers of the president. The announcement of the election results was delayed until Thursday, then until Sunday, and at that point the nation understood yet again that something was going on behind the scenes and millions of Egyptians – Brotherhood members and others – went out on the street in an attempt to rally pressure against anyone trying to falsify the will of the electorate.

History one day will uncover what took place before the election results were declared but stories have abounded all pointing to one truth. Despite the fact that the legal system in Egypt is not independent but falls under the executive authority, we do have some independent judges who possess the conscience and courage to speak the truth whatever the price may be.

Zakariya Abd el-Aziz and a group of other judges formed an association called "Judges for Egypt" to monitor the elections. They confirmed the victory of Mohamad Morsi over Shafik by a margin of almost one million. Judge Zakariya Abd el-Aziz does not agree with the philosophy or the politics of the Brotherhood, but he is a much-respected judge whose only motivation is to do what is correct. The report of the independent judges was a brave initiative that embarrassed those who attempted to falsify the results.

The Egyptian revolution realised a great achievement in voting Shafik out of office and electing Mohamed Morsi. Regardless of my political differences with him, he is the first civilian elected president in the history of modern Egypt. This victory of the will of the people will not just affect Egypt but it will push the wheel of change in the wider Arab world, and will hopefully rid it of the corrupt dictators who have been holding the people down for decades.

It is our duty to congratulate President Morsi, but it is also our duty to remind him of a few truths.

First: The new president was not elected with Brotherhood votes alone as these would not have been enough to ensure him victory. He was elected by millions of Egyptians who thought that supporting him was the only way to stop the Mubarak regime coming back, and consequently President Morsi is accountable to all Egyptians and we demand that he should sever his ties with the Muslim Brotherhood immediately, and, as he promised, form a transitional government whose ministerial appointments should include revolutionaries as well as people from other political trends.

Second: For a year and a half the military council has refrained from realising the aims of the revolution and has rejected any change to the Mubarak-regime structure. Now, after the elected president's victory, change can not be put off any longer: we expect President Morsi to help ease the passage of the Judiciary Authority Law to uncouple the judiciary from the executive authority. We expect him to rescind the constitutional declaration that set the military council above all other authority in the country. Those accused of corruption must be put on trial, first and foremost Ahmed Shafik. The police must be purged of the corrupt and murderous elements who have killed demonstrators. The state security service must be shut down and intelligence operatives must not be allowed to intimidate citizens. Civilians must not be tried in military courts and the 12,000 civilians being held in military prisons must be released and their cases sent for trial at a regular court. A minimum and a maximum wage must be set and poverty and unemployment must be ended. This revolution came about for freedom, dignity and social justice. The president's credibility or lack thereof will depend upon how true he remains to the ideals of the revolution.

Third: Mohamed Morsi would not have been able to become president had 1,200 young Egyptians not sacrificed their lives during the revolution or without the ongoing disappearance of a thousand Egyptians mostly killed and buried in unknown graves, or the thousands of people injured with many of them losing their eyesight to bullets. They are the people Egypt should thank, after God Almighty, for without their sacrifice we would not have been able to experience this moment. President Morsi must see to it that those who killed people get their just reward. He should see to it that the families of those killed are looked after, and the highest level of medical treatment inside and outside Egypt should be provided at the state's expense to people who have been injured. The new president should not let the injured of the revolution become charity cases. He should not allow those who killed demonstrators to stay free and in their jobs, as if they had not spilt the innocent blood of young people whose only crime was that they rose up for the sake of the dignity of their fellow Egyptians.

Fourth: The president has just two options in front of him: he can either realise the aims of the revolution for Egyptians in general, or he can realise the interests of the Muslim Brotherhood by means of secret agreements with the military council. I hope that the Brotherhood do not repeat their historic mistake in thinking, as they unfortunately have done since the establishment of the organisation in 1928, that the interests of the Brotherhood are those of the nation; something which always put them into alliances with the ruling power and which did much harm to the national movement. The most recent of these is their alliance with the military council after the revolution, which lost us the opportunity to draft a new constitution and has left us in this dire situation. Morsi's task will not be easy because he is confronting the Mubarak regime which still controls the state and which I expect to put up stiff resistance to any change. In its fierce battle with the Mubarak regime, the president will need the support of all Egyptians, something he will only get if he is seen to be fighting for all of Egypt and not just for the Muslim Brotherhood.

Fifth: President Morsi has always promised a civil state. This phrase can be explained in several ways. In my opinion what he meant by civil state can be summed up in four cardinal points:

Citizenship rights. An Egyptian citizen must have full rights regardless of religion. The Copts must have restored to them under the new president all the rights that were subverted in the Mubarak era, as true Islam would dictate.

Protection of the personal freedoms established centuries ago in Egypt. One of the foremost markers of Egyptian way of life has been that you alone define the course of your life within the confines of the law. Any attack on personal freedoms in the name of some moral programme turns citizens into no more than the wards of overarching authority, as is the case in Sudan and Saudi Arabia. That would be a return to the dark ages and a disaster for all of Egypt.

Protection of freedom of thought and expression. On this, we should warn the president not to listen to the voices of the anti-culture and anti-art extremists. Egypt has always been a citadel of art and thought in the East. We will never agree to creativity being censored by the puritanical, as that would only lead to the loss of our artistic heritage and the end of the Egyptian creativity we are all so proud of. The way to confront thought is with thought and only the law can be used to set a limit to creativity. That is the golden law for the protection of Egyptian culture.

Any attempt to implement the corporal and capital Sharia punishments will lead to a rift in Egyptian society, and president Morsi knows well that he cannot implement Sharia punishments until he has brought an end to poverty, ignorance and illness. He cannot have thieves' hands cut off before he has provided them with a decent life. This was a basic rule of humanity before it became one clad in the wording of a religious-juridical opinion.

The Egyptian people who have just elected Mohamed Morsi expect much from him and will support him provided he works for the interest of Egypt and realises the aims of the revolution.

Democracy is the answer.

RH

Hold Your Ground

2 July 2012

I am writing this article from my hotel bedroom in Toulouse, and through the window I can see a large square filled with people attending the "Marathon des Mots", which is one of the largest literary festivals in France. The festival is organised by Olivier Poivre d'Arvor, director of radio France Culture, and a team of young French people, as well as the Egyptian, Dalia Hasan. This year, the festival decided to choose me as a guest of honour, and for this I am truly grateful. The management organised an evening of readings to celebrate my work, during which the famous French actress Ariane Ascaride read out excerpts from my one of my novels. On top of my personal delight at this great honour, I am proud that an Egyptian author has been chosen as the guest of honour out of a group of the most important authors in the world. The French follow what is happening in Egypt with great interest and believe that it is Egypt which will shape the future of the whole Arab world. Mohamed Morsi's election as president caused huge controversy in France with some people considering the accession of Islamists to power, even if elected, in any country, to be a catastrophe. Many French people worry that Morsi will turn Egypt into Iran by replacing the military dictators with a theocratic dictatorship. In a theocratic state, it is often the minorities, women and the artistic community that pay the highest price. Other French people, and they are mostly liberals and rightists, are of the opinion that Morsi will have to respect the will of the people whatever the results, and that he must be treated as an elected president and given a chance before judgement is passed on him. They think that the Islamists' entry into democratic politics will be a moderating influence on the Egyptian people and will stop them veering to violence. I defended the opinion of this latter group and told them that the existence of an Islamist president does not necessarily mean the establishment of a theocratic state, and that the Islamist parties within the democratic system will be somewhat akin to the right-wing Christian parties in Germany and Switzerland. I had listened to President Morsi's speech in Tahrir Square and I admired it for its clarity and sincerity. However, I was shocked when I saw the celebrations at Cairo University because the president appeared to go back on his previous political stances. The president had already promised to see justice done for the those killed, not just during the revolution but also those killed in the massacres that took place under the rule of the military council, such as at Abassiya, Mohamed Mahmoud, Maspero, outside the cabinet office, and in Port Said.

Seeing justice done for those killed does not just mean paying out compensation for them, but holding fair trials for those involved in their deaths. The military council cannot be absolved of political accountability for all these massacres. I was astonished to hear President Morsi demanding that the members of the military council be honoured for the way they ran the government during the transitional period. Under this "wise" administration, young revolutionaries were shot with bullets, crushed to death by armoured cars, blinded by rubber bullets, dragged along the ground and abused – all crimes that have been documented and filmed. How can Morsi restore to the dead their rights, whilst simultaneously calling for those politically responsible to be honoured? The president is on the horns of a dilemma. Furthermore, the president has already declared his utter rejection of the constitutional declaration and has thereby handed authority to the military, denuded democracy of its content and made the president something akin to the secretary of Field Marshal Tantawi. However we were surprised to see the president swearing his oath of office in front of the Constitutional Court just as it passed the constitutional declaration that he rejected. Then he went to speak at Cairo University where he uttered not one word about his rejection of the constitutional declaration against which millions of Egyptians have been staging protests for days.

We should not rush into judgement of President Morsi, but nor should we remain silent as we notice him shifting his political positions. There is a real problem with the political behaviour of the Muslim Brotherhood in that they can see no difference between the interests of the Brotherhood and those of the state. Consequently they always try to realise their own political interests regardless of the effect on the people and the country. This concept has led to the Brotherhood forging alliances with all the rulers of Egypt without exception, from King Farouk to the military council. The Muslim Brotherhood by nature is a conservative, reformist and non-revolutionary political force that avoids any clash with authority in any form. Its leadership is beset with fears that a clash with the ruler will bring about the end of the organisation, so they have always tended to forge alliances to further the organisation's interests, just as, in the presence of the sultan, they bend with the wind and behave within the limits of what the ruler allows them. We saw just that in the celebrations at Cairo University with the appearance of Saad el-Katatni, who made such a huge fuss over Field Marshal Tantawi's dissolution of the People's Assembly, not only stating his rejection of this decision but trying to enter parliament to challenge it, only to be stopped by the security police. After this bitter war of words, el-Katatni did an about-turn at Cairo University, and the moment he saw Field Marshal Tantawi his face lit up and he jumped for joy as if nothing had happened.

We saw the same political contortions in parliament when the Brotherhood MPs tried to placate the military council at the expense of the revolution. We all remember how the Brotherhood applauded when a member accused the revolutionaries of being thugs and drug addicts. We also remember how the Brotherhood let revolutionaries be cut down on Mohamed Mahmud Street, so keen were they to placate the military council, and how they levelled obscene accusations against female demonstrators who had been abused. In addition there is a singular scene, which I do not think has occurred in the history of parliaments, when members of the

People's Assembly discovered that a secret police agent had been inciting the masses to attack the People's Assembly. There was a total uproar in parliament, with so much shouting that the rafters shook. They demanded that the minister of the interior come immediately to explain the matter. When he arrived, the distinguished members of parliament rushed over to embrace him and have their photograph taken with him. I do not know the definitive reason for all these Brotherhood contortions, but it is a phenomenon that has been a feature of the whole history of the Brotherhood since the organisations establishment in 1928 and is actually the thing that most threatens President Morsi's position at the moment. President Morsi made definitive and clear promises when he told the people that he would carry out the following demands:

1. To cancel the constitutional declaration and to take back full presidential powers, to exercise full, rather than symbolic, authority, meaning that the army should return to its barracks, restrict itself to the task of defending the nation and not interfere in politics in any form or pretext.

2. The immediate release of 14,000 people from military detention centres, the transfer of their cases to regular judges and an end to civilians being tried by military courts.

3. Reforming the Constitutional Assembly to better express the will of the people but without a Brotherhood majority, so that they cannot impose their own constitution on the people.

4. The formation of a transitional government with an independent, nationalist prime minister, the appointment of a woman and a Coptic deputy prime minister and the appointment of revolutionary ministers, so that Brotherhood ministers do not make up more than 30 per cent of the cabinet.

5. The preservation of the civil state, respect for legally-guaranteed personal freedoms and the non-imposition of dress rules on women under any pretext.

6. The protection of the Copts and the realisation of their legitimate demands which were ignored in the Mubarak era.

7. The preservation of freedom of expression and the protection of legally-guaranteed creative freedom. No reactionary or retrogressive attempts to rein in the arts aimed at destroying the cinema industry or restricting literary creativity.

President Morsi made these promises more than once to the Egyptian nation, and he is now at a crossroads. Ahead of him he has only two choices: either to behave like a legitimate elected president who represents the revolution and to wage a political battle against the military council in order to snatch back his full powers and restore authority to the Egyptian people who suffered from military rule for sixty years. Then it will be incumbent upon us to support the president with all our might in order to achieve the essential aim of the revolution which was to put an end to military rule and to transfer power, in a real form, from the military to the Egyptian people so that they can rule themselves in a democratic manner for the first time in sixty years.

The alternative, which I hope will not happen, is that the Brotherhood pressures President Morsi into appeasement and political contortions and that the president cuts a secret deal with the military council granting the Brotherhood only as much power as allowed by the military council, which will continue to rule from behind the scenes with the president's power being only figurative. If the president chooses this option he will have failed the people and broken his promises, and before he becomes merely Field Marshal Tantawi's secretary any position which President Morsi takes will not just affect the course of the revolution but the whole Arab world. It is the president's right to be granted the chance to fulfil his promises, and it is incumbent upon us also to communicate our fears to him. I hope that he stays in the nation's favour by carrying out what he promised to do regardless of the pressures he may be subjected to. The best I can do here is to quote an eloquent sentence, which everyone who participated in the Egyptian revolution knows. When the security police and Mubarak's thugs were attacking and beating up demonstrators, those in the front lines used to shout at their fellow demonstrators: "Hold your ground!" This cry was heard time and again as we became ever more certain of our power and determination to defend the revolution to the end even if they killed us. This shout drummed into us that if we retreated we would lose, and if we ran for our lives this would only give those thugs the chance to finish us off. Every time we used the call "Hold your ground!", we managed to face attacks and many times even to chase off the attackers. It is this firmness that has made the revolution, by God's grace, victorious in the end and enabled it to force Mubarak from power. I hope that President Morsi will realise the demands of the revolution, whatever pressures he is exposed to, either from the military council or from the Brotherhood organisation.

President Morsi, hold your ground!

Democracy is the answer.

RH

Are We Repeating el-Senhouri's Mistake?

9 July 2012

Abdel Razek el-Senhouri was one of the greatest jurists in the history of Egypt and the Arab world. It was he who drafted the constitution and civil law for many Arab countries including Libya, Iraq, Sudan, Kuwait, Syria and the United Arab Emirates. This great man made an unfortunate mistake almost sixty years ago, whose price we are paying to this day. El-Senhouri was well known for his hostility towards the Wafd Party, which held a majority in parliament at that time. In 1952, the Free Officers carried out a military coup, which later became a revolution, forcing King Farouk to abdicate in favour of his son, the young Prince Ahmed Fuad. A Regency Council had to be formed, and according to the 1923 Constitution, the Regency Council had to take the oath in front of the Wafd-majority parliament.

Gamal Abdel Nasser, in my opinion, was a devoted and great leader but he was also one of the first to establish military rule in Egypt. Nasser was very much aware of the overweening popularity of the Wafd Party and went to seek advice from el-Senhouri, then president of the Council of State. El-Senhouri was so blinded by hatred for the Wafd Party that he came up with a legal loophole to enable Nasser to exclude them from parliament. Shortly after, Nasser issued a decree that dissolved all political parties and abolished parliamentary government. At that point el-Senhouri realised by excluding the Wafd Party he had unwittingly participated in the destruction of the democratic system itself.

El-Senhouri attempted to correct the mistake, opposing Nasser, defending democracy and demanding the return of the army to their barracks, but it was too late. The Free Officers were irritated by el-Senhouri's opposition to them and sent its hirelings to beat him up severely in his office. Then the Revolutionary Command Council[1] issued an edict abolishing the Council of State from the outset. El-Senhouri was humiliated by his actions and died a broken man in 1971. The significance of the incident is that our political differences with any party or association should not blind us to the truth.

We must defend our principles even if our political opponents profit from them. In Egypt there is now a fierce struggle raging between the Mubarak regime, which still controls the state, and Mohamed Morsi, the first elected civilian president. His position as a member of the Muslim Brotherhood means

1 The Revolutionary Command Council (RCC) was the body established to supervise Egypt and Sudan after the Revolution of 1952. It initially selected Ali Maher as Prime Minister, but forced him to resign after conflict over land reform. The RCC controlled the state until 1954, when the Council dissolved itself.

that many people are unwilling to give him a chance; objecting to what he says even before he says it. I have always opposed the Muslim Brotherhood in both theory and practice. In theory, because they believe in an Islamic caliphate and I consider that to be a fascist, dictatorial system that led to Egypt falling under the first Ottoman occupation, just as I oppose them because they believe that Islam is both religion and state. I do not believe that Islam offers a definitive system of government, but rather general principles and that it allows Muslims to choose their own political system. On the practical level, I oppose the politics of the Brotherhood, which do not see any difference between the association's interest and that of the country, something which has turned them into opportunists who have forced alliances with dictatorial authority against the will of the people. An example being the Brotherhood's renunciation of the revolution and their alliance with the military council, which deprived Egyptians of writing a new constitution. As for the Salafists, I oppose them because they insist on the Wahhabi-Saudi version of Islam, which contradicts the moderate Egyptian version. I am also against the Salafists' extremism, their short-sightedness and their politics, which are anti-freedom, anti-women's rights and inimical to the arts and literature. Thus my relations with the Brotherhood and the Salafists are not, shall we say, the most cordial, and people associated with the Salafist movement have attacked my private clinic twice and tried to attack me because of my views. I have attempted to bring them to justice for this but the case is still pending.

This violent feud with political Islam however should never stop me from helping them if they are injured or from supporting them if they wage a nationalist and legitimate campaign. The conflict is now between two parties: the president, who has been elected by the will of the people, and the military council that imposes its will on us through the barrel of a gun. This conflict forms the essence of the Egyptian revolution, which arose first and foremost in order to put an end to military rule and to restore power to the people, who are the legitimate authority. The slogans of the revolution, "life, freedom and social justice", will never be realised unless the people regain control of the country. President Morsi is now confronting the full force of the Mubarak regime, which has control over public institutions, as well as secret branches that have pervaded all aspects of the Egyptian state.

These secret branches, which are sometimes referred to as the "deep state", have been responsible for a number of the crises in Egypt since the fall of Mubarak. The Mubarak regime operates according to the following principle: the Egyptians have risen up against unfair conditions and if the situation is much worse than the one they revolted against, they can always restore the old regime in a new form. Evidence for this can be seen in the scores of incidents orchestrated by the Mubarak regime, from the defamation of revolutionaries, to the creation of ongoing shortages of basic foodstuffs. This has all been done with the aim of turning Egyptians against the revolution and making them suffer from the deterioration in the standard of living. Then they put forward an old regime candidate in the guise of a devoted hero who will restore order and put an end to the suffering of Egyptians.

The Mubarak regime tried to suggest Omar Suleiman as the man to take on this role but the popular opposition was strong enough to force them to withdraw his candidacy a few days later. Then they put forward Ahmed Shafik, who had the full support of the Mubarak regime. Pro-Mubarak businessmen showered him with millions of pounds from their coffers. He gained mass support from senior figures in the Ministry of the Interior, leading figures in the National Democratic Party, officers in the state security service and the media, all educated in the corridors of the Ministry of the Interior, in addition to the four million names which were added to the electoral roles and who all voted for Shafik. Moreover, educated opportunists, in the belief that Shafik was the forerunner, quickly abandoned the revolutionary ship and declared their support for him.

Millions of Egyptians went out to vote for Morsi, not out of love for him, but in order to bring down Shafik as the representative of the old regime. Although Morsi's victory was clear from the start, the declaration of the election results was delayed for a week and there are indications that the intention in doing so was to fix the results in favour of Shafik. Al Faraeen TV broadcast a document issued by the Supreme Presidential Electoral Commission (SPEC) purporting to show Shafik's victory over Morsi, and strangely the judges who were signatories to this document did not present any charges against the channel. The Mubarak regime stepped back from changing the results and also withdrew temporarily in front of the elected president. At the same time the military council issued an illegitimate constitutional declaration which snatched powers from the president of the republic. Then the full machinery of the Mubarak regime swung into action to foil the elected president and defame him even before he had taken office.

The same old method – the ever-worsening breakdown in law and order – is taking place in full view of the civil and military police which has not intervened to protect the Egyptian people. There have also been continuous attacks on citizens by Islamist extremists. Some of these attacks have been spontaneous, but others have involved officers and thugs connected to the state security apparatus. Moreover, the incidents have received enormous coverage in the media in an obvious attempt to cow citizens. However, we must not forget the relationship between the state security service and some of the extremist organisations, which the Islamists have themselves admitted. The speaker of the Nour Party, Nader Bekar, named four clerics as agents of the state security service. What is the truth about the Committee for the Command of Virtue and the Prevention of Vice, which has been renounced by all the religious parties and associations? Why does it always appear and disappear according to political circumstances?

Any reading of the communiqués of this association shows that its first aim is to terrorise the people, as it speaks of mounted patrols day and night, canes, electricity cables and guns. Why have officials in the Ministry of the Interior not been monitoring its website and arrested its members within hours? The answer is that the Mubarak regime is continuing to terrorise Egyptians until the time is right to take the next step.

Yesterday a female judge close to the military council declared that President Morsi must resign once the constitution has been drafted. The plan thus becomes clear. The operations to terrorise civilians will continue and the elected president will continue to be defamed until the military council announces his dismissal after the constitution has been drawn up, and citizens will then feel a deep sense of ease at the removal of the evil of the Brotherhood. There will be further elections and the Mubarak regime will throw its support behind a candidate who might be Shafik, or Omar Suleiman, or anyone from the military establishment. Thus we must organise our priorities. The attitude of some Egyptians towards the Brotherhood has turned into an animosity so deep that it has blinded them to the truth and pushed them into accepting military rule in order to spite the Brotherhood; just as el-Senhouri took the side of the Free Officers against the Wafd Party and then regretted it bitterly when the whole democratic regime came tumbling down. On the other hand, some of the Islamist hardliners are incapable of comprehending what is happening as they try to impose their puritanical ideas with force, unwittingly helping the Mubarak regime in its vain conflict with the elected president. We must defend the principles of democracy and the aims of the revolution regardless of who might profit from it. When we reject the authority of the military council to govern, and demand full powers for the president of the republic, we are neither doing that for Mohamed Morsi, nor for the Muslim Brotherhood, but for the sake of the revolution and Egypt.

Our main battle is now with the Mubarak regime, which is fighting tooth and nail to abort the revolution and to return to full power. If the alternatives are military rule or rule by the people, then it is our absolute duty to support the elected president even if we oppose his politics diametrically. However, our support for the president is not unconditional: if he confirms that he is in fact the president of all Egyptians, and if he fulfils his promises and carries on the battle to put an end to the Mubarak regime and to restore power to the people, then we must support him with all our might. However, if his Brotherhood membership takes priority over his duties to the people, if he carries out cheap horse-trading to further the interests of the Brotherhood, we will discard him, like he has discarded the revolution. At that time, the revolution will have to confront both the military and the Brotherhood. Whatever the case, the revolution will eventually win and will realise its aims so that Egypt can have the future it deserves.

Democracy is the answer.

RH

A Future Imagined

16 July 2012

Fourth Unit: Lesson Seven

Following the rigged parliamentary elections and due to the widespread corruption, unemployment and poverty, in addition to the brutality practiced by the state security service against citizens, the revolution against Hosni Mubarak broke out on 25 January 2011 with the participation of millions of Egyptians. The state security service tried to put the revolution down savagely, killing and wounding thousands of demonstrators, but the revolution continued for 18 days until Mubarak was forced out of office and handed over power to the military council which, due to pressure from the people, had to arrest Mubarak and put him on trial. However, the military council, instead of working to realise the aims of the revolution, preserved the Mubarak regime and carried out an elaborate scheme to bring an end to the revolution by the following methods:

1. By bringing about a breakdown in law and order across the country with total civil and military police indifference, leaving Egyptians terrorised.

2. By deliberately defaming the revolutionaries in the corrupt state media.

3. By creating a series of artificial crises in the standard of living, such as price hikes and shortages of basic foodstuffs, which plunged Egyptians into greater misery and turned many of them against the revolution.

4. By committing a series of horrendous massacres of revolutionaries in which demonstrators were killed with live ammunition, in which they lost eyes to rubber bullets and in which women were abused, dragged along the ground and sexually molested. All that was done

with the intention of breaking the will of the revolutionaries and making them submissive again.

5. By the military council forging an alliance with the Muslim Brotherhood, who snubbed the revolution in which they had participated and became the political wing of the military, helping them pass amendments to the old constitution instead of drafting a new constitution for the revolution.

The scheme was carried out over a period of 16 months during which Egyptians suffered horribly, and then the alliance between the Brotherhood and the military council broke down. The ensuing dispute led to the military council dissolving the elected People's Assembly and calling for presidential elections. The revolutionaries committed a grave error in not uniting around a single candidate, which led to run-off elections between Mohamed Morsi, the Brotherhood candidate, and Ahmed Shafik, Mubarak's prime minister and devoted disciple who was protected from multiple charges of corruption by the military council. Remnants of the Mubarak regime spent millions of pounds supporting Shafik, who was also helped by all the institutions of state, such as the police, the ministries and the state security and secret services. It was a great surprise when the results where declared and the winner was Mohamed Morsi. Historians ascribe his victory to the fact that it would have been impossible to fix the results in Shafik's favour as millions of Egyptians would have rejected vote-rigging.

Additionally, a group of independent judges announced the results before they were officially revealed. The military council grudgingly accepted Morsi's victory and issued a constitutional declaration that grabbed back many of the president of the republic's powers, making him akin to the military council's secretary. From the very first day that the elected president Morsi took on his presidential duties, the Mubarak regime started up a violent campaign to unseat him with the media launching a massive defamatory and degrading campaign against the elected president and alarming the population with secret schemes being carried out in the Brotherhood's interest. The Mubarak regime, which still controls the apparatus of state, acerbated both the breakdown in law and order and Egyptians' daily struggle to get by. The following groups of Egyptians participated in the campaign against the elected president:

Remnants of the old regime who want to topple him in order to impose a president loyal to them.

Some Copts who have been so struck with terror at the presence of an Islamist president that they want to see him gone even at the cost of aborting the revolution and having the old regime come back into power.

A group of opportunist intellectuals who worked in the service of Mubarak and then went on to work in the service of the military council in their greed for position and hand-outs.

Some liberals and rightists who did not realise that the core of the conflict is between the elected president and a dictatorial power and whose hostility to the Brotherhood has pushed them into supporting the military council against the elected president.

However, President Morsi bears the lion's share of the responsibility for his failure for two reasons: firstly because he took no clear steps to soothe public opinion and to show that he is the president of all Egyptians and not just a Brotherhood emissary, and secondly because President Morsi showed no mettle when he needed to be robust. Had Morsi demanded full powers the people would have backed him in this legitimate nationalist battle, but the president avoided the clash, hesitating, manoeuvring, retreating and handing out greetings and platitudes to the point that the military managed to topple him after less than a year. The president was forced to submit his resignation after a constitution was drafted by a committee under the influence of the military council that called for presidential elections in which it proposed a new candidate, Abdel Zaher Sherkas, former commander of the Signal Corps. The old regime exerted all its energy promoting him, with songs composed in praise of his heroism and strategic experts appearing on television stating that he is such a military genius of unprecedented ability that his Signal Corps tactics are studied in military academies across the world. Egyptians were so confused, frustrated and exhausted that they accepted and supported the military council's candidate in the hope that things would get better and Abdel Zaher won the presidential elections by a large margin over the rightist candidate Hamdeen Sabahi and the Brotherhood candidate Mohamad el-Beltagy. Thus the first wave of the revolution was aborted and the old regime returned to power with full force. Abdel Zaher managed to restore order within a few days and then ordered a one-off salary hike for civil servants, which led Egyptians to think the future augured well. However, within a few weeks of President Abdel Zaher assuming office, the state security services launched a campaign of terror during which thousands of revolutionaries were arrested and thrown into prison on trumped-up charges. Corruption continued, as did the plundering of the state's resources in a manner worse than in the days of Mubarak. Abdel Zaher slammed the door shut on any bringing to account of the former regime, resorting to legal ruses which allowed him to grant Mubarak an amnesty on health grounds and to release Mubarak's cronies who then left the country for Europe to enjoy the riches they had plundered from the people.

All these practices aroused the anger of the Egyptians, leading them to believe that if Abdel Zaher remained in power, the blood of those killed would have been shed in vain. After two years of Abdel Zaher's rule, a second wave of the revolution broke out, stronger than the first wave. The revolutionaries were well aware of the lesson and Islamists and liberals united as one and formed the Revolutionary Leadership Council to mobilise millions of Egyptians throughout the country.

The military council resorted to the most powerful methods of repression to confront this second wave of the revolution and hundreds of people were killed, but the revolutionaries this time stayed out on the streets until the military council agreed to step aside and hand over power. An agreement was drawn up and signed by revolutionaries and the military and the Egyptian revolution took power on 4 August 2015. This was the date of the inception of the Second Republic. Egyptians started working enthusiastically and seriously, and Egypt flourished like it never had before. The illiteracy of 30 million Egyptians was eradicated in less than two years, a call was made to Egyptian intellectuals in Western universities and many of them came back home and undertook an important role in revitalising the country. The state started providing free medical treatment and education to the poor, and housing and jobs for graduates. The level of education was raised to the point where Egyptian universities could match any in the world, and the national product increased considerably, adding millions to the state budget. The name of Egypt stood out as one of the most important countries for military production. The fame of the Egyptian Fajr machine gun spread, as well as that of the Egyptian October tank. Egypt restored its agricultural productivity in a way unknown since the time of the Romans, becoming self-sufficient in cereals and exporting the surplus. In less than ten years Egypt became a major player in regional and world politics. However, the greatest advance was made in the field of human rights.

The judicial system achieved complete independence from the executive, and it is now common place for a president's representative to be summoned for questioning. The police apparatus is now in the service of the people and not a tool to oppress them, and the prisons and headquarters of the state security, where millions of Egyptians were tortured, have all been turned into museums visited by groups of schoolchildren to see the implements with which their fathers and grandfathers were tortured. The position of women in Egypt improved to such a degree that Egyptians now see women working in all professions, from civil servants to airline pilots. The democratic system took root so firmly that the presidency has been occupied by a member of the Muslim Brotherhood, a communist and a liberal, who were all elected in unsullied elections and who have all completed a single term in office. In 2035, the twentieth anniversary of the Second Republic, a Coptic woman called Mary Abdel Nour, was put forward for the presidency by the Socialist Party and ran against the Wast Party's [sic] Muslim candidate, Ahmed Abdel Hafeez. It should be pointed out that the Muslim Brotherhood and the Salafists (who updated their political philosophy) declared their support for the female Coptic candidate because, in their opinion, she is the better-suited candidate and regardless of her sex or religion they felt it their legitimate duty to support her. Mary Abdel Nour won the elections, becoming the first female Coptic president of Egypt. And how has the wonderful rebirth of Egypt impacted on the neighbouring Arab countries?

That is the topic of our next lesson. Homework exercises can be found below:

1. Give a detailed account of how the Mubarak regime managed to abort the first wave of the revolution, and why did the second wave succeed?

2. Fill in the missing words:

Democracy means the _____ of the people and no institution, such as the military council should _____ the constitution beyond the _____ of the people.

The aim of the Egyptian revolution was the restoration of _____ from the military establishment and handing it over to _____ where legitimate power lies.

3. Put a tick or a cross against the following sentences:

[ ] The military council protected the revolution.

[ ] President Morsi is not responsible for his failure as president.

[ ] Some rightist Copts and liberals caused the failure of the first wave of the revolution by rejecting the elected president because he was an Islamist.

[ ] Islam does not allow a woman or a Copt to be president.

Quoted from the third year history text book for the school year 2050-51.

Democracy is the answer.

RH

Truth is a Virtue

23 July 2012

A few months ago, Naguib Sawiris[1] travelled to Canada and took part in a number of television interviews, in which he reasserted his demand that Western countries should intervene in Egypt to protect the Copts and to help the liberals build a civil state. When the interviewer raised objections to Western interference in Egyptian affairs, Sawiris barked back: "Why do you allow Qatar and Saudi Arabia to fund the Muslim Brotherhood? Either put an

1 Naguib Sawiris, who founded the Free Egyptians Party in the wake of Egypt's uprising against President Hosni Mubarak in 2011, pushed for the removal of Mohamed Morsi by helping a rebel group lead a petition seeking his ouster.

end to that funding or intervene for the sake of Egypt."

In another interview with the Canadian journalist Cristina Freeland, Sawiris again demanded that the West intervene to protect the Copts and the liberals from the Islamists, but when Freeland challenged him on Western intervention in Egyptian affairs, Sawiris replied: "When the West intervenes to support us, they should do it openly."

Freeland was astonished and asked him: "So you are demanding open support from the West?"

These interviews are available online and Sawiris cannot deny his words. It is not my right to cast doubt on Naguib Sawiris's patriotism, but I completely reject his demand for the West to interfere in our affairs. The only way to counter the financial support provided by Qatar and Saudi Arabia is to monitor all payments through the Central Auditing Organisation and to criminalise any secret funding, whatever its form or source. As for Sawiris's call for Western intervention to protect the Copts, I am in no doubt that the Copts, with their history of nationalism, will be the first to reject such scurrilous intervention. I am a leftist who defends the civil state in which citizens are equal regardless of their religion, but I reject any foreign intervention in the affairs of our country and I would ask Sawiris what sort of democracy would Western, [former] colonialist governments create for us? Name me one Arab country in which Western governments have protected the minorities. Has the US protected the Christians and Shi'a in occupied Iraq? Has the West protected the Christians in Palestine from being murdered by the Israeli occupation or from having their churches destroyed?

Egypt fought for decades for its independence and national sovereignty, with thousands of Muslims and Copts dying for the cause. Consequently, Sawiris's call for Western intervention in Egypt undermines what all these people died for and I would call upon Naguib Sawiris to read a little about the history of the Egyptian church and to take pride, as I do as an Egyptian, in the nationalist positions [of the past] which put the interests of Egypt above any other consideration. I would also call upon Sawiris to read about Father Serguis, one of the leaders of the 1919 Revolution, who spoke at Al-Azhar and declared that Copts rejected the protection of the British Occupation and demanded Britain's immediate evacuation of Egypt. The odd thing is that Sawiris called upon the West to intervene in his country and requested their open support, but when the American secretary of state came on a public and official visit to the elected President Morsi, Naguib Sawiris condemned the visit and stated that he considered it interference in Egypt's internal affairs. Who is being inconsistent, Naguib Sawiris?

What is Sawiris's attitude towards the revolution? Did he support of oppose it? I have been astonished as I watched his many recorded interviews because he oscillates from one position to its diametric opposite without the least embarrassment. Before the revolution, Naguib Sawiris declared time and again that he supported Hosni Mubarak and considered him a national hero. At the start of the revolution, Mehwar TV showed him crying in public out of sympathy for Mubarak at which point the anchor, Sayyid Ali, comforted him: "Mr Sawiris, we are all so moved to see you shedding tears for Egypt."

In subsequent interviews during the revolution, Sawiris confirmed that he did not want Mubarak to step down. Not only did he avoid going to Tahrir Square, but he went to Mustafa Mahmud Square where Mubarak supporters carried him aloft shouting slogans that called for Mubarak to remain in power. This position was completely reversed with the success of the revolution but Sawiris stated, in a recorded interview, that he had supported the revolution from the very first day and that he was over the moon about its success. He went on to say, in an interview with Canadian media, that his forthright support for the revolution had brought down upon him the ire of members of his family who feared for his safety due to his revolutionary bravery. These contradictory positions have all been documented and are easy to find online. If he allows me, I will even send CD copies to his office so that he can look over his political positions at his leisure so that he can see how much he has chopped and changed.

Naguib Sawiris became angry with me, accusing me of racism because I wrote the following sentence: "Some Copts have been so struck with terror at the presence of an Islamist president that they want to see him gone, even at the cost of aborting the revolution and having the old regime come back into power."

First of all I shall clarify the meaning of racism in Western law: "Racism is the belief that differences in race or sex lead to differences in human capability." I would advise Sawiris to write out this definition and to try and understand it so that henceforward he does not use concepts of whose meaning he is ignorant. As for the sentence that made him so angry, he did not quote it correctly as I wrote "some" Copts, whilst he quoted me as saying "the Copts". Whatever the case, let's talk frankly. Does he deny that a large segment of the Copts voted for Shafik as they would have voted for Omer Suleiman had he submitted his candidacy? The prominent Coptic author, Suleiman Shafik, recently stated that 80 per cent of Copts voted for Shafik. Does he deny that the accession of Shafik or Omar Suleiman to power means putting an end to the revolution, or at the very least, the end of the first wave of the revolution? I can understand the position of those Copts who support the old regime out of fear of the Islamists, but I cannot concur with their stance.

Furthermore, Naguib Sawiris has stated that ONtv played an important role in the revolution, something with which I am in complete agreement, having had the good fortune to have some familiarity with this channel. I saw the enormous effort made by the channel's director, Albert Shafik, and its outstanding journalists, such as Yosri Fouda, Reem Maged and others, to follow the strictest journalistic standards. I was proud of the way ONtv fought bravely to broadcast the truth, but what happened then? The moment Ahmed Shafik announced his participation in the run-off elections for the presidency against Mohamed Morsi, Naguib Sawiris started employing the logic of "whoever owns the ball" – a game we used to play as children, in which whoever owned the ball had the final word and we had to do as they said or they would go home and there would be no match at all. Sawiris forced ONtv to support Ahmed Shafik, disallowed any criticism of him in any of their programmes and vetoed the appearance of many of Shafik's critics. At the same time he scrapped most of the discussion programmes and then, as a result of all these pressures, the leading journalist Yosri Fouda suspended his talk show, issuing a statement to viewers as follows: "I've stopped my show because I respect you." He refused to return to the channel as a matter of principle. Not only can Sawiris not deny all these facts, but his fervent support for Shafik, which he now denies, was witnessed by scores of people. I can recall that a great Egyptian, one of the most important figures of the revolution in Egypt, told me once: "Just imagine, Sawiris called me three times asking me to support Shafik."

Examples of Sawiris's inconsistencies are endless. He has accused me, on several occasions, of having changed my position and forged an alliance with the Muslim Brotherhood. I do not know what has led him to believe that, but I understand that it must be difficult for Sariwis to understand my position because I am not biased towards any group, or party or group interest. As a matter of principle I defend the rights of everyone, be they Brotherhood members or Salafists, with whom I disagree philosophically and politically. I defend their rights as citizens just as I defend the rights of the Copts. I was one of the few voices who rejected military trials for the Muslim Brotherhood and demanded that they be allowed to form parties. I expressed these opinions at the height of the Mubarak regime's oppression. However, I have also been one of the Brotherhood's greatest critics after the revolution because it put its own interests ahead of those of the revolution and forced an alliance with the military council to the detriment of the revolution. I did not vote for Mohamed Morsi and I called for an election boycott as a protest against the candidacy of Shafik until the 35 cases of corruption filed against him were investigated.

So how can Sawiris accuse me of having made an alliance with the Brotherhood? Is it because I received an invitation from the elected president of Egypt to discuss the methods of realising the aims of the revolution? I went to see him in the company of the great figures of the revolution such as Wael Ghoneim, Asmaa Mahfouz, Wael Qindil, Hasan Nafea, Seif Abdel Fattah, Hamdi Qindil, Abdel Galeel Mustafa, Omar Ali Hasan and others. We told Morsi what we expect from him in order to be the real president of all Egyptians and not just a Brotherhood face in the presidency. And what was wrong with doing that? Should I have turned down an invitation from the elected president in Egypt just to keep Sawiris happy? I do not care whether Sawiris is happy or angry, but I always do what my conscience tells me to regardless of the consequences. It is odd that Naguib Sawiris, who has had many meetings with Israeli officials and businessmen regarding his projects in Israel, should be angry with me for meeting the elected president of Egypt. The reason is that he is an Islamist president and that is what seems to be an unforgivable crime to Sawiris. This is not the first time that Sawiris has shown his true colours. Some time after the Party of Freedom and Justice was established, I took part in a televised debate with Mohamed Morsi as the head of the party, on the talk show of the great journalist Yosri Fouda. I discussed my reservations about political Islam with Morsi and I registered my complete opposition to the Brotherhood's philosophy. The discussion was held in a constructive and civilised manner. Two days later I happened upon Naguib Sawiris at the home of a common friend and we had a private conversation during which he stated that we view the Islamists differently.

Naguib Sawaris, I differ with the politics and philosophy of the Brotherhood and the Salafists. However, your hostility towards the Islamists has unfortunately turned into enmity. You should never take such a hostile position that you do not recognise the rights of your opponents or defend them if they are correct. Your enmity has stopped you from treating them equitably and has driven you to a position of bias and cruelty. I build my position on justice as I see it, whereas yours is built upon your enmity towards the Islamists. The result is that I, thank God, have adopted a coherent and upright position which I will defend no matter what the price, whereas you have unfortunately strayed so far from the path that you have ended up taking the same position as Mubarak's followers, and regrettably as Tawfik Okasha.

Naguib Sawiris, please stick to the truth. That would be a virtue.

Democracy is the answer.

RH

Should We Support the Brotherhood or the Military Council?

30 July 2012

The Qur'an incites hatred and calls for murder and mayhem. I don't hate Muslims. I hate Islam.

These foul words were spoken by Geert Wilders,[1] an extreme right-winger from the Netherlands. He stirs up waves of Islamophobia wherever he goes, deeming Islam a danger to Europe, which must be fought aggressively. He made a film called *Fitna*, so replete with ignorant and unjust attacks on Islam that many people called for him to be put on trial. Geert Wilders is not a rare example but part of a phenomenon which is now spreading across Europe, with the extreme right gaining between 5 and 20 per cent of the seats in parliaments. Every European country has an extreme right wing party with an anti-immigrant platform. There are many reasons for the surge in the extreme right: the fall of the Soviet Union and the negative effect that had on parties of the left; the economic crisis which has left some Europeans feeling xenophobic because they feel that foreigners have taken their jobs, not to leave out the September 11 attacks on the United States and the many terrorist operations in which Islamist extremists have been involved.

Most mosques in the West are funded by Wahhabi individuals or organisations based in the Gulf. Hence they present an extremist Wahhabi version of Islam which both creates a distorted and untruthful image of Islam. The rise of the extreme right in the West is a negative phenomenon, which is a concern to people in the West because these extremist parties are not just anti-Islam but mostly anti-Jewish and anti-people of colour. They mostly cling to the racist principle of white superiority, which presupposes that the genes of a white man make him a more superior being than a man of colour. These extreme right parties generally have reservations about women's rights, and often display open admiration for Nazi and fascist philosophy, both of which are un-democratic. These extremist parties have led to the appearance of groups of extreme right-wingers who shave their heads and wander around European cities attacking immigrants or setting their houses on fire. These groups have also carried out horrendous terrorist operations, the last of which was the attack in Utøya, Norway, carried out by a right-wing extremist, in which 77 people were killed.[2]

Western democracy thus faces a unique dilemma: in the name of democracy, parties have been formed with racist platforms, inciting hatred and adopting positions that do not recognise democracy at all. Thus we have the question: why do Western governments not pass legislation closing down these parties and arresting their members, so that people can relax and feel calm again? The answer is that the principles of democracy prevent the taking of exceptional measures because all citizens have the right to express their views provided they are not against the law. If members of the extreme parties say or do anything that contravenes the law, they will be arrested and tried.

---

1 Geert Wilders is a Dutch populist politician and the founder and leader of the Party for Freedom which currently is the fourth-largest party in the Dutch parliament.

2 On 22 July 2011, Anders Behring Breivik carried out a bomb attack on government buildings in central Oslo before heading to the island of Utøya, where he shot at least 85 people. Breivek harboured radical right-wing views and had railed against what he saw as a Marxist Islamic takeover of Europe.

Even if a Western government were to take authoritarian measures and close down the extremist parties, the first people to defend those parties would be their political opponents, because in such a case they would be defending the rules of democracy even if the beneficiaries were the very people they oppose.

The old democracies have learnt that withdrawing freedom of political expression from extremists does not put an end to their philosophy, but feeds it. Even if they were to pass legislation closing down the extremist parties, within a few months they would turn into secret armed organisations and carry out scores of attacks on citizens and property. The only way to counter extremism is by strengthening the democratic system. Extremist thinking is like bacteria attacking the body. The body's defence system must be strengthened in order to overcome it. Society's defence system is the democratic system. The more we defend it and strengthen its foundations, the more we will be able to counter extremism. Imagine if the army in a European country seized power in a coup d'état, abolished the democratic system, and told the people: "The military have taken power because if we were to hold elections, the extreme right parties will be voted in."

The people would have two alternatives: either to accept military rule with all the authoritarianism that entails and all the subsequent catastrophes, or to demand a return to democracy under which even the extremists can function.

I have no doubt that if that were to happen in a Western country all the citizens would unite in order to put an end to military rule and to restore democracy. A democracy is capable of preventing right-wingers from causing damage. Over the course of thirty years the Egyptian nation was presented with the dreadful alternatives of the Muslim Brotherhood or the military and was Mubarak's permanent excuse for autocratic rule.

Many are the times I heard officials of the Mubarak regime stating: "We have to fix the election results otherwise the Brotherhood will win."

That is why such a large segment of the Egyptian population put up with dictatorship as a substitute for extremism and all sectors of the country were poisoned. Then the revolution came along and succeeded in dislodging Hosni Mubarak, but it has failed so far in replacing the Mubarak regime, which still rules Egypt under the aegis of the military council. The day after Mubarak stepped down, the Mubarak regime started putting the other alternative in front of us: the Muslim Brotherhood and the army went into an alliance at the expense of the revolution. The Brotherhood wanted to realise their aim of getting into power, and the military succeeded in using the Brotherhood as a bogeyman to pressure the people into bringing back the old regime. A grand scheme was played out on the Egyptian people with an intentional breakdown in law and order, anarchy, and thugs hired by the intelligence agencies attacking all and everything including hospitals and primary schools. The Mubarak regime picked the Copts out for special treatment, burning many of their churches in full view of the civil and military police, and allowing attacks on the homes and properties of Copts by men with beards who were not put on trial even though they can be clearly identified in video recordings. The campaign of intimidation reached its apogee in the Maspero massacre, where people were shot dead and crushed by armoured cars.

The message they were sending was: "You Copts have lost Mubarak, who used to protect you from the Islamist extremists, and now you have to pay the price for having supported the revolution." That is what makes us understand why a majority of the Copts voted for Shafik, the representative of the Mubarak regime, to stop an Islamist candidate winning the presidency. Today we are facing the dreadful alternative itself which has plagued Egypt for decades: whether to recognise the legitimate elected president even though he is a member of the Muslim Brotherhood, which many people consider an extremist and dangerous organisation. We do not know who funds the Brotherhood, nor do we know if they have an armed wing. These are all legitimate and reasonable fears about the Brotherhood and are what make many people err on the side of caution when dealing with President Morsi. The other alternative is for us to help the military council stay in power to protect us from the Brotherhood. But that would mean us dismantling the revolution with our own hands.

In my opinion, the revolution came about in order to put an end to sixty years of military rule (with the greatest of respect to the great leader, Gamal Abdel Nasser). If we cling on to military rule out of fear of the Brotherhood, then why did we have a revolution at all? In that scenario, we would have to apologise to Hosni Mubarak and bring him back to power, because he has the most experience in suppressing and arresting the Brotherhood.

In my opinion, the best option is to reject military rule, recognise the legitimacy of the elected president and then pressure him to bring the Brotherhood into line. We should demand that the president makes Brotherhood finances public and subject to state supervision. We must stop the Brotherhood usurping power and refuse to allow Egypt to be turned into a theocracy. All that should be done within the democratic system and not outside it.

We have seen how the Muslim Brotherhood has lost almost half of their voters since the parliamentary and presidential elections. President Morsi himself did not succeed on the Islamist vote alone, but because ordinary Egyptians decided to support him in order to prevent the return of the old regime in the person of Shafik. You cannot protect democracy from extremism by handing power to the military, but democracy can always protect itself with people power and by honouring the election results as unpalatable as they may be. In Egypt we now have a president elected by the will of the people who is confronting the Mubarak regime that still rules under the aegis of the military. The Mubarak regime is launching a vicious campaign against the president, playing on Egyptians' fear of the Muslim Brotherhood, but the aim of this campaign is not to protect Egyptians from extremism but to ensure the continuation of military rule.

All the demands of the revolution are now being presented in the media as if they are the Brotherhood's demands. If the president demands the resignation of el-Adly's men in the Ministry of the Interior who are responsible for the killing of demonstrators and the breakdown in law and order, the media represent this as an attempt by the Brotherhood to take over the Ministry of the Interior. If someone demands an investigation into Ahmed Shafik, who is refusing to cooperate in the 35 charges of corruption levelled against him more than a year ago, the media present this as a litany of grievances concocted by the Brotherhood against Shafik. The Mubarak regime hides behind the bogeyman of the Brotherhood in order to stop any change taking place and to ensure the continuation of military rule in Egypt. For those who do not agree politically with the Brotherhood, including me, there are two ways of keeping the Brotherhood out of power: either to support the military council in order to control the Brotherhood, even though that would mean aborting both the revolution and democracy, or to get the military council out of power and support the democratic system which alone is capable of defeating the Brotherhood at the ballot box.

I can almost hear some people objecting: you are comparing Egyptian voters with their European counterparts who are more educated and politically astute. The truth is that you do not need a doctorate to practice democracy, proof of that being India, a country which suffers from poverty and illiteracy, but which has managed to be the largest democracy in the world. There is also a proof from our own history in 1950 and the last free and fair elections before the revolution of 1952. The Muslim Brotherhood at that time were at the peak of their power, but they failed to win a single seat in parliament, because the Wafd Party swept the polls and won the majority of seats. For decades we have been trapped between the Brotherhood and the military and, in my opinion, the only way out is to consolidate a real democracy that is capable of protecting Egypt from both extremism and dictatorship.

Democracy is the answer.

RH

What is Egypt Waiting For?

6 August 2012

Should we attack someone who is carrying out a religious duty? Should we attack someone as they pray, be they Muslim, Christian or Jewish, or the follower of some other religion? Should we attack someone who is fasting and who is getting ready to break their fast and say their prayers? This is a contemptible and foul crime under any legal system or set of norms. Some terrorist groups, who falsely claim to be religious, attacked Egyptian soldiers and policemen in Rafah as they were preparing to break their fast. They opened fire on them as they were doing their duty of protecting their country's borders. The attack caused the death of more than 16 Egyptian soldiers and policemen, and wounded many of their colleagues. Then the terrorists made off with two Egyptian armoured cars and used them to smash their way across the Israeli border where the Israeli air force attacked them, announcing that they had destroyed one of the armoured cars but not mentioning what became of the second. The incident is suspicious and dangerous; it raises a number of questions and makes us see the scene in Egypt differently.

Since the success of the revolution in deposing Mubarak, the military council has taken over the powers of the president of the republic until a constitution is drafted and a new president elected. The revolutionary forces have many times demanded the formation of a civilian, presidential council made up of independent nationalist personalities with the presence of a representative of the army so that it can perform the duties of the president of the republic during the transitional period.

The proposal for a civilian presidential council was backed by two truths: firstly, the military leaders, for all their military experience, have not a shred of experience in running the country and this will only lead to more crises and problems for the Egyptian people. Secondly, the task of military leaderships the world over is to concentrate on the basic task of defending the country, steering clear of matters of state or political disputes. However, the military council rejected this proposal and has insisted on taking over political issues and the generals on the council have been preoccupied with writing the constitution, holding elections and dissolving the People's Assembly. Unfortunately the army leadership's preoccupation with political matters has had a marked effect on the performance of their military role. The terrorist incident betrays a woeful shortcoming on the part of the various branches of the armed forces.

Israel had publicly warned that a terrorist incident would take place in Sinai, and even alerted Israelis visiting southern Sinai. If a warning of a terrorist attack was publicised a few days in advance, why did the military leaders in Egypt not take the necessary precautions to prevent this attack and to defend our soldiers? Why were no instructions given to prepare against an attack that Israel confirmed would take place in Sinai? This shortcoming led to the death of 16 Egyptians and there must to be an immediate, far-reaching and robust internal investigation within the armed forces so that this cannot happen again.

From the very first day of the revolution, Israel stood firmly in line with Hosni Mubarak whom Israeli officials described as a strategic treasure for the

Hebrew state. For the first time in the history of Israel, the prime minister convened three press conferences in less than three weeks for one purpose: to support the Mubarak regime against the revolution. Moreover, the Israelis exercised unprecedented pressure on the American administration to prevent Mubarak from being toppled, but the revolution won and deposed Mubarak. It would be naïve to imagine that Israel would be happy at the success of the revolution or that it would stand idly by while a democratic transformation takes place in Egypt. Israel is well aware of Egypt's gravity and leverage in the Arab world. It knows that Egypt has great capabilities and that, if it completes its democratic transformation, within a few years it will regain its position of leadership in the Arab world. Israel knows that if the revolution succeeds in Egypt, the whole Arab world will be revitalised and Israel will do everything in its power to prevent this.

On the other hand, Israel operates according to a Zionist ideology which holds that the borders of greater Israel are from the Nile to the Euphrates, and consequently all the accords Israel has signed are just tactical steps to control the Arab world, accords which can be renounced at any time. This terrorist operation benefits no one except Israel, and indeed there are grave suspicions regarding Israel's role in the attack. How did Israel predict the terrorist operation days before it was carried out? What drove the terrorists to crash the armoured cars into the Israeli border? Did they think they would be able to carry out an operation inside Israel with armoured cars alone? Were the terrorists not fully aware that the Israelis were monitoring them? That the terrorists got into Israel just increases suspicions regarding Israel's role in the attack.

I should add that the Israeli attack on the two armoured cars inside Israel ends any Egyptian hope of identifying the terrorists or their backers. For a while now, Israel has been making a hue and cry in the Western media about the danger of the security vacuum in Sinai. The US secretary of state, Hillary Clinton, has warned more than once that an anti-Israeli terrorist operation might be carried out in Sinai. The Israeli minister of defence issued a statement blaming the Egyptian army for having failed to protect the border and alluded to commissioning international forces to protect Israel's security. Israeli precedents show that it will attempt to exploit any event in Egypt or the region to achieve its expansionist and aggressive aims, and it has used this act of terror to achieve two aims: the internationalisation of a section of Sinai by putting it under international supervision, and/or an Israeli drive to occupy a section of Sinai on the grounds of protecting itself from attacks.

We hope that Israel does not exploit this terrorist event to vilify our Palestinian brethren in Gaza and to re-impose a siege. The Mubarak regime committed a horrendous crime against the Palestinians when it cooperated with Israel in putting the Palestinian people under siege and starving them.

We hope that members of the military council and President Morsi do not get swept up in Israel's plan to re-impose a siege on our brethren in Gaza. The ordeal of the Palestinians in Gaza is not just an Arab issue, but also a humanitarian issue. Cutting off water, electricity and foodstuffs from civilians is a crime against humanity, regardless of who the perpetrators or the victims are. The flotillas, which attempted to break the siege on Gaza, were mostly manned by Christian and Jewish foreigners who considered the siege a crime against humanity.

The military council has taken over the duties of the president of the republic during the transitional period, even though we still believe that the military council committed serious mistakes which have led Egypt into deep and treacherous waters. The military council preserved the Mubarak regime, which was responsible for the problems now facing Egypt post-revolution, from the breakdown in law and order and the economic crisis, to the outbreak of chaos intended to restore the old regime at any price. The military council bears political responsibility for the wounding and massacre of scores of people, as well as the hundreds of civilians tried in military courts and thrown into military prisons. We have continued to criticise the actions of the military council while at the same time emphasising that the criticism directed at the policies of the military council in no way applies to the Egyptian armed forces which is the army of the Egyptian people. There is not a family in Egypt that does not have someone serving as a soldier or an officer in the armed forces. We have always affirmed our pride in the army although we object to the policies of the military council and reject the involvement of the army in politics.

Despite our criticism of the military council and our objections to its policies, at this delicate time we find that we must support it in order to defend Egypt. It is time for Egypt to revise the Camp David Agreement which gives it the right to revise its clauses from time to time. The Egyptian forces in Sinai are too few to guarantee Egypt's borders. It is now time for the Egyptian army to retaliate against anyone who attacks an Egyptian soldier. We do not want the military council to behave the way it did last year when Israeli forces attacked the Egyptian border, killing six Egyptian soldiers, and the Egyptian authorities at the time accepted a half-hearted apology from Israel.

On the domestic front, there must be an immediate end to the breakdown in law and order which has been brought about intentionally by the Mubarak regime and is a crime against Egypt, and which, if it continues in the same dangerous vein, will be an act of high treason against the nation. When Egypt is exposed to danger, we all have to take responsibility. We must now act, not out of a specific political logic, but rather out of a sense of national belonging. At this moment, we are not Salafists, Brothers, liberals or right-wingers, but just Egyptians whose duty it is to whole-heartedly support the leadership of the Egyptian army, whatever political differences we have. It is our duty now to come together, step up to the responsibility and put all our energies into the service of the homeland. Of course that does not mean backing down and ceasing democratic transformation.

Egypt is being reshaped now after the revolution, and we have to share our views and efforts while remaining aware that the country is going through a dangerous moment which has room for differences of opinion, provided they do not get out of hand. We hope that the military council will respond to our demands and return to its core duties of defending the country and that it will leave political affairs to the elected president and his cabinet. However much we disagree with President Morsi, and however negative our opinion of the cabinet he formed, it is the interest of Egypt that makes us back the leadership of the armed forces and help the elected president to keep our country secure and to solve its crises, because at any moment we could be exposed to another attack by Israel, which now has the pretext for military intervention in Sinai. Egypt expects us all to rise above our differences and to put Egypt's interest above all other considerations. May God preserve Egypt and may God have mercy on the martyrs.

Democracy is the answer.

RH

Heartfelt Joy and Rightful Concerns

13 August 2012

If you participated in the Egyptian revolution, supported it, or even understood the reasons why it happened, the latest decisions made by President Morsi must have filled you with hope and joy. Despite all the attempts of the old regime to abort the revolution, the people were able to appoint an elected, civilian president for the first time in 60 years and this elected president was able to fulfil a basic demand of the revolution: the end of military rule. By dismissing Field Marshal Tantawi and General Sami Hafez Enan,[1] and annulling the complementary constitutional declaration,[2] Morsi has established himself as an elected president capable of building a truly democratic state for the Egyptian people.

1 General Sami Hafez Enan was the chief of staff of the Egyptian Armed Forces and deputy chairman of the military council during the transitional period. Both Tantawi and Enan were appointed as presidential advisors by Morsi and were awarded the Order of the Nile. General Abdel Fattah el-Sisi replaced Tantawi as defence minister and general commander of the army. *See* Glossary.

2 The complementary constitutional declaration was issued by the military council before the presidential elections in an attempt to restrict presidential powers.

Indeed, the announcement brought the revolutionaries much joy, but their celebrations have also been tainted by fear of what's to come. Many Egyptians are asking themselves: should we be rejoicing because military rule – whose downfall we have been calling for – has fallen, or should we instead be worrying about Egypt's future now that the Brotherhood has consolidated its control of the state? These concerns are understandable because Morsi belongs to an organisation whose structure, behaviour, and funding sources are unknown and often unpredictable. The organisation is unregistered and unlicensed, and its huge budget is not subject to scrutiny by the Central Auditing Organisation. The first duty of the president should be to persuade or compel the leadership of the Brotherhood to open their organisation's coffers and also to subject it to state supervision so as to assuage the rightful concerns of the Egyptian people.

With the annulment of the complementary constitutional declaration, President Morsi gave himself the right to form a new Egyptian Constituent Assembly, which would be able to amend the constitution in the event that the present committee was unable to complete its work. This decision was undemocratic and unacceptable because the Constituent Assembly must express the will of the people and not that of the president, even if he has been elected. We were expecting President Morsi to give the people back their rights, for it is the people's right to choose a Constituent Assembly for the amendment of the constitution through free elections. We were expecting him to act on his promise to reform the current assembly, so that the Islamist movement would not control the assembly and direct it according to its ideologies.

It is well known that the Ministry of Information is a failed tool of oppression found only in totalitarian regimes. These regimes try to direct public opinion by creating a ministry whose function it is to deceive and mislead the public by glorifying the despotic ruler and justifying all that they do, even if they have committed crimes. One of the demands of the revolution was the disbanding of the Ministry of Information and the establishment of a "Supreme Council for the Media", which would monitor professional standards in the media sector. The president has so far ignored these demands and appointed a prominent member of the Muslim Brotherhood as minister of information.

The only explanation for keeping the Ministry of Information intact is that the president wants to regulate the media rather than free it. Indeed, the minister of information got to work immediately and launched a vicious campaign against privately owned television channels, scrutinising statements made by presenters about President Morsi. As a result, the privately-owned Al-Faraeen satellite channel was abruptly closed down by the authorities and its owner, Tawfiq Okasha,[1] was arrested. Of course, I could never defend a station that has deliberately defamed and attacked people associated with the revolution, myself included, but the Ministry of Interior will set a dangerous precedent if it continues to attack independent media outlets.[2] Undoubtedly, Tawfik Okasha and his ilk deserve to be held legally accountable for their actions, but shutting down a television channel in a democratic system must be done through the courts rather than being implemented by government edict.

If we allow the government to shut down Al Faraeen without adhering to the correct process and procedure, they will continue to close down any channel that criticises Mohamed Morsi. Furthermore, Tawfik Okasha is not the only media personality guilty of spreading hatred and intolerance; Sheikh Khaled Abdullah, of Al-Nas TV channel, publicly condemns anybody who dares to disagree with him. The question is: to what extent is Tawfik Okasha being brought to account because of his disreputable media outlet, or is it because of his insolence towards President Morsi? If Okasha is being punished for overstepping the mark, then Sheikh Khaled Abdullah must also be brought to account. However, if Okasha is being punished because he angered President Morsi, then we must wake up to the fact that the president is no better than Mubarak or the military council. Morsi pushes his government to make an example of his opponents, but no such action is taken when the same infractions are committed by members of the Islamist movement.

In all democratic systems of government, the media devotes a lot of time to criticising the president or leader of the nation. But the law rarely brings anybody to account for such criticism, because it pertains to the ruler's ability to carry out their duty and is therefore of public interest. However, it is also true that the law does not tolerate libel and defamation when it concerns ordinary people, and has put in place laws to protect its citizens. In France, a well-known satirical newspaper, *Le Canard enchaîné*, has published weekly cartoons since its founding in 1915 that ridicule the president of the French republic and other senior officials. Ordinary citizens would not tolerate being depicted in such a way, but public officials must do so. Harry S. Truman, former president of the United States, gave voice to this sentiment when one of his ministers came to him complaining about the harshness of the attacks on him by the media. Roosevelt smiled and said sarcastically: "Those who work in the kitchen can't complain about how hot the stove is."

The point of this comment is that bearing harsh or wounding criticism is one of the duties of public office in a democracy. This is the kind of

1 Tawfiq Okasha is a controversial media figure who is a vocal critic of the Morsi administration. He has reportedly been the subject of a number of defamation cases.

2 During his year in office, Morsi complained about the influence of private television channels owned by business tycoons, holding them responsible for increasing opposition to Muslim Brotherhood rule.

democracy we want to build in Egypt, but unfortunately Morsi is attempting to seize control of the media and constrain Egyptian journalists. The newspaper *Al-Dustour* was recently seized by the authorities and its editor sent to court on charges of insulting the president of the republic, in addition to the well-known trumped-up charges of "causing sectarian strife" and "incitement" – the kinds of charges that can be directed at anybody with whom President Morsi is not satisfied. I hope that President Morsi will refrain from prosecuting journalists and convince Egyptians that he is still committed to building a true democracy.

Most of Egypt's national newspapers are corrupt organisations failing both in their management and in their journalistic integrity. They have debts of hundreds of millions of Egyptian pounds that have been relinquished and stolen from the Egyptian people. By law, the Shura Council owns these news organisations and was formerly in charge of appointing their editors, with the help of the security services. The result was that most of the editors were hypocrites and many journalists grew accustomed to dishonest practices. They were prepared to bend to the will of the state security services in order to guarantee promotion, far above their level of competence.

After the revolution, journalists demanded an end to the Shura Council's ownership of news organisations so that they could become completely independent of the state. Sound, comprehensive proposals were prepared in order to advance the cause, but the Shura Council – in which the Brotherhood control the majority of the seats – rushed to announce that they would be holding elections to appoint new editors-in-chief for the national newspapers. This proposal, along with the committee who oversaw it, raised a lot of objections and questions.

So, the results were announced and new editors-in-chief were appointed for all the national newspapers. Some of the new editors are well-known for their competence, such as Sulaiman Qanawi and Thuna Abu al-Hamid amongst others. However, our grievances do not pertain to the individuals, but to the system that has kept in place the Shura Council's right to control the editors-in-chief. Thus, however competent a new editor-in-chief may be, we cannot forget that they were appointed with the consent of the Muslim Brotherhood, who control the Shura Council. If an editor-in-chief were to oppose the Brotherhood, they would be immediately dismissed from their position and so, naturally, they will be cautious when dealing with any subject involving the Brotherhood or the Islamists. Here we see that the Brotherhood, instead of creating a free and independent media, has devised a new system for controlling the Egyptian news organisations through the Shura Council.

The question remains: is Morsi determined to dismantle the tools of despotism and return power to its legitimate owner, the Egyptian people? Or is he a president who merely tames the tools of despotism to serve his own interests, stripping power from the military council only to establish the control of the Brotherhood? If this president's plan is to spread the Muslim Brotherhood's influence over every facet of the Egyptian state, then it is a plan doomed to failure. The people that defied Mubarak's rule, toppled his regime, and prosecuted him in court will never allow Egypt to be transformed into a state of the Muslim Brotherhood. If the President truly wants to bring an end to despotism and establish a true democracy, then he must put do right by the Egyptian people and prove that he is a president of all Egyptians citizens. He must release all the revolutionaries held in prison just as he has released imprisoned Islamists. If it were not for the sacrifices of the youth of the revolution, who are now being held in military prison, President Morsi would never have set foot in the presidential palace.

The president must carry out his promise to appoint Copts to influential and active positions as a demonstration of his respect for the principle of equality between citizens. He must change the structure of the Constituent Assembly so that it represents all sectors of society and is not dominated by the Islamist movement. If this assembly gets into difficulties, it must be reformed through holding free elections, not through a committee chosen by the president at his discretion.

Congratulations are in order to President Morsi for his brave decision to end military rule, but we await further decisions from him to convince us that he is a president of all the Egyptians who truly wants to bring an end to military despotism and, rather than to found in its place a religious absolutism, form a true democratic system that would give Egypt the future it deserves.

Democracy is the answer.

PN

Do Egyptians Resent Success?

27 August 2012

If you were an Egyptian who had emigrated to the West and then completed your education in one of the best universities in the world and obtained a degree, as well as a well-paid job, what would your relationship with Egypt be? You would have two alternatives: either to enjoy your success and lifestyle in the West, coming to visit Egypt with your family on your holidays to enjoy its beaches and warm sun, or, you feel a sense of obligation towards your country and you would use your knowledge and experience for the benefit of Egyptians.

This second alternative causes many problems for you, as you are exposed to inaction, personal attack and distrust. You discover to your astonishment that there are Egyptians willing to attack you and work against you, people who will not rest until you despair of being able to make a difference and you go back whence you came. That is exactly what is happening now to the great Egyptian scientist Ahmed Zewail, who won the Noble Price for Chemistry as well as having 50 honorary doctorates from the best universities and being the recipient of many honours from governments around the world. The US administration named him as one of the most important brains in America; Zewail considers himself indebted to his country and wants to do something useful and pass on his superb knowledge to the new generations in Egypt.

Ahmed Zewail wanted to establish a new scientific foundation consisting of experienced scientists seconded to Egypt from specialist institutions. This city of science would be unique in the whole Arab world and the East, and would help Egypt move forwards in the fields of scientific research, technology and manufacturing. Any country in the world would have rushed to place all its resources at Zeweil's disposal so that he could bring about a scientific renaissance. But in Egypt Zeweil has been fighting strenuously over the course of 15 years to establish a city of science.

Hosni Mubarak honoured Ahmed Zeweil by awarding him the Order of the Nile. He was keen on his project and awarded him a plot of land for the building, but the state security service sent Mubarak reports warning him that Zeweil enjoyed such immense popularity amongst the younger generation that some of them wanted him to be a candidate for the presidency. Mubarak then turned against Zeweil and the land for the project was repossessed after the prime minister had laid the foundation stone. Zeweil spent years as *persona non grata* of the Mubarak regime until the revolution took place and, with Mubarak deposed, Zeweil started up the great project again. And here we have to review the details:

Mubarak's prime minister was Ahmed Nezif, founder of the Nile University. As prime minster, he allowed this university to rent 126 *feddans* at one Egyptian pound a *feddan* for 30 years. The government funded some of the buildings from the state budget because the prime minister was the patron of this private university.

When the revolution took place and ousted Mubarak, the board of trustees of the Nile University met on 17 February 2011 and decided unconditionally to waive their rights to the land allotted for the university and to hand it back to the state. Two days later the government issued a statement accepting the land back from the Nile University and re-categorising it as state property.

After the state got the Nile University land back, following the trustee's unconditional waiver, the Egyptian government decided to apportion the very same land to Zeweil's city of science. Zeweil set to work and formed a board of trustees made up of the greatest scientists in the world, headed by six Nobel laureates, Magdi Yaqoub, Mohamed Ghoneim, Mustafa al-Sayyid and others, in addition to a number of Egyptian laureates who left their jobs in some of the best universities in the world to come and work in the city of science. Zeweil wanted the project to be built by Egyptians and he set up a fund to which millions of Egyptians gave donations in a manner reminiscent of how Cairo University was built by public subscription in 1908. Then came the blow. Officials from the Nile University turned up to demand the land back that had been taken from them against their wishes. They then instigated a systematic and shameful campaign in the media to discredit Zeweil. How did officials of the Nile University permanently waive their rights to the land allotted to the university and then change their minds and demand it back? And what has Zeweil got to do with this whole issue? Why did the Egyptian government not intervene and state that it was the party responsible for allotting the land to Dr Zeweil? And why did the government not make public the official land waiver signed by officials of the Nile University?

Is the president of the republic not aware of the long-term benefit of establishing Zeweil's city of science in Egypt? Does the army leadership not realise that it would bring about outstanding advances in the field of military production? Does it make any sense that a Nobel Prize laureate should come to establish a city of science which will turn his country into a great power only to find himself prevented from doing so by his fellow citizens? The answer to all these questions is that we are in Egypt, a country without laws or regulations, where might is right. Most officials at the Nile University were influential men during the Mubarak era, and until the fall of the Mubarak regime they continued to enjoy great influence over the media and in government circles. Buoyed by their power, they thought it their prerogative to waive their right to the land whenever they wished and then to take it back whenever they wished, even at the cost of wasting a great opportunity to realise Egypt's scientific renaissance. The most important question is thus: do Egyptians resent success?

What happened to Ahmed Zeweil has happened to most Egyptians who studied in the West and then came back to give their country the benefit of their education. They were so frustrated that they left Egypt and went back whence they came. Laureates are honoured first in their own country and then they receive international recognition, except in Egypt. Egyptians receive global recognition and then come back to their homeland where they are subjected to vicious attacks and a wave of negative reactions. Any country in the world makes great efforts to help one of its citizens get the Nobel Prize, and Egypt is the only Arab country whose citizens have won the Nobel Prize, four times. However, Egyptian Nobel laureates are the people most subjected to disparagement and distrust by their fellow citizens.

Egyptian society is plagued by a sickness that drives Egyptians to drag down people who have been successful, to defame them and to belittle their achievements. Some Egyptians resent anyone who has been a success and show them such open hostility that they flee or are so beset by despair that they give up. These people who resent success have caught the disease of self-destructiveness that makes them self-harm. The resentment displayed by some Egyptians towards their compatriots who have achieved some worldwide success is engendered by the following reasons:

First: Most prizes and honorary awards in Egypt are apportioned by nepotism and favouritism, with the result that they are awarded to people who do not deserve them, something which has caused many Egyptians to lose faith in the success realised by any Egyptian and which makes them suspect him and accuse him of having received such recognition by underhand methods. These doubters forget that most awards and prizes in the West are decided according to objective criteria. Moreover, any Egyptian or Arab who achieves prominence in the West has to prove that he is twice as good as his Western counterpart.

Second: With the spread of extremist religious thought, many Egyptians have started seeing the West as anti-Arab and anti-Muslim, and consequently they suspect that anyone who receives an international award must have placated their enemies – a mistaken view stemming from rank ignorance. Indeed, Western governments have often pursued policies that have caused great damage to the Arabs and Muslims, but it is also true to say that the West is not a monolithic whole. People, universities and establishments in the West often take positions that are at odds with, or even against their governments. People in the West helped and supported the Egyptian revolution from afar, whereas Western governments oscillated between warning and helping Mubarak. Whereas most Western governments supported and participated in the war on Iraq, public opinion in the West was against it, and the anti-war demonstrations in Western capitals were much larger than any that took place in the Arab capitals.

Third: Egypt experienced thirty years of corruption and injustice under Mubarak's rule and in the end this led to widespread frustration amongst Egyptians. The Egyptian people feel that they deserve a much better life and that each and every one of these frustrated individuals believe that their failings and shortcomings are a result of circumstance rather than their own lack of ability or motivation. In many cases this is the truth, but the danger is that they compare themselves permanently with other people. As a consequence the frustrated Egyptian, should he come across an Egyptian who has realised worldwide success, must be irritated by that success because it proves to them that their own failure is not due to their own ability or a result of difficult circumstances, but has been caused by their own failings. It then follows that an Egyptian living with his own frustration will launch a fierce attack on an Egyptian who has succeeded in order to prove to himself that the other person's success is neither real nor deserved.

I am acquainted with Ahmed Zeweil and have seen for myself how patiently and consistently he has been working to realise his dream of a science city in Egypt. I have seen how he has met scores of officials and attempted to deal with Kafka-esque Egyptian bureaucracy, and how he has had to put up with all variety of scheming, abuse, and scare tactics which would frighten off anyone of a lesser fortitude. I have often wondered what makes one of the most important scientists in the world put in so much effort and cope with so much disparagement and so many insults, in order to realise a project from which he will gain no profit or position. The answer is that Zeweil, as with other people like him, believes that success brings with it the responsibility to help others, and, because he loves his country, he wants it to benefit from his enormous learning, whatever the effort or the cost to his nerves. I hope that the change for which the revolution came about will be realised so that a cure can be found for Egypt's self-destructiveness in resenting success. I also hope that all Egyptians will stand behind Ahmed Zeweil so that he can bring Egypt what it deserves.

Democracy is the answer.

RH

Are Egyptians Civilised?

3 September 2012

There was a young man who worked in an office in Cairo. The man had to go on a business trip to Alexandria so he arranged for his female colleague to wait for him outside the office to give him some documents he needed to take with him. The woman was waiting for him in the street when a strange man approached her and whispered in her ear: "You're very cute."

The stranger started groping her. He groped her in the middle of the street in broad daylight. She called for help and tried to push him away, but he would not relent. The woman's colleague arrived, saw what was happening and tried to get the man away from her. The stranger was physically stronger than the young man and hit him so hard that he broke one of his ribs and gave him a black eye. He gave the young man such a hard shove that he fell into the road and was almost run over. People crowded around and the police were called. This altercation took place after the revolution when law and order had completely broken down. In this instance, the officer in charge at the police station acted in a responsible manner and ordered the molester be remanded in custody for four days pending investigation.

The stranger was Muslim and the victim was a veiled Muslim woman called Rahma Mohamed. The young man who so desperately tried to defend her is a Copt by the name of Michel George, and the officer who threw the book at the molester was also a Copt, Colonel Hani Girgis, who was the duty officer at the Qasr el-Nil police station. The question is what would drive a young Coptic man to put his life in danger to rescue a veiled Muslim woman? And what drove the Coptic police officer to remand in custody a Muslim who attacked a Muslim woman? The answer is that the young man and the police officer did not treat the woman as a Muslim or a Copt but as a human being who was being molested and whom it was their duty to protect.

This incident embodies civilised behaviour: we should defend the rights of others regardless of their religion or gender. In the midst of the sectarian incidents during the attacks on Coptic churches and homes, civilised Muslims would often turn up to protect the Copts. They do not think of them as Copts but as flesh and blood with human rights, whom it is their duty to defend. These noble acts which take place from time to time beg the question: are we really civilised? My opinion is that we are civilised but that we live in an uncivilised country. We have to differentiate between being modern city-dwellers and being civilised. We can look modern to all intents and purposes, but being civilised is something deeper. If the state makes economic progress, raises the standard of living of its citizens and establishes a strong army – these all make it a strong, modern state, but they only make it a civilised state if it declares the value of human life and defends the rights of its citizens, regardless of religion or social class. A state cannot be considered civilised if the following concepts do not prevail:

First: A humane understanding of religion. Do we consider ourselves first and foremost human beings or are we Muslim and Copts? Does our religious affiliation take precedence over our humanity or vice versa? The answer is that it is our true understanding of religion that makes us more human. A deep sense of religiosity should make you defend the rights of others even if they differ from you in their religion or thinking. This real meaning of religion was completely undervalued by the Mubarak regime. For thirty years, the Wahhabi version of Islam, funded by oil money, spread an extreme vision of the religion amongst Egyptian society, judging people by their beliefs and considering the Copts as a misguided community. Some months ago, I wrote a story in which the people killed during the revolution, Muslims and Copts alike, ascended to paradise. Many readers sent me negative reactions, blaming me for imagining that Copts go to heaven for, in their minds, heaven is restricted to Muslims.

Second: Ascertaining personal responsibility. A civilised state considers people responsible only for their individual behaviour, and not as members of a group or community. If we generalise the way we treat other people, this is the first step towards bigotry. As Arabs, do we oppose Israel because of its politics or its religion? If we oppose unjust and aggressive Israeli policies, this is a reasonable humanitarian standpoint shared by millions of people throughout the world. However, if we are against Israel simply because it is a Jewish state, that is sectarianism and intolerance. We have no right to oppose a group of people on the basis of their religion. If we were to hate Jews in general simply for being Jews, we would have to allow other people to treat us with the same intolerance and to resent us simply for being Muslims. It is also patently wrong for us to hold someone responsible for the actions of others just because they are of the same religion. There is a long list of names of Western Jews who have made public their opposition to Israel and have condemned its aggressive policies. The late Jewish Austrian president, Bruno Kreisky, the Jewish American Noam Chomsky and many others, not to mention the young Jewish American woman, Rachel Corrie, who left the United States to go to Palestine and defend the rights of Palestinians. On 16 March 2003, as Israeli bulldozers were demolishing Palestinian homes in the town of Rafah, Rachel Corrie tried to stand in their way. The driver of one bulldozer drove straight at her and she was crushed to death. So here we have a young Jewish woman sacrificing her life to defend Muslim Palestinians. Hence it is wrong to be against any group of people based on their sex or religion. People have to be held individually responsible for their actions.

Third: The establishment of a civil state. In a civil state, religious affiliation does not confer any political rights on citizens, as they are all equal before the law, regardless of their religion. In a civil state, citizens have the right to embrace any religion they wish to and to practice its rituals without this detracting from their rights as citizens. Unfortunately, freedom of belief in Egypt has been held back due to the state's weakness in protecting it. Last month an Egyptian citizen was tried and imprisoned for being Shia, thus making this a crime under Egyptian law. In 1939, Princess Fawzia, sister of King Farouk, married the crown prince of Iran and the whole of Egypt celebrated the royal wedding with not a thought about the groom being Shia and the bride Sunni. The Egyptian state tenaciously refuses to recognise the rights of Baha'is, something that has led them to have to lie on official documents by stating that their religion is Muslim. It is unfortunate that the newly-drafted constitution restricts state recognition to the three main monotheistic religions. This provision undermines the concept of freedom of belief, as there are Egyptians, such as those of the Baha'i faith, who do not belong to the three main religions and it is their right to have the state, if it is a civilised one, recognise their religious rights. So we come to the following question: what if states with a Buddhist or Hindu majority decided to treat us similarly? What if an Egyptian resident in China or India, be he Muslim or Copt, went to say his prayers only to find the authorities waiting to arrest him, telling him that they do not recognise Islam or Christianity, just as the Egyptian state has refused to recognise Buddhism or Hinduism? A state is only civilised when it affords its citizens complete and unconditional freedom of belief.

Fourth: A culture of tolerance and the criminalisation of hatred. Religion is not a matter of personal opinion but an exclusive belief. Thus the followers of any religion believe that theirs is the only true religion and that all other religions are false or distorted. Islam recognises Christianity and Judaism, but considers that these two religions have been subject to a distortion that has set them aside from the path of truth. Christians do not recognise the prophethood of Muhammad, the Jews do not recognise Christianity or Islam, and believe that the true messiah has not yet appeared. This clash of religions has caused so many wars and horrendous massacres over the course of human history that civilised states have learnt to respect all religions and they have passed laws preventing the followers of one religion from offending other religions. It is your right to practise your beliefs but it is not your right to offend the religions of other people. Under Egyptian law it is illegal to show contempt for religion, but action is only ever taken against people who offend the beliefs of Muslims. When it comes to some of the extremist clerics who despise the Copts and state that they are unbelievers who are not to be given greetings for their festivals, the state does not consider this to constitute the crime of contempt for religion.

The Egyptian people are a civilised nation, but the state is not civilised in allowing discrimination to be practised against those not of the majority religion, just as the state also does not respect the humanity of Egyptians whether Muslim or Copt. Then the Egyptian revolution came about and we had the first democratically elected head of state and we expected him to set about establishing a just and civilised state which values human worth and dignity regardless of a person's religion or political affiliation. However, the signals being sent out by President Morsi are worrying and bode ill for the future of the revolution. President Morsi has been releasing the Muslim detainees who, like him, belong to Islamist political groups, while refusing to use his power of amnesty for the revolutionaries tried and jailed by military courts, because they are not Islamists. There is an Egyptian woman, called Nagla Wafa, who was sentenced to 500 lashes after a dispute with a Saudi princess. There is also the lawyer, Ahmed el-Gizawi, who made an appeal for help after being tortured in a Saudi prison, as well as the scores of Egyptians in custody. However, President Morsi's relations with the Saudi ruling family, it would seem, are more important to him than the dignity of those Egyptians, just as Mubarak used to foster a close friendship with the kings of the Gulf with nary a thought for the conditions of Egyptians working there. Egypt will not be a civilised country unless it considers that one of its most important duties is preserving the dignity and rights of Egyptians.

Democracy is the answer.

RH

How to Make a Dictator

11 September 2012

> Since swearing the constitutional oath on 30 November, President Morsi has not been on any private holidays with his family. President Morsi has even spent bank holidays in the presidential palace, running the country and holding meetings with visitors and officials. Finally, President Morsi managed to spend the two days of Eid el-Fitr with his family in Burj el-Arab, away from his official work responsibilities, but he still could not escape from the 22 telephone calls from Arab and Western leaders wishing to consult him on the regional and international situation.

This is from a front-page article published in *Al-Ahram* newspaper. It was an attempt to garner sympathy for the president, claiming that he had such a great workload that he couldn't even take one day off to be with his family.

The truth of the matter is that President Morsi has only been in his job for a few weeks, and that is generally not a long enough period for someone to need a holiday. In addition, it is not as if the president dials the international telephone calls himself. His staff would arrange this on his behalf, and the president could take the calls in the comfort of his own home. This sort of mendacious and hypocritical reporting is being repeated time and again within the framework of an operation to create a dictatorship. President Morsi has inherited the Mubarak regime in totality: the apparatus of repression is ever ready to carry out torture, arrests and murder and to put out false stories showing their loyalty to the regime regardless of how it is performing. The institutions of state are long used to carrying out any and all instructions from the president and to singing the praises of his wisdom.

We expected the first elected post-revolution president to establish a real democracy but unfortunately he has kept in place the machinery of dictatorship that he inherited from Mubarak and has since used it for his own benefit.

In place of the national newspaper editors who pandered to Mubarak for so long, the Shura Council via some arcane process, appointed new editors who owe their positions to the Muslim Brotherhood. Instead of a minister of information with the rank of general preventing criticism of the military council, we now have a Brotherhood minister of information who is banning television programmes which criticise the Brotherhood.

Instead of appointing provincial governors loyal to Mubarak, governors loyal to the Muslim Brotherhood have been appointed, and in place of the Emergency Law, in whose shadow Mubarak committed horrendous crimes against Egyptians, a new Emergency Law is being drafted in the service of President Morsi.

I have learnt from trustworthy sources that the top officers in the state security apparatus are getting in bed with the Muslim Brotherhood, apologising for the crimes they committed against them during the Mubarak era and offering their services to them. The state security apparatus, which has not changed after the revolution, could at any moment become the tool that the Muslim Brotherhood use to oppress us.

However humble an individual might be, when they attain power they are often weak in the face of obsequiousness and gradually start believing that all praise directed at them is well deserved.

In his excellent book, *Whatever Happened to the Egyptian Revolution?*, the great professor of economics, Galal Amin, speaks of his experience at the American University of Cairo. When he was still giving lectures there, students would throng to his office to ask him questions or request course material. The students would often thank him effusively and heap praise on him for having helped them so much. Of this, Galal Amin wrote: "I noticed that in situations like that I was given to a not insubstantial degree of self-admiration and pride, because I believed what was being said of me and thought it was true merely because I wanted it to be." However most people do not enjoy the same degree of self-awareness or resistance to pride as Galal Amin.

We have seen how President Morsi went on a routine visit to China to study means of cooperation and how the media portrayed his visit as a great success, with professors of political science vying with each other to expound on the great benefits which would come flooding to Egypt and its people as a result of Morsi's historic visit.

There suddenly popped up an unknown group that called itself the World Peace Organisation and announced that it had awarded President Mohamed Morsi the World Peace Prize for 2012. We have to ask ourselves why this organisation did not wait until the end of the year to make sure that the president was indeed eligible for the prize, and above and beyond that, what has President Morsi actually done to deserve any prize? So far he has failed to propose any solution for Egypt's chronic and complex problems.

The process of creating the dictator is in full swing and unfortunately President Morsi is showing signs of responding well to flattery. We have seen him request a large loan from the International Monetary Fund (IMF) without consulting the Egyptians who are the ones who will have to pay the cost of the loan and the interest thereon. At a time when the police have refused to protect the people, and hospitals have been forced to shut their doors out of fear of attacks by [paid] thugs, the president has no qualms about going around with an entourage of three thousand soldiers and scores of officers and marksmen, and neither does he seem embarrassed, as an Islamist president, to see the presidential guard stopping people from entering a mosque if he is praying there.

This tells us that the president's security is much more important than a citizen's security; the same notion prevalent in Mubarak's days have been dragged out again for President Morsi.

Mohamed Morsi was elected president by the Egyptian people, despite the fact he belongs to the Muslim Brotherhood, which had previously been an underground organisation. How many Muslim Brotherhood members are there? Do they have a military wing and how do they get the enormous sums they have spent on their election campaign? These are all unanswered questions because the Muslim Brotherhood refuses to regularise their organisation and hence Egyptians have an elected president who is partially beyond their ken.

We do not know where the boundary lies between the presidency of the republic and the office of the supreme guide, or what the relationship is between the president and the supreme guide. Hence the Muslim Brotherhood is still the secret arm of the president, spying on the people and holding the country to ransom. We have seen how organised groups have attacked Media City in Cairo and anti-Brotherhood journalists and senior members have rushed to condemn such attacks. As long as the Brotherhood remains illegal and rejects any state oversight, President Morsi has under his command a secret organisation which can intervene in myriad ways to keep the president in power.

As President Morsi is an Islamist, he refers to the Islamic heritage in all of his speeches and statements. The problem is that the ruler-citizen relationship in Islamic history can be understood as two contradictory concepts. Islam brought in the democratic conception of authority which was epitomised during the caliphates of Abu Bakr and Omar. Upon taking power, Abu Bakr gave a resounding speech that started as follows: "I have been given the authority over you, and I am not the best of you. If I do well, help me; and if I do wrong, set me right."

That statement was a democratic constitution that treated the ruler as an ordinary man in the service of the people whose right it was to criticise him, set him right or dismiss him from office. However, this exemplar quickly became no more than an obscure incident in Islamic history as jurists started opining that a Muslim ruler had the right to absolute authority, even if he was corrupt or unjust.

The revolution broke out, toppling Mubarak, putting him in custody and sending him for trial, but some Egyptians are still fond of Mubarak, generally those who profited from the Mubarak regime. It is odd, however, that there are some Egyptians who suffered severely from the injustice and corruption of his regime, but who defend him and show sympathy to him. In my opinion they are suffering from Stockholm syndrome.

In 1973 a group of thieves raided a bank in Stockholm and held four bank employees (three women and a man) hostage for six days. The ironical aspect was that after their release it appeared that they had formed such an emotional attachment to their captors that they were hostile to the police. Just as Stockholm syndrome can affect individuals, it can also affect a whole nation which has been subjected to dictatorship over a long period with some people becoming attached to the tyrant, and even though they are aware of his injustice and corruption they feel safer with him in power, paternalistically protecting them from the evils of the world. They remain attached to him, no matter how much he wrongs or brutalises them. This group of Egyptians, whose number is unknown, are incapable of dealing with the president who is a civil servant and they hanker for a tyrant to protect and oppress them, someone in front of whom they can feel weak and insignificant.

These people, who are suffering from Stockholm syndrome, having first ascertained that Mubarak is not coming back, started bonding with President Morsi, justifying everything he has done, rightly or wrongly. They see him as a great and inspiring leader who has come along to save the nation with his wisdom and bravery.

In the shadow of all of these elements, a new dictatorship is being created in Egypt. President Morsi has stated many times that he rejects dictatorship, but experience has taught us that every ruler of Egypt started out as a good and decent man, defending the rights of the people, and then gradually turned into a tyrant or an oppressor. President Morsi, in front of our very eyes, is turning from a normal man who won the elections by a tiny majority into that great, wise inspiring leader, man of the revolution, hero of peace, and all those other epithets of obsequious flattery which people have always showered on the rulers our country.

During the Egyptian revolution thousands of people were killed and injured for the sake of dignity, freedom and social justice, and these principles can only be realised after we acknowledge that the president is just a civil servant whose job is to serve the people, and that he must be held closely to account for his mistakes, just as he must be able to take criticism, no matter how harsh, because criticism is constructive.

In my opinion, the revolution must try and stop the creation of a new tyrant. Then we can build the democracy for which so many people have died.

Democracy is the answer.

RH

In Defence of the Prophet

17 September 2012

Regardless of your religious denomination – whether you are a Muslim or a Christian – you have the right to practice your religion freely and to ask others to respect your beliefs. Therefore, the Muslim community was within its rights to be angry when a provocative and poorly-made film was released that ridiculed the Prophet.[1] Muslims were also within their rights when they objected to the cartoons of the Prophet published in Denmark a few years ago.[2] Similarly, they were within their rights to get angry about *Fitna*, the film produced by the Dutch bigot Geert Wilders in 2006, which vilified the Islamic faith and presented it as the source of terrorism in the world.[3]

Muslims were justifiably angered by those who slandered the Prophet, because it is their right, as human beings, to enjoy complete respect for their religious beliefs. But unfortunately, in all of these instances, the Muslims forfeited this right, and instead contributed to the negative image of Islam by letting their anger get the better of them. They also overlooked several important factors:

First: The nature of freedom of expression in the West. People in Western societies abandoned the concept of the sanctity of religion a long time ago. In fact, they consider criticising religion to be a legitimate part of freedom of expression. In the West, for every film that is considered offensive to Islam, there are a dozen films which insult Christianity. Christian fundamentalists call for these films to be banned and appeal to the courts in order to stop them being shown, but they are very rarely successful. In the West, there are atheists who appear in the media describing the Messiah as an illusion and deriding the very notion that God sent prophets to Earth. These atheists also savagely

1 The trailer for the film triggered protests across the Muslim world with Western embassies being targeted in North Africa and the Middle East.

2 The twelve caricatures of the Prophet Muhammad were first published in the Danish newspaper *Jyllands-Posten* on 30 September 2005 to accompany an editorial criticising self-censorship in the Danish media.

3 Geert Wilders, a right-wing Dutch MP, was taken to court on charges of inciting hatred against Muslims, but was later acquitted.

attack the Church, calling it a corrupt capitalist institution. However, people in the West are rarely mobilised against these opinions as they have the right to believe and say what they like within the confines of the law. Western law does not consider "criticising religion" a crime, but it does have a crime for "inciting hatred".

In the West, there is no punishment for not believing in religion or denying the Prophets, but punishment is directed against those who incite people to hate the followers of a particular religion and this charge must, of course, be proven in court. If only the Muslims had realised the nature of Western society, they could have benefitted from this freedom of expression and produced a film presenting the true face of Islam to Western audiences, who are interested in understanding more about Islam. They could have fought a legal battle to prosecute the filmmakers for inciting hatred by portraying Muslims as savage barbarians who spill the blood of innocents.

Instead, many Muslims surrendered to anger and took to the streets in a violent rage. Their actions only served to reinforce the negative image that the film attached to Muslims. How will the world be convinced that the film was misleading when Muslims in Libya killed four American diplomats, including the American ambassador in retaliation?[1] Is it Islamic for us to kill innocent people who were representing their country and who had no relationship whatsoever with the film or the filmmaker?

Second: The nature of power in the West. In the Arab world, we live in tyrannical and oppressive societies, in which those in power can do as they wish. For example, if you had a dispute with your doorman, you would contact one of your acquaintances in the security forces to intimidate him and forcefully put him back in his place. If you then had a dispute with this officer, you would look for someone who knows the director of security to discipline the officer. But as for the president of the republic, or the king, or the sheikh of the emirate, they have complete and unrestricted power. They are able to shut down television channels and newspapers, or throw citizens in jail without evidence of wrongdoing. Taking into account this absolute control, the ruler is undoubtedly responsible for everything that is disseminated in the media or produced in the cinema, because they have the power to put a stop to it.

Whenever the Arab media launches a campaign against officials in another Arab country, the officials who have been targeted usually complain to the ruler of the country whose media attacked them. Then, the ruler is able to stop the campaign against them with a click of their finger and perhaps – if they want their respect – order said channel or newspaper to be shut down. Unfortunately, many Muslims believe that Western society functions in the same way. Therefore, they hold Western governments responsible

1 Armed militants in Libya, apparently prompted by the Egyptian protest, attacked the US consulate in Benghazi, killing Chris Stevens, the American ambassador to Libya.

for all the films that are produced and all the articles that are written in the West. This naïve belief regarding the Western political system pushes many to commit wrongdoing. Western society is democratic, so every state official has only limited powers that cannot be overstepped without risk of dismissal or prosecution.

In the West, a president of the republic cannot interfere with the content of what is published in the media directly, and they cannot shut down a newspaper or television channel on a whim. In fact, it is often the newspaper that is able to remove the president, if it can convince the electorate that they are not fit for their position. Many Muslims are not aware of this fact, so they storm Western embassies, burn them down and kill innocent diplomats presuming that they are putting pressure on governments to stop the showing of the film insulting to Islam.

Third: The double standards of Arab countries. We cannot demand that our principles be respected when we are the first to break or challenge them. When a film is released insulting to Islam, or Muslims are subjected to discrimination in the West, we get angry and demand that the right of Muslims to practice their religion be respected. But in our own countries, unfortunately, we don't respect the rights of our citizens who belong to different religions. Does the Saudi government have the right to protest against the banning of the niqab in France, or to advocate for the respect of minorities, when it oppresses the Shia in its own country and has sent its troops to kill Shia citizens in Bahrain because they were protesting and demanding their rights?[1]

Do Egyptian Salafists have the right to demand the respect of Muslim rights in the West when they consider the Copts in Egypt second-class citizens, who are not permitted to accede to the presidency or lead the army, and when they consider the Baha'is apostate infidels and call upon them to repent or be killed? In Egypt, the state refuses to acknowledge the right of Baha'i citizens to register their religion. How many times have Muslim extremists attacked the Copts because they wanted to build a church? How many times have extremist sheikhs come out and vilified the beliefs of the Copts and branded them infidels whose deaths should not be mourned?

In Egypt, the charge of blasphemy is only applied to those who attack Islam. As for those who speak badly of the Copts or Shia or Baha'is, they are safe from punishment. A few days ago, a young Egyptian Copt called Alber Saber posted the trailer for the film insulting to the Prophet on his personal Facebook page. Local residents in the area where he lived surrounded his house and attacked him. When his mother called the police for help, they came and, instead of protecting Alber from the attack, they arrested him and

1 During the Bahraini Uprising, the Saudi Arabian government and other Gulf region governments strongly supported the King of Bahrain. Saudi Arabia deployed about 1,000 troops with armoured support to quell the protests.

put him on trial for blasphemy. The other prisoners – with the encouragement of the officer in charge – attacked Alber until he was dangerously injured with a cut to his neck. What crime has Alber committed? That he watched the film and posted it on Facebook? Millions of Egyptians have seen the film and done the same, but none of them have been arrested. In fact, Sheikh Khaled Abdullah was the first to show the film, on the Al-Nas TV channel, to millions of viewers. The difference here is that Alber is a Copt, and therefore unworthy of fair treatment. But as for Sheikh Khaled Abdullah, he is an Islamic sheikh and is above reprimand. Is this the justice that Islam commands of us?

Demonstrations broke out in Egypt protesting against the film insulting to the Prophet, in which both Copts and Muslims took part. The Egyptian Church and Coptic associations released statements condemning the film in a wonderful show of Egyptian unity in defence of the Prophet, but what did the extremists do? They carried banners deriding the Copts and describing them as "worshippers of the cross" and Sheikh Wagdy Ghoneim said that Coptic priests were homosexuals and that all Copts living abroad were prostitutes. Is this the kind of Islamic behaviour we are showing the world? One sheikh, Abu Islam, burned and tore up the Bible in public, in front of the cameras, and said that next time he would urinate on it. Do we have the right to demand the respect of our religion and the things we hold sacred if this is what we do to others?

Ultimately, our battle to defend Islam is legitimate, and we would be successful if we did the following:

1. Muslims must present a civilised model for respecting the beliefs and rights of others (which Islam in fact prompts us to do anyway). We must give every citizen in our country freedom of belief. Every citizen chooses the religion they wish and the state remains at all times a guarantor and protector of the rights of all citizens concerning their religion. When we respect what is sacred to others, then it will be our right to defend what is sacred to us. Our firm moral position will convince world public opinion to join with us and forbid any offence to Islam.

2. We must present the truth of Islam to the Western public. It is my wish that a fraction of Arab wealth – accumulating from the profits of oil – be used to produce world class films presenting the truth about the Prophet – may the peace and blessings of God be upon him – so that the world will know the humanitarian essence of Islam.

3. We must uncover exactly who is behind the production of films insulting to Islam, and get the help of the Muslim community in the West to boycott the products of any company or foundation funding the offensive films.

4. We must seek recourse to specialist legal firms in the West to prosecute the makers of the offensive films, because they committed the crime of inciting hatred towards Muslims – a crime recognised by all Western legal systems.

No matter how great our anger, we must defend the Prophet in a civilised and rational manner reflecting the civilisation of Islam, which has taught the world tolerance, justice and freedom.

Democracy is the answer.

PN

Where is the President Taking Us?

24 September 2012

I did not vote for President Morsi. In fact, I called on the Egyptian people to boycott the elections in protest of Ahmed Shafik's candidacy. Shafik should not be able to run for preseident before the 35 counts of corruption brought against him have been investigated. The call to boycott the elections was not successful, and millions of Egyptians came out to vote for Mohamed Morsi, not out of conviction for the ideas of the Brotherhood, but to prevent the return of the Mubarak regime in the form of Ahmed Shafik. As a result, Mohamed Morsi was declared Egypt's first democratically elected president. I called for the will of the people to be respected, and considered it unfair to attack President Morsi without first giving him a chance. After three months in power, we are now in a position to read his political manoeuvres, which have so far been disconcerting.

One of the most important demands of the Egyptian revolution was to stop the brutal repression carried out by the Ministry of the Interior against ordinary Egyptians. The revolution demanded, from the very beginning, that the state security service be disbanded and the Ministry of the Interior be purged of the corrupt bastions of the Mubarak regime. But the military council vigorously refused to carry out any change to the Ministry of the Interior during the transitional period, a decision which was later upheld by Mohamed Morsi when he appointed Ahmed Gamal El Din[1] as minister of the interior. There seems to be an implicit agreement between the Brotherhood and the leadership of the Ministry of the Interior, which protects the old guard from criminal prosecution and maintains their privileges, in exchange

1 Ahmed Gamal El Din was one of the major members of the National Democratic Party (NDP) during the Mubarak era. *See* Glossary.

for them returning the country to security and protecting the interests of the Brotherhood. Security returned in a limited fashion, but with it returned all the hallmarks of oppression, such as police violence and brutality. Last week, a young engineer called Mohamed Fahim was driving through Mansoura in his car when he was stopped by a police officer. The officer asked him to produce his driving licence, but Mohamed realised that he had left it at home. He politely asked the officer to allow one of his squad to go with him to his house nearby to get his driving license. "Tell that to your mother," replied the officer. Mohamed Fahim took objection to this insult, at which point the officer savagely beat him and ordered his colleagues to push him to the ground. They then took him to the police station, where they subjected him to torture and abuse, before bringing him before the attorney general's office, which ordered that he be held in custody pending investigation.

There are many other examples of incidents in which the rights of ordinary citizens have been disregarded. President Morsi, like President Mubarak before him, has shown no remorse for the cruel and inhumane treatment of Egyptians. And the truth is, that the dignity of Egyptians abroad is no better than at home. It is well known that the Saudi legal system does not apply international standards of justice. The Saudi authorities can do no harm to Westerners, whereas there are hundreds of Egyptians in Saudi prisons either held without trial or held as a result of unfair trials. amongst them are Nagla Wafa, who is flogged weekly because she had a disagreement with one of the Princesses, and the lawyer Ahmed al-Gizawi, prosecuted on a fabricated charge because he dared to bring a legal case against the king of Saudi Arabia and stand up for the rights of Egyptians.

On his first visit to Saudi Arabia, President Morsi exchanged greetings and commemorative photographs with officials, but did nothing to help the Egyptian citizens being detained there. In addition, there are thousands of Egyptian currently detained in military prisons as a result of their involvement in the revolution. The April 8 Officers,[1] who joined the demonstrations in Tahrir Square, are still being held in custody and have been subjected to torture at the hands of the authorities. In the run up to the elections, President Morsi promised to free all of these people as soon as he got into power – he has not fulfilled his promise.

When the president announced the formation of his cabinet, we were surprised to see so many ministers that belonged to the previous regime. The indication of this is simply that there are no significant differences between the policies of Mubarak and Morsi. President Mubarak was biased towards the rich, maintaining their comfort and increasing their profits, and he cared

1 Fifteen Egyptian soldiers and mid-level army officers joined the demonstrations in April 2011, flouting a ban issued by a military spokesman. They were subsequently arrested and taken into custody.

nothing for the suffering of the poor. Unfortunately, we do not find Morsi to be any different from Mubarak. Morsi, who has allied himself with businessmen from the Mubarak regime and takes them to foreign countries on his private plane. Morsi, who is apparently trying to combat the economic crisis but never thinks of cutting government spending or dismissing the corrupt consultants who are being paid millions of Egyptian pounds unnecessarily. Morsi, who never thinks of imposing cumulative taxes on the rich, or reducing energy subsidies to factories that sell products at the global market price.

President Morsi did not consider these solutions because they would threaten the interests of the rich. Instead, President Morsi (like Mubarak) thought of borrowing money from abroad, and so presented a request for a heavy loan to the tune of 4.8 billion dollars to the International Monetary Fund (IMF), without revealing to the public the conditions that came with securing the loan. Here we must mention that former Prime Minister el-Ganzouri wanted to borrow from the IMF, but at that time the Brotherhood opposed it vehemently, saying that the loan would put Egypt into greater debt. They also emphasised that loans with interest were not permissible in Islamic law. But now here the Brotherhood is, praising the loan that President Morsi has requested. They have suddenly discovered that loans are permissible when it is a necessity, and ends apparently justify means.

The Mubarak regime used its control of the media and the national press to paint a false picture of Mubarak as being an inspirational leader and a wise ruler. Then came President Morsi, and instead of making the national press independent and shutting down the Ministry of Information, the president appointed a member of the Brotherhood as minister of information, while the Shura Council appointed the editors-in-chief of the national newspapers; the same Shura Council who owe their positions to the Muslim Brotherhood. Day after day, the influence of the Brotherhood on the media becomes more apparent. State television continually broadcasts images of President Morsi, just as it used to do with Mubarak. Even private television channels owned by businessmen are taking care to strengthen their relationship with the Brotherhood, starting by getting rid of media figures well known for their opposition to the Brotherhood and making new contracts with their supporters. We saw recently a televised discussion with President Morsi that was an exact copy of one of Mubarak's interviews. The president sits proudly and seems completely at ease with himself, while in front of him is a presenter almost shaking with fear, because he knows that one word out of line could ruin his career. The presenter asks the president vague, indulgent questions, which he answers with empty phrases that don't mean anything. Then the presenter suddenly looks into the president's face with admiration and says: "Your Excellency, you have worked so hard for Egypt ... when do you ever take a rest?" So we see, President Morsi has maintained the corrupt media of

Mubarak, and is beginning to use it to serve his own interests.

The Constituent Assembly, in its present form, is governed by the Muslim Brotherhood as they hold the majority of the seats. This means, however long the hearings and debates go on for, the supreme guide of the Muslim Brotherhood is the one responsible for the drafting of the Egyptian constitution. President Morsi promised, before his election, that he would reconstruct the Constituent Assembly with a view to making it representative of all sections of society. But, as usual, he did not fulfil his promise and left the Constituent Assembly as it was, and the document that emerged contains unacceptable violations of public liberty, women's rights, and freedom of the press. What we can expect now is that the Constituent Assembly will produce the constitution that best serves the interests of the Brotherhood, which is then put to the public in a sudden poll. Again, the Brotherhood will call upon preachers at the mosque to persuade ordinary people that voting in favour of the constitution is a religious duty for which they will be rewarded in Paradise.

President Morsi promised that public liberty would flourish under his rule. But in fact we are seeing the opposite: newspapers have been seized, Al Faraeen TV channel has been shut down and whatever our opinion of it may be – we do not accept its closure by government edict. There is an Egyptian citizen named Bishwi al-Buhairi who will spend two years in prison with the charge of insulting President Morsi on his Facebook page, in addition to two senior journalists now on trial for the same charge. The charge of "insulting the president" is not found in any democratic system, but it seems President Morsi leans towards punishing his opponents with jail time while also refusing to scrap prison sentences for crimes of defamation. Leading Brotherhood member Mahmoud Ghozlan stated that the imprisonment of journalists would not be scrapped, because journalists are "no better than other people". This statement reveals Ghozlan's ignorance about what happens in civilised countries, where a writer or a journalist is not imprisoned because of his opinion or his writings but, if he is found guilty, is ordered to pay a monetary fine. In terms of civil liberties, the Morsi era will be no better than the Mubarak era, if not worse.

President Morsi was elected by the people, but at the same time he belongs to the Muslim Brotherhood. A secretive and obscure organisation whose funding sources are unknown. Many times we have demanded that the Brotherhood be regulated, and made subject to state supervision, but it seems that President Morsi prefers the Brotherhood to remain a secret organisation that supports him from behind the scenes. Indeed, the President's attachment to the Brotherhood has resulted in actions that would be unacceptable in any democratic state. Khairat el-Shater, a senior figure in the Brotherhood who is not a government official, makes statements about legislation, meets officials of other countries, holds negotiations and concludes agreements with them.

In what capacity does he conclude these agreements? In fact, do we really know who governs Egypt: is it President Morsi, or is it the supreme guide of the Brotherhood?

It is a worrying picture, as if nothing in Egypt has changed after the revolution except for the president: Mubarak stood down and Morsi came to power. And here is President Morsi, moving with a 3,000-strong guard of infantry to protect him, besides officers and snipers. Then President Morsi goes to Rome and stays in the same luxury hotel which Mubarak used to stay in, costing the state thousands of Egyptian pounds for one night and paid for by the money stolen from the impoverished Egyptian people.

The revolution achieved something incredible when it deposed Mubarak, brought him to trial and threw him in prison with his own kind. The priority of the revolution is now to prevent the Brotherhood controlling the state. If nationalist forces do not unite immediately to save the Egyptian nation from the hands of the Brotherhood, we will pay a heavy price, both now and in the future. The people who made this great revolution are able to save it.

Democracy is the answer.

PN

When Will the West Respect Us?

1 October 2012

I write this article from Cosenza, a city in Southern Italy, where I have come to receive the Mediterranean Cultural Award, which I won this year. The award is organised by the Carical Foundation, under the sponsorship of the Italian Ministry of Culture and is one of the major literary prizes in Italy. It was awarded to many internationally renowned authors before me, including two major Arab writers: Amin Maalouf and Tahar Ben Jelloun. This is the fourth award I have received in Italy and it is the fifteenth time I have won an international honour or prize. It always happens in the same way: a letter or a telephone call from the judging panel congratulating me on the prize; there is no influence, or exchange of favours, or pressure on the judging panel, as would happen in Egypt.

In the West, writers usually only put themselves forward for an award if they are at the beginning of their career. In this case, the real prize is that their work gets published. Writers do not put themselves forward for prizes, but are nominated either by the judging panel, or by the publisher of their work. The judging panel of the Mediterranean Cultural Award is comprised of distinguished professors of literature in Italy. I found out through one of them, informally, that the final choice was between myself and a Spanish writer. At the awards ceremony, when I went up to the stage to receive the prize, I was overcome with strong but conflicting emotions; I was thankful to God the Almighty, who brought me this success, but also proud that I, as both an Egyptian and an Arab, am being given such an accolade. After the ceremony, I asked myself: how can Arabs and Muslims project a possitve and respectable image of themselves to the rest of the world? The answer, perhaps, can be summarised by the following:

First: Our knowledge of the West. What would you do if you lived in one country and had the opportunity to travel to another? Wouldn't you ask about the climate in the other country, so that you could take the necessary clothing? What if you assumed the other country would be hot like your country so packed light clothing, only to find that it was covered in snow? Is this not foolish behaviour? Well, we are always making these kind of foolish mistakes in our dealings with the West. Many of us make certain presumptions about the West which have no basis in fact. Every day in the Arab world, dozens of articles are written about the West, claiming that it is at war with Islam. We have started to believe that this statement is true, building our future actions and ideas upon it.

I lived and studied in the West for many years, and I found that in their dealings with Arabs and Muslims, Westerners can be divided into three types: the first is Western governments, who are, more often than not, opportunist and colonial, caring only for their own interests. They have always supported despotic Arab rulers and ignored the crimes they committed against their own people for profits and oil. The second type are those bigoted, racist Westerners who hate Arabs and Muslims, and every race except the white race. However, the third and most numerous type of Westerner is the ordinary citizen, who differ from us only in faith and their acceptance of sexual relations outside of marriage. These are the majority of Westerners, and they usually know nothing about Islam; just as the majority of us Arabs know nothing about Buddhism or Hinduism.

How has Islam been presented to these Westerners? The answer is unfortunate, because it is Osama bin Laden and other extremists like him, who have made many Westerners believe that Islam is a religion of violence and killing. The word "sharia" is beginning to be used in Western languages to mean cutting off the hands and slaughtering people by the sword, while "jihad" in the West is a synonym for "killing". Thus, through the crimes of some Muslim terrorists, the image of Islam has been distorted in the minds of millions of Westerners. What can we expect, when there are some amongst us who consider bombing innocent, peaceful civilians to be a sort of jihad that brings them closer to God?

Some may disagree with my words, saying: "Why do you talk about the terrorist Bin Laden and not talk about the crimes of the American army in Iraq and Afghanistan?" The answer is that we must punish the killing of innocent people, regardless of who killed whom. Likewise, human accountability should be individual, not collective. So, those killed by Al Qaeda in Madrid and New York were not responsible for the crimes of the American army. Otherwise, by the same logic, every Arab in the West would become responsible for the attacks of September 11. The voices of protest in the West against the crimes of the American army are loud and numerous. What is more, if it wasn't for Western media, we would not have known anything about what happened in Abu Ghraib and Guantanamo Bay. In fact, the demonstrations opposing the war on Iraq held in Western capitals were bigger than those in the Arab world.

We cannot combat a crime with another crime. Anybody who has read history knows that the first Muslims did not respond to the crimes of their enemies with similar crimes. Instead, through their sense of justice and tolerance, they presented a civilised, Islamic model which convinced millions of people to embrace Islam. It suffices here to compare the tolerance showed by the Muslims towards the Copts of Egypt at the time of its conquest, and the brutal massacres perpetrated by the Christian armies with the support of the Catholic Church against Muslims and Jews after the fall of Al-Andalusia. The killing of innocent people is an atrocious crime which cannot be excused under any circumstances and which undermines the legitimacy of a cause, even if it is a just one.

A few years ago, I won the Bruno Kreisky prize for political literature. At the award ceremony, I said a few words to the audience – all of them foreigners – in which I spoke of the Prophet having taught us truth and justice and freedom and equality. I told them how the Prophet was kneeling in prayer, when his two grandsons Hassan and Hussein jumped on his back in jest. The Prophet continued to kneel until they had finished their game, stopping his prayer so as not to upset the children. Is it conceivable – I then said – that a man so mild-tempered would agree with the bombing of innocent people in a restaurant or a train station? I remember that the audience clapped for a long time, and many people came to ask me where they could find some reliable sources to read about the Prophet and his works. Before blaming Westerners for their fear of Islam, we must ask ourselves what picture we are presenting of our religion.

Second: Outstanding and creative people. In the West, individuals are given the opportunity to excel, even if you come from a different culture. There are many distinguished Muslim scientists in the West, but our governments have failed to make use of their expertise and success. Likewise, in Egypt and the Arab world, we have some exceptionally creative people who are unknown in the West. If we were to translate their works, and present them in the correct manner, surely they would gain the recognition they deserve, which in turn would greatly enhance our reputation and image. The question is: who has benefitted Islam the most? Is it Ahmed Zewail[1] and Naguib Mahfouz, or Osama Bin Laden and Ayman al-Zawahiri?[2] Is it not best to present our culture to the world through scientific and literary achievement, rather than through extremist groups and murderers?

Third: Human rights. Humanity has made great progress to arrive at a collection of basic human rights forming the essence of civilisation. It follows that anyone who violates these human rights is considered savage and uncivilised. How strange it is that Islam introduced the concept of human rights centuries before the West, but some Muslims are now going against these rights. We have extremist clerics who believe a husband is allowed to discipline his wife by beating her. This violation of women's rights effectively removes us from the civilised world, because a woman is a person and to hit a woman is to disregard her dignity and destroy her self-respect.

There are clerics calling for the marriage of young women as soon as they have reached puberty, even if they are only ten years old. This perverted, depraved appeal considers a woman nothing more than an object to be used and abused by men, and completely denies women the ability to make autonomous decisions. Anyone who finds a child sexually desirable is a criminal and should be arrested, brought to trial and imprisoned. What is more, documented studies have proven that the noble Prophet married Aisha when she was nineteen or thereabouts, not nine years old as is generally believed. Some clerics talk of their contempt for the great heritage of Ancient Egypt and their intense hatred of the arts. They are incapable of having an imagination or of deriving pleasure from art, and deliberately deprive themselves of music. It is very unfortunate that all of these backward and ignorant views have been broadcast all over the world, and have reinforced Islam's negative image in the minds of Westerners.

Fourth: What we give to the world. Most Arab and Islamic countries are dependent on the West. It is an unfortunate truth that for centuries, we have contributed very little to humanity. We have thousands of scientific experts, but they either work in universities in the West, or are restricted in their own countries from contributing their efforts due to despotism, corruption and bureaucracy. No Arab country contributes anything to the world; neither industry, nor agriculture and scientific research. Even the rulers of rich, oil-producing countries put their wealth away in Western banks. Instead of using the money from oil to produce a true renaissance, many of them simply

1 Ahmed Zewail is an Egyptian-American scientist who won the 1999 Nobel Prize in Chemistry for his work on femtochemistry. He was the first Egyptian scientist to win a Nobel Prize in a scientific field.

2 Ayman al-Zawahiri, who helped found the Egyptian militant group Islamic Jihad, is the current leader of Al Qaeda. He was named leader a few weeks after Osama Bin Laden's death.

purchase the hard work of others. They recruit people to work instead of them, and enjoy a life devoid of any meaning but the pursuit of pleasures. How can the world respect us when we, with 22 Arab nations, are incapable of making anything of use to humanity? Those religious zealots who curse the West from the pulpit are shouting into microphones manufactured in the West, leading the prayer knelt upon prayer mats made in China, and living their whole lives using the tools of Western civilisation towards which they are so hostile. The world will not respect us until we start to carry out respectable scientific research, until we start to manufacture the products we need, so as to contribute seriously and effectively to human progress.

Islam has given to humanity a great civilisation, which Muslims, Christians and Jews helped to build, and which led the world for eight centuries. It established the values of love, justice and mercy, but some Muslims are guilty of bringing shame on their religion. If we want to restore the image of Islam, we must be must work hard, make progress, and respect human rights. Only then will the world respect us.

Democracy is the answer.

PN

The Art of Putting on Shoes

8 October 2012

In 1948, King Farouk, in the company of Prime Minister Mahmoud an-Nukrashi,[1] was driving to the celebration of the sighting of the crescent moon, marking the beginning of Ramadan. Following protocol, the prime minister was sitting next to the king on the back seat, while the king's servant was sat next to the driver. As soon as the car stopped, it was the servant's duty to spring from the car and open the back door so that His Majesty, the king, could get out. At this point, the king's servant discovered that the door handle had broken; he frantically tried to open the door but to no avail. As the minutes past, the situation became embarrassing. The car had stopped, but the king had not emerged. Standing next to the door was an officer in the Royal Guard and a major general in the police. "Open the door for His Majesty, the king," shouted the major general to the young officer.

"You open the door, sir," replied the officer in a loud voice. "You're closer." The king brought this embarrassing situation to an end by opening the door himself and stepping out to attend the celebration.

1 Mahmoud an-Nukrashi (1888–1948) was the second prime minister of the Kingdom of Egypt. He was assasinated in 1948 after outlawing the Muslim Brotherhood.

That day, at the presidential palace, talk was only of the officer of the Royal Guard who publicly refused to open the door for His Majesty, the king. The palace staff were convinced that the young man would be dismissed from service immediately. Perhaps he would be court-martialled and spend months, if not years, in military prison. The following day, as soon as the young officer arrived at the palace, the captain of the Royal Guard summoned him to his office and there passed between them the following dialogue:

Captain: "Why did you disobey the orders of the major general of the police and refuse to open the car door for His Majesty, the king?"

Officer: "The major general was closer than me to the royal car, so I told him to open the door."

Captain: "And why didn't you open the door for His Majesty yourself?"

Officer: "Sir, I am an officer of the Royal Guard, not the king's servant. My duty is to protect the king, not to open doors."

The captain looked at the young officer with incredulity, then escorted him to the office of the grand chamberlain and left him to wait outside. A few moments later, the captain emerged, patted the young man on the back and told him to return to his duties; he would receive no punishment.

This is the true story of Al-Gharib Al-Husseini, who would later become the personal bodyguard of King Farouk. As a young officer, he stood up for himself and refused to be a servant of the king. Even though he would have been prepared to sacrifice his life for the king, Al-Husseini would not stoop so low as to open the door for him. This position was understood by the captain of the guard and after him the grand chamberlain, who sent him away without punishment.

A few days ago, the renowned TV personality and journalist, Ibrahim Eissa,[1] broadcast a recording of the supreme guide, Mohammed Badie, giving a religious lecture to a crowd at a mosque. When the supreme guide rose to leave, a group of Brotherhood members swarmed around him, bowed down and helped the supreme guide put on his shoes. Everyone who saw the recording of the incident remarked that the supreme guide did not object, and that he allowed a young man to fawn over him and help him into his shoes. This suggests that the supreme guide accepts this kind of behaviour and, moreover, he enjoys it. Viewers also noticed how proud and honoured the young man appeared, as if he had performed an exceptional and noble feat.

1 Ibrahim Eissa is an Egyptian journalist, television personality and political apologist best known for co-founding the popular Egyptian weekly *Al-Dustour*.

These two events present two contradictory rationales: the young officer, who refused to open the door, valued his own dignity more than his loyalty to the king. As for the young man who bent down to help the supreme guide into his shoes, he is a submissive wretch who takes pleasure in his own servility. He does not understand the difference between loyalty and indignity. He sees himself as inferior to the supreme guide to such a degree that he is not ashamed to perform a task that even a servant might refuse to do. The first rationale – that of the young officer – results in a strong, dignified personality, able to think independently and make decisions. The second rationale – that of the shoe carrier – produces a servile follower, who can't form an opinion or think in a way independent from that of his master, the supreme guide.

The Muslim Brotherhood is founded on blind obedience and servile loyalty. It has only one mind, and that is the Guidance Office, headed by the supreme guide. As for the thousands of Brotherhood members, unfortunately they are nothing but tools used to carry out the will of the supreme guide. They have no right to disagree or criticise, or even to express ideas contrary to the orders of the supreme guide. All members of the Brotherhood give the same opinion on any topic and take the same stand in any affair.

If the supreme guide is satisfied with you, then all of the Brotherhood will immediately be satisfied with you and will praise your wisdom and bravery. Days or hours after this heavy praise, if you disagree with the supreme guide and anger him, then the Brotherhood will heap insults and curses upon you and your family. They will discover that you are a Western agent, an immoral enemy of Islam, and a hater of God's laws. If you disagree with the supreme guide, then you will be ostracised and punished because his is the only opinion that matters. In the Brotherhood, defending the opinions of the supreme guide is a sacred duty.

We have observed how all those who have split from the Brotherhood possess strong, commanding personalities which were not compatible with this brand of servile obedience. We have observed also how, as soon as these people have left the Brotherhood, they are subjected to a barrage of vile insults. The Brothers do not take into account the previous comradeship or shared history between them and have shunned many former members, including Abdel Moneim Aboul Fotouh, even though he did a great deal of good for the Brotherhood. Indeed, the concept of absolute loyalty practiced in the Brotherhood undoubtedly hinders the ability of a person to think creatively and independently.

If we chose the closest companion of Mohamed ElBaradei or Hamdeen Sabahi, or indeed Abdel Moneim Aboul Fotouh, and then suggested that they help their party leader into their shoes, there is no doubt that they would refuse, and take offence at the insolence of the request. In fact, not one of these eminent personalities would ever allow another person to put their shoes on for them. However, they may argue that it is a person's right, if they wish, to kiss the hand of the supreme guide and help him into his shoes, and that this is their own business. The answer to that is that it was their own business in the past, but now that the Brotherhood governs Egypt, it is no longer only their business, but the business of all Egyptians.

We have a president who belongs to the Muslim Brotherhood for which millions of Egyptians were obliged to vote, not out of love or respect for Morsi, but to prevent the collapse of the revolution and the return of the old regime at the hands of Ahmed Shafik. This elected president spent his entire life in the Muslim Brotherhood. Isn't it our right to ask the president if he agrees with a young man helping the supreme guide into his shoes? Will the president see this practice as demeaning and detracting from the dignity of the shoe-bearer, or will he consider it an ordinary occurrence? If he considers it an ordinary occurrence, then what is the meaning of dignity in President Morsi's view?

One hundred days after President Morsi came to power, we have discovered three facts:

1. The president is a man who promises but does not deliver. He promised Egyptians he would reform the Constituent Assembly to make it balanced and representative of all sections of society, instead of being controlled by the Brotherhood. The president promised to look after those who were injured in the revolution, seek justice for the martyrs and release all those imprisoned, and many more promises besides, of which the president has not acted upon a single one. It is strange how the president does not seem to be showing the slightest shame or embarrassment about breaking these promises.

2. President Morsi does not possess a political vision that goes beyond that of Hosni Mubarak. The president has made no effort to bring about real changes to the structure of the Mubarak regime. He has chosen ministers from the remnants of the previous regime and kept the old guard of the Ministry of the Interior, who are responsible for the killing and torturing thousands of thousands of Egyptians. Like Mubarak, he favours the rich at the expense of the poor. He has negotiated to obtain a loan from the International Monetary Fund (IMF) without publicly revealing the conditions of the loan. He has appointed a minister of information from the Brotherhood to repress his opponents and control the national press through the Shura Council, which selects editors-in-chief which are loyal to the Brotherhood. President Morsi allows Egyptians to be prosecuted and imprisoned on

the charge of "insulting the president"; a ludicrous, imaginary charge not found in any respectable nation. He has let Egyptians be treated with disdain inside and outside Egypt, just like Mubarak. It seems now as if after the revolution we have simply swapped President Mubarak for President Morsi, without any accompanying change in ideals or policies.

3. President Morsi is a member of the Muslim Brotherhood. This is an illegal and enigmatic organisation, with questionable funding sources and working practices. It is our right to ask whether the president is making administrative decisions of state independently of the supreme guide, or simply following instructions from him on how to run the state. There are many worrying signs: senior Brotherhood figure Khairat el-Shater is meeting with officials in foreign countries to discuss joint ventures with Egypt. Nobody asks him in what capacity he is negotiating in the name of Egypt, since he does not hold an official position authorising him to do so. Furthermore, when President Morsi decided to dismiss Field Marshal Tantawi and General Enan (and this is his singular achievement to date), another senior Brotherhood leader, Essam el-Erian,[1] made a statement in which he said: "The president took the decision to dismiss [Tantawi] without the consent of the supreme guide, who, in the final days of Ramadan, was occupied with spiritual matters."

The meaning of this is clear: had the supreme guide not been thus occupied, he would have contributed his opinion to a political decision of this gravity. And whether he accepted or rejected it, would the president find it in himself to go against the orders of the supreme guide? President Morsi's duty compels him to force the Muslim Brotherhood to adjust their status in accordance with the law and immediately disclose their sources of funding.

Egyptians, after starting a great revolution for which they paid the price in blood and gave thousands of martyrs for its sake, will never allow their human rights to be compromised, even though the Brotherhood continue to exploit them, as Mubarak once did. The revolution will continue until it has fulfilled all its aims.

Democracy is the answer.

PN

1 Essam el-Erian is an Egyptian physician and politician. He is the vice chairman of the Freedom and Justice party and former member of the Guidance Office.

A President Who Serves Two Masters

15 October 2012

Was the Egyptian Revolution legal? Was the act of millions of people demonstrating to depose Mubarak constitutional? At the outset of the revolution, was Hosni Mubarak a legal and legitimately elected President?

Everything that took place before the Egyptian revolution was against the law. The revolution was started principally against Mubarak's fraudulent elections, unjust laws and corrupt constitution. If Mubarak's constitution had expressed the will of the people and if his laws had been just, then Egyptians would not have needed a revolution in the firast place.

A revolution always starts in order to bring down an unjust regime, along with its laws and constitution. It also works to transfer power to the people so that they can – with constitutional legitimacy – start to purge the state of corrupt figures. Then, a Constituent Assembly is elected to write a new constitution embodying the aims of the revolution. After that, a set of new laws are enacted to deliver the justice demanded by the revolution. Throughout human history, this is what all revolutions have done.

As for the Egyptian revolution, it succeeded in deposing Mubarak, but to this day it still has not succeeded in toppling the Mubarak regime. The military council colluded with the Muslim Brotherhood to keep the old regime intact. Instead of revoking the old constitution, the same constitutional amendments, which Mubarak himself suggested, were brought forward. The military council appointed a committee tasked with making these amendments, which was comprised of jurists loyal to the Mubarak regime and supporters of the Muslim Brotherhood.

I remember calling one of the members of the committee, a legal specialist well known for his affiliation with the Brotherhood, and asking him directly why he wanted to amend the old constitution? I argued that a new constitution that embodied the ideals of the revolution would be better for Egypt. He initially agreed with my view, but then spoke at great length in order to justify the constitutional amendments. After a long discussion, he got to the bottom of the matter by telling me clearly: "Legitimacy has passed from the revolution to the military council, and now it can do as it pleases."

Little by little, the deal between the Brotherhood and the military council became clearer. The military council, self proclaimed enemy of the revolution, found in the Brotherhood a well-organised ally, able to mobilise the common people through religion and common bribes. The Brotherhood, thirsty for power by any means, allied with the military council to guarantee their getting into government. The Brotherhood overturned the revolution and abandoned its aims, calling for elections first and foremost to enable them to write the constitution they wanted. Meanwhile, to break the will of the revolutionaries, the military council carried out a number massacres in which hundreds of martyrs died. These massacres had the complete blessing of the Brotherhood, to the extent that Brotherhood figures cursed the revolutionaries and accused them of thuggery.

In the end, there was a dispute between the military council and the Brotherhood; parliament was dissolved and Egyptians found themselves going into presidential elections forced to vote for President Morsi not out of devotion tothe Brotherhood, but to preserve the revolution and depose Shafik, devoted protégé of Mubarak. Three months into President Morsi's rule, we see that, unfortunately, he is moving ever further away from fulfilling the aims of the revolution. Instead he is allying himself with the remnants of the Mubarak regime to serve the interests of the Brotherhood.

In the midst of this came the crisis of Egypt's attorney general, Abdel Meguid Mahmoud. President Morsi's advisors spoke with him and politely suggested that he hand in his resignation to assume the position of Egyptian ambassador to the Vatican. The attorney general agreed, but on condition that he was made ambassador to an Arab country, since he was not gifted with languages. By the following day, the attorney general had changed his mind and announced that he would remain in his current position. He now considered that the call from the president's advisors had been to intimidate him and was a direct threat to the independence of the judiciary. Many people sided with the attorney general. While some of them were revolutionaries, afraid of the Brotherhood gaining control over the judiciary, the majority were remnants of the old regime. For them, the attorney general remaining in his place was the best guarantee of protecting them from any accountability for the things they had done under Mubarak.

Abdel Meguid Mahmoud was chosen by Hosni Mubarak, who transferred him from the state security service, where he had worked for many years, and appointed him as attorney general. I shall quote here from a statement issued by the El Nadim Center for the Management and Rehabilitation of Victims of Torture, in which it said:

> The El Nadim Center has received thousands of torture cases where in one case after another the office of the attorney general, Abdel Meguid Mahmoud, continues to close the files by irrevocable order. Therefore, these cases are discontinued for lack of evidence, depriving thousands of victims from access to the courts in search of justice.

This is aside from the dozens of other cases which the attorney general has subjected to political accommodations, such as the sinking of the

MS al-Salam Boccaccio 98, the killing of demonstrators, the allegations of corruption against Ahmed Shafik, and many others. We should therefore stop making any connection between the attorney general and the independence of the judiciary. For him to stay in his position is not a victory for the independence of the judiciary, it is a victory for the Mubarak regime, which has managed to prevent any revolutionary change or any serious accountability for corrupt figures. Where were these angry defenders of the judiciary's independence when the United States violated Egyptian sovereignty? The military council complied with them while the chairman of Cairo's Court of Appeal, Abdel Moaz Ibrahim, held a special hearing to release the American suspects. It is strange that those who applauded the attorney general for staying in his position are the same ones who prevented the dismissal of Chairman Abdel Moaz Ibrahim and stopped him being held accountable for the escape of the detainees.

Why did we not hear the views of these champions of judicial independence when judges were given assignments in ministries in exchange for generous rewards when deciding on cases which may have concerned the self-same ministries they were working in? What is their opinion about those judges that were involved with vote-rigging in the elections? What did they think about the children of some advisors being appointed to the attorney general's office ahead of those with better qualifications from ordinary Egyptian families? Most judges in Egypt are honourable and free to act in line with their consciences, but the judicial system in Egypt is not independent and the attorney general, who disregards the rights of martyrs, cannot be a spokesman for any independent judiciary.

Changing the attorney general was one of the key aims of the revolution. So why, when President Morsi tried to get rid of the attorney general, did the world turn against him and everyone – including some revolutionaries – attack him? The reason is an absence of trust between President Morsi and the revolutionary forces. The revolutionaries remember very well the history of the Brotherhood's opportunistic deals and their abandonment of the revolution to serve their own interests. Likewise, the relationship between the president and the Muslim Brotherhood organisation is completely ambiguous. Nobody really knows whether the president makes his decisions by himself, or merely follows the instructions of the Brotherhood's supreme guide. Why did President Morsi honour Abdel Moaz Ibrahim, when he is connected to the scandal of the release of the American suspects? Why did President Morsi honour Field Marshal Tantawi and Lieutenant General Enan, instead of prosecuting them? Is it to ensure himself a safe exit? And why has there been no investigations into the massacres that were carried out by the military council?

Why has President Morsi refrained from purging the senior officials from the Ministry of the Interior, and appointed Ahmed Gamal El Din as minister of the interior? Why did President Morsi keep the security service and not disband it or make it into an intelligence-gathering unit, as the revolution asked? Why did President Morsi choose General Khaled Tharwat to head the security service? The majority of the decisions taken by President Morsi do not benefit the revolution, but disregard its aims and tie the Brotherhood ever closer to the Mubarak regime. Are people not within their rights to have doubts about the intent of the president's decisions?

The dismissal of the attorney general was a popular demand. How could President Morsi fulfil it with one hand, while disregarding the aims of the revolution with the other in order to serve the interests of the Brotherhood? It is not possible for President Morsi to – as it says in the Gospel – serve two masters. The president cannot be faithful to the aims of the revolution and the interests of the Brotherhood at the same time. What happened last Friday is the biggest indication of this contradiction. While President Morsi was trying to dismiss the attorney general, the Brotherhood amassed thousands of their supporters and attacked the revolutionaries in a savage, fascist manner. It was this blunder that lost the president popular support and made him lose the battle with the attorney general,. It is my opinion that his defeats will come thick and fast if he does maintain a clear position. The president must choose to govern the republic as the deputy of the supreme guide, working only in the interests of the Brotherhood, or be a president of all Egyptians and vow to fulfil the aims of the revolution. The President still has a chance – although it may be his last – to correct his course and adhere to the revolution. We ask the president to implement the following steps:

1. Regulate the affairs of the Brotherhood, making its budget public and disclosing its funding sources, in addition to forbidding the leadership of the Brotherhood from interfering in affairs of state, unless they hold official positions.

2. Carry out a complete purge of state institutions, starting with the Ministry of the Interior, which is still controlled by el-Adly's old guard, who are responsible for corruption, killing protesters, and breakdowns in security.

3. Prosecute Field Marshal Tantawi, General Enan, General Hamdi Badeen and General Hassan al-Ruwaini, who are responsible for the successive massacres in which hundreds of revolutionaties became martyrs.

4. Create special courts for the revolution in coordination with the Supreme Judicial Council, to launch an investigation into the massacre and killing of demonstrators. Its members from the judiciary would be

given the power to investigate military personnel and civilians so to achieve true justice.

5. Rebalance the Constituent Assembly to include a sufficient number of democratic and revolutionary forces and give them the right to vote, so as to produce a constitution expressing the will of all Egyptians.

6. Achieve social justice by setting a minimum and maximum limit for wages, adding the wealth of private funds to the state treasury, adopting a policy of cumulative taxes on the rich, and cutting subsidised gas, electricity and water for factories that sell their products at the global market price. These steps will generate billions of Egyptian pounds for the state and may spare the president from borrowing money from abroad.

7. Disband the Ministry of Information and promote the independence of journalistic institutions, instead of their subordination to the Shura Council, as well as removing the charge of "insulting the president" which is used to scare the opposition.

These are examples of practical steps to achieve the aims of the revolution. If the president follows them, he will enjoy the support of all Egyptians. However, if the president continues to appease the old regime to the benefit of the Muslim Brotherhood, he will lose everything, and much more quickly than he imagines.

Democracy is the answer.

PN

On State Prestige and National Symbols

22 October 2012

After graduating, I worked as a resident physician in an oral surgery at Cairo University Hospital, training in surgical procedures. While I was operating on one of the patients, a teacher in the department, well-known for his temper, passed by and told me that the technique I had used during the operation was wrong. I got into a long discussion with this teacher and tried to defend my decision to the best of my ability. During our conversation, I called over another professor from the department and asked him to intervene and judge which one of us was right. I gave the professor our two points of view, without specifying whose opinion was whose, and was surprised when the professor turned to the teacher and asked him: "Which was your opinion?" The teacher stated his opinion. "Your opinion is correct", replied the professor.

Feeling angry and despondent, the next day I brought with me a famous book on surgery and went to the professor's office. As soon as he saw me come in with the reference book, he said sarcastically: "You brought me this book to prove you were right? I know that you were right."

"But professor, you said I was wrong," I replied.

The professor looked at me and said, in a tone meant to suggest deep wisdom: "You are still only a resident, and he is a teacher at least ten years your senior. I can't tell him that he is wrong in front of you, I must maintain his prestige."

Realising it was pointless to continue this conversation with the professor any further, I thanked him and left.

A few months later, I had the opportunity to go and study at the University of Illinois in the United States. There, I was lucky enough to study under one of the most important histology professors in the world, Professor Denis Weber. Two weeks after the start of term, Professor Weber asked us to share our opinions on his course. He wanted to know if he had hindered our learning in any way or if we had any criticisms of his mistakes.

I was baffled by his question and kept silent. But a number of my colleagues criticised Professor Weber, and provided evidence and examples from the course. All the while, the great scientist remained silent, recorded all the comments and then promised to address his shortcomings. During the weeks that followed, I observed Professor Weber's relationship with the students and found that his kind treatment of them had not changed.

I always recall these two events together. In Cairo University Hospital, the professor is always right, so as to maintain his prestige before the junior doctors. Meanwhile, in Illinois University Hospital, a senior professor asks for criticism and feedback and then acknowledges his mistakes and promises to address them.

This is the difference between tyranny and democracy. If you searched in the Western media for the phrase "the prestige of the state", you would struggle to find it because the sole prestige is the law. However, in Egypt, the term "prestige" is widespread and often used to cover up iniquity and abuse. The "prestige of the state" means ruling despotically over the lives of citizens, and the "prestige of the police" means the repression, abuse and torture of citizens. The "prestige of the judiciary" means not daring to criticise a judge, even if they are involved in electoral fraud, or it is proven that they have a connection with the security services. The "prestige of the president" means that the head of state can prosecute and imprison any person for "insulting the president".

Now that we have a president that belongs to the Muslim Brotherhood, the concept of prestige has spread to the leadership of the Brotherhood, for they have started to treat God's creations with arrogance and condescension. A few days ago, Essam el-Erian, a leading Brotherhood figure, was being interviewed by Jihan Mansour, one of Egypt's most notable television personalities. When the discussion heated up, el-Erian accused the presenter of taking a bribe, and threatened her with arrest for attacking the Brotherhood.[1]

In the democratic world, there is nothing called the "prestige of the state" or the "symbols of the nation". These are terms of tyranny. In a democracy, the only prestige is the prestige of law, and the only symbol of the nation is the citizens; the people whose rights and dignity the state was founded to uphold. However, the ruler in a tyrannical society is the symbol of the nation, because they serve as would the leader of a tribe. They know better than any of us what is in the public's interests, and make decisions on our behalf. They order and we obey. They are usually unjust and corrupt, but the people are afraid to bring them to account because it would compromise the prestige of the nation. In a democratic country, a leader is the servant of the people in the true sense of the word. The humblest citizen, even if they are a street-sweeper, has the right to bring the president to account and to criticise without being punished for doing so. In fact, in a democratic country the law protects the ordinary citizen from slander and abuse, but does not protect the president of the state.

If you said to your neighbour in the presence of witnesses, "you are a liar and a cheat", your neighbour could take you to court and demand compensation for defamation. However, if you appeared on television and criticised the prime minister, the law would protect you because your comments would be perceived to be in the public interest. In Egypt, it seems that the president is content to prosecute Egyptians and imprison them on the charge of "insulting the president". There is one citizen, named Bishwi al-Buhairi, who will spend two years in jail because he insulted President Morsi on Facebook; as if the president of the nation is a sacred relic that cannot be touched. President Morsi is a long-standing member of the Muslim Brotherhood, and was brought up to be completely obedient to the supreme guide. We have seen the video which shows members of the Brotherhood jostling with each other to put win the chance to help put the shoes on the supreme guide's noble, pure feet. Whoever grows up in this environment is able to adapt to a culture of tyranny.

After President Morsi succeeded in removing the military council from power, he invited some public figures – myself included – to the presidential palace. That day, I asked the president a very specific question: "Why did you honour Field Marshal Tantawi and Lieutenant General Enan, when the

1 The court ordered Jihan Mansour to pay LE 10,000 in compensation for "insulting and defaming" the Muslim Brotherhood's Essam el-Erian on air.

revolutionary forces demanded for them to be put on trial for the massacres which took place during their time in power? Could giving them these honours be considered some sort of "safe exit" agreement with them, in which you guarantee they will not be legally prosecuted?"

The president answered forcefully: "I want to assure you all that after the revolution, nobody is above the law, not even Field Marshal Tantawi or General Enan."

Over the last week, there has been a flood of complaints against Field Marshal Tantawi and General Enan, accusing them of unlawful gains and inflation of wealth, being as they are public employees with fixed salaries. They were also accused of being responsible for the killing of Egyptians in the massacres that took place during their time in power. All of these are serious accusations, demanding a court case, but the army issued a statement condemning any attempt to bring Tantawi and Enan to trial. They considered that any such trial would compromise the prestige of the armed forces, and constitute an insult to the symbols of the nation.

At this, President Morsi announced that he would never permit any insult to the armed forces, or its leadership past and present. The president also added that he wished to reassure the army that its allocations, budget and enterprises would not be touched by anyone. This statement accurately demonstrates that Egyptian citizens are not equal before the law. As long as you are a senior officer in the army, you have the right to do as you wish, and nobody can bring you to account because you have become a "national symbol". Thus, any commander in the army has the right to order his troops to kill demonstrators and throw their corpses in the rubbish, or crush them with tanks, or indecently assault Egyptian women and drag them through the streets. An army commander has the right to acquire palaces and large tracts of land and amass huge amounts of wealth and nobody can question them because they are a national symbol and thus above questioning and criticism. In Egypt, where half of the inhabitants live below the poverty line, the armed forces start projects costing billions of pounds about which the Egyptian people know very little. We can tell that some army commanders have huge amounts of money, but we never know the exact quantity or how it was acquired. It is as if the army has become a state within a state.

Of course, our respect for, and pride in the armed forces is firm and profound, but to protect individuals because they belong to the military is odious behaviour, unacceptable in a democratic country. If President Morsi thinks that prosecuting Field Marshal Tantawi and General Enan infringes the prestige of the army, then why did he agree with the prosecution of Ahmed Shafik, who was a commander in the air force? Why, too, did he agree with the prosecution of Mubarak? Was he not also considered a national symbol? And should Gamal and Alaa Mubarak be prosecuted? Or are they also to be considered (minor) national symbols like their father?

From now on, let's agree that the nation has no symbols. The only symbol of any nation is the citizen. Likewise, a nation in itself has no prestige, but it derives its prestige from the power of the law, not from protecting murderers and corrupt figures.

The picture of President Morsi is clearer now than ever before. President Morsi is a man who promises and does not deliver. He may use fine words but he delivers ugly actions. President Morsi is determined to make the Brotherhood an organisation outside the law and not subject to accountability. We do not know the Brotherhood's budget, we do not know whether they are receiving funding from inside or outside Egypt, and we do not know whether President Morsi is making decisions himself, or receiving his instructions from the Brotherhood's supreme guide, who may well be the de facto ruler of Egypt.

But now something more dangerous has surfaced, namely that President Morsi has concluded a "safe exit" agreement with the military council, which guarantees that none of its members will be brought before the courts. President Morsi has snubbed the blood of the martyrs and given amnesty to those who do not deserve it. Once more, the Brotherhood have abandoned the revolution and traded their principles to gain power.

The Egyptian revolution was started for the sake of truth and justice. The revolution will not allow anyone to be above accountability, whatever their position in the state. The revolution will continue until it has fulfilled its aims completely.

Democracy is the answer.

PN

In Defence of Women

5 November 2012

I know a young woman in her twenties who wears the veil and always dresses modestly. She was walking down the street in broad daylight, when a young man attacked and molested her. She tried to push him away but the attacker was much stronger than her. Lucky for her, a policeman was standing close by and he arrested the young man and escorted him to the police station. The young women was eager to press charges and was shocked when other people asked her to consider his future and drop the case against him. In fact, one of the women who saw the incident shouted at the young woman: "Shame on you! Let the boy apologise to you and leave him to go on his way, instead of ruining his future!"

Those citizens are well aware that the young man sexually harassed the woman, and they must have daughters and sisters whom they would protect from harassment. But none of them believed that this matter called for legal action against the molester. In fact, they consider saving his future much more important than punishing him for the crime he committed. If this young man was a robber or a murderer, would the citizens show the same capacity for tolerance? If this young man was a Copt or a Baha'i, or a Shia, and said something they considered to be critical of Islam, would they have been so tolerant? Or would they have beaten him up and called for his prosecution?

The answer is obvious, and Egyptians do not usually tolerate any kind of crime except sexual harassment. They show pity on the molester, considering him to be "just a misguided youth" and often resort to generalisations such as "It turned out OK in the end" or, "It's not worth getting upset about". Egyptian's tolerance towards those who sexually harass women does not stem from an innate good-heartedness, but is related to the way they view of women. We say that women are half of society; they are our sisters, daughters and wives. Yet, women in Egypt are rarely show any real respect.

Those citizens who asked the young woman to show forbearance towards her attacker do not consider harassment a real crime. In their view, all the young man did was touch the body of a woman. They do not view the young woman as a human being deserving of respect; she is a body which has been rubbed, over the clothes, once or twice, and the matter stops there. The important thing is that the young woman has kept her virginity, so the man who is going to marry her can be sure no one has used her sexually before him.

Indeed, sexual assault is the practical application of our contempt of women. In Egypt, we no longer respect women. I say "no longer" because women in Egypt used to live alongside men and experience relative equality. Egyptian women were pioneers in education, employment and public services until Wahhabism arrived on our shores, reducing women to their biological functions. Generations of Egyptians have grown up to think of women as nothing but a tool for pleasure, which must be covered up and hidden away so that no men can fall victim to their temptations. Furthermore, we are now seeing Salafist Wahhabi sheikhs objecting to a minimum marriageable age for women in the constitution, because they consider that it is a man's right to marry a woman at any age as long as she is able to physically bear copulation, as one of their sheikhs put it. These people don't think that marriage requires mental and psychological maturity. In their mind, a woman is a machine for pleasure that men can use as long as it does not get damaged or break down.

These violations dehumanise women – denying them respect for their dignity and their individuality – and contribute to the rise of sexual harassment across Egypt. During holiday periods, groups of young men roam the streets like predatory animals, ready to harass any woman they come across. According to a 2008 study conducted by the Egyptian Centre for Women's Rights, which involved 1010 women: 98 per cent of foreign women and 83 per cent of Egyptian women were subjected to sexual harassment in Egypt. This uncivilised phenomenon is totally at odds with the values of Egyptian society and it cannot be explained away with arguments about the way women dress. The accusation that women are to blame because they wear provocative clothing is ludicrous, as it blames the victim rather than the perpetrator of the crime. The fact that a woman wears clothes revealing her arms, for example, does not excuse her being attacked, nor does it remove her right to be treated with respect. The difference between a human and an animal is that humans are able to control their desires. The logic that justifies sexual harassment by the wearing of provocative dress could well be employed to justify all crimes. Using the same logic, why do we blame someone who steals other people's money? He is poor and can't resist the temptation of money. Why do we blame someone who steals a luxury car? He longed for a car such as this, but was unable to acquire it himself. When he sees it in front of him, he is not able to resist.

Whatever clothing a woman wears, sexual harassment is a base, barbaric crime. The majority of women in Egypt are Muslims who wear the veil, so in any case there are no grounds for this argument. The type of clothing a woman wears has absolutely no relation to the spread of sexual harassment. For several decades, as recently as the 1970s, Egyptian women did not wear the veil. Women used to wear modern, revealing dresses, and go to the coast to swim in the sea wearing bathing costumes, which revealed their legs. Despite this, there were few incidents of sexual harassment. So why have men in Egypt started to sexually assault women who wear the veil, whereas in the 1970s and before, they were able to fight the urge to harass women who wore miniskirts?

The answer is that we used to respect women and consider them equals. We cannot respect a womank, acknowledging that she has a mind, a consciousness and feelings, and then sexually harass her. Whoever sexually harasses a woman considers her body a commodity which is owned by a husband or a father. If the attacker is not able to buy a body with a marriage contract to slake his desire, then as soon as he finds an opportunity to grope a woman in the street, he will not hesitate from doing so.

Another common explanation for harassment is that it is the result of interaction between men and women. But this is also untrue. Egyptian society has seen the interaction of men and women for many long years. Closed societies, which segregate men and women, have more instances of sexual harassment than mixed societies. When society forbids men from seeing and interacting with women at school, university and in the workplace, a man can grow up without knowing the proper way to treat a woman because he is not used to seeing her as an equal.

According to Reuters, Saudi Arabia has the third highest number of cases of sexual harassment in the workplace out of 24 countries. The study, which included 12,000 women from various countries, showed that 16 per cent of female employees in Saudi Arabia were subjected to sexual harassment by their male colleagues at work. Furthermore, the study revealed that the percentage of sexual harassment in Saudi Arabia (16 per cent) was far higher than the United States (8 per cent), Spain (6 per cent), Germany (5 per cent) and Britain (4 per cent). France and Sweden came at the bottom of the list, where the percentage of women who were sexually harassed at work was no more than 3 per cent. This demonstrates that open societies witness far less sexual harassment than closed societies.

Of course, followers of political Islam will retaliate and ask each other indignantly: how can Western countries, which permit sexual relations outside of marriage, have less instances of sexual harassment than our Islamic societies where people by their nature are religious? The answer is that tolerance of sexual relations outside of marriage certainly does not mean tolerance of sexual harassment and other sexual offences. Western society gives every person, whether male or female, married or unmarried, the right to have sexual relations. It considers sexual relations to be a part of one's private life, for which people cannot be punished or judged.

As for the argument that the Egyptians are by nature a religious people, we need to rethink this idea. If 83 per cent of women in Egypt are subjected to sexual harassment, how can we claim that we are a religious people? We are the people most obsessed with upholding the outward appearances of religiosity; while simultaneously denouncing religious principles through our actions. Before the Wahhabi influence, we were less concerned about manifesting religiosity, and more concerned about following religious principles by our actions. Now, we have taken the form and procedure of religion, but abandoned its essence. Many Egyptians strictly observe prayer, fasting, go on Hajj and perform Umrah, but in their financial dealings they are known to be untrustworthy. They lie and dissimulate to their bosses at work, do not speak the truth when they see it, and work to serve their own interests, with a disregard for morality and common decency.

Sexual harassment is one of the symptoms of cultural malaise, which manifests itself as contempt of women. It limits a woman to her body, attaching no importance to her feelings, her mind, or her capacity as a human being. It commodifies women, reducing them to something to be obtained through a marriage contract. What is amazing is that during the Egyptian revolution, our civilised view of women came back to us. Millions of women took part in the revolution, and over three weeks neither Tahrir Square nor the squares of the revolution in other provinces witnessed instances of sexual harassment. It is as if when Egypt revolted, all of our civilised characteristics came back to us automatically. We cannot get rid of sexual harassment unless we regain our respect for women, unless we start to see them her as human beings equal to a men in abilities, rights, feelings and dignity. Only then will we discover what is much more important: that she is a person.

Democracy is the answer.

PN

A Great Writer and a Good Friend

12 November 2012

It was thirty years ago and I had just taken my first tentative steps into the literary world. I had written a short story which I wanted to get published in the *Sabah el-Kheir* magazine. I made an appointment with Louis Greiss, the editor-in-chief who passed me on to his features editor, Alaa el-Deeb. I was awestruck at meeting one of Egypt's greatest writers but Alaa greeted me warmly and set about reading my first short story. When he had finished reading, he looked up at me and said: "It's a good story, but I have a few comments if you'd like to hear them."

"I certainly would," I replied.

For a whole hour Alaa gave me a useful lesson about writing. He told me that the problem with Arabic writing was fuzziness. We have to write precisely what we intend. He advised me to use punctuation more carefully. I have not forgotten his very words: "We write the way we speak. Every time you make a pause, or slow down or speed up the rhythm of the words, there has to be a reason."

I left Alaa's office astonished that a great writer like him would have so much time for a budding and unknown author.

My story was published in Sabah el-Kheir, with my first collection of short stories appearing a few years later. I sent a copy to Alaa and he gave it a glowing review in the magazine. I was over the moon. Alaa's glowing review was a springboard for any young writer. We got to know each other better and I became his honoured friend for a quarter of a century. Alaa was a great novelist who wrote of a uniquely humane world in a beautiful crystalline language which was matched by no other author. His most important books were his famous *Lemon Flowers*, and his superb trilogy *Tearless Children*, *Moon over the Morass* and *Eyes of the Violet*, which dealt with the alienation of Egyptians during the period of "opening up" in the 1980s. As well as all his novel-writing, the great man also continued practicing applied criticism for fifty years in his column in the weekly Book Juice.

Every week he would publish a straightforward yet deep essay on a literary text which aimed at educating the general reader and drawing them to the mysteries of literature. Generation after generation of Egyptians and Arabs became literary aesthetes due to Alaa el-Deeb. I can remember reading Book Juice every week and than dashing off to get whatever it was Alaa had written about in his column. Another major role played by Alaa el-Deeb was discovering and publicising new literary talent. The moment he read something by a gifted author, he would be writing about it, contacting the author and doing all he could to promote him. Most of the glittering names in the literary world were first presented by Alaa and cut their first teeth with him. He is one of the few people I have met in whom there is no contradiction between what they say and what they do. He lives just as he writes.

I learnt from Alaa how to separate the private from the public. I saw that more than once. If a friend of Alaa published a book Alaa did not like, he would not review it. If someone with whom Alaa had had an argument published a book which he liked, he would give it a glowing review. I saw how he did his utmost to avoid pettifogging literary squabbles. Alaa was a great example of an author who was not in search of fame or fortune. He disliked the limelight and anything affected or artificial. There was one famous incident when an editor convinced him to take part in a televised discussion on his great novel *Lemon Flowers*. Just after recording started he was surprised to be asked by the programme host: "Could you give us a quick synopsis of the novel?"

Alaa looked at her and replied: "Miss, are you telling me that you plan to discuss a novel you haven't read?"

Without waiting for a response, he unclipped the microphone from his jacket and left the studio to the astonishment of everyone there. Alaa considered writing a duty he performs and not a commodity. I saw many times how Alaa turned down positions that other great writers were gagging for. I saw how he treated with dignity and respect the most senior state officials and millionaires to whom everyone else was subservient. He is an example of a man devoted to art above all else, whose dedication gave him a strength that others do not have. He summed up his philosophy of life as follows: "All the glamour and limelight are meaningless. We all die and nothing of us remains except the things of value we leave for posterity. If you write your whole life long and only add one useful sentence to the corpus of Arabic literature, then you have achieved something great."

It should be pointed out, however, that Ala el-Deeb has left more than one sentence behind, he left us a towering building, a garden which he had planted and tended with love and which has produced wonderful varieties of flowers. Arabic literature will remain indebted to this man for his timeless works of beauty, for the critical essays which have educated generations of people, and for his having promoted the greatest literary talents in Egypt and the Arab world for over a half century. Had Alaa el-Deeb been French, or English, and only achieved a quarter of what he did for literature, he would have been given the highest honours.

What has the Egptian state done for Alaa el-Deeb? One time, the Ministry of Culture wanted to lend some credibility to the state awards which it handed out to cronies and acolytes, and chose a few respected names such as those of Alaa el-Deeb and Galal Amin. Apart from that, the state has only caused problems or irritations for Alaa. For years he needed heart surgery, and some officials stated that this would be carried out at the state's expense (the most basic rights of a citizen). The operation was a failure as a result of negligence on the part of the hospital, and he had to undergo two further operations which have had a deleterious effect on his health. In a disgraceful act, those same officials neglected to cover the cost of his treatment and the director of the hospital got Alaa, while he was still recovering, to sign the hospital bill. When the Ministry of Culture did not pay up, a criminal charge was filed against Alaa and he was threatened with prison. Students of Alaa battled it out with the Ministry of Culture and in the end the ministry paid for his treatment.

That is how the Egyptian state treats one of the most important Arab writers. Another time the editor of the *Al-Qahira* newspaper pressed Alaa to write a weekly review piece and to edit the literature section. As Alaa writes as a cultural duty and not as a means of generating income, he acceded to Salah Isa's insistence and agreed to take on the job. In addition to writing his weekly article, he reads scores of pieces by young writers. I have seen how every week he puts them all in a large file, reading them carefully and noting which are publishable. For years Alaa has devoted himself to the *Al-Qahira* newspaper for a paltry wage, which is less than a secretary would put up with in a government office, even though he could earn a fortune if he agreed to write for a magazine in the Gulf or the non-state owned press which has been after him for years. It is not Alaa's nature to be interested in money and he feels true satisfaction in making a useful contribution to culture.

Then the managing director of *Al-Qahira* was replaced by a man with whom Alaa did not feel comfortable and he tendered his resignation. When he told me this over the telephone with a laugh, I congratulated him upon his resignation because I had been urging him to leave *Al-Qahira* for a long time. Apparently Alaa's resignation irritated the new managing director, who, like all directors, wants to be the one in control of events. The managing director issued statements claiming that it was he who had decided to no longer make use of Alaa's services. Why would the managing director attempt to insult this great author? There is no need to answer this question, because someone who does not realise the value of Alaa el-Deeb knows nothing about Egyptian culture. However, we can ask why it is that the cultural sector is treated with great honour in a democracy whereas it is marginalised and harassed in dictatorial regimes?

I would add that a dictatorial regime usually treats its artists with trepidation, only trusting them when they sing from the ruler's hymn-sheet. When an author dices with danger by sticking to his principles, as Alaa has done, this arouses the resentment of various state officials. Alaa el-Deeb does not need the Ministry of Culture, its jobs or rewards, because his acclaim stems from the people and not from the managing director of the *Al-Qahira* newspaper or those of that ilk. When Victor Hugo was eighty, the French came up with the best way of honouring him. The French press requested everyone who had read his work to pass under his balcony and the whole day long thousands and thousands of people went there to express their love for him. Were we to copy this notion and call upon Alaa el-Deeb's students and admirers, the whole of Maadi, where he lives, would be choked by the throngs of people this great author has educated and affected.

May no harm ever come to you, Alaa.

Democracy is the answer.

RH

Before You Chop Off Our Hands

19 November 2012

"Are you a Muslim? If you are a Muslim, why do you oppose the application of the law of God? All those who oppose the application of Islamic law are liberals and communists, agents of the West and enemies of Islam. So are you one of them?"

These are the kinds of questions the Brotherhood and the Salafists are asking fellow Egyptians to stir up their religious sentiments and mobilise them to form demonstrations. They also want to force them to adopt positions that will consolidate the political gains of political Islamist groups.

The truth is that this way of discussing Islamic law is dishonest, because every Muslim wants to follow the law of Islam. First we must explain to people the difference between sharia (Islamic law) and *fiqh* (Islamic legal interpretation). Islamic law constitutes the solid principles sent down to us by God, whereas its interpretation (*fiqh*) is the knowledge that enables us to understand this law and apply it to our daily lives. Islamic law is divine, fixed and never changing, whereas legal interpretation is a human process, changing with time and place. Certainly, Islamic law calls for truth, justice and equality, but what the Brotherhood and Salafists are calling for is not the principles of Islamic law sent down to us by God, but interpretations thereof. These interpretations have been written by humans and are consequently susceptible to error. Furthermore, many of these interpretations were written in the tenth century are are no longer appropriate for modern times.

The Brotherhood and the Salafists control the Constituent Assembly and readily apply these old interpretations of Islamic law to the constitution. After the liberals, the Copts and the Islamists had agreed on Article 2 of the constitution, which states that the principles of Islamic law are the primary source of legislation, the Brotherhood and the Salafists came back and added another article which stated that the principles of Islamic law include the entirety of the evidence, principles both fundamental and interpretive, and sources adopted in the Sunni doctrines.

This article quite simply sets the principles of Islamic law on a par with legal interpretations of it, and leads Egypt towards certain danger. I have searched for one of the sources adopted in Sunni doctrine, and I could find no better than *Sunni Jurisprudence* by the late Sheikh Sayyid Sabiq. This book is commonly recognised as one of the most important works on Islamic legal interpretation. Sheikh Sayyid Sabiq was one of the Muslim Brotherhood's historic leading figures, and the preface to *Sunni Jurisprudence* was written by the late Sheikh Hassan al-Banna, the founder of the Muslim Brotherhood. In it, al-Banna praises the book as an excellent achievement for which its author deserves a reward from God, so it follows that no one from the Muslim Brotherhood can challenge *Sunni Jurisprudence*. In his book, Sheikh Sayyid Sabiq presents the opinion of the Sunni doctrine on various aspects of life. (Here, I apologise because I will use the term "infidel" to refer to our Coptic citizens, because the majority of interpreters of Islamic law refer to them as such, as did Sheikh Sayyid Sabiq himself.) Let's imagine that a Muslim thief robs a pharmacy owned by a Copt. In this instance, if the witnesses to the robbery were Copts, they cannot legally testify because the Sunni scholars of Islamic law agree that the testimony of a non-Muslim is not accepted against a Muslim. Sheikh Sabiq says that: "A condition for the acceptability of a testimony is that the witness must be a Muslim. The testimony of an infidel against a Muslim is not permitted, except in the case of making a will when travelling (according to Imam Abu Hanifa)."

That is to say, if a travelling Muslim was on his death bed, and the only person he could find to convey his last Will and Testament was a Copt, then this would be the only situation in which their testimony would be acceptable in the eyes of the law. It would be virtually impossible to apply this legal interpretation to modern day Egypt as it would grant any Muslim the right to attack the property and churches of the Copts, confident that all of witness testimonies would be scrapped. Following the opinion of the Islamic legal interpreters, their testimony against a Muslim would be unacceptable, even though they committed a crime.

It is forbidden for Muslims to drink alcohol and the punishment is 80 lashes of the whip (although some Islamic legal scholars say only 40 lashes). This ruling is well-known, but some scholars try to make the law prohibiting alcohol applicable to non-Muslims as well. Sheikh Sabiq writes:

> Applying the punishment for drinking alcohol is not made obligatory to Muslims [only], but also to Jews and Christians who hold citizenship in a Muslim country, such as the Copts in Egypt, and likewise those Jews and Christians who are residing there (temporarily), such as foreign nationals, who will receive the punishment if they drink alcohol in the Islamic lands.

Again, it would be impossible to apply this ruling in modern Egypt. If a Copt who drinks a beer were to be arrested and receive 80 lashes; this would have catastrophic repercussions to tourism in Egypt. When we invite European or American tourists to visit Egypt, we must warn them that they are unable to enjoy a glass of wine with their meal as they may be arrested, stripped of their clothes and flogged, in accordance with this legal interpretation. In Islamic legal interpretation, the term "defamation" means (falsely) accusing somebody of adultery, or seeking to tarnish their reputation. It is an offence punishable by 80 lashes. Strange that the legal interpreters consider the aggrieved party's being a Muslim an essential condition for carrying out the punishment for defamation of his honour. Sheikh Sabiq says:

> To be a Muslim is a condition for the defamed person (the aggrieved party). If the defamed person is non-Muslim, in the opinion of the scholars there is no punishment for his defamer. In the opposite case, that the Christian or the Jew defames the Muslim, then he must receive 80 lashes as a Muslim would.

After this, who can talk about the rights of citizenship or equality before the law? If a Copt insults a Muslim they are given 80 lashes, but if a Muslim insults a Copt, they will not. It is as if human dignity is reserved exclusively for Muslims. As for the Copts, they are beasts of burden without reputation or honour.

The term "blood money" refers to a monetary fine paid by anyone who commits manslaughter or second-degree murder. This blood money, according to Islamic legal scholars, differs according to gender and religion. The blood money paid for a murdered Muslim woman is half the blood money for a murdered Muslim man, as is the blood money for a murdered Coptic man. As for the amount paid for a murdered Coptic woman, it is half that of a murdered Muslim woman, that is to say, a quarter of the blood money paid for the murdered Muslim man. This is the judgement of the Islamic legal scholars. If we applied this Islamic legal ruling, we would be saying that human life does not have the same universal value for all people. The life of a Muslim man is worth more than the life of a Muslim woman; the life of a Copt is cheaper than the life of a Muslim, and the life of a Coptic woman is the cheapest of all. In the twenty-first century, can we really accept this obsolete concept? Would the Egyptian state be able to bear the international sanctions set against it if it tried to apply this judgement, which goes against every consecutive human rights treaty the Egyptian government has ever signed?

For the crime of first-degree murder, the death penalty must be applied to the killer. However, one of the conditions for this punishment to be enacted is that the victim was a Muslim. If the victim was a Coptic infidel, then the killer receives no such punishment. Sheikh Sabiq says:

> One of the conditions for punishment to be enforced in a capital crime, is that the victim be equal to the killer in religion and status. So there is no punishment for a Muslim who has killed an infidel, or a free man who has killed a slave, because there is no mutual correspondence between the killer and the victim. On the other hand, if an infidel kills a Muslim or a slave kills a free man, then they will both receive the punishment.

Some Islamic legal scholars disagree with this opinion, but the predominant opinion amongst Sunni scholars is that a Muslim is not killed for killing a non-Muslim. If we enforced this interpretation of Islamic law and an Egyptian Muslim killed a Copt by shooting him, or beating him to death, in this instance it would not be permissible to execute the Muslim killer. What state would our society be in if we enforced this interpretation of Islamic law? How could they Egyptian people claim to live in a country whose citizens are equal.

The Brotherhood and the Salafists want to adopt some of these forms of Islamic legal interpretations in Egypt; all of which were written by scholars who worked hard to make them relevant to the society in which they lived. If we applied them in Egypt today, they would irreversibly bring an end to society as we know it and would lead to a civil war between the Muslims and the Copts, as happened in Sudan. I am not against the law of Islam, because it is God's law, one of justice and truth, but I am against the application of these anachronous interpretations. If we want to apply Islamic law in a correct fashion, our Islamic legal scholars must first devise new interpretations of Islamic law suitable for the modern era. Otherwise, by applying old interpretations of Islamic law, which are completely at odds with religion and ourselves, we lead our society towards fragmentation and our country towards destruction, pushing Egypt several centuries back into the past.

So, you extremists impatient to cut off hands and stone and flog, I hope that you reconsider your actions. The revolution supports the application of Islamic law, but these ancient interpretations of it no longer suit the age we are living in. With your extremism and your intransigent ideas, you are offending Islam and pushing us towards certain catastrophe. It is our duty, as Muslims and Copts, to prevent you from doing this, and, by God, we will prevent you and save our country from your extremism. We will never recognise the deformed constitution you are imposing on the Egyptians.

The revolution will continue until it achieves a modern, civil nation. We will march on towards the future and never return to the darkness of the past.

Democracy is the answer.

PN

Some Questions and Answers about the Crisis

26 November 2012

1. Why do you oppose the constitutional declaration issued by President Morsi?

The constitutional declaration gives the president quasi-divine powers, allowing him to suspend the law and do as he so wishes, without the slightest scrutiny or accountability. With this announcement, President Morsi has nullified the will of the people who carried him into the presidency and turned into a dictator. Every dictator is automatically an enemy of the revolution, which was started fundamentally to found a country on rule of law.

2. Why can't you allow the president to have these absolute powers temporarily, for a few short months?

There are no "temporary dictators". All despotic rulers claim that they are forced to take exceptional measures temporarily, then go on to monopolise power forever. Let us recall how in 1952 the Free Officers pledged to return to their barracks after six months, but remained in power for many years. If we allow any ruler to suspend the law for one day, he will turn into an eternal dictator.

3. Isn't it possible that President Morsi has been obliged to adopt these exceptional measures to fight the old regime and protect the revolution?

Freedom, the rule of law, and respecting the will of the people; in themselves these are all principles of humanity. Any achievement that comes through tyranny is unacceptable, as every tyrannical regime throughout history led in the end to failure and tragedy. We are suffering from disorder in all aspects of life as a result of the tyranny of Mubarak, so we cannot accept any tyranny from Morsi.

What is more, President Morsi and the Muslim Brotherhood did not fight the old regime, they colluded with it for their benefit at the expense of the revolution. Who was it that mobilised people to agree to Mubarak's amendments to the 1971 constitution? Who was it that allied with the military council and refused to put the constitution first, rushing instead into elections so that the Islamists would then be able to write the constitution at their discretion? Who was it that accused the revolutionaries of thuggery and made fun of the women indecently assaulted by soldiers in the massacre at the Council of Ministers? Who was it that described those calling for a new constitution, then elections, as "devils in human form" and described the military council members as "darlings"?

This was all the Muslim Brotherhood's doing; it colluded with the military council and made deals signed in the blood of the martyrs. What has President Morsi done during his five months in power? He has appointed Ahmed Gamal El Din as minister of the interior; a man responsible for the Mohamed Mahmoud Street massacre, which claimed the lives of 70 people. President Morsi has offered a safe exit to Field Marshal Tantawi and General Enan, who are responsible – at least politically – for consecutive massacres, in which hundreds of innocent people were died. President Morsi has appointed the remnants of Mubarak's as ministers despite the fact they have stolen from the Egyptian people and amassed huge riches by improper or unlawful means.

If President Morsi had wanted to carry out the aims of the revolution, he would have done so upon his election. In reality, he is working in the interests of the Brotherhood and therefore against the revolution. There is no reason for the Egyptian people to place their trust in President Morsi as he has gone back on his word time and again.

4. Why did President Morsi make this constitutional declaration?

President Morsi is following the instructions of the Guidance Office to placate the old regime instead of fighting it. The Muslim Brotherhood wants government institutions to remain as they were in the days of Mubarak, on the condition that their allegiances change to the Brotherhood, instead of to the military council and Mubarak. Therefore, President Morsi has kept the state security apparatus and appointed General Tharwat to oversee its operations. Likewise, he has kept the Ministry of Information intact and appointed a Brotherhood official to run it, managing the media in the Brotherhood's favour.

The supreme guide of the Muslim Brotherhood estimated that making a deal with the old regime would enable the Brotherhood to hold onto power indefinitely. But he then discovered that the old regime was in fact conspiring against him. The supreme guide discovered that there were agencies working to spread chaos across Egypt in order to get rid of President Morsi. At this point, the supreme guide encouraged Morsi to make the constitutional declaration so that he could suspend the law at any time and maintain control.

Then there's the Constituent Assembly, which the Supreme Constitutional Court will surely annul for the second time, which should lead to the forming of a balanced assembly that will write a new constitution for Egypt. However, the Brotherhood's supreme guide wants to keep the present Constituent Assembly so it will write a constitution that will enable the Brotherhood to stay in power for the long term. The revolution, in my opinion, has no part to play in this struggle between the Brotherhood and the old regime. All we are trying to do is to stop the creation of a new dictator.

5. How can the president get out of this dilemma?

The only solution is for the president to revoke the constitutional declaration and return to respecting the law. If the Supreme Constitutional Court dissolves the Shura Council and annuls the Constituent Assembly, the president must respect the law and get on with implementing the judicial ruling immediately. If the president sticks by the constitutional declaration, he will have lost his legitimacy. A president who tramples the law under his feet is not legitimate, even if he was elected.

But who is responsible for the Brotherhood's rise to power? Wasn't it those revolutionaries who supported Morsi against General Ahmed Shafik?

I personally did not vote for Morsi; I called for the boycotting of the elections. However, at the same time I show complete solidarity with those revolutionaries who voted for Morsi. They wanted to safeguard the revolution and prevent the return of the old regime in the person of Ahmed Shafik, faithful servant and protégé of Mubarak. The choice was between the Brotherhood and the old regime. The revolutionaries chose the Brotherhood, knowing full well the extent of their opportunism, because it was the only choice available to safeguard the revolution.

Morsi won with the votes of Egyptians who did not belong to the Brotherhood, but who voted for Morsi in order to bring down Shafik. This was the only way to stop the Mubarak regime from returning and does not require apology. In my opinion, the ones who should be apologising are those revolutionary presidential candidates who refused to agree on a single candidate to represent the revolution. They caused the revolutionary vote to be split and all failed to get past the first round of voting.[1] Those who still think that Ahmed Shafik would have been suitable for the presidency of Egypt, while I respect their opinion completely, do not recognise the Egyptian revolution. It is inconceivable for us to start a revolution against the Mubarak regime, then vote for one of the pillars of that selfsame regime.

6. Twelve million Egyptians voted for Shafik. Do none of them recognise the revolution?

Those who do not recognise the revolution are more numerous than those that voted for Ahmed Shafik. Twenty million people were involved in the Egyptian revolution, and if we add to them another 20 million sympathisers, we find that those who belong to the revolution are less than half of the Egyptian population. This is the case in all revolutions, because only 10 per cent of the population is required to cause a revolution. In Egypt, that figure was 20 per cent but we still must understand that for 40 million Egyptians, the revolution took them by surprise. Many of them did not understand the revolution and were not prepared to make the smallest sacrifice on its account.

Therefore, I believe that those who voted for Shafik do not care about the revolution. I cannot imagine that anyone who took part in the revolution could have voted for another Mubarak. The exception to this judgement is the Copts, a minority who have been terrified – whether deliberately or inadvertently – by the political Islamist movements. It is natural that their fear for their lives and human rights should push them to vote for any party that would prevent the Brotherhood from gaining power. For most Copts I know, Shafik was not the first choice, and they had voted for a revolutionary candidate in the first round. When the choice became between the Brotherhood and the old regime, they chose the old regime because understandably they were in a state of fear, which nobody except a religious minority, living in a repressive country suffering from religious sectarianism such as Egypt could feel.

7. What do we do now?

Egyptians must all struggle to overturn the constitutional declaration. We must use every form of pressure to make President Morsi turn back from tyranny.

1 Egyptian presidential elections follow the US model of a first round of voting followed by a second in which only the two frontrunners remain.

But at the same time we must refrain from violence completely, because it will lead us to disaster. This great revolution must remain peaceful. We must also examine this complicated situation with clarity and see that there are two types of Egyptians who oppose the constitutional declaration: revolutionaries, and the remnants of the Mubarak regime. They may repeat the same mistakes and take the same positions, but they have completely different objectives. The revolutionaries want the constitutional declarations to be revoked so as to build a country with rule of law, for the sake of which the revolution was started. But the remnants of the Mubarak regime want to see the destruction of everything in Egypt in order to cause an unstable situation, as a precursor to the intervention of the army and a return of the old regime.

8. The remnants of the old regime are still Egyptian citizens. Why do we deny them political participation?

I am not calling for them to be denied political participation, but I am reiterating that they are enemies of the revolution and that they are currently working to return the Mubarak regime to power. As for them being Egyptians, that does not make them immune from political accountability. Those who tortured, killed and blinded innocent people, and indecently assaulted their wives in front of them, were all Egyptians. Can we forget their crimes?

9. Has the Egyptian revolution failed?

A revolution is essentially a change in human behaviour leading to political results. A revolution means putting concepts above personal gain. A revolution means that a group of people, at a specific moment, are prepared to die for the sake of dignity and freedom. This noble behaviour is rare, which explains the fact that throughout human history there have been very few true revolutions.

A change in human behaviour is the true achievement of the revolution. Egyptians have broken the barrier of fear never to return behind it again. However, the political achievements of the revolution come slowly and with difficulty, as a result of the collusion of the military and the Brotherhood and the fragmentation of the revolutionary forces. But revolutions usually take many long years to form a democratic country. We deposed Mubarak in less than three weeks, and if we compare this achievement to other revolutions throughout history, we should be proud of our revolution.

The revolution will continue, until it is victorious and fulfils its aims.

Democracy is the answer.

PN

Who Can Cure the President?

10 December 2012

The meeting took place in the villa of the supreme guide. President Morsi and Kheirat el-Shater arrived before the dawn call to prayer. They did their ablutions and the supreme guide led the prayers and then he invited them to stay for breakfast. The table was groaning under the weight of *ful mudammes*, eggs, omelettes, flaky pancakes with honey and a variety of cheeses. The three ate heartily and then went off to the supreme guide's luxurious office where they started their meeting as they sipped their coffee. The supreme guide stated: "I want to hear your evaluation of the situation."

El-Shater began: "With regard to the international situation, the American administration is giving us their support. They telephoned me to say that they will be issuing a statement condemning the violence which took place in front of the presidential palace, and I told them it was crucial that the statement should be general and not just a condemnation of the Brotherhood. The Americans agreed. The youth wing of the Brotherhood is ready to deal with any gatherings against the president."

The supreme guide touched his spectacles and knitted his brow: "Is their state of readiness sufficient?"

El-Shater laughed and said: "Of course. The youth wing of the Brotherhood is full of animals. One of them can beat up twenty secularists."

The supreme guide looked satisfied, and continued: "And you, Morsi, what's your opinion?"

The president sighed: "supreme guide, you can always see what we cannot see. God Almighty inspires you to do the right thing for Islam and Muslims."

The supreme guide smiled and continued: "I have the feeling, Morsi, that you are trying to say something!"

"Well it's just that I did not expect the constitutional declaration to cause all these demonstrations. I tried to stem all the anger by issuing a new constitutional declaration, but the demonstrations are just continuing everywhere."

The supreme guide interrupted him: "That is just so much misplaced anger, Morsi. We are right and they are wrong. God has enabled us finally to govern Egypt. We will never allow those activists who hate religion to take power. Egypt is now entering the period of the blessed caliphate."

El-Shater nodded and added: "They are fighting against God's law and by God we will never let them get their hands on the constitution even if we all die in the process. Do you know who is creating all this uproar? It is the remnants of the Mubarak regime, along with a number of Copts, communists and atheists; none of them worth a hoot. Whatever they do, we will win any elections and any referendum will go our way. People in Egypt want religion. Religion is behind us. Whatever the subject of a referendum, people will look to support religion."

President Morsi smiled and mumbled: "Of course. Of course."

The supreme guide leafed through the documents in front of him and said: "The police are neglecting their duty of protecting the offices of the Brotherhood, Morsi."

The president replied: "I have had a meeting with the minister of the interior and he has promised me to do all he can, please God."

The supreme guide turned angry at this point and shouted: "Empty words! More than twenty Brotherhood offices have been set on fire. The minister of the interior is either useless or in cahoots with them"

President Morsi then asked him: "Do you think that we should appoint a new minister of the interior?"

The supreme guide wiped his hands over his face, as he always does when getting excited, and then sighed: "No. A cabinet reshuffle would give a negative message and might create animosity within the Ministry of the Interior. Wait a little and then as soon as things calm down, replace him. Now, your brothers have prepared a plan to secure the Brotherhood offices. I want to hear your comments."

The supreme guide handed out copies of the plan to President Morsi and el-Shater. They examined it in silence and then el-Shater spoke up: "The numbers required are quite large. We will have to call up reserves."

The president nodded. "Do whatever you think necessary," he said and continued reading. He passed a sheet of paper to the supreme guide and commented: "I think there is a mistake in the name of the person responsible for Tanta."[1]

As the supreme guide took the sheet from him, he noticed the president's hand and asked: "Have you had an accident, Morsi?"

President Morsi looked at his right hand and noticed a spot of blood. He seemed irritated and said: "That's strange. I don't remember cutting myself."

El-Shater made light of it by saying "You probably bumped into something without noticing."

The dark, dry blood stain was the size of a coin right in the middle of his palm. El-Shater jumped up and fetched some cotton wool and disinfectant. The president took a piece of cotton wool, dipped it into the disinfectant and started wiping away at the blood stain but it would not shift. He made his excuses and rushed to the bathroom and tried to wash it off with soap and warm water, but it would not disappear. Nothing had any effect on it

1 Tanta is a city in Egypt. It is the country's fifth largest populated area

and he started to get worried. He asked the supreme guide for permission to leave and then asked his driver to take him as quickly as possible to a private hospital owned by one of his colleagues in the office of the supreme guide. When the chauffeur informed the presidential guard, they rushed over to check on the president's well-being, but he kept his right hand hidden, forcing out a smile and telling them that it was nothing important and that he was alright, thank God.

Half an hour later the president rushed into the office of the doctor and informed him: "There is a blood stain on my hand and I don't know how it happened."

The doctor put on his surgical gloves and examined the president. Then he took his hand and examined it carefully under the lamp. Finally, he dipped some gauze into a solution which had a pungent odour and started wiping away at the blood stain, but to no avail.

The doctor threw the gauze away and said: "This is a very strange thing, indeed. The blood has not come from a wound on your body. It seems to be glued on and won't come off."

The president sounded worried: "I am really astonished!"

"Me too. I cannot work out what it is."

"And what should I do?"

"Leave it as it is until tomorrow morning. I am going to call a vascular specialist in Germany because in all truth this is the first time I have seen something like this."

At this, the President started getting agitated: "I can't wait. I have a cabinet meeting at seven o'clock, and then I have to record a speech for the television. I cannot deal with people with blood on my hand."

The doctor gave him a sympathetic look and said quietly: "Mr President, what is on your hand is very puzzling. We shall run tests here and abroad until we understand what has happened to your hand."

The president felt that there was no further use talking about it. He thanked the doctor and went off to his office in Qasr al-Ittihadiya. After that the day passed as normal – meetings with Egyptian and foreign officials, a cabinet meeting and then recording his speech to be broadcast the next day. During all those meetings, the President kept his right hand out of sight, but when he went home it was more difficult to hide the matter from his wife. He gave her an account of what had happened and she became distraught. She took his hand and kept turning it this way and that, trying to wash the blood stain off with warm water and a pumice stone, but nothing had any effect. There it remained, dark, round and stuck firmly in the middle of the president's palm as if scoffing at all attempts to remove it. Eventually she gave up trying, calling upon God's help and resorting to reading the Qur'an, so overcome that tears started running down her face.

The president took a hot shower to try and forget about the blood stain, but he could not help looking at it from time to time hoping that it might have disappeared or reduced in size a little, but there was no change. The president could not sleep that night out of anxiety. He did not fear death, because that was preordained by God. If the blood stain was the symptom of some horrible illness, then there was nothing he could do about it, but he was worried about news of it spreading. If this blood stain remained on his hand people would notice it and it would give his opponents a chance to attack and damage him. The president kept going over everything that had happened the previous day and could not recall coming into contact with anyone who had a wound, and had not been in contact with blood in any shape or form. When he heard the dawn call to prayer, he made his ablutions and said his prayers. Then he had his chauffer and members of the presidential guard woken and he put on his robe and headed for the supreme guide's villa where he found Kheirat el-Shater. The president greeted both of them quickly and took a seat.

The supreme guide looked at him and asked: "What news? Please God your hand has healed."

President Morsi responded in a low voice: "Something is wrong with me, supreme guide. The blood stain on my hand just will not disappear. The doctor told me he has never seen anything like it."

The supreme guide said nothing for a while, seemingly lost in thought, then he said: "I think you could go and see a doctor in America or Europe."

The president did not seem enamoured of the thought, and he added in a low voice: "I'm afraid that God is punishing me for the people who have died."

El-Shater then asked him with incredulity: "Why would God be punishing you?"

"The people who died," the supreme guide stated firmly, "include some Brotherhood members."

"That's true, supreme guide. May God have mercy upon them and may we consider them martyrs, but I feel that I am the reason. If we had acted differently, they would still be alive."

The supreme guide appeared to be trying to staunch his irritation, and he retorted: "Understand this, dear president – the decisions which we have taken were necessary to get us into power and to frustrate the schemes of anti-Muslim agitators."

El-Shater added: "Do you think we should have let them take power, Morsi?"

He nodded and replied: "Of course not. You are right."

The supreme guide smiled and continued calmly: "All the decisions we have taken have been in order to satisfy God and his Prophet. We have never been interested in power like other people, thank God."

President Morsi nodded and said no more. Then he looked at his right hand. The blood stain was still there.

Democracy is the answer.

RH

In Secret

17 December 2012

This location is only known to the first man and some of his intimates. It refers to a large basement in a building on the outskirts of the El-Tagamu El Khames district of new Cairo. The basement has a separate entrance which means that the building's inhabitants do not see who goes in and out, as well as having various emergency exits so that people holding meetings there can escape at a moment's notice. The first man uses this location for his important secret meetings. He used it, for example, when he was negotiating with Omar Suleiman, Mubarak's deputy, to put an end to the revolution and disperse the demonstrators who were in Tahrir Square in exchange for some privileges demanded by the Brotherhood. He used it to conclude a deal for the safe exit of members of the military council. Yesterday, the first man went to this secret location, turned on the lights and walked down the long corridor with the second man behind him. When they entered the main room, the first man sat down at his desk with the second man taking a seat in front of him. The following conversation took place:

First man: "I have brought you here so that we can talk about the catastrophe."

Second man: "What a catastrophe it is!"

First man: "How could the referendum results show that in ten governorates half of the Egyptians rejected the constitution."

Second man: "I am deeply shocked."

First man: "Yes. Deeply shocked because you failed."

Second man: "I reject that statement."

First man: "Well you did fail. That cannot be denied. We selected you for your job and apparently we made the wrong choice."

Second man: "I didn't ask for the job. Your Excellency charged me with it. I cannot continue a discussion along these lines. Please excuse me now and I shall come back when Your Excellency is a little less agitated."

First man: "Sit down!"

Second man: "I insist on leaving."

First man: "And I insist that you remain seated. Don't get angry. You and God both know how much I love you. Forgive me if I say some harsh things, but the situation is critical."

Second man: "I can take anything from Your Excellency, but the accusation of failure is too much. God be my witness that I have done all I can. We made all the arrangements – I supervised them personally. We left the referendum forms unstamped. We had our Brotherhood members stationed at all the polling booths and female members went from door to door offering financial and other assistance. We spent huge sums of money on the poor voters, handing out sugar, rice and top-up cards. We had our own employees, rather than judges, positioned in many voting stations. We hired thousands of buses to transport people to come and vote for us. We carried out the plan of action with great precision."

First man: "So what went wrong?"

Second man: "It was a surprise result, strange and inexplicable. Millions of people turned out to vote against the constitution."

First man: "Must have been the Copts."

Second man: "Not just the Copts. Unfortunately, it was millions of ordinary citizens. They were fired up against us in a way I have never seen. People who really resent us. We did all we could to discourage them. We made them queue for hours, but they just stood there insisting on entering the polling stations and raising a ruckus."

First man: "I can't believe it. How can 50 per cent of Egyptians reject us when we represent Islam. We are Islam. How can Egyptians reject Islam? Do Egyptians not believe the mosque preachers whose hands they rush to kiss?"

Second man: "Thank God, the clergy are still held in great reverence. Had it not been for the preachers, the results would have been worse. And we shouldn't forget that the results were in favour of the constitution."

First man: "Yes, but by a tiny majority, and if we consider the arrangements we made and the sums we spent then it has been an abject failure."

Second man: "Media bias had a bad effect."

First man: "I have asked you here so that we can make some decisions. We must go over the situation and come up with some solutions. We are not leaving here until we agree on the action to be taken."

Second man: "As you wish."

First man: "I have a digest of foreign press comment for you. Take as much time as you want to read it. The Western press are all reporting that we have been politically defeated as a result of the referendum. We present ourselves to the world as a majority who can get the people to do whatever we want. We tell the world that the liberals have no presence on the street. After the results of the referendum, no one will believe us. If 50 per cent voted against us, that means that the liberals are as popular as us. Do you appreciate the seriousness of the situation?"

Second man: "I do."

First man: "On the internal front we have another serious problem. We convinced the Brotherhood youth that anyone who rejected the constitution was a secularist and an enemy of Islam. But now that half of the voters rejected the constitution, they must be feeling confused and suspicious."

Second man: "Well the Brotherhood youth are quite frustrated about the referendum result. This morning one of the youth leaders came and asked me if it was plausible that half of the electorate were against religion. I didn't know what to tell him."

First man: "If we don't dispel their sense of frustration, they may lose confidence in us."

Second man: "God forbid."

First man: "I have drawn up a general outline of the tasks we need to carry out before the second round of the referendum. It's a life and death struggle. If the result is the same as the first round, it will be a crushing blow for us and it will take us years to recover from it. Firstly, we have to counter the corrupt and misleading media coverage."

Second man: "We have taken a few steps on that matter. The minister of information has stopped dealing with those elements of the media who are hostile towards us. With regard to the privately owned television channels, we have been withdrawing their operating licenses. If we find that any of them are operating illegally, we will take immediate legal steps against them."

First man: "That's not enough. We've got to stop those journalists at all costs."

Second man: "I agree, Your Excellency. They are not just out of line, but they are anti-Islam and hostile to the law of God. We have sent out a strong message to them. Of course Your Excellency has heard about the last sit-in and the attack on the *Wafd* newspaper. That's just the start of it, please God."

First man: "I have followed the sit-in, but I was not happy. Firstly, the people in the sit-in beat up well-known people and attacked the *Wafd* newspaper, making us all look like thugs and that was a big mistake. If you want to make someone wise up, do it in a way that cannot be connected to us. Secondly, I am not at all convinced by the man who led the sit-in."

Second man: "I think he's as good a man as any on God's earth."

First man: "As good as you say he is, he has unfortunately caused us more damage than good, because he is reckless and idiotic. Every time he calls for a sit-in, he then goes home to sleep and lets the people get beaten up."

Second man: "He says that his bad knee doesn't allow him to spend the night on the street."

First man: "Of course his knee hurts from having to support all that weight! It's clear to all that he eats voraciously. Why does he have to have a fresh sheep slaughtered every day to eat with his friends in a sit-in? Let him stuff his face at home and just be seen eating a sandwich during a demonstration. Why should the hungry poor who see him eating mutton every day have any sympathy for him at all?"

Second man: "Our brethren are in contact with them and I will convey Your Excellency's remarks to him."

First man: "Listen: I want you to get intelligence reports for me on the newspaper and satellite channel owners. They are all businessmen and you will find that they have all contravened some law. Get someone to contact them and use some plain talking. Either they stop attacking us or we'll serve charges on them and the attorney general will definitely have them hauled into court."

Second man: "Good thinking."

First man: "The main thing is to act quickly. And another important thing regarding the second round of the referendum – you have to double the number of Brotherhood youth in all the polling stations."

Second man: "The Human Rights Council issued permits to a large number of the Brotherhood to be present inside polling stations even though it is against the law. It will be a sensitive matter to issue more permits."

First man: "Tell the Brotherhood members on the council that it is my wish. They have to double the number of permits. We'll deal with the repercussions."

Second man: "Of course."

First man: "The third matter is that of arrangements on the ground. We have to redouble our efforts. Brother Fahd sent us 2 million dollars today."

Second man: "We need much more than that."

First man: "You have carte blanche. Everyone has to get out and support the constitution. We have to get to every home. We have to help the poor. We'll give them hand-outs and they'll never let us down. Spend whatever it takes."

Second man: "I shall take steps to increase the quantities."

First man: "We have a map of every district in Egypt. If we can get people out to the polling station first thing in the morning, we will get the necessary votes. After that, anyone who turns up to vote can be left queuing. That way we will achieve a majority, please God."

Second man: "Please God. Are there any other tasks Your Excellency would like me to carry out?"

First man: "I want you to go on television and welcome the results, saying that you are ready to accept the choice of the people whatever it is. We need our brethren in the media to inform public opinion that in any country a constitution can be passed by a very narrow margin."

Second man: "They have already started preparing public opinion, may God reward them."

First man: "You know what you have to do and may God be with us. I will contact the Americans personally. I am going to call Hillary Clinton and will explain to her that we are still in the majority and that we can still control the street. I need to reassure her that we are keeping to our side of the agreement. If I don't convince the Americans of our strength, they could stop supporting us at any moment."

Second man: "I hope the call goes well, please God."

First man: "Don't be angry with me for having spoken to you harshly."

Second man: "Your Excellency knows I cannot be angry with him. Please would you excuse me now as I have a meeting at the palace."

First man: "Of course. Good luck to you, please God."

This is the transcript of a conversation which took place between the two men in the secret location.

Democracy is the answer.

RH

How to Lie and Maintain Moral Purity

24 December 2012

The minister of information, a member of the Muslim Brotherhood, went to cast his vote on the day of the referendum. The queue of voters snaked out of the main door and out on to the street. The minister entered the election commission building through the back door, casting his vote in moments, while the voters were waiting outside for hours to enter the commission. As the minister was leaving, one brave journalist asked him: "Why didn't you enter the commission through the main door, like the rest of them?"

With no hesitation, the minister replied: "I entered through the main door. I did not enter through the back door."

The minister of information was able to lie in front of cameras and journalists, without any visible signs of regret or embarrassment. In a democratic country, this lie from a minister would have caused a scandal and would perhaps have led to his dismissal. In Egypt, under the rule of the Brotherhood's supreme guide, the minister will stay in his position as long as the Guide is satisfied with him. The minister is a religious man, who observes his prayers, and performs the ritual ablutions beforehand – yet he lied. The question is, does lying invalidate purity? Does this supposedly religious minister know that lying is wrong, and that God does not accept prayers uttered by liars?

This question does not just concern this lying minister, but all the leading figures of the Muslim Brotherhood, including Mohamed Morsi. They do not practice what they preach, and never deliver what they promise. They are prepared to do anything in order to maintain power. The lies of the Brotherhood have no limit, and the latest of them was the referendum, the results of which were blatantly falsified in in order to pass the Brotherhood's constitution. All types of infraction happened during this referendum, from preventing the Copts from casting their ballot, to intimidating voters and buying the votes of the poor, to collective voting and cutting electricity to the electoral commission buidling. All this was done by a group of people calling themselves "Muslim Brothers", people who failed to consider for a moment that lying, deceit and interfering with the will of the people are behaviours that contravene the most fundamental tenets of Islam.

Just try, dear reader, to criticise the Brotherhood's supreme guide on Facebook or Twitter and you will be bombarded by obscene curses and abuse. Those slandering you are young religious men specifically tasked by the guidance office with insulting the opponents of the Brotherhood on the internet.

How can liars and slanderers have the audacity to call themselves "Muslim Brothers", when Islam exhorts us to be honest, sincere and polite? What is the secret behind this flagrant contradiction between belief and practice? It is that the followers of political Islam (the Brotherhood, the Salafists and the jihadists) do not understand religion in the same way as an ordinary Muslim does. Their understanding of religion is based on the following principles:

First: Absolute obedience to the supreme guide. The Brotherhood and the Salafists only acknowledge as correct that which is said by the supreme guide or the Salafist sheikhs. A Brotherhood member pledges complete obedience to the supreme guide and a Muslim Brother is expected not only to carry out the instructions of the supreme guide, but to do it with full conviction. A soldier may carry out the orders of his commander, but he doesn't have to show conviction. How can you ask thousands of people to believe every word uttered by a fellow, and therefore fallible, human being as true? That they must support everything he does and must find no fault with his opinions. In effect, they are being asked to do away with their own minds and thoughts entirely. You have taken away their capacity to judge for themselves and rendered them tools of obedience in the hands of the supreme guide.

Many of these young men are well educated, amongst them engineers and doctors, but they are in a state of intellectual subordination to their sheikh, which has made them lose the ability to discern and think independently. The evidence for this is how Sheikh Hazem Abu Ismail treats his followers. This sheikh made headlines recently when it emerged that his mother was an American citizen, contrary to what he had said. Each time he calls his followers to hold a sit-in, he leaves them to go back to his house, where he relaxes in the warmth and tucks into the delicious meals he is so fond of, while his followers receive beatings from the police. None of Abu Ismail's followers would dare to query his repeated escapes, or question him on his mother's nationality because, in their view, whatever he does is completely correct.

I mentioned before that when the supreme guide left the mosque, the Brotherhood members bowed at his feet and competed for the honour of helping him into his shoes. This portrays the extent to which the Muslim Brotherhood are subordinate to their supreme guide, and their inability to think for themselves.

Second: An exclusivist understanding of religion. With the Brotherhood and the Salafists, there is no room for debate, or presenting different views on religion. For them, Islam is whatever the sheikh or the supreme guide says and nothing else. Strange that most of their comments on the internet contain major spelling mistakes, which goes to show that they don't read, and that their culture is a purely oral one, sitting at the feet of the sheikh only to hear his words and repeat them. There is no point in debating with them because they will reject any opinion not belonging to the sheikh, even if it came from a senior Islamic scholar. If you were to engage them in debate, they would treat you with animosity. They have built their lives on the sheikh's words being true. If you said something that made them doubt this, then they would attack you to defend their practices which, if they are shaken, will mean having to rethink their whole life.

Third: The demonisation of opponents. The supreme guide of the Brotherhood and the Salafist sheikhs normally attempt to dehumanise their opponents. The Brotherhood and the Salafists do not consider their opponents individuals, each with his own human life, but put them all under collective pejorative categories, such as "secularists", "followers of the West", and "enemies of God's law". They do not consider that somebody who opposes them politically merely holds a different opinion, but that they are immoral, an infidel, or an agent of Zionism.

Of course, this contempt for their opponents makes it much easier to do them wrong. If you consider that you are the only one who possesses the absolute truth, while your opponents are agents and enemies of religion, logically you could not possibly afford them the same rights as yourself, because you are better than them. You carry the word of God, while they are followers of the devil. You are pure, fulfilling God's will; they are impure, enemies of Islam. It follows that doing them wrong is acceptable, and perhaps necessary at certain moments. We saw that when Morsi called for the Brotherhood's militia to attack demonstrators outside the presidential palace.

Here the contradiction between belief and practice appeared most prominently: groups of bearded men who would not allow themselves any leniency in observing prayer, committed disgraceful crimes without the slightest feeling of guilt. They hit women, attacked demonstrators and brutally tortured them, and savagely beat a citizen whose only "crime" was to be Christian. Due to their understanding of religion, the Brotherhood and the Salafists are always in a state of war with all those who disagree with them. In war, anything is permissible, from lying and rigging elections, to beating and torture.

Fourth: Searching for the grand conspiracy. When the American ambassador came to Cairo to inspect the referendum, a crowd of young Brotherhood members and Salafists gathered around her angrily shouting "Islamism! Islamism!" These young men had been convinced by their sheiks that there was a grand conspiracy against Islam led by America. Due to their mental subservience to their sheikhs, they were unable to discover that the truth is quite the opposite. The United States is not preoccupied with Islam at all, but rather with protecting its own interests and the security of Israel.

America welcomes Islamic government so long as these interests are kept secure, and there are numerous examples of this. For the last 50 years, the biggest ally of America has been the Saudi regime, which the Brotherhood and the Salafists consider a model for Islamic government. Likewise, the Taliban were founded by American intelligence, and in Pakistan, General Zia-ul-Haq was installed with Saudi funding to give the United States a loyal ally in the region. The Brotherhood understood this formula, and has kept open channels of communication with the US administration since the days of Mubarak. Morsi has attempted to guarantee the security of Israel through his influence with Hamas, and whoever follows the international press will find that many Western officials are praising Morsi in the same way they used to praise Mubarak.

The US administration would prefer the ruler of Egypt to be a compliant dictator, keeping his people under control and fulfilling American interests. It does not want a democratic system to emerge in Egypt because it would make Egypt an immensely powerful nation, deciding the path of the whole region, and this could threaten Israel. Yet the leading sheikhs of political Islam continue to convince their followers that the United States is conspiring against Islam, while they themselves meet with American officials and try to satisfy them in any way possible. The existence of a grand conspiracy against Islam, in as far as it is a delusion, is important for the sheikhs, as it enables them to sharpen the religious sentiments of their young followers and employ them to carry out their orders.

These are the four bases of political Islam which have turned the meaning of religion on its head. Instead of being a vehicle of justice, freedom and equality, it has transformed into a tool for inciting hatred. In this vein, the first elected president of Egypt has transformed himself into a dictator, suspending the law and imposing upon Egyptians a distorted constitution, running a rigged referendum and sending thugs to lay siege to the Supreme Constitutional Court and intimidate the judiciary, so it does not annul the constitution.

Nevertheless, Morsi's tragic transformation has had some positive effects. For the first time, it has brought the patriotic and revolutionary forces together, who have unified to save the nation from the Muslim Brotherhood trying to extinguish it. The ascension of the Muslim Brotherhood to power was a long-postponed test for Egypt and there is no doubt that she will pass it. The revolution succeeded in deposing Mubarak and bringing him to trial, and getting rid of military rule. Only the Brotherhood remain, who failed the test of government. In only a few short months, their unpleasant side was revealed.

If I was to stop any Egyptian in the street, whatever their level of education, and asked them what they think of the Brotherhood, they would be aware of the difference between true Islam, and the Islam of the Brotherhood which permits lying, deceit and hostility to people. Every day the Brotherhood are losing their popularity, to the extent that not one of their leadership (including Morsi himself) is able to appear in a public place without being met by hostile jeers from passers-by. The crimes perpetrated by the Brotherhood over the past few months have lost them their popularity, and the more they are aware of this, the more violent and aggressive they become. I expect that in the near future there will be more instances of repression, attacks and murders against all who oppose the Brotherhood.

It is our obligation to bring down the illegitimate, distorted constitution by all peaceful means. The rigged referendum was made on a void constitution produced by a void, illegal Constituent Assembly. And if Morsi hadn't suspended the rulings of the judiciary in his dictatorial declaration, the judiciary would have dissolved it a second time.

The revolution is ongoing, until the rule of the Brotherhood is overthrown completely as Mubarak was overthrown. Only then will Egypt be set free towards the future it deserves.

Democracy is the answer.

PN

Where Does Your Money Come From?

31 December 2012

Imagine that you work as a doctor or an engineer and you own a private clinic or business, are you allowed to call up the tax authority at the end of the year and inform them that as you made a loss in your work this year, you won't be paying any taxes? Or does the law require you to present a file of your earnings and expenses to be reviewed by the tax authority, who will calculate your profits, and how much tax you need to pay? Is it acceptable to consider presenting your accounts a violation of your privacy? Is it acceptable to deny the tax authority their right to know how much you earned at work?

The answer to these questions is obvious: it is the right of the state to know the amount of money earned by citizens in order to calculate the tax they need to pay, and to collect from them. If the state has this right over professionals, who use their income to pay for the upbringing of their children, then what about the politicians who work in the public sector, who run for positions in the People's Assembly and who are selected for top state positions? Is it not the right of the state – and its duty – to scrutinise the funding of these politicians and their parties and organisations? Is it not the citizen's right to know the funding sources of any individual running for a position in parliament or as prime minister or president.

Revealing the funding sources of parties and politicians is a basic right for a state and its citizens. In Egypt, a strange situation has emerged after the revolution. All Egyptian political parties are subject to state supervision, and must announce their funding sources and publish their budgets in the press, that is all except political Islamic organisations. Their officials vehemently refuse to announce their sources of funding, while every day they are spending millions of Egyptian pounds on their campaigns. The Brotherhood and the Salafists are building hundreds of regional headquarters around Egypt with money from an unknown source. It's enough to know that the Brotherhood has 1375 regional headquarters in Egypt and that their main headquarters in the Mokattam district of Cairo alone was built at a cost of 30 million Egyptian pounds. Throughout the elections we saw how the Brotherhood and the Salafists were distributing thousands of tonnes of food supplies to the poor for free in order to buy their votes. Every day, we see conclusive evidence that the budget of the Brotherhood and the Salafists is in excess of hundreds of millions of Egyptian pounds. But they never say how they came to acquire these vast funds.

We have asked the leadership of the Brotherhood and the Salafists repeatedly to reveal their funding sources, and each time they get angry and reply with a torrent of curses and accusations. If you come forward to demand this information, the Brotherhood and the Salafists are quick to call you an immoral secularist, and enemy of Islam who rejects the law of God, and an agent of the West and of global Zionism. By refusing to reveal their funding sources, they are opposing the state and disregarding its laws. One leading figure of the Brotherhood had this to say on the topic: "Yes, we have billions of Egyptian pounds and we will not say how we obtained them. Our funds have nothing to do with anybody, so go to hell."

This attitude is odd, and unacceptable. We are not talking here about a minor infraction, but a political and criminal offence. The question is: has the state simply been careless in ascertaining how the Brotherhood and the Salafists obtained their funding, or did it turn a blind eye to them and was in fact their accomplice? There are some indications of clear collusion from the state. Before the revolution, Salafist groups used to ask the Ministry of Social Solidarity for permission to receive funding from certain individuals and organisations in the Gulf. The ministry often refused these requests for reasons of security, and because they believed that this funding was being used for political purposes.

After Mubarak stepped down, the Brotherhood and the Salafists allied themselves with the military council for their mutual benefit. The military council needed an organised faction to support them and guarantee the continuation of their privileges, while the Brotherhood and the Salafists wanted elections to be held first, to give them the majority in parliament so that they could write an Egyptian constitution along their wishes, side-lining the other political parties. As a result of this alliance, the military council agreed not to monitor or investigate the funding sources of the Brotherhood and the Salafists.

On 21 February 2011, the Ministry of Social Solidarity sanctioned 296 million Egyptian pounds of funding coming from the Gulf to be received by a Salafist organisation. This huge amount was totally inconsistent with the aims of this charitable organisation, and what is more, officials from the organisation failed to explain where they spent the money. According to the officials, the organisation had spent 30 million Egyptian pounds for the purpose of providing support to orphans and caring for the poor. As for the rest of this amount, the officials said that they had put it towards "various development purposes." This is a vague and flexible term, and it doesn't require a great deal of intelligence to realise that these "various development purposes" could well include supporting Salafist parties during the elections.

Let us recall that this 296 million Egyptian pounds – a huge amount of money – came from some well-known individuals in the Gulf. It is only one of a number of payments made to this single Salafist organisation. We can only estimate the billions of pounds sent to the Brotherhood and the Salafists during the transitional period while the Egyptian state closed its eyes, so that the military council did not embarrass its allies; the Brotherhood and the Salafists.

Only once did the state attempt to monitor the funding of the Brotherhood and the Salafists, when former justice minister Mohammed al-Jundi formed a judicial committee to investigate foreign funding. Amazingly, after it had uncovered the 296 million Egyptian dollars obtained by the aforementioned Salafist organisation, the committee suddenly decided to permanently close the cases on funding of Islamic political organisations, turning its efforts to monitoring the funding of civil society organisations instead. The committee transferred its officials to the famous trial in which the American suspects escaped under the direction of Chairman Abdel Moaz Ibrahim (who was subsequently honoured by Morsi).

The floodgates were thus left open for huge amounts of money to pour into the Brotherhood and the Salafists from undisclosed sources. As we have all seen, this money is being used to buy the votes of the poor and in need. This huge funding happened during the transitional period under the military council, but now that the Brotherhood has taken power the situation has become more complex. We can't imagine that Morsi will order that the funding of the Brotherhood – to which he belongs – be subjected to scrutiny. We are not accusing anybody of betrayal or doubting anybody's patriotism. However, the matter is an extremely dangerous one and cannot be ignored for the following reasons:

First: In any democratic country, receiving funding from abroad for political purposes is categorically and without exception a crime. If it is proven that a politician has received funding from abroad to use in his election campaign, his fate is sealed: he will be stripped of his position and imprisoned. The cases under investigation involving officials of democratic countries accused of receiving funds from abroad for political purposes are too numerous to mention here. If all the democratic nations are aware of the seriousness of this political and criminal offence, then we cannot allow it to be committed here in Egypt if we want to build a healthy democracy.

Second: The flow of anonymous funds into the Brotherhood and the Salafists' coffers contravenes an important principle of democracy, that of equal opportunities. Fair elections are not only achieved with the absence of any electoral fraud, but are achieved when all the candidates are given a fair, equal opportunity to present their program and their ideas. They are achieved when the voter chooses his candidate freely, far from the influence of any bribery during the electoral process. They are achieved when the voter knows each candidate's source of funding and how it has been obtained. We cannot accept the results of any election if the Muslim Brotherhood and the Salafists continue to use millions in anonymous funding used to take advantage of Egypt's poor and buy their votes. In light of these circumstances, even if there is no rigging at the ballot box, elections will never be democratic because they will not express the true will of the people. Instead, they will express the fact that the Brotherhood and the Salafists' have exploited people's needs for the sake of gaining power by any means and at any price.

Third: That Islamic political parties use anonymous funding inhibits state sovereignty and dignity and exposes it to danger. It allows foreign parties to govern the course of affairs in Egypt. Here we should bear in mind the case of Lebanon and remember what has happened to that great country since the 1970s. Money flowed in from foreign parties to re-design Lebanon – along the lines of those providing funding – until the country descended into civil war. We are not accusing the Brotherhood or the Salafists of being any kind of agent for foreign powers, but we need to ensure the legitimacy of their funding. Why do they refuse to reveal their budget in public and make it subject to state control? If we assume that funding for the Brotherhood and the Salafists flows in from organisations or governments in the Gulf, are we naïve enough to believe that these funding sources are charitable organisations? As the American saying goes, "I pay, I say."

Do these organisations that fund the Brotherhood and the Salafists have political objectives they are keen to achieve in Egypt? If we assume that these funds flow into Islamic political organisations from the countries of the Gulf, we must bear in mind that some ruling families in the Gulf have taken, and maintain, a hostile position to the Egyptian revolution. These Gulf regimes view the revolution as a grave danger to their power. They know that if the revolution succeeded in Egypt and established a healthy democratic state, the model presented by Egypt would lead inexorably to the fall of many regimes in the Gulf also. Can we imagine that these Gulf regimes are funding Islamic political organisations for the sake of helping the revolution succeed? Or are they paying the Islamists millions of pounds so that they can tighten their grip on power, putting the revolution in danger?

It is a duty and a basic right of the state and the citizen to demand that the Brotherhood and the Salafists reveal their funding sources. If the revolution has matured and learned from its mistakes, it cannot enter any future parliamentary elections while not knowing who is paying who and at what price. Otherwise, once again we will see the Brotherhood and the Salafists buying the votes of the poor in public, with money of unknown origin.

The Brotherhood and the Salafists must set an example of honesty and integrity and publicly reveal their funding sources. Before participating in any future elections, the other political parties must find an answer to this question: what are the funding sources for political Islam in Egypt? Brotherhood, Salafists, where does your money come from?

Democracy is the answer.

PN

Being a Muslim in Britain

7 January 2013

Being Muslim in Britain means knowing from an early age that you are different. At school, you are treated with contempt by your fellow classmates and you are often the subject of unwelcome looks and comments during your religious studies lesson. Thereafter you become friends with other Muslim pupils and feel safer because people are less likely to make fun of your religion or bully you if you are a part of a group.

Being a Muslim in Britain is difficult because the majority of people disapprove of your religion and refuse to recognise it. Just saying your name reveals your religion and gives rise to prejudice and ill-treatment. Being a Muslim in Britain means living on the margins of society and being regarded with suspicion and contempt. It is rare that you will be treated as an equal and your rights and dignity will be, for the most part, ignored. Being a Muslim in Britain means having to study or work on your religious festivals because the state, with sublime indifference, only recognises one of your festivals as an official holiday.

Being a Muslim in Britain means studying as hard as you can but realising that often you will not get the final grade you think you deserve. During oral examinations at university, the examiner only has to read your Muslim name for their face to turn ashen and for them to give you a lower mark than your fellow students. Even if you get the highest grades, the university administration will try to prevent you from being appointed as a lecturer because you are Muslim. The people who stop you getting a job are mostly religiously observant people who think that you should not enjoy the same rights as they do. Being a Muslim in Britain means that you must prepare yourself to emigrate at any moment, because you are constantly at risk of being attacked by extremist groups. Being a Muslim in Britain means that you will never get to a senior position in the civil service. No matter how qualified you are; you will never be president, prime minister, head of the army or a senior manager in the intelligence agency. But why are you thus disadvantaged?

Because you are Muslim and some people from the majority religion believe that it is God who has forbidden your appointment to senior jobs in Britain. You are considered untrustworthy and therefore unworthy of promotion. In the eyes of the state, you are a fifth columnist and a potential threat to security. They consider Muslims "enemies of the state" and treat you accordingly. Being a Muslim in Britain means going through great difficulties in order to obtain permission to build a mosque to practice your religion. The state and extremists work together to prevent construction linked to your worship. The state passes complicated regulations to make building a mosque almost impossible; you cannot redecorate or renovate without the approval of a number of authorities. Moreover, extremists in Britain consider the building of a mosque an open act of hostility with serious consequences. If you do eventually manage to start building a mosque, hundreds of extremists will attack you and attempt to burn it down. The police will turn a blind eye to these attacks and the reports will be written long after the troublemakers have left, making justice impossible. Being a Muslim in Britain means that you might be chased out of your home and neighbourhood at any moment by the extremists. At that moment, you will forced to leave your home and move your family to a far away place of safety. If you call the police for help, they will tell you: "We would advise you to leave your house in the meantime, because we just do not have the resources to protect you."

Being a Muslim in Britain means that you risk death and persecution on a daily basis. You might be coming out of the mosque one feast day with your friends and be set upon by extremists that will beat you to within an inch of your life. The extremists will attack and set fire to Muslim homes, often killing the residents. The police will turn up after the event and arrest some people, but the perpetrators will often escape justice. If you are a Muslim and you live in a small or deprived area of Britain, all it takes is for one of your neighbours to stand under your window and shout: "This disbeliever has denigrated our religion on Facebook!"

This false accusation will anger and rile your religious neighbours. They will surround your house and attack your family, while chanting religious slogans. After every new massacre, the authorities will come out and explain away the blood of the innocents with platitudes, stating that investigations are taking their course and that the perpetrators will not escape justice. They will make grand statements about national unity and insist that Muslims are part of the fabric of Britain and that they live there in complete safety. Being a Muslim in Britain means hearing anti-Islam slurs everywhere, on television, in the street, and even on public transport. Those of the majority religion will warn their followers not to have dealings with you, not to mix with your family or to console you when someone dies. Moreover, they warn their followers not to give you good wishes on your religious festivals because that would imply that they recognise your religion. Being a Muslim in Britain means watching an extremist rip up your holy book on camera and state that he will get one of his grandchildren to urinate on it. You have to accept all this public humiliation with good grace. After a formal trial this extremist will walk free from the court into a crowd of his supporters who all ridicule and defame your religion.

In Britain anyone has the right to challenge your religion because you are a Muslim, but if you should criticise the majority religion you will be arrested immediately and thrown into prison for defaming religion. At that point you will discover that defaming religion in Britain only applies to those who challenge the majority religion. Being Muslim in Britain means that you have to ask a girl's religion before falling in love with her just in case it ends in tragedy. If you fall in love with a women from another religion, thousands of extremists will consider your love a serious blow to their honour and they will call for your blood. Extremists will violently attack you and set fire to your house because you dared to love a woman from their religion. They consider you a disbelieving Muslim who should never be allowed to pollute one of their own.

Being Muslim in Britain means not expressing your beliefs in public. You will take the tube and find that many passengers are reading their holy book aloud, but if you were to do the same, you would be subject to scorn and abuse. You will find other people using religious exclamations to confirm their statements, but if you swear by your God people get upset and reproach you. You will find other people plastering their religious slogans all over their cars and windows, but if you were to affix a religious slogan to your person or property you would be met by looks of resentment and hatred. Being a Muslim in Britain means seeing a sector of the population demand that their religious law be applied to you, and if you object or try to explain that you have a different religion and that it is not acceptable to impose on you the laws of a religion you do not believe in, they will retort: "Britain is our country and we can apply our law. If you don't like it, go and live somewhere else."

If you are a Muslim in Britain, you have to accept that freedom of belief is restricted to one religion. If a Muslim converts to the majority religion, the state celebrates their decision. The convert will find that henceforth life is much easier. However, if the opposite takes place and someone converts to the minority religion, they will have to flee abroad as quickly as possible because in Britain they are immediately in danger of being killed by people who consider this a religious duty.

Finally, if you are a Muslim in Britain, please do not get too overwrought by all this injustice. Do not hate or leave your country. Remember just how beautiful Britain, your country, is. Remember how tolerant it was before the extremists arrived on its shores. Remember that in Britain we have always lived together, that we have eaten, drunk, gone through good and bad times, and defended the country with our souls and our blood. Remember that for every extremist there are scores of tolerant people who have grown up to respect the beliefs of others and that they suffer from the attacks of extremists just as you do. Do not emigrate from the Britain you love. Stay there and defend the country. Hold your ground and work with us to free our civilised country from the extremism that is trying to take over the country.

Dear reader, there is a deliberate mistake in the preceding article. Please replace the word Britain with the word Egypt, replace the word Muslim with the word Copt, and replace the word mosque by the word church. Then read the article again to understand what it means to be a Copt in Egypt now. Then I hope that you will contact all the Copts you know and send them Christmas greetings.

Democracy is the answer.

RH

A Conversation Between a Revolutionary and a Good Citizen

21 January 2013

This conversation took place by chance. A young revolutionary was sitting in a cafe in central Cairo with political banners laid out before him. At the next table sat a bald man in his fifties, drinking mint tea and smoking a water pipe with great gusto.

Good citizen: "Excuse me, can I ask what those banners are for?"

Revolutionary: "They're banners which we're going to hold up on Friday 25 January at a demonstration to mark the second anniversary of the revolution."

Good citizen: "Are you a revolutionary?

Revolutionary: "I'm one of the 20 million Egyptians who brought about the revolution."

Good citizen: "I did not participate in the revolution. I watched in on television. I am one of those people they call the 'Armchair Party'. Naturally I was against Mubarak and I was glad to see him fall, but I have never been involved in a demonstration. I tell you, son, I think we've had enough demonstrations. We need stability; we need the wheel of productivity to start turning again."

Revolutionary: "Stability will only come when people feel that justice has been served, and it is everyone's right to demonstrate peacefully. You can find demonstrations all the time in democratic countries and their economies have not been affected. The Brotherhood tries to lay the blame for everything on the demonstrations."

Good citizen: "Alright then. Can you tell me the purpose of the demonstration on Friday?"

Revolutionary: "We're demonstrating because two years after the revolution, nothing has changed. On the contrary, things have got much worse. Brotherhood rule is exactly the same as the Mubarak regime; the Egyptian people are facing the same injustice, oppression, inflation, poverty and unemployment. Writers and journalists are still being terrorised and sent to court on trumped-up charges such as defaming religion. Civilians are still being tried by the military courts. People are still being arrested and tortured in police stations. Tell me one thing that has changed since the days of Mubarak."

Good citizen: "But President Morsi has only been in power for six months and he has told us to be patient and give him a chance."

Revolutionary: "Listen, hajji.[1] When someone makes a promise, are they not obliged to come good on it?"

Good citizen: "Of course."

Revolutionary: "If I promised you something ten times and then broke my promise each time, would you keep on believing my promises?"

Good citizen: "No. I'd be an idiot to do so."

Revolutionary: "You've said it yourself. The Egyptian people are not idiots. In the presidential elections, even though I am against the Brotherhood, I went with my gut feeling and voted for Mohamed Morsi rather than Ahmed Shafik.

1 A term of address to an older Muslim man.

Whatever the faults of the Brotherhood, I thought they would be better than the Mubarak regime, but unfortunately it was six of one and half a dozen of the other. I hoped that President Morsi would live up to his promise to be the president of *all* Egyptians, but he has turned out to be no more than a Brotherhood president who cares not a whit for anyone else."

Good citizen: "The Brotherhood have said that we should wait four years before passing judgement on President Morsi."

Revolutionary: "Well, sir, just suppose that I had agreed to drive you to the northern coast but then headed south to Upper Egypt. Would you have to wait until we reached the deep south before raising any objection?"

Good citizen: "Of course not. I would ask you to turn the car around immediately and take me to the coast road as agreed, or I would get out of the car."

Revolutionary: "That's exactly what Egypt is like. Morsi, instead of carrying out his promises, is just carrying out the orders of the supreme guide and he is only out for the interest of the Muslim Brotherhood. Morsi is just working to entrench his organisation so deeply in power that it will be impossible to remove them. We cannot wait four years for him to carry out the supreme guide's scheme. Either Morsi governs fairly or he should go."

Good citizen: "Don't forget that he is an elected president."

Revolutionary: "Well he might be an elected president, but he has violated the conditions of his election. You elect a president according to the law, but then he comes along and tramples the law underfoot, puts his own decrees above the law, and puts so much pressure on the Supreme Constitutional Court that it never rules against the useless drafting committee which he formed. If the president imposes on us an attorney general in contravention of the law, and if this attorney general asks the prosecutor general to imprison innocent citizens in order to save the president from embarrassment, how can we trust the attorney general or the president for that matter? What if the president imposes on the people a constitution which only represents the Muslim Brotherhood by means of a rigged referendum? If the elected president does all that, he loses all legitimacy because his legitimacy stems from a respect for the law, and if a ruler rides roughshod over the law, he has no legitimacy."

Good citizen: "Can I ask you something without you getting angry at me?"

Revolutionary: "Go ahead."

Good citizen: "Are you a bit of a secularist?"

Revolutionary: "What exactly do you mean by saying secularist?"

Good citizen: "Well, the imam of the mosque where I pray says that those who oppose President Morsi are secularists who reject the law of God and are enemies of Islam."

Revolutionary (smiles): "If the first Muslims could criticise the actions of [the caliphs] Abu Bakr and Umar ibn Al-Khattab, then why should we not be able to oppose Morsi? Secularism just means the separation of religion and politics and you can be a secularist and a devout Muslim. Of course you have heard of Saad Zaghloul, Mustafa el-Nahhas and Gamal Abdel Nasser?"

Good citizen: "All great Egyptian leaders."

Revolutionary: "They were all secularists, but that doesn't mean that they were against religion. They were proud of Islam, but they believed that Egypt would not be able to build a democratic state based on religion. We are Muslim, thank God, and we want to apply God's law, but Egyptians were not disbelievers before the Brotherhood took power. Most of the laws in Egypt accord with Islamic legislation – that's the opinion of the minister of justice, Ahmed Makki, whose thinking is in line with the Brotherhood. What's more, the Brotherhood's aim is to wield power and not to institute Islamic law."

Good citizen: "What do you mean?"

Revolutionary: "The plan to issue Islamic financial bonds. Have you heard about this?"

Good citizen: "Well, I didn't give it much attention."

Revolutionary: "The Brotherhood want to put Egypt up for sale to the highest bidder. Any foreigner who can afford it can purchase anything in our country, even the Aswan Dam or the Suez Canal."

Good citizen (incredulous): "Good Lord"

Revolutionary: "The plan to institute Islamic bonds was rejected by the Islamic Research Authority, who stated that it is against Islamic law. But even so, the Brotherhood are planning to institute it. So are the Brotherhood really that interested in observing Islamic law?"

Good citizen: "Lord above! I never thought of it like that. You should do all you can to frustrate this scheme because it is dangerous. How can we go around selling off the country?"

Revolutionary: "The Islamic bonds scheme is just one of the many catastrophes caused by Brotherhood rule over the last six months. The Brotherhood have attacked the rights of Egyptians and imposed on them the supreme guide's constitution by means of a rigged referendum. Two years after the revolution, Egyptians are still dying on the trains,[1] houses are still falling down

1 A train in the Manfalout area of Assiut has collided with a school bus, killing dozens of children.

because they were built without permission and people are still being tried in military courts and tortured in custody. Egyptians abroad still have no value or dignity. Naglaa Wafaa, Ahmed el-Gizawi and many others have been thrown into prison and given the lash in Saudi Arabia. Morsi turned the world upside down over 11 Muslim Brothers arrested in the Emirates, whereas he doesn't lift a finger to protect ordinary citizens in Egypt or the Gulf."

Good citizen: "Then why don't you vote the Brotherhood out of office?"

Revolutionary: "All democratic elections in the world have to take place according to certain conditions, the most important being transparency and equality of opportunity. Where is the transparency when we have the Brotherhood and the Salafist spending millions of pounds during the election campaign? They refuse to place their finances under state supervision and the origins of this money are unkown. If we don't know the source of the Brotherhood's or the Salafists' funding, then the elections have no legitimacy. And how can we have elections when they are run according to a law passed by the useless upper house according to instructions from the office of the supreme guide?"

Good citizen: "So you think that we should boycott the elections?"

Revolutionary: "We have stated what we believe to be the conditions for a fair election, and if these are not put in place, we'll boycott it."

Good citizen: "Well what you say is convincing, but do you think that demonstrations will bring about any results?"

Revolutionary: "It was demonstrations that brought down Mubarak, sent him for trial, and had him remanded in custody."

Good citizen: "So you are trying to get Morsi out of office?"

Revolutionary: "We want what is our right. And it is our right to have a constitution for all Egyptians. It is our right to be treated with dignity and respect. It is our right to have justice and freedom. We will continue with the revolution until we achieve our aims. Morsi has to respect the Egyptian people, annul the one-sided constitution and allow Egyptians to draft their own constitution. If Morsi refuses to do that, he'll be ousted."

Good citizen: "How old are you?"

Revolutionary: "I'm 28-years-old. I graduated from the College of Engineering in Cairo University in 2007."

Good citizen: "Well, son, you seem to be spending a lot of your time in demonstrations and protests and are exposing yourself to danger. You could get beaten up or, God forbid, killed, or at the very least arrested and tortured. Haven't you ever thought of putting all that heart-ache to one side and getting a well-paid job in the Gulf? You could go there, earn a packet, and then come back and live like a king here."

Revolutionary: "Listen, hajji. I took part in the revolution from the very first day and have seen young Egyptians shot and killed at my side. I have carried the dead aloft and have seen many people lose their eyesight to bullets aimed at us by snipers. The dot from a laser would circle around us and then someone would be shot in the head and drop dead right in our midst. I could have died at any moment, but God wanted other people do die and let me live on so that I could finish what we started. Those martyrs died dreaming of justice, freedom and dignity, and I shall continue the revolution until I realise their dream."

Good citizen: "You and your colleagues are very brave. You are right to demonstrate."

Revolutionary: "If you are convinced by our words, come and join us on Friday."

Good citizen: "I have never been involved in a demonstration."

Revolutionary (laughing): "Don't worry. Come along to the demonstration with me and I'll keep an eye out for you."

The two men laughed and then sat discussing where and when to meet for the Friday demonstration.

Democracy is the answer.

RH

Why Is Morsi Killing Egyptians?

28 January 2013

Mohamed Morsi cannot claim that all the millions of Egyptians calling for his downfall are remnants of the Mubarak regime, or liberals and leftists, opposed to political Islam. The truth is that the Brotherhood vote was not enough to guarantee a victory for Morsi in the presidential elections. It was in fact the eight million ordinary citizens that voted for him in the second round run-off that secured his seat. This included a large number of revolutionaries, liberals and leftists who gave him their support to prevent the return of the old regime at the hands of Ahmed Shafik.

All his grumblings about a liberal, leftist conspiracy is therefore nonsense. Likewise, it is ludicrous to imagine that the millions of people who oppose the Brotherhood are remnants of the deposed regime. If the Mubarak regime really had millions of supporters, it would not have fallen in the first place. All of these myths are being invented by the Brotherhood in order to conceal the truth about their mounting unpopularity.

On the day after he was elected president, Mohamed Morsi called a meeting with the revolutionary forces at the presidential palace which I myself took part in. In attendance were representatives from all across the political spectrum, from far left to far right. Before we were joined by the president, I perceived a great optimism amongst the group for the first civilian, elected Egyptian president and an earnest readiness to help the president succeed and see the renaissance of Egypt achieved under his government.

But President Morsi moved towards failure with a rapidity neither his supporters nor his opponents were expecting. After a few short weeks, Egyptians were surprised to learn that Morsi was a part-time president, a president detached from the events of the real world. It was made clear to everyone that Morsi was not the one responsible for presidential decisions. Instead, they came to him pre-prepared from the Guidance Office. All he had to do was open the envelope and read them out, as if he were the one issuing them.

The Egyptian people soon discovered Morsi was not the president of Egypt, but a representative of the Muslim Brotherhood in the presidency. There is a video and a photo that reflect this situation. The video shows some Muslim Brotherhood members bowing down to the ground, rushing to help the Brotherhood Guide put on his shoes, as his eminence stands, extending his foot to his followers so that they can carry out their solemn mission. The photo shows Morsi standing up to kiss the head of Khairat el-Shater (the real leader of the Brotherhood). This acutely demonstrates Morsi's relationship with his guide, Mohammed Badie, and his boss el-Shater.

Egyptians have since lost hope in their subordinate president. They have been let down by Mohamed Morsi, and indeed the Brotherhood. Morsi has gone back on almost all of his election promises and has shown little or no remorse for his actions. It has become increasingly apparent that the "Renaissance Project"[1] trumpeted by the Brotherhood's media machine was nothing but empty words and Morsi has lost his credibility extremely quickly.

Piece by piece, the true picture emerges: the Brotherhood, along with the Salafists and the repentant terrorists from Al-Gama'a al-Islamiyya,[2] do not consider Morsi's coming to power as a victory for democracy. In their view, it is a divine triumph against the enemies of Islam (seemingly the rest of the Egyptian people). What is more, the Brotherhood decided to use democracy

1 That project comprises two core points: to draw lessons from the experiences of all successful countries such as Italy, Germany, South Africa, India and Norway; and to cooperate with those countries in the economic field.

2 Al-Gama'a al-Islamiyya began as a dissident group of former members of the Muslim Brotherhood. Since the late 1980s it has moved to replace Egypt's government with an Islamic state.

like a ladder to climb to power and then kicked it from underneath them so so that nobody else could follow. What the Brotherhood is trying to achieve is quite simply a re-ordering of the conditions of the Egyptian state so that they can stay in power indefinitely. They have no intention to restore the Islamic Caliphate.

It is enough for anyone to read about the atrocities committed when the Ottoman armies occupied Egypt and the barbaric crimes perpetrated by the Umayyads and Abbasids, to know that rightly-guided Islamic rule only existed for 31 years (for 29 years under the rightly-guided caliphs and two years under Umar ibn Abd al-Aziz). The Islamic Caliphate – while it may be an attractive idea – would be impossible to restore because it did not actually exist. However, the leaders of political Islam amass followers under the banner of the caliphate, exploiting their ignorance of history and their impassioned religious sentiments. The Islamic caliphate is like the windmills with which Don Quixote did battle, imagining that he was routing armies of enemies existing only in his imagination.

So, the Brotherhood plans to stay in power forever and Morsi has transformed himself into a dictator. He has made an unconstitutional declaration to give himself unfettered powers, allowing him to do anything he wants, including dismantling the judicial system to make himself and his decisions immune from any prosecution. Morsi has urged his followers to surround the Supreme Constitutional Court until the defunct Constituent Assembly has finished writing the defunct constitution prepared by the Guidance Office.

President Morsi has shown his true colours and the Egyptian people gathered together and held peaceful demonstrations outside the Federal Palace.[1] Then Khairat el-Shater sent his armed militia to attack the demonstrators at the palace, arrest them and brutally torture them. There were deaths on both sides but the responsibility for all of them lies on the shoulders of Morsi and his boss, el-Shater. Resistance to the new dictator mounted for one simple reason: Egyptians started a revolution in which they lost hundreds of people and tens of thousands were wounded. After all this, they cannot allow one dictator to be exchanged for another.

However, the tyranny of the Brotherhood is not as bad as their failures in running the state. After children were killed in the train disaster in Assiut, Morsi failed to adopt the simplest measures to prevent a repeat of the disaster. A series of train disasters followed which killed and injured many Egyptians, prices rose and the economic depression continued. Meanwhile, Morsi was pleading with the Internatinal Monetary Fund (IMF) to grant him a loan while el-Shater put forward the idea of Islamic bonds,[2] which would result in

1 The residence of President Morsi.
2 Islamic bonds, structured in such a way as to generate returns to investors without infringing Islamic law (that prohibits riba or interest).

Egypt being sold to the highest bidder. But then, something really surprising happened: the Islamic Research Academy rejected the idea of bonds because they are against Islamic law. Despite this, the Brotherhood was still determined to put this plan into action, a plan that contravened the Islamic law they pay lip service to.

This goes to show that staying in power is more important to the Brotherhood than religion itself. In this way, the opportunism and lies of the Brotherhood and its failure and inability to govern was brought to light for everyone to see. The only tool it has left is repression. The solution was for Morsi to use the minister of the interior to terrorise and intimidate the Egyptian people, insofar as Habib el-Aldy had done under Mubarak. All those who witnessed the killing of Egyptians in recent days may be asking themselves: did Israel ever kill fifty Palestinians on the same day? Did Israel ever shoot Palestinians while they were bidding farewell to their dead by their gravesides? The Muslim Brotherhood has outdone Israel in killing, but the difference is that Israel kills whom it believes to be enemies and terrorists. Morsi kills Egyptian citizens, many of whom voted him into the presidency.

Why is Morsi killing Egyptians? The standard response is that they were attacking state facilities. Isn't it possible to protect state facilities without killing people? Does the law not lay down incremental measures for dealing with demonstrators, starting with gas canisters and water cannons, then warning shots in the air, and lastly shooting around the edges of the demonstrators so they are stopped in their tracks but not killed? Was it too difficult for the police officers to aim their guns at the feet of the demonstrators instead of their chests and heads? Couldn't we have spared the lives of Egyptian citizens by arresting them and putting them to trial, as would happen in any respectable country? Dozens of civilians and two police officers have lost their lives over the past two days, and the blood they shed will stain the hands of the Brotherhood forever. But however many Egyptians Morsi kills, the Egyptian people who rose up in revolution will never comply, and never fear.

After killing his own citizens, Morsi emerged to deliver a weak, futile speech. He did not apologise for the loss of human life, nor did he make an effort to surmount the catastrophe he had caused. Instead, he threatened the Egyptian people with more killing and even thanked the perpetrators in the police force. It is unfortunate that this disregard for the lives of the Egyptian people comes from Morsi, who presents himself as a religious man who reads the Qur'an and prays regularly in the mosque. Morsi has proven that the true Islam, which we embrace and cherish, is completely opposed to the Islam adopted by the Muslim Brotherhood.

After the bullying and threats, Morsi ended his miserable announcement with a call for dialogue. What is the point of dialogue when all decisions are dictated by the Guidance Office; from suspending the law and rigging the referendum, to the continued killings of Egyptians? With whom should we debate Brother Morsi, and what for?

The truth is that Morsi does not plan to open a dialogue, but he does need to give the impression of opening a dialogue. The Muslim Brotherhood have lost their reputation and credibility inside and outside Egypt, and in order to court public opinion they need to hold these false, superficial meetings. In them, they will show the world that they are open to the revolutionary elements.

Morsi, if you want to save yourself from the catastrophe you inflicted on Egypt, first you must see reason and annul the distorted constitution you have imposed on Egyptians against their will. If you want to save yourself from the fate of Mubarak, you must bring those murderers of Egyptian citizens to trial, whether they are in the police, the army, or they are civilians. You won't be able to achieve stability unless you are just; and justice won't be achieved except by returning power to the people who elected you. They trusted you, but you have turned against them and have become a tyrant and dictator, using the most fascist and brutal of policies to stay in power.

Muhamed Morsi is responsible for the blood of the martyrs who fell in cities all over Egypt. Strange that we bring Mubarak to trial on the charge of killing demonstartors, while Morsi commits the same crime. Morsi, you and your organisation belong to the past, and the revolution belongs to the future. Neither you, nor your boss Khairat el-Shater, nor your guide Mohammed Badie, have the capacity to stop the future and bring the revolution to an end. You have conspired against the revolution from the very beginning. You lied and set up the deal with the military so you could monopolise power indefinitely, at the expense of all the martyrs.

Keep on killing, Morsi; kill to your heart's content, but know that killing won't save you from your fate, nor will it stop the revolution.

Democracy is the answer.

PN

Six Ways to Keep Hold of Power

4 February 2013

First: Take leave of your voters and focus on your target. Now that you have won, you must take one last look at the millions of people who voted for you and rejoiced in your victory. Henceforth you must not think of them.

Focus on your target precisely so that you can keep hold of power for as long as possible. Your party has spent years struggling for power and now you have finally assumed your rightful role. You must stay in power and ensure that you are able to pass on your title to someone within the organisation when the time comes. Don't worry too much about the economy, tourism or development. These are all less important matters which can be solved later. Your first priority is to change the structure of the state in order to realise the permanent empowerment of your party. You must draft a new constitution and impose it on the people by whatever means possible. You must pass laws which are in your party's interest and which are deleterious to others. If the judiciary stand in your way, beat them back. Put your own people in the judiciary and try to buy whichever judges you can. Some judges may refuse, but you will be able to find a hundred ways of getting rid of them. Remember that a judge, at the end of the day, is a just one individual and you have the whole state behind you. If you make an example of one judge, a score will fall into line.

Second: Make use of your followers and servants. In order to guarantee your power, put individuals from your party in all the important places. Give every last influential position to your own people, leaving the less desirous positions for the civil servants. Don't judge people by their actions while in government. Power has a very strong lure which can change a person utterly and completely, such as those political science professors who have bent to your every will. They have obediently defended your every decision, and formulated political theories to prove that you are a great ruler. There are also the servants of the former regime, who are all eager to please you; from university professors, journalists and authors, to artists and politicians. Do not drive them away or lose them, because their experience may prove useful. You will need to have enough funds to pay your supporters. You will have to have a source of funding at home and abroad. Even if you have to bankrupt the state, you must have enough personal wealth to reward all your supporters, if you want to stay in power.

Third: Rape and be efficient. Did you know that the pelvic muscles in a woman are the strongest in the body? No one can rape a woman unless she stops resisting [sic]. An efficient rapist has to crush the will of his victim until they have no choice but to submit. You must carry out the same thing on the people. They must realise that you are more powerful and vicious than your predecessor. The people have to understand that anyone who goes out onto the street to oppose your rule will pay a horrendous price. When necessary, get your followers to teach the demonstrators a lesson by torturing them, provided that they leave no trace of your connection to them. Do not get on the wrong side of the police because they are at your service. Some of the men in the upper echelons of the police are hired killers and they can be bought for the right price. You will find someone amongst them who, for a million Egyptian pounds per month, will be willing to kill hundreds of people. These men are your real soldiers so be careful not to ignore them if you want to stay in power. However long the economic crisis goes on, you have to find the funds to purchase new weaponry for them. Body armour is much more important to the police than bread on the table. Tear gas, bullets and ammunition are more important than food. If God provides you with an efficient and heartless minister of the interior, it will make your life much easier. Give him the green light and let him do what he wishes but make sure that he has protection.

The state security apparatus has an infinite variety of tricks to control the streets. At every demonstration they will infiltrate the demonstrators and throw Molotov cocktails to provide the police with ample justification for attacking demonstrators. Anyone arrested at a demonstration has to be taught a harsh lesson and their dignity has to be completely crushed. If a detainee dies while being beaten or electrocuted, you must never punish the killer as this may demoralise the police force. The killing of demonstrators must be carried out in an efficient and professional manner. One shot in the neck or the head will suffice. There will never be any proof, because the investigations will be carried out by the killer's colleagues in the police force. In addition to this, there will be groups of thugs who specialise in sexual abuse and rape. They will work their way into a demonstration and set upon the female demonstrators, and violently assault them. The benefit here is twofold: the attacks will be used to discredit the demonstrators, and the recurrent incidences of molesting and rape will terrify every woman into thinking twice before joining another demonstration. You will only manage to hang onto power if the people are afraid to demonstrate. If someone knows that joining a demonstration represents a threat to their life and honour, they will desist and stay at home. During the campaign of terror, you have to divert the ordinary citizen's attention away from the deonstrators. The ordinary citizen is not interested in who is in power, but they are concerned with the cost of living. You have to take a loan out from an international organisation in order to be able to increase wages and pensions. What then happens to the demonstrators will be of no interest to the ordinary citizen and you will be able to crush your opponents.

Fourth: Always dress up the truth. Make a lot of easy promises and don't fulfil any of them. Never stop defending your position even though your words bear no relation to reality. Whenever someone is killed in a demonstration, express your deep sorrow and send your thoughts to the family of the deceased. Promise to track down the perpetrators and have them sent for trial as quickly as possible. After every massacre, ask your supporters to form a supreme investigative committee whose work will remain ever unfinished.

If you sign a decree raising prices, prattle on about the importance of social justice. After imposing on the people a constitution drafted by your party, talk openly about the necessity of a national consensus. Do not think that a lie can hurt you. On the contrary, a lie repeated often enough will confuse the people and work in your favour. Call upon the people to join in a broad national debate, which will cement your image as a democratic ruler, both at home and abroad. Let the participants in this debate get together and talk. Display your interest and then have them issue recommendations which you will naturally do nothing about. And don't forget about a plot; there must always be a plot against you in order to garner sympathy from the electorate. You will remain in power if you manage to convince the people that enemies of Islam or the state are plotting against you. If you want them to be convinced that you are the victim of a plot, you need to control the media. Choose a minister of information who is one of your supporters. It is not a difficult job to control the state media as the remnants of the old regime are still in their jobs. The channels loyal to you will discreetly ensure that your opponents are discredited. Have your security service review the CVs of the businessmen who own the private channels and newspapers. They are bound to find some illegal activity which they can use to threaten the owners into ceasing their opposition and backing you.

Fifth: Worship in front of the cameras. Don't forget to make use of religion. Religion is a force which moves people greatly. You must be filmed dutifully performing your prayers in a mosque so that millions will see you humbly supplicating God. During Friday prayers, you should be visibly moved to tears by the imam's sermon to create the impression that you are a devout and god-fearing ruler. The clerics must support you. There are some stubborn, trouble-making clerics who will refuse to help you but have them taught a lesson by the security services. There are clerics who will be ready to cooperate, who consider religion a service offered to the highest bidder.

There are also those who pandered to the former regime and who will no doubt do the same for you. They will say whatever you want them to, and justify whatever you do in religious terms if you cross their palms with silver. Be careful not to lose those clerics because they have a great affect on the general population. You will manage to stay in power if you convince the people that you do not represent yourself, but religion itself. Then the religious will defend you, thinking that they are defending Islam. They will accept whatever you do and justify it so forcefully that, even if you stole the whole state budget, they will delude themselves and deny the truth even though it might be plain as daylight. These good people will not only be prevented from recognising your injustice and monopolisation of power but they will deem your opponents enemies of the religion, avowed atheists or foreign agents. If your police should drag a female demonstrator along the ground, molest her or even rape her, they will transfer the blame onto the victim, asking what brought her down to the demonstration when her natural place should be in the home. If the police attack a man in front of the cameras with the world watching the crime, they will justify their action by saying that the man had been throwing Molotov cocktails at government installations, and the world will sympathise with the difficult job the police have to do.

Sixth: Keep calm and let time take its course. No matter how many protests or demonstrations flare up, leave the matter to the police and keep calm. Rebellion cannot go on forever. Whatever they are rejecting or demonstrating about today, the people will learn to live with it. Once you have secured yourself in power and your party has imposed its will, the people will go back to their old obedient ways, the way an abused wife goes back to the marital home.

Democracy is the answer.

RH

Exercises Upon Seeing the Sun

11 February 2013

Imagine that an Egyptian newspaper published a news item about a leader of the Muslim Brotherhood sexually abusing one of the younger Brothers. How do you think the Brotherhood would react? Would they rush off to investigate the crime and demand that the perpetrator is punished or would they try to cover up the crime in order to shelter the Brotherhood from embarrassment? Would the Brotherhood thank the journalist for having published details of the crime, or would they treat him with scorn and contempt?

All these questions popped into my mind whilst reading what happened this week in the United States. Some years ago the American press exposed a scandal involving Catholic priests who had sexually abused the children in their congregation. The American press aggressively pursued a number of cases of sex abuse, and the Church were forced to make an apology. The accused priests were put on trial and the Church introduced a new system of checks to prevent it ever happening again. The Catholic Church then appointed a new sexual crimes prosecutor, Father Robert Oliver, to look into any allegation of sex abuse within the Church. Father Oliver began by holding a press conference in which he stated that the US media "did a service" to the Catholic Church through its aggressive reporting on child abuse and that it helped the Church "confront the truth".

His words reflect a psychological and intellectual maturity and betray great media savvy. This is in stark contrast with the way in which the Brotherhood treat the media; they have been waging a fierce war against the independent media since they assumed power. Freedom of expression was greatly restricted in the days of Mubarak, but the way the media have been shackled under Brotherhood rule is even worse. Many journalists have been put on trial on charges of defaming President Morsi, a foolish and unreasonable charge which can be levelled against anyone who criticises the president. Respected journalists, such as Dina Abdel Fattah and Wael el-Ibrashi, have been put on trial for having dared to invite members of the Black Bloc party[1] onto their programmes. It is well known throughout the world that inviting someone onto a television programme, even if he is wanted by the law, does not impose any legal onus on the journalist. However, the Brotherhood is fighting a dirty and violent war against the independent media. At Morsi's suggestion, or agreement, supporters of Abu Ismail[2] besieged Media Production City, attacking journalists and celebrities.

On the second anniversary of the revolution, millions of Egyptians joined in demonstrations denouncing Brotherhood rule. They demanded the annulation of the worthless constitution, and the holding of early presidential elections. Under the leadership of the new minister of the interior, the police responded to the demonstrators by opening fire on them, killing 53 people in one week, as well as arresting hundreds of demonstrators, who were later tortured. An Egyptian television channel also broadcast a video of an Egyptian man, Hamada Saber, pleading with police as they dragged his naked body along the ground and physically and verbally abused him. After these events, the prime minister, rather than speaking about all these instances of criminal abuse, surprised us by releasing a statment about the importance of breast feeding.[3] The prime minister became a laughing stock all over the world and the Brotherhood promptly sacked the journalist who had broadcast the prime minister's press conference because the producer should have stopped the broadcast

1 A black bloc is group of demonstrators that wear black clothing, scarves, sunglasses, ski masks, motorcycle helmets with padding, or other face-concealing and face-protecting items to conceal their identity and therefore hinder criminal prosecution. In 25 January 2013, on the second anniversary of the Egyptian Revolution, black blocs made an appearance in the Egyptian political scenes where they have reportedly attacked various Muslim Brotherhood headquarters and government buildings and stopped traffic and metro lines in more than 8 cities.

2 Supporters of former presidential candidate Hazem Salah Abu Ismail

3 The prime minister stressed the need for a nursing mother to clean her breasts before feeding in order to avoid the baby developing diarrhea.

when the prime minister started prattling on. According to the minister of information, the duty of the media is not to broadcast the truth, but to stifle anything that might damage the Brotherhood. The same logic was adopted by the Brotherhood minister of justice, Ahmed Makki, when *al-Watan* newspaper reported that his son, a judge, had been seconded to Qatar on a high salary, and that this most definitely created a conflict of interest between the minister and the state of Qatar. The minister confirmed that his son had gone to work in Qatar and then let loose a stream of abuse against the rotten media. In Makki's opinion, a decent media should cover up anything that might harm him, even if it is true. The Islamists and the Salafists control a surprising number of religious television channels, funded by Wahhabis in the Gulf, which broadcast clerics not so much speaking about religion as flinging obscene curses at opponents of the Brotherhood and inciting people to commit murder. Although the Brotherhood regularly insult their opponents, they will not countenance criticism being raised against them pubicly in the media. What is it about the independent media that worries the Brotherhood so much? The answer is that the Brotherhood does not understand the difference between the media and propaganda. For them the media are not a means of exposing the truth but a means of spreading propaganda which can be used either in their service or against them. Consequently, they consider a journalist who criticises them a tool in the propaganda war against them who must be silenced by any means. I do not think that this misconception is a result of a widespread ignorance or stupidy on the part of Brotherhood because many members of the Brotherhood are well educated. So why do they not understand that the media do not create the truth but report it, or that the fundamental task of the media is to report on wrongdoing and criminality?

And here we come to the crux of the matter. We first have to admit that only rarely do people choose a religion of their own free will. We are generally born into a religion, predefined by our forefathers. We learn from an early age what to believe and how to observe the practices of our religion. Religion can enrich our lives immeasurably, and God has bestowed on us religious emotions which can comfort us in our darkest hours, whatever religion we embrace. We embrace religion first with our hearts, and then with our heads, that is, we believe first with our emotions and then we use our intellect to seek out evidence to underpin our belief. Religion is a belief based completely on feeling. Believers always think that their religion is the only true religion and that all others are wrong. Muslims hold that the Christians and the Jews altered their scriptures and both have erroneous beliefs; the Christians do not accept Mohammad as a prophet or as a messenger of God, and the Jews reject both Christianity and Islam and believe that the real messiah is yet to come.

That is the nature of religion. And there is no harm if citizens in a democratic state learn how to live alongside other religions. The problem arises when politicians start dabbling in religion. A Muslim Brother does not have to think independently in order to form an opinion. They receive the truth ready-made from the supreme guide and they are ready to embrace and defend it. It is most dangerous when a Muslim Brother believes that they are the only group to represent Islam and the word of God. Consequently, anyone who opposes the Brotherhood is offending Islam. If you try to tweet comments or criticisms of the supreme guide on social media, you will immediately be flooded with abuse and the foulest of curses, sent by supposedly religious individuals. They will urge you to stop criticising the supreme guide, and to return to God before death comes and flings you into to hell.

The state of identification between the Brotherhood and Islam has prevented them from acknowledging their own mistakes and criminality. Perhaps the most recent example of Brotherhood aggression was the attack on demonstrators in front of the Trade Union building, when supposedly religious and pious men savagely attacked female demonstrators. These same men would not be able to salve their consciences if they missed evening prayers, but they can torture other people without the slightest feeling of guilt because they believe that they are representing Islam. The Brotherhood considers its opponents religious traitors and infidels. They accuse them of being against Islam and call them disbelievers, promiscuous adulterers, degenerates or agents of those foreign powers which are conspiring against Islam.

The Brotherhood justify their acions by claiming to be performing a religious duty. The Brotherhood will never confess to the countless acts of brutality, even though videos of these attacks have been broadcast around the world. They will just continue to bolster opinion and deny the truth. Asking any Muslim Brother to admit that the supreme guide has incited violence is just like asking a religious man to admit the existence of inconsistencies in his religion.

Mohamed Morsi, who started off as an elected president and turned into a dictator, has trampled roughshod over the law, and imposed a biased and illegitimate constitution on the Egyptian people without their consent. He is also responsible for the torture and murder of peaceful demonstrators who dared to speak out against him. These crimes are the same as those committed by Mubarak, crimes for which he was arrested and thrown into prison. Despite this obvious point of comparison, the brotherhood refuse to admit any wrong doing as it would undermine their belief that the Brotherhood is interchangeable with Islam. The battle in Egypt at the moment is not between the opposition and the government, but between Egypt and the Brotherhood, between the revolution, which has not achieved its aims, and the Brotherhood who colluded against the revolution and betrayed it for their own interests. The revolution belongs to the future and the Brotherhood to a deep and distant past. Can anyone stop the future? The revolution goes on and will be victorious, with God's will.

Democracy is the answer.

RH

How Can Flexibility Kill Us?

18 February 2013

Imagine that you were renting out your furnished apartment and were living from the income. One day, a religious bearded man comes and asks to rent the apartment and you sign a four-year lease with him. The new tenant immediately sets about handing out all of your elegant furniture to his relatives, pulling down interior walls and remodelling the whole interior. You would be angry because the tenant has contravened the terms of the lease and because what he has done indicates that he is planning to expropriate the flat and stay there indefinitely. Suppose that you went to your lawyer and had an eviction threat sent to the tenant for contravening the terms of the lease and you receive back from him a photocopy of a forced lease which you did not sign permitting him to do what he wants to your apartment. At this point you would realise that you have happened upon a mendacious tenant who is trying to take over your apartment. You will insist upon him vacating the apartment immediately, but he resorts to violence. When your friends go round to try and convince the tenant to leave the apartment, they are met by a gang of thugs who open fire and kill some of them. The lying, falsifying tenant has now become a murderer. It will no longer suffice just getting him out of the apartment; you want to see him charged with the murder of innocent people. Oddly, the tenant who has committed these crimes now sends an intermediary to talk with you, and he intimates that you should just raise the rent a few pounds. The law is clearly on your side against the lying homicidal tenant, but he, unfortunately, makes a great show of being religious and going to pray in the mosque with his clique of bearded associates. They all defend him whether right or wrong and talk down any accusations of criminal behaviour. One of his associates approaches and asks: "Why do you hate Islam so much?"

"How can I hate Islam when I'm a Muslim," you answer.

"You want to evict our friend from your apartment just because he is an observant Muslim."

"If I hated him for being observant, as you claim, I would not have agreed to rent the apartment to him in the first place. Your friend, moreover, is not observant. He is a shame-faced liar. He always says what he is going to do and then reneges on all of his promises. On top of that, he is a murderer responsible for the death of martyrs."

"Even if that were the case, if you evict him from your apartment, you will be going against the sharia. He has the right to do what he wants in your apartment for four years."

"Putting my signature next to his on a contract does not mean that I condone his criminal behaviour. The legality of a contract is conditional upon its clauses being honoured, and your friend has broken the law and produced a dummy contract with my name on it. He has also killed innocent people and must be put on trial."

"Good lord! Why is your heart being eaten up by hatred for Islam?"

"I will evict your friend because he has killed, lied, cheated and broken his word, not because he has a beard and prays regularly."

"Why won't you accede to our invitation to go and talk with our friend?"

"How can I sit down and talk with someone I wish to see on trial? And what is there to say except that I demand he leaves the flat immediately."

"Why did you reject the rent increase he offered?"

"Because if I accepted the increase in rent, that would mean accepting the current situation which has been imposed on me by your lying, murderous friend."

"So you refuse to talk or come to any terms. You must be a foreign agent paid to sow dissent. Are you an agent of the Church or of world Zionism?"

"I am an agent of no one. I am just demanding my rights."

"Islam is on its way, notwithstanding your ire. Muslims will be the masters of the world, you will see, and you can take your fury to the grave with you."

This short scenario highlights the contradictions of the situation in Egypt at the moment. Egptians elected Mohamed Morsi, according to the law, but he has monopolised power with his party, appointed a loyal attorney general, and put himself and his decisions above the law. He legally ring-fenced the sham Constitutional Committee and the equally useless Shura Council. Then he imposed on the Egyptians a constitution they had no hand in drafting. He permitted the deaths of scores of demonstrators, and the hideous torture of hundreds of innocent people with electrocution, and the sexual abuse and rape of both men and women. The person who bears prime responsibility, criminal and political, for all these crimes is Mohamad Morsi. This president lost his legitimacy when he made the constitution declaration which made a mockery of the law.

The president's legitimacy falls away, even if he is an elected president, merely by dint of him having broken the law by killing his own citizens. Demonstrations are taking place all over Egypt at the moment to demand that the rotten constitution imposed on the nation by the Brotherhood is annulled and that a new constitution is drafted which expresses the will of the people followed by early presidential elections. At that time, Morsi will be able, should he so wish, to declare himself a presidential candidate anew, but only after he has been tried for the torture and murder of Egyptians. The annulation of the constitution, early presidential elections, the resignation of the attorney general and the trial of people who have killed others – these are clear revolutionary demands which cannot be ignored or only half-accepted. History teaches us that half measures are the death of revolutions. At a time of revolution, we should not be practising politics. Politics and revolution are opposites that ne'er do meet. Politics is about implementing practicalities but revolution is about principles. Politics deals with what is possible, but revolution dreams of the future. Politics preserves the existing system and uses it for its own interest, but revolution turns a corrupt system on its head in order to replace it with a just system. The Egyptian revolution took 18 days to become victorious, but it preserved its dream and did not compromise with the current situation. It won out because it demanded the departure of Mubarak and refused to accept the half measures offered by Mubarak or to negotiate with him and his cronies.

In the history of Egypt there have been moments which represented real opportunities to build a democracy – had the participants only been able to act in a democratic manner, but their political procrastination led to wasted opportunities and regrets. When the 1919 Revolution succeeded, and Britain was forced to recognise Egyptian independence, the time was ripe to draft the first post-revolutionary constitution. The Wafd Party, which led the revolution, demanded that the Constitutional Committee should be an elected one, but King Fuad I rejected this and appointed his own committee to draft a constitution because he knew that an elected Wafd committee would restrict the king's powers.

Saad Zaghloul, then leader of the Wafd Party, could have mobilised Egyptians against the committee of appointees and brought it down. He could have forced the king to accede to the demand, but for some reason Zaghloul's political will softened and he did no more than refer to the committee of appointees as the "committee of stooges." The committee produced the 1923 Constitution which had in it an article allowing the king to appoint and dismiss ministers and to dissolve parliament. The result was the Egyptian democracy was a hollow sham for thirty years with the majority party governing for less than seven. Another example took place when Gamal Abdel Nasser decided to abolish democracy.

At that time the Wafd Party still enjoyed popularity and authority throughout Egypt. The Wafd leader, Mustafa el-Nahhas, managed to mobilise Egyptians to defend democracy, but yet again he chose political compromise over revolutionary action. He withdrew to his house, and watched as Gamal Abdel Nasser set up an authoritarian system in Egypt which led Egypt into catastrophes for which we are still paying the price today, with all due respect to Gamal Abdel Nasser's love and devotion to his country. There was a third incident when political compromise lost us the opportunity to institute reform: in September 1981, Anwar Sadat ordered the arrest of approximately fifteen hundred of his political opponents. A few weeks later Anwar Sadat was assassinated and Mubarak took over the presidency. He released the detainees and had them brought to a meeting in the Qasr el-Uruba presidential palace.

This was a turning point. Most of the detainees were big names who were well known for their participation in the nationalist struggle. If they had only insisted, when they met Mubarak, on him instituting real democratic reforms, or if they had refused to be released until true democracy was instituted, Mubarak would have had to concede to them because, it can be argued, the circumstances at the time were not conducive to authoritarianism. However, the activists who had been released, with all due respect, chose political compromise over revolutionary ideal. They had a pleasant meeting with Mubarak, who apologised for their detention. They thanked him warmly and wished him success and then went back to their homes. There are numerous similar examples in our history.

There comes a crucial moment when a revolutionary stance is needed but when the actors show misplaced political compromise. That is what has lost us opportunity after opportunity. We are now passing through a similar phase.

The Muslim Brotherhood is re-shaping the state in a manner which ensures their permanence in power. They have tortured, killed and brutalised innocent people, trampling the law underfoot, and now, having taken what they want from the revolution, they are trying to find a political basis to cover up their crimes. They want to hold televised discussions and invite a token opposition in parliament. I am afraid that the leaders of the Salvation Front[1] will fall into the trap. I am speaking of the widely-respected personalities, who played a large part in the revolution, but who are now being subjected to pressure from inside and outside Egypt; I fear that they will give in to political pragmatism rather than sticking to their revolutionary stance. Agreeing to discussions with

1 National Salvation Front is an alliance of Egyptian political parties, formed to defeat Egyptian President Mohamed Morsi's 22 November 2012 constitutional declaration. *See* Glossary.

Morsi before he has been tried for torture and murder is no more than a betrayal of the revolution and the rights of the murdered demonstrators. Agreement to enter into elections for the People's Assembly under the law issued by the sham Shura Council, based on the sham constitution, just gives credence to the sham constitutional situation imposed on us by the Brotherhood.

The parties who agree to participate in the elections for the People's Assembly may win a few seats, but it means foregoing the aims of the revolution and helping the Brotherhood to cover up their crimes. What sort of elections can they be when the authority running them belongs to an illegal organisation which is not subject to the law? What sort of elections are they when the Brotherhood and the Salafists spend millions buying the votes of the poor and when we have no knowledge of the sources of their funding? I would direct one question to my friends in the Salvation Front: do we want the democratic state, for which the revolution came about and for which all those people have died, or do we want those few seats in parliament which the Brotherhood might charitably grant us? Accepting half measures means betraying Egyptians, helping the Brotherhood to abort the revolution and leaving Egypt under autocratic rule forever. The revolution will continue, God willing, until all of its goals have been achieved.

Democracy is the answer.

RH

What Do You Do With Blood?

25 February 2013

Last year, I received an invitation to a Christmas celebration at the Qasr al-Dubara church. This church played a huge role in the revolution. It set up a hospital to treat the wounded, collected donations and its officials behaved with rare courage in protecting revolutionaries from being killed and arrested. I went into the church hall and was greeted by a group of personalities connected with the revolution. My seat was behind that of Ahmed Harara and his mother. Harara is a young dentist from a well-off family who graduated from the College of Dentistry and opened a private clinic. He had a life of comfort, and like many other dentists, he could have gone to work in one of the Gulf states and earned a fortune there, but he believed in the revolution and took part in it. On the Friday of Anger,[1] a policeman shot him in the eye and he lost the sight in it.

1 The "Friday of Anger" protests began, with hundreds of thousands demonstrating in Cairo and other Egyptian cities after Friday prayers on 28 January 2011. *See* Glossary.

That sacrifice should have been enough to make Harara one of the heroes of the revolution, but even after losing one eye he continued to take part in demonstrations with the same zeal. That is, until the Mohamed Mahmoud incidents when he was hit in his good eye and lost sight in it also. Harara went to France where doctors informed him that there was almost no hope of doing anything for him. The heroic Harara has paid an enormous price for the revolution, but it remains a fierce advocate for the movement. If you want to be assured that the revolution will win, you just have to sit with Harara for a few minutes. There can be no defeat for a revolution in which a young man has sacrificed his eyes and his profession, but whom, for all that, is still optimistic about the revolution. I sat down behind Harara and his mother. His mother sat with her hand on his shoulder, explaining to him what was going on around him. She described how the hall looked, the way people were moving around and as someone came over to greet him, she whispered the man's name in his ear. It looked like something she had been used to doing for years.

She was describing the world around him with the same way she must have looked after him when he was sick as a child. She whispered with the same tenderness with which she must have cooked dinner for him when he was doing his studies. I thought how happy she must have been when he got good grades in his final school examinations, how proud she would have been when he was accepted by the College of Dentistry and how happy she would have been when she visited his clinic for the first time. And now, at the end of all that, she has gone back to the starting point, hugging him and telling him what she could see, just as if she were cradling him as a child. Harara, Malek Mustafa and many others are the real heroes who lost their eyesight so that their country might see the light of the future.

It is mothers who have paid the greatest price during this revolution. I take my hat off to the mothers of the murdered demonstrators. The sorrow of a mother over her martyred son cannot be described in words. If a friend of yours is killed, you will grieve for him, but his mother does not so much grieve as die. She dies every day when it is time for him to come home and he does not arrive. She dies every time she sees his clothing or books when she goes into his bedroom, whenever she meets his friends, whenever she makes food which he used to love. The mothers of the murdered demonstrators all have a singular characteristic which is beyond anything we understand about grief. Their heartache takes them to another world. It is as if they live in our midst but they belong to a world we cannot know. I have often heard the mother of a murdered demonstrator speak of him as if he is still alive. The mother of Mohamad al-Gindi appeared on television boasting that he could speak three languages and describing in great detail how he insists that she should share his desert with him even though she is diabetic. One time, the mother of a murdered demonstrator told me in a neutral and calm tone of voice: "Thank

God I was the one who wrapped him in a shroud and buried him with my own hands. I was the first to receive him into this world and the last one to bid him farewell."

During the Saad Zaghloul sit-in in Alexandria, a woman dressed in black came over to me and said: "I am the mother of Amira, the youngest person killed in Alexandria. Amira was 13-years-old and standing next to me on the balcony and when she saw an officer shooting at demonstrators she picked up her mobile telephone and started filming it. The officer noticed and shot her in the head. He could have just confiscated her telephone instead of killing her."

I could not find any words to say to her. All the usual words of consolation seemed meaningless when faced with a mother who had lost her daughter. The officer that killed Amira was acquitted. He was promised, and received, a 300 per cent pay rise. To this moment, no one knows the exact number of people killed in the revolution. The numbers issued by the Ministry of Health are not correct and hospitals have succumbed to pressure from the security forces and issued false documentation to exculpate the killers. And, as we saw with the case of Khaled Saeed, the coroner also dances to the government's tune. According to unofficial estimates, the number killed is approaching 3,000 in addition to the 2,000 missing (most likely killed and buried in secret locations) and the 18,000 who have been wounded.

This is the price Egypt has paid to get rid of Mubarak. Mubarak stepped down, but the killing continued. The military council carried out many massacres whose victim's number in the hundreds. Then they left and the Muslim Brotherhood took power and the killing continued. Mohamad Morsi, who presents himself as a devout Islamist president has killed a record number of Egyptians with the help of his murderous interior minister. In one month alone, almost 70 people were killed. For the first time in the history of Egypt, snipers opened fire at the funeral of dead demonstrators in Port Said, making martyrs of the mourners.

Young revolutionaries have been kidnapped, horribly tortured and then their bodies have been flung out onto the street as part of a clear plan to eliminate anyone who might play an active role in uncovering the crimes of the Brotherhood. In any country in the world, if the president kills his citizens he loses his legitimacy immediately, or is put on trial, even if he has been elected a hundred times. In Egypt, however, we have people who still consider Morsi the legitimate president as if those who have been killed are flies or cockroaches whose lives have no value. Islam to the young Muslim Brothers is personified in the supreme guide and they will support him enthusiastically if even that means killing everyone in Egypt.

The situation in Egypt is clearer now than at any previous time: we have a president who was elected and then turned into a dictator who has decided, following instructions from the supreme guide, to hang onto power forever.

He started by having a constitution drafted by illegal committee which he has put beyond any possibility of legal redress. He then appointed a loyal attorney general whom the judiciary accuse of interfering on behalf of the Brotherhood. Then he put gave legal protection to the sham Shura Council against any attempt by the judiciary to dissolve it. He turned the Shura Council into a legislative authority, in spite of it only having been elected by seven per cent of the population and got it to pass legislation to keep the Brotherhood in power. Since the start, the Brotherhood have colluded with the military council in a deal of mutual benefit in which the military allowed the Brotherhood to hold elections before the constitution has been drafted, and to ignore the way they buy the votes of the poor, in order to enable them to impose the constitution which the Supreme Guide wants. In exchange, the military council can preserve its members' privileges and huge fortunes and is protected from any accountability for all the deaths they have caused. The Brotherhood has done whatever it wanted and has achieved whatever it desired. The only thing it is lacking is an empty frame to give legitimacy to its crimes.

Mubarak was an autocrat who ruled the Egyptian state as he wished but he covered up his authoritarianism with ridiculous play-acting involving the People's Assembly, the Shura council, discussions and talks and slogans, all giving the regime the veneer of democracy while he alone wielded power. The Brotherhood is now following Mubarak's footsteps. Having imposed their constitution and laws on us, as well as its own attorney general, and having prevented the judges from doing their jobs, it will now hold elections so that it can form the majority of People's Assembly and control it. It will allow the opposition to have a few symbolic seats in parliament to complete the democratic farce. What value is there to elections held according to an invalid law passed by the sham Shura Council according to a sham constitution produced by a sham Constitutional Committee? What legitimacy is there to elections held in the shadow of a government controlled by an illegal association with funding from who knows where and under the supervision of a president responsible for torturing and killing his own citizens. How will anyone who stands alongside the Brotherhood feel able to demand the annulation of the sham constitution under whose aegis they have achieved their seat in parliament? Some people will of course say that they are participating in the elections in order not to leave the field clear for the Brotherhood, to uncover vote rigging or to express the voice of the revolution in parliament. These are all hollow excuses which reflect shallow thinking or even tasteless political greed which is inconsistent with the moment which Egypt is currently passing through. The truth is staring us in the face: anyone who takes part in these elections is betraying the revolution, disregarding the rights of those killed, enabling the Brotherhood to cover up their crimes, and according legitimacy to a president who has killed his own citizens, and rejigged the law to the benefit of his own party. The constitution must be annulled and the illegitimate attorney general fired. There must be early presidential elections and a fair trial given to those officials accused of murdering demonstrators, first and foremost being Morsi himself and Mohamed Ibrahim, the murderous minister of the interior. These are the clear demands of the revolution for which millions of people all over Egypt have mobilised and these demands are clearly not served by elections run by a murderous and illegitimate regime.

The revolution will not achieve its aims by cutting deals with murderers. The correct way is what the people of Port Said are doing at the moment. A general strike leading to peaceful civil disobedience will make it impossible for the Brotherhood to govern. Then the Brotherhood will be compelled, in spite of themselves, to accede to the demands of the people. The Brotherhood control gangs of killers who are loyal to them or to the police, and they can always murder their opponents, but they will never be able to cope with civil disobedience.

They will not be able to arrest millions of Egyptians who decide to stay away from work. The mere thought of civil disobedience strikes terror into the hearts of the Brotherhood. In just two days, 40 people have been killed in Port Said, but despite that, Morsi went out to thank those responsible and to threaten the Egyptian people with more killing. However, on the first day of the civil disobedience, he rushed to re-establish the free zone in Port Said in a sorry attempt to bribe the locals.Morsi imagines that the people of Port Said will just forget about the blood of their sons in exchange for money from the free zone.

Civil disobedience is a legal right of Egyptians, protected by the law and the international accords signed by Egyptian governments. We must boycott these elections because they are drenched in the blood of martyrs who have sacrificed their lives so that we can live in a modern democratic state which respects the humanity of its citizens and protects their rights. Blood will be on the hands of anyone who participates in these sham elections. Let us boycott the elections and join in the civil disobedience so that Egypt will be freed from the grip of murderers. The revolution will continue, God willing, until all of its goals have been achieved.

Democracy is the answer.

RH

An Angry Discussion in Mokattam

4 March 2013

The office of an important man in Mokattam occupies the second floor of a luxury block which reportedly cost 40 million pounds to build. This man usually goes to his office straight after performing his dawn prayers. Members of his association receive him with love and enthusiasm, gathering around him to kiss his hand, while he greets them, smiling, and bestows paternal affection upon them. He always has a schedule full of meetings and appointments, not to mention the reports which he receives from everywhere in Egypt. Today, as he walked into his office, he asked for a large glass of salep in milk with sprinkles, a beverage he likes because it gives him energy for the rest of the day. He immersed himself in the lengthy reports written by his officials in the various sectors. He had an hour-long meeting with a foreign ambassador and then at around eleven o'clock, the voice of his office manager came over the intercom: "The brigadier has arrived."

A stocky man in his sixties came in. His serious mood was somehow emphasised by his harsh features. The important man shook his hand warmly and then sat down opposite him and the two had the following conversation:

Important man: I have invited you because I am concerned. There are still disturbances taking place in Port Said, Mansoura and many other cities."

Official: "It will take a little time, but we will restore order soon, please God."

Important man: "I thank you for all of your efforts. May God reward you and your men manifold. But I need more from you."

Official: "We are only doing our duty. We are at your service, sir, and you will see the results soon."

Important man: "Bear in mind we don't have much time. The country has to be calm before the elections."

Official: "It has been good of you, sir, to give us so much trust."

Important man: "Had I not been sure of your capabilities, I wouldn't have chosen you for the job. I want to hear the outline of your plan and then I'll be able to feel more relaxed."

Official: "I have served for 40 years. I have had positions in most of the governorates in Egypt and I have a large amount of experience with the people. Our people are good and obedient, but most importantly, they yearn for stability. Our people are cowardly by nature and they hate problems. Out of pure fear, most Egyptians would run a mile before confronting authority. What happened during the January revolution was exceptional. Wham! A few kids on Facebook and Twitter started writing some offensive comments and the security forces dealt with them in a most stupid manner. God forgive me if I display vanity in saying that had I been an official when the revolution was going on, I would have known how to finish it off in two short days. After Mubarak stepped down, most Egyptians thought they were revolutionaries who could change anything they did not like by having a demonstration about it. They need to wise up now. They have to be made to go back to living in fear. They have to be their old selves again. They all need to be made aware that there is a swingeing price to pay for opposing authority. Anyone going out to take part in a demonstration has to learn that they might be killed, arrested, or beaten to within an inch of their life. Any young woman who demonstrates has to know that she might be pushed around or kicked along the street, she might get her clothes ripped off, and our guys might sexually abuse or even rape her."

Important man: "Fine."

Official: "We know the names of the ring-leaders. Our plan is to track them down one by one. We have already put this into operation, as you have seen, sir. One bullet in the brain in the thick of a demonstration and we're shot of them."

Important man: "God grant you success."

Official: "As for the hooligans in the second category, we take them into custody and get heavy with them. We do things to them to make them compliant again and unable to further oppose authority."

Important man: "Make sure there are no cock-ups."

Official: "We're professionals. None of the places where we hold people can be connected to us. Even the forces that arrest the hooligan elements are in plain cloths, and they transport them away in microbuses. There is no evidence of state responsibility. The hospitals collaborate with us, and the coroner writes whatever we ask them to in their reports."

Important man: "There isn't much time left. The country has to calm down before the elections. If this hooliganism carries on it will embarrass us in front of our friends abroad. You know that the US administration trusts us. The secretary of state was here with me two days ago and told me clearly that the Americans will agree to any steps we take against the hooligans, provided that we restore order quickly."

Official: "I hope you will take my opinion in the manner in which it is intended. The Americans are well-known for deceit. I would ask you, sir, not to trust them or to rely on them. The Americans supported Mubarak when they needed him and when things got too hot, they dropped him and turned against him."

Important man: "Don't worry. This time the Americans will support us properly. Your men were out killing demonstrators while the secretary of state was in Cairo, and he did not utter a word of protest. How much more support than that do you want?"

Official: "They did the same in Mubarak's time."

Important man: "Our organisation is not Mubarak. We have thick skins and we know how to deal with America."

Official: "Please explain, sir."

Important man: "Imagine you are a doctor working in a hospital. It is normal that you will try to stay on the right side of the hospital director. What if you discover that the director fell in love with his secretary and married her in secret? Thus, if you keep the secretary happy she will put in a good word for you with the boss. True or not? That's exactly our situation with regard to America. America is the director and Israel is the secretary. We have come to an understanding with Israel. They are reassured about us and have confirmed that it is in their interest for us to stay in power. It follows that the Americans can never turn against us. At the same time, however, if you take too much time getting the country back under control that will make us all look bad."

Official: "I am committed to handing you a calm country before the elections, sir."

Important man: "God bless you."

Official: "I have a request sir."

(The official stands up and passes some documents across the desk.)

"We need new weapons. I have written down the required types, sir, and I hope that we will be able to receive them as soon as possible."

(The important man picks up the documents and starts poring over them.)

Important man: "Didn't we send you new gas canisters a week ago?"

Official: "Yes, sir. But the gas we requested is not tear gas. We requested something much stronger – the gas with the nerve agent in it. Within moments it makes a demonstrator lose consciousness, go into convulsions, and sometimes causes death."

Important man: "Alright then. We'll get you the gas if it does the job. Do you also want more sniper rifles?"

Official: "Using sniper rifles against demonstrators is most efficient. We tried it in Port Said and the results were impressive. The snipers take up their positions and pick off the demonstrators without leaving any evidence behind them."

Important man (smiling): "Sniper rifles are really expensive, but never mind. Please God we'll find the money for them."

Official: "I have a second request, sir. With regards to our officers. They want to grow their beards, according to the custom of the Prophet. I have no objection to that, naturally. You know, sir, that I am an observant man. I have made the pilgrimage twice not to mention the numerous minor-pilgrimages God has permitted me to make. I would never stand in the way of a religious man. The issue is that beards are against police regulations. I would ask you to meet the bearded officers, sir, and try to convince them that they put off the issue until we have managed to control the country again."

(The important man said nothing for a few moments and his face became ashen.)

Important man: "If I did not know that you were a man who feared God, I would deem your faith suspect. How can you come to me and ask me to go against a confirmed custom of the Prophet, may He be blessed?"

Official (meekly): "I am just asking you to tell the officers to wait a little so as not to rock the boat."

Important man: "Go and read some Islamic jurisprudence before you speak. Do you know what it would mean if I gave an order forbidding something allowed by the Sharia? By God, I'd rather have my hand cut off or die before trying to suppress a custom of the Prophet, may He be blessed. Having a beard is a religious duty in all four legal schools. The officers with beards are doing their best to follow their religious duty, and they should be role models for their colleagues. I hope to see all officers growing a beard, you first and foremost. Have you done your ablutions?"

Official: "Yes, sir."

Important man: "Then let's go and do the noon prayers and remember, you have promised to hand me a demonstration-free country before the elections. I have made myself clear. I don't want those saboteurs in the country. Those demonstrators have put themselves outside the law and therefore their death is permitted according to religious law. Under Islamic law they can be subjected to the punishments for making war on God, which means that their hands and legs can be cut off. Anything you do to them will definitely be less than Islamic law dictates for them. Even if you kill them, you'll be carrying out Islamic law. I want you to send a clear message to all your officers. I have given them full authority to do what they want to the demonstrators. Don't even think of hesitating. Don't let your hands tremble on the trigger. I have given you my word of honour: no single officer will be tried even if he kills a thousand demonstrators. If the price for stability means killing up to a hundred thousand demonstrators, do it. You have my consent. All those saboteurs have to be thrown in prison or killed so that the people can live in peace."

The official nodded and then scurried out behind the important man who walked down the stairs rather than waste time waiting for the lift. The noon call to prayer sounded and the important man rushed to the mosque where he was greeted warmly by men from his association who kissed his hands, with more than one of them kneeling down to help him take his shoes off and put them on the shoe rack for him. Within minutes the important man was standing in front of the *mihrab* and leading the prayers. He closed his eyes and whispered verses from the Qur'an with total submissiveness.

Democracy is the answer.

RH

When Will Morsi Go?

11 March 2013

The following incident was witnessed by an acquaintance of mine, a young man who is prepared to testify to it.

Saturday 9 March. Four o'clock in the afternoon. The young man found himself in front of Shepherd's Hotel on the Nile Corniche, where demonstrators had gathered on one side of the street. Opposite stood a group of officers and soldiers of the central security force, flanked by a large group of young men who were throwing stones and gas canisters at the demonstrators. It was clear that the young men were being given orders to provoke the demonstrators. The situation escalated, but the young man managed to convince an officer that he was simply a passer-by and had not taken part in the demonstration. He quickly sped away from scene of the disturbance, but was approached by two men who asked him: "How do we get to Bab el-Louq?"

The young man gave them directions and, noticing that they were not speaking with an Egyptian accent, he asked them what country they came from. One of the men smiled and said: "We're your brothers from Gaza."

The young man bade them welcome and pointed them in the direction of Bab el-Louq.

This incident has two implications: firstly, the police forces use plain clothed mercenaries, who, upon receipt of orders, will attack demonstrators and set buildings on fire, framing it as the work of the demonstrators, as the police look the other way. The more important question is what are our brethren from Gaza doing in the middle of a clash between demonstrators and the police? I am not accusing anyone of wrongdoing and I always welcome our relatives from Gaza, but I have to wonder: is it normal for a non-Egyptian to put themselves at risk by standing in an area where clashes are taking place, in the midst of rubber bullets and live gunfire? Why would they endanger their lives for a cause that is not their own? Why were the two men from Gaza going to Bab el-Louq where, at that time, everything was closed off because of the violent demonstrations which had led to the burning of a number of shops and restaurants? Is it true that the Brotherhood have called upon Hamas elements for help in carrying out their plans in Egypt?

There is no point formally investigating an incident like this because the leanings of the attorney general are well-known. Events in Egypt have taken a violent turn under Morsi and the Brotherhood. The minister of the interior, Mohamed Ibrahim,[1] has carried out a number of fatal and violent attacks on the Egyptian people in attempt to prove his credentials to the Brotherhood. These attacks, in Port Said and elsewhere, have left more than 80 people dead in a single month, as well as the detention of hundreds of people who have been tortured in the prisons of the central security service. All these crimes have been documented on video and in scores of reports, both inside and outside Egypt. The supreme guide of the Brotherhood wanted to control the Egyptian state and impose his will on it by resorting to policies even more oppressive than those used by Mubarak. However, the revolution has changed the way all Egyptians think, including the police officers themselves. Some police officers obediently followed the orders given by the minister of the interior to kill and brutalise people, to blind them with rubber bullets and to subject detainees to electrocution and rape. However, a large number of police officers have refused to be used by the Brotherhood as a tool to oppress the Egyptian people and they have declared a strike.

They have demanded the resignation of the minister of the interior because of his links with the Brotherhood and his refusal to acknowledge the crimes he has committed. The minister of the interior has also threatened Egyptians saying that if they continue demonstrating the police will withdraw and leave them to deal with the consequences. The whole world over, if an official fails in their duties, they hand in their resignation and leave the job for someone more capable. In Egypt, the minister of the interior, having committed all these crimes, threatens the people with the withdrawal of the police, giving the people the choice between submitting to the will of the supreme guide of the Muslim Brotherhood or chaos. It does not stop there; the Ministry of the Interior has put forward a proposal to the Ministry of Justice which suggests giving juridicial authority to private security groups. Simply put, this means empowering the Brotherhood to establish scores of private security companies with firearm licenses and authorising them to arrest Brotherhood opponents and abuse them legally. At the same time, the Islamist association, which has a long history of terror and bloodletting, announced that it was forming militias to preserve law and order.

Meanwhile, Sheikh Hazem Abu Ismail suddenly appeared and announced that his supporters would go out onto the street and do everything to protect Brotherhood rule. Even odder than this, the attorney general, who was

1 Mohamed Ibrahim Moustafa succeeded Ahmed Gamal El Din to take a place in the Qandil Cabinet in January 2013.

appointed by Morsi, came out to announce that every citizen has the right to arrest saboteurs. So it is my right, and the right of any citizen, to arrest any other citizen they believe to be a saboteur. Who are the saboteurs and what are the criteria that define sabotage? What sort of legal system is it that grants individuals state authority to arrest other people? What if people use the right granted to them by the attorney general to eliminate their personal enemies? The words of the attorney general are a clear declaration to the militias of the Muslim Brotherhood to take over from the state police. It is a particularly dangerous manoevre that can only lead to chaos and civil war because, if Brotherhood militias go out onto the street, then the opponents of the Brotherhood will also have the right to form armed militias. The Brotherhood are interested in imposing their rule on the Egyptian people even if it results in a gruesome civil war, for which our children and grandchildren will pay the price.

The Brotherhood's lust for power has blinded them completely. They believe that the millions of people who oppose their rule are remnants of the former regime, agents of Zionism or anti-Islam agitators motivated by their hatred of religious law. At the same time, the Brotherhood speak fondly of their relationship with Israel and also make use of, and strike deals with, the remnants of the former regime who pillaged Egypt. It has become clear that the Brotherhood have nothing to do with Islam.

The supreme judicial authority in Egypt has rejected the Islamic bonds scheme put forward by the Brotherhood, removing the word "Islamic", and insisted on putting the scheme into action even though it contravenes religious law. Are the Brotherhood's crimes consistent with the principles of Islam? Does Islam stipulate death, torture, lying and vote-rigging? Islam does not present a definitive model of rule, but general humanitarian principles: freedom, equality and justice which are themselves the principles of democracy, whereas experiments in political Islam in Iran, Afghanistan, Somalia and Sudan have produced fascist autocratic regimes which allow injustice, oppression and even murder in the name of religion.

Morsi was given a golden opportunity to unite the whole nation around him and to realise the aims of the revolution. He could have been a shining example of a rightly-guided and just Islamist president, but he squandered the opportunity by placing the office under the control of the supreme guide. Egyptians accepted and celebrated Brotherhood rule by voting them into office. But those who praised Morsi's victory were soon surprised to find that he is incapable of keeping to his word, saying one thing then doing the exact opposite. He is an eccentric president, detached from reality, incapable of taking a decision unless it is handed down by the supreme guide. He made the constitution declaration in order to destroy the democratic system, placed himself above the law, gave political immunity to the sham Constitutional

Committee and the useless Shura Council, and imposed a Brotherhood constitution on Egyptians.

It is Morsi who has ruined his relationship with the Egyptian people and not vice versa. The millions who went out onto the street to celebrate Morsi are the ones who went out to demonstrate, a few weeks later, calling for an end to government by the supreme guide. Under Morsi's orders, the police have killed the very citizens that voted for him to become president. It is Morsi who has stymied the law, broken his oath to respect the constitution, killed scores of innocent people and lost every shred of legitimacy. He must resign and call for early elections.

However the United States will continue to support Mohamed Morsi as president even if he kills every last Egyptian. The US Secretary of State visited Egypt especially to help Morsi stay in power despite all his crimes. The US has the impudence to state that it supports Morsi because he is an elected president, while at the same time they have treated the Hamas movement in Gaza with hostility since the very first day. The US also supported Hosni Mubarak and one of its closest allies is the authoritarian Saudi regime which belongs politically to the Middle Ages. The US supports Morsi because it is in their interest, and the interest of Israel, to do so. If Israel felt threatened by the Brotherhood, it would turn against them and then, and only then, condemn the crimes it has been committing daily against the Egyptian people. The Brotherhood has not learnt the lesson of Mubarak's fall. They have not learnt that the US only plays with the winner and that it will continue supporting a dictator until he falls, only to then wash its hands of him. The Brotherhood has not learnt that a ruler shored up by external support cannot do without the support of his own people. It is using old, discredited tools to deal with the current situation. Using terror against Egyptians is pointless. Neither murder nor torture can make Egyptians stop demanding equality, justice and freedom, and the revolutionaries cannot be paid off with a few paltry seats in parliament.

The police can no longer commit crimes against the Egyptian people like they used to under Mubarak. Those methods lost their validity when Mubarak fell. The big question now is no longer what Morsi decrees or does, but when will he leave power. Who can we deal with a president who kills his own citizens?

Mubarak is in custody, charged with killing demonstrators, which is the same crime which Morsi has committed. Morsi must step down and be put on trial, just as Mubarak stepped down and was tried. The general strike must include all sectors of society and become total civil disobedience. This is the only way to get the Brotherhood to submit to the will of the people and to accede to the demands of the revolution, which are to the annulment of the constitution, early presidential elections, the dismissal of the attorney general, the prosecution of those who have killed demonstrators, first and foremost amongst them being Mohamed Morsi and Mohamed Ibrahim, the minister of the interior. The revolution will continue until its aims have been realised. The Muslim Brotherhood will fall and will pay the price of its crimes – sooner than they think.

Democracy is the answer.

RH

Who Respects Women?

18 March 2013

Do you have a daughter of marriageable age? What if she presented to you a well-bred, well-off, well-educated and well-mannered young man? Even though he is a wonderful candidate for her hand, the young man has been married before. If it is plain to you that he has nothing to hide, you agree to his marrying your daughter and you justify your agreement by saying: "His first marriage failed, but he was not to blame." What if the situation was reversed? If your previously unmarried son decided to marry a divorced woman, you would most probably refuse to grant them permission before knowing the reasons for her divorce. You would not be able to bear the thought of your son wedding a previously married woman, because you would rather see your son marry a virgin untouched by male hand. What is the reason for this contradictory behaviour you evince towards your son and daughter even though the situation is the same? The reason is that, in your mind, marriage implies using a woman's body. A man is not harmed by getting married and divorced, but a divorced woman is a second-hand woman, who has been deflowered by a man who used her body and then left her to be used by another man. You do not want your son to marry a second-hand woman. The thought that another man kissed your son's bride before he did, caressed her body and had sex with her, would make you uneasy. You would like your son to marry a virgin so that he will be the first man to take pleasure from her body. In fact, you approach your son's marriage as you would approach buying a car. If he had the money to buy a new car, why would he buy a second-hand model?

The conception of a woman as a body to be used is deep rooted in Egyptian society. However much we speak of the rights of women, however educated we may be, most Egyptian men are incapable of seeing a woman as separate from her body, as something more than the sum of her femininity.

The same goes for the men who run after women, as well as for the men who try to cocoon them. Whether we try to catch a glance of her naked body or oblige her to wear modest dress, we still treat women as nothing more than an object. In this, the womaniser and the religious man are one and the same. They are both unable to see the human side of a woman. If any man tries to dispute this fact, he should ask himself: how many times has he seen a woman and not thought of her body, even if just for a moment? How many times has he seen a woman and managed to be interested in her education or professional capabilities without casting a furtive glance at her breasts or posterior? The reduction of a woman to no more than her body has nothing to do with what she is wearing, but results from a depraved attitude towards women which strips women of their individuality and sees them just as tools for men's pleasure. Covering up a woman's body does not help men to be more virtuous; it is we men who have to stop objectifying women and reducing them to the sum of their body parts.

In the cosmopolitan, tolerant Egypt that existed until the 1970s, Egyptian women wore modern, short skirts and could wear swimsuits to the beach. In spite of that, cases of sexual harassment were rare. In Egypt now, where people make a great show of religiosity, most women wear the hijab and the niqab but sexual harassment has reached greater proportions and woman are subjected to it on a daily basis. The unfortunate side to this is that society lays the blame on the victim, considering a woman responsible for any harassment because she is wearing provocative clothing. But this is so far from the truth. The incidence of sexual harassment in closed societies where women have to cover their bodies is much greater than in societies where women wear what they want. In a study carried out under the supervision of Reuters, the numbers of professional women who experience sexual harassment in 24 countries were compared. Saudi Arabia came third with 24 per cent, a number much higher than any Western country. Spain showed 6 per cent, Germany 5 per cent and Britain 4 per cent.

That is to say that the average percentage of women who are subjected to sexual harassment in a closed countrym, which makes women cover their body completely, is seven times greater than in a developed country. These statistics prove that sexual harassment has nothing to do with what a woman wears, but with the way men view women. At this point we need to ask ourselves whether Islam offers a modern or reactionary attitude towards women. Has Egyptian's attitude towards women not always been one of objectification? Islam is truly a great religion, but like all religions it can be interpreted in various ways. A correct reading of Islam affords rights and individuality to women, but an erroneous and retrograde interpretation of Islam restricts women to their physical role alone.

Egypt has seen both interpretations. A religious reformist movement appeared in Egypt in the nineteenth century which reached its apogee in the person of Mohamad Abduh, who offered a modern reading of Islam and freed the Egyptian mind from superstition, setting Egyptian society free to innovate in all fields. Egyptian women won rights, which women in most Arab countries still do not have today. Egyptian women discarded the Turkish-style veil and became pioneers in the field of education and in the workplace. In 1933, Egyptians celebrated the graduation of the first Egyptian woman pilot, Lotfia El Nadi, as a national triumph. This modern, progressive attitude towards women lasted until the end of the seventies, when the Wahhabism came to Egypt.

After the 1973 war, the price of oil rose steeply, giving the Gulf states unprecedented economic power. As most of the ruling families in the Gulf are allied with the Wahhabi religious establishment, the worldwide spread of Wahhabism provides them with political support, which is why the Gulf rulers spend millions of dollars in order to spread it far and wide. Moreover, millions of Egyptians went to work in the Gulf, only to return steeped in Wahabbi ideology.

Just as an enlightened reading of Islam led to the liberation of Egyptian women, the spread of Wahhabi thought encouraged a reactionary attitude towards women. The Wahhabis deem women intellectually inferior, religiously deficient and incapable of controlling their own desires. Women are above all objects of temptation who must be completely veiled from view. Some Wahhabi clerics have even called upon women with beautiful eyes to draw their niqab over one of their eyes to reduce their attractiveness.

Some Wahhabi clerics allow marriage with a girl as young as ten provided that she is physically capable of consummating the union. Some believe that a husband is only obligated to care for a wife as long as he can enjoy her. If she becomes ill, then he is not obligated to pay for her treatment. We thus have two mutually contradictory views of Islam – a modern and humane outlook – versus a back-ward looking Wahhabi interpretation of religion. The modern version considers women to be human first, and female second; an attitude which accords them all their rights and encourages women to study and work. The Wahhabi version reduces a woman to her biological function as an object to be used for enjoyment and as a childbearer.

Wahhabism spread from the Gulf to the Egyptian people, and then to the governing power. Everyone who has taken power in Egypt, before and after the revolution, has shared this reactionary attitude towards women. The Mubarak regime, the brigadiers of the military council and the leadership of the Muslim Brotherhood may well differ on many things, but they have all shared the same condescending and reductive attitude towards women. They are opposed to women in the workplace and are deeply troubled by women's participation in anti-regime demonstrations.

They have all resorted to the politics of sexual oppression to prevent women from taking part in the revolution; they have tried to intimidate and humiliate the women of Egypt through beatings and harassment. They have a narrow-minded view of the role of women, believing that they should stay at home and look after the children. The systematic sexual harassment of female demonstrators is the same today as it was under Mubarak. The attacks correspond in substance to the crimes of the military council, which had women kicked along the ground, stripped naked and subjected to virginity tests. Religious fascism is like military fascism in its enmity towards women and its fear of the concept of their liberation.

A few days ago the United Nations published a report on the use of violence against women. The Brotherhood pre-empted the report by issuing a statement rejecting it before it was published, accusing the report of things it did not contain. The Brotherhood cannot renounce violence against women because they simply do not see women as having full legal rights. How can they renounce violence when they permit child marriage and disregard the psychological and physiological damage it could cause to a child? They do not accept that there can be rape within marriage because it is a man's right to enjoy his wife's body whenever and however he wants.

The revolution liberated the thinking of Egyptians and reawakened the modern attitude towards women. Egyptian women have played a great and fundamental role in the revolution. Had it not been for the women, the revolution would not have lasted a single day. The crux of the struggle going on in Egypt at the moment is between reactionary thought, which keeps people down and belittles their dignity in order to preserve autocratic rule, and the freedom-inclined philosophy presented to us by the revolution which deems that we are deserving of our humanity. In my opinion one of the most important aims of the revolution is the granting of freedom and rights to women.

The crux of the struggle is between the future and the past, between the dream of a democratic society in which women are masters of their own fate, and the reactionary view of women which considers them legitimate objects for men's sexual pleasure. Egypt will not be liberated from authoritarianism until women are freed of all shackles of oppression. Only when we learn how to respect women will we be capable of realising the aims of the revolution so that Egypt can embark on the future it deserves.

Democracy is the answer.

RH

How Did the Faithful Muslim Become a Torturer?

25 March 2013

During the clashes that erupted last Friday between demonstrators and the Muslim Brotherhood in the Mokattam district of Cairo,[1] the Brotherhood arrested left-wing activist Kamal Khalil and held him captive in a mosque. There, he saw for himself a number of demonstrators who had been stripped of their clothes and savagely flogged until most of them lost consciousness. The Brothers were using a large whip to beat their victims. Kamal questioned the owner of the whip who turned to him with pride and said: "I've been soaking this whip in oil for a long time. One hit from this takes off the skin."

Kamal Khalil was lucky. amongst the Brotherhood members he recognised one of his neighbours, who intervened to stop his torture. Afterwards, he published his account of the Brotherhood's slaughterhouse on the *Al-Bedaiah* news site. Soon after, a flurry of witness accounts appeared in the press confirming that they had been brutally tortured. As for one of the demonstrators, Amir Ayad, the Brotherhood found out that he was a Copt so they beat him twice as hard until he almost died, all the while calling him a "Christian dog".

The Brotherhood committed the same savage crimes in Mokattam as they did previously outside the Federal Palace and at the bases of the Central Security Forces. As I was reading the testimonies from the victims of the Brotherhood, I recalled the Muslim Brotherhood member boasting about his oiled whip and his associates who flogged their victims so mercilessly until they lost consciousness. These are all faithful Muslims, observing their prayers and fasts, and striving to avoid doing anything that is prohibited in Islam. How then did they turn into torturers?

Let us remember that committing atrocities in the name of religion is a universal phenomenon that has occurred in all religions. For example, the Catholic Church – which has given the world great values of love and tolerance – also launched the Crusades and established the Inquisition and killed hundreds and thousands of Jews and Muslims. Any religion that we understand in the correct way makes us better human beings, but it is also possible to interpret it an extremist fashion that leads to atrocities being committed. The question is: how did the faithful Muslim become a torturer? I believe that no true believer would be able to commit such crimes. The

1 Intense clashes took place between hundreds of Muslim Brotherhood supporters and opponents near the group's Cairo headquarters after Muslim Brotherhood members and guards reportedly attacked a group of anti-Brotherhood demonstrators and graffiti artists. Meanwhile, buses transporting Brotherhood supporters to Mokattam were torched by demonstrators.

extremist is the one who can turn into a torturer, and the process of his transformation is as follows:

First: Monopolising the truth. Religion is not a point of view that can be debated or changed. People often use their intellect to support their faith, but rarely discover their faith by using their intellect. Furthermore, one's religion is an exclusivist belief. Despite this, history has proven that those who understand their religion correctly show tolerance towards those who believe in other religions. However, the extremist always believes that they alone have a monopoly over the correct understanding of religion. As for the others, in their view they are all impure infidels or immoral degenerates, living in sin. The extremist believes that they are at the centre of the world, and all those who differ from them occupy the abandoned corners. This certainty with which they monopolise truth and denigrate all others does not originate from Islam, which in its essence teaches tolerance of all humankind. What is more, the presumptuousness of the extremists ignores the fact that Muslims only constitute about one fifth of the world's inhabitants. This means, in effect, that the extremist despises four fifths of humankind.

Second: Practicing religion to distinguish oneself from others. The extremist has not had a profound religious experience. For them, religion is not a spiritual relationship with our God Almighty but a means to distinguish themselves from others. The extremist enjoys exhibiting their religiosity because it makes them feel superior to others who are less committed to religion than they are. Usually, the extremist suffers from an inferiority complex that they are able to silence by surpassing others in religious practice. Their religiosity does not afford them any tranquillity or peace. Instead, they use it to get the better of others and to control them. Perhaps the extremist feels that others are more educated than they are, or have been luckier in life, but they compensate for that by lording over them with their religiosity. What is more, the extremist is not satisfied with just distinguishing themselves above others. This is usually accompanied by contempt for those who are different, allowing the extremist to take more pleasure in their religious superiority.

Third: Restoring the glory of religion through holy war. It is beyond doubt that the extremist lives in an imaginary, hypothetical world and they are comfortable in the delusional notion that they are a brave soldier fighting to exalt God's word. They believe that there is a big, nasty, multilateral war being waged against Islam and it is their duty to fight the enemies of religion with ferocity for the sake of exalting God's word. This extremist who clings to this imaginary world is exactly like the character created by famous Spanish novelist Cervantes, Don Quixote. They want to be a knight long after the age of chivalry is over and end up doing battle with windmills.

The leaders of political Islam have succeeded in creating a delusional concept of the Islamic Caliphate. Hundreds of thousands of followers of political

Islam – who have learnt an erroneous version of history from their sheikhs – believe that Muslims ruled the world when they followed the commands of their religion, but when they abandoned religion they were weakened and were then occupied by the West. They await the return of a new caliphate whose leaders will rule over all the Islamic countries. Of course, there is nothing preventing Islamic countries – and indeed all human kind – from cooperating with each other. However, a restoration of the justly governed Islamic Caliphate is a great delusion for the simple reason that there was no such thing in the first place.

It is not difficult to see that what these leaders of political Islam call the Islamic Caliphate was neither a caliphate, nor was it Islamic. Over the many centuries of states founded by Muslims, there were only 31 years of just and rightly-guided rule: 29 years during the period of the four rightly-guided caliphs and two years under the rule of Umar ibn Abd al-Aziz. As for the Umayyad and Abbasid states, like all empires they committed horrific crimes and killed thousands of innocent people to keep the sultan on the throne. As for the Ottoman caliphate, it was nothing but a horrible occupation of our country. Anyone who disputes this fact should read the works of the Egyptian historian Mohammed Bin Ayas al-Hanafi al-Qahiri who describes the horrors Egyptians endured at the hands of the Ottoman troops (who were Muslims). In fact, the Ottoman Caliph – who is so revered by the followers of political Islam – was one of the reasons behind the colonial occupation of Egypt. On 9 September 1882, he made the decision to publicly declare the insubordination of Colonel Ahmed Urabi.[1] This led many to desert Urabi's resistance army which resulted in the defeat of the Egyptian army and the British occupation of Egypt.

Fourth: Dehumanising their opponents. When Kamal Khalil condemned flogging the demonstrators so brutally inside the house of God, the Brotherhood tried to convince him that their victims were not rebels but criminal thugs. They were supposedly drug addicts who were so intoxicated that they could not feel the torture they subjected them to. This was an attempt by the Brotherhood to vilify their victims in order to vindicate them of wrongdoing. The Brotherhood immediately attacks anyone who objects or brings attention to their crimes. In their opinion, all their opponents are either the remnants of the Mubarak regime, agents of global Zionism or else secret Freemasons, or in the best case scenario, simply immoral and promiscuous people whose basic aim in life is to spread immorality in society and legalise gay marriage.

The most senior leading figures of the Brotherhood repeat this hogwash without feeling the slightest embarrassment or asking themselves just once: what has made the millions of Egyptians who celebrated when Morsi won

1 For a few months previously, Urabi – the prime minister of Egypt – had been actively supporting the protests against the governor (the Khedive), who requested the assistance of the Ottoman Sultan, still technically the ruler of Egypt.

the elections now demand that he stand down? The mind of the extremist is completely unable to see reality. Likewise, the leadership of the Brotherhood could not have convinced their young recruits to flog people with whips if they had recognised the slightest virtue in their victims. This is how the Brotherhood can commit the crimes they do, enthusiastically shouting, "God is great" to preserve their hypothetical world and stave off any remorse. They are working tirelessly to convince themselves that they are not committing crimes, but are in fact fighting a sacred, religious war.

Fifth: Denying anything that threatens their hypothetical world. During the massacre at the Council of Ministers in which army troops killed dozens of demonstrators, one of the female protesters was stripped of her clothes and – in front of the cameras – a group of soldiers stomped on her naked body with their boots. But the Brotherhood, which at that time was allied to the military council, made fun of this woman and doubted her morals. In Morsi's presidency, the Egyptian police returned to their crimes, killing 80 demonstrators and torturing many more. These incidents were recorded and broadcat around the world, but the Brotherhood denied their involvement or made excuses for all of these crimes.

It is typical behaviour of all extremists to deny everything that threatens their hypothetical world, even when it is clearly the truth. The extremist who bases their whole life on a delusional world in which they see themselves as a soldier on the path of God, will never allow themselves to be persuaded that it is any other way. You will be amazed to see how this person, who boasts of their religiosity, turns nasty and insults you with the vilest of curses (as happens on Facebook) because you place doubt on things that they consider to be universal truths. The fact of the matter is, they have built a delusional world around them and they will never allow anybody to bring them back to reality. To do so would mean the collapse of the principles upon which they have built their life.

After these five steps, the faithful Muslim has turned into an extremist and is prepared to commit any crime asked of them. They will hit women and drag them around the streets, they will flog any opponents with whips and shock them with electricity. They may have turned into a torturer, but they are still convinced that they are undertaking a sacred duty. They alone hold the true faith and have been tasked by God to restore the glory of religion. They believe that their opponents are not deserving of respect and dignity. They are either foreign agents or enemies of Islam who must be swept from their path, so that the banner of Islam can be raised across the whole world.

The crimes committed by the Muslim Brotherhood are increasing by the day. Despite their brutality, at least the Brotherhood has been exposed for what they are. Egyptians have discovered that the Brotherhood have no relation to religion and have come to know their lies and treachery, and their betrayal of the revolution. The Brotherhood is another manifestation of the Mubarak regime. We have exchanged the Mubarak regime for another repressive system, and this time it deals in religion; we have exchanged military fascism with religious fascism.

Soon the Muslim Brotherhood will fall, and they will be judged for all these crimes. The revolution will continue, God willing, until it fulfils its aims.

Democracy is the answer.

PN

Having a Divine Mandate from God

1 May 2013

In the year 1492, the city of Grenada – the last bastion of Islam in Spain – fell when the last of its Arab rulers, King Boabdil, was defeated by the army of the Catholic king and queen, Ferdinand and Isabella. Although the king and queen signed an agreement in which they pledged to respect the beliefs of the country's Muslims and Jews, they reneged on it, and instead, they took the decision to expel the Jews from Spain – King Juan Carlos I would make an official apology five centuries later. As for the Muslims, they were given a choice: either convert to Christianity, or die. Thousands of Muslims who refused to become Christians were beheaded – men, women and children. Fearing for their lives, however, many Muslims did convert to Christianity. In order to humiliate those who did, the Spanish adopted a pejorative term for referring to these new converts: *los Moriscos* (the Moors).

However, forcing the Muslims to convert to Christianity was only the beginning of their ordeal. Those in power then imposed increasingly severe measures to restrict, oppress and impoverish them, and thereby, to obliterate Islamic culture and customs. Because of this, the converts rose in rebellion on several occasions and it was at this time that the authorities realised that many of the converts were continuing to practise Islam secretly. This presented a problem of some complexity, because although these converts were legally recognised as Catholic Christians, in reality, they were merely concealing their true belief in Islam. The authorities feared that such converts would teach their children the principles of Islam, which would result in a new generation of Muslims that the authorities did not want. The Catholic Church also had serious doubts about the validity of the converts' beliefs. Would Christ accept their faith or would they remain outside the fold of His flock?

It was around this time that a strange and mysterious figure appeared who would play a key role in how these events played out. Jaime Bleda was a monk of the Dominican Order, famed for his piety and his zeal for the purification of the Catholic faith. After much consideration, Bleda concluded that it was impossible for the Church to know for certain whether the converts truly believed in Christ or whether they were simply pretending to be Christians for fear of being killed. Thus, the only solution would be to put these converts before Christ and let him judge whether they were sincere in their faith or liars. Of course, they could not face Christ unless they were in the next life. Bleda, therefore, proposed that they all be killed forthwith, and thereby, their souls would ascend to Christ after death that he may judge the sincerity of their faith.

Strangely, the Catholic Church enthusiastically agreed with Bleda's plan; the clergy were fully prepared to kill hundreds of thousands of converts in order to serve God and purify of the Catholic faith. The Spanish government, however, was against killing the converts, who were vast in number; were they to meet with resistance then the authorities may not be able to contain the problem. Instead, the government decided to expel the converts from Spain. Although Bleda's preference was for the immediate killing of the converts, he accepted this alternative solution. The French historian Gustave Le Bon describes these events in his book *The Civilisation of the Arabs*, writing:

> In the year 1610, the Spanish government ordered the expulsion of the Arabs from Spain and most of them were killed en route. The monk Bleda expressed his satisfaction that three quarters of these migrants were killed as they went into exile; 100,000 Muslims from a convoy of 140,000 were killed on their way to Africa.

Here one has to wonder: how can a man of religion endorse the murder of this number of innocent people simply because they differ from him in their beliefs, without experiencing the slightest sense of guilt. How is it that Bleda could reconcile his faith in Christ – who taught mankind peace and love – with a bloodthirsty and unnecessary massacre? The answer is that faith, in any religion, does not necessarily make us more humane; it is the way in which we understand religion that determines our behaviour. The way in which we interpret religion can teach us tolerance, fairness and compassion, but it can also push us towards fanaticism, hatred and aggression. If we consider that all religions are just different paths leading to knowledge of God Almighty, then it follows that we are not better than others whether we are Muslims, Christians or Jews; indeed, what credit can we take for this when most of us simply received our religious creeds from our parents? We should remember that God will judge people by their actions before He will judge them for their religious beliefs. If this was how we understood religion, then we would be tolerant of those who have different religious beliefs. We would defend the rights of all humans, regardless of their religion.

However, if we believe that our own religion is the sole and absolute truth, and that is transcends all others, if we believe that we are the only true believers and that people who follow other religions are impure infidels living in error, then, logically, we would not acknowledge that those who differ from us should have the same rights as we do; our fanaticism will lead us to believe that we have a divine mandate from God to elevate His word and carry out His will. This false divine mandate would lead us to believe that we are superior to others, and consequently, lead us to violate their rights. It could cause us to commit the most heinous of crimes without experiencing any feelings of guilt, since we would believe that we were carrying out the will of God. Bleda had a clear conscience when he endorsed the killing of innocent people, because he felt that he was carrying out God's will; he believed that God wanted Spain to be a purely Catholic country, in which there was no place for Muslim or Jewish infidels. The belief that one has a divine mandate occurs repeatedly in Spanish history and often led to horrific crimes being committed in the name of religion. In this sense, there is little difference between Bleda and the terrorist Osama bin Laden. Although their eras and circumstances are different, the way they view the world is the same. Each felt that they had a mandate from God to implement His will and to defend religion. They both viewed those who differed from them as inferior, and they both believed in collective responsibility. In Bleda's eye, all Arabs were collectively responsible for the actions of any individual Arab. Similarly, in Osama bin Laden's eyes, all Westerners were responsible for the crimes committed by American and Israeli troops against Arabs and Muslims.

When it comes to the concept of a divine mandate, there is no place for individual responsibility. It would have been impossible to convince Osama bin Laden that there are millions of people in the West who condemn the crimes of the American army; just as Bleda could not have been convinced that, in all likelihood, there were upstanding citizens amongst his Muslim victims. The value of others' lives and their rights are not even a consideration in the minds of those who believe they have a divine mandate. The lives of non-Muslims were unimportant to bin Laden, just as Bleda was little concerned for the lives of Arabs. Both killed thousands of innocent people in the belief that they were doing something good that would be rewarded by God with their entrance into heaven.

When you feel you have a mandate from God, you will never allow others to criticise your actions or question you. You will neither respect those who differ from you, nor will you recognise their rights. You will feel that you are always right because you are carrying out the will of God. You will never be able to engage with reality properly because you have been blinded by your own delusions. You will deny the truth no matter how obvious it is, and you will treat anyone who questions you with hostility. You will behave in this way because you have built your entire life around this delusion and without it you would fall apart.

This concept may help us in understanding the behaviour of the Muslim Brotherhood and many others who are affiliated with political Islam. The Brotherhood have been in power for some months now and Egyptians are asking: how can the Muslim Brothers claim to represent Islam when they continually lie, break their promises and collude with others to save their own interests, even when the price of this entails the blood of martyrs and the collapse of the state itself? Why do the Muslim Brothers not feel any guilt when they assault and kill those who disagree with them?

The answer to this is that the Muslim Brothers do not view themselves as ordinary politicians who make decisions on behalf of the people; rather, they believe that God has sent them to save Egypt from irreligion and ungodliness. They think that they are carrying out the will of God, and thus, they are above the law and should not be judged according to the standards of ordinary people. They believe that God has entrusted them with promoting His word and carrying out His judgment. It follows that anyone who criticises them or argues with their style of politics is an enemy of Islam, because the Brothers believe that they represent Islam.

Every time a situation arises, the Brotherhood likens it to some event in Islamic history – viewing themselves as the Muslims and their opponents as the enemies of God. A few days ago a member of the Brotherhood wrote an article in which he likened the clashes in Mokattam to the Battle of Uhud.[1] Naturally enough, the Brothers were portrayed as the companions of the Prophet Muhammad, peace be upon Him, while their adversaries were portrayed as the infidels. This is the mentality that the Brotherhood has towards political dispute.

The situation in Egypt is perfectly clear: an elected president has turned into a dictator in order to serve his own organisation. He has trampled on the law and imposed the will of the supreme guide of the Brotherhood on all of the people. He has employed an illegitimate attorney general to make an example of all those who oppose him, while his security agencies have been implicated in the killing of hundreds of people and the torture of thousands.

Despite all this, however, the Brotherhood, due to their belief that they have a divine mandate, are incapable of seeing the truth; they are always ready to deny, argue and deceive. There is absolutely no point in trying to persuade the Brotherhood of the truth. Even if the their leader was to kill thousands of Egyptians, and even if his policies were to bring disaster, his followers would

1 The Battle of Uhud was fought between the Muslims, led by Prophet Muhammad, and the Meccans, led by Abu Sufyan ibn Harb. For the Muslims, the battle was a significant setback: although they had been close to routing the Meccans, the Muslim soldiers went against Muhammad's orders, which resulted in a defeat.

continue to defend everything he does, because in their view he is carrying out God's will. The supreme guide of the Brotherhood is just like Osama bin Laden and Bleda the monk: he is a man who feels that he represents God's will and is fully prepared to violate the rights of others without batting an eyelid, because he believes that God has willed that his organisation be in power, and that the will of the people counts for nothing.

So what can be done? History teaches us that there is no hope of coming to a mutual understanding with religious fanatics who view themselves as instruments of God's will. There is no point in entering a dialogue or negotiating with the Muslim Brotherhood. The solution is to apply pressure until this fascist regime is overthrown. The revolution cannot afford to lose its way in the maze of politics or the corridors of futile negotiations. We demand early presidential elections, the dismissal of the illegitimate attorney general, the repeal of the invalid constitution and the prosecution of those who are responsible for murder and torture – first and foremost amongst these should be Mohamed Morsi and Mohamed Ibrahim. These are the just demands of the revolution and we must not give them up, or accept compromises of any kind. The revolution will continue until it triumphs over fascism and achieves all its goals.

Democracy is the answer.

AB

Will Mubarak Keep His Smile?

15 April 2013

There was once a poor Jewish man who had a large family. They were so poor that he, his wife and their ten children had to sleep in two rooms. When his suffering became too much he went to the rabbi and said: "I can no longer bear this miserable life. Rabbi, pray for me and tell me what I should do."

The rabbi listened to him calmly and told him to come back the following day. When he returned he found the rabbi holding a pig. "God wants you to take this pig to live with your family," the rabbi said. The man was shocked, because pigs are regarded as unclean in Judaism and, furthermore, his house was filled with children, so how could he also accommodate a pig?

The man tried to get out of taking the pig, but to no avail; the rabbi assured him that this was the irrevocable will of God. He eventually gave in and took the pig home with him. Now his life truly became a hell. The pig rampaged through the house, it broke the furniture, and it defecated all over the house making it stink. After a week the man appealed to the rabbi to rid him of the pig, but the rabbi firmly refused. Another week went by and the man returned to the rabbi, he kissed his hand and sobbed: "Rabbi, have mercy on me. The smell of the pig is unbearable, all the furniture is destroyed; we cannot live in the house because of this pig."

The rabbi then gave him permission to get rid of the pig. A week passed and the man turned up again. When the rabbi asked him how he was, he smiled and said: "Praise God, although I live with my ten children in two rooms and although we are very poor, nevertheless, we have been living in a state of bliss since we got rid of the pig."

This well-known story is frequently told to remind us that we shouldn't complain when our circumstances are hard, because they could always be much worse. Yet, whenever I read it I have to ask myself, why does the man in the story have to choose between poverty and living with a pig? Why does he have to choose between bad and worse? Is it not the man's right to live like a human being with his family in an adequate house?

The story of the rabbi and the pig represents our situation now in Egypt. When the January 25 revolution started, millions of Egyptians took part in demonstrations to oust Mubarak, and to this end, they paid a high price. At that time a feeling of optimism prevailed; the Egyptian people felt that they were beginning a new era in which they would rid Egypt of oppression and tyranny, in which they would bring about justice and live in dignity. However, two years on from this, things have deteriorated drastically, with the breakdown of the rule of law, inflation and unemployment. Anarchy is rife, so much so that many Egyptians have now grown nostalgic for Mubarak's corrupt and oppressive regime, just as the Jewish man in the story grew nostalgic for his miserable life before the arrival of the pig in his house.

Most likely it was this deterioration of conditions in Egypt that caused Mubarak to smile in the first session of his retrial. He appeared confident and at ease in the courtroom, greeting his supporters as though he were a presidential candidate. It was as though he wanted to say to Egyptians: "You rose against me and you forced me out of power, but what have you gained from the revolution other than chaos and misery? You thought my rule was bad, but now you know just how much worse the rule of the Brotherhood is."

Mubarak considers himself a national hero; he actually believes that he achieved great things for the country. He refuses to acknowledge the crimes and the corruption of his regime, which caused Egypt to fall behind in every field of accomplishment. This self-deception has been practised repeatedly by all tyrants throughout history. They live oblivious to their crimes, they are lost in a world that is divorced from reality. With Egyptians growing increasingly frustrated with the deterioration of conditions, the ideas which formed the basis of the Mubarak regime have unfortunately started to spread across Egypt.

Hosni Mubarak believes that the Egyptian people are unfit for democracy, and consequently, they will always have to choose between either authoritarianism or chaos. This theory, which has long been used to justify fraudulent elections and to subdue opponents, is entirely without basis; it also reveals the ignorance of those who advance it. The Egyptian people began practising democracy a long time ago. Between 1923 and the revolution of 1952, seven out of ten elections resulted in landslide victories for the Wafd Party. At that time they represented the popular will; the simple peasants would vote in opposition to the landowners and junior officials would vote in opposition to senior officials. Perhaps we should recall the vast numbers of Egyptians who took part in the referendum of March 2011. And let us not forget that millions of Egyptians, especially women, that queued up to vote in the last referendum to reject the illegitimate constitution imposed on us by the Muslim Brotherhood. Never in our history have the Egyptian people failed to perform their duty, provided that the elections are fair and legitimate. But the chaos which we are now suffering from has been deliberately created by the Mubarak regime, which remains in power. The military council preserved the repressive elements of the police force, and when the Brotherhood came to power they joined forces with them against the people. Many police officers still refuse to restore law and order because they believe that the Egyptian people should be punished for rising up in the first place.

Mubarak views dignity, freedom and other such things as empty concepts to be mocked. This is because he believes that the only purpose of the Egyptian people is to eat, drink and work for money in order to raise a family. The Egyptian revolution, however, demonstrated that this idea is no longer valid because 20 million Egyptians took to the streets risking their lives for the sake of freedom and dignity. Indeed, most of the young revolutionaries who were either killed or injured in the revolution could have gotten jobs in the Gulf countries; many Egyptians have gone there to work and come home wealthy. They could have looked abroad in order to escape the crises at home; instead, however, they decided to change Egypt, from the bottom up. They chose revolution over a life of abject safety.

While Mubarak believes that the principles of human rights and the rule of law can be applied in Western countries, he does not believe the same is true for Egypt. He believes that Egypt has a cultural specificity which makes the relationship between its citizens and the government different from that which exists in the West. He adopted this logic during his time in power in order to justify the repression of the Egyptian people, and, regrettably, this notion has trickled from the top of the regime down to the lower levels of the governing structure. Many police officers, for example, hold the belief that there are certain types of Egyptians (such as thugs and political opponents) who can only be dealt with by repression and torture. This reprehensible mentality is, of course, in error; it does not even deserve to be discussed with any seriousness, because it is a basic right to be treated humanely in any country of the world, irrespective of that person's crime. Mubarak and his supporters may respond to this by saying that the repression of Egyptians continued after his overthrow and that this demonstrates that any government in Egypt will necessarily have to repress the citizens in order to control them. It is true that the military council was responsible for numerous massacres – these involved both the torture and killing of citizens. Similarly, under the rule of the Muslim Brotherhood, the police killed a hundred citizens and tortured thousands. But the continued use of repression after Mubarak had stepped down does not prove that it is a necessary practice for governing the Egyptian people, on the contrary, it confirms that the Mubarak regime has not yet fallen.

Despite any shortcomings of his regime, Mubarak believes that it was the last obstacle preventing the Brotherhood from coming to power. Mubarak promoted this idea both here in Egypt and abroad, so that the world would endorse his corrupt and authoritarian regime as a more desirable alternative to the Brotherhood being in power. It was as though fate had decreed that the Egyptians would forever remain caught between the hammer of the military and the anvil of the Brotherhood, as though forever destined to choose between military fascism and religious fascism. This too is also a huge fallacy because the growth of the Brotherhood's influence was the direct result of the restrictions placed upon political freedoms during Mubarak's reign. In 1950, the Muslim Brotherhood were at the height of their power; one year prior to this they had assassinated the prime minister of Egypt, Mahmoud Fahmi al-Nuqrashi.[1] Yet, as soon as fair elections were held, the Wafd Party, as usual, won a landslide victory taking over 90 per cent of the seats in parliament. The Mubarak regime did not protect us from extremism; rather, the regime created it. Authoritarianism does not prevent extremism; it helps it to spread. Furthermore, the relationship between the Brotherhood and the Mubarak regime was not always one of mutual hostility, but rather, it was punctuated by many deals and periods of truce. There isn't room here to go into the public statements made by the leaders of the Brotherhood, in which they have expressed their esteem for Mubarak as the father of the Egyptian people and the symbol of the nation. The Brotherhood's rise to power was an unfortunate but necessary lesson for the Egyptian people. They have now learned how to distinguish between religion and those who strive to exploit it. Egyptians had to experience the Brotherhood's lies and misconduct, which are completely divorced from the morals of religion, so that they could forever understand what the Brotherhood is really like. Look at how the people who elected the Brotherhood in parliamentary elections have now voted them

1 In 1948, Mahmoud Fahmi an-Nuqrashi outlawed the Muslim Brotherhood due to rumours of a Brotherhood coup against the monarchy and government The assets of the group were seized and many of its members incarcerated.

out of the student unions and trade unions[1] – and there is more of this to come. The Mubarak regime did not protect us from the Brotherhood; on the contrary, it strengthened them. Were it not for the tyranny of Mubarak, the Brotherhood's influence would not have spread, nor would they have come to power at all.

Thus, there is no reason for Mubarak to gloat over the mishaps of Egyptians. The revolution, which we made, shows that our country is still living, and that we can still demand freedom and dignity. The Egyptian people did not make a mistake when they removed Mubarak; their mistake was letting his regime remain in power. They made a mistake when they called on the military council to carry out the aims of the revolution, forgetting that it was composed of Mubarak's followers. Egyptians made a mistake when they trusted the Brotherhood and expected Morsi to fulfil the aims of the revolution. They soon discovered, however, that the president was nothing but an agent of the Brotherhood and that the Brotherhood sought to carry out a plan that would give them control of the state forever. Egyptians have made mistakes, but they have quickly learned from these mistakes. A revolution is not just a single moment; it is a phase in the history of a people. A revolution implies human change, and once this has taken place there is no going back to how it was before. Those who made the revolution and made sacrifices for freedom reject the Brotherhood's tyranny now, just as they rejected the tyranny of Mubarak. The Egyptian people must not be limited to a choice between the military and the Brotherhood. We must not think like the Jewish man in the story, accepting what is bad in order to avoid what is worse. The revolution is our dream and we will not give it up until it has been realised. Peaceful pressure must continue to be applied in order to force the Brotherhood to hold early presidential elections; this is a legitimate democratic demand. The revolution shall continue, God willing, until it achieves all its aims. And when that happens, Mubarak will no longer have reason to smile.

Democracy is the answer.

AB

When Will Don Quixote Come to His Senses?

22 April 2013

Dear reader, I suggest that you carry out the following experiment. Log into Facebook or Twitter, write something sharply critical about Mohamed Morsi

1 On 23 April, Independent candidate Mohamed Badran won the presidency of Egypt's Student Union, winning 24 votes to the 22 of Mostafa Mohamed Mounir, who is affiliated with the Muslim Brotherhood.

and then simply wait a few minutes. You shall receive a barrage of slanderous insults from Brotherhood supporters. They will use the filthiest language, insulting your mother and father in imaginatively obscene ways. After this, visit the profiles belonging to these vitriolic individuals and you will find that they have posted verses from the Qur'an as well as sayings of the Prophet Muhammad. When I did this, I found that some of them had even written prayers wherein they beseech God's favour with utmost humility. The irony here is that this profound sense of religious faith does not prevent them from insulting people in the most obscene manner. In this way, the Muslim Brothers lie, slander and oppress, without their own religious sensibilities ever being disturbed. We have seen the Muslim Brothers – dozens of instances have been recorded on video – beating up their opponents, savagely torturing them, dragging women along the ground and assaulting them. The strange thing about all this is that when they commit these crimes they cheer and shout "God is great", as though they were fighting an army of infidels.

There are only two ways to explain this strange contradiction between belief and behaviour: either the Muslim Brothers are a bunch of hypocritical scoundrels who lack conscience and who consciously commit these evils while pretending to be pious, or, the Muslim Brothers really are sincerely religious, but they are driven to criminal behavious because of a major flaw in their interpretation of religion. As a matter of fact, I am inclined towards the second explanation. In my opinion, the Muslim Brothers are not intrinsically evil people; they are neither liars nor swindlers in the typical sense. Rather, they have a mistaken impression of themselves and they suffer from a real flaw in their perception which leads them to commit the most heinous crimes all the while believing that they are doing the right thing and fulfilling their religious duty. They do not see themselves as ordinary citizens who are simply engaged in politics but rather, they consider themselves to be the knights of Islam and its protectors who have dedicated their lives to religion and made the decision to sacrifice everything of value in order to raise the banner of Islam and restore its glory. Indeed, in their eyes they have devoted their lives to fulfilling a sacred task. In light of this, they view those who are not members of the Brotherhood as having less faith and as being less committed to religion.

That the Muslim Brothers believe that they and Islam are one and the same might help us explain their actions. The Brothers think that they represent Islam and that outside of them, Islam does not exist. They consider people outside the Brotherhood – whether they are merely unconcerned about religion or more actively secular – enemies of Islam and agents of the West who seek to extinguish the light of Islam. As for non-Muslims, they consider these to be nothing but infidels that have strayed from the path of God.

Because the Muslim Brothers do not consider others as equal to them in religion, naturally, they therefore do not accord people, who have strayed from the true path, the same rights that they themselves enjoy. Indeed, the concept of equality between people can only be realised when we assume that all people are equal. However, if one group amongst the people is convinced that they are superior to others, then this will inevitably lead them to violate the rights of those who differ with them. In light of this, the Muslim Brothers are notable for two contradictory types of behaviour: they are utterly loyal to each other and show upright moral character amongst themselves, but when they deal with others they exempt themselves from any moral obligation.

Amongst themselves the Muslim Brothers display honesty, loyalty and other noble qualities. However, in dealing with others, every deceit, injustice and treachery is permissible as long as it furthers the interests of their organisation. If necessary, the Muslim Brothers permit themselves to beat up their opponents and elctrocute them in order to extract confessions. Nor do the Muslim Brothers have any qualms about dragging women along the streets, torturing them and insulting them with the most obscene language. They commit all these crimes with a perfectly clear conscience because they see their victims as being less faithful to Islam than they are. The Muslim Brothers believe that God has chosen them to restore the glory of Islam, thus, anyone who opposes them is an enemy of God and His prophet and consequently deserves neither dignity nor rights. In fact, one must strive to punish such people for being enemies of God.

The Muslim Brothers live in the shade of this delusional reality and they would sacrifice their lives in its defence. If they were to see the truth and to perceive reality, just once, then they would realise that the reality which they inhabit is false and unfounded. If the Muslim Brothers realised that the Islamic caliphate – and by that I mean a just and rightly-guided government – only really existed for 31 years, [and was followed by] many centuries of despotic states which carried out massacres and oppressed the people; if they realised that Islam is a great religion but that it does not give precedence to any particular form of government; if they realised that the only way to revive Islam is to establish a modern democratic state in which all citizens are equal regardless of their religion, not one founded upon tyranny in the name of religion, as has happened in Sudan, Afghanistan, Somalia and every other country that has been plagued by religious fascism. Then their dream world would collapse and they would lose their sense of superiority over others. Their organisation would disintegrate and their mission would lose its relevance and meaning. Thus, in order to preserve their delusions the Muslim Brothers have no option but to deny the truth, even if it is as clear as day. In a television interview, one of the Brotherhood's leaders asserted that his organisation had never taken up arms except against the British occupation, but one of the other guests objected, saying: "How can you say that when the Brotherhood killed

Egyptians, Judge Ahmad Khazendar,[1] for example, in 1948?" When he heard this, the Brotherhood leader smiled and said: "Khazendar and the English are the same thing."

These fallacies that dismiss reality in order to preserve their dream world can be seen in all the actions of the Muslim Brothers; they deny reality to protect their delusion and to preserve the pleasing image they have of themselves. Egypt has hit rock bottom in every sector; Mohamed Morsi is the model of an impotent and failed president but the Brotherhood will never admit it. In the space of a week the Brotherhood had two books printed that discuss the amazing achievements of Morsi – no one can see these achievements, of course, except the Brotherhood. Morsi himself, in his speeches, just uses forced rhetoric, refusing to acknowledge his failures as a president. He seems to be divorced from reality, living in a fantasy world where he sees himself as a great leader. As for the distressing conditions which afflict the Egyptian people, Morsi does not see these as anything other than the result of conspiracies on the part of remnants of the Mubarak regime and the enemies of Islam.

There is a famous novel called *Don Quixote*, written by the great Spanish author Miguel de Cervantes. The protagonist is a man who was born after the age of chivalry but is obsessed with reading the old books which describe the heroic deeds of knights. He continues to dream of being a knight until, at some point, this delusion that he is a knight takes possession of him. Thus, he decides to live the life of one, even though the age of chivalry has ended. He dons an old suit of armour, takes hold of a worn-out lance and takes part in imaginary battles. When he sees the dust stirred up by a flock of sheep he imagines they are enemy soldiers and without hesitation he rushes in to kill them. The shepherds, however, pelt him with stones which break several of his teeth. On another occasion, Don Quixote sees a windmill and never having seen one before he imagines it to be a giant [lit. a satan] with enormous arms. He rushes towards the windmill to strike it with his lance; however, the spinning blades of the windmill knock him to the ground, leaving him with broken bones. Don Quixote continues to cause himself harm in pursuit of the this delusion. He cannot see reality until he finally comes to his senses in the end and recognises the truth; he realises that he cannot possibly be a knight because the age of chivalry has passed and shall never return. He admits that the "dark shadows of ignorance" had taken possession of him due to his reading so many books from long ago.

In my opinion, Don Quixote represents the closest literary parallel to the Muslim Brotherhood. Like him, they want to restore a past that will never

1 In 1948 the Muslim Brotherhood is thought to have assassinated appellate Judge Ahmad Khazendar in retaliation for his passing a "severe sentence" against a member of the Brotherhood who had been involved in an attack on British soldiers at a nightclub.

return, and like him they think they are on a holy quest which is actually a dangerous and unnecessary fabrication. Like him, they are completely unable to see reality and they are driven to commit the most heinous crimes while at the same time believing that they are carrying out a glorious task. The important lesson to be drawn from this great novel is that it is the force exerted by reality, and not the power of reason, that makes Don Quixote come to his senses. Thus, there is no hope in having dialogue with the Brothers; they listen only to the instructions of their own leaders, who, like Don Quixote, are deluded by the belief that they are carrying out a noble mission. There is no point in trying to reach any agreement with the Brotherhood because they will later go back on their word if it goes against their interests; their promises cannot be trusted.

The current political scene in Egypt is now clearer than ever before. It is not a political struggle between a government and an opposition, as some like to portray it; rather, it is a widespread popular resistance against a fascist organisation that came to power through elections and which is now relentlessly pressing forward with its plan to take over the Egyptian state once and for all. Mohamed Morsi started out as an elected president but he lost legitimacy when he violated the law and the constitution, when he placed himself above the law, bolstered an illegitimate Constituent Assembly with his own supporters, which then produced an illegitimate constitution. He lost legitimacy again when his minister of the interior had a hundred Egyptians killed, in addition to being responsible for the well-documented torture of hundreds of others. If we prosecute Mubarak and his minister of the interior, Habib el-Adly, for their part in the killing of demonstrators, then the same charge must now apply to Morsi and his minister of the interior, Mohamed Ibrahim. Indeed, in order to be fair, it is incumbent upon us to prosecute Morsi and Ibrahim for the same crime as Hosni Mubarak and Habib el-Aldy. The worst thing that could happen now would be for us to accept any compromise whatsoever with the Brotherhood. Is there a single reason for us to trust the promises of the Brotherhood? When has Morsi ever made a promise which he has fulfilled? Whoever takes part in the coming elections, which are based upon an illegitimate constitution and an illegitimate president, is aiding, however good his intentions, the Brotherhood in their permanent takeover of our country. Egypt has now reached a defining moment – a moment of confrontation with religious fascism that demands that the revolutionaries take a stand and reject political accommodations. Our demand must be for early presidential elections; this is the democratic right of the people. No democratically elected president in the world can maintain their legitimacy if they fail to recognise the law and they are responsible for the killing of a hundred citizens. It is our duty, in my opinion, to boycott the elections so as not to give an illegitimate president political cover. The people must continue to apply peaceful pressure in order to force the Brotherhood to hold early presidential elections. God willing, the revolution will continue until it achieves all of its goals.

Democracy is the answer.

AB

How the News Will Look in the Future

29 April 2013

The Parliament of Egypt Agrees to Send Aid to Qatar

On Monday the parliament agreed, by a large majority, to provide financial assistance to the state of Qatar, offering a grant worth 4 billion dollars. Furthermore, in addition to this amount, the government of Egypt will also come to the aid of the Qatar Central Bank by providing it with a deposit of 6 billion dollars. As we know, the financial crisis in the oil-producing Gulf States has been ongoing for years due to the widespread use of solar power throughout the world, which has reduced the need for oil and led to the fall in its price. The president of Egypt, Khaled Ali, had requested that the parliament debate the proposed financial aid for Qatar. During the requested debate some of the members of the house opposed granting aid unless the Qatari government offered an apology for Qatar's support of the Muslim Brotherhood during their time in government, prior to the second wave of the revolution which overthrew the organisation. However, the majority of the house believed that Egypt, being the most powerful Arab state, had a higher duty to help Qatar and that this duty should not have conditions attached. Today, the Central Bank of Egypt began the process of transferring the aid to the government of Qatar.

Saudi Government Offers an Official Apology for the Jeddah Airport Incident

A spokesman for the Saudi Royal Court has issued an official apology to the Egyptian government concerning the Jeddah airport incident. The incident, which occurred a number of weeks ago, involved an altercation between an Egyptian citizen, Hassan Khafagi (a laundryman by occupation), and the manager of the airport, who in the course of this altercation slapped Khafagi, whosubsequently filed a lawsuit with the Saudi courts against this manager; he was supported in this action by Egypt's Ministry for Foreign Affairs, which insisted that Khafagi receive an official Saudi apology in addition to the 250,000 Saudi riyals awarded by the Saudi courts in damages. The incident had threatened to cause a diplomatic rift between the two neighbouring countries, but the issuance of an official Saudi apology yesterday put an end to the crisis. In his first comment on the incident, the Egyptian Minister of Foreign Affairs Mohamed Effat said: "Everyone must understand that we will not permit any Egyptian citizen to be insulted, however lowly they may be, because the dignity of Egyptians is the dignity of Egypt." Mohamed Effat is the son of Sheikh Emad Effat, who was killed in the massacre outside the Council of Ministers when the military council was in power. It was the death of Sheikh Emad Effat and dozens of others that led to the prosecution of both Field Marshal Tantawi and General Enan after the fall of the Muslim Brotherhood, which had been obstructing their being brought to trial.

Unemployment Benefits to Continue

Alaa Abd el-Fattah, the minister of labour and well-known leftist, has stated that unemployment benefits will remain at their current level and that there is no plan to reduce them. A number of businessmen have argued that the benefits are too high, stressing that each unemployed claimant receives 10,000 Egyptian pounds per month while the minimum salary is 15,000 Egyptian pounds. They argue that this encourages low-salaried workers to be lax in their work, since they know that they can always claim generous unemployment benefits should they lose their jobs. However, Alaa Abd el-Fattah struck back against the views of the businessmen, saying that Egypt's economy has never been so strong and that this obligates the state to fulfil its important commitment towards the unemployed. The minister also stressed that the current policy regarding unemployment benefits is in accordance with the law passed by parliament, and that no one individual can overrule it.

The Salafist Symphony Orchestra Begins European Tour

Tomorrow, the musicians of the Salafist Symphony Orchestra will set off for their European tour. Beginning with a concert in Paris, the will travel on to a number of other cities, performing in Lyon, Frankfurt, Berlin, London and finally Liverpool. Sheikh Maamoun al-Sayyid, the conductor of the orchestra, has stated that the concerts will include works by Beethoven, Tchaikovsky and Mozart. The Salafist Symphony Orchestra was set up by the Salafist Daawa Organisation ten years ago after Salafist sheikhs set out to revise their long-standing judgment which prohibits music. There are one hundred musicians in the orchestra; they are all bearded salafists except for seven foreign musicians. As for the conductor, Sheikh Maamoun al-Sayyid, graduated from both the Faculty of Islamic Law, as well as from the Cairo Conservatoire. He then studied at the Vienna Conservatory where he received his degree in conducting. For a number of years he worked in the Vienna Philharmonic Orchestra as well as the Stuttgart Philharmonic Orchestra before returning to Cairo to lead the Salafist Symphony Orchestra, which under his direction has won numerous international awards.

"Our Treatment, Our Right" Plan to Start on 1 November

Minister of Health Ahmed Harara has announced that all hospitals throughout Egypt will be ready to start implementing the 'Our Treatment, Our Right' plan from 1 November. The plan will provide free health care to all Egyptian citizens. He also stated that the plan would place Egypt amongst the few countries in the world that provide completely free health care, such as Sweden and Norway. Harara, who lost both of his eyes during the January 25 revolution, is a dentist and is considered a national hero. From his first day in office, Harara has promoted the free health care plan and he was able to win parliamentary agreement for the plan's budget when he made his now famous statement: "Illness does not discriminate between the rich and the poor, so health care should not discriminate between them either."

Al-Gama'a al-Islamiyya supports Abdel Massih

After a meeting, which lasted two hours, the political leadership of the al-Gama'a al-Islamiyya decided to support Mary Abdel Massih as the group's candidate in the upcoming presidential elections. Mary Abdel Massih now enjoys the support of all the major Islamist parties except the Muslim Brotherhood. Mary Abdel Massih, who is 57, holds a doctorate in economics from Cairo University. She took part in the January 25 revolution, and along with her colleagues she set up the Maspero Youth Union. She suffered serious injuries during the Maspero demonstrations when a massacre was carried out on the orders of the military council. Former president Mohamed ElBaradei selected her for the post of minister of finance after he won the presidency in the elections that followed the fall of the Muslim Brotherhood. She was subsequently reappointed to the same position by the former president Hamdeen Sabahi, and again by the current president, Khaled Ali, who insisted that she continue in her post, throughout both his terms in office. Over the course of her 16 years in this position Abdel Massih has been able to boost Egypt's economy, making it one of the strongest in the world, both in terms of GDP and per capita income. Because she has demonstrated such competence in government administration, broad sections of the Egyptian people support her for the presidency, now that Khaled Ali's second and last term is expiring in accordance with the 2015 Constitution. Officials from the Islamic parties have explained their support for Mary Abdel Massih, who is both a woman and a Christian Copt, by saying that: "The correct understanding of Islam obligates us to elect the person who is most qualified for the presidency, regardless of that person's religion or gender." Commenting on al-Gama'a al-Islamiyya's backing of her, Abdel Massih said: "I am indebted to our great people for everything I have achieved, and the revolution has taught us that we are all Egyptians first, before we are Copts or Muslims."

State Security Facilities To Be Maintained as Museums

The governor of Cairo has said that the use of state security facilities as museums will continue, in accordance with the law. As we know, the second wave of the revolution led to the overthrow of Morsi through early presidential elections in 2014. It was subsequently decided that state security facilities would be turned into museums so that visitors and school children could see the instruments of torture used against opponents of the regime during the eras of Mubarak, the military council and the Muslim Brotherhood. Recently there was a heated debate about the benefits of maintaining this tradition; some members of parliament argued that it would be better to use the buildings for the government's own administrative purposes, especially since the use of torture is no longer practised in Egypt. However, the majority of the members of parliament said it was beneficial for Egyptian children to visit the state security museums in order that they learn about the hard battle that their parents and grandparents fought for freedom.

Amun Spaceship Is Ready for Launch

A spokesman for the Egyptian Space Agency has announced that the Amun spaceship will be launched into space next Thursday at 5.15 am. The spaceship will be carrying three Egyptian astronauts: Abdel Kader Hassan, George Michel and Fatima Kamel. The spokesman refused to give any details of the spaceship's itinerary; he said only that it would carry out critical missions in outer space. The youngest of the three astronauts is Abdel Kader Hassan. This is his first time going into space; nevertheless, he expressed that he felt confident about the trip because of the excellent training that he received at the Space Flight Centre in Alexandria. Astronaut George Michel has flown into space numerous times, however, the most experienced of the three is Fatima Kamel, who is the commander of the spacecraft and responsible for the safety of her two male colleagues.

The Crisis in the Muslim Brotherhood Continues

A security source has stated that the 'Brothers, But Honest Ones' movement staged a mass sit-in yesterday, with thousands of young Muslim Brothers gathering outside the organisation's headquarters in the Mokattam. The demonstrators set up hundreds of tents and began shouting "Down with the rule of the guide!" Some of them tried to storm the building and seize members of the Guidance Office. However, the security forces intervened to protect the offices and ensure the safety of the besieged members of the Guidance Office, who were taken out by the back door under heavy guard. The youth of the Brotherhood announced, however, that their sit-in would continue until their demands are met. In brief, they are asking for the abolition of the organisation's present rule which requires that the youth of the Brotherhood swear their allegiance and give their obedience to the supreme guide. According to them, this makes them mindless tools in the hands of the guide, who uses them to gain power. The young Brothers are also demanding new regulation and genuine elections that will enable young members to hold positions of leadership in the organisation. A spokesman for the group 'Brothers, But Honest Ones' stated that:

> The current leaders of the Brotherhood are the ones responsible for the organisation's troubles. The people elected a president that was a member of the Brotherhood in the first elections following the revolution; this demonstrates that the people had confidence in the Brotherhood at that time. But Morsi, and the members of the Guidance Office who backed him, abandoned the people and betrayed their trust. Instead of carrying out the goals of the revolution, Morsi took his orders from the Guidance Office. He neutralised the law, he imposed an illegitimate constitution, and under him the police force killed hundreds of demonstrators and tortured thousands. This is what caused the second wave of the revolution which imposed the early elections that ousted Morsi and ended the rule of Brotherhood.

The spokesman also said that the youth of the Brotherhood would continue their struggle until they get rid of the Guidance Office members who would 'lie and misguide the people', as he put it, and until they have elected respectable members in their stead.
Dear reader, these are some of the news articles you will read in 2030, God willing.

Democracy is the answer.

AB

Morsi and the Three Fish

6 May 2013

There were once three fish that lived in a pool connected to a river. One day they overheard a fisherman talking to a friend saying he would return the next day with his net to catch the fish. The three fish discussed the matter but they could not agree collectively on the best course of action. One of the fish acted decisively; he saved himself by leaving the pool and swimming off towards the river. As for the other two fish, however, they remained indecisive and confused about what to do. The next day the fisherman came back carrying his net. Now, as soon as the second fish saw him, he took off for the river and, luckily, saved his skin. The third fish, however, remained indecisive until it was too late; the fisherman cast his net, caught him, and he perished.

This fable appears in the book known as *Kalila wa Dimna*[1] and it conveys an important lesson about human behaviour. As soon as the first fish learns what the fisherman intends to do, he does not hesitate for one moment; he makes the decision to save himself. He represents a person who is resolute, someone who makes decisions and quickly carries them out. The second fish symbolises a person who is indecisive, who is slow in their response to danger but who makes the right decision at the last moment. The third fish, however, represents an indecisive person who is unable to grasp what is happening because reality is obscured by his delusions or desires – because of this he ultimately loses everything. So what is the connection between the tale and what is happening in Egypt?

Firstly, Mohamed Morsi is the first civilian to be elected president in the history of Egypt. He had a historic, golden opportunity to rally the Egyptian people around him and to achieve the goals of the revolution, for which thousands of Egyptians were either killed or injured. By themselves, the Muslim Brotherhood were unable to secure victory for Morsi in the first round of the elections; credit for his success must go to the millions of Egyptians who voted for him in the subsequent run-off, even though he was not their candidate of choice in the first round. Whether these people voted for Morsi because they had a good impression of the Brotherhood, or whether they did so in order to prevent the old regime from returning to power – as represented by Mubarak's former associate Ahmed Shafik – the Brotherhood is lying, as usual, when they say Morsi's opponents hate his Islamic project. In fact, Morsi has neither an Islamic project nor a un-Islamic one: his sole plan is to enable the Brotherhood to take control of the state. Morsi won in the second round of

1 *Kalila wa Dimnah* is an Arabic translation of the Panchatantra, which is an ancient Indian collection of animal fables written in Sanskrit.

the elections through the votes of millions of people who have no inclination towards political Islam. These same voters, however, quickly turned against Morsi when they realised that he was merely a tool being used to carry out the decisions of the Brotherhood's Guidance Office. And they also turned against political Islam when it became clear that Morsi was implementing a definite plan to dismantle the Egyptian state and reconstruct it in such a way that it would be fully under the Brotherhood's control.

In this case we should not cloud the distinction between government and state. Any elected authority has the right to extend its control over the government; however, it does not have the right to subject the state to its authority. If the elected president were a socialist, for example, he would have the right to appoint socialist advisers and ministers in order to assist him in carrying out his political programme, but he does not have the right to take control of the judiciary, the police and the office of attorney general. According to the democratic system, the agencies of law enforcement must be kept separate from the interference of politics, because they play a pivotal role as independent authorities, and therefore, they act as the lawful arbiter between the various political currents.

In order to enable the Brotherhood to take control of the state, Morsi issued his constitutional declaration in which he suspended the law, violated the constitution and placed his own will above that of the judiciary. He followed this up with a number of illegitimate resolutions: he appointed an attorney general from amongst his supporters in violation of the law and he fortified the illegitimate Constituent Assembly with his sympathisers. As for the Shura Council, which is illegitimate under the law, only seven per cent of Egyptians actually bothered to vote in the election of its members, since it was considered a body that lacked any clearly defined agency. Morsi secured the council's immunity from the rulings of the judiciary and turned it into a legislative assembly subject to the Brotherhood, which passes the laws they require to consolidate their grip over the state.

With the constitutional declaration Morsi lost his legitimacy as president. Were any elected president in France, the United States or any other democratic state, to issue a constitutional declaration placing their will above the rule of law, the people would have withdrawn their support for them immediately because they would have changed from being an elected president into being a fascist despot. The constitutional declaration represented the termination of the lawful, mutual contract between Morsi and the Egyptian people. Now that a hundred people have been shot dead by the police, our demand should not merely be for Morsi's dismissal from office, but also for the prosecution of both him and his minister of the interior on charges of orchestrating the killing of demonstrators – the same charge brought against Mubarak and his own minister of the interior.

The Brotherhood has persisted in carrying out its planned takeover: they kept the illegitimate attorney general in his position, and they were able to form an alliance with the senior officers in the police force, who have reverted back to their old criminal ways. A hundred Egyptians have been killed, hundreds more have been detained and tortured in ways more repulsive than anything during the time of Mubarak: for the first time reports have come out about men being raped by police while in detention.[1] All these crimes have taken place during the term of a president who claims to stand for Islam. The Brotherhood secured complete control of the office of the attorney general and the police force as the essential instruments employed in the service of despotism. They then began a relentless war against freedom of expression, with a barrage of denunciations against people in the media who opposed them. Followers of the Brotherhood have twice besieged Egyptian Media Production City; the goal of which was to terrorise the media outlets that were exposing the crimes of the Brotherhood. The Brotherhood then began levelling trumped-up charges against their opponents and detaining the youth of the revolution, such as Hassan Mustafa[2] in Alexandria and Ahmed Douma[3] members of the April 6 Youth Movement and others.

Behind all of this is the attorney general, working with the full cooperation of the police in order to mete out punishment against those who oppose the Brotherhood. The Brotherhood seeks to break the will of the revolutionary youth because they know they are sincere, principled and cannot be bought off with positions or seats in the parliament, unlike other opponents. The revolution belongs to these brave and noble young men; they opposed Mubarak when he was at the height of his power, they rose up against him and they overthrew him at a time when the supreme guide of the Brotherhood paid homage to Mubarak as "the father of Egypt" and "the symbol of the nation".

The Brotherhood's next step was a move to take control of the judiciary. The Shura Council presented new legislation on the judiciary that would lead to the removal of thousands of judges who stand in the way of the Brotherhood's plan to take control of the Egyptian state. At the same time the Brotherhood entered into secret negotiations with senior members of the old regime; many of the latter were released from prison as a result, in exchange for financial settlements about which we know nothing. Some senior members of the

---

1 One of the most shocking cases documented by Amnesty International was that of M.R.S , 23, a student arrested in February 2014 near Nasr City in Cairo. He said he was held for 47 days and was tortured and raped during his interrogation.

2 Hassan Mustafa is an Alexandrian activist. He was arrested in January 2013 for assaulting a police officer, and sentenced to two years hard labour in March 2013. He was released in July 2013 when the police officer withdrew his complaint

3 Ahmed Douma is an Egyptian activist who has been arrested under each consecutive Egyptian government in recent years. In April 2013 he was arrested for calling Morsi a killer and a criminal, and on 3rd June 2013 sentenced to six months in prison. He was released on 6 July 2013 following appeal

Brotherhood have travelled abroad in order to meet with businessmen, who had left Egypt, and entice them back by offering financial contracts, though we do not know whose interests these contracts would ultimately serve. In doing this the Brotherhood are operating in the knowledge that these wealthy businessmen only care about their own interests; they worked with Mubarak and, equally, they will work with the Brotherhood provided that the Brothers can guarantee a steady flow of profits back to them. The clearest evidence that the Brotherhood has betrayed the revolution is that Ahmed Douma, Hassan Mustafa and their fellow activists are in prison while Fathi Sorour, Safwat el-Sherif and Zakariya Azmi are still at large.

It should be noted here that the Brotherhood never give any ground once they have taken a step towards increasing their control, no matter what problems or disasters result from it. Division within the national forces and their inability to project a united position have provided the Brotherhood with a golden opportunity; the Brotherhood has been able to manoeuvre in order to buy itself time and advance its plan to take over Egypt.

What is happening now in Egypt is not an ordinary political contest between a government and an opposition. It is a popular resistance, which is both necessary and legitimate, against a fascist organisation that came to power through elections but subsequently decided to subject the state to its will by violent and oppressive acts. It is futile to negotiate with the Brotherhood and there is no hope of a national reconciliation with them. When have the Brothers ever told the truth? And when have they fulfilled their promises? So why should we believe their new pledges now? Those who take part in the elections are playing into the hands of the Brotherhood; they will end up as bit players in a play, the plot of which is the Brotherhood's takeover of Egypt, and we will all pay the price.

Now is the time that we must unite under a single goal. Immediate steps must be taken to withdraw confidence in Morsi because he is a president who has lost legitimacy and is responsible for crimes for which he must be tried. In democratic states, when the elected president breaks the law and is responsible for the death of dozens of people, the parliament will immediately hold a vote of no confidence, whereupon early presidential elections will be held. Right now there is no elected parliament in Egypt, therefore, the procedure devolves to the people. Parliament represents the people, but if there is no representation, i.e., parliament, then recourse must be had in the will of the represented, i.e., the people themselves. Collecting signatures of Egyptians in order to demonstrate the popular withdrawal of confidence in Morsi and a legitimate demand for early presidential elections is, in my opinion, the right course to save our country from this fascist organisation. This is precisely what the Kefaya movement began to do, and it is my hope that all of us will join the their Tamarod campaign. If we are able collect a number of signatures which is greater than the number of people who voted for Morsi, then we will undermine his legal and political legitimacy, both at home and abroad. After that, according to the most basic rules of democracy, early presidential elections must be held, under the supervision of the armed forces and with rigorous monitoring by both Egyptian and international organisations in order to provide proper guarantees against electoral fraud, which the Brotherhood would commit without hesitation.

The campaign being led by the Kefaya movement is a real opportunity to save Egypt and take back the revolution from the Brotherhood, who usurped the revolution and betrayed it. We must seize the last and only opportunity like the second fish in the fable. If we do not, then we will meet the same fate as the third fish. Some people might ask: what would compel Morsi to defer to the will of the people? Here we must reaffirm our confidence in the people. The Brotherhood's scheme to seize control of the state has been accomplished quickly and with ease in other countries; however, so far they have failed to impose their will on Egypt because it has resisted them with courage and firmness. A people that was able to remove Mubarak, put him on trial and throw him in prison can also force Morsi to accept early presidential elections, which he will certainly lose in light of all the crimes that have taken place during his rule and all the disasters which he has caused for Egyptians. The battle that the Kefaya movement is fighting is legitimate, necessary and a move in the right direction. A campaign to collect signatures from citizens has begun in order to demonstrate a withdrawal of confidence in Morsi and, thereby, hold early presidential elections in all governorates. There can be no compromise and no dialogue with a president who tramples on the law and the constitution and whose hands are stained with the blood of Egyptians. If we want to put an end the rule of the Brotherhood peacefully and democratically we must join the Kefaya movement in order to show that we have withdrawn our confidence in Morsi and his fascist organisation. The revolution shall continue and, God willing, we shall triumph.

Democracy is the answer.

AB

A Conversation Between a Young Revolutionary and a Frustrated Citizen

20 May 2013

It was late in the afternoon. A man in his fifties was sitting in front of a cafe drinking tea and smoking a water pipe. He appeared relaxed as he watched the people and cars passing by. A slender young man approached him and asked if he could speak with him for a moment. The man smiled, and asked the youth to sit down at his table. The young man looked around him and grabbed a chair from a nearby table .

Revolutionary: "My name is Tamer Aqil. I'm an engineering student at Cairo University and I support the revolution. Might I know your name, sir?"

Citizen: "Nice to meet you, Tamer. My name is Hassan Abdel Bari. I work for the Ministry of Agriculture."

Revolutionary: "I wanted to ask you Hassan, if I may, are you happy with the state of the country?"

Citizen: "Of course not. The country is in ruins; we can't go on like this. Prices are soaring, the state is failing, and thugs roam the streets. I have two daughters in university and I'm in constant fear for them. When one of them has a lecture in the evening, I have to go and pick her up from the university myself. You say you're a supporter of the revolution? No offence, but can you tell me what the revolution has done for us? It's true that Hosni Mubarak was corrupt and despotic; I was happy and optimistic the day he stepped down, but two years on things have become worse than they were under him. All of Egypt has fallen into chaos and ruin. We're living in a nightmare, so much so that many people are now saying that life was much better in the days of Mubarak"

Revolutionary: "You mustn't be so harsh on the revolution, Hassan. You can't really judge a revolution unless it's the revolutionaries themselves who take power. The revolutionaries don't govern Egypt, so we can't hold them responsible for what's happening. After the fall of Mubarak, it was the military council and the Muslim Brotherhood that came to power. They are the ones responsible for the decline we are now seeing."

Citizen: "The Muslim Brothers say that they cannot govern because you persist with demonstrations and strikes."

Revolutionary: "Strikes and demonstrations take place all over the world; a decent government could not be brought to a standstill by a demonstration. People who hold demonstrations are demanding their rights because, like you, they cannot live like this any longer. If the government treated them with respect by sitting down with them, and promising to address their demands according to a plan with a time frame for implementation, then the demonstrations would cease."

Citizen: "Then what do you see as the cause for this mess we find ourselves in?"

Revolutionary: "We began the revolution in order to bring down a despotic regime and create a new, just system. Unfortunately, however, the military council took power and kept the old regime intact. After this, the Muslim

Brotherhood joined forces with the old regime so that they could take control of the state and, ultimately, monopolise power forever."

Citizen: "It's hard to believe, but I actually voted for Mohamed Morsi, and was overjoyed when he won the presidency. I said to myself, 'Here is a man who has memorised the Qur'an and is devoted to God.' But, unfortunately, my hopes were dashed."

Revolutionary: "Morsi worked to further the interests of the Brotherhood, not the interests of the country. You know, of course, that when he issued his constitutional declaration he placed himself above the law; that is to say, his decisions were absolute, and not subject to legal challenge. I'm sure you are also aware that he intended to force 3,000 judges into retirement so that he could replace them with judges affiliated with the Brotherhood and, thereby, seize control of the judiciary. And no doubt you also know that he is going to create an independent zone around the Suez Canal. He alone will control the funding for this project, which won't be accountable to any regulatory bodies – not even to the People's Assembly."

Citizen: "In all honesty, sometimes I think that Morsi is divorced from reality; it's as though he's living in another world. He has caused all kinds of disasters yet he claims that he's implementing the goals of the revolution."

Revolutionary: "The Muslim Brothers are liars. Morsi takes his orders from the Brotherhood's Guidance Office. How can abolishing the law accord the revolution, when the whole reason for the revolution was to get rid of dictatorship? Morsi imposed an illegitimate attorney general on Egypt. And he also imposed an illegitimate Shura Council on us – only 6 per cent of Egyptians took part in the vote. Morsi has destroyed Egyptian pride. Remember how our soldiers were killed in Rafah? A whole year has passed and we are still waiting for justice for them. And what about the soldiers that were abducted in Sinai, did you see how they were humiliated?"

Citizen (shaking his head): "I feel very sad for them. God help their families."

Revolutionary: "Morsi detains the youth of the revolution, tortures them and kills them. Do you know how many have been killed since the January 25 Revolution? One hundred Egyptian citizens have been killed by Morsi, not to mention the thousands who have been detained and brutally tortured by the police."

Citizen: "It's exactly the same thing that went on under Mubarak."

Revolutionary: "Now you're getting it. Mubarak is locked up on the charge of killing demonstrators; Morsi is also responsible for killing demonstrators. So, logically, we should either prosecute Morsi or release Mubarak."

Citizen: "But how can we put Morsi on trial if he's the president of Egypt?"

Revolutionary: "Well, if I may, what is your job at the Ministry of Agriculture?"

Citizen: "I'm the deputy director for human resources."

Revolutionary: "So that means your boss is the undersecretary of the ministry?"

Citizen: "Not quite, the undersecretary is the boss of my boss."

Revolutionary: "OK, let's suppose that the ministry undersecretary broke a number of regulations or committed a crime. Say, for example, that you witnessed the undersecretary smoking cannabis in his office, or harassing female employees, or taking bribes from officials; would you keep silent or speak out against him?"

Citizen: "I would have to speak out, of course."

Revolutionary: "Well, what if someone told you that the undersecretary had received his position legitimately, does that mean that he can act outside the law once he holds the position?"

Citizen: "No, of course not. There are laws. Anyone who commits a crime should be held to account."

Revolutionary: "This is exactly what we are trying to do in the case of Morsi. He came to power legitimately through the elections, but he has since lost his legitimacy when he issued the constitutional declaration and began killing demonstrators."

Citizen: "You mean you want to depose Morsi?"

Revolutionary: "We don't want to depose him, exactly. We want to pass a vote of no confidence against him."

Citizen: "What's the difference?"

Revolutionary: "A vote of no confidence is an entirely legal procedure, it happens in many democratic countries. When an elected president breaks the law or commits a crime, the parliament can pass a vote of no confidence and hold early presidential elections."

Citizen: "But right now we don't have a parliament."

Revolutionary: "In the absence of a parliament, power devolves to the people themselves. Let's say you are involved in a legal trial and you appoint a lawyer to take your case before the judge. Now, let's suppose your lawyer does not show up on the day of the hearing. In this case, you have the right to speak for yourself in his absence. Similarly, the parliament is the representative of the people, if the representative is absent, then power reverts to the people. If we can collect a greater number of signatures than the number of votes that Morsi received in the elections, then we have the legitimate right to demand early presidential elections. Our campaign is called Tamarod and we are collecting signatures in all the governorates of Egypt. There has been huge interest in the campaign; we've collected more than 4 million signatures in three weeks."

Citizen: "That's all very well, but instead of collecting signatures, why don't you run as candidates in the elections yourselves; if you succeed in getting into parliament then you can advance your cause?"

Revolutionary: "To enter elections at this point would lend legitimacy to a president who has lost all legitimacy. Everything that has taken place in Egypt since the constitutional declaration is invalid. The Constituent Assembly is invalid, the Shura Council is invalid, the constitution is invalid – and everything they have done is invalid. How can we still say we don't recognise the constitution, but then enter parliament and swear an oath to uphold the same constitution that we reject?"

Citizen: "What do you intend to do once you have collected the signatures?"

Revolutionary: "When we have collected 15 million signatures this will show, decisively, that the people have no confidence in Morsi; the whole world will know that he has lost his legitimacy as president. Once this happens, nobody, whether in Egypt or abroad, can rightly treat Morsi as the legitimate president of Egypt, because the number of those who have no confidence in him will exceed the number of those who actually voted for him. We intend to present these signatures to the Supreme Constitutional Court and demand that it call for early presidential elections."

Citizen: "Young man, your words seem logical enough, but actual success in all this will be very hard to achieve. Have you forgotten that the Brotherhood besieged the Supreme Constitutional Court and prevented it from issuing legal rulings?"

Revolutionary: "Even if the Supreme Constitutional Court refuses to assist us we will still have 15 million citizens who have shown they have no confidence in Morsi. If we were to amass in front of the presidential palace then we could force Morsi to hold early presidential elections."

Citizen: "Very well, but if the Muslim Brothers do the same and start beating you and killing you, as they have done before, then what will you do?"

Revolutionary: "When there are millions of us it will be difficult for them to kill us. And even if they were to kill us, we are ready to die as martyrs for the revolution. Our lives are not more valuable than those of our companions who have been killed. We have truth on our side; the same people who elected Morsi have the right to declare they have no confidence in him. He must hold early elections. Would you like to support us by signing our petition of no confidence?"

Citizen (hesitantly): "I'll sign it, may God protect us. Although, to tell you the truth, I hesitate; I'm a stubborn old man with enough problems as it is already."

Revolutionary: "Mr Abdel Bari, you yourself said that we are living in a nightmare, and you complain that the country has gone to ruin. But instead of simply complaining, you need to act in order to save it. Let me reassure you that by signing the petition you are acting entirely within the law; no one can take action against you. As a citizen, you have the right to withdraw your support from any elected official. Take heart, and don't forget the thousands that were injured or killed in the revolution. Most of them were heroic youths who sacrificed their lives so that Egypt could be a country where there is justice and freedom."

(Hassan reached out his hand and took the paper from Tamer, who explained to him how to sign it. Hassan took out his national identity card and carefully filled in his details. He then signed his name.)

Revolutionary (smiling warmly): "Thank you, Hassan. I have another small request. How do your neighbours and work colleagues feel about Morsi?"

Citizen: "Most of the people I know have come to reject Morsi's presidency."

Revolutionary: "Excellent, take twenty of these forms and give them to people you know. Have them to sign them and then call me on this number. I can come meet you anywhere you like and get them from you personally."

Tamer gave Hassan no time to think about it; he quickly handed him a large envelope full of forms. When Hassan took the envelope Tamer smiled and then warmly shook his hand. Then he turned around and went about looking for new people to sign the petition.

Democracy is the answer.

AB

Who Will Drive Out the Sheep?

27 May 2013

This took place in a dense and lush jungle ruled by a corrupt and unjust elephant that relied on the bears and boars to keep the animals under control. The wolves would attack the animals each night and dine on their carcasses, leaving the scraps for the boars. The animals had no stability of life or food and the dreadful stench of the boars spread throughout the whole jungle.

When the animals could take no more, they declared a revolution against the elephant and the ensuing battle led to the deaths of hundreds of animals. In the end, they won out over the elephant and drove him out of the jungle. The animals authorised the giraffe to negotiate on their behalf and it went off to meet with a noble lion.

"O great lion. You are the leader of a pride of brave lions, and as you defend the jungle from anyone who brings you harm, I would ask you to look after us also, for we love and trust you."

The lion accepted to rule the jungle and an atmosphere of optimism and contentment swept through the jungle. But, as the days passed the animals noticed that the lion relied on the sheep so much that it became apparent he would hand power over to them. At that point the animals all got together to consult with each other. The hoopoe stated: "Be careful, colleagues. The lion obviously intends to hand power over to the sheep. The sheep are lying creatures and they will not keep their promises or maintain our rights. They will do whatever it takes to look after their own interests."

The ostrich shrieked: "We rose up against the unjust elephant with his wolves and boars so that we could live in peace and dignity. The lion is going to hand power over to those good-for-nothing sheep. What a waste of all the blood we have shed!"

However, the donkey had a different opinion and he brayed: "Animals! Why do you try and second-guess things? Who said that the sheep are going to rule the jungle?"

The hoopoe replied: "Listen, donkey. All the signs suggest that there is an agreement between the lion and the sheep. We had a revolution against rule by the elephant and his injustice and now we are living in peace. You will see for yourself that rule by the sheep is no better than rule by the elephant."

Day after day their fears were realised as the sheep took over governing the jungle completely and the lion withdrew to his den. The animals soon discovered that rule by the sheep was the same as rule by the elephant; the same injustice and the same lies. On top of this, the sheep also invited the ferocious wolves back into the jungle and they attacked the animals with the same immunity as they had in the days of the elephant. The animals were frustrated and one night, as the giraffe was walking around sad and lonely a boar stood in his path and said: "Good evening, giraffe. I know that you are saddened by the way the sheep are treating you. We boars also resent what has happened to the jungle. You rose up against the great elephant and ejected him, and now you are paying the price."

"The elephant was not great," the giraffe reported. "He was corrupt and unjust. He is the cause of all our difficulties. You boars were his partners in injustice, rapine and corruption."

The boar sighed and answered: "Let's forget the past, dear giraffe. I come bearing a message of friendship from the boars. I know that you are preparing yourselves for a new revolution against the sheep. I would warn you that the sheep have made an agreement with a large pack of wolves who will rip you to pieces if you rebel."

The giraffe snorted loudly and swung his long neck to the left and right: "Don't make fools of us, O boar. There are more animals living in the jungle than all the sheep and wolves put together. We are brave fighters and prepared to defend our rights to the end even if it should cost us our lives."

"I do not doubt your bravery. The only thing I would ask of you is that you let your brains win out over your brawn. The age of the old elephant is over, and he is now down by the river calmly awaiting death. We are hundreds of well-organised boars, and if you make an alliance with us we will finish off the sheep in one single day. O giraffe, I would ask you to agree to our request to join forces with you to drive the sheep out of the jungle."

The giraffe snorted again and said: "I am not authorised to speak on behalf of the animals in this matter. Give me a day, O boar."

"This is a golden opportunity, so don't let it slip through your claws. We boars are just waiting for the signal from you to come and join you in the right against the sheep."

The giraffe nodded his head as if in agreement, and said: "Tomorrow I will come here and tell you what the animals think."

The giraffe did not sleep that night. He went off to see all the animals and explained the situation to them and then listened carefully to their opinions. While he was speaking with the donkeys, the oldest one said: "I accept the boars' offer. The most important thing is for us to expel the sheep by any means. We have to make use of the boars' strength in our battle with the sheep."

The monkey did two somersaults, clung to a tree trunk as he thought, and then stated: "O giraffe, I reject this offer. How can we rely on the boars when we rose up against them because they killed hundreds of our colleagues during the first revolution? I can never accept that."

The ostrich bent its long neck and rubbed its beak in the ground. Then it raised its head and exclaimed: "O giraffe, you have forgotten what the boars did to us in the days of the tyrannical elephant, but I have not forgotten. I prefer death to cooperating with those criminal boars."

Finally the giraffe went off to the lion's den. He stood in front of it, bowed his long neck in a gesture of respect, and stated: "O great lion that, along with your cubs, has defended the jungle scores of times. We have always been happy to have your presence here with us and everyone fears your anger and your power. Speak. Tell us what to think. We have risen up against the unjust and corrupt elephant and now God is testing us with rule by the sheep who are no less corrupt or unjust than the elephant."

The lion yawned and replied: "What do you want from me, giraffe?"

"I want you to tell us where you stand, O lion. It's unclear to me whether you are with us or with the sheep?"

"I am with anyone who is good for the jungle," said the lion.

"That is neither here nor there. Will you help us to get rid of the sheep? Please give me a clear answer, O lion."

The lion yawned again and then said: "I'll give you my answer later, O giraffe. Now I want to have a sleep."

The giraffe went off saying to himself: "The lion is no use at all. We cannot rely on him. It's clear that he is in cahoots with the sheep."

At the appointed hour, the boar turned up and said: "Have you consulted with the animals, O giraffe?"

The giraffe answered calmly: "With the exception of some of the donkeys, the animals want nothing to do you with the boars because you were the helpmates of the elephant in his injustice. We rose up against you so how can we now collaborate with you? That will never happen."

"That is stupidity itself," the boar squealed in anger. "You are destroying the jungle with your idiocy. We are all living in such a state of upheaval that we just want the great elephant to come back and take over things again."

"As far as you boars were concerned, the elephant was marvellous because he gave you privileges you did not deserve but we animals can still see the truth. You boars and sheep are just as unjust as each other. We will have to get rid of both of you."

"May you and your animals be cursed," squealed the boar.

The giraffe lifted one leg threateningly and said: "Get out of here if you value your life."

The boar ran off in fear. At the crack of down, the animals all convened as they had agreed. They knew that the sheep did not stir before first light and hence the animals decided to launch a pre-dawn attack.

The giraffe proclaimed: "O brave animals. Remember our colleagues killed by the elephant by means of the wolves and the boars. They died dreaming of justice. Now you are rising up again for the sake of justice. You have refused to collaborate with the boars, and the lion has washed his hands of you because he is in cahoots with the sheep. Your fate is to fight by yourselves, but your bravery will win the day."

The hope and enthusiasm in the giraffe's voice affected the animals and spurred them on to attack the sleeping sheep who woke up terrified and called for the savage wolves to come and attack the rebellious animals. The wolves grabbed their victims by the throat and with their sharp teeth despatched them with one bite. Many animals were killed and as noon approached it became clear that the revolution was on the verge of collapse. As so many animals had been killed, they started to weaken and despair, but then they heard a terrible roar, which was soon followed by the appearance of the enormous lion, which had brought a whole pride with him. They attacked the wolves, ripping them to shreds with their claws. About ten wolves were killed and the rest took to flight. When the sheep realised that the they were defeated, they all lay down submissively on their sides to assuage the lion who roared loudly: "You sheep! I put up with you until the animals thought I had lost my mind. I gave you the chance to return to justice, but you just went and created more injustice and animosity, using the wolves to kill completely innocent animals the way the elephant did. Thus, I had to intervene to protect the animals from your wrongdoing. Our duty as lions is not just to defend the jungle from attack, but also to defend innocent animals from the injustice of an oppressor."

The animals all raised their voices in deep gratitude to the leader of the pride who roared again as if returning the greeting and stated: "Now I have done my duty and driven the sheep out of power, I shall return to my den with my pride. Fellow animals, I leave it to you to choose whoever is the right one to rule over you in place of the sheep. So who is it you want to rule the jungle?"

The animals all started calling out for the giraffe. He seemed embarrassed by this, lowered his head and started shifting around and scratching the earth with his hooves. Then he looked up at the animals and stated: "Thank you, my brethren, for having so much faith in me. I also wish to thank the great lion for having beaten the savage wolves and helping us to get rid of the evil sheep. I promise you the long dreamt of justice for which we have fought."

Cries of joy went up throughout the jungle as the animals felt for the first time that their revolution had succeeded and that they were entering into a new era.

Democracy is the answer.

RH

How to Break Free from Fascism

3 July 2013

In ancient Rome, the term *fasces lictoriae* referred to a bound bundle of wooden rods, sometimes including an axe with its blade emerging. The symbolism of the *fasces* suggested strength through unity and they were often carried at celebrations after a military conquest. The *fasces* reminded the subjects of the magistrates, as well as the emperor's, power and authority. This term disappeared for many centuries until it was brought back into currency when the Italian leader Benito Mussolini founded the fascist movement in 1919. Later, the influence of fascism spread beyond Italy with similar movements emerging, such as Nazism in Germany and Spanish fascism in Spain under the leadership of General Franco. Thus, derived from a historical context, the word "fascism" became a modern political term.

Fascist groups do not respect the will of the people. They believe that they possess the absolute truth and that they have the right to impose what they believe on others by force. As soon as fascists come to power, whether through free elections or by military coup, they demolish the democratic system and implement a plan for absolute control over all aspects of the state. Fascists despise those who oppose their ideology; they oppress them, they violate their rights and dignity, they interfere in people's lives in order to make everyone conform to one model of behavior. Fascists are inherently hostile to culture and the arts, to public and private freedoms. They do not hesitate in committing the most horrific crimes with a clear conscience, as they believe they have been chosen for a sacred task, one which justifies their infringement on others people's rights, their possessions and their lives.

Fascism can be military in nature; its aim being to restore the glory of empire by fighting other countries and occupying them. But it can also have a religious character; in such cases, fascists believe that they are not ordinary politicians but, rather, that God has appointed them to carry out a divine mission. Egypt has experienced both military fascism and the religious kind. Despite our respect for Gamal Abdel Nasser as a great leader and a patriot, it must be said that the regimes that has ruled Egypt since 1954 was a fascist, military one. In order to maintain itself, it depended on the power of the army and the police – not on free elections which would reflect the will of the people. Then the January 25 revolution happened and the military council and the Muslim Brotherhood made a deal with each other to further their own interests at the expense of the revolution. The first civilian, elected president, who was a member of the Brotherhood, came to power, and in the space of a few short months he put aside the rule of law and the constitution and imposed on the Egyptian people whatever the supreme guide of the Brotherhood decreed. This involved issuing an invalid constitution through the Constituent Assembly, exploiting the illegitimate Shura Council, appointing an attorney general who is a supporter of the Brotherhood, and electing an unknown person as the minister of culture in order to ruin Egyptian culture and purge it of artists and intellectuals who have ideas that the Brotherhood does not approve of.

Egypt is now ruled by a fascist organisation that came to power through elections. The Muslim Brotherhood decided to exploit democracy as though it were a ladder to power and thus, they cannot truly be described as

Islamists because they are liars and deceivers. They have committed crimes that are unacceptable in Islam and all other religions. Does Islam allow the shooting-dead of more than a hundred demonstrators by the police, or the torture of detainees with electric shocks, or the rape of men in Morsi's prisons? The Brothers are certainly not Islamists; they are fascists in every sense of the word. When a nation is afflicted with a fascist government, all citizens must put aside their political differences; their primary task must be to liberate their country from the grip of fascism. What we are dealing with here is not some ordinary politician whose performance has not lived up to our expectations; we are in the presence of a fascist organisation that came to power through elections but which is now carrying out its scheme to exclude others from power and to hold a monopoly on it forever. The fascist Brothers are living in an imaginary world; they think they alone represent Islam, and in their delusion they believe that they have been chosen by God to restore the glory of Islam. They talk about liberating Jerusalem and regaining Al-Andalus when they are not even capable of maintaining control over Sinai. Nor are they able to protect the waters of the Nile from the infringements of some African countries.[1] They have failed even to secure an adequate supply of fuel for Egyptians. However, the very worst failure of the Brotherhood is that they do not even recognise failure, ever. This is because they are simply unable to see reality. They are tireless in stubbornly maintaining their opinions, in their ability for deception, and their ability to deny facts which are crystal clear, all in order to preserve that seductive illusion in whose shade they were raised, namely: that they are the ones chosen by God to restore the Islamic caliphate[2] (which only really existed in the true sense for three decades before it was followed by centuries of despotism). The Brotherhood will not delay their plan to take over the country for one moment no matter how disastrous this is for the Egyptian people. They will never fulfill their promises, nor show due deference to the law; they will continue to show disdain for the legal rulings of the courts, and to relentlessly wage war against anyone who tries to stop them taking over the state.

It is our duty to resist this fascist rule, because with each passing day that they remain in power we are being led one step closer to destruction and ruin. Everywhere in Egypt now people feel frustrated and anxious. This is causing heated discussions which have sometimes turned into violent altercations. There are those who hate the revolution and blame it for allowing the Brotherhood to come to power; they long for a return to the days of Mubarak. The revolutionaries, however, are the ones who have suffered most from

1 There are 10 countries on the Nile, but the Nile Water Agreement (1929) allocates most of the water to Egypt and Sudan. However there remain disagreements and tensions frequently rise over the Nile River Basin

2 The Rashidun Caliphate lasted from Muhammad's death in 632 CE to 661 CE.

the Brotherhood's treachery and opportunism. They faced a dilemma in the presidential run-off: either to elect Ahmed Shafik, and thereby bring back the regime they had risen against, or to elect the Muslim Brotherhood's candidate. Some people, including myself, boycotted the elections; others voted for the Brotherhood, believing it to be the lesser of two evils. It is not true that the revolutionaries are the ones who brought the Brotherhood to power. Rather, the revolution empowered Egyptians to take part in free elections for the first time in decades. It was natural for the Brotherhood to win because they were the most organised and they used religion to appeal to ordinary people. Egyptians quickly learnt their lesson, however, and discovered the truth about the Brotherhood which has successively lost at the polls since. The rule of Brotherhood was a necessary experiment for Egypt that had been delayed until the current time. Now that Egypt has experienced their rule we can move on. But how do we first break free from the fascism of the Brotherhood? I believe there are three essential step to be taken:

First: Defend the institutions of the state. One of the rights of an elected president is that he may appoint his own followers to positions in the government and thereby take control of the government in order to ensure that his policies are implemented. However, the state must remain neutral. The Brotherhood is attempting to take control over the state itself in order to make it impossible for them to be overthrown. The Brotherhood's urge to involve Egyptian society in endless political and legal struggles is understandable when one considers how exhausted Egyptian society currently is; such a situation aids the Brotherhood in their goal to impose their will on the state through illegal means. The Brotherhood's claims that it is making reforms are false. While the Egyptian legal system does need to be reformed, the Brotherhood do not actually want to improve it; rather, they want to gain control of it by dismissing thousands of judges which will then be replaced by judges who support them. It is true that the former attorney general was in collaboration with the Mubarak regime, but the Brotherhood did not dismiss him so that he could be replaced by someone who would represent the people, rather, they did so in order to give the position to one of their own followers. Thus, our duty must be to defend institutions of the state against the Brotherhood's plot, even though we realise that these institutions have committed errors and excesses. We must observe here how the wrecking ball of the Brotherhood has attempted to demolish the judiciary, the media, culture and, yet, the Supreme Constitutional Court has not even touched the police force whose crimes against Egyptians were a direct cause of the revolution. The reason for this is that the Brothers need a strong oppressive force in order to ensure that the Egyptians submit to their planned takeover of the country.

Second: Reject compromise. Fascism always relies on the element of surprise and on imposing its will as a fait accompli. Afterwards, it takes on the first violent wave of protests, until little by little the voices of opposition die down and the people start to feel exhausted. In the end they just get on with their everyday lives, they grow accustomed to the new situation and, perhaps, even accept it. Accepting compromise is an act of complicity with a fascist regime; it represents a tacit acknowledgement of the new reality that it has imposed. If we accept the actions of the attorney general then we are essentially acknowledging his legitimacy, and whoever takes part in the parliamentary elections will subsequently lose their right to object to the illegitimate constitution, since by doing so they are tacitly supporting it.

We must not let a fascist regime lure us into negotiating with them over smaller issues lest we lose sight of the main issue at stake. The issue, as I see it, is that Morsi started out as a legitimate, elected president, but he lost his legitimacy when he issued the constitutional declaration and thereby trampled over the constitution and the rule of law. His legitimacy was further undermined when a hundred demonstrators were shot dead by police under his authority. Morsi must leave without any further delay. Every passing day that he remains takes our country further towards destruction and ruin.

Why are some politicians requesting guarantees from the Brotherhood that elections be free and fair? Have they not yet realised that the Brothers are liars who never keep their promises? Why do some politicians acknowledge that Morsi lost his legitimacy but then rush to meet with him as soon as he calls on them? Compromise greatly benefits the Brotherhood; it acts as an endorsement for the unlawful policies that they impose on us. We will not be able to break free from fascism unless we join together under one single demand: Morsi must go.

Third: Continue to resist peacefully. The Tamarod campaign emerged as a revolutionary idea to achieve the people's demands in a legitimate manner. In a democratic system the parliament can withdraw its confidence in the president and this will be followed by early elections. In this case, he will either win re-election and remain as president, or lose, in which case he will have to quit the presidency and be replaced by whomever is chosen by the people. In a democracy there is no power without accountability and there can be no accountability without the right to withdraw confidence. Egypt is presently without an elected parliament. Since there is no parliament to represent the people, therefore, it is natural that this power should revert to the people themselves. Those who gave their signatures in support of the Tamarod campaign are not anarchists; they are citizens who are practicing one of their fundamental political rights. They are requesting that confidence be withdrawn from a president who has trampled on the law and the constitution, who has detained innocent people, tortured them and killed them – not to mention his utter failure in managing the state. When the number of signatories for the Tamarod campaign is greater than the number of people who elected

Morsi, the entire world will see that his legitimacy has been lost, and when that happens the people will take to the streets. Millions will march on the presidential palace in order to force Morsi to accept the will of the people. Right now Egypt is occupied in the true sense of the word. It is not only foreign powers that occupy countries; fascist rule is a kind of internal occupation that is no less reprehensible or dangerous than one committed by a foreign country. On 30 June, God willing, millions of Egyptians will take to the streets to show their rejection of the Brotherhood's rule and demand early presidential elections as their right. The Egyptian people will triumph over fascist rule.

Democracy is the answer.

AB

The Importance of Cinema

10 June 2013

Do you remember the first ever time you went to the cinema? Do you remember the feeling of excitement mixed with awe when you gave your ticket to the usher and he led you into the darkness directing you to your seat? Do you remember how, when you sat down, you entered a new, magical world? Have certain scenes in a film ever affected you to the extent that they remained in mind afterward and took root in your imagination? If you are of an older generation then you will no doubt be fond of Farid Shawki, Ahmed Ramzy, Nadia Lutfi, Hind Rostom and Hoda Sultan. No doubt Soad Hosny represented the epitome of the sweet Egyptian girl – like the one who lived near you, or who you met at university, and fell in love with. And no doubt you adore – like all Egyptians – Umm Kulthum, Abdel Wahab, Abdel Halim, Mohamed Mounir, Ali El Haggar and others.

The question here is, what happens when a person is deprived of art? The fundamental difference between a primitive human being and one who is civilised is the latter's ability to overcome his or her base desires. Primitive humans are unable to comprehend anything beyond their immediate senses. Their enjoyment is found only in sensual pleasure, whether this be eating, drinking or the pleasures of sex. The civilised person, however, has the ability to know happiness that goes beyond the sensual; he or she can find enjoyment in music, literature and the arts. It is our creativity and appreciation of art that makes us civilised human beings.

In light of this we should be proud to be Egyptians. Egypt is a third-world country that suffered long decades of occupation and tyranny. Yet, in terms of culture, Egypt is a major player. The cinema, for example, arrived in Egypt in the year 1896, one year after its invention by the Lumière brothers in France. The Egyptians were aware of cinema before many people in the West, and Egypt is the only Arab country that has had an established film industry since the beginning of the last century. Egyptians who have made notable contributions in the fields of literature and the arts should be considered national treasures. Although despotism has left Egypt in a state of utter decline, nevertheless, Egyptian art remains at the forefront in the Arab world. No Arab artist can achieve great success unless he or she comes to Cairo; no Arab country has a comparable number of outstanding artists as can be found in Egypt.

This great treasure trove of Egyptian art and culture is currently under threat. The Muslim Brotherhood came to power through elections, but they soon revealed their fascist and repressive character. First, they issued the constitutional declaration that placed the will of the president above the rule of law, and thereafter, they began carrying out their plot to take over the state. They appointed an illegitimate attorney general who is loyal to them, and now they are using the illegitimate Shura Council to pass a law against the judiciary in an attempt to get rid of thousands of judges so that they can fill the vacancies with judges that are loyal to them.

The latest episode in the Brotherhood's takeover of Egypt is happening in the field of art and culture. The Brotherhood appointed Alaa Abdel Aziz as the minister of culture and his first ruling was to purge the administration; he fired all of the senior officials. Then, for reasons known only to him, he began insulting famous artists – a practice which he seemed to derive enjoyment from. For example, he sacked the internationally renowned flute player Inas Abdel Dayem from his position as head of the Cairo Opera House in a most disgraceful manner. And when notable intellectuals such as Bahaa Taher[1] and Sonallah Ibrahim[2] objected to his behaviour, the minister accused them of being uneducated. The minister then declared that he had been appointed to eradicate corruption in the Ministry of Culture. Of course, the Ministry of Culture does, in fact, suffer from endemic corruption and routinely wastes public funds on certain beneficiaries. But do the actions of the Abdel Aziz actually assist in the fight against corruption? Is it conceivable that, in any other country in the world, a minister could take up his position and to sack all of the senior officials in his ministry, then tarnish their reputations by repeatedly making accusations against them in the media, all without any legal action being taken as a result? Is Alaa Abdel Aziz unaware that ministries of culture throughout the world knowingly accept financial losses for the sake

1 Bahaa Taher is one of the most respected living writers in the Arab world. He was awarded the inaugural International Prize for Arabic Fiction in 2008.

2 Sonallah Ibrahim is an Egyptian novelist and short story writer who is known for his leftist and nationalist views. In 2003, he refused to accept a prestigious literary award worth 100,000 Egyptian pounds from Egypt's Ministry of Culture.

of promoting access to culture for those who would otherwise be unable to afford it?

It is quite clear that the minister's talk about fighting corruption is a pretext to persecute leftist artists and intellectuals who do not support the Brotherhood. Minister Abdel Aziz wants to erode Egyptian culture in order to pave the way for the imposition of new modes of culture that the Brotherhood views as being more compatible with Islam. This is not a matter of conjecture; whenever the Brothers talk about art they demonstrate their disdain for it as well as their ignorance of its meaning. The Brothers do not believe that art is a reflection of the imagination, which inevitably involves representations of both moral goodness and deviance. They fail to understand that it is not the role of art to pass moral judgments on others, but rather, to create empathy for them and to offer insight into their behaviour, regardless of the wrongs they commit. Like all fascists, the Muslim Brothers want art to act as propaganda in the service of their ideology. They do not want art to represent the lives of thieves, prostitutes, the marginalised or the deviant; rather, they want art to promote a model of pure and righteous living, as they see it. They do not comprehend the meaning of art and they don't derive pleasure from it, because they are extremists. Art and extremism are antithetical to one another; it is impossible for someone who appreciates art to be an extremist, just as an extremist can never appreciate art.

In March 2012, the newspaper *Al-Ahram* published the draft of a law proposed by Sheikh Al-Sayyed Askar, the head of the Religious Committee in the former People's Assembly. The draft proposed the introduction of what it termed as "moral regulations with regard to cinematic film". It proposed that any satellite channel that broadcast a pornographic scene should be closed down and a five-year prison sentence handed down to the owner of the channel. Now, while I am not here to defend pornography, we have to ask Sheikh Askar what constitutes, in his opinion, a pornographic scene. Is it pornographic when an actress puts on an evening dress that reveals her back and arms? If this is the case then we will have then to rid ourselves of thousands of Egyptian films that have been made since the 1930s right through to the present day. Sheikh Askar's proposal also bans other vices on the screen; if the protagonist is an alcoholic he is not permitted to make an appearance while drinking alcohol. Thus, the best way to avoid the penalties proposed by the sheikh is to only write righteous or pious characters. However, this would turn the film into an absurd religious lecture. Artists must enjoy complete freedom to be creative. Any restrictions placed upon their imaginations will completely spoil their art.

The Muslim Brothers may ask: what if an artist produces something that offends public taste? The answer to this is that, in civilised countries, when an artist displeases the public it is they who sanction him, not the authorities.

If the artist offends his audience then they will ignore his work as a form of reprimand. The Brothers might say: what about children, we do not want them exposed to certain films? The answer to this is that the only censorship in democratic countries is the classification system that is based on age. It's not a problem if some films are made for adult viewing only, nor does the classification of films require the work of art to be interfered with.

Restrictions only undermine the very essence of art. Drama is all about struggle, and struggle cannot be believable unless both good and evil are portrayed in a natural and convincing way. The Brotherhood thinks that the portrayal vice in art is in opposition with the virtue that religion is calling for. But this is a naïve way of thinking because art and religion both work to promote human values, it's just that they do this in different ways. While religion adopts the method of direct preaching, the power of art lies in its ability to convince through representation. We turn the light out in film theatres in order to forget the real world and completely merge ourselves inside the world we see on the screen. We must give the artist complete freedom to portray human life as they see fit – in the end we will discover that the positive impact of art on morality is no less than that of religion.

An example of this is the scene in the film *Al-Karnak* where Soad Hosny is raped. This scene symbolised the rape of Egypt by dictatorship. The scene can only evoke feelings of shock and pain in the viewer. Despite the actress' legs being bared, this scene performs a moralistic function; it demonstrates to the viewer how repulsive the crime of rape is. Another example is the way in which marital infidelity is condemned by religion; the wife that is unfaithful can be regarded having committed a crime for which she should be killed. In the history of literature, however, there are two great writers who characterised unfaithful wives sympathetically. One was the French writer Gustav Flaubert who did so in his novel *Madame Bovary*, and the other was the Russian writer Leo Tolstoy in his book *Anna Karenina*. The sympathy shown by these two writers for their unfaithful heroines compel us to understand the motivations behind their infidelity. Little by little, we discover the torment suffered by an unfaithful wife when she cheats on her husband. And while both novels are sympathetic towards the unfaithful wife, nevertheless, through their portrayals they ultimately highlight the moral dissolution that leads to the act of infidelity. The moral outcome is arguably that women readers would think long and hard before committing infidelity herself.

Thus, art and religion share many high-minded objectives, it's just that the ways in which they achieve them are different. The Egyptian art that we have cherished for so long, and which has helped shape our conscious for generations is now under attack from the fascist Brotherhood. The Brothers seek to eradicate our great Egyptian culture and replace it with the teaching programme that Hassan al-Banna [founder of the Brotherhood], imposed on his followers.

Yesterday I went to join a demonstration at the Ministry of Culture in order to show my solidarity with the artists and intellectuals who were protesting there. They were not there in defence of anyone in particular, nor were they hoping to be granted positions. Instead, they were there to simply do their duty: to defend Egyptian culture against the Brotherhood's fascism. Like millions of Egyptians, these protestors support the Tamarod campaign because it seeks to demonstrate that the people have lost confidence in Morsi, so that early presidential elections can be held. What Alaa Abdel Aziz is doing to culture is merely one aspect of the Brotherhood's plan to take complete control of the state and scupper any possibility that power will be shared. Right now, Egypt is under the occupation of a fascist organisation that will not rest until it has fulfilled its plan of turning Egypt into a Taliban-like emirate. There can be no dialogue or compromise with the Brotherhood. Experience has taught us that they are deceitful liars who never keep their promises. If you love the cinema, the theatre, literature and music, and if you don't want Egypt to be like Afghanistan or Sudan, then hurry out to sign the Tamarod petition. Join us on 30 June so that we save our country from the rule of a fascist organisation that exploits religion and commits, in religion's name, acts that are in direct contradiction to its teachings.

Democracy is the answer.

AB

How Can the President Sleep at Night?

17 June 2013

The plan had been carefully thought out by the head of the Republican Guard and senior officers from Homeland Security. Members of the security forces had been amassed outside the presidential palace in Heliopolis in order to create the impression that President Morsi was still inside. The number of guards outside his home in Al Sharqia Governorate was also doubled, which led people to think that the president's family was in residence there. In reality, however, the president and his family had secretly been taken to a two-story villa located on the north coast. This villa had been selected for its seclusion, safety and its proximity to El Alamein Airport; thus, the president could board his jet and flee the country should events require him to do so. The entire ground floor of the villa was allocated to the president's wife and their children, while the president had the first floor all to himself.

President Morsi was tired when he entered his suite. He had spent the day in endless meetings preparing for 30 June; all of the security agencies had informed him that on this date millions of Egyptians would take to the streets in all of the governorates of Egypt to demand early presidential elections. Morsi undressed and put on his white *jellabiya*, which he wore for going to bed. He performed his ablutions and the evening prayer. Then he phoned the supreme guide of the Brotherhood and spoke with him for almost an hour. They discussed both internal and foreign affairs. The supreme guide asked him to take certain decisions, and the president, fearing that he might not remember these instructions, wrote down what the supreme guide told him on a piece of paper which he carefully put next to the bed. At last, he could get some rest. He reached out his hand to turn off the lights, then, as was his habit, he turned onto his right side and recited some prayers, closed his eyes and slowly drifted off into sleep. Morsi did not know how long he had been asleep, but after a while he was woken by whispering voices that echoed through the room. He kept his eyes shut and tried to ignore what he was hearing but the whispering only grew louder. Frightened, he opened his eyes and reached out his hand to turn the light on. Before him was a strange scene; he looked on unable to believe his eyes. A large group of people surrounded him; they were all young people and their faces all bore the same sarcastic expression. They gazed at him with intense, searching eyes and the president's fear now turned into anger. He rushed to his feet and shouted: "Who are you, and how did you get in here?"

"Lower your voice, you're in no position to speak like that." The response came from a young man in his twenties. He was slender, his hair was combed back and he wore glasses. Morsi looked at the young man and suddenly noticed that there were very serious wounds on his face and body. He noticed that the others also bore similar injuries; they appeared to have gunshot wounds through their foreheads and their chests. Astonishingly, however, despite these wounds, they all smiled and appeared perfectly serene.

Morsi again shouted: "God protect me from Satan! Who are you?"

They all looked at one another, then the young man answered: "We are the hundred martyrs whom you killed, Morsi."

"I did not kill anybody."

"You are the one who gave the orders to the minister of the interior to kill us."

Morsi fell silent for a moment, then, with a stifled voice he said: "I didn't order the minister to kill anyone. The country was in a state of disorder and trusted religious scholars issued a fatwa ruling that Islamic law permits that resolute measures to taken as means for restoring order."

The young man smiled and said: "Morsi, we know our religion better than you; it forbids the killing of innocent people. You consulted no one except the supreme guide of the Brotherhood whose orders you carry out. You will answer to God for killing us, and the supreme guide will be of no help to you on the Day of Judgement."

Morsi tried to speak but the young man motioned with his wounded hand and said: "We did not come to listen to your empty words. Each one of us is a witness to your crimes. Do you know me, Morsi?"

Morsi did not answer, so the young man continued. "My name is Mohamed Nabil Abdel Aziz el-Gendy.[1] I worked as a tour guide. I took part in the revolution and was arrested at a demonstration on 25 January. An officer said to my face that my mother was a whore, and when I told him that he had no right to speak about my mother, he became furious and sent me to the central security camp in el-Gabal el-Ahmar, saying to his fellow officer: "I don't want to see him again." I was tortured so brutally that they ended up killing me. Afterwards, my body was thrown in front of a car so that the ministry could say that my death was a result of a car accident. Standing here before you are my fellow martyrs: Kirsty,[2] Jika,[3] El-Husseini Abu-Deif[4] and all the others; you killed us, and our blood is on your hands."

"What do you want from me?" Morsi shouted, his voice shaken.

As calmly as before, the young man answered: "Of course, you do realise that your days in power are numbered?"

"Impossible! I was elected to be president and I will complete my rightful term in office."

Now, el-Gendy raised his voice defiantly, and said: "You twice lost your legitimacy, Morsi: first, when you made your constitutional declaration and thereby trampled on the constitution and the rule of law; second, when you committed these crimes. Any president who kills his people loses his legitimacy. On 30 June millions of Egyptians will take to the streets to force you to step down so that early elections can be held."

"No one can force me out of office."

"You stubbornly resist the people just like Mubarak did and soon you will meet the same fate."

"I am not like Mubarak! The people love me and always show their support for me!" shouted Morsi.

The martyrs laughed loudly at this, and then el-Gendy said: "Where are all these people who love you? Fifteen million Egyptians have joined the Tamarod campaign to show they have withdrawn their confidence in you.

1 Muhamed el-Gendy, was an Egyptian activist who died after being beaten unconscious during interrogation at a security camp where he was detained for three days.

2 Mohamed 'Kristy' Hussein was an activist and one of the founders of the anti-Brotherhood Ikhwan Kazeboon Facebook page. He was killed in recent violent clashes at the presidential palace.

3 Gaber 'Jika' Salah, was a member of the April 6 Youth Movement. He was killed in November 2012 during protests on the first anniversary of the Mohammed Mahmoud Street massacre.

4 Egyptian journalist El-Husseini Abu-Deif, who died in hospital after being injured in clashes in December 2012, was probably killed by a bullet fired by a "professional".

You mobilise your followers into buses so that they can come and cheer for you in front of the cameras; have you no shame in using the same absurd performances as Mubarak? If the people love you so much then why are you in hiding here?"

"I am not hiding. These are just security measures against the conspiracies being hatched by members of the old Mubarak regime."

"Enough of your nonsense. Who are you trying to fool, yourself, or us? You allied yourself with members of the old regime, and thanks to your help most of them have been freed from prison, while on the other hand, you had the revolutionaries locked up. The people despise you, Morsi, and they despise the Brotherhood. They now know the truth about your organisation, how you exploit religion."

"You should show some respect when you speak."

"If you had honoured the promises you made than we would have shown you respect. Listen Morsi, we didn't come here to depose you; this is not our task. It is the Egyptian people who will depose you. We are your victims; it is we who will bear witness against you on the Day of Judgement and God will punish you severely, and justly, for your crimes."

"Enough! Get out, I don't want to see you!"

"But we shall never leave you, Morsi. We are your punishment in this world for the crimes you have committed. Wherever you go you shall see the bullet holes through our heads, our lacerated chests and the marks of torture on our skin. Always you shall hear the crying of mothers whose children you have killed, and the screams of you victims being tortured in your prisons."

At this, terrible screams, groans and pleading were heard all around. Morsi put his hands over his ears and started screaming: "Stop! Stop!"

El-Gendy now spoke with emotion in his voice: "Look at these people, look what you have done to them. Look at the bullet holes in their chests and their heads; you gave the order for them to be shot."

"Enough! Be quiet!"

"We shall never be silent, Morsi. We'll remain with you for the rest of your life. You'll hear the screams of the victims whom your subordinates electrocuted and raped. The screams of those who were tortured shall not leave your ears for a single moment."

"This is madness! I do not permit you to do this, do you understand me?" This time Morsi's voice alerted the guard who knocked on the door who rushed into the room with his gun at the ready. He had a look around and said: "Everything alright, sir?"

Morsi looked at him and said: "Some people got into my suite. Arrest them!"

The guard looked around in amazement and said: "Mr President, there's no one here except you, we have very tight security measures in place."

The martyrs burst into derisive laughter. Then Mohamed el-Gendy said: "Morsi, part of your punishment is that nobody can see us except you. If you don't keep quiet the guard will think that you are having hallucinations."

Morsi forced a smile and said to the guard: "Thank you. I seem to be tired, I'll try to get some sleep."

The officer saluted and left. But no sooner had he shut the door than the screams of the tortured echoed out once again – piercing screams of unbearable pain, followed by cries for help. Morsi began to hear the pleading voices with their broken expressions: "No, please don't do that! Please sir, I beg you. Have mercy on me!" and, "Don't torture me. I'm a human being with dignity. I beg you not to do this to me! Please kill me!" The screaming continued and the martyrs began circling Morsi, all the while they motioned to their lacerated bodies and the gunshot wounds to their heads.

Morsi trembled and covered his ears with his hands, then he screamed: "What do you want from me? Leave me alone! Leave me alone!"

At this point Morsi's nerves appeared to give way. He furiously pressed the bell to summon the guard, who rushed in looking anxious. Morsi hesitated at first but then said: "Call the doctor immediately."

The guard rushed out and returned with the doctor who appeared to have just woken up. The martyrs kept circling around Morsi showing their wounds while the screaming continued. Morsi yelled: "Doctor, I want a strong sleeping pill, and don't leave until I am asleep."

The doctor was somewhat perplexed. He took a triangular pill from his bag and gave it to Morsi who snatched it from his hand and swallowed it with a glass of water. There was no immediate effect, however. He still saw the martyrs and still heard the screams of the victims. After less than a minute Morsi shouted again: "Doctor, the pill is not working! Give me an injection, I must sleep immediately, I don't want to hear or see anything!"

The doctor hesitated, but he complied, shaking his head. He took a syringe from his bag and asked Morsi to lie down on his side; he then administered the injection. Morsi closed his eyes but he could still see the bodies of the martyrs and he could still hear the screams of those being tortured.

How can Morsi sleep at night?

Democracy is the answer.

AB

Revolt or Die

24 June 2013

Imagine that you find yourself in a legal dispute. You find yourself a lawyer who will represent you before the courts. Well, what if, subsequently, you find out that your lawyer is useless, or, that unconscionably, he has colluded with your opponents against you, then what do you do? Well, you will not allow him to represent you and you search for another lawyer who is honest and capable. In such a case, is it right for anyone to deny you the right to withdraw this lawyer's power of attorney? Is it right for anyone to demand that you continue to employ a useless and dishonest lawyer until your case, which he is taking before the judge, has been decided? Is it reasonable for anyone to say to you: "You chose this lawyer, so you must continue with him until the end, even if it leads to the loss of your case and the loss of all your rights"? Of course not. Your relationship to the attorney is not obligatory; it's optional and based upon mutual consent. It continues by the agreement of both parties. It's your case and it's your right to choose whomever you please to defend you. Furthermore, you have the right to replace a lawyer with another one at any time. This clear and straightforward logic is what gives a people the right to withdraw their support for an elected president.

One of the principles of a democratic system is that authority cannot be handed over to anyone without there being the power to hold that same person accountable. And there can be no real accountability where this power is absent. In all democratic countries the president is elected according to the will of the people through the ballot box. He shall be entitled to complete his term of office according to the constitution. However, were he to commit crimes, or make decisions that endanger the country and harm society, then it is the right of the parliament to hold a vote of no confidence, and to announce early presidential elections. In this instance, the president would face two possible outcomes: either he would win in the fresh elections and remain in power, or, he would lose the support of the voters, and, thereby, his position as the president. Withdrawing support from a president or from an elected prime minister is an established tradition amongst democratic systems. It has occurred many times before in France, Britain, the United States, Italy, Greece, Spain, the Netherlands, Venezuela, Argentina and Brazil. The people's election of a president is very similar to the power of attorney which one grants to one's lawyer; it is neither an obliging contract that lasts forever, nor is it a blank cheque. Just as you have the right to cancel a power-of-attorney, likewise, the people have the right to withdraw their support for their president.

This is what is going to take place on 30 June, God willing. Millions of

Egyptians will take to the streets to demand early presidential elections. The Muslim Brotherhood will refuse to see sense and will accuse the demonstrators of either being linked to the old regime or else secular infidels who are anti-Islam. The Brotherhood repeats these lies because they do not want to acknowledge their failure or their crimes. The Brothers consider themselves as holy, divine beings chosen by God to uphold His word and to restore the glory of Islam. Because of this, they take upon themselves the right to lie, to misguide and cheat, to abuse and kill the people. They convince themselves that these crimes are necessary for the cause of Islam, but even the enemies of Islam have never harmed Islam as much as the Brotherhood. If the Muslim Brothers reflected a little, and reconsidered the events of their rule over the past year, they would know that it is they who have divided the nation, neglected its interests and destroyed their own reputation.

When a member of the Muslim Brotherhood was elected as president, millions of Egyptians cheered in the streets. In large part, their joy was not because of the election of Morsi per se, rather, most of them were jubilant because Ahmed Shafik, the representative for the old Mubarak regime, had been defeated. Egyptians were optimistic about the election of the first civilian president after the revolution, and they welcomed Morsi's call for dialogue with representatives from the national forces and the revolutionaries. And although these parties were ideologically at odds with the Muslim Brothers, they showed a willingness to support Morsi so that he could succeed in realising the goals of the revolution. Regrettably, however, only a few weeks after his election the Egyptians discovered that the man they had elected was not the real president; rather, he is a junior subordinate of the Muslim Brotherhood's Guidance Office. In reality, it is not Morsi that presides in Egypt, but Khairat el-Shater. Egyptians discovered that the Brotherhood was not a political party, nor are they a pressure group; it is a secretive and fascist religious sect.

They raise their children to be fanatics who consider themselves superior to others, they teach them to despise others and to deny others their rights. Because of this they are prepared to commit every crime, from lying and breaking promises, to committing murder. To the Brothers everything is permissible as long as it is in the interests of their organisation, which take precedence over the interests of even the country itself. Everything the Muslim Brothers have done over the past year has demonstrated this truth. They say one thing and then they do something else; they use flashy, seductive slogans but then they harm the people and the country whenever it serves their own interests. They dismissed the attorney general who had links with Mubarak, but instead of replacing him with an independent candidate, who would act on behalf of the people, they appointed one of their own followers. They did this so that they could use him as an instrument with which to punish those who stand in their way, and at the same time to aid members of the Brotherhood who have committed horrible crimes to escape prosecution, even though their crimes have been recorded and documented by the revolutionaries.

They use the slogan "purifying the media" but then they appoint a minister of information who verbally harasses women and forces the state media to carry out the will of the Brotherhood.[1] They use the slogan "purifying of the judiciary" and then they abuse the law in order to get rid of thousands of judges so that they can replace them with judges who are loyal to the Brotherhood. They talk about the rule of law but then they trample on it whenever it gets in the way of their own interests. For the first time in the history of modern Egypt, a president has issued a declaration that places himself above the law and the constitution. He has invalidated the legal rulings of justice and has strengthened the illegitimate Shura Council with his supporters, as well as the illegitimate Constituent Assembly so that it can issue a illegitimate constitution. He then pushed through a referendum on this constitution in order to grant it legitimacy despite the rulings of the Constitutional Court which confirmed that referendums do not validate procedures which are themselves illegitimate.

Since the Brotherhood have been in power, a hundred people have been shot dead by the police. Thousands of innocent people have been detained and horrifically tortured; there are 20 documented cases of rape of detained men. None of this matters to Morsi, the Islamic president; on the contrary, when people were killed by the police in Port Said, and when their loved ones were still mourning them, Morsi spoke out thanking the killers and threatening the victims with further bloodshed. After this incident there was the killing of Copts: one of them was burned alive in Al Khusus, and bullets and bombs were used to attack a Coptic Cathedral in Cairo.[2] All that Morsi did was to offer his condolences by phone. On the other hand, when a Muslim Brotherhood cell was detained in the United Arab Emirates, he sent his deputy to smooth things over, as well as the head of the intelligence services.[3] He did not do this because they were citizens, but because they were Muslim Brothers. When Egyptian soldiers were kidnapped and killed in Sinai the Brotherhood put little effort into arresting the culprits; rather, they sought to appease the extremist groups in case they need to call upon their aid later on should the need arise. If you're not a member of the Brotherhood, they consider you misguided, unimportant and undeserving of either rights or dignity.

The Muslim Brothers are undertaking a development project in the Suez Canal region. Councillor Tarek el-Bishry has come out to say that he will strip

1 Minister of Information Salah Abdel Maqsoud faced allegations of verbally sexually harassing a reporter, Nada Mohamed, at an event organised by *Akhbar Al-Youm* and Cairo University's Faculty of Mass Communication.

2 The Ministry of Health said at least 90 people, including 11 policemen, were wounded around the cathedral, seat of the Coptic pope, in one of the worst sectarian flare-ups since the fall of autocratic President Hosni Mubarak in 2011.

3 UAE officials put 30 Egyptian and UAE suspects on trial for alleged coup plots linked to Egypt's Muslim Brotherhood.

the state of its control there and put a part of the country outside of the state's dominion; state law will not apply there and no one will govern it except the president and whomever he appoints from amongst his friends and followers. The truth is clear as day: this is not a failing president who merely needs us to give him a chance so that he can address his faults; rather, this is a fascist conspiracy to take over the Egyptian state so that it may rule in perpetuity. Every day that the Brotherhood remains in power leads Egypt closer and closer to ruin.

In the midst of all this darkness, however, the Tamarod campaign emerged. It represents an innovative, revolutionary idea that will hopefully lead to the removal of the Muslim Brothers by peaceful and democratic means. Withdrawing confidence in the president is one of the basic rights of the parliament, however, because Egypt does not currently have a parliament, the right to withdraw confidence devolves to the people who elected him. The Tamarod campaign has succeeded in collecting 16 million signatures; this number is greater than the number of votes Morsi received in the second round of the elections. With the campaign's success Morsi must now, according to political and democratic perspectives, hold early presidential elections. If Morsi were an ordinary president, he would be embarrassed by this rejection of his leadership and take measures to step down or call for early presidential elections. But Morsi is a member of the Muslim Brotherhood and they are more than willing to kill Egyptians and ruin the country in order to maintain power by any means and at any cost. Thus, there is nothing left for the Egyptians to do except take to the streets across Egypt and voice their discontent on 30 June. They will occupy the squares and will not return to their homes until Morsi announces his resignation so that fresh elections can be held. All sections of society have announced that they will participate in these demonstrations: artists, students, workers, trade unions, political parties, the national forces, and, most importantly, ordinary citizens who have not previously taken an interest in politics. They will all join in because the rule of this ruthless and immoral gang has made them fear for their lives and for their children's futures.

The Muslim Brothers try to terrorise the Egyptian people with the threat of assault. But we shall not be afraid, we shall join the demonstrations and exercise our democratic right to withdraw our confidence in an illegitimate president who has killed and tortured Egyptians, who has lied and broken his promises and who has violated the dignity of the country and the rights of its people. On 30 June we will have two choices: either we stand firm, showing that we care about our country and the future of our children by ousting this tyrannical gang, or, we submit – and if we do this we are finished, and the country will be lost forever.

We only have one demand: early presidential elections. There is no point in negotiating with the Brotherhood; they would only offer temporary compromises in order to escape being brought to account, then they will renege on the promises as they always do. When did the Muslim Brothers ever keep their promises before? So why should we believe them this time? If you love Egypt and you want to save it from the claws of this fascist gang, if you want Egypt to be a respectable country that is not discriminative against some sections of its society, if you honour the 3,000 martyrs who died so as we may live in a free country, if you honour the 18,000 wounded who paid with their blood for our dignity, then take to the streets on 30 June and do not leave until this affliction has been chased from our country. If you fail in your duty to protest then you will no longer have any right to complain later on about the injustice, the humiliation and the oppression. Either you rebel against the rule of the Brotherhood or you accept the humiliation they will impose on you: revolt or die.

Democracy is the answer.

AB

Candid Thoughts on a Wonderful Scene

8 July 2013

No matter how hard the Muslim Brothers try to deceive themselves, the truth is clear: more than 30 million Egyptians took to the streets, and the rule of the Brotherhood was overthrown by the will of the people. The question is this: was the ousting of Morsi, by these means, democratic?

In any democratic system it is within the rights of the parliament to withdraw its support for the elected president prior to the end of their term. When this happens the president will resign and early presidential elections will be held. In the exercise of its power, it is the duty of the parliament to act as representative for the people, but if there is no parliament then it is for the people themselves to exercise this power. Morsi became president with 13 million Egyptian votes; however, the Tamarod campaign collected the signatures of 22 million people demanding his resignation. Following this, more than 30 million Egyptians took to the streets to demand that he step aside. The General Assembly of the Egyptian People[1] demanded an end to the Brotherhood's rule. General Abdel Fattah el-Sisi, commander of the armed forces, had no choice but to carry out the will of the people in order to save Egypt from civil war – the threat of which was becoming apparent. The army, therefore, did not stage a coup d'état; rather, it carried out the will of the people in difficult and exceptional circumstances that almost led to the collapse of the state. By definition, a coup d'état is when the military uses

1 In the absence of a parliament to represent the people in matters of government, power must revert to its source: the people. The General Assembly of the Egyptian People is used here to illustrate this.

force to seize power. However, the army declared, right from the outset, that its aim was not to seize power, but to intervene in order to carry out the will of the people by removing a president who had lost his legitimacy.

Morsi's legitimacy was thrice lost. The first instance was when he issued a declaration that put his own will above the constitution and the law. He set about strengthening an illegitimate Constitutional Committee [i.e., with his own supporters], which then issued an illegitimate constitution. He strengthened the illegitimate Shura Council to better use it as a legislative tool to issue whatever laws the Brotherhood wanted. Second, he lost legitimacy due to the killing of more than a hundred people during his term in office. Thirdly, he lost legitimacy when millions of Egyptians signed the petition of the Tamarod campaign and took to the streets to show they had withdrawn their support. Thus, the ousting of Morsi in this manner was an entirely democratic procedure. The will of the people triumphed and the rule of the Brotherhood was overthrown. Nevertheless, it is useful to remember a few facts:

First: Since the referendum in March 2011, the revolution has been pushed in the wrong direction and led astray. But now the Egyptian people have taken their revolution back; the time has now arrived to achieve the aims for which revolution was initially carried out. The leadership of the army has changed, and the new leadership has proven that its desire to serve the country's interests comes before compliance with international pressure or compromise with the Brotherhood. Likewise, the police force has learned lessons from the revolution; thousands of police officers have refused to serve an authoritarian regime. All of the state's institutions united with the people to liberate Egypt from the Brotherhood, and a road map for the transition to democracy has been produced in the presence of representatives from different sections of the population: the Coptic Pope, the Sheikh of Al-Azhar, representatives from the Tamarod campaign and the Salafist Al-Nour Party. We need a national consensus but we should not show lenience towards those who broke the law, nor should we yield to political blackmail by any group, regardless of its influence. Change will not be forthcoming in Egypt unless those who made the revolution enter government.

Second: Over the past thirty years, the Muslim Brotherhood has been used as a scarecrow in order to justify despotism. According to the logic of Mubarak, the Egyptian people were not ready for democracy. He believed that any fair election would result in the Muslim Brotherhood coming to power, and if this were to happen, no one would be able to overthrow them because they would use religion as a weapon, and religion will always hold an influence over the Egyptian people. This logic shows a disdain for the people; it considers them ignorant and incapable of making informed decisions. Yet, since the Muslim Brotherhood has come to power the Egyptian people have surprised everyone by recognising the difference between Islam and political Islam. The Egyptian people discovered that the Brothers exploit religion for political ends, that they do not adhere to religious principles, and that for them, everything is permissible in order to increase their power.

On 30 June, 30 million Egyptians gathered in city squares and streets to oppose the Brotherhood and denounce its attempt to exploit religion for political gain. Although the rule of the Brotherhood was a painful experience, it has been an important lesson for Egypt and for the revolution because it revealed the truth about the Brotherhood. The Egyptian people suffered under the tyranny of the Brotherhood and the organisation should be disbanded. If the Brotherhood renounces the use of violence in the future, then they can form a right-wing party like all the other conservative, right-wing parties in the world.

Third: Perhaps General el-Sisi will now understand that the strong criticisms leveled against the military council never lessened our respect for the national army. The former members of military council that are responsible for crimes against the Egyptian people cannot be excused, but this cannot influence our attitude towards the army going forward, especially when the army is acting in our best interests. Similarly, although we are pleased that the relationship between the people and the police has been restored, this does not prevent us from demanding justice for the martyrs who were killed by police officers. Comprehensive national reconciliation cannot be achieved without justice, and there can be no justice without fair trials.

Fourth: The leadership of the Brotherhood never imagined that the people would turn against them so quickly, in light of this, their fall from power came as a great shock to the organisation, which explains their violent reaction. They know that Morsi will not return to power, yet, their supporters continue to attack state institutions in order to create anarchy. By doing so they believe that they are providing their ally President Obama the opportunity to intervene. The continual criminal acts perpetrated by the Brotherhood and their allies confirm their terrorist nature. For many years they concealed it behind their lies about how they reject violence. We are not demanding exceptional measures; the revolution happened so that the rule of law would be established. Therefore, the institutions of the state must be fully committed to punishing anyone who terrorises and attacks Egyptians.

Fifth: In the second round of voting in the presidential elections – the run-off between Ahmed Shafik and Mohamed Morsi – Egyptians found themselves stuck between a rock and a hard place. Those who had taken part in the revolution did not want to vote for Shafik, because he was seen as another Mubarak. For this reason, some of the revolutionaries boycotted the elections while others gave their vote to the Brotherhood candidate because they did not want a return to the rule of Mubarak's regime. This position is illustrated by the activist Abdel Halim Qandil[1] when he said: "The choice was between

1 Abdel Halim Qandil was a Nasserist activist and political columnist. He was involved in the establishment of the Kefaya movement and was former editor-in-chief of *Al-Arabi al-Nasiri*.

the shame of voting for Shafik who would return the old regime to power, or for the flames of the Muslim Brotherhood whose danger I was aware of. In the end, I favoured the flames over shame." However, there was a section of the population whose fear of the Brotherhood was greater than their zeal for the revolution and so they voted for Shafik.

Over the past year, those revolutionaries who voted for Morsi, or those who abstained, have been blamed for Egypt's ruin at the hands of the Brotherhood. A sarcastic name was coined to make fun of them: "the lemon squeezers", i.e., those who flavored their decision to vote for Morsi with lemon juice, in order to make it more palatable. The lemon squeezers were all revolutionaries, while most of those who blamed and ridiculed them were linked to the old Mubarak regime. In truth, they didn't hate the lemon squeezers for voting for the Brotherhood, they hated them for taking part in the revolution in the first place.

Those who brought down the Brotherhood were not just one group of people. There were the ordinary citizens who trusted the Brotherhood initially, but later began to realise the error of their ways. There were also those who felt anger and bitterness towards the Muslim Brotherhood because it turned its back on the revolution in order to further its own interests. The final group was made up of remnants of the old regime that saw an opportunity to take advantage of public anger. The military council managed to preserve the Mubarak regime; then the Brotherhood came to power and, with their usual opportunism, decided to ally themselves with the old regime in order to gain support for their plan to take over the state. The remnants of the old regime, however, never trusted the Brotherhood, instead they pursued their aim of restoring the Mubarak regime. Indeed, those linked to the old regime spent millions of Egyptian pounds on utilising the media; this played an important role in exposing the crimes of the Brotherhood and encouraging Egyptians to rebel against them. However, in their legitimate war against the Brotherhood, their message was also hostile to the revolution. It is no coincidence that Mubarak's supporters, both politicians and journalists, are now leading Egypt's current struggle against the Brotherhood. Nor is it a coincidence that the voices that portray Mubarak and his regime in a positive light, in comparison to the Brotherhood, are growing louder. These are the same voices that now seek to cleanse the old regime's reputation as it prepares to regain power.

The gains of the revolution are manifold. It taught us not to be afraid. It taught us that when the people come together they will triumph. The revolution saved us from Mubarak, from military rule and from religious fascism. It was able to unify the state institutions with the people against the Brotherhood. The revolution now has an opportunity to build a modern democratic state with the support of the national army. However, as the revolution moves forward in this direction it will face two dangers. Firstly, there is the threat of the military returning to power, and secondly, the return of the Mubarak regime to government. In my opinion, the former is not a threat because the army does not want to rule; its motivation for supporting the people in achieving their will was purely patriotic. The latter is more dangerous and the supporters of the revolution must draft a new constitution that will implement legal and constitutional precautions so as to prevent those who oppressed, plundered and degraded the Egyptian people from returning to power. The revolution was carried out to put an end to tyranny and corruption, wherever these arise. The future belongs to the revolution alone.

Democracy is the answer.

AB

A Conversation Between a Revolutionary and a Muslim Brother

15 July 2013

The encounter took place within a middle-class Egyptian family after they had broken the fast [i.e., during Ramadan]. Most of the younger members of the family had taken part in the revolution, but there was one amongst them who was a Muslim Brother. He was an engineer who had joined the Brotherhood while studying at university and had remained an active member after he had graduated. When they were drinking tea after the meal, a young man who was known for his revolutionary zeal approached the Muslim Brother.

Revolutionary: "I didn't expect to see you here today; I thought you would be at Rabaa Al-Adawiya."[1]

Muslim Brother: "I was. I left the sit-in to break the fast with you, but I'll return there later."

Revolutionary: "Can you tell me why you are having a sit-in?"

Muslim Brother: "We are staging a sit-in so that the legitimate president of Egypt will be restored to his rightful position."

Revolutionary: "Morsi is no longer the president; the people removed him."

Muslim Brother: "Not so, he is the legitimate president of Egypt; he was overthrown by a military coup."

Revolutionary: "You parrot the words of your leaders without so much as a thought. By definition, a coup d'état is when a group from within the military

1 The square in Cairo where the famous massacre would later take place.

moves to seize power by force. This scenario is the complete opposite of what happened here in Egypt. Twenty-two million Egyptians gave their signatures in support of the Tamarod campaign and 30 million Egyptians took to the streets to remove Morsi. Egypt was on the verge of civil war, so the army intervened on the side of the people to save the state. How then can this be a military coup?"

Muslim Brother: "The Tamarod campaign, of which you are speaking, is an instrument of the old Mubarak regime."

Revolutionary: "It's a shame that you just parrot the words of the supreme guide. The youth who started the Tamarod campaign belonged to the Kefaya movement and to the Egyptian Popular Current;[1] they were some of the fiercest opponents of Mubarak. According to the democratic system, the election of a president is a contract that is made between the people and the person they elect. If the president violates that contract, then parliament has the right to hold a vote of no confidence. If this succeeds then the president is forced to step down and early presidential elections will be held. Parliament exists to represent the people in exercising its powers, but because Egypt currently lacks a parliament, it is the right of the people to exercise such powers themselves. Thus, the Tamarod campaign is entirely legal and democratic."

Muslim Brother: "How do you know that the signatures of the Tamarod campaign are even genuine?"

Revolutionary: "The organisers of the Tamarod campaign asked the Supreme Constitutional Court to verify the authenticity of the signatures, some of them even asked the United Nations to review the signatures. However, before this could be done, millions of Egyptians took to the streets in protest – the largest protest in the history of Egypt. Because this happened, there was no longer any need for verification; it was perfectly clear that the people wanted Morsi's removal. It is simply impossible to defend him."

Muslim Brother: "You misunderstand me. I am not defending Morsi; I am defending democracy. The removal of Morsi in such a way simply means that the people will now have the right to depose any elected president in the future; all they have to do is protest."

Revolutionary: "In a democratic system there is no power without accountability, and no accountability without the right to withdraw one's support. It is the right of parliaments all over the world to hold a vote of no confidence against an elected president at any time. Morsi had fundamentally lost his legitimacy. He lost it last November when he issued his constitutional declaration by which he suspended the rule of law and the constitution. Can you tell

1 The Egyptian Popular Current is a movement in Egypt, created after the 2012 presidential elections by former presidential candidate Hamdeen Sabahi. Many of its leading members formerly belonged to theMuslim Brotherhood's youth wing and the April 6 youth movement, along with several independent young activists involved in the January 25 Revolution.

me of any elected president in any democratic country that has issued such a declaration and managed to stay in power after doing so? And what kind of democracy are you talking about? Are you joking? Your president gave his own decrees immunity from prosecution."

(After these words there was a tense silence.)

Muslim Brother: "Please be more careful with your words; they are giving me a headache. You and your fellow revolutionaries have double standards; you talk about democracy while at the same time you sided with the military in order to depose an Islamic president, all because of your hatred for the Brotherhood."

Revolutionary: "No offence, but I don't really understand the Brotherhood's relation to Islam. Does Islam advocate lying, deception, breaking agreements, oppression and appointing incompetent people simply because they are loyal to your organisation? Does Islam encourage you to seek help from the United States so that you can remain in power? Does Islam recommend that you invite the European Union to interfere in our country? Does Islam tell you that you should incite armed groups in Sinai to kill Egyptian soldiers?"

Muslim Brother: "You're just throwing around random accusations."

Revolutionary: "You know very well that I am speaking the truth. Didn't one of the Brotherhood's leaders say that the violence in Sinai would continue until Morsi was returned to power? Do you know what we call a person who incites attacks against the soldiers of their own country?"

(The Muslim Brother was silent, as though trying to maintain his composure.)

Muslim Brother: "So you're glad that Egypt is back under military rule?"

Revolutionary: "You still insist on distortions. The army aligned itself with the will of millions of Egyptians and prevented the country from sliding into civil war. Any given army in the world has two main tasks: defending the nation against invasion and preventing it from internal collapse. The Egyptian army performed its national duty. In a few months, God willing, Egypt will have a new constitution – not the current, illegitimate one that was rushed through in the middle of the night and then imposed on us by the Brotherhood. We will also have a new elected president and an elected parliament that expresses the will of the people. So how is this military rule?"

Muslim Brother: "Wasn't it your people that called for the end the military rule? Why have you changed your tune so easily?"

Revolutionary: "Changing a position is not necessarily to one's discredit; in fact, it's natural, because new circumstances necessitate new positions. The important thing is that someone does not alter their principles or surrender them to further their own selfish interests. In the early days of the revolution we would shout, 'The army and the people are one hand.' However, when successive massacres against Egyptians started taking place under the military council, we then called for the end of military rule. The leadership of the army has changed and this new leadership took a great, patriotic stand and so we strongly supported them. Despite this, however, we will continue to demand the prosecution of those who were responsible for the massacres under the military council. We adapt our positions according to changing events but we never alter our principles. As for the Muslim Brothers, however, you drop your principles whenever it serves your interests. Who was it that awarded Field Marshal Tantawi and General Sami Hafez Enan the Order of the Nile? Who prevented the reform of the police force? Who prevented the prosecution of the officers who killed demonstrators? Who cheered and clapped for the military council when the revolutionaries were being killed on Mohamed Mahmoud Street? Who mocked the female demonstrators that were sexually assaulted in front of the Council of Ministers? Who failed to make a successful appeal to overturn the acquittal of those who were responsible for the bloodshed at the Battle of the Camel until the courts had given them a final verdict of innocence?[1] The people rejected the Brotherhood on 30 June because you betrayed the revolution."

Muslim Brother: "Those who took to the streets on 30 June were supporters of the old Mubarak regime."

Revolutionary: "If Mubarak had had 30 million citizens supporting him then he wouldn't have been deposed in the first place."

Muslim Brother: "Do you deny that Mubarak's supporters joined the Tamarod campaign?"

Revolutionary: "The Tamarod campaign did not discriminate; it was directed at all Egyptians. But who is actually responsible for the reemergence of those who support the old regime? A number of writers, who for a long time had pandered to Mubarak and served his son Gamal, kept a low profile after the revolution – to the extent that they adopted pseudonyms in order to continue writing in the press. Now, however, they have reappeared attacking the revolution and shamelessly defending Mubarak. Who is responsible for their return? It is the Muslim Brothers who are responsible, because the Egyptian people wanted to get rid of the Brotherhood so much that they have forgotten, for the moment, how bad the crimes of the Mubarak regime were. But this

1 Mohamed Morsi had promised to deliver justice for early victims of the 2011 uprising when he was elected in June. However, the Court of Cassation issued a final ruling in support of the Cairo criminal court's decision to acquit all defendants in the case of protester killings during the Battle of the Camel.

forgetfulness won't last; just as the revolution swept away the Brotherhood, so too it will prevent a return to the old regime."

Muslim Brother: "The police against whom the revolution erupted have now joined with the demonstrators in Tahrir Square. Does this not show that the old regime has returned?"

Revolutionary: "The most basic principle of justice is individual culpability, not collective. The revolution cannot denounce the entire police force. Individual officers who oppressed, tortured and killed Egyptians must be handed over to receive a fair trial. However, when thousands of police officers refuse to be used as a tool of oppression against the Egyptian people then we should show our solidarity with them. You talk as if Morsi bears no responsibility for any crimes! Who's responsible for the torture and killing of Mohamed el-Gendy? Who's responsible for the killing of 134 martyrs within six months? Who killed innocent people in Port Said during the funerals for their martyrs? Who detained 3,400 citizens and tortured them horribly? Do you know that there are 20 cases of male detainees being raped in the prisons of your president who calls himself a Muslim?"

Muslim Brother: "I don't understand why you are all so hostile towards Islamification."

Revolutionary: "Where is this Islamification? If the Egyptians were hostile to it then why did they elect Morsi in the first place? And why did they celebrate his victory in the streets but one year ago? Have you never asked yourselves why Egyptians have come to despise you so much in such a short space of time? You really have lost touch with reality. What kind of Islam justifies shedding the blood of the people? Who killed and tortured people outside the Heliopolis Palace and Bein El Sarayat?[1] Who incited people to violence and murder? Who threw children from the rooftops?"[2]

Muslim Brother: "Did you not hear about the massacre committed by the Republican Guard?"[3]

Revolutionary: "I did hear of it, and I was deeply saddened that there were so many casualties – regardless of their political persuasion. I believe there should be an independent investigation in order to establish whether the

1 On the afternoon of 2 July 2013, thousands of Muslim Brotherhood supporters gathered near Cairo University for a rally on behalf of Morsi's presidency. Both local residents and demonstrators supporting former President Mohamed Morsi died in clashes, with 18 people reported dead.

2 Mahmoud Hassan Abdel-Naby and Abdullah el-Ahmady were arrested after a video showing them throwing children from the rooftop of a building in Alexandria's district of Sidi Gaber went viral. The footage showed one of the defendants stabbing a child and throwing him off the rooftop of the building.

3 In the early hours of 8 July 2013, security forces killed 51 Muslim Brotherhood supporters camping outside the Republican Guards' club in Cairo. The Egyptian military claimed the demonstrators had attempted to break into the building with the aid of armed motorcyclists.

Brothers were out to demonstrate peacefully or to launch an armed assault on the Republican Guard."

Muslim Brother: "So you agree with the detention of Muslim Brothers and the shutting down of religious television channels?"

Revolutionary: "I disagree with the detentions; I want to see Morsi properly brought to trial as soon as possible on charges of treason and the killing of demonstrators. The same goes for your leaders who incited people to commit murder at Rabaa Al-Adawiya; they should be arrested and prosecuted immediately. I'm against any extraordinary measures but I do demand proper application of the rule of law. As for the religious channels I'm against them being shut down without a proper court order. However, you know very well that these channels were continually inciting hatred and violence, and this made it very easy to procure the necessary court order to get them shut down."

Muslim Brother: "I must now return to the sit-in but I want to remind you of the danger of excluding the Brotherhood; we represent a significant section of society."

Revolutionary: "I'm against excluding any section of the population, but you won't have a place in our society as long as you carry arms against us. Only when you respect others and stop accusing them of being infidels will you have full rights as citizens. In democratic systems, those who take up arms against citizens and the state are sent to prison."

The Muslim Brother shook his head, he stood up, shook everyone's hand and departed.

Democracy is the answer.

AB

The Case of Fujimori

22 July 2013

Alberto Fujimori was the president of Peru during the 1990s. He came to power through democratic elections, and then, two years into his presidency, on 5 April 1992, he issued a presidential decree by which he dissolved parliament, and suspended the law and the constitution. By doing so he effectively granted his presidential decrees immunity insofar as they could not be overruled by the judicial system. As soon as Fujimori issued this dictatorial declaration the international community came out in strong opposition against him: the United

States quickly severed diplomatic relations with Peru and put an embargo on economic and military aid; they condemned Fujimori's declaration as an assault on the democratic system, since it effectively transformed Fujimori from an elected president into a dictator. Most countries followed the example of the United States: Venezuela cut its relations with Peru, Argentina and Chile withdrew their ambassadors, and Germany and Spain cut their aid to Peru (with the exception of humanitarian aid). The Organisation of American States[1] also condemned Fujimori's overthrow of democracy and threatened to revoke Peru's membership. Fujimori could not hold out against all of this international pressure; after a few months he repealed the constitutional declaration and took measures to restore democracy, and thereby, Peru was able reestablish its relations with the international community. This incident confirms a simple truth: when an elected president abolishes the law and places their individual will above the judicial system, granting their decrees immunity from legal challenge, they are no longer an elected president; they are a dictator. When they take such a step they lose all legitimacy, because if they destroy the democratic system by which they were elected then they also destroy their own legitimacy.

Perhaps you will notice, dear reader, that what Alberto Fujimori did is exactly the same as what Mohamed Morsi did last November when he issued a declaration in which he abolished the law and the constitution, and granted his decrees immunity against legal challenge. Morsi committed the same crime as Fujimori; both started out as elected presidents and then turned into dictators. It would have been the duty of parliament to hold a vote of no confidence in Morsi immediately after he issued his declaration, but Egypt had no parliament. In the absence of a parliament to represent the people in matters of government, power must revert to its source: the people. This is why the Tamarod campaign was so significant: 22 million Egyptians signed it to show that they had no confidence in Morsi's presidency. Then came 30 June, when more than 30 million Egyptians took to the streets to demand that Morsi step down and that early presidential elections be held. With Morsi's rejection of these demands, Egypt was put on the brink of civil war. This led the army to make a great, patriotic stand to save the Egyptian people and Egypt from ruin. Thus, it was not the military that sought to overthrow democracy; it was Morsi who did so when he issued his dictatorial declaration.

Thus, we can observe how Morsi's declaration – in both the form and content – corresponds with that of Fujimori. The curious thing here, however, is that while the United States raised a storm of protest against Fujimori's declaration, it completely ignored that of Mohamed Morsi. The reason for this

1 The Organisation of American States, or the OAS or OEA, is an inter-continental organisation founded on 30 April 1948, for the purposes of regional solidarity and cooperation amongst its member states.

is that the US foreign policy is never motivated by higher principles; rather, it acts only in accordance with US interests. For 30 years the United States supported Hosni Mubarak, all the while knowing he was a corrupt dictator. They knew he rigged the elections, they knew about the oppression and the torture of thousands of Egyptians by the state security service, and yet, they still considered Mubarak a good leader. Why? Because he cooperated with them in furthering US interests. The United States worked with Morsi just as they did with Mubarak. Fujimori's actions conflicted with US interests and, therefore, on this occasion they deemed his actions an overthrow of the democratic system. However, US interests led the United States to side with the Muslim Brotherhood; they bet on the Brotherhood because of its popularity, its organisational strength and its ability to keep Hamas under control. This latter asset offered Israel an opportunity to counteract acts of resistance carried out by Hamas. Thus, when Morsi issued his dictatorial declaration, the US didn't utter a single word in condemnation of him. On the contrary, both President Obama and his ambassador to Egypt, Ann Patterson, continued to support the Brotherhood even though this went against the will of the Egyptian people.

I urge all English-speaking Egyptians to go onto the White House website and ask them the following question: why did the United States condemn Fujimori when he overthrew the law and the constitution in 1992, yet not utter a single word of condemnation when Morsi did exactly the same thing in Egypt in 2012?

The hypocrisy of US politics is nothing new. The truly astonishing thing, however, is that, even as we speak, the Brotherhood remains incapable of seeing what has actually taken place. It is astonishing that the leadership of the Brotherhood persists in denying the truth, and even now, it is out rallying their followers to prosecute an absurd jihad that only exists in their imaginations. It is astonishing that the leaders of the Brotherhood are actually trying to create chaos in their own country, and that they would even consider an attack on the army in Sinai as an acceptable response to Morsi's removal. It is astonishing that their leaders would appeal to the United States for help when they were the ones who so frequently accused the Copts, the liberals and the leftists of seeking support from abroad. It is astonishing how the sheikhs of the Brotherhood curse the US in their sermons as the greatest enemy of Islam and as the murderer of Muslims in Iraq and Afghanistan, but then turn round and publicly ask the US to restore them to power.

The leadership of the Brotherhood has demonstrated that they are prepared to do anything for power: from sending their supporters to certain death, to asking the West to intervene in the affairs of Egypt. The question is this: many of the members of the Brotherhood are educated and intelligent, so why is it that even now they are incapable of seeing what has actually taken place? How can they not comprehend that what General Abdel Fattah el-Sisi did was not a coup, but that the real coup was carried out by Morsi when he abolished the law and the constitution, and granted his decrees immunity against legal challenge (exactly as Fujimori had done)? Why were the Muslim Brothers incapable of seeing the millions of protesters calling for Morsi's removal?

All of these questions have one simple answer: the politics of the Muslim Brotherhood proceeds from a religious perspective. Most people can deal with criticism regarding their ideas and behaviors, but cannot accept criticism when it is directed at their religious beliefs. This is because religious belief is based upon sentiment rather than reason. Those who are religious often use reasoning to prove the veracity of their beliefs, but they also tend to disregard any rational, objective assessment of them. Religion involves the rejection of differing religious beliefs, and while one's religion may allow for coexistence with people of different religions, nevertheless, one will not acknowledge that their beliefs are true. This is because everyone who adheres to a certain religion believes that it alone is the correct one and that other religions are either false or defective. Thus, even the most intelligent people, and those who are the most open to criticism when it comes to general matters, are infinitely capable of holding erroneous ideas when it comes to matters of their religion. Indeed, such people may even commit acts of aggression in order to protect their religion from skeptical criticism. Such has been the case with religions since earliest times. Religious conflict has long been the cause of disasters, wars and horrific massacres that have claimed millions of lives throughout history. In light of this, permitting the formation of religious parties is the biggest mistake a society can make, because those whose politics stem from a religious perspective will automatically claim that they are defending religion and thereby deny that any of their decisions might be in error.

This is the problem facing Egypt at the moment. Those who are holding sit-ins for the purpose of returning Morsi to power refuse to acknowledge that most Egyptians wanted his removal. Instead they will continue to support him and esteem him as a great president even though he has killed thousands of Egyptians and committed every kind of crime. The reason for this is that they believe they are supporting Islam by supporting Morsi. It's just as pointless trying to persuade the Muslim Brothers that Mohamed Morsi lost his legitimacy as it is trying to persuade someone that their religion is wrong. It's no coincidence that the Brothers at the sit-in call themselves "Mohamed's Army" and consider the rest of Egyptians as enemies of their plan for Islamification. In their opinion, only the Guidance Office has the right to decide what best serves the interests of Islam, and anyone who opposes the Brotherhood is, in their opinion, opposing Islam itself.

The Brothers did not view Morsi's coming to power as just a political victory; rather, they saw it as a victory sent down by God Almighty to enable them to promote the word of God and restore Islam's former glory. The

Brothers' separation from reality, and their preoccupation with this delusional jihad, is precisely the same problem that afflicts the Salafists. For that matter, this inability to see reality will be a problem for any political party that bases its politics on religious doctrine; they will always be prepared to justify the mistakes and crimes committed by their leaders, because, according to what they believe, they are carrying out the commands of God.

What happened on 30 June is one the greatest achievements of the Egyptian people. After just one year under their rule, Egyptians (even the least educated amongst them) were able to discern the real nature of the Brotherhood and discovered that Islam is one thing and Islamism is another thing altogether. Islam is a great religion that defends truth, justice and freedom, whereas Islamism is nothing more than a political tool that exploits people's religious sentiments for the sake of gaining power. Egyptians rejected Islamism but became more devoted to the Islam they know and love. The sight of millions of Egyptians praying together and calling for the removal of Morsi throughout the public squares of Egypt had a profound significance for me. In that moment, it was as though the Egyptian people wanted to show how much they love their religion, and in this way repudiate those who would exploit it for the sake of power.

It is my hope that those who will now develop the political road map for democracy will not let the Egyptian people down this time, as happened with the March 2011 referendum. I hope that the committee responsible for amending the constitution will prohibit the formation of parties that are essentially religious in nature. If we want to build a democratic state then there can be no place for parties that believe that they alone speak on behalf of God. The former military council made the mistake of permitting the formation of religious parties and Egypt paid a high price – it is now time to remedy this mistake. As we have seen, allowing the formation of parties that discriminate against Egyptians on the grounds of religion only ever leads to the division of the country, to the spread of extremism, sectarianism, chaos and ruin. Placing a ban on religious parties does not mean preventing the Muslim Brothers and Salafists from exercising their political rights. As long as they do not break the law, and as long as they do not commit crimes, then the Muslim Brothers and Salafists should have their full political rights as Egyptian citizens – including the right to form political parties. However, these parties must be democratic in character. They must promote equality and not discriminate against Egyptians on the basis of religion. Over the last two years the great revolution lost its way, but right now we have a real opportunity to put it back on the right track. Now is the time for a fresh start. The revolution will continue, God willing, until all of its goals have been achieved.

Democracy is the answer.

AB

Thoughts on the Course of the Revolution

29 July 2013

It's been a long time since I've seen the Egyptian people as happy as they were last Friday. Egyptians were in a state of joy and optimism for the future, more so than when Hosni Mubarak stepped down on 11 February 2011. In every part of Egypt, millions of people took to the streets to support General Abdel Fattah el-Sisi, commander-in-chief of the Egyptian armed forces, in the task of fighting the malignant terrorism that is now facing the country in the Sinai region and in most Egyptian cities. The people rejoiced that the rule of the Muslim Brotherhood had ended – the terrible nightmare that they had endured for a year. They were glad to see the Egyptian state was functioning again for the first time since the January 25 Revolution in 2011. Everyone stood in solidarity – the armed forces, the police and ordinary civilians – united by one purpose: to remove the Brotherhood from power and put its leaders on trial for the crimes they have committed. Egyptians were happy because they felt that their armed forces were protecting them against a criminal, fascist organisation whose sheikhs had been threatening Egyptians with bloodshed and death for a number of weeks. I should restate here that what has happened earlier this month was not a military coup d'état; rather, the people rose up in a great wave of revolt; and the army, taking a patriotic stand that the history books will celebrate, came to their side. I should also restate that Mohamed Morsi lost his legitimacy the moment he issued his constitutional declaration, which placed his own personal decisions above the law and the constitution, and granted them immunity from legal challenge.

When President Alberto Fujimori did the same thing in Peru in 1992, most of the international community severed relations with his country; they did this because they saw that an elected president had effectively staged a coup, and that he had become an illegitimate dictator. Morsi had already lost legitimacy when those millions of Egyptians took to the streets to remove him; he had lost it even before 22 million Egyptians signed the Tamarod campaign to show their lack of confidence in him. In order to show their rejection of Morsi's government, unprecedented numbers of Egyptians came out in protest on three successive occasions. In this way they showed their endorsement for the army to step in and defend Egypt from the terrorist threat to which it was exposed.

With complete appreciation for the stance taken by our great national army, it may be useful to now discuss the following points:

First: What happened on 30 June was truly a massive, popular uprising. It was a new wave following on from that of the January 25 Revolution, that is to say, 30 June was not unconnected to its predecessor. One may hold a demonstration that lasts for a day, but no matter how large it may be you cannot call it a revolution. To have two actual revolutions, however, in just over two years is something truly extraordinary. A revolution is not an isolated and fleeting event; rather, it takes place over an extended period in which the people struggle to completely tear down an old corrupt system in order to replace it with a new and just one. Revolution is a process by which society remodels its culture, its political structure, its economic policy and its entire worldview. It will take years, and perhaps even decades, for the revolution to build the kind of state that it set out to achieve. The events of 30 June, in my opinion, represented the third wave of the Egyptian revolution. The first wave led to the removal of Mubarak and to his subsequent trial. The second wave lasted a year and a half, during which time the young revolutionaries fearlessly and heroically defended the spirit of the revolution. In taking up this fight they were vilified, beaten, mutilated and shot dead in several massacres that were deliberately orchestrated – and for this the former members of military council should be prosecuted in a court of law. The third wave of the revolution, however, came on 30 June, when millions of Egyptians rose up to show their rejection of Morsi and demand the Brotherhood's removal from power.

It is necessary to understand the nature of the relationship between the January 25 Revolution and the 30 June uprising in order to realise what now needs to be done to fulfil the goals of the wider revolution. Of these two events, one should not necessarily be given more significance than the other; there have been repeated attempts to portray 30 June as the true revolution and to denounce the January 25 Revolution as a plot devised by the United States and the Muslim Brotherhood against Mubarak. The aim of this false representation is to restore the reputation of Mubarak's corrupt and authoritarian regime in order to absolve it of its crimes and reposition it for a return to power. The January 25 Revolution showed the world how the people can triumph over tyranny through peaceful protest. That phase has passed, however, and our concern now should be to prevent the revolution from being stolen from us again. The Muslim Brotherhood stole it once; we should not let Mubarak's associates steal it this time. Those loathsome faces, that were for so long linked to Mubarak's corrupt regime, have reappeared on the scene once again. Now they are out brazenly singing Mubarak's praises: extolling his alleged sagacity, patriotism and virtues. There are other worrying signs which indicate that the Mubarak regime is preparing for a return to power: reports have been leaked concerning a return to emergency law, which had been abolished thanks to the revolution. Furthermore, some of the disgraced officers of the state security services have been reinstated to the positions that they held prior to the revolution. These are the executioners who degraded and tortured thousands of Egyptians, and instead of prosecuting them for their crimes they have been rewarded with their old jobs – as though the revolution never even happened. In order to justify this shameful policy, it has been argued that the state needs their knowledge and expertise. But what expertise do these executioners have other than in torturing, sexually assaulting and electrocuting people? If these are the kind of experts needed by the current government – one that includes a number of important figures from the revolution – then government should openly state its intention to once again torture Egyptians, in which case, it should reinstate the chief executioner, Habib el-Adly, to his old post as minister of interior. After all, there is no one more qualified than him when it comes to repressing Egyptians.

The army sided with the people and the Muslim Brotherhood has been overthrown. New possibilities for the future have opened up for Egypt; however, the way forward has not yet been clearly defined. There are two choices before us: one option is for us to let the Mubarak regime return to power; its capabilities have remained intact throughout. This is so because the former military council maintained these capabilities, as did the Brotherhood; indeed, the Muslim Brothers sought to co-opt these capabilities for themselves. The other option, and the correct one in my opinion, is for the supporters of the revolution to push for the realisation of its goals and to avoid any compromise with the Mubarak regime. In the new Egypt, that the revolution is trying to build, there can be no place for those who worked in the service of Gamal Mubarak and his mother, those who plundered Egyptians, oppressed them and denied them their voice.

It was actually the former military council that first used the term *fuloul*, meaning "remnants", to describe those with links to the old regime. The *fuloul* are those things that break away from the main bloc and disperse, like iron filings or sparks from the fire. The fuloul of an army are its scattered remnants after a defeat. In my opinion, the fuloul are all those who took part in plundering the people and oppressing them under the Mubarak regime. The only legitimate arbiter in this matter can be the law. Whoever is proven to be guilty of committing crimes should have no place in the new state, and whoever is proven to be innocent – no matter what their political persuasion may be – should be allowed to exercise their political rights.

Second: The January 25 Revolution occurred in order to establish the rule of law, to prevent arbitrary detention, killing, torture and the humiliation of Egyptians. The 25 January was specifically chosen because it is National Police Day,[1] and thereby, to highlight the revolution's opposition to the repressive practices used by the police force. General el-Sisi sought a mandate from the

1 National Police Day is a public holiday that commemorates and is a remembrance for 50 police officers killed and more wounded when they refused British demands to hand over weapons and evacuate the Ismaïlia Police Station on 25 January 1952.

people to combat terrorism, and millions of Egyptians responded by taking to the streets in order to show their support. They demonstrated their support for el-Sisi, but they by no means endorsed the use of repressive practices and the killing of innocent people.

Right now, Egypt is offering the whole world a model for how to struggle peacefully to achieve the basic human rights of freedom, justice and equality. Other than the Egyptians, I cannot recall a people who were able to remove, by peaceful protest, two dictators in two consecutive years. The fight against terrorism should be conducted within the boundaries of the law. The violation of human rights should not be permitted in the process because when this happens the fight against terrorism loses its meaning; it becomes a form of terrorism itself. In relation to this, it should be pointed out that the job of the army and the security services is very difficult, because the Brotherhood is not an ordinary political party; it is a misguided religious sect that uses groups of armed criminals to attack innocent people and their property. Our national duty calls us all to fully support the army in its war against terrorism. However, I call upon security services to act with the utmost transparency, fairness and self-control, and to refrain from shooting except under conditions where this is lawful; the excellent image of the people united with the army, which has been seen by the world, must not be tarnished.

Third: The Egyptian revolution lost its way over the past two years, but now, following the 30 July uprising, we have a great opportunity to get it back on the right track. We need to learn from prior mistakes and not repeat them, otherwise we will end up enduring the same awful outcomes as before. What would be the point of simply amending the pathetic and illegitimate constitution that the Brotherhood single-handedly came up with, using a committee [i.e., the Constituent Assembly] that was itself judged to be unconstitutional by the Supreme Constitutional Court?[1] Why was the drafting of a new constitution that would reflect the aspirations of the people and represent the will of all Egyptians, in all their diversity, ruled out? Even now I cannot fathom why the interim government continually yields to the pressure of the Salafist groups. What is the connection of these groups to the revolution, when they have always prescribed dissent against ruling authorities? It is my hope that the interim government will not surrender to pressure from the Salafists, like the former military council did with the Muslim Brotherhood. The new constitution must prohibit the formation of political parties that are fundamentally religious in nature. The former Supreme Council made a grave

1 On 2 June 2013, Egypt's Supreme Constitutional Court ruled that the Shura Council and the Constituent Assembly, which drafted the December 2012 Constitution, were unconstitutional. The court found that the electoral law under which the Shura Council was elected violated the principles of equality and non-discrimination because party members were allowed to contest the two-thirds of seats reserved for parties as well as the one-third of seats allotted for independents.

mistake when it permitted religious parties to enter into politics – and all of Egypt paid the price for this. In a civil, democratic state there can be no place for parties that discriminate against Egyptians on the grounds of religion. I am not advocating an absolute political ban on the Brotherhood or the Salafists; as long as they are not guilty of crimes they have the right to establish whatever parties they want. However, if they want to engage in politics they must give up the idea of having a divine mandate and comply with the rules of civil society.

There should also be a ban on political propaganda in all places of worship, and this law must be strictly applied. During recent times we have seen how mosques have been used as venues for inciting violence – the Brotherhood even tortured their opponents inside them.

Before elections can be held, a new constitution must be drafted which contains provisions to counteract electoral fraud. How can elections be fair if voters can be bought with money, fuel or sugar? This is how the Brotherhood bought votes time and again. And how can elections be fair if there is no transparency regarding the sources of political funding? Transparency is a fundamental requirement in a democratic system. Before going to the polls we need to know who is funding the candidates and why they are doing so.

In the space of just one year, the Egyptian people, with their civic values, have come to recognise the failure of political Islam. Egypt rose up on 30 June in order to remove the Muslim Brotherhood from power, and our great army took the side of the people. Now we must build a new state on the foundations of justice and transparency, so that the revolution will achieve its goals – goals that thousands of Egypt's finest died for. The revolution will continue, God willing, until all of its goals have been achieved.

Democracy is the answer.

AB

An Emergency Meeting at the Zoo

5 August 2013

On 30 June millions of Egyptians took to the streets to show that they had no confidence in Morsi's presidency and to demand an end to the rule of the Muslim Brotherhood. The army acted in response to the will of the people; they deposed Morsi, took him into custody to await trial and set out a new road map to put the revolution back on track.

On the other hand, however, the Muslim Brothers and their supporters lost their minds when they lost power. There have been recurrent terrorist attacks in Sinai, and Egyptian soldiers are being killed daily. The Brotherhood have amassed their supporters at Rabaa Al-Adawiya and at Al-Nahda Square, where they are holding sit-ins. Unfortunately, however, the Brotherhood sit-ins are not peaceful: dozens of people have been tortured where they are taking place. There have also been random shootings at innocent passersby when armed supporters have ventured beyond the confines of the sit-ins. A whole month has passed, but the crimes of the Brotherhood still continue. The people living in and around Rabaa Al-Adawiya have made complaints that the sit-in has turned their life into a living hell, while at Al-Nahda Square, the inhabitants of Bein El Sarayat have been suffering savage attacks from the Brothers – these attacks have led to the killing of dozens of Egyptians, and the injuring of hundreds.

It is easy to forget, in the midst of these tragic events, that the Brotherhood sit-in at Al-Nahda is located right next to the zoo. Giza Zoo was established in 1891 and is the oldest zoo in both the Arab world and Africa. The animals of the zoo have suffered a great deal because of the Al-Nahda sit-in, some reports stating that depression has spread amongst them. The elephants, giraffes, lions, tigers, zebras, ostriches and all of the other animals are going through the hardest days they have ever known.

Yesterday the monkeys had had enough: they came out from their pens to the open space of the enclosure and began crying out loudly in the most heart-rending way, as though they were pleading for help. Out of sheer frustration, they somersaulted and struck the sandy ground with their hands and feet. The monkeys continued like this for a quarter of an hour or so – as though railing against their suffering – until their elder appeared. He was the oldest monkey in the enclosure and all of the other monkeys revered and respected him. He walked unhurriedly on his hands and feet with his tail raised proudly. The monkey elder climbed up to the highest point of the enclosure's rock and ran his eye over the other monkeys. Little by little, they quieted down until silence reigned. Then he raised his husky voice saying: "My dear children, believe me when I say that I know your suffering and I feel as you do, but I council calm so that we can think clearly and act in the best way."

A monkey who was standing near to him cried: "But we can no longer endure this hell!"

Another monkey leaped into the air and said: "It's been a whole month and not one person has visited us. For a whole month we haven't been able to sleep; we haven't had a moment's peace because of all the terrible noise. Those people at the nearby sit-in never stop shouting into their microphones; the noise is deafening! And then there is the sound of gunfire during the clashes. When some of them come out from the sit-in they shoot at innocent people. We saw them torturing people to death against the walls of the zoo."

Hearing this, one of the female monkeys screamed in dismay. Gripped by emotion she put her face in her hands and said: "I saw them cutting the bodies of their victims with knives. They're criminals! Savages!"

The elder shook his head, unable to comprehend such actions. There was another monkey who spoke up; he seemed to be clever, even if a little rash in his manner. He said: "Elder, all we do is talk. Is there nothing we can do to stop these criminals? Isn't it the government's responsibility to protect the Egyptian people?"

The elder replied cautiously saying: "It is clear that General el-Sisi and the members of the interim government are hesitant to break up the sit-in for fear of the casualties that will result."

Hearing this, the monkeys began raising their voices in opposition. No individual voice could be heard through the shouting, so, with a movement of his hand, the elder restored calm. The clever monkey now said: "Casualties will result from the sit-in itself, not from its being shut down. If the sit-in continues then the number of victims will grow on a daily basis, whether they are killed by gunfire or from torture. I can't understand General el-Sisi's hesitation; millions of Egyptians have entrusted him with the task of fighting terrorism. Besides, it's possible to break up the sit-in without there being casualties; this is done all over the world. If a thousand soldiers were to storm the sit-in armed only with water cannons then they could break it up without anyone being killed."

The monkey elder responded to this, saying: "Don't forget that there are armed people at this sit-in. We have seen Muslim Brothers carrying automatic weapons with our own eyes. Were this to happen, the first thing the Brothers would do would be to open fire on the soldiers."

The clever monkey replied: "In this case the soldiers would have the right to defend themselves and shut the sit-in down. With all respect to you, as our elder, the issue is this: every day we gather here to complain and shout, but then we return to our pens and do nothing. Tonight we came here determined to find a solution."

Overcome by emotion, the monkeys began shouting. The elder bowed its head in silence, then calmly he said: "Listen, my boy, the matter does not only concern us. There are also our fellow animals in the zoo to consider. I will go ask them for their opinion, but I will return quickly. Do not disperse."

The elder monkey leaped high and disappeared behind the thick trees; he appeared strong and graceful in his movement despite of his advanced age. The other monkeys remained tense, they talked and shouted for about half an hour until the elder returned; he raised his voice and said: "My children, I consulted with our fellow animals. They all agree with you that this criminal sit-in must be shut down as soon as possible. This is the view of the lions, the tigers, the elephants, the ostriches and the zebras. As for the gentle giraffes, never in my life have I seen them so angry!"

The monkeys were swept up in a wave of enthusiasm. But the clever monkey interrupted this saying: "Respected elder, please tell us what we should do."

The elder answered: "The animals asked me to send a message to General el-Sisi. Do you agree with this idea?"

Cheers of assent rose up from the monkeys, but the clever monkey questioned this: "Do you really think General el-Sisi will care what the animals in the zoo think?"

The elder answered: "Of course. General el-Sisi has a duty to care about us; he must relieve our suffering. We, the animals of the zoo, are important to Egyptians. There's no one in Egypt who doesn't have fond memories of us. Is there an Egyptian who didn't come to see us as a child on a school trip? Is there an Egyptian who didn't take his girlfriend to the zoo when he was a young man? General el-Sisi has to know that we love Egypt as much as he does. He sought a mandate from the people for the task of combating terrorism. Millions of Egyptians took to the streets to show their support for this, but now he seems hesitant to confront the Brotherhood; this is because the Brothers have the protection of the United States. America pressures General el-Sisi and the members of the government to allow the Brotherhood's sit-ins to continue and to spread. As soon as clashes between Egyptians and the Muslim Brothers have spread throughout the country, America will intervene to restore the Brotherhood to power."

All of the monkeys shouted in opposition to this plot, and the clever monkey said angrily: "The people will never allow the Brotherhood to return to power. But General el-Sisi must take the necessary steps to protect Egyptians, and us, the animals of Giza Zoo."

The elder said in a loud voice: "Listen, you know Mr Kadry, the zookeeper. He has looked after us for the last 30 years and in this time he has come to learn our language. He has told no one about this because no one would believe him. But I sit with Mr Kadry every day; we talk together and we understand one another. I both like him and trust him. I propose that we now think about what we want to say to General el-Sisi, and I am confident that Mr Kadry will faithfully convey our message to him. I received some ideas from our fellow animals but I want to hear yours as well. Whoever wants to speak should raise their hand."

The monkey elder invited the female monkey to speak. Her voice trembled with emotion as she said: "I would like to ask General el-Sisi why he has abandoned the Egyptians, who put their trust in him, to be tortured and killed in the streets."

The monkey elder replied: "My dear, let's not forget that some Muslim Brothers have also died."

The female monkey said: "We grieve for anyone who is killed unjustly, whether they belong to the Brotherhood or otherwise. But I don't understand why the government doesn't apply the law to everyone equally. Anyone who commits a crime must be put to trial immediately. The first point of order should be to break up these illegal armed sit-ins."

The elder gestured to another monkey at the far end of the rock formation. This monkey jumped in the air twice, and said: "I would like to ask General el-Sisi why the Egyptian government gives in to pressure from America. When has America ever wanted what is best for Egypt? America wants to restore the Muslim Brothers and use them to achieve its aims regardless of what is best for Egypt."

The elder said: "Listen, I will now share with you the message that Mr Kadry will bring to General el-Sisi for us:

Dear General el-Sisi,

We are the animals of Giza Zoo. We ask you to take a decisive stand concerning the Brotherhood's criminal sit-ins taking place in Rabaa Al-Adawiya and Al-Nahda Square. We, General el-Sisi, are Egyptians, and we love Egypt as much as you do. You are our leader; you called upon Egyptians to entrust you with the task of dealing with the terrorists, but weeks have passed and you have not done anything about them. The zoo has become a living hell. We are tormented; we can't sleep or eat, and we simply can't go on like this. In a few days the Ramadan fasting will end and the festivities will begin. This is a happy occasion for us because we normally receive thousands of visitors; we as the animals of the zoo bring our visitors happiness and they bring us happiness. But no one will come during the festival this year because the people are frightened to go anywhere near this criminal sit-in; they would risk being abducted and brutally tortured to death at any moment. What kind of state allows these crimes to continue? The Egyptian people support you, General el-Sisi, so don't worry about America. The destiny of our country will not be decided by America; only the Egyptian people will decide it."

As the elder spoke the final sentence he was overcome by emotion and his voice trembled. The other monkeys were swept away by excitement; they started to cheer and do summersaults. The elder waited until the uproar had calmed down and said: "This is our message to General el-Sisi. Do you agree with it?"

The zoo resounded with the cheers of the monkeys. Then the elder smiled, turned around and departed.

Democracy is the answer.

AB

Who Is Letting Egypt Down?

19 August 2013

Last year the prime minister of the United Kingdom, David Cameron, paid a visit to the city of Plymouth. While there, he went into a cafe to get a cup of coffee, but he had to stand in a queue. Ten minutes passed and no one offered him their place, so he asked the waitress if she could speed things up. However, she reprimanded him, saying: "You have to wait your turn like everyone else."[1]

In a separate incident Cameron made a visit to a hospital in London. As he was talking to patients, the doctor stormed in angrily and expelled the photographers who were in his entourage. It seems that they had not taken the proper hygiene precautions before entering the patients' ward.[2] This is how the British behave towards their prime minister. The reason for this is that, in a culture of democracy, the leader is not considered to be the divinely chosen; they are not regarded as the symbol of the nation. In a democratic system, presidents, or prime ministers, are considered public servants that can be criticised and held to account. Furthermore, demonstrations are given protection by the police so that no one can attack them. A democratic state guarantees the political rights of all its citizens. However, these rights will be promptly taken away from citizens if they take up arm and attack others. In this case, the citizen becomes a criminal, to be prosecuted and punished.

Last May, in London, two Islamist terrorists butchered a British soldier in front of distraught passersby.[3] A few minutes later the police arrived and promptly opened fire on the killers, who sustained serious injuries as a result. In July 2005, three bombs were denoted on the London Underground, and a fourth on a double-decker bus in Tavistock Square. As well as the four bombers, 52 civilians were killed and over 700 more were injured in the

1 Sheila Thomas, who was behind the counter, failed to recognise the prime minister and told him she was busy serving other customers.
2 *See* https://www.youtube.com/watch?v=EPa7GXYvW6Y
3 On the afternoon of 22 May 2013, a British Army soldier, Fusilier Drummer Lee Rigby of the Royal Regiment of Fusiliers, was attacked and killed by Michael Adebolajo and Michael Adebowale near the Royal Artillery Barracks in Woolwich, southeast London. Two men ran him down with a car, then used knives and a cleaver to stab and hack him to death.

attacks.[1] These events put the police force on high alert. Tragically, they chased and shot dead a Brazilian man called Jean Charles de Menezes, believing him to be a terrorist. Afterwards, it was discovered that the man was innocent, so the police force had to apologise to the family of the dead man and pay them compensation. Last year in Toulouse, a French terrorist of Algerian origin, Mohammed Merah, confessed that he had killed seven people.[2] The French police surrounded his apartment, and when he opened fire on them they shot him dead. In another incident in France, the police conducted an extensive search for terrorists in the city of Strasbourg. When a suspect opened fire on them, the police shot and killed him on the spot. The French president, François Hollande, commented on this incident saying: "The state is determined to protect citizens from all forms of terrorism."

The European authorities dealt just as firmly with a number of terrorist groups that became active there in the 1970s – groups such as the Red Brigades in Italy,[3] the Baader-Meinhof Group[4] in Germany and ETA in Spain.[5] Democratic states do not tolerate terrorism; they counteract it in order to protect the nation and the people. Despite the difficult conditions in Egypt we should not confuse terrorist activity for political activism. The Muslim Brotherhood has a long history of terrorism, from its inception in 1928 through to the 1960s when Nasser's security services severely cracked down on it. The Brotherhood adapted, however; it reemerged in the 1970s, presenting itself as a peaceful, political organisation that believed in democracy.

In the wake of the January 25 Revolution the Muslim Brothers came to power through elections. Having achieved this, they then abolished the democratic system by means of the constitutional declaration of November 2012. They revealed their true fascist character by restructuring the Egyptian state so that they could stay in power indefinitely. On 30 June, however, the people rose up against them, and the army came to their side. It was at this point that Egyptians discovered that the Brotherhood had never really turned its back on terrorism, but rather, the Muslim Brothers had been assembling

1 The 7 July 2005 London bombings (often referred to as 7/7) were a series of coordinated suicide attacks in central London, which targeted civilians using the public transport system during the morning rush hour.

2 The Toulouse and Montauban shootings were a series of three gun attacks targeting French soldiers and Jewish civilians in the cities of Montauban and Toulouse in the Midi-Pyrénées region of France in March 2012. In total, seven people were killed, and five others were injured, four seriously.

3 The Red Brigades (Italian: Brigate Rosse, often abbreviated BR) is a paramilitary organisation, based in Italy, which was responsible for numerous violent incidents, including assassinations, kidnapping and robberies during the so-called "Years of Lead".

4 Baader-Meinhof Group were a West German far-left militant group founded in 1970 that described itself as a communist and anti-imperialist "urban guerrilla" group engaged in armed resistance against what they deemed to be a fascist state.

5 The ETA is an armed Basque nationalist and separatist organisation. The group was founded in 1959 and has since evolved from a group promoting traditional Basque culture to a paramilitary group with the goal of gaining independence for the Greater Basque Country.

a secret armed organisation that would carry out terrorist attacks should the need arise. The crimes now being committed by the Brothers are beyond the pale of any democratic system. They can no longer be considered as a political group; they are a terrorist organisation.

The state should dissolve the Brotherhood and criminalise membership to it, just as European countries have done with every other terrorist organisation. The only difference between the Brotherhood and the aforementioned terrorist groups is that the Brothers' acts of terrorism stem from a religious ideology. Those Muslim Brothers who have taken up arms against the state are basically just the pawns of their leaders who have portrayed events not as a mere political dispute, but as a holy war against the enemies of Islam. It's truly saddening to see the Brothers and their allies committing such despicable crimes; they believe that they stand for Islam, but their actions could not be further from its great principles, which call for truth, justice and freedom. Right now we need to learn from what has happened. We must have a new constitution that prohibits the forming of political parties that are essentially religious in nature. After the Brotherhood has been disbanded, and criminalised, those members of it that did not commit crimes should have the right to set up whatever parties they want. However, such parties should only be permitted on condition that they do not go against the rules of civil society, that they do not speak in the name of religion and that they do no present themselves as being the sole representatives of God's will.

However, no matter how passionately you may disagree with the ideology of the Muslim Brothers, it is impossible not to feel deeply saddened by the sight of those who were killed or injured when the Brotherhood sit-ins at Al-Nahda Square and Rabaa Al-Adawiya were broken up. No doubt you asked yourself: would it not have been possible to break up the sit-ins without so many casualties? In all fairness, we have to bear in mind the dozens of police and army personnel who were killed, in the most despicable way, by the Muslim Brothers or their extremist allies in Kerdasa,[1] Sinai and other governorates in Egypt. We have to remember that the Brotherhood sit-ins were not peaceful: time and again armed demonstrators shot and killed innocent people in the streets. It happened at Al-Manil, Bein Al Sarayat, Giza and most of the cities in Egypt. Here we can refer to the report issued on 2 August by Amnesty International that confirmed that protesters possessed weapons at the sit-ins in Al-Nahda and Rabaa Al-Adawiya. The same organisation also documented a number of criminal acts committed by the Brotherhood, including holding captive anti-Morsi protesters, their torture and their murder by the Muslim Brothers.[2] The report included the testimony of victims of the

1 The Kerdasa massacre refers to the killing of fourteen security personnel in August 2013 in Kerdasa's main police station, a town in Giza.

2 *See* Amnesty International, [Egypt:] Evidence points to torture carried out by Morsi supporters, AI Index: PRE01/390/2013, 2 August 2013.

Brotherhood including Mastour Mohamed Sayed who was taken, along with 20 others, to the sit-in at Rabaa Al-Adawiya where they were all held and horribly tortured by Morsi's supporters – a woman who was amongst them was sexually assaulted. In the text of his testimony Mastour states that:

> Morsi's supporters aimed their guns at me and I felt very frightened. They led me, and the others, underneath the podium at the Rabaa Al-Adawiya sit-in. It was there that they began to beat us, shouting that we were infidels. Then they started electrocuting us – several times I lost consciousness. They had tied my hands and covered my eyes, but the blindfold was not tight and I was able to see some what was happening. I saw the blood on the ground and heard the screams of a woman as she was being tortured with electric shocks. Then I heard the voice of another woman who ordered her to undress. The victim shouted, "Shame on you!" She was beaten again. Then I saw two bearded men rape her and I heard her crying out the whole time. The torture continued until the following day. They would ask us, "Why do you support General el-Sisi?" Then they threw me out of the sit-in, but they kept my identity card.

This is just one of the many accounts detailed in the report by Amnesty International. No one can accuse this organisation of fabricating reports or of being biased towards the army and the interim government. The conclusion is this: the Brotherhood sit-ins at Al-Nahda Square and Rabaa Al-Adawiya were not peaceful protests; they were more akin to armed camps where the Brotherhood brutally tortured anyone they suspected of being in opposition to them. Furthermore, every night armed Brothers would emerge from these sit-ins and randomly shoot and kill innocent people. They would take citizens hostage, as though they were prisoners of war, beat them, electrocute them and violate them. So the question is: if these criminal acts been committed in London, would the British government have considered these sit-ins lawful? Would it have waited for a month and a half to break them up?

This is by no means an attempt to justify the killing – and again, I offer my condolences to the families of all the victims, irrespective of their political affiliations. However, we must also remember that the Muslim Brothers rejected every political solution that was put to them. They ignored repeated requests for them to shut down the sit-ins. Their demonstrators refused to exit from the sit-ins through the security corridors that had been put in place for them by the police. Indeed, they began shooting at the police, and they killed four officers before the police returned fire. If the police were guilty of using excessive force, that is, if the level of casualties was unnecessarily high, then the officers responsible should put on trial. However, what happened in this case is not the same as the killing of peaceful protesters, as happened in the January 25 Revolution; rather, this was a clash between the state and armed terrorists that involved casualties on both sides. In taking up arms against the state, the Brotherhood must bear the primary responsibility for the outcome of these events.

What's happening now is not a political dispute; Egypt is waging a war against a criminal organisation committed to terrorizing and killing innocent people, to bringing down the state and spreading chaos. Rocket-propelled grenades have been used in coordinated attacks on police stations in most of Egypt's governorates, state properties, such as the Giza Governorate headquarters, have been set alight, dozens of churches have been burned down and there have been widespread attacks on Copts in Upper Egypt. All such acts can only be described as terrorism – their purpose is to overthrow the state of Egypt and restore the Brotherhood to power, even though the Egyptian people have rejected them. Furthermore, the Brotherhood have continually, and cruelly, attacked the Copts, their property and their churches. They do this in order to provoke a response that would plunge Egypt into a sectarian war – one that would sow destruction throughout Egypt. Here we must pay tribute to the Egyptian Copts for their considerable political awareness and their loyalty towards Egypt; they saw their churches burn before their eyes, yet, not once did they respond with violence – they refused to play into the hands of those who would like to see Egypt plunged into a sectarian war.

Right now all of Egypt is waging a war against terror, for its present and its future. Lines are drawn in times of war. There is no room for those who hesitate, sit on the fence or abandon Egypt in its time of need. We all have a duty to support the state of Egypt in this fight against terrorism, with all our strength. The revolution will continue until it achieves its goals and the people of Egypt have the country they deserve.

Democracy is the answer.

AB

Mistakes Made in the Midst of Battle

26 August 2013

Imagine that your country's army was fighting a war to defend you and the nation, but in performing this task you saw that it was committing serious errors. Would you openly criticise the army while it was in the middle of fighting or hold your tongue until the war had ended? There are two different ways of looking at this question. Some people are of the opinion that criticising the army while it is waging war can demoralise and weaken it, thereby playing into the hands of the enemy. The second opinion, which I hold, is that loyalty to your country and solidarity with its army obliges you to promptly confront it with its mistakes. In this way, it can quickly correct its errors and go on to win the war.

I believe that writers should not hold back from expressing their thoughts under any circumstances or for any reason. Indeed, covering up the facts, and neglecting to criticise mistakes, in order to try and preserve a unified front, is precisely what has led to countless defeats in our modern history. Right now the state of Egypt is prosecuting a real war against terror. Ever since the terrorist Muslim Brothers were ousted from power by the people and the army on the 30 June they have tried to spread chaos and destroy the state with no thought for the mounting dead amongst Egyptians. In my opinion, all Egyptians have a duty to support the state in its war against terrorism. However, this does not preclude us from bringing the following errors committed by the state to its attention:

Firstly: What would happen in a democratic country if a political party controlled a secret, armed organisation whose members went out and killed army soldiers, attacked police stations with rocket-propelled grenades and automatic weapons, who abducted police officers, killed them and mutilated their corpses, who then burned down courts of law, ministries, governorate offices, and churches, and whose members shot randomly at passersby, kidnapped them and tortured them to death? If a political party were to commit such acts in any other country, the state would immediately declare it a terrorist organisation, it would be criminalised, its premises closed down and its assets seized. All of the above terrorist crimes have been committed by the Brotherhood, yet, until now, the Egyptian state was hesitant to designate the Brotherhood as a terrorist organisation. As for those members who were not involved in terrorist activities, they should be treated as Egyptian citizens and given their full political rights in accordance with the law. However, the new constitution must prohibit the forming of political parties that are based on religious ideologies, rather than on the notions of civil society.

Second: On 17 August the *Los Angeles Times* published an article concerning the sit-in at the Al-Fateh Grand Mosque. It featured a big picture of an Egyptian soldier aiming his gun at a group of people, and behind him was a young man who had a beard. Now, if you are Egyptian then you will understand that the soldier was trying to prevent the angry crowd from killing this young man who belonged to the Brotherhood. But the newspaper published this picture without comment, and of course, this only encourages American readers of the newspaper to arrive at a wrong conclusion, that is, that the soldier was threatening a group of the Brotherhood's followers with his weapon before killing them. This is just one example of the bias in the Western media against the Egyptian revolution and their portrayal of it as a military coup.

I had expected the Egyptian state to be more proactive in publicising the truth about what is happening in Egypt to people in the West. Unfortunately, however, apart from the favourable press conference with Mustafa Hegazy, advisor to the interim president, the government's use of the media at this defining moment in Egypt's history has been disappointing. Indeed, an important series of events took place that the government did not even pass comment upon. The protagonist of this episode is Volkhard Windfuhr, one of the oldest and most distinguished reporters in the world. He is 77 years old and for decades he has worked for the German magazine, *Der Spiegel*, as its correspondent in Cairo. He has achieved great acclaim in the field of journalism and was on good terms with President Gamal Abdel Nasser, Yasser Arafat and other international political leaders. This is a man who loves Egypt and always tries to report accurately for his German readers. He was disturbed by the bias in the Western media concerning its attitude towards the wider revolution in Egypt, so he publicly appealed to his fellow foreign reporters to strive for greater accuracy in reporting on the events in Egypt and to report on the terrorist crimes being perpetrated daily by the Muslim Brothers against the Egyptian people. Windfuhr's appeal, however, was met with outrage. The German newspapers organised a vicious campaign against him that sought to ruin his reputation – even *Der Spiegel*, his own magazine, joined in with the others to attack him. I was expecting the interim government to give support to this courageous man, who was going out of his way to defend the rights of the Egyptian people, more so than many Egyptians. I thought that the government would seek to profit from his considerable journalistic experience in combating the malicious campaign being mounted by some Western media against the revolution. It seems, however, that either the government does not concern itself with international opinion, or is unable to distinguish between supporters of the revolution and enemies thereof.

Third: In the midst of everything that's happening, a ruling has been issued for Mubarak's release from prison.[1] The Muslim Brotherhood has used this ruling to their advantage. It lends credence to their assertion that the freeing of Mubarak is conclusive proof that what happened was a coup carried out by members of the old regime. Such nonsense does not even deserve a serious response, of course. If Mubarak had been able to mobilise 30 million Egyptians around him, then his fate might have been different. The task of convicting Mubarak is not so much the responsibility of the current government as it

1 Hosni Mubarak was released from prison after appealing against his detention. He was taken by helicopter from Cairo's Tora prison to a hospital and was later put under house arrest. He still faced charges of corruption and complicity in the killing of demonstrators during the revolution.

was that of the military council. Ofcourse, the Muslim Brothers themselves controlled parliament for a period of six months as well as the presidency for an entire year. In all this time the Brotherhood did nothing to get justice for the martyrs of the revolution.

The problem, in my opinion, is not only Mubarak; the prosecution services, and the ways in which they carry out judicial investigations, are not fit for purpose. They are incapable of producing the evidence required to prosecute those who committed crimes against the demonstrators. For a period of almost three years – from the beginning of the revolution until now – thousands of people have been killed and not one of the killers has received their just punishment. The prosecutor in the Mubarak case, for example, openly stated that state institutions had deliberately destroyed evidence that could secure the conviction of Mubarak. Egypt will never be able to move forward until justice has been done. In light of this, we should seek to benefit from the experience of other nations that have gone through similar ordeals. We should hasten the process of transitional justice which implements both judicial and extra-judicial measures in order to uncover the truth about human rights violations, which prosecutes killers and compensates victims so that a spirit of reconciliation and justice can prevail amongst the members of society. Strangely enough, there is a government ministry in Egypt whose task it is to implement the process of transitional justice; unfortunately, however, in the weeks since it was formed it has not begun to carry out its work.[1]

Fourth: When the esteemed German journalist Volkhard Windfuhr stood alone, courageously defending the truth and being subjected to harsh abuse from the powerful Western media, the only concern of many Egyptian satellite channels was to increase their viewers in order to generate greater profit from their advertisers, and thereby, increase their own incomes. That a channel seeks to increase its viewers is not bad in and of itself; however, it is deplorable when it seeks to achieve this through unprofessional and unethical means. Egypt is the only country in the world where, when you switch on the television, you will see the presenter threatening to hit with his shoe anyone who disagrees with his opinion, or accusing any adversary of either being part of a Muslim Brotherhood sleeper cell or a fifth column working for US intelligence. Nowhere in the world will you hear verbal abuse on the television like you will in Egypt; it has become the norm to hear base insults, and accusations of adultery and homosexuality, being made against public figures. Some people are hired by certain television programs precisely because they excel in using obscene language. One such individual was invited to appear on a programme a few days ago. For three hours he slandered people using language that you would not even hear in the street, and the whole time the presenter looked

1 Interim President Adly Mansour appointed Judge Mohamed Amin el-Mahdi as Egypt's first-ever Minister of Transitional Justice and National Reconciliation.

at him with affection. In the rest of the world people submit accusations to the prosecution services, in Egypt however, people make their accusations on television. All that a guest on a programme needs to do is take a piece of paper out of his pocket and announce that it is a report by some authoritative body, then he can start wildly accusing someone of all kinds of things ranging from being a pimp to being an Israeli spy. Many television programmes have now become nothing more than vulgar instruments for spreading slander. Nor is this slander randomly directed, however; individuals that opposed the Mubarak regime and took part in the January 25 Revolution are specifically targeted. The aim of this is moral character assassination, so that Egyptians turn against them and the revolution itself. The wider goal of these media campaigns is to pave the way for the return of Mubarak's old associates to power. This degenerate farce must stop because is unbecoming of a people that made a glorious revolution and presented a model of upright character to the world. The worst thing about all this slander on the airwaves is that the Western media believes that the army leadership is responsible. Even *The New York Times*, for example, issued a report under the title: "Military Dominates Airwaves in Egypt."[1] One report suggested that the military had complete control of the official state media, as well as private satellite channels, and through this control it prevented Egyptians from knowing the truth.

Fifth: Along with all the slander in the media there is a parallel campaign of fabricating charges against political opponents and carting them off to the offices of the state security prosecution service. Two notable activists, Israa Abdel Fattah[2] and Asmaa Mahfouz, were charged with spying for foreign countries. Similarly, other charges have been leveled against respected activists such as Belal Fadl[3] and Alaa Abd el-Fattah.[4] The charges of spying on behalf of foreign countries, spreading confusion, threatening the social peace or inciting hatred of the regime, are all sham charges; they have no real basis in the laws of democratic states. They are used as simple expedients to be leveled at anyone who antagonises the regime. They were leveled at those who opposed Mubarak, then those who opposed the military council, then the Brotherhood, and now they are being leveled at those who oppose the new authorities in Egypt. The continuing harassment of political opponents by

1 *See* http://www.nytimes.com/video/world/middleeast/100000002397509/egypts-military-dominates-its-airwaves.html

2 Israa Abdel Fattah, also called Facebook Girl is an Egyptian internet activist and blogger. She was arrested by Egyptian security in 2008. She drew the attention of few Egyptian newspapers challenging by this the state's censorship policy, turning her into an overnight symbol for resistance and resilience against corruption and injustice.

3 A leader of Egyptian political satire, Belal Fadl has inspired a generation to voice its dissent more vividly than Egyptians had dared during Mubarak's rule.

4 Alaa Abd el-Fattah was arrested for allegedly encouraging a demonstration against the new constitution outside the Egyptian Parliament. Twenty policemen raided Abd el-Fattah's home, broke the door down, and proceeded to confiscate the family's computers and mobile phones.

slandering them in the media and trumping up charges against them represent negative, worrying signs concerning the nature of Egypt's commitment to becoming a truly democratic state.

The great January 25 Revolution was able to oust Mubarak and put him to trial. Then, on 30 June of this year the revolution got back on track and ousted the terrorist Muslim Brotherhood. The revolution will never allow the corrupt Mubarak regime, nor the terrorist Brotherhood, to return to power. The Egyptian people will not accept anything short of true democracy. Egyptians demand a just state where everyone's rights are respected, where no one will be slandered, where the authorities will not trump up charges against political opponents simply because they have a different point of view. The revolution will continue and, God willing, it will prevail.

Democracy is the answer.

AB

The Tragedy and Farce of Egypt's Democracy

2 September 2013

A few years ago I was having dinner with a group of friends when I was introduced to a woman who boasted that she was an NGO expert. I asked her what her work involved and she said proudly: "I have the know-how to write a proposal in such a way that the sponsor will immediately agree to provide funding for the NGO."

Then I asked her: "Do these NGOs do charity work to help the sick and the poor?"

Confidently the lady smiled and said: "Some NGOs are charitable organisations, of course. But there are many others whose aim is to promote democratic values and support transitions towards democracy. In the case of these NGOs, there are a great many institutions that are keen to provide them with very generous funding."

"And who are these institutions that provide the funding?"

She answered: "There are many sources of funding. Some are wealthy countries such as the United States and those in the European Union. There are also funding institutions within these countries, such as the Swedish International Development Cooperation Agency, for example. And there are similar institutions that support development in other countries. Then there are the non-governmental institutions that seek to fund projects that promote civil society, there's the Ford Foundation, Freedom House and many others."

I said to her: "I can understand foreign funding for charitable work such as providing treatment for people with disabilities and financial support for the poor or unemployed. But funding NGOs that have a political agenda, such as promoting democracy, seems a bit suspicious to me. Would that not amount to foreign interference in the affairs of Egypt, as an attempt by the West to gain control over the country?"

The woman looked at me contemptuously and said: "You talk as though we are still living in the 1960s. The concept of national sovereignty has radically changed since then; the world has become a small village. Moreover, the funding of NGOs that promote civil society has become a perfectly normal and accepted practice."

When I departed that evening I wondered to myself: what makes the governments of EU countries or that of the US spend millions of dollars teaching the poor in Imbaba or Upper Egypt about the difference between proportional representation and the first-past-the-post voting system? Have officials in the West become so kind-hearted that they now spend millions of dollars on teaching Egyptians about the principles of democracy?

I studied in the West and worked there for a number of years. Culturally speaking, I know how careful the West is when it comes to spending money. In my experience, if a Western friend invites you to dinner; it is not the done thing to invite another person, because normally the food will be prepared with the precise number of guests in mind. People from the West will not spend a single dollar frivolously or unnecessarily; they carefully calculate what their expenses will be in relation to the income, and they save some of their salary every month so that they can take their annual vacation with their family. Similarly, the parliament of any Western country will call the government to account for every dollar it spends of the taxpayers' money. So, how did it happen that Western governments suddenly became stricken by this extraordinary generosity, one that induces them to spend millions teaching Egyptians about the principles of democracy? Certainly there must be a motive behind this generous foreign funding because Western governments are not charities.

Now, I'm not criticizing anyone who works for these NGOs that receive foreign funding. The people who work for them are all patriotic Egyptians. Most of the human rights organisations in Egypt – and most of them do receive foreign funding – have played a significant role in defending the rights of Egyptian citizens, as well as exposing human rights violations and crimes committed by the authorities, both before and after the revolution. My critique, therefore, is not directed at the good people working for NGOs and human rights organisations; rather, I want to discuss the reason behind the funding. I understand, of course, that there are kind-hearted people all over the world who help the sick and the poor, but why do Western governments fund Egyptian NGOs with the aim of promoting democracy? Are we to believe that

Western governments are enthusiastic to support democracy in Egypt when they are the ones that have given support to so many despotic regimes in the Arab world? And why does the struggle for democracy need foreign funding in the first place anyway?

Throughout Egypt's modern history, there are excellent examples of movements and parties that played a great patriotic role without having the need for foreign funding. The Wafd Party, for example, contended with the king's despotism and resisted British occupation for decades without receiving any foreign aid whatsoever. Nor did the Kefaya movement, which was the first to confront Mubarak's despotism and demand that he step down from power. Then there is the National Association for Change;[1] it paved the way for the January 25 Revolution. And, of course, the Tamarod campaign, which rallied the people to get rid of the Muslim Brotherhood. All the above nationalist movements relied on self-funding; none of them received a single Egyptian pound from abroad.

The struggle for democracy does not require foreign funding. Furthermore, the funds that are lavished upon these NGOs come with strings attached; the funding binds the interests of activists to the political goals of Western governments. There's no such thing as funding without conditions attached. Sometimes the conditions for receiving funding are explicit, but mostly they're just implied. To speak plainly, if you work for an NGO that receives funding from a foreign government, are you free to act contrary to the interests of the government that funds you? The foreign governments that pour funding into Egypt do so because this serves a political purpose designed to benefit them. The question is this: why has the Egyptian government kept silent about foreign funding? It has not prohibited it, nor has it sought to prevent it. It has been content to simply look on as it happens. The truth is that Egyptian authorities simply yielded to the blackmail of Western governments – governments that have fiercely defended their giving funds and that consider any move against this practice as an act of aggression against democracy and human rights. In this way, the West has thus succeeded, over the last decades, in establishing this underhanded practice as something that is perfectly normal and acceptable. That is to say, Western governments and organisations spend millions of dollars on Egyptian citizens as a means of securing political influence over Egypt itself.

The hypocritical thing here is that Western countries themselves block funding entering the West from abroad. When Islamic charitable organisations in the US and Europe receive donations from abroad, their spending is closely monitored in order to ensure that these donations are used for charitable work

1 The National Association for Change is a loose grouping of the various Egyptian of all political affiliations and religion, men and women, including representatives of civil society and young people aims to change Egypt.

and not to further political objectives. If it is suspected that a Western official has received financial support from abroad, he will be put on trial immediately. The former French president Jacques Chirac, for example, was involved in a scandal over the so-called "African briefcases".[1] He was investigated after being accused of receiving money from African leaders that was then used to fund his presidential campaign. Furthermore, last November another former French president, Nicolas Sarkozy, was also accused of receiving illegal funding for his own campaign.[2] French law puts a limit on the amount that individuals can donate to a presidential campaign – such donations cannot exceed 4600 euros. Sarkozy, however, was accused of receiving a donation of 150,000 euros in support of his bid for the presidency from Liliane Bettencourt, who is one of the principal shareholders of L'Oréal, the well-known, French cosmetics company.

In Western countries it is strictly illegal for politicians to receive foreign funding. In Egypt, however, our politicians receive lavish funds from abroad right in front of our very eyes. On several occasions, the media has reported that the attorney general investigated cases in which a number of presidential candidates were believed to have received financial support from foreign countries in the last year. But the matter never went any further than this; Egyptians were left in the dark as to who these candidates were and who gave them the financial support.

In order to present a fair case, two things should be states. Firstly, those activists that support the revolution and who also work for NGOs receiving foreign funding are very few – they are less than ten in number. That some activists do work for foreign-funded NGOs has been repeatedly exploited by political opponents to discredit the revolution itself. Secondly, foreign funding is not only received by those NGOs promoting civil society, it is also received by organisations that seek to promote political Islam. Religious parties spend large amounts of money on their infrastructure and their elections campaigns, yet we do not know where this money comes from. After the revolution, the former minister of justice, Mohamed el-Gendy, formed a judicial committee to investigate the funding behind organisations seeking to promote civil society as well as these Islamic organisations. The findings were astonishing. The committee revealed that one Islamic organisation had received 296 million

1 A lawyer who worked as an African emissary for Jacques Chirac claimed that that he had handed tens of millions of dollars in secret cash payments from African leaders to the ex-president and to the former prime minister, Dominique de Villepin in the period 1995–2005.

2 A criminal investigation was opened last month after it emerged that more than €10 million spent on Sarkozy's 2012 campaign – in which he was defeated by the Socialist Francois Hollande – had been fraudulently passed off as UMP party expenses. Sarkozy denied any knowledge of, or role in, the apparent fraud which meant his campaign spent nearly 50 per cent more than it was legally entitled to.

Egyptian pounds from two Gulf states in one month alone.[1] When the people running this organisation were questioned about the money they said that they spent 30 million pounds on support for orphaned children. As for the remaining 226 million pounds, however, they said that they had spent this on what they referred to as "various development projects".

This raises suspicions that funding for these Islamic organisations is used to provide financial support for religious parties. On the other hand, the committee revealed that one of the NGOs promoting democracy had received 522,000 dollars while one of the centres for human rights had received 907,000 dollars, and another had received 245,000 dollars. These are just some examples amongst the hundreds of organisations that receive foreign funding. Strangely, however, after their report, the judicial committee suddenly decided to exclude Islamic organisations from further investigation, and instead focused only on the NGOs. That the Islamic organisations were allowed to avoid investigation might be explained in light of the alliance that was formed between the previous military council, the Muslim Brotherhood and the Salafists. In the end, the judicial committee turned a number of NGO workers over to be tried for being in receipt of foreign funding.[2] The foreigner defendants amongst them were allowed to leave Egypt and tried in absentia; however, the Egyptian defendants were convicted and sent to prison.

The Egyptian state must criminalise foreign funding for political activities, as is the case in civilised countries throughout the world. It is no longer acceptable for an Egyptian citizen to receive funding from Western governments to undertake political activity in Egypt. Our national struggle doesn't need outside funding; it is based on the work of volunteers and donations from the Egyptian people. Some people argue that these organisations have expenses to cover in order for them to be able to carry out their work, but why don't they ask for financial aid from Egyptian businessmen instead of foreign governments?

Millions of Egyptians took to the streets on 30 June in order to bring down the rule of the Brotherhood and put the revolution back on the right track. The army responded by siding with the people and announced a political road map for transition to democracy. If we want to build a truly democratic state then we need to ban all foreign funding for political activities. The Egyptian state must not give in to the blackmail of Western governments; these governments seek preserve a means by which they can exert influence over Egypt. Right now we are fighting a battle for autonomy; Egypt should be able to make its

1 A report said that Egyptian Salafis received 296 million Egyptian pounds from the Arabian Gulf states, including 181.7 million pounds from Qatar and 114,493,643 pounds from Kuwait. According to Kuwait's ambassador in Cairo, the Islamic Heritage Revival Association sends its donations through Egypt's social solidarity ministry and the Kuwaiti embassy in Cairo.

2 A Cairo criminal court has convicted 43 NGO workers of operating without a licence and receiving foreign funding. Twenty-seven of the defendants, all of whom were tried in absentia, received prison sentences of five years. According to Egyptian law, NGOs have to be formally registered with the government. However, critics argue that the relevant legislation is ambiguous.

own decisions without being blackmailed. If we don't put an end to foreign funding then Egypt will become a stage performance of puppets controlled by the wealthy from behind the scenes.

With this great revolution we must establish a genuine democratic state with complete sovereignty – a state that does not permit foreign interference in its decision-making, or in its affairs, one that will not permit any organisation to receive foreign funding for political activities, whatever country this may come from. The revolution will continue until it achieves its aims.

Democracy is the answer.

AB

What Have We Learnt from the Disaster?

9 September 2013

Regina is an African-American woman who worked as a secretary in the College of Dentistry at the University of Illinois, where I studied in the eighties. We struck up a friendship and I used to stop by her office from time to time to drink coffee and chat. One day she said to me all of a sudden: "Do you know that I converted from Christianity to Buddhism?" I smiled but didn't say a word, so she went on. "Buddhism is a great religion that is embraced by more than 500 million people worldwide. Every week I meet with my Buddhist friends to exchange our spiritual experiences and meditate. Would you like to join one of our meetings?"

My curiosity got the better of me and I agreed. At the end of that week, I went with Regina to a small house in a poor neighbourhood in the south of Chicago. The light was dim and the narrow room was full of men and women, all of them African-Americans. I shook hands with all of them and sat down. It became clear that Regina had told them about me because they gave me a warm welcome. They began to discuss the ways in which faith in Buddha had changed their lives for the better: the alcoholic gave up drink, the unemployed found a job, and a woman who could not bear her husband came to be happy living with him.

After this, it was the turn of a woman in her fifties to speak. "Before I knew the Buddha," she said, "I was an extremely miserable person. The man I loved left me to live with a younger woman, then I lost my job and got into debt. I even thought about suicide. There was one morning when I didn't have a single dollar to pay the gas bills, the rent and the electricity. I sat and prayed with strong devotion to the noble Buddha and asked him to save me. Do you know what happened?" The whole room was looking at her as she smiled and said: "As soon as I had finished my prayer to the Buddha, I heard a knock at the door. I opened it to meet the postman who handed me a cheque for ten thousand dollars; this was my share of the inheritance coming from my aunt in Boston who had passed away."

Everyone in the room cheered and the woman said, holding back her tears: "So I say to you, my friends, love the Buddha from the depth of your hearts. Place your trust in him and he will never let you down." The room was in awe, and before we went, Regina said in a loud voice, as she stood by the front door of the house: "Don't forget to take the Buddha with you. We have statues of the Buddha in different sizes, starting with this small statue for only 5 dollars right up to this large statue for 30 dollars."

I thanked Regina, said goodbye to everyone and left while some of the others rushed to buy statues of the Buddha. I thought to myself: this woman, who had spoken about the miracle, seemed like an educated and intelligent person. How could she not recognise that the cheque had been made out days before her prayer to the Buddha? In fact, there is no doubt that the procedures for the division of the inheritance had been finalised many weeks before her prayer to the Buddha. How could this woman not realise that the arrival of the cheque, at that moment, was a coincidence that could happen to millions of people who would not consider it a miracle or an act of divine benevolence?

The answer is that this woman experienced and understood the events through the eyes of a believer. She is a Buddhist who has faith in her religion and is therefore ready to believe anything that confirms her faith, and even more ready to deny anything that might make her question it. This attitude is not uncommon amongst people of religion the world over. However, very few people choose their religion by their own free will. We are usually born into the religion of our parents and we grow up believing that this religion is the only true religion. We use our minds to prove the validity of our conviction while at the same time stridently refusing to believe anything that undermines our faith or causes doubt. In fact, people of faith will fiercely attack anyone who subjects their beliefs to criticism.

Religion, by its very nature, is an emotional, absolutist and exclusivist belief. The followers of any religion believe that only their religion or belief system is true. Muslims, for example, consider Christianity and Judaism to be distorted religions, while Christians do not recognise Islam and Jews recognise neither Islam nor Christianity. Religion, in as much as it fulfils human spiritual needs, can sometimes be used to justify persecution and harm. We need religion because it brings us closer to God and provides us with an explanation for the origin of life and a comforting vision of what happens after death. It also imposes a strict dress code and a system of punishment that makes us put aside any injustices that we experience in our lifetime because we know that justice will ultimately be done in the hereafter.

History, however, teaches us that religion, at the same time as being a great source of human values, has often been the cause of deadly wars and the horrific massacres of millions of innocent people. How can religion turn from being a tool used for good into being one used for evil and destruction? Here the matter rests on our understanding of religion. As long as we practice a modified form of exclusivism, in which other faiths are recognised as legitimate, then we will follow religion correctly. However, if we consider our own religion to be superior to other religions, then we will turn into intolerant and hateful people. Whenever we give ourselves the right to interfere in the lives of others and force them to do what we believe is best for them, we lose this correct understanding of religion. Whenever we consider that we alone comprehend God's will and that He has chosen us to carry it out, we become misguided and incapable of seeing the truth; we may even commit the most savage of crimes while continuing to recite our prayers and worship God in order to get closer to Him.

In light of this, it is important that religion is kept seperate from politics, especially in a multi-faith society. Religion and politics are polar opposites. Politics involves human concepts and practices that can be criticised by ordinary citizens. These practices can be shown to be at fault and consequently reformed and changed for the better. On the other hand, religion reflects firm, definitive beliefs that must be believed in and surrendered to, and whose credibility cannot be debated. Anyone who governs in the name of religion inevitably turns into a tyrant, who rules despotically over their people, repressing them and robbing from them. During the Middle Ages, the Catholic Church ruled over Europe and people's lives became a living hell because of extreme injustice, corruption and repression. In Islamic history, Muslims enjoyed rightly-guided and just rule for a period of 31 years (29 years under the rightly-guided caliphs and two years under Umar ibn Abd al-Aziz). Aside from this short period, Muslims suffered for centuries under cruel and unjust tyrants who ruled in the name of religion, from the Umayyads, who destroyed the Ka'aba during their struggle for power with Abd Allah ibn al-Zubayr, to Abu al-Abbas as-Saffah, the founder of the Abbasid Caliphate, who ordered a group of Ummayad princes to be massacred and then ate and drank upon their writhing bodies. Later we have the Ottomans, who occupied Egypt and killed 10,000 inhabitants of Cairo in a single day, apart from the women and children, whom they raped.

No society in the world progresses until religion has been made separate from politics. In democratic countries you have the right to embrace any religion you wish and to practice the rituals of your religion, but you do not have the right to impose your religion on others. In a democratic country, you are a citizen with full rights regardless of your religion. It is not possible to establish a true democracy if the political parties are based on religious principles. Democracy is based on diversity, whereas religion is founded on an absolute truth; democracy means equality between citizens, whereas religion dismisses non-believers as infidels. Democracy puts ideas forward for debate, which may be right or wrong, whereas religion lays down beliefs and demands acquiescence. Whoever practices politics from a religious perspective, however nicely they speak, will see their political rivals as enemies of religion. They will defend the behaviour of sheikhs and their leadership with the same ferocity by which they defend their own religious beliefs. They are prepared to commit crimes and will use religion to justify their actions because they believe themselves to be engaged in a holy war to uphold religion. We Egyptians have paid a heavy price for mixing religion and politics, and it is time for us to learn from this hard lesson.

The military council allowed political parties to be formed on the basis of religion and the result was the emergence of fanatical groups who vilified and despised those who differed from them politically. They accused their opponents of being infidels, whose blood could be spilt. They were unable to engage in the reality of the situation because they consider themselves warriors fighting for the cause of Islam. Dozens of churches, government buildings and police stations have been burned to the ground; dozens of innocent people have been killed, our soldiers were killed in Sinai, and there was also an attempt to assassinate the minister of the interior.[1] Yet, even after all of these terrorist acts, the Muslim Brothers still consider themselves to be heroic victims, because in their imaginations they are fighting a holy war to make Islam triumph over the infidel secularists. Only this complete detachment from reality can explain the spectacle of the Brotherhood's killings, and their mutilation of the bodies of their victims while declaring: "There is no god but God" and cheering for Islam. I saw a video in which one Brotherhood member was shouting: "I am godly and I do what God has ordered. You all oppose God and his Prophet."

A few days ago, Tharwat el-Kherbawy (who was a member of the Brotherhood who left when he discovered how misguided they were) wrote about a discussion he had in the seventies with Mahmoud Ezzat, a leading figure in the Brotherhood. Ezzat argued that assassinating the Brotherhood's rivals was completely acceptable behaviour in the context of Islam, because the opponents of the Brotherhood are throwbacks to the pagan society that tried to prevent the establishment of Islamic rule. Therefore, killing them is

1 A powerful bomb blasted through a convoy of cars carrying the interior minister along a residential street, raising fears of a widely predicted turn toward terrorist violence by opponents of the military ouster of President Mohamed Morsi.

religiously acceptable. Do we need any more proof that the Brotherhood is a terrorist organisation and that we must ban the establishment of religious parties in the new constitution? On 30 June millions of Egyptians took to the streets not only to announce their rejection of the isolated president and the rule of the Brotherhood, but also the rejection of all religious parties.

After this great revolution it is very strange to see the interim government courting and chasing after the Salafist Al-Nour Party and practically begging it to agree to participate in the writing of the new constitution. I don't understand how we can talk about getting rid of religious parties and then involve one of the most religiously fanatical parties in the committee that will draft the constitution. We ask the members of the Constituent Assembly – all of whom are respected national personalities – to learn from the lesson we all lived through under the rule of the Brotherhood and write a new constitution that will be the basis for a modern, democratic, civil state that respects civil liberties and the equal rights of citizens irrespective of their religions, one that respects religion but does not allow it to be used in politics. Then and only then will Egypt's future begin.

Democracy is the answer.

PN

Who is Iskandar Tus?

16 September 2013

Do you know Iskandar Tus? I imagine that not many people have heard of him, apart from his family and his customers. However, Iskandar Tus played an important role in the events currently being covered by the media. Despite this, I was unable to find a personal photograph of him or any details about his life. Of course, the media has its priorities: if a film star gets a sprained ankle, or if a minister has secretly married his secretary, or even if a famous football player has decided to get some respite and is spending a few days in his villa on the north coast, then it will be in the news. As for Iskandar Tus, never in his life had he done anything newsworthy. All that we know about Iskandar Tus is that he was over 60 years old and was a barber. But the barbershop he owned was not in a classy neighbourhood in Cairo or Alexandria amongst the rich and famous, but in a remote, forsaken town called Dalga in Minya Governorate.

In all honesty, Iskandar Tus was an unimportant person. He was one of millions of ordinary Egyptians who are fated to live and earn their bread, engaged in a constant struggle just to stay alive and, despite this, nobody feels anything for them at all. Iskandar is one of the millions of impoverished people strategic analysts talk about at length on satellite TV and whom all politicians put in their election manifesto but in reality no one cares about.

What was the life of Iskandar Tus like? At over 60 years old, he had reached the age when people start to think about death and hope their end will be a happy one, and they consider the fate of their children after they have passed away. No doubt Iskandar kept good relations with his neighbours – after all they were also his customers. I can picture old Iskandar working all day, perhaps resting a little when business was slow and taking out a simple lunch prepared for him by his wife. I can imagine he would open his shop for Muslim and Christian festivals when fathers take their sons to get a "festive haircut". Old Iskandar often used to cut the hair of state security personnel and policemen for free so they would do him no harm and to endear them to him because they could be useful to him in times of need, especially because Iskandar was a Copt in a town with a Muslim majority.

The inhabitants of Dalga number 120,000: 20,000 are Copts and the rest are Muslims. But these are not ordinary Muslims. The majority of them are supporters of the Muslim Brotherhood; they believed that Mohamed Morsi was the long-awaited caliph who would restore the glory of Islam and make the Brotherhood masters of the whole world. When Egyptians rose up against Morsi, deposed him with the help of the Egyptian army, the Brotherhood supporters in Dalga became deeply angry. Thousands of them travelled to take part in the sit-ins in Rabaa Al-Adawiya and Al-Nahda Square, and when the sit-ins were broken up by the security forces, the Brotherhood's supporters in Dalga considered this a declaration of war on Islam, of which they considered themselves the sole representatives.

The Brotherhood supporters went to the town's mosques and climbed the pulpits to announce a holy war. All the Brotherhood's supporters in Dalga, including women and some children, were armed and they left the mosques imbued with religious fervour and the courage to fight a blessed battle. They attacked the local police station, burned it to the ground and took complete control of the town. Because they considered the Copts to be cross-worshipping infidels, and because Pope Tawadros II had approved of Morsi's dismissal and participated in the transitional road map – just as a sheikh from Al-Azhar and 33 million Egyptians had done – the Brotherhood supporters decided that their sacred war was against the Copts. They attacked and looted all the churches in Dalga then burned them to the ground, including an ancient monastery of priceless archaeological value that was founded in the 1400s. After that, they turned on the Copts themselves, forcing them out of their own homes before setting them on fire.

These horrifying attacks led ten Coptic families to flee the town, but many Copts were not able to escape and were forced to submit to the Brotherhood supporters; they had to witness their churches and houses looted and burned down without saying a word in protest. In fact, they agreed to pay a levy to the supporters not to do them harm.

Here it must be said that sectarian violence against the Copts has continued unabated for 30 years. It happened during the rule of Mubarak, continued throughout the rule of the military council as well as the Brotherhood, and now it is spreading all over Upper Egypt since the fall of Morsi. Those who attack Copts usually escape punishment, because the Egyptian government prefers to pressurise Copts into holding reconciliation meetings with those who attacked them, which always end in a noble speech about national unity and exchanges of kisses and smiles in front of the cameras. Afterwards, everybody leaves and forgets all about what happened until a new wave of violence requires new reconciliation meetings to be held.

After the fall of Mohamed Morsi, his supporters attacked the Copts in most of the governorates in Upper Egypt. Their aim was not only to take revenge on the Copts and to terrify them, but also to provoke them to fight back so that Egypt would slip into the sectarian war that the Brotherhood wanted and strived for so perniciously. However, the Copts conducted themselves with a noble national conscience and did not fight back. They watched as their churches burned down in front of their eyes, but refused to fight the extremists and stoop to their level.

But what happened in Dalga was more serious than incidents elsewhere, because the Brotherhood supporters had driven the police out of the town and put up an armed resistance when the army attempted to retake the town. Therefore, they alone had undisputed rule. The Copts living in Dalga had only limited options: either flee the town, or pay an exorbitant amount of money every day to protect their houses and their families. Iskandar Tus, the barber, behaved differently. He could never imagine leaving the town in which he had lived his whole life and he knew no other place to go. Being poor, he could not pay for his family's protection. The Brotherhood supporters came and demanded that Iskandar take his family and leave his house so that they could loot and burn it like they had done to dozens of Copts. What did Iskandar do then exactly? Perhaps he stood his ground and protected his house, refusing to leave; perhaps he shouted in protest or gave his attackers a look of defiance, or perhaps he said something they did not like. Whatever it was that Iskandar Tus did or said, the Brotherhood supporters understood it as a blatant challenge to them from an infidel Christian. In their view, this Christian had to be severely punished as a warning to any infidel after this who would dare defy Islam and Muslims.

The Brotherhood supporters grabbed old Iskandar, covered him in punches, kicks and slaps and dragged him out into the street. Some of them knelt on him while others grabbed his sides, then they slaughtered him, yes, slaughtered him with a knife right across his throat, as a butcher slaughters sheep on Eid al-Adha. Did it ever occur to Iskandar that he would pay with his life for his objection to the looting of his house? What did he say to them when he realised that they were going to slaughter him? Did he beg them to keep him alive for the sake of his children? What was Iskandar thinking when he received the first cut to his neck? Was he in pain throughout, or did he give up his soul at the first cut? These are questions we will never know the answer to. What we do know is that when the Brotherhood's supporters slaughtered Iskandar, they intentionally did not sever his head completely; they made arrangements with the owner of a tractor, then they tied the slaughtered man to it by his feet and had him dragged through the streets. In this way, the whole town saw Iskandar Tus, the barber, for the last time; slaughtered and dragged behind a tractor while his partly-severed head flapped back and forth, the blood flowing copiously from it and making a trail on the ground behind.

After the Brotherhood supporters had finished the procession of his body through the town, they threw the corpse of Iskandar into the street. Nobody from the town dared to approach the body fearing that they would meet the same fate. In the end, a good Muslim man came and buried Iskandar in the Christian charity tombs. However, after a while, the supporters of the Brotherhood, realising that they had forgotten to film the slaughter of Iskandar, went to the graveyard to find the body. They set about digging the body up and then they filmed it with their mobile phones until they were satisfied. One of them was about to amuse himself by firing bullets into the corpse but his colleagues prevented him, perhaps to save ammunition.

This is how the life of Iskandar Tus from the town of Dalga ended. Now he lies in the charity tombs after being beaten, slaughtered and dragged around for all to see, and then filmed after his body had been desecrated. What did Iskandar do to deserve such a fate? True, he was a poor and unimportant person, from a humble background and with no prestigious connections. But he was also a noble and hardworking man; he worked earnestly to gain a few pounds a day to spend on his children. Did Iskandar not have the simplest rights to respectful and humane treatment? Was it not his right that the state to which he paid his taxes should protect his life, his house and the few simple possessions he had? If he was indeed fated to die, did Iskandar not have a right to die with dignity and leave the world in a way that any human being deserves?

How did his children feel when they saw their father slaughtered and his body being dragged through the streets, as people came to watch it and take pictures with their mobile phones? In what kind of country is a citizen slaughtered and paraded through the streets because he objected to his house being looted? In what religion is a human life so cheap that a person is slaughtered because he said something or gave a look that did not please the supporters of the Brotherhood? Didn't the Brotherhood supporters hear about the value Islam places on the human soul? And has Dalga turned into an emirate of the Brotherhood? And were the police force unable to enter Dalga, or did they prefer to stay out of danger and leave the Copts to their fate?

A few years ago, when the Egyptian Marwa el-Sherbini[1] was killed by an extremist in Germany, the whole German nation rose up and did not rest until Marwa's killer received just punishment. Meanwhile, Iskandar Tus was slaughtered in his own country in the middle of his own town and no one in a position of authority did anything, even the papers only mentioned it briefly. The difference between Marwa and Iskandar is that Marwa was killed in a country that respects a person unequivocally, while Iskandar was killed in Egypt, where a person's value is defined according to their religion, wealth and social status.

Goodbye, old Iskandar Tus. We are sorry we were not able to defend you as we should have. I call on all Egyptians, and especially Muslims rather than Copts, to start a campaign to look after the sons of the martyred Iskandar Tus and bring those who killed him to justice.

The revolution is ongoing, until Egypt beats terrorism and creates the just, civilian state in which citizens are not harmed due to their religion or the views they hold, or because they are poor.

Democracy is the answer.

PN

A Piece of Candy

23 September 2013

Dear reader, let's imagine you have a daughter of marriageable age and a young man has proposed to her who is excellent in many ways: he's rich, educated and has a bright future ahead of him, in addition to being good-mannered and religious. His only fault is that he has been married once before and divorced his first wife without having any children. Would you accept this young man as a husband for your daughter? In most cases, you would ask about the reasons for his divorce in order to be certain that he was not to blame for the failure of his first marriage. Then you would accept him as

1 Marwa Ali El-Sherbini was an Egyptian woman and German resident who was killed in 2009 during an appeal hearing at a court of law in Dresden, Germany. She was stabbed by Alex Wiens, a German immigrant from Russia against whom she had testified in a criminal case for verbal abuse. Sherbini's funeral took place in her native Alexandria in the presence of thousands of mourners and leading government figures.

a husband for your daughter and say: "This man got caught up in a doomed marriage, and that could happen to any person. It's no fault of his."

Now what if the opposite happened? What if your young son who has never been married before told you that he had fallen in love with a divorced woman and went into rhapsodies about her personality and her morals? In most cases, you would refuse to even consider the thought. Your anger might get the better of you. "Are you crazy?" you might shout at your son, "are you going to pass over a virgin to marry a divorcee?"

Unfortunately, this discrepancy in behaviour reflects our attitude towards women in Egypt. However much we talk about women's rights, in defining moments like these, our true feelings are laid bare. The father loses his temper with his son because he, a young man who has never been married before, wants to marry a divorcee. The father asks himself what could compel his son to marry a woman by whom another man has been pleasured. It's as if you gave your son the money to buy a new car and, to your horror, he comes home with a second-hand one for the same price. Certainly you would get angry, because you wanted him to enjoy a new car that nobody had driven before. This is how we truly see women, whatever we may claim to the contrary.

Whenever we praise someone for their strength or bravery we say that he's a "true man", as if bravery is a male phenomenon. On the other hand, if we threaten a man we tell him: "By God, we'll make you wear the veil!" Similarly, when policemen are torturing a male prisoner they enjoy humiliating him by calling him by a woman's name, as if masculinity is evidence of nobility and bravery, while femininity is a sign of humiliation and submission. The whole world has moved on from these backwards ideas; masculinity is no longer a mark of distinction and femininity is no longer a sign of weakness. Progressive peoples consider a woman to be simply a person who happens to be female, just as a man is a person who happens to be male.

Ther have been over 30 female heads of state around the world and often the countries that are governed by women do a lot better than those governed by men. Let us remember that meeting between the German Chancellor Angela Merkel and our deposed president, Mohamed Morsi. How powerful and brilliant Merkel seemed that day, next to the weak, bumbling Morsi.[1] In 1982, war broke out in the Falklands, and Britain, led by Margaret Thatcher, dealt Argentina a humiliating defeat, which was at that time governed by a group of supposedly virile generals.

The reality is that the men of Egypt always swing between two views of women: the progressive view that the woman is an autonomous human

1 Morsi had travelled to Germany to discuss funding and debt relief with the German chancellor. Germany had earlier hinted that it might consider forgiving some of Egypt's loans (€240 million), but Morsi came away from his visit empty-handed.

being whose capacities match those of a man, and the other, backwards view that equates a woman with her biological and domestic role. According to the latter view, she is to be a source of pleasure for her husband and a means of bearing children; a house worker who washes, cooks and sweeps the floor – that she is capable of other things is considered less important.

These two views of women have been competing in our society for decades. At the end of the nineteenth century, the great thinker Muhammad Abduh appeared in Egypt and presented Muslims with an open-minded, contemporary interpretation of Islam that rid the Egyptian mind of its superstitions and did justice to women, considering them complete human beings. After this, religion turned into a catalyst for renaissance; it moved society forwards and Egypt progressed in all areas – despite the British occupation – and Egyptian women were liberated from everything that restricted their humanity. For the first time, Arab women were receiving an education, getting jobs, driving cars and even flying planes. They went to university, got into parliament and then into government. Under Gamal Abdel Nasser, women advanced in all areas – that is, until the seventies when the price of oil rose significantly after the October War. Millions of Egyptians were forced to go abroad to work in the oil-producing countries. When they returned, many brought with them a Wahhabi interpretation of Islam: a narrow-minded, backwards interpretation contrary to the Egyptian one presented by Muhammad Abduh. Millions of dollars were spent on new preachers, most of whom had not studied theology in a proper academic way but had been the disciples of Wahhabi sheikhs. All they did was simply repeat their backward views, which returned to popularity in Egypt despite being expulsed almost a century before. Regarding the Wahhabi view of women, I can find no better example than the view of one Wahhabi preacher who had this to say on his television show:

> Let's imagine that a man craves something sweet and there are two pieces of candy in front of him: one of them is completely wrapped in cellophane and the other has been left open and is collecting flies. Which of them would he choose? Of course, the man would prefer to eat the candy that is wrapped and would be disgusted by the open candy covered with flies. Therefore, a man should prefer to marry a veiled woman, because she is like the wrapped candy: she saves her sweetness for her husband. An unveiled woman is like the uncovered candy: she is available to all and collects flies.

As well as inciting hatred towards unveiled women (including Christians), the words of this preacher reflect the Wahhabi view of women. For them, women are like candies created by God for men to enjoy. Candies have no mind or feelings or free will. Therefore, men must guard the candy in their possession so that another man doesn't eat it. The predominant view amongst Wahhabi sheikhs is that it is permissible to marry a woman as soon as she starts menstruating, even if she is a girl of ten. One of their sheikhs said: "A man can have intercourse with a ten-year-old girl as long as she can physically bear it." Of course, the man does not know if she can bear it until after he has slept with her. Last week, an eight-year-old girl from Yemen died after she married a forty-year-old man. When he entered her, he tore her womb and she bled to death.

The "piece of candy" mentality explains why sexual harassment is increasing all over Egypt. Until the end of the seventies, it was not common for women to be veiled. In fact, they often went to the sea in bathing costumes and wore short, revealing modern clothing. However, at that time, sexual harassment was extremely rare. Then the Wahhabi ideology spread and most Egyptian women started wearing the veil, with many wearing a full face veil, and despite all of this modesty, sexual harassment spread like the plague. Egypt now ranks second in the world, behind Afghanistan, for instances of sexual harassment.

Many attribute the spread of sexual harassment to women wearing provocative clothing, but this is clearly untrue, since the majority of the victims of sexual harassment are veiled. Many others would argue that sexual harassment is down to the harassers being unmarried – as if their sexual deprivation justifies them committing crimes – or because they did not receive a good upbringing, as if implying that upbringing is completely separate from culture and social conditions. In my opinion, however, all of these are secondary reasons and the spread of sexual harassment stems essentially from the change in the way Egyptians view women. If you consider a woman to be a piece of candy which you long to eat but do not have the means to buy – that is, to marry – and the chance comes along to snatch a bite of a piece of candy owned by somebody else and escape punishment, you certainly would not hesitate. Whoever harasses a woman on the street sees her as nothing but a body. If he considered her a human being with feelings and dignity, he would not harass her.

In Egypt, the progressive, humanistic view of women fell out of favour only to be replaced by the backwards, Wahhabi view. That is, until the January 25 Revolution came and changed everything. A revolution is not only a political change, but a comprehensive human transformation resulting in radical changes in every area. A revolution means that people have changed their view of the world and discovered things they had never thought of before. An example of this is that the Egyptian, whom some had previous accused of cowardice, submissiveness and passivity, suddenly turned into a brave creature confronting bullets with his chest and more than willing to die for the sake of freedom.

One of the biggest achievements of the revolution is that Egyptian women have reclaimed their rightful role in society after decades of regression in the face of a backwards ideology. Anyone who participated in the revolution will know that women made up around half of the revolutionaries; they were always in the front lines and, were it not for the bravery of Egyptian women, the revolution would not have lasted a single day. The reaction of the authorities was especially violent against women. The truth is that the Mubarak regime, the military council and the Muslim Brotherhood, despite differing in many ways, share one thing in common: their backwards view of women. During the demonstrations, the security forces cracked down on the women twice as hard. The female demonstrators suffered attacks and indecent assaults; the authorities dragged them through the streets in order to send an explicit message to every woman in Egypt: their natural place is in the home and if they come out into the streets to protest, they will be shamed and their bodies will be exposed in front of the cameras.

The struggle of Egyptian women did not end with the outbreak of the revolution in January 2011, nor with the great revolutionary wave of 30 June; it is ongoing. When the Committee of 50 was formed to amend the deplorable, sectarian constitution imposed on Egypt by the Brotherhood, we were surprised and saddened to see that the number of women on the committee was very small indeed. It was not proportional to their percentage of the population, nor was it representative of their role in the revolution. The members of the Committee of 50 are all revolutionary, patriotic figures, but the limited number of female members means that whoever formed this committee considers the writing of a constitution a serious and precise task of which only men are capable. Here again we run into the piece of candy mentality.

I compel the members of the Committee of 50 to do all that is necessary to secure Egyptian women their rights. We must have a constitution that makes provision for a quota or a specific proportion of seats in parliament, and all elected bodies, that is reserved for women. This kind of positive discrimination in favour of women is, in my opinion, necessary, at least temporarily, because the prevalent culture now does not trust women and this will lead to them being sidelined in any future elections. The new constitution must reflect the principles of the revolution concerning the rights of women and Copts, social equality and the banning of any political party which is formed on religious grounds or that has any association with religion.

The revolution will continue until it fulfils all of its aims. One of the most important of these is the right of a Egyptian women to be treated as human beings that have full rights and a free will; they are not like pieces of candy, whether they are covered or not!

Democracy is the answer.

PN

The Disadvantages of Expediency

30 September 2013

Twenty years ago, I hired a decorator named Saeed to paint my apartment. He told me he had learnt his trade from an Italian decorator in Alexandria. I had never met anyone before who had perfected his work to the degree that Saeed had. He painted walls as if he were painting a canvas. He used to sand down the wall with emery paper and cover it with paste. Next, he would sand it again and then paint it, then he would wait for the paint to dry completely before applying a second coat. At the end of his day he would sweep where he had been working and scrub it with water and soap so that he would find it clean again in the morning.

Strangely, Saeed's perfection in his trade did not lead to his promotion within it. In fact, it brought him serious problems. Amongst his fellow decorators, Saeed became known for the slow pace of his work; sometimes it could take days for him to finish a job that another decorator could finish in just one day. This reputation led contractors to be reluctant to hire Saeed for their projects and soon he had no work at all. Saeed tried time and again to convince the contractors that his perfectionism in his work, even though it took time, would in the end save them from additional costs further down the line, but it was all in vain. The contractors were all convinced that Saeed would bring only delays and headaches. Once I spoke with Saeed and he said bitterly: "The contractors can never understand me. I want to do it properly, and they want me to do everything expediently."

Saeed left the decorating trade and worked as a travelling salesman until he died in poverty last year, leaving behind a wife and children. I was sad when he died and reflected that in any country in the world, people would lose their jobs if they didn't do them perfectly – apart from in Egypt, where, on the contrary, a person can lose their job if they try to perfect it. I looked up the term used by Saeed, "expediently", and found that in Arabic, the expression is derives from the verb "to expedite", which means "to do quickly". So, were you to say: "The man expedited his work." This would mean that he did it in a rush, without precision, or, if you said: "The man grilled the meat expeditiously." This would mean that he didn't cook it for long enough.

If there is one term to describe Egyptian society, it is expeditious. Very rarely do we take the time to perfect our work or do it according to the proper specifications. How many lawyers do you know who read over the case thoroughly and carefully prepare points for the defence before making their appeal to the judge? How many doctors take the time to examine the patient and compare their test results and scans with the symptoms in order to come to the right diagnosis? Egypt must be the only country in the world where a person has surgery and discovers months later that the doctors have left a pad or some scissors in his bowels. The reason for this is that the nurse rushed her work and did not count the tools before and after the operation.

In addition to expedience in our professions, we Egyptians also suffer continually from political expedience as well. Professional expedience is a result of greed or lack of patience, but the authorities do what is politically expedient in order to cheat the people and deny them of their rights. In January 2011, Egyptians started a great revolution in which they ousted Mubarak. Then, they handed the revolution over to the military council and returned to their homes. The military council made a show of siding with the revolution and then rushed through policies while keeping the Mubarak regime intact and preventing the changes for which the revolution took place in the first place. The military council allowed the formation of political parties on the basis of religion – in contradiction of every Egyptian constitution – then allied with these parties and covered up their crimes in the election because it wanted them to control parliament. The military council did not apply the law to the religious parties, nor did it call for them to declare their sources of funding or ask them about the millions they had spent on purchasing regional headquarters and election campaign materials. It then founded the Supreme Presidential Electoral Commission (SPEC), which was presented with video evidence capturing the Muslim Brotherhood and the Salafists buying the votes of poor people in broad daylight; yet, nothing was done.

As for the presidential elections, the extent of political expedience was considerable. The SPEC announced that the winner was Mohamed Morsi, who had acted president for a whole year before it was revealed that his competitor Ahmed Shafik had presented an appeal accusing Morsi of rigging the votes to his advantage.[1] In the end, the judge presiding over the case stepped down and refused to make the results of the investigation public, apparently because he had reservations about the trial. Of course, the issue here has nothing to do with Ahmed Shafik – whom I still see as a loyal follower of Mubarak, and who should not be allowed to assume the presidency after the revolution had ousted his master. The issue here is this: a whole year had passed before Egyptians discovered they had been cheated and that the result of the presidential elections had been brought into question. Furthermore, certain documents have been appearing in the media from time to time that appear to show that Shafik was, in fact, the true winner. Each time we are told that the attorney general will launch

---

1 On 27 May, Ahmed Shafik's lawyer lodged an appeal request with the SPEC, claiming the results had been rigged. Morsi narrowly defeated Shafik, garnering 51.7 per cent of the votes in a hard-fought final runoff round. Morsi had allegedly received 110 million Kuwaiti dinars from "Islamists in Kuwait" for use in his electoral campaign. By law, each presidential candidate is allowed to spend LE10 million on his/her campaign, along with an additional LE2 million in the event of a runoff vote.

an investigation, but we never hear the outcome of any of these.

The question is this: how could the SPEC have publicised Morsi's victory before investigating the appeals brought against him? And if this is how the SPEC acted in the second round of the presidential elections, then how can we be certain that it acted any better in the first round. Indeed, the presidential candidate Hamdeen Sabahi presented a complaint in which he recorded that gross violations had taken place which benefitted Shafik. The SPEC received the appeal, but it didn't take any action.

Every time the people have a real chance to change things, we find this political expedience by which Egyptians are cheated in illegal elections involving behind-the-scenes negotiations which we don't see, but whose existence can be deduced from the events that follow. On 30 June of this year, millions of Egyptians took to the streets in a great revolutionary wave. Their aims were crystal clear: end the rule of the Brotherhood, ban religious parties and found a truly democratic state in which there is social justice and the rule of law. The army sided with the will of the people and Morsi was forced to step down and the road map for a transition to democracy was made public.

Egyptians became optimistic and breathed a sigh of relief when they had got rid of the Brotherhood and its cronies. The Committee of 10 was formed and they received suggestions for amending the Brotherhood's constitution, which were then passed on to the Committee of 50. However, we began to see suspicious, worrying signs. Instead of banning the religious parties in compliance with the revolution's demands, we saw the interim president approach the Salafist Al-Nour Party and insist that they be part of the Committee of 50. For its part, the Al-Nour Party – which was complicit with the Brotherhood in all its crimes but then fell out with it only over the spoils – played hard to get and laid down conditions for its participation in the Committee of 50 only to leave the sessions in protest, warning that amending the constitution would lead to devil worship and orgies.

Brotherhood supporters are committing acts of terrorism and killing our soldiers on an almost daily basis, but the government is hesitant to brand them a terrorist organisation. Half of all Egyptians live below the poverty line and one of their most basic rights is that there should be an upper and a lower limit on wages, as there is in every respectable country. However, the government has cheated Egyptians by setting a minimum wage but not putting a cap on higher salaries. This, of course, is to the benefit of senior officials who are raking in millions of Egyptian pounds every month – their salaries being paid for by Egyptian taxpayers.

These days, we have begun to hear speculations about the new presidential elections and some politicians have announced their candidature, while others have announced that they would not run if General el-Sisi were to put himself forward, insofar as he is bound to win because Egyptians consider him a national hero after supporting the people against the Brotherhood. They want us to engage in this debate, while, at the same time, forgetting the past so that we can make the same mistakes time and again. They want us to be convinced that this time we will have elections that are truly fair. But, in Egypt, we do not use a single one of the safeguards that democratic countries use in their elections. Do people know the size of the presidential candidates' fortunes and how they have been obtained? Do we know where the millions of pounds, which they are spending on their election campaigns, comes from? How can we guarantee that the SPEC will not bury the complaints brought against a certain candidate and announce the victory of this candidate before investigating them sufficiently, as has happened before?

The presidential and parliamentary elections in Egypt have been nothing but political expedience with an absence of equal opportunities, transparency, rules or means to apply the law. But this expedience is not random; it has been adopted as a practice in order to smother the aims of the revolution and prevent the change for which it erupted in the first place. The members of the Committee of 50 – all of them respected national figures – now bear the historic responsibility of implementing the demands for which millions of people came out and demonstrated. The most important of these are:

1. Banning any political party that is formed on a religious basis or that has an association to religion, and disbanding the current religious parties. If the members of these parties wish to work in politics, they must form civilian parties and serve the interests of Egyptians without using religious symbols for political purposes.

2. Setting out in the constitution a lower and upper limit for wages in the state sector, as in every democratic country. The upper limit should be no more than 50 times the lower limit.

3. Subjecting the economic activities of the armed forces (vis-à-vis their public service companies) to monitoring by the state so that the correct taxes can be collected.

4. Subjecting all stages of the parliamentary and presidential elections to international supervision and applying proper conditions to ensure the integrity of the elections. Such conditions include: transparency with regard to funding, disclosing the candidates' assets, disqualifying any candidate who transgresses the upper limit of campaign spending and making vote-buying a criminal offence.

5. Enforcing positive discrimination in all elected bodies by specifying a quota for Copts and women. This measure gives a fair chance to groups where the prevailing culture prevents them from being represented in parliament.

6. Appointing an attorney general through the Supreme Judicial Council who will be completely independent of the president, in accordance with the principle of the independence of the judiciary.

7. Appointing the heads of the regulatory bodies independently of the president in accordance with the principle of regulation. In no democratic country does the president have any choice concerning the regulatory bodies that monitor his practices.

8. Comprehensive free medical treatment and free education at all levels are amongst the rights of the citizen that the state must provide. The expense will be paid for by the collection of taxes imposed on the wealthy.

9. Collecting all special funds[1] – which have created a secret economy amongst the luckiest of state employees – and adding the funds within them to the public treasury. It should not be permitted to collect any fees that are not then added to the public treasury.

10. It should not be permitted for civilians to be tried before military courts for whatever reason. In addition, state security courts and public prosecutions should be disbanded. The duties of the state security apparatus should be restricted to making inquiries and presenting them to the attorney general's office which will then investigate the accused.

These are the principles that will fulfil the demands of the revolution. If they are ignored, the amended constitution will only serve to reproduce the Mubarak regime and we will find ourselves back to where we started. The revolution will continue, God willing, until all of its goals have been achieved.

Democracy is the answer.

PN

Are We Building a State or an Authority?

7 October 2013

Who should take credit for Egypt's victory in the October War of 1973? Firstly, mention must be made of Egypt's military leaders and, most importantly, Chief of Staff General Saad el-Shazly, whose military genius was a driving force behind the victory, even though Anwar Sadat would later fall out with him and dismiss him from service. Mubarak continued the unfair treatment

1 Special funds are monies raised by state institutions through means other than customs or taxes, such as revenue accruing from hospital fees or parking tickets.

of el-Shazly and tried to wipe his name and the role he had played from the history of the war. However, with all due respect to the military leadership, those who really brought Egypt the victory were the soldiers from poor backgrounds who came from Egypt's towns and villages to do their military service after the defeat against Israel in 1967. Their military service went on for more than six years and their lives remained on hold until war broke out. Many of them were killed or injured and the rest left the military, going back to their lives only to find that the Egypt they had known before their conscription had completely changed.

The open-door economic policy of President Sadat had pushed society into an intolerable economic condition. During this period, prices skyrocketed, corruption was widespread and a new class of the super-rich was created whose wealth came mainly from estate agencies and brokerages. The state ended its national plan for Egyptians and the country transformed from an intellectually and psychologically unified nation to a collection of individuals who were bound only by proximity of location – each one caught up in their own personal problems and interests. Egyptians learned to concern themselves only with family affairs; they came to realise that their opinions were of no value, because the authorities would always do as they wanted, regardless of whether one agreed or disagreed. Egyptians fought furiously to pay for their children's education, then, as soon as they graduated, they would join the long queues in front of the Gulf embassies in order to look for a work contract, because the state made it clear that it was not obliged to find employment for its graduates. Under the rule of Mubarak, the state changed from a moral entity with a duty to fulfil the needs of its citizens into a tyrannical authority that monopolised power by means of repression, vote rigging and by turning its back on millions of impoverished Egyptians, who had no access to medical treatment, education, work or housing.

If you want to see an example of the crimes of Mubarak, you only have to drive to a cemetery in Egypt to find whole families living and raising their children amongst the bodies of the dead. Millions of Egyptians have been living in cemeteries for decades, for religious as well as economic reasons. On top of this, if you go beneath any bridge, you will find street children living in meagre conditions; in Egypt such children number between two and three million. After 30 years of Mubarak's rule, Egypt has divided itself into two separate countries which, even though they share the same name, are opposed in every way. There is prosperous Egypt: Zamalek, Mohandessin, El Tagamu and the Northern coast, where the rich live in palaces and drive luxury cars with many acquiring private planes. Aside from their businesses, these people have no need of the state since; if they fall ill they are treated abroad and they send their children to private foreign schools and universities with exorbitant fees. Then there is the other, forgotten Egypt that is drowning in extreme poverty, in which over half of the population now live. Millions of impoverished people have been left out in the cold and the authorities deal with them as if they are a caste of untouchables. They do not provide them with jobs, medical treatment or a real education. Whether they live or die is of no concern to the state. These people get kidney failure and cancer from polluted food and water, and if they go for treatment in a public hospital they often die of neglect. The private hospitals, who charge thousands of Egyptian pounds for treatment, will refuse to help them. These people burn to death in third-class train carriages, or are drowned in boats and ferries in their desperate attempts to escape the country. Meanwhile, the state watches on and treats the deaths of a few thousand of them as merely an unfortunate event.

The slogan of the Mubarak regime was: "Those who have not, want not." In the view of the Mubarak regime, the poor were nothing but a bunch of apathetic failures, who were entirely responsible for their own poverty. The reason they couldn't find work was simply that they weren't fit for work and were, therefore, sponging off the state and bringing only problems and crime. When impoverished Egyptians emigrated to Iraq searching for a livelihood, the war started between Iraq and Iran and the Egyptians were forced to sign up with the Iraqi army to fight a war that had absolutely nothing to do with them. Those who died during the war returned to their homeland in coffins. At this point, protests mounted in the media about the killing of Egyptians in this way and Hosni Mubarak did nothing but defend Saddam Hussein and ridicule the Egyptians who died in Iraq saying: "Saddam Hussein is calling for Arab solidarity and we must support him. Anyway, we know that most of those who died in Iraq had a screw loose." By this, he was referring to the fact they were destitute and running from the law.

In 2006, the *MS al-Salam Boccaccio 98* passenger ferry sank (due to negligence and corruption) and more than a thousand Egyptians died. Central Security Forces attacked the families of the victims while Mubarak was attending a training session for the national football team to witness the players' fitness prior to the African Cup. The Mubarak regime's neglect of the poor stemmed not only from disregard and corruption, but from a form of social philosophy based on the vilification of the poor for failing to make money. The poor must find their own solutions to their problems, solutions that do not involve the state. Across the whole world, the duty of a state is to provide a decent life for its citizens, except in Egypt, where the state disregards the poor and applies a lash to repress them if they rebel.

In the Mubarak regime, the state became merely an authority, and the distinction between the two terms is huge. The state is a moral entity responsible for looking after its citizens, while an authority monopolises power and remains there only as long as it is able to repress its citizens. Therefore, it is not overly concerned with their views or interests. After 30 years of Mubarak's rule, the dream of most young Egyptians is to escape from their homeland by any means: either to receive a work contract in one the Gulf countries where they usually face all kinds of injustice and abuses in order to provide for their families, or, to emigrate to Europe illegally, many of them drowning en route on the so-called "boats of death". A few years ago, Egyptian television broadcast an interview with one of the survivors from the boats who swore he would try to escape again by the same method as soon as possible. When the presenter warned him he might die, he smiled bitterly, saying: "Do you think I'm alive in Egypt? I'm already dead!"

This was the situation of the poor in Egypt, that is until the revolution started and millions of Egyptians took to the streets to demand the ousting of Hosni Mubarak, raising the slogan: "Bread, freedom and social justice". Then the military council worked to preserve the old Mubarak regime, after that power was transferred to the Brotherhood and it became quite clear to Egyptians that the Brotherhood were just as corrupt and tyrannical as the Mubarak regime – they simply did it all under the banner of religion. On 30 June, millions of Egyptians came out in a great revolutionary wave to end the rule of the Brotherhood. The army sided with the people, a political road map was announced and a constitution formed to amend the Brotherhood's constitution.

It was here that a real opportunity came about to build a modern nation providing jobs, a decent life, fixed abodes for everyone and free medical treatment for all citizens without exception. In democratic countries, social justice is achieved by two means. The first is to connect the lowest and highest salaries of state employees together, the idea being that the state derives these salaries from taxpayers' money and thus it cannot reflect an unfair disparity between employees. For example, a doctor or engineer cannot be employed on a salary of 500 Egyptian pounds a month when successful senior civil servants are getting one or two million a month from the treasury. The second means to achieve social justice by using cumulative taxes. This means that taxes rise in line with the profits of individuals and companies to provide the state with adequate resources, guaranteeing a decent life for the poor. This system for social justice is used in most democratic countries and it is this system that Mohamed Ghoneim – in his capacity as member of the Committee of 50 – is trying to have adopted in the new constitution.

Ghoneim is one of the world's leading urologists; he founded the famous urology centre in Mansoura which has treated thousands of impoverished people for free. Ghoneim played a great, patriotic role in the Egyptian revolution and has contributed suggestions to the committee, including tying the lowest salary to the highest salary for state workers and adopting a system of cumulative taxes on the rich so that the state can provide a dignified life for the poor. This caused a huge uproar and an organised campaign was started against the suggestions of Ghoneim. Behind the campaign were a group of millionaires who owned media outlets, factories and companies who naturally did not want to pay cumulative taxes on their huge fortunes. These people see nothing wrong with giving to charity every once in a while, but they ardently reject the state seizing their riches in order to benefit the poor. Some of Ghoneim's opponents have accused him of promoting communist ideas and this accusation betrays a saddening ignorance. There are no cumulative taxes in a communist system because the state has abolished private property full stop. It gives to citizens according to their needs and demands that they work according to their capabilities.

Tying the lowest salary to the highest salary and cumulative taxes are both policies that are applied in the majority of democratic countries. Even though in Egypt taxes go no higher than 20 per cent, skilful accountants can always fill out tax returns proving that their wealthy client has recorded a loss or meagre gain. We find that in most countries in the world, taxes rise in line with increases in earnings, and individuals can pay up to 57 per cent in Sweden, 50 per cent in Japan, 45 per cent in Britain, 55 per cent in Belgium, 52 per cent in Spain, 51 per cent in Denmark, 50 per cent in Austria, 45 per cent in Germany, etc. These are only some examples of different countries, not one of which is communist. In fact, most of them are based on the principle of the free market.

Egypt is now at a crossroads: either the state continues to ignore its basic duties and remains merely the ruling authority, leaving its citizens drowning in ignorance, poverty and illness, or the state does as it should and imposes cumulative taxes on the assets of the super-rich in order to provide a decent life for the poor. It is every Egyptian's right to be treated humanely: to live in a fixed abode, to find a school for their children in which they receive a free, quality education. A state must look after the health of its citizens and provide medical treatment irrespective of their financial capabilities. The new constitution must include the cumulative tax system and the tying of the lowest and highest wages so that the state has the necessary resources to give a decent life to millions of the less well-off.

The revolution is ongoing until it fulfils all its aims, and the most important of these is social justice.

Democracy is the answer.

PN

Reflections From a Chambre de Bonne

21 October 2013

"Chambre de bonne" is a French term which means the "maid's room", but French hotel staff very rarely employ it. Since the seventeenth century, the wealthy in France have reserved the top floor of their homes for their maids. Each maid would be given a narrow room under the roof of the house and there would be a few shared bathrooms. Over time, things changed and these rooms came to be used by students, who rented them at a low price. Then owners of property and hotels began to incorporate some of the chambres de bonne into their developments. They installed toilets and washrooms, and fitted them with stylish furniture before letting them out to guests. Chambres de bonne became a sign of luxury, with a rent sometimes higher than other rooms in the building. When staying in the hotels of Paris, I always love to stay in chambres de bonne because I can look out onto the city from above. Also, they are usually stylish, and the old wooden beams that hold up the roof give the room a beautiful historical touch.

I recently visited France at the invitation of a literature festival in Marseille and the festival management reserved two seminars for me to talk about my latest novel, *The Automobile Club*, with readings of some sections in French. Before the festival, I decided to spend a few days in Paris and booked a chambre de bonne in one of the hotels overlooking the Place de l'Odéon in central Paris. Whilst in Paris, I conducted a number of press conferences and held a seminar at the French-Egyptian Parliamentary Friendship Group, in which I clarified what I believed to have happened in Egypt during the past few months. I said what every Egyptian would have said, that is apart from the Brotherhood and their supporters. That on 30 June a great revolutionary wave swelled and the people came out to withdraw their confidence in the president, as has happened in numerous democratic countries. I found out, unfortunately, that the French were not aware of many important details. They did not know, for example, that Morsi had suspended the law and the constitution in November 2012. Nor were they aware that Egypt is currently without a parliament, which made the collecting of signatures, to demonstrate a lack of confidence in the president, a sound democratic procedure.

My last appointment in Paris was for the purpose of a literary exchange; I had been invited to a symposium by Jack Lang, director of L'Institut du Monde Arabe (Arab World Institute), to talk about my latest novel. Jack Lang is a world-renowned French intellectual and has held the positions of minister of culture and minister of education more than once. We agreed that Gilles Gauthier, a novelist, former diplomat and also the translator of all my books into French, should chair the symposium. I had an inkling that the Brotherhood would not allow my literary symposium to proceed without disruption but I never thought of cancelling it because I was defending the truth, the revolution and the right of Egyptians to choose who governs them, as well as their right to oust whomever they elect should they want to.

The Brotherhood obtained permission to hold a demonstration against me for two hours outside L'Institut du Monde Arabe. For their part, the French police mobilised a large number of officers to protect the institute in the event that the Brotherhood resorted to violence. Surprisingly, the Brotherhood did not hold their demonstration and we later realised that their objective in asking permission was to trick the French police by diverting their attention away from what they planned to do inside the symposium. As soon as I entered the room where the symposium was to take place, I noticed that something was amiss. Sitting in the first row were a few bearded, sullen-looking men, accompanied by their veiled wives and their children. The rest of the room was mostly French, in addition to a large group outside who had not been able to get a seat. Gauthier asked the officials from the institute to allow the group to enter, even if they spent the symposium standing at the back of the room.

I spoke for around half an hour about literature and about *The Automobile Club*, but I noticed that only those on the back rows were taking an interest in what I was saying. As for the Brotherhood members in the front rows, they were looking at me in disgust. Suddenly, a bearded man stood up and shouted: "We want to talk about what is happening in Egypt!" Gauthier told him that this was essentially a literary symposium but promised to give him an opportunity to discuss whatever he wanted with me after I had finished talking about the novel. Suddenly, another Brotherhood member from the other side of the room stood up and shouted: "What is all this?" This must have been the secret trigger, for they all stood up at once and took off their shirts to reveal the t-shirts they were wearing with the four finger rabia sign[1] and they started directing vile curses at both me and the Egyptian army. I replied that they were traitors because they had betrayed the revolution and were killing Egyptian soldiers. They had begun the attack even before I had replied to them. I noticed that they had weapons and had set about using them to break everything in the room from windows, tables and chairs; they even took Gauthier's phone and they would have trampled my small bag if a policeman had not have rescued it, after great effort.

The worst thing about this incident was seeing the French audience rushing from the room in terror. What is the crime of those who had come to attend a literary symposium, and why were they beaten and terrified in this way?

1 A hand gesture of an open palm showing four fingers with the thumb folded, used by protesters, activists and politicians who oppose the recent coup d'état in Egypt. Named after Rabia (fourth) Square, where the Brotherhood held a sit-in before being dispersed.

A policeman came to our aid and pulled us into the basement underneath the stage. We stayed there for quarter of an hour listening to the sounds of crashing and chanting from the room above. Afterwards, I learned that some audience members had resisted the Brotherhood and were beaten severely. Amongst them was a French woman who had shouted: "What you are doing is uncivilised. We came to a literary symposium to listen to an Egyptian author." The woman paid for her remark with a hard punch to the face that brought her to the floor, while the Brotherhood continued cursing everybody. We were evacuated by the back door of the institute and Jack Lang came to make sure we were OK. It was clear that he was extremely upset and annoyed about what had happened.

My friend Olivier Poivre d'Arvor, director of Radio France Culture, invited me to his house for dinner where I found a group of French intellectuals, all of whom expressed their sadness and regret at what had happened. Poivre d'Arvor told me: "It saddens me that this has happened in France, the country of liberty and the arts. Never before in France has a novelist been prevented from talking about his novel in this barbaric fashion." Jack Lang and Gilles Gauthier went on to condemn what happened in two statements to the press, which had a deep influence on French public opinion. I was greatly affected by the many expressions of solidarity that reached me from Egypt and France and, in fact, from other Western countries.

The following day I went to Marseille and was welcomed by a large number of Egyptians, led by the Egyptian Consul General Tarek Youssef. Seeing them as they stood in the street singing "Great, Oh Egypt"[1] was wonderful and very touching. The festival management made sure that these symposiums were made totally secure. First, I attended an open seminar in which I talked about the novel. After that, some parts of the novel were read by Philippe Caubère, one of the most important actors in France, who played the leading role in a famous film about Molière. This was the first reading of the French translation of *The Automobile Club* and the French audience received it with enthusiasm, clapping for several minutes after Caubère had finished reading.

In Marseille, I also met my friend, Thierry Fabre, a noted French writer and thinker. He was one of those who took on the task of initiating cultural exchanges between France and the peoples of the Mediterranean, and worked to establish the fantastic Museum of European and Mediterranean Civilisations in Marseille. I hope that the heads of museums in Egypt will visit it to benefit from this great achievement. It was then that a pressing question came to my mind that I didn't know the answer to, so I put it to Fabre, saying: "As soon as they found out the truth of what happened in Egypt, most of the French people I have met showed their solidarity with the

1 A patriotic poem by Ahmed Alam, famously put to music by the Lebanese singer Wadih El Safi.

revolution. But I don't understand why some French politicians are eager to help the Brotherhood, knowing very well that they are a fascist, terrorist organisation."

"These Western politicians view Egypt through the theory of Eastern despotism," responded Fabre. "This theory was put forward by some European politicos in the nineteenth century, and it boils down to the view that Egyptians, and the peoples of the East, in general, are not fit to practice democracy because their Islamic culture is incompatible with democracy and glorifies tyrannical leaders. For years, these politicians insisted to decision-makers in the West that a revolution would never happen in Egypt because Egyptians do not understand democracy and do not have use for it. When the Egyptian revolution happened, these politicians were shocked because their views about Egyptians were revealed to be untrue. They are defending the Brotherhood now, just as they defended Mubarak before, because they consider that the continuation of tyranny in Egypt is the biggest indication of the validity of their theory, which states that democracy is only suitable for Westerners and that Egyptians are fit only to be governed by a tyrant like Mubarak or a fascist organisation such as the Brotherhood."

Fabre's opinion reminded me of a dispute started by Taha Hussein[1] in the 1930s. He requested that Latin and Greek be taught in Egyptian Faculties of Arts, since it was not possible for any learner to be familiar with the heritage of mankind without mastering these two languages. Strangely, the person who was most opposed to the teaching of Latin and Greek was an English professor named Copeland, an expert on the Middle Ages. When the dispute became heated, Taha Hussein asked Professor Copeland: "Why are you opposed to the teaching of Latin and Greek in Egyptian universities? Do you know one British university that does not teach these two languages?"

"It's true that Latin and Greek are taught in all British universities," replied Copeland, "but Egyptian universities are not like British universities, and Egypt is certainly not anything like Britain."

I found a similarity between the logic of some Western politicians and the logic of Professor Copeland, who knew the importance of teaching Latin and Greek in university but saw Egyptians as unworthy of having a prestigious university. This is just like the Western politicians who are well aware that the Brotherhood is a terrorist, fascist organisation, but promote their rule of Egypt, which, in their opinion, is only fit for Eastern despotism.

The Egyptian revolution is at a defining moment. Successive terrorist operations carried out by the Brotherhood make it necessary for us all to stand up and confront them together. But our duty now is to build true foundations

1 One of the most influential twentieth century Egyptian writers and intellectuals, and a figurehead for the Egyptian Renaissance and the modernist movement in the Middle East and North Africa.

for a state of law and a new constitution. The forthcoming elections must be transparent and fair, and must be held under the watchful eye of international supervision. The steps towards transitional justice must begin at once: the holding of a fair investigation into all the incidents resulting in people being victimised since the beginning of the revolution in January 2011 up to now. We must prove to the world that the Egyptian revolution is capable of building the democracy for which it called for in the first place.

Democracy is the answer.

PN

Citizens or Tribesmen?

29 October 2013

During the time I studied in the United States, I was living in the University of Illinois' halls of residence. My roommates were from all over the world, and amongst them were some Arab students with whom I used to exchange greetings and occassionally chat with. One day one of these Arab students approached me and told me about a female Arab student at the university. He informed me of her name and nationality and then said: "She is having a relationship with a Polish student. Have you seen them?" I had seen them before, in the garden of the halls of residence and in the canteen. It seemed to me they were totally infatuated with one another. "This girl is morally out of control," he continued. "She kisses him in public without any respect for the feelings of the other Arabs in the university. It is making our blood boil and we will never accept this dishonour. We've found the contact details of her father and have decided to warn her that if she doesn't leave her Polish boyfriend and sort out her behaviour, we will inform her father of her obscene actions."

"Don't you realise that by doing so you are obtruding on a person you do not know and poking your noses into her personal life?" I replied. "She isn't a child, and you aren't her guardians."

"Brother, are you not an Arab?" he shouted, clearly taken aback by my words. "How can you watch an Arab girl kissing her foreign lover in front of your eyes without getting angry or offended?"

"I am responsible only for myself," I said, "and not for all Arab women. Anyway, if you consider yourselves responsible for this woman, why didn't you help her with anything before? Why do you interfere now with the intention of repressing her and threatening her on account of her personal behaviour?"

After an absurd debate, I made it clear to him that I would not be joining their "morals police", so he left, giving me a look of pure contempt. I later found out that they had confronted the girl as planned and told her how angry they were with her behaviour. She replied that she was free to do as she liked, then submitted a complaint against them to the management of the university which summoned them for questioning. After this, the Arab students desisted from following the girl out of fear of punishment.

In my opinion, this incident shows how some people, despite receiving the best education, do not behave as free citizens but as members of a tribe. Those Arab students only felt angry because the woman – whom they didn't even know personally – was an Arab, and they consider all Arabs as members of one big tribe. Thus, if any Arab woman loves a foreign man it is their duty to deter her or take revenge on her. The spread of a tribal mentality in our Arab societies constitutes a real obstacle to building a democracy. Tribal culture is at odds with democracy because it gives rise to despotism, oppression and favouritism, since it is founded on the following elements:

First: Collective responsibility. Whereas democratic culture maintains that responsibility lies with the individual, in that every citizen is responsible only for their own actions arising from their own free will, tribal mentality is based on the concept of collective responsibility. For example, it considers that all police officers are responsible for the crimes of torturing and killing demonstrators that some amongst them committed. It considers all Americans responsible for the crimes of the American army in Iraq and considers all Jews, wherever they are in the world, responsible for the crimes of Israel – even if they spoke out against them. It considers all Copts responsible for the actions of a single Copt, and when a Copt living abroad produced a film offensive to Islam, the sheikhs of political Islam uttered curses and insults against all Copts, insofar as they considered them all responsible for the offensive film. The principle of collective responsibility jeopardises the establishment of a modern nation, which is built on the notion that every citizen has rights and responsibilities that do not change according to religion, profession or gender.

Second: Professional cliquishness. When it was decided to turn my novel, *The Yacoubian Building*, into a film, I was astounded when a number of journalists presented a complaint against me to the Egyptian Syndicate of Journalists (ESJ). They considered the homosexual journalist character in the novel offensive to all journalists and demanded that the character be removed from the film or given a profession other than journalism, so that the masses wouldn't assume that all journalists were gay. Galal Aref, then chairman of the syndicate, promptly withdrew the complaint and assured me that the ESJ was a stronghold of freedoms and could never punish a novelist for his imagination.

But what happened to me has recurred dozens of times. Whenever a bad person appears in a film or television series, whoever shares the same profession as them makes a strong public protest. If the deviant character is a lawyer, the lawyers protest. If he is a doctor, the doctors call for the film or television series to be banned. This professional cliquishness is an aspect of the tribal mentality and places a disturbing limit on creative freedom. It may also assume an anti-democratic nature when professionals are only concerned with gaining what is best for their profession, as is happening now within the Constituent Assembly. The judges are refusing to subject the budget of the Egyptian Judges' Club to scrutiny by the Central Auditing Organisation and want to make it the one thing that cannot be discussed before the People's Assembly. Meanwhile, the military are insisting that the practise of trying civilians in military courts be allowed to continue; this has been a weapon used by those in authority to punish and repress their opponents since 1954 to the present day. Furthermore, they refuse to acknowledge the right of the president to appoint the minister of defence (as happens in all democratic countries) because they believe that a civilian, even if he is a president elected by the people, cannot decide who heads the army.

Third: Justice being relative. Whereas a democratic culture places emphasis on the notion that all citizens are equal before the law, tribal culture demands members of the tribe show solidarity towards one another if the conflict is with people outside the tribe, irrespective of who is right in the dispute. Therefore, the tribal mentality is unable to see things objectively, because in any situation it decides who is right depending on where it stands on the matter. In Egypt, it is very clear of late that justice is relative. Whereas the deposed Morsi is on trial – and rightly so – for insulting the judiciary, after he accused some judges of fraud in a public speech, we also see a lawyer who is famous for his foul language appearing on satellite TV channels and subjecting public figures to a torrent of vile accusations of treason, being a foreign agent and bribery; yet, nobody brings this foulmouthed lawyer to account because he is condoned by the current authorities. Also, while members of Judges for Egypt are rightly being prosecuted for practicing politics, which contradicts the presumed impartiality of judges, we see another team of judges announcing their political views at press conferences. However, nobody is prosecuting them for what they have done. If justice is relative, this negates the democratic concept that is founded on complete equality amongst citizens regardless of their relationship to those in power.

Fourth: Creating national symbols. In a democratic country, people consider the president of the republic a public servant whom it is their right and duty to liberally criticise and rebuke should they make a mistake. If they do not amend their conduct, parliament can pass a vote of no confidence and kick them out of office. In this vein, in the West there are hundreds of comedy programmes and satirical magazines making fun of politicians, first and foremost the president, who is forever resigned to be the butt of jokes, because they are aware that any criticism directed at them, however painful or wounding, is always for the public good and not to be taken personally.

In Egypt, however, the tribal mentality obliges us to raise our president above the level of ordinary people. The ruler, in relation to us, is not a public servant but a father figure, before whom we must all bow down and obey. The ruler is a national symbol and it is considered impolite and even treasonous to criticise them. The evidence for this is the case of Bassem Youssef, famous for presenting caricatures satirising public figures in his excellent, well-known show *Al Bernameg*. Previously, the show has dedicated whole episodes to making fun of President Morsi, and when Brotherhood supporters protested, everybody stood up in support of Bassem Youssef, in defence of freedom of expression. Then Egyptians rose up against Morsi and deposed him and the army sided with the will of the people. Bassem Youssef's programme returned to its usual ways and he made some jokes about General el-Sisi. This time, the whole country was in uproar; *Al Barnameg* was dropped by its producer, CBC, and many people objected to jokes being made about General el-Sisi because he is "the leader of the nation", "the nation symbol", and many more of these kinds of expressions which have been spouted insincerely about all the former presidents of Egypt without exception.

General el-Sisi performed a great national duty, averted Egypt from civil war and upheld the will of the people. All of this is true, but General el-Sisi must not be a national symbol because the only symbol of a nation should be the citizens, since the state was founded primarily to fulfil their interests and protect their rights. Sir Winston Churchill (1874–1965) led Britain to victory in the Second World War and the British took their courage from him in the most difficult of circumstances. Despite this, the great Churchill lost in the first general elections held after the war. The British may love Churchill and consider him a national hero, but they did not compose songs for his love and glorification and did not consider him a national symbol. On the contrary, they kicked him out in the elections because they believed that after the war Britain needed another politician, one that wasn't Churchill, who had new ideas and different, innovative policies. Meanwhile in Egypt, making pharaohs, an art in which some Egyptians are, sadly, all too proficient, is the one thing responsible for all the tragedies we have been caught up in.

Gamal Abdel Nasser was a great leader, but we made him into a pharaoh and we suffered the humiliating defeat against Israel in the Six-Day War of 1967. We made Sadat a pharaoh, then the disastrous war of 1973 took place and Egypt was held in the clutches of his open-door economic policies that left millions of Egyptians in poverty, or forced them to emigrate for work. If some Egyptians had not made Mubarak into a pharaoh, then there would not have been such a rise in corruption during his era, he would not have stayed in power for 30 years through corruption and vote rigging, and would not have dared to pass Egypt down to his son.

A revolution is not merely a political change; it involves a fundamental human change, casting a new look at the world and puts long-held assumptions up for discussion so that people come to find a new vision that leads to radical changes in all aspects of life. The revolution will not achieve any changes as long as the tribal mentality is present in our minds, because a tribal mentality blurs our vision, preventing us from looking to the future. We will not be able to build a modern nation unless Egyptians believe that they are all equal, and that they do not need a leader who is above accountability or sarcastic criticism, even if it is General el-Sisi himself.

Democracy is the answer.

PN

The Story of the Hall of Mirrors, the Lord and His Servants

4 November 2013

The following event happened at a hall of mirrors in an amusement park, where people go with their friends and relatives to look at themselves in the mirror. When they find their reflections strange and distorted they laugh and exchange humourous comments, and in the end they leave, having had some amusement. One evening, the Lord entered the hall of mirrors unannounced. There were eight people with him: four servants, two drummers and two pipers. The servants surrounded the Lord at all times and rushed ahead of him when he walked so as to clear the way for him. It seemed as if they were always reading his facial expressions so that they could satisfy his every want before he had even asked for it. They enthusiastically agreed to everything he said, and competed to show their fascination in everything he did.

In addition to the servants there were two men who each beat a drum and two other men who each played a pipe. The drumming and piping around the Lord was incessant and did not bear the slightest resemblance to music. Instead, it was a kind of noise intended to create a sense of awe around the Lord, or to prevent him from hearing what people said to him. As soon as the Lord and his entourage entered the hall of mirrors, people stopped their laughing and gazed at him. It seemed that as though they respected and loved him. Some of them even shouted warm greetings, while others waved at him. The Lord replied with a smile, but the servants rushed to surround him so as to prevent people coming close to him, while the drumming and piping grew louder still. The owner of the hall of mirrors hurried over and bowed before the Lord.

"We are honoured, my Lord. I am the owner of the house of mirrors, at your service," he said. The Lord smiled and shook his hand affectionately, then walked a little until he arrived at the first mirror, his entourage following behind. He looked at himself in the mirror and found that his body had become extremely tall but his head had shrunk to the size of a lemon. The Lord's face showed some displeasure.

"This mirror is defective. My Lord, please move away from it. I can't bear to see Your Grace in this form," one of the servants remarked. The Lord moved away from the mirror shaking his head. He came to the next mirror and when he looked into it he saw that he had become very short. His body was less than a metre tall, and his eyes were bulging very strangely. "My Lord, this mirror is more accursed than the first. What is with these defective mirrors?" shouted the servant angrily. The owner of the house of mirrors smiled and tried to explain but his voice was lost amidst the drums and pipes. The Lord walked slowly to where the third mirror was, on the opposite wall. He looked in it and found himself extremely rotund, like a barrel, while his face was bent to the right and completely flattened. At this point, the servants erupted with fury and expressed their condemnation of the mirrors in pantomime fashion.

"I can bear no more to see the Lord in these despicable mirrors. By God I will break them all!" shouted one of them.

"We must know who is responsible for this farce," added another.

"This is not a farce, it is a conspiracy by the agents of a fifth column who are trying to lure us into the hands of our enemies!" shouted a third.

The drumming and piping grew more intense. The owner of the hall of mirrors, however, waited for the noise to die down and then went up to the Lord, saying: "Sorry, my Lord, I beg you not to be displeased with your reflection in these mirrors. They do not show a true picture, but present an exaggerated image. A person sees himself short or tall or twisted. That is why they call them "the laughing mirrors". People come here to see this strange image of themselves; they laugh and are entertained by it, but they know very well that the laughing mirrors do not show the truth."

The Lord was about to say something, but then stopped because the drumming and piping started up again. Then a servant approached the owner of the house of mirrors determinedly. "How dare you put up these vile mirrors which present a deformed image of the great Lord!" he shouted.

"You must be either part of a fifth column or part of a sleeper cell!" shouted another.

"Whoever dares to insult our Lord must be severely punished!" shouted a third.

The owner of the hall of mirrors smiled sadly, then said: "God forbid that I would try to insult the Lord. I am one of those who admire him greatly and belive him to be very brave. But this is what a hall of mirrors is like all over the world. In the mirrors, a person's form is changed in an amusing way. This happens all over the world and never before has anyone considered their image in the hall of mirrors to be insulting." Meanwhile, the Lord continued looking at the owner of the hall of mirrors with a blank expression.

"This place of ill-repute must be closed immediately. I will summon the police," cried a servant as he was hurrying out of the door.

"Anyone who insults our Lord shall have his tongue cut out," shouted another, as the drumming and piping returned.

"Lord, this matter is a grave and dangerous one," said another servant, bowing reverently before the Lord. "Insulting ordinary people, whatever the circumstances, is an ordinary matter. But insulting you, Your Grace, is an insult to the nation as a whole. Your Grace is our leader, our teacher, our symbol and our saviour, and we are your soldiers and your sons. What is more, these villainous insults never occur by chance, because they come at a time in which the enemies of the nation are lying in wait."

"Thanks be to God a thousand times," cried the fourth, his voice breaking with emotion, "that no photographers were here. What if one of them had taken a photograph of Your Grace as you appeared in one of these accursed mirrors and was then circulated it in the press? They want to tarnish the image of Your Grace so that people lose confidence in your leadership and feel at a loss. Their aim is to weaken our morale and tear the home front to shreds, in addition to causing confusion and disturbing social peace."[1]

"Listen everybody," said the owner of the hall of mirrors, growing anxious, "why do you insist on blowing this issue out of proportion? The matter is simple. This is a place for laughter and amusement, no more and no less. Every day, dozens of people visit the hall of mirrors, see their distorted reflections and laugh. They do not consider that anyone has insulted them in the slightest. All of us know that the reflections these mirrors show are distortions. There is no conspiracy and nobody feels offended. By God, I didn't even know about the Lord's visit, and even if a picture of His Lordship thus distorted appeared in the media, that would not be insulting to him at all. In fact, it would do quite the opposite. This picture would prove that His Lordship is an ordinary, humble man, who goes to the hall of mirrors at the amusement park like everybody else."

"You mean to say that you agree with the Lord being photographed in this insulting fashion?" shouted a servant. "You really are a fifth columnist. By God, you've been found out!"

The owner of the hall of mirrors said something, but his voice was lost

1 The usual allegations made against any pro-democracy demonstrators before, during and after the revolution

once again amidst the drumming and piping. A servant returned with three policemen and a determined-looking officer. "Bring me the license for this place immediately," said the police officer, as he approached the owner of the hall of mirrors. The owner of the hall of mirrors hurried to his office at the end of the hall and returned with the license, which the police officer scrutinised carefully. Finding it to be sound, he thought for a while then asked him: "How many fire extinguishers do you have in this place?"

"Praise be to God, I have six fire extinguishers, all of them in excellent condition," replied the owner of the hall of mirrors confidently.

The police officer smiled and said: "The law states that you must have four fire extinguishers, not six."

"But I installed two supplementary fire extinguishers as a precaution. Where is the fault in that? In any case, if you like I can get rid of the additional fire extinguishers right away."

The policeman shook his head. "No, my good man. The law says only four fire extinguishers, and you have just told me that you have six. We must shut this place down."

The owner of the hall of mirrors tried to object, but it was in vain, because the officer had already signalled to the policemen to start removing the customers and finally gestured to the Lord, who was heading for the exit surrounded by his servants and drummers and pipers. The owner of the hall of mirrors walked quickly to intercept the Lord, taking no notice of the servants who tried to push him away and in a raised voice said: "My lord, it is not correct for my rights to be violated in your presence. This place is legal and licensed and is merely for entertainment and humour. The police only closed it at the instigation of your servants." The Lord looked at him silently, as the owner of the hall of mirrors went on with emotion in his voice: "Why do you not reply to me, Lord? Don't I have a right to hear your opinion?"

The drumming and piping rose and the servants pushed the owner of the hall of mirrors roughly aside as the Lord's procession moved on. The policemen finished clearing out the customers then escorted the owner of the hall of mirrors outside. It seemed that the police officer found enjoyment in closing the hall of mirrors with a red wax seal. The owner of the hall of mirrors shouted at him in a defiant tone: "Even if you close the hall of mirrors, I will open it again somewhere else and if I am not able, then the world will still be filled with halls of mirrors. It is ridiculous to ban people from imagination and laughter!"

The police officer shook his head sarcastically and took one last look at the red wax, feeling it with his hand to make sure it had dried. Once again the owner of the hall of mirrors saw the Lord's procession and shouted: "Lord, I love you and respect you and ask God to keep you safe. The picture people have of you is respectable and will not be influenced by how it appears in the laughing mirrors because everybody knows they do not show the truth. A hall of mirrors is not a threat to you, Lord. The real threat will come from those who surround you and try to convince you that you are unique for your time, and that conspiracies are being plotted against you and that everyone who disagrees with you is an agent and a hireling. Beware of the servants and drummers and pipers. They do not love you, but love only their privileges. They are playing the hypocrite with you, just as they have done with your predecessors and will do to all who come after you. Get rid of these hypocrites if you want to maintain your good relations with the people who love you."

It seemed that the Lord heard him this time, because he looked at him with sympathy. But as usual, the drumming and piping grew more intense and the servants hurried to move the Lord on and so he moved away. The owner of the hall of mirrors was still standing in the street when the police officer came up to him and said, in a decisive tone: "Listen, brother. The hall of mirrors contravened the terms of its licence. It had to be closed in the interests of public safety. Rest assured, the Lord had nothing to do with its closing. I warn you against getting confused or misled, for we will counteract that with a firmness you cannot even begin to imagine. You know, as everyone knows, that the Lord is the biggest champion of freedom and he would never allow any person to be prevented from expressing himself here.

Democracy is the answer.

PN

An Altercation at Maadi Hospital

11 November 2013

You will not read this story anywhere else because it is banned from publication. After the deposed president, Mohamed Morsi, had attended the first hearing of his trial, he was transferred to Burj al-Arab prison. There, his family brought him one of his favourite meals: a whole duck stuffed with delicious onions, served with rice and bread pudding with cream for dessert. Morsi ate with a great appetite, performed the evening prayer and settled down to sleep. All of a sudden, he felt severe chest pains. The prison doctor was called, who diagnosed his condition as a heart attack. Morsi was transferred by private plane to Maadi Military Hospital and immediately admitted to intensive care where he was kept under supervision for several days; all of the media outlets continued to claim that he was in Burj al-Arab prison.

At the other side of the hospital is Hosni Mubarak, living in a wing of his own, where he has spent the period of his house arrest after his time in preventive detention had elapsed. The presence of Mubarak and Morsi in the same place did not escape the notice of the hospital staff. Indeed, many thought it remarkable: here are two presidents who took power and who were both deposed by the Egyptian revolution. Mubarak's wing is big and luxurious; it includes an office and a sitting room. He eats whatever he likes, wears his civilian clothes and receives visitors, with the permission of the authorities. Suzanne Mubarak, his wife, spends all day with him and doesn't leave until he goes to sleep.

There was one doctor who used to look after Mubarak, but a week ago the hospital management exchanged him for a new doctor. Suzanne was not happy with this new doctor because he seemed a strange and reckless young man. More than once he had used the expression "the January 25 Revolution" in conversation, something for which Suzanne had not forgiven him. When she told her husband what she thought of the doctor, he told her that his main concern was that he was of officer rank. In the military, it is not possible for an officer to do anything without the permission of his superiors. Therefore, he considered that the appointment of this young man as his attendant was a bad sign of the army leadership's estimation of him.

It was approaching seven o'clock in the evening. Mubarak had taken a shower and was wearing a silk dressing gown, watching television. His hair had been styled and dyed with care. However, despite all this, he appeared exhausted and absent-minded. Suddenly, the door opened and the doctor appeared. "Sir, there is a patient in the hospital who has asked to visit you," he said.

"He is very welcome," said Mubarak, who always welcomed visitors, convinced that he still had his admirers.

"The person who has requested to visit you is Mohamed Morsi," continued the doctor.

Mubarak's face betrayed his utter astonishment. He looked towards Suzanne. "What cheek!" she said. "Tell him that the president refuses to meet him."

Mubarak, however, raised his hand and said in a faint voice: "It's OK, let's see what he wants. Show him in."

The doctor quickly left the room in a state of excitement, perhaps at his good fortune to be present at an unforgettable meeting between the two deposed presidents. The door opened and in came Morsi. Looking pale, he smiled and extended his hand to greet Mubarak, who held Morsi's hands by the ends of the fingers as he does with anybody whom he considers to be beneath him. Morsi ignored this cold reception and took a seat opposite him.

"I said to myself, it is not at all fitting for us to be in the same hospital and that it would bring Your Grace no contentment," said Morsi. "But whatever our political differences, the Brotherhood's estimation for you has always been boundless. Your Grace will surely recall that the Brotherhood said, on more than one occasion, that you were the father of all Egyptians and a symbol of the nation, and I think you will have noted, in the period of my presidency, my strict instructions regarding Your Grace's good treatment. You should also recall that I complied immediately with all of your requests. In fact, throughout my presidency, we came to satisfactory arrangements with senior officials such as Safwat el-Sherif, Fathi Sorour and Zakaria Azmi. Also, we were on the cusp of reaching an arrangement with Gamal and Alaa Mubarak, and Ahmed Ezz the engineer. We reached a solution concerning the Battle of the Camel, and were close to a solution regarding the assets smuggled abroad. We would have solved all these problems completely but then the coup d'état happened and brought everything to a standstill."

"All this is true, Morsi," said Mubarak, as Suzanne stared at Morsi with disapproval, "but truth be told I am tired and need some rest. Is there something specific you came here to talk about?"

Morsi remained silent for a moment, as if searching for the right words. "With God as my witness, sir, all my life I never coveted power or prestige."

"Never, you say?" said Mubarak, smiling sarcastically.

At this point the doctor interrupted: "You both destroyed your country for the sake of power."

"We were fighting to defend the law against the military coup," said Morsi.

"What happened in Egypt was a revolution, not a coup," replied the doctor. "You were the ones who made the real coup when you suspended the law with the constitutional declaration and made whatever you decided law. Egyptians withdrew their confidence in you of their own volition because they didn't have a parliament. The army did its duty and upheld the will of the people."

"I wouldn't think any citizen wants Egypt to be ruled by the military," said Morsi, glaring at the doctor.

"You are the one who honoured Tantawi and Enan, awarding them the Order of the Nile instead of bringing them to trial for the crime of killing revolutionaries," said the doctor with a derisive smile. "Young revolutionaries were killed on Mohammed Mahmoud Street and you, the Brotherhood, sent out a declaration in which you said the revolutionaries were a gang of thugs and the female revolutionaries were harlots. Weren't you the ones in Tahrir Square shouting, "Tantawi, you are our chief"? Weren't you the ones who supported the military trials of civilians through your representatives in the People's Assembly?"

Morsi looked to Mubarak uncomfortably, as if asking for him to intervene. He waved his hand at the doctor, who fell silent.

"Mr Morsi, I can't see this discussion being of any use," said Suzanne.

"I just ask for your patience," said Morsi, smiling. "Despite my determination to uphold the law," he said, turning to Mubarak: "I feel responsible before God and the people. I came, to ask Your Grace to intervene and stop the bloodshed. Undoubtedly you know the leaders of the coup and you are able to convince them that all this division is doing nobody any good. Young men are dying every day and the country has come to a standstill. The leadership of the Brotherhood are all in prison and our members are being locked up and put on trial on a daily basis."

"Mr Morsi, the greed and treachery of your organisation is the only reason for this," replied Mubarak. "During the events in January, you spoke with Omar Suleiman and you promised to remove the young men from the square. You made an agreement that I could stay in power in exchange for allowing you to form a political party. However, as usual you did not go through with your promises and were too greedy for power. Now you are paying the price."

"I object to the term 'greed'," said Morsi. "We are the Muslim Brotherhood; we are endowed with the morals of Islam. Our role model is the Prophet of God, peace be upon him. These are our morals and are our characteristics, this is how we were raised and educated, this is how we live and shall die."

"Do stop pontificating," said Mubarak. "I am on medication and very tired."

"Very well," said Morsi, smiling, "I'll get to the point. Can Your Grace intervene to prevent the bloodshed? I made contact with His Eminence, the supreme guide of the Muslim Brotherhood, this morning and he assured me that the Brotherhood are prepared to come to an understanding with the leaders of the coup, on condition that the leadership of the Brotherhood and all those imprisoned are immediately released. If we can reach an agreement, the Brotherhood would be content and will stop the demonstrations and the attacks against the army in Sinai immediately."

Here the doctor stepped in: "Anyone who launches attacks against the army is a traitor," he said.

"I am old enough to be your father and I don't like your tone of voice," said Morsi, turning angrily to the doctor. "Those who launched the attacks on the army and the police are not members of the Brotherhood."

"But since you are able to stop the attacks, you must be responsible for them."

"I don't have the power to control the people's anger."

"The Brotherhood members act on orders with blind obedience. You released terrorists from the prisons and refused to punish them for the killing of our soldiers. In fact, you used them to your advantage. Did you forget about all those who you imprisoned and tortured when you were in power? Did you forget the slain al-Jundi,[1] Kristy and Jika, and the martyrs of Port Said whom the police killed on your orders?"

1 Mohammad al-Jundi was an opposition activist who died from wounds sustained as a result of brutal torture in a police camp.

Morsi shot up from his seat and shouted at the doctor: "Listen, my boy, I don't wish to speak with you." He then looked to Mubarak and said: "Sir, I came to put the matter to you, and Your Grace can think about it in his own time."

"You and the Brotherhood conspired against Egypt in January 2011 and the people of Egypt were taken in by you," said Suzanne. "They recognised the value of President Mubarak when they saw what you were really like. Now the people are saying that they miss the days when he was president."

"I'm sorry, madam," said the doctor, "but these words are not true. Firstly, the January 25 Revolution was one of the greatest revolutions that the world has ever witnessed. Secondly, the Brotherhood did not make the revolution, they stole it. Thirdly, the rule of the Brotherhood and the rule of the National Democratic Party were as bad as each other. Who else forced Egyptians to live in cemeteries and slums and drink water mixed with sewage?"

"At least President Mubarak stood down from power of his own free will, to prevent more bloodshed," replied Suzanne.

"Wrong again," said the doctor. "It was, in fact, the revolution that forced him to stand down, after he had caused thousands of Egyptians to be killed."

"Listen, doctor," shouted Suzanne, "you are here only on account of your work; you are not to speak without permission. Is that understood?"

"I am not one of your servants who needs to ask your permission to speak. I am a military officer and a doctor and I have the right to say what I think about the affairs of my country. The Brotherhood committed a crime against Egyptians and you also committed a crime against them. The Brotherhood live in a fantasy world and think they are the protectors of Islam, whereas, in fact, they are criminals. You live in a fantasy world where you don't see the swamp of corruption and injustice Egypt has sunk into under your tenure. You and the Brotherhood are two faces of the same bad coin."

"I shall call the manager of the hospital and he will deal with you," shouted Suzanne, raising the volume of the television.

"Do your worst!" shouted the doctor, who had seemingly lost control of himself, marching out of the room and slamming the door behind him.

The room fell silent as the deposed presidents exchanged confused looks.

"Never mind that boy, sir," said Morsi to Mubarak, "he seems unhinged. Let's get back to our topic. I hope Your Grace will think about the idea of intervention. God willing, I will come by in the morning and take your opinion to His Eminence, the supreme guide."

Mubarak looked at Morsi and shook his head.

Democracy is the answer.

PN

How to Build a Modern Democratic State

18 November 2013

Consider the following questions:

1. What if I told you that God created 360 chosen ones, holy and beloved, and gave them the ability to create thunder, lighting and rain, and to control the sun and the pattern of day and night? What if I told you that these chosen holy men would marry equally as holy women, and make them pregnant by whispering a certain word in their ear? Would you believe me?
2. What if I told you that God wants you to wear a certain pair of trousers, and that you must wear a steel bracelet and use a specific comb to brush your hair? What if I told you that you have to hang a dagger round your waist and never remove it from there, would you believe that these are God's commands and that you'll be cursed if you disobey them?
3. What if I told you that God created you in the lowest human rank and that you will be despised and rejected by all you come across because your soul inhabited the body of a bad person in a past life, who committed several sins and crimes? What if I told you that you must accept this mistreatment as a fair punishment, and believe that when you die your soul will be resurrected in the body of a kind person so that you can experience love and respect?

If you are a Muslim or a Christian, you may find the above practices unusual and disregard them as superstitious. However, these rituals and beliefs belong to the Mandaean,[1] the Sikh and the Hindu religions respectively. These three religions have millions of worshippers all over the world. Hinduism claims around 950 million followers, i.e., almost 14 per cent of the world's population, making it the world's fourth largest religion after Christianity and Islam. It would be a grave error to consider such a large group of people stupid or charlatans based on the unusual nature of some of their religious practices. The majority of Hindus are well-educated and intelligent human beings that choose to align themselves with this particular religion. Even though we may consider some of their beliefs and practices strange, we must accept that both Muslims and Christians also have their

1 The Mandeans are an ethnoreligious group indigenous to the alluvial plain of southern Mesopotamia and are followers of Mandaeism, a Gnostic religion.

own set of practices which would seem alien to other religions, such as a strident belief in miracles and religious truths that cannot be proven.

We must note here that those who witnessed the emergence of religion, in ancient times, are the only ones that were able to choose their religion at will and reject others. Their successors, on the other hand, rarely get to choose their own religion, but tend to inherit it from their family or tribe. Had they been born into other religions, they would have believed in them with equal zeal. Had the Christian been born Buddhist, they would have believed that Buddha was the only truth in the world. Had the Muslim been born Hindu, they would have considered Hinduism the true religion. We have to admit that, to a certain extent, religiosity is an emotional belief in the first place and that we very rarely use our minds to acquire religious beliefs. The religion of any person is usually determined by their parents. We inherit religion and then invest in it emotionally, using all the intelligence granted to us by God to prove that our religious beliefs are founded. Religion is an absolute and exclusivist belief; each person believes that their religion is the only true religion and that all the other religions are unworthy imitations.

Islam considers both Christianity and Judaism altered religions. Christianity, in turn, doesn't consider Mohammad a Prophet and Judaism does not acknowledge Christianity or Islam. Religious people are always ready to passionately defend their own beliefs and refuse to listen to criticisms, regardless of how open-minded they are in other aspects of their life. This defense of religion can often lead to violence if the believer is pushed to the limits of their tolerance. That's why religious strife, more than any other factor throughout history, has been the root cause of brutal wars and horrible massacres, in which millions of people have been killed. The killing of others in defense of religion is much easier than killing them in defense of a nation or a person's honour. If you consider your religion to be the only true and pure religion, it's difficult to acknowledge the rights of people belonging to other religions. You think of them as sub-humans, living in darkness and sin. You consider the poor treatment of these heathens as part of your religious duty.

All religions in their essence call for freedom, justice, truth and goodness. Religion presents an interpretation of the evolution of the universe and a clear conception of what happens after death. It also accords our actions to a strict system of reward and punishment which encourages us to carry out good deeds and to avoid wrong-doing. Religion may be indispensable for humanity but mixing religion with politics always leads to catastrophe. Whoever practices politics from a religious perspective will inevitably turn into a fanatic who hates and despises whoever disagrees with them. They use religion as an excuse to justify their political policies which may well be right or wrong.

What happened in Egypt while the Brotherhood was in power can be seen as evidence of this. The followers of political Islam mixed the acts of their sheikhs with the sacred commands of religion; we see them defending the deposed Mohamed Morsi as if they were defending their own religious beliefs and so they deceive, argue and deny facts. Many of the followers of the Brotherhood go as far as to endow Morsi with a holy nature and assert that he's supported by God and that overthrowing him is a sin against God and His prophet. In reality, Mohamed Morsi was the puppet of the corrupt Khairat el-Shater, and was responsible for the unlawful detention of 4,000 Egyptian citizens and the killing of 143 martyrs. While in power, this supposedly religious man issued a constitutional decree in which he suspended the democratic system, and turned himself into a dictator whose orders were above the law and the constitution. All these crimes would be enough to topple any president and to put him on trial, but the followers of the Brotherhood practice politics through their religious belief, which warps their perception of reality. They consider the revolution that overthrew Morsi a conspiracy against Islam. They seek to avenge this betrayal by killing and tortuting innocent people who opposed Morsi's rule. They consider their opponents immoral non-believers or Zionist agents, which makes persecuting them sacred jihad for the sake of God.

Here we have to learn a lesson: the millions of Egyptians who created the great revolutionary wave on 30 June were not just calling for Morsi to be ousted. Their message was definite and clear: Egypt can no longer accept parties of political Islam. After 30 June, the revolutionaries assumed that all political parties based on religion would be dissolved and banned, as was written in all Egyptian constitutions since 1923. Yet, we were surprised to find that the Salafi Al-Nour Party, one of the most backward and fanatical religious parties, was invited to play a role in the writing of the constitution. We were astonished to hear that the people in power were talking about reconciliation with the Brotherhood as if what had happened in Egypt was not a public revolution against the rule of a fascist terrorist group, but just a quarrel between two friends. After seeing the problems associated with ruling in the name of religion, we must separate religion from the state in the new constitution. Otherwise, Egypt will fall anew into the grip of religious fascism.

What do we actually want for Egypt? Do we want it to be a modern democratic state, or do we want it to be ruled by a fascist religious regime similar to the ones ruling in Afghanistan, Somalia or the Sudan? Separating religion from the state is by no means the same as fighting religion or eradicating the religious nature of the people and society. The civil state respects all religions and protects the rights of the people, but it doesn't position itself with one religious group and doesn't claim to rule in the name of God. Religious parties have no place in a democratic system, but this doesn't mean that the system excludes certain groups or treats them unfairly. If a Muslim Brother or Salafist wants to work in politics, they must establish a civil political party that lacks a religious agenda. If they are elected, they have to carry out their policies on the understanding that they are merely human efforts that can be right or wrong, rather than acting under religious commands that they impose on us in the name of God, so that they can label whoever objects to them as infidels. If they want to preach for religion, they have the right to found religious societies that have nothing to do with politics. This separation between religion and politics should be extended to worshipping places; mosques and churches should not, under any circumstances, be used for political purposes. The total separation between the state and religion will be proof that we have learned from our mistakes, and that we have learned the lesson well. It is a first step that is indispensable in the building of the modern democratic state which the revolution sought to establish, and for which thousands of Egyptians offered their blood and their lives. The revolution will continue, God willing, until all its goals have been achieved.

Democracy is the answer.

Our Justice, May God Protect It

2 December 2013

This is the story of Rasheed Rafie, a 37-year-old Moroccan man living in France. Rafie was recently accused of being associated with a terrorist organisation by the French authorities, and a call was made for his immediate deportation. Rafie appealed to the French courts against this verdict, but all his appeals were rejected. In a last ditch attempt to remain in France, Rafie presented an appeal to the European Court of Human Rights, which intervened to prevent his deportation to Morocco. The French government appealed against the decision, but it was overturned on 5 November 2012 by the European court. The French government is now prohibited from handing Rafie over to Morocco because he would be in danger of being tortured if he was sent back to his country. The European court based its verdict on the reports commissioned by the United Nations and Amnesty International which explore the use of torture in Moroccan prisons.

This is just one example of recent verdicts issued by the European Court of Human Rights in recent years. They have rejected calls for Arab citizens, accused of committing terrorist acts, to be sent back to their countries on the grounds that they would be subjected to torture or injustice. Dear reader, I can imagine your astonishment in reading that a European judge would protect a terrorist from torture. You might be wondering: doesn't the judge know that this criminal terrorist would not show the same mercy to others? Why isn't he handed over to his country to be tortured as a punishment for his terrorism?

The verdict of the European Court of Human Rights teaches us two important lessons. Firstly, the law must protect the rights of any person regardless of their deeds. Even those who have broken the law are deserving of a fair trial. The second lesson is that the law should be applied to all, regardless of their nationalities; the European Court protected the Moroccan man in the same way it would protect a European citizen.

This noble concept of the law exists only in democratic countries. In the Arab world, we consider committing a crime justification for depriving someone of their human rights. For example, look at what people do when they find a pick-pocket on a bus: they often beat them and torture them until the pick-pocket begs to be handed over to the police. I'm sure no one will forget what happened in Abou El Nomros a few months ago, when residents lynched and killed four Shi'a citizens and dragged them along the ground amidst the jeers of men and women alike.[1] The European judges who protect terrorists from torture don't sympathise with terrorism but know that it is their duty to protect a person's rights and dignity, even if they are a terrorist, until they are brought to a fair trial and punished within the confines of the law. Fair trials are the difference between a tribe and a state, between savagery and civilisation. In 1906 when the British occupation unfairly sentenced four Egyptian peasants to death in the famous Denshawai incident, the great writer George Bernard Shaw wrote:

> If [England's] empire means ruling the world as Denshawai has been ruled in 1906 then there can be no more sacred and urgent political duty on earth than the disruption, defeat, and suppression of the Empire.

If we are a civilised people, then we should defend the rights of all people without exception. I'm not suggesting that the West is a paragon of virtue and justice; we know that there are many instances of corruption and wrongdoing in the West but there is also a law that is applied to all citizens equally. When the American army was involved in crimes against humanity in Guantanamo Bay detention camp and the Abu Ghraib prison, it was Western journalists that exposed these crimes as they believed in equality and human values above all else. Nobody accused the journalists of being traitors or agents. Nobody brought them to trial for tarnishing the reputation of the American armed forces. On the contrary, they enjoyed people's respect for defending human values pertaining to all individuals without discrimination. The symbol of justice has always been the famous Greek statue of a blindfolded woman holding a sword

1 Residents in the Egyptian village of Abou El Nomros lynched four Shi'a citizens on June 23 and injured many others in an assault that extended over several hours. The attacks illustrated the potentially tragic consequences of Islamist endorsement of sectarian policies.

in one hand and a scale in the other, meaning that justice should be blind; the law should not discriminate. This noble and refined perception of justice has been absent from Egypt for decades. During the past few weeks, hundreds of Syrian refugees and their children have been wrongfully detained in the police stations of Alexandria, where they have been abused and harassed on a daily basis. Certain journalists even publicly accused the Syrian refugees of supporting the Brotherhood, and the Egyptian authorities have continued to violate their human rights in order to persuade them to go back to their country. Notice the sad difference: European judges protect an Arab terrorist from torture while Egyptian security forces savagely abuse peaceful, helpless refugees who have fled from persecution and death at the hands of Bashar al-Assad.[1]

Justice in democratic countries is blind; it doesn't discriminate between people, whereas justice in Egypt categorises people according to several considerations. Social class, power, religion and wealth are all elements that may determine your fate if you are put on trial in Egypt. The compromised judicial system in Egypt was one of the driving forces behind the Egyptian revolution. But alas, even though Mubarak was toppled, many instances of injustice were repoted under both the military council and the Muslim Brotherhood. The biased execution of law is still a reality in Egypt; the new authority is using the same methods and the same tools to persecute and suppress its critics. In democratic states, the authorities strive to uphold justice, while in dictatorial regimes justice is selective and the law is used as a tool of persecuting and disciplining the opposition.

During the rule of the former military council, I criticised its policies severely and called for the immediate trial of those who were responsible for the killing of hundreds of Egyptians – from the Mohamed Mahmoud massacre, to those in Maspero Square, Port Said and Abbasiya, amongst others. I was shocked when, as a consequence, I was put on trial in a military court and charged with insulting the armed forces, even though I was only criticising the political performance of the military council and had always been vocal about my support of the Egyptian armed forces as an institution. I sent my attorney to the military court and there the officer told him: "We are aware of your client's case, and we will get round to it as and when we feel like it."

The message here is that the law in Egypt is not used to achieve real justice; it is used as a tool to oppress opponents and discipline them in order to silence them. Legal discrimination is prevalent in Egypt and is used by the state to maintain power. Every day we see sorrowful instances of injustice: the deposed president Morsi is presented to court with the charge of killing demonstrators in front of the Ittihadiya presidential palace in Heliopolis. This trial is welcomed, of course, but Morsi is also responsible for killing 52 citizens in Port Said. Yet, he

1 Bashar al-Assad is the president of Syria, general secretary of the Ba'ath Party and regional secretary of the party's branch in Syria.

wasn't put to trial for this crime because his accomplice was Mohamed Ibrahim,[1] the present minister of interior. The officers who killed countless demonstrators during the revolution all pleaded innocent and many managed to avoid trial and sentencing. I recall one case in which an officer, who shot and blinded tens of demonstrators, was sentenced to just three years in prison. Meanwhile, the daughters of the Brothers who demonstrated by holding balloons at the Corniche of Alexandria were sentenced to 11 years of prison each.[2]

Egyptians have struggled for a long time for the right to demonstrate. But the illegitimate interim government issued a law that prohibits demonstrations unless they are approved by the authorities. The interim government does not represent the will of the people and it does not have the right to change the law as it is not an elected body. Some young revolutionaries organised a peaceful demonstration in front of the Shura Council in objection to this legislation, and as a result, they were beaten and dragged along the ground by officers. The female demonstrators were sexually harassed and later released on a desert road in the middle of the night.[3] Ahmad Maher and Alaa Abd el-Fattah were amongst those arrested for inciting demonstrators to protest without a license. At the same time, demonstrations supporting General el-Sisi were taking place across Egypt without permission, but the authorities made no attempt to punish the organisers. When a young man from the Brotherhood attacked a female supporter on 30 June, the aggressor was brought immediately to court and General el-Sisi made a point of meeting with the woman to offer his apologies and comfort her. On the other hand, not a single officer was punished for attacking the daughters of Egypt who were beaten, dragged along the ground and sexually harassed in front of the Shura Council. An officer even hit the wife of Alaa Abd el-Fattah while arresting him, knowing that he wouldn't be punished because Alaa and his wife do not support General el-Sisi. The state actively encourages people to practice cruelty, injustice and terrorism so that they can silence and punish those that call for a fairer judicial system. If you refuse to sing the praises of the present power, you are immediately accused of being a fifth columnist or part of a sleeper cell that belongs to the Brotherhood.

Egyptians took to the streets on 30 June to get rid of the rule of the Brotherhood. All sections of society participated in that revolutionary wave, but we have since discovered that, although the demonstrators had similar goals, they had different intentions. The revolutionaries wanted to remove the

1 Mohamed Ibrahim was one of the ministers who kept his cabinet place after July 2013; he was re-appointed to Hazem el-Beblawi's interim cabinet, formed later in the same month.

2 An Alexandria court sentenced 21 women to 11 years in prison for blocking the Corniche Road while participating in a demonstration to support ousted President Mohamed Morsi. The defendants were charged with disrupting traffic and vandalising public property during their protest.

3 Nearly two dozen Islamist women and girls, some as young as 15, were handed heavy prison sentences for demonstrating in a court ruling that came a day after police beat and terrorised prominent female activists in a crackdown on secular demonstrators under a tough new anti-protest law.

Brothers from power in order to achieve the aims of the revolution, whereas people belonging to the old regime wanted to get rid of both the Muslim Brothers and the revolutionaries. It is true that Egypt is defending itself against terrorist groups that commit the basest of crimes every day. It is true that it's our duty to support the Egyptian state until it achieves victory over terrorism. But it is also true that this fight against terror should not be a pretext to oppress people, to apply the law selectively or to revive an oppressive state. The new state will never be established until justice prevails.

Democracy is the answer.

What Disturbed Rocca?

9 December 2013

When Rocca first came to the zoo in Giza she was greeted by the eldest giraffe who had been expecting her for some time. "Welcome, dear Rocca. How wonderful it is to look upon you. I was once as beautiful and graceful as you, but I have grown old and tired, and each moment brings death a little nearer."

Rocca rubbed her long neck against the elder giraffe to show her gratitude.

"Inasmuch as your presence pleases me," continued the elder giraffe, "I must be frank with you about life in the zoo. We have many problems and crosses to bear. Some of the visitors are kind and thoughtful people, but there are also those that throw pebbles and stones at us out of malice. The director of the zoo and his assistants are careless and cruel degenerates that neglect us and force us to live in squalor. They often forget to feed us or steal the money set aside for our food. Had we not discovered that we could eat the leaves that fell nearby, we would have starved to death."

Rocca was shocked to hear about life in the zoo, and looked at the elder giraffe with worry in her eyes. The elder giraffe shook her head and pushed out her long tongue and caressed Rocca's face with it, saying: "What's really strange is that, in spite of our great suffering, we all prefer this zoo to any other place. I think there's something in Egypt that drives our attachment to it."

The elder giraffe introduced Rocca to the other giraffes; ten females and ten males. Rocca exchanged greetings and platitudes with them all and felt happy to be amongst them.

Day by day, Rocca got more and more accustomed to her new life in the zoo. She would spend the whole day playing, until the guard would lead her to the front of the cage so that the visitors could look at her. With the passing of time, Rocca began being able to recognise the good visitors from the bad, and was able to avoid stones and pebbles thrown at her. Rocca would sleep for three hours each night and would wake up active and cheerful. She was very beautiful; her graceful body had perfect orange and dark brown spots all over, and her eyes were a dazzling green. Like all female giraffes, she knew that she would be forced to marry one of the male giraffes so that they could breed. But Rocca had much more important things on her mind.

During the revolution, Rocca would watch the violent conflicts between the demonstrators and the police from behind the bars of the fence surrounding the zoo. She sympathised with the demonstrators who fell; their blood staining the ground outside the zoo. She pushed her nose hard against the bars, imagining herself breaking through to protect the youth against the violations of the police. Rocca wasn't scared of the tear gas or the bullets that surrounded her. She was completely preoccupied with the revolution and started eavesdropping on the small black and white television that the guard kept in his office. Rocca slowly started to piece together what was happening outside the walls of the zoo. She knew that a corrupt and unjust ruler had been in power for many years and that he wanted his son to inherit power. Egyptians thus revolted against him and managed to overthrow him. Rocca knew that a group of officers took over after Mubarak, and that there was now a president who belonged to a group called the Muslim Brotherhood. What surprised Rocca was that the demonstrators were consistently attacked throughout this time, as if the corrupt rulers were all united by their hatred for the young revolutionaries. On 30 June, Rocca watched the mass demonstrations, which were unlike any she had seen before. She knew from television that the people gathered in the street managed to overthrew the Brotherhood and this filled her with a great joy.

Rocca's enthusiasm for the revolution was often ridiculed by the other giraffes, especially the female ones. Whenever the demonstrations broke out the guard would push the giraffes to the other side of the zoo so that they were safe from bullets and tear gas. Rocca was the only giraffe that disobeyed the guard, sticking firmly to her place near the fence to watch what was happening. The male giraffes were attracted to Rocca and all vied for her attention, much to the envy of the female giraffes. One day, another demonstration broke out in front of the zoo, and the guard managed to push Rocca to the other side of the zoo along with the other giraffes. The males fought and rubbed their necks against each other competing for the females. Three males competed for Rocca and fought hard till one of them was eventually victorious. He was a graceful and strong male that approached Rocca to claim his prize. However, when the male giraffe tried to mate with Rocca, she jumped away and kicked him as hard as she could. The male giraffe reluctantly withdrew, breathing heavily with shame and anger. The giraffes talked about this incident at length. One of the female giraffes said: "Did you see what happened with Rocca? The male giraffes all fight for her yet she denies the winner her body." Another female giraffe jumped and said passionately: "I envy her. He was a strong and handsome giraffe. If I were in her place, I wouldn't waste that opportunity."

The female giraffes did not understand Rocca and thought her unusual. The male giraffes were kinder but they thought that her head was full of strange ideas that would eventually undo her.

The elder giraffe was saddened by Rocca's enthusiasm for the revolution. "Rocca, honestly, I don't understand you. Your head is filled with revolution and you think little of anything else. A beautiful giraffe like you should be thinking of her future and of finding a mate. Don't you see that males follow you wherever you go? If I were you, I would choose a male and settle down." The elder giraffe's words fell on deaf ears. Rocca continued to follow the revolution and became more and more preoccupied with events outside of the zoo. She estranged herself from the group and expressed no interest in finding a mate. She thought only of the demonstrators whom she saw being killed and tortured out on the streets. Last week, Rocca looked sad and silent, the elder giraffe asked: "Dear Rocca, what's wrong?"

Rocca hit the floor with her feet, lowered her head and said softly: "I'm saddened by what is happening outside these gates. The youth who made the revolution and sacrificed everything for their country are now oppressed by the present authorities; they're beaten up, dragged along the ground and thrown in prisons."

The elder giraffe asked her: "Do those youth belong to the Brotherhood?"

Rocca replied: "Had they been from the Brotherhood, I wouldn't have sympathised with them. Have you forgotten what they did to those poor demonstrators? They killed and tortured them in front of the zoo. The young revolutionaries don't belong to the Brotherhood; they are loyal only to their country and don't want anything for themselves. They have been killed, blinded and imprisoned by the authorities because they dared to demand change.

"I don't understand why the authorities continue to attack them when the real enemy is the Brotherhood," said the elder giraffe, rubbing her neck tenderly against Rocca.

"Is it the fate of Egyptians to live forever between the Mubarak regime and the corrupt rule of the Brotherhood? Is it their fate to always have to choose between two sorts of scoundrels?"

The elder giraffe closed her eyes a little to avoid the strong light of the sun and said: "You're right, but don't forget about the people. It was not the remnants of the Mubarak regime that toppled the Brotherhood. Moreover, the Brothers continue to tear the country apart and kill people every day, and it is the authorities that fight against them. If we are to attack the authorities, then surely this would aid the Muslim Brotherhood, even if unintentionally."

Rocca said fervently: "I'm against the Brotherhood but I'm also against the old regime and those that oppress the youth of the revolution. The people should have the right to demand change and declare what they believe in regardless of the consequences."

Suddenly, a big row occurred just outside the gates of the zoo. Rocca rushed to the fence and saw a group of demonstrators setting fire to a police car. When the driver of the vehicle jumped out, the demonstrators attacked him and kicked him to the ground. The demonstrators blocked the fire engine from tending the flames and raised their hands to form the Rabia sign. The elder giraffe turned to Rocca and said: "Did you see what the Brothers just did? Isn't it a duty to support the government against those villains?"

Rocca thought a little and then said: "Of course it's a duty but I don't understand why the authorities follow the revolutionary youth. Aren't they the ones who created the change and ousted the Brotherhood?"

Mother Giraffe came closer and rubbed her neck against Rocca's body and said gently: "Calm down my dear, Rocca. Go have your lunch and try to think of other things."

Rocca headed towards the big tree at the end of the zoo as was her habit. She stretched her neck and ate some leaves, but could not shake the sadness which hung heavy around her neck. She was torn between her sadness over the youth of the revolution and her feeling towards the Muslim Brothers, who want to set the whole country on fire. Rocca was overcome with sadness and was paying little attention to the things around her. When she stretched her neck to reach more leaves, she became trapped in between two bars. Rocca panicked and thrashed her neck from side to side to try and free herself, but it was no luck. She could not break free from the bars and choked and died, alone by the big tree in Giza zoo.

Democracy is the answer.

Should We Approve the Constitution?

16 December 2013

Imagine that you have just moved house. You quickly discover that your neighbour, living in the apartment opposite, is an unbearable person. He consistently refuses to pay the electricity bills for the elevator and the outside lighting, and throws his rubbish bags in front of your apartment to avoid paying the rubbish collection fees. His negligence has caused water to leak from his bathroom into the walls of your apartment, but he refused to have the pipes inside his flat repaired even when you offered to pay the bill. In sum, this neighbour is continually impinging on your rights. So, what do you do? Of course, you try to solve the problem amicably, but this infuriating neighbour continues to attack you, so you have no choice but to resort to legal action. You make a formal statement at the police station, noting all the infractions your neighbour has committed. This statement will lead to a case brought before the courts.

Let's imagine that a fire breaks out on the floor on which you and your neighbour live. The flames grow higher and higher, and threaten the whole building. Of course, you rush to put out the fire and are astounded when you see your neighbour coming out to help you extinguish the blaze. What do you do now? You have two ways to behave: either, you say to yourself: "This neighbour is my enemy and has violated my rights; I will not cooperate with him and will not join hands with him, even to put out the fire that threatens us all," or, you think in another way, and say to yourself: "The danger of the fire is much bigger than my problems with my neighbour. I must put my feelings aside and work with him, otherwise the whole building will be detroyed; along with all the things we were arguing about in the first place."

The first way of thinking – refusing to cooperate with your neighbour to put out the fire – is, in my opinion, very short-sighted; it will no doubt end in disaster. As for the second option, which treats the feud with the neighbour as a secondary harm – with the fire that threatens the whole building as the primary harm – it is the more mature and objective path because it adopts a suitable position according to real circumstances.

But what does this story have to do with what is happening in Egypt? On 30 June, Egyptian people of all denominations rose up against the rule of the Brotherhood. The army sided with the people and implemented their will. They dismissed Mohamed Morsi and drew up a road map for the transition to democracy. To this end, the Committee of 50 drafted a constitution and put it to a general referendum. I have read a copy of this constitution and found it to be really one of the best constitutions I have seen in Egypt in the areas of citizenship, anti-discrimination, civil liberties and the rights of minorities, women, children and the handicapped. It also curtails the powers of the president and makes their decisions subject to scrutiny by the House of Representatives, which represents the will of the people.

Truly, this constitution marks the beginning of a democratic system for Egypt, if it wasn't for two flawed articles. The first one obliges the president to seek the consent of the leadership of the army before appointing a minister of defence. This article is not in keeping with a democratic system, the basis of which is that a president who is elected by the people has the power to appoint the minister of defence and dismiss them without the consent of another party. Despite its flaws, this article is acceptable, principally because it is only temporary and will be annulled automatically after eight years. Also, the makers of the constitution had taken into consideration the exceptional circumstances Egypt is going through and wanted to maintain the stability of the Egyptian army, the only Arab army that has come out unharmed from the vicissitudes of the Arab revolutions.

However, the other article is not at all consistent with a democratic system, and cannot be accepted under any circumstances. This is the article that allows civilians to be tried before military courts in specific circumstances outlined by the constitution. Democratic systems do not recognise military trials of civilians in any shape or form because the military courts are not independent, since the judges who preside over them are officers with military ranks, who must follow the orders meted out by their superiors. Furthermore, under military law, the Supreme Commander of the Armed Forces has the right to issue a pardon to any accused person or demand a retrial. This puts the fate of a civilian defendant in the hands of the chief of the army, irrespective of whether they are innocent or guilty.

According to standards of international justice, military courts lack the legal safeguards that would guarantee a fair trial for civilian defendants. In November 1954, for the first time in Egyptian history, leader Gamal Abdel Nasser had civilian defendants brought before a military court following the famous attempt to assassinate him in Al-Manshiyya, Alexandria. Since that time, military courts ceased to be a means to deliver justice to civilians and were instead largely a tool to repress anyone whom the authorities sought to take revenge on, or to silence voices that opposed their policies.

Specifying particular circumstances for bringing civilians before military courts will not help to rein in these courts, because the ambiguous charges could be applied to anyone. For example, any article published that the military establishment does not like could be interpreted as tarnishing the reputation of the armed forces and its writer could be brought before a military court. In our unpleasant experience of the military judiciary during the period of the military council's rule, thousands of civilians were tried in military courts lacking the most basic principles of justice. Members of the No to Military Trials campaign[1] have documented the testimonies of hundreds of peaceful demonstrators who were arrested by the military police and dragged to the military judiciary on trumped-up charges. During

1 The campaign to end the military trials of civilians is made up of several active members of the ongoing Egyptian revolution. They believe that ending the military trials of civilians is a key requirement on the road to freedom and democracy.

these trials, Molotov cocktails were presented as evidence to prove that the demonstrators had attacked military installations and personnel. They were given long prison sentences after brief trials lasting no more than a few days, during which they were unable to defend themselves in a just and legal way.

Some of you may be asking: what are we to do about the terrorist groups who attack army installations? There is only one answer: if we are to live in a true country of law, anyone who has committed a crime – no matter how brutal – must have a fair trial and the conditions for this fair trial are not provided by the military judiciary. The war on terror must not be a reason to deprive the accused of being tried by a regular, civilian judge who, after all, is able to hand down the harshest of punishments, even death by hanging. Sentencing, however, should only take place after a fair trial, one in which there are plenty of safeguards to ensure that the sentence is just. We cannot bring civilians to military courts and then ask the world to believe us when we claim that Egypt is a democratic country. Military trials for civilians will continue to serve as a thick baton in the hands of the authorities, which they bring down on the heads of whomever they want, whenever they want.

Egyptians' fears of a return to a Mubarak-era state are understandable and legitimate. The present government is transitional and unelected by the people. Therefore, it has no right to issue laws. Nevertheless, it issued an anti-protest law that restricts civil liberties and gives officers in the Ministry of the Interior the authority to prohibit demonstrations. This goes against the right to protest law which can be found in democratic countries, where demonstrations cannot be banned except by court order. In addition to this, the Ministry of the Interior has returned to its repressive practices. We saw how officers pounced on the peaceful demonstrators in front of the Shura Council, beat them and dragged them to the ground before putting them on trial. Meanwhile, not one of the police officers who was caught killing demonstrators during the revolution has been punished.

The remnants of the Mubarak regime have reappeared: those who worked in the service of Gamal Mubarak and sought to help him to inherit the rule of Egypt from his father have come back. Those business men who made their riches by virtue of their closeness to Mubarak, who own the satellite television channels and the newspapers that play a vital role in directing public opinion against the revolution, have returned. These are the media outlets which launched a huge campaign to defame everyone who took part in the January 25 Revolution, an event they are keen to assert was a Brotherhood conspiracy, despite the fact that the Brotherhood – as history has proven – did not participate in the revolution and initially condemned it before joining the cause once certain of its success. As we can see, there are legitimate fears concerning a return to power of the Mubarak regime and the repression of its opponents by means of military trials. But are these fears sufficient to reject the constitution or boycott the referendum?

I cannot find a better answer to this question than the story I gave at the beginning of this article. As the neighbour accepted working together with his enemy because the danger of the fire was larger than his feud, we must agree to this constitution because to refuse it would have punishments far more severe than those that a military court could give to civilians. The referendum on the new constitution, to take place in a few days, is in essence a referendum on the deposition of Morsi and the end of Brotherhood rule. The day of the referendum will be the first opportunity for Egyptians to prove that what happened on 30 June was a revolutionary wave that brought an end to the rule of the fascist Brotherhood and not a military coup against democracy, as the Brotherhood and their followers keep claiming. The Brotherhood will continue to scream and shout that the recent action was a coup against an elected president, even though it was this same president who launched a coup against democracy when he issued the constitutional declaration by which he suspended the law and placed his decisions above the rulings of the judiciary.

There can be no democracy when a parliament does not have the right to hold a vote of no confidence against the elected president, but Egypt does not have a parliament, because the Supreme Constitutional Court decided to dissolve it. In the absence of a parliament, it is the people's right to assume the powers of parliament themselves. To this end, the Tamarod campaign – which gathered millions of signatures for Morsi's dismissal – undertook what can be called a completely democratic procedure, after which millions of people came out to demand that Morsi stand down and the army stepped in to implement the will of the people.

Agreeing to this constitution means that the people approve of Morsi's dismissal and the fall of the Brotherhood. Even if we oppose a few articles of the constitution, we must agree to it with a large majority in order to complete the path of the revolution, which began on 25 January and which corrected its course on 30 June. If the constitution is rejected, or if there is a low turnout in the referendum, this will cast backwards and make what happened on 30 June appear like a coup d'état, giving the Brotherhood a legitimacy that they do not deserve.

Our duty is to agree to and vote for the constitution in order to push our country forward onto our next struggle: building elected institutions to achieve fairness and freedom, preventing the old regime from returning and outlawing the trial of civilians in military courts. Our duty today is to forget our differences and gather together to support this constitution by a large majority. Our duty is to prove to the whole world that the Egyptian people are the ones who decided to end the rule of the Brotherhood and who will now get on with forming their democratic nation.

Democracy is the answer.

PN

Will you Detain All of Egypt?

23 December 2013

I knew about the demonstration planned for 25 January 2011 weeks before it was due to take place, but I wasn't very optimistic about its success. I knew from previous experiences that such events, no matter how widely publicised on Facebook and Twitter, don't reach much of the population. They always end up drawing only a few demonstrators that the authorities contain with a huge number of riot police, rendering the demonstration totally ineffective. On 25 January 2011, I woke up early and started work on my novel, *The Automobile Club*. I had planned to drop in on the demonstration in the evening, but at about four o'clock in the afternoon a friend called me and said that the demonstrations were massive. I rushed to Tahrir Square only to be struck by the awe inspiring scene: tens of thousands of Egyptians had crowded into the square. Thrilled by the success of the demonstration they started chanting and discussing the demands for change. In Egypt's governorates, the police had been killing demonstrators since the early morning, but in Tahrir Square the police seemed to be taken aback by the great numbers of demonstrators; they waited on the margins for instructions from their superiors about what action to take. It was not until a huge group of demonstrators from Imbaba neighbourhood arrived and entered the square from the side of the Ministry of Foreign Affairs that the riot police began attacking them with clubs. The demonstrators, however, did not withdraw; on the contrary, they attacked the riot police and, for the first time in my life, I saw security forces running away from demonstrators. Cheers of joy were raised in support of the new arrivals coming from Imababa and the square was filled to capacity with hundreds of thousands of people.

I started roaming the square talking to demonstrators. There was a wonderful mix of people: students, middle-class professionals, labourers, peasants, as well as veiled and unveiled women of all classes. A little after midnight we noticed strange movements amongst the soldiers and police officers and, suddenly, the gates of hell opened: soldiers shot a lethal barrage of tear gas. Hundreds of canisters were thrown at us from three directions and the square disappeared in a cloud of suffocating gas. Dozens of people passed out – even some members of the security forces. Plain-clothed police were waiting on side streets to arrest demonstrators who fled from the gas. I ran from the square with a group of demonstrators and, because I was familiar with downtown Cairo, I took a shortcut that led to Maa'rouf Street and we kept running till we reached Talaat Harb Street. We stopped to catch our breath now that we had escaped – albeit temporarily – the gas and arrest. An old street-sweeper man passed by us with a broom in his hand and he shouted loudly at us: "Don't toy with Mubarak. Never draw out a serpent and then turn your back on it – either you kill it or it will kill you!"

His voice was unsteady but enthusiastic, and his statement sounded almost too eloquent for his simple appearance. I directed my speech to the young people surrounding me, saying: "My friends, this has been a historic demonstration. Let's leave now and return in the morning."

They raised their voices in objection to my suggestion, so I said: "Do you really think we will overthrow Mubarak with one demonstration? It's going to take time and perseverance."

A slim, young man with a dark complexion came closer to me and said: "Listen, I'm from Ismaïlia. I have a university degree. I'm 30, but my father still supports me; I have no job. I can't afford to marry or travel. I came here and I'm not going back to Ismaïlia until Mubarak is gone. Let him kill me if he wants. What kind of life do I have anyway? I may as well be dead."

At this point his voice cracked and he started weeping. Silence prevailed and it seemed that the decision was already made. These youth went back to Tahrir Sqaure and I with them.

That's how the greatest experience of my life began. For 18 days I lived in Tahrir Square, except for a few hours when I went to my home in the mornings to reassure my family that I was still alive. Tahrir Square was experiencing a miracle. Half a million men and women were at the sit-in during the day, and the numbers increased in the evening to reach a million or two million demonstrators. There were no incidents of theft or sexual harassment in the square, not a single one. There was a strange intimacy amongst the diverse types of people who wouldn't necessarily have gotten along under normal circumstances. I saw upper-class girls eating and having friendly chats with simple, female peasants. I saw young Copts protecting Muslims as they performed their prayers. One day a young man with a beard took the floor to say: "I want to apologise to all of the unveiled women and those who don't wear headscarves. I was raised to hate and despise them. But in Tahrir Square I have learned that they are often more noble and courageous than many bearded, Muslim men."

I still remember Abdel-Hakkam, the square's very own minister of information. He was man in his forties who worked for a bank. He bought a microphone and loudspeakers and, spending nights without sleep, would invite people to talk to the revolutionaries. The mothers of those who were killed sat beside the platform, each holding the picture of their martyred children close to their chests. Every night I gave a speech, and I will never forget the scene of thousands of demonstrators thundering: "Down with Mubarak!"

On 28 January, the Mubarak regime deployed snipers on the roofs of the Ministry of the Interior and all other buildings close to the square. In daylight the snipers put on white handkerchiefs over their heads to ward off the sun's rays. In the evenings, the laser sights of their guns would circle the square and, when it stopped moving, a bullet would hit one of the demonstrators, blowing their head clean off. The astonishing thing is that, even though the bullets were raining down, tthe demonstrators did not withdraw or run away; on the contrary, whenever a martyr fell they would carry them on their shoulders and continue the demonstration.

I once read a psychology paper which claimed that when a person is caught up in a state of revolution, they will lose their feelings of individuality and become a member of a group whose only aim is for the revolution to prevail. All of the negative characteristics of the Egyptian personality disappeared in Tahrir Square, a space opened up for the performance of dazzling and noble acts. I remember, for instance, that even though the demonstrators were being repressed and killed by Mubarak's security forces, nevertheless, they totally rejected the idea of chanting any slogans that would insult the reputation of Suzanne Mubarak, because insulting women did not become the revolution's high-mindedness, as I was told by one of the revolutionaries.

I remember feeling exhausted one morning. It was around four o'clock. I smoked a cigarette and threw the empty packet on the ground. A woman wearing a headscarf, who was about seventy years old, approached me and said in a firm but friendly manner: "Please pick up the packet you threw on the floor and put it in the bin over there." I felt ashamed and did as she had asked. When I came back she smiled and said: "If we are to build the new Egypt that will be fair and respected, then it has also to be clean."

During the days of the revolution, I ate dozens of times with the revolutionaries, yet I didn't know who brought the food. A person would come with lots of food, put it in the middle of the square and leave. I'll never forget the sight of a certain old man whose clothes were torn and who wore slippers in the cold of January. Despite his poverty, he used to bring a great number of broad bean sandwiches, and then leave them in the middle of the square for other people. Once a friend of mine, Yehia Hussein, was wandering in the square when a man from Upper Egypt approached him and asked for help with selling his cell phone. The man was a simple salesman who earned his living day-by-day, but he had run out of money during the days of the sit-in. Yehia Hussein pressed the man to accept some money saying that he could think of it as a loan to be paid back when he was able. It was then that Yehia realised that there must have been hundreds or even thousands of people at the sit-in who had lost their sources of income just so that they could take part. Hussein talked to Dr Abdel Galil Mostafa, one of the fathers of the revolution, about his worry. Mostafa agreed to give Hussein 17,000 Egyptian pounds, from his own money, to spend on the poor who were living in the tents of the sit-in. From evening prayers till dawn, Hussein walked between the tents, looking for somebody to take some of this money, but he eventually came back with the whole sum intact, not having given away a single pound; the poor in the tents simply refused to take any money.

There simply isn't enough space to cite the dozens of incidents that confirm the high-mindedness of those who took part in the revolution. According to Western media, 18 to 20 million Egyptians participated in the revolution; these people are, in my opinion, the most courageous, noble and enlightened amongst all Egyptians. They are what remains of all that is clean in the body of our nation – a nation that had sometimes seemed hopelessly polluted and dead. Unfortunately, the revolution is now fighting an opposition that would see all of its achievements erased from memory. The considerable forces of counter-revolution are now showing their ugly faces and are seeking to efface one of Egypt's most glorious moments from the history books. They are the remnants of the Mubarak regime, as well as swathes of corrupt businessmen, who now fear for their own interests. They are the security officials who have tortured ordinary Egyptians for years. They are those in the media who lied and deceived Egyptians on the instruction of the state security officers who still control them. They are the politicians who worked as servants for Gamal Mubarak and who convinced him that he would inherit Egypt as if the country were his father's personal estate.

All of the above insult our revolution, mock it and falsely claim that it is an American or Muslim Brotherhood conspiracy. This accusation is nonsense, of course; it isn't even worth responding to. In any case, the Muslim Brothers didn't even join the revolution until they were certain that it would be successful, then they betrayed it several times over for the benefit of their own organisation. The revolution also represented a severe blow to US foreign policy; it toppled Mubarak, who was a strategic asset to the Jewish state, as Israeli leaders had themselves asserted on more than one occasion. Slanderous campaigns against the revolution have continued, accompanied by a strong crack-down on revolutionary activists. On 30 June, the people took to the street to get rid of the Brotherhood and, while I realise that it's our duty to support the state in its war against terrorism, the following question has to be asked: what has the war against terror got to do with the oppression of revolutionary activists? The imprisonment of Ahmad Douma, Alaa Abd el-Fattah and their colleagues will not end the revolution; they participated in the revolution but they didn't create it by themselves. The revolution belongs to the millions of high-minded Egyptians who took to the streets and risked their lives for the sake of freedom, justice and dignity. You, who have links with the former regime, if you want to end the revolution, then try imprisoning the millions of Egyptians who created it. Detain the whole of Egypt if you can. Our revolution will continue and it will prevail; the future belongs to us and you belong to a past that will never return.

Democracy is the answer.

AB

Old Realities Impact the Future

30 December 2013

Mustafa the singer was over forty years old, but he still had the appearance of a much younger man. He used to meet with me and my friends in a cafe downtown. He always carried an *oud,*[1] which he never parted with. Whenever somebody asked him about it, he would tell them that he was a civil servant in the Ministry of Supply and Internal Trade, but at the same time, he was also a singer who had been applauded for his talent by the greatest composers of Egypt, which caused other famous singers to envy his talent and plot against him. Mustafa would then recount many incidents to demonstrate that he was a victim of the conspiracies of these singers who were jealous of his artistic genius.

Oddly enough, when we listened to Mustafa's singing, we found his voice to be rather mediocre. It would even break while he sang and he used to lose his breath as a result of being a heavy smoker. Still, one of our friends got excited and used his connections to secure Mustafa the opportunity of a lifetime: he got him the chance to perform on a live radio broadcast. Mustafa was extremely happy; he thanked our friend warmly and kept regaling us with daily reports about how he was getting himself ready for the live performance. On the night of the performance, we sat beside the radio waiting for Mustafa's number. When the concert ended, however, we had still not heard Mustafa sing. We called him the next day but he didn't answer, so we called our friend at the radio station to ask what had happened. Mustafa had called him before the concert to apologise for not participating. We were puzzled by his strange behaviour; Mustafa had been waiting for years for the opportunity to perform before such an audience, yet when he got the chance

1 The oud is a pear-shaped stringed instrument, similar to a lute.

he pulled out. I concluded to myself that Mustafa must fear the audience. He had lived for so long in the comfort and safety of his imaginary world – one in which he believed himself to be a great singer who had been victimised by the plotting of his opponents who envied him – that when the time came for him to prove himself, he became scared of failing. Had he sung badly in front of an audience, his imaginary world would have shattered around him and he would have been forced to face the painful truth: that he was not talented and that his voice was not great. In this case, he would have only himself to blame for his failure.

What happened to Mustafa the singer has happened to many of us. We often refuse to see the truth and invent a fantasy world, which absolves us of responsibilities and creates reassuring, illusory images in our minds in which we are noble victims of others' villainy. A virtual world saves us from facing the truth, which might cause us pain or guilt. The Muslim Brotherhood is causing havoc in Egypt by killing innocent people and burning down places of worship, as well as attacking the police and the army. Do the Muslim Brothers realise how horrendous their crimes are? We saw video footage of the followers of the Brotherhood slaughtering police officers in Kerdasa while chanting the name of God. The Brothers live in a fantasy world in which they think of themselves as good and pious believers, as the heirs of the prophets and as victims of plotting by the enemies of Islam. They believe they lost power because of a military coup that was staged by the old guard of the Mubarak regime in collusion with secularists who are enemies of Islam, and all under the auspices of international Zionism, of course. It's pointless to remind the Brothers of their betrayal of the revolution, of how Mohamed Morsi violated the democratic system when he issued the constitutional declaration, which made his decrees unanswerable to the law. There's no use reminding them of how the United States supported them or of the millions of Egyptians who took to the streets to oust Morsi before the intervention of the army. There's no use discussing anything with the Brothers because they refuse to see the reality of the situation, preferring instead to hold on to the illusions of their virtual world. It's difficult for anyone who has spent years of their life imbibing the beliefs of the Brotherhood to then turn around and admit that they have wasted their time defending ideas that are unfounded and fake, or admit that their sheikhs – whom they obeyed as though they were obeying God – are, in fact, a group of power-hungry criminals. The only choice a member of the Brotherhood has is to hold on to a comforting delusion that absolves them of responsibility and portrays the Muslim Brothers as victimised *mujahideen*, no matter how horrible the crimes they commit are.

But the phenomenon of the virtual world is not exclusive to the Brothers. The remnants of the Mubarak regime are also guilty of living in a dream world. They believe that the revolution that toppled Mubarak was a conspiracy orchestrated by the Muslim Brotherhood and the United States. They keep inventing tall tales to prove that this plot was orchestrated by the CIA against their beloved leader, Mubarak. There's no use asking them to present evidence for their claims so that authorities can investigate them, instead they spout their ludicrous claims on television and people's reputations get tarnished. There's no use reminding them that the Egyptian revolution had been in the air for ten years before it finally happened, and that the 20 million citizens who took part in the revolution cannot all be plotters or foreign agents. The remnants of the Mubarak regime, just like the Muslim Brotherhood, don't want to face reality because it will condemn and harm them. This is why they retreat into their fantasy worlds. The businessmen who made their fortunes by exploiting their relationships with the Mubarak family find it difficult to admit that they're thieves who robbed Egyptians, and some of the state security officers who tortured thousands of innocent people find it difficult to admit that they are just brutal criminals. Only in a virtual world can the corrupt businessman consider himself to be a patriot and the sadistic officer consider himself to be a hero confronting enemy agents. The most dangerous development of recent times is that there is no longer one truth in Egypt, but many; truth has become something relative because of the deliberate obfuscation that obstructs a clear vision. Both the Brothers and the remnants of the Mubarak regime are incapable of seeing the truth, and each camp tries to impose its own deluded version of reality. Do we need to discuss such delusions while the state is fighting a war against the terrorism of the Brotherhood? Right now we have a greater need to see the truth clearly than ever before, no matter how painful or condemning it may be. Can a doctor find a treatment to an illness if the tests are not accurate? Can an economist find a solution to an economic crisis if he or she relies on false statistics? It's the same with we Egyptians; we can't take a step forward unless we acknowledge the following truths:

First: The Mubarak regime was corrupt, incompetent and oppressive, and because of this, the country declined significantly during his rule. Mubarak oppressed thousands of Egyptians and caused the death of many due to negligence and corruption; deaths occurred in public hospitals, aboard faulty ships and trains, and from cancerous foods and fertilisers. In January 2011, Egyptians revolted against Mubarak, and the revolution was a model of civilised values that showed the whole world how an unarmed people can oust an oppressive ruler who has the protection of a huge security apparatus. Unlike what his supporters claim, Mubarak didn't step down to save people's blood. In just 18 days, he was responsible for the deaths of 2,000 citizens, and the disappearance of a further 1,000 who have yet to be found – they are believed to have been killed by Mubarak's police officers and buried in unmarked graves. Furthermore, 18,000 people were injured by the police, many now suffering partial or total disability.

Second: Although the former military council refused to oppress the revolutionaries at the beginning, it later turned against them, and under its rule many horrible massacres took place in which hundreds of Egyptians were killed. The military council is the institution that must bear responsibility for these massacres, which were never investigated and for which none of the perpetrators were punished.

Third: The revolution is not responsible for the Brotherhood coming to power; it's the Mubarak regime that shut down political life, giving the Brotherhood the opportunity to be the only group that was organised; it was their organisation that enabled them to win in non-rigged elections that took place during the Mubarak era, such as elections for trade unions and the first round of the parliamentary elections in 2005. It was natural for the people to grant the Brotherhood their trust, but when the Brotherhood failed the test, and its criminal character was revealed, the people withdrew their support and ousted it within only one year.

Fourth: There's no longer any doubt that the presidential elections that were conducted last year were anything but a silly piece of theatre designed to deceive Egyptians and secure victory for the Brotherhood candidate. No rules to guarantee the validity of the elections were put in place: there was no transparency concerning funding, which would have allowed the general public to know who funded the campaigns of the candidates, a maximum limit on spending in elections campaigns was not imposed, and the results were not made void in many constituencies where violations were confirmed. Even more serious is the fact that the Supreme Electoral Committee (SPEC) didn't investigate the appeals presented by candidates against each other. In the first round, the Hamdeen Sabahi campaign presented several complaints claiming that a great number of police officers voted for Shafik in violation of the law, yet the SPEC ignored these complaints. In the second round, Shafik made a complaint in which he accused Morsi of misconduct but, again, the committee ignored this and declared Morsi the new president. How can we trust an electoral committee which declares a candidate to be the winner before investigating the complaints levelled against him?

Al Watan recently published an interview with Judge Abdul Moaz Ibrahim, a member of the Supreme Electoral Committee, in which he maintained that he alerted Major General Mamdouh Shahin that the elections law was unconstitutional. Shahin, however, replied, saying: "I know, and so does General Tantawi. Get on with your job." This incident confirms Tantawi's control over the committee and proves that the elections were improper. There was a political will working behind the scenes to ensure that the Brotherhood candidate took the presidency. Now, many people are once again nominating candidates for the presidency as if the Egyptian people are simply going to fall for the same trick again. The result of any elections that are conducted under the same circumstances as the previous ones will be a foregone conclusion; the winner will be the one who is backed by those working behind the scenes. In order to avoid this outcome, we need to make sure that conditions for fair elections are put in place before we even begin debating the credentials of the various candidates.

Finally, 30 June was a great revolutionary wave made up of millions of Egyptians who took part in it in order to get rid of the fascist rule of the Brotherhood. Despite the mistakes committed by the transitional government, it's our duty to support it as it undertakes a war against the terrorism of the Brotherhood, the aim of which is to cause the fall of the state. Moreover, the draft constitution written by the Committee of 50 – excluding its provision for allowing civilians to be tried in military courts – is one of the best constitutions Egypt has ever seen. Regardless of our reservations concerning the constitution, we should all understand that our vote is not so much about approving the constitution as it is about showing approval for the ouster of Morsi and the Brotherhood. Whoever participated in the events of 30 June has, in my opinion, a duty to endorse the constitution in order to prove to the world that the will of the people that brought down the Brotherhood, and that the army didn't stage a coup but acted on behalf of the Egyptian people

Democracy is the answer.

Does General el-Sisi Like Poetry?

6 January 2014

Your love is like a small garden growing within me.
Its leaves grow around my sorrow, shading it from the heat of pain.
If my fingers become interlocked with yours,
Roots will grow and keep my garden safe from the rains and the winds.
I feel your love growing inside me like an unborn child,
It touches my soul, making me want to cry out.
But I'm scared. I know that these times are an enemy to my heart.
At night, I will sit with a sleeping child in my arms, thinking of you.
I will think of how spring comes while your heart and mine are not together like two apples
On a happy branch that fills the earth with its scent.

I see a distant winter. I walk with my grandson, we are surprised by rain, and I talk to him about you without reason.
I hear your voice around us, the light movement of a wing.
I see everything passing in front of my eyes, I see a dream, running and hiding like a squirrel amongst the branches,
And I tell him: "Son, they were graceful steps that walked the streets of my heart and disappeared."
I feel your love throwing a dream away, and I rush to win it back between two questions:
How can a dark tomb contain you without me? And how will I enjoy – alone – a beautiful morning like this one?

Were I to attribute this poem to one of the famous Arab poets, nobody would have suspected the deception; it's such a tender poem and the beauty of its imagery reveal a real gift for, and mastery of, poetic language. Yet, the truth is that this poem was written by a young man from Alexandria called Omar Hazek. I was introduced to him some years ago, and admiring his talent, I presented him at one of my literary seminars, after which we became friends. I have found him to be a gentle, cultured young man with a sound moral compass and the courage to do the right thing; this, however, has brought him a lot of problems.

Despite the corruption so prevalent in official cultural institutions, Omar Hazek has managed, by his talent alone, to get the recognition he deserves. Several well-known critics have praised his gifts, to the extent that he has become one of the most famous poets of his generation. And in spite of the difficulty of translating poetry, Hazek, with his beautiful poems, managed to gain international recognition when he was awarded the first prize for poetry at the Love, Justice and Peace in the World festival in Italy. He then issued a volume with the Portuguese poet, Tiago Patrício, and the Italian poet, Nikki Datoma, under the title *Spaces of Freedom*. If Omar Hazek were French or English, his country would take a keen interest in him and state institutions would seek to nurture his gift – in democratic countries an artist is considered a national treasure to be valued and aided. But Omar Hazek is an Egyptian, and in Egypt only hypocrites are given the spotlight, while prestigious positions are distributed amongst followers and lackeys to the exclusion of the competent and the talented.

Omar Hazek took part in the Egyptian Revolution of 2011; he faced the police bullets and carried the dead and injured on his shoulders. He then continued the struggle against religious fascism by participating in the events of June 2013 that led to the Muslim Brotherhood's removal from power. Hazek also fought against administrative corruption in the Bibliotheca Alexandrina, where he worked as a civil servant. As a result, he was persecuted and dismissed from his job. He was then reappointed after pressure was exerted by his colleagues in the administration of the library. Ismail Serag El Din – a friend of Suzanne Mubarak and head of the Bibliotheca Alexandrina – accused him of slander, but when he was tried, the judiciary ruled that he was innocent of the charges. Why does a talented poet involve himself in such struggles? Why didn't he simply ignore the injustice and corruption around him, and instead, focus on writing poems, winning awards and achieving personal success? The answer is this: the nature of art is such that it acts in defence of justice and freedom – an artist cannot defend higher human values in his literary works but then keep silent when these values are attacked in front of his eyes. The history of art details hundreds of artists who fought for justice and freedom and paid dearly for taking a stand. Today, Omar Hazek is paying a price for the high-minded stance that he took.

On 2 December, there was a court hearing for the killers of Khaled Saeed; he was murdered by the Mubarak regime and, as a result, became the icon of the revolution. A number of young activists stood in the courtroom holding banners calling for the killers of Khaled Saeed to be punished. Suddenly, however, a police officer began to violently beat one of these protesters. One of the victim's friends tried to stop the attack, which led to the police officer arresting both of them. Hazek approached this officer and asked him: "What have they done that would warrant you beating them up and arresting them?" The officer took this question to be a disrespectful challenge to his position; in his mind prestige can only be gotten by bullying and humiliating citizens. He then arrested Hazek as well and had him referred to the state security prosecution service to be tried on charges of "vandalising buildings, burning police vehicles, assaulting soldiers and police officers, attacking public property, defying the authorities, demonstrating without a permit and jeopardising public security."

Such trumped-up charges are – as every Egyptian knows – typically levelled at anyone who angers a police officer. Anyone who has seen the slight figure of Omar Hazek will find it impossible to believe that this man could have miraculously turned into some sort of giant capable of beating up soldiers and officers with one hand and destroying police vehicles and buildings with the other. But the authorities treated Omar Hazek like a dangerous criminal, both he and the two others were handed over to the courts for a speedy trial. Their bail was set at 50,000 Egyptian pounds, and then they were sentenced to two years in prison. Court verdicts are to be respected, of course; but the imprisonment of the talented poet Omar Hazek is part of a wider, organised campaign against the young activists of the revolution. It's now clear that the recent anti-protest law issued by the interim authorities is aimed at suppressing and silencing the young revolutionaries so that they realise that the era of protest is gone forever and submit to whatever the authorities dictate – either they do so or they will go to jail. This oppressive campaign, which makes full use of the anti-protest law, has also been accompanied by a hostile campaign in the media, which is supported by the security agencies and aims to sully the reputation of the revolutionary youth. It seeks to achieve this by using such tactics as accusing them of being agents in the pay foreign powers, and it make such claims without a shred of proof, or any investigation of the facts.

How can some of these people in television call themselves media professionals when all they do is broadcast whatever they are told to by the state security officers who manage them? When a serious accusation is made against any citizen, the office of the attorney general must record such claims so that they can be used as evidence of slander in a court of law. Searching for dirt on people – let alone broadcasting it on television – is an immoral deed and a crime punishable by law. However, those with ties to the former regime don't seem to care about laws or morals. Rather, they seem to be motivated by the desire to take revenge on the Egyptian revolution for putting their leader in prison. They are plotting to take back the power that they lost because of the revolution and this is why they make every effort to defame and oppress the revolutionaries. Their calculations are worthless and naive, however, for it is not only Omar Hazek, Hassan Mustapha, Alaa Abd el-Fattah, Mona Seif, or Ahmad Douma who were behind the revolution, but millions of Egyptians. It was they who took to the streets against Mubarak in January 2011 and forced him to step down. It is they who demanded his trial and imprisonment. Vilifying the revolution will prove to be futile because the millions of Egyptians that carried it out it remember very well the crimes that were committed by the Mubarak regime for which nobody has yet been punished.

It is regrettable that this persecution of the revolutionaries continues even though we have been making calls for the army, the police and ourselves, the supporters of the revolution, to put our differences behind us and stand together as one against the Brotherhood's terrorism. It is our duty to support the state in its war against terror, but, unfortunately, many of those in positions of power have adopted the use of oppression and slander against the most high-minded of Egyptians. The young revolutionary activists are the ones who took to the streets and toppled Mubarak in January 2011, and it is they who again went out on 30 June in order to overthrow the Muslim Brotherhood. These same young activists, who have been slandered and defamed, have never bowed like the servants of Suzanne Mubarak. And unlike the sycophants who are now returning to the fore, they never praised the genius of Gamal Mubarak or welcomed him as his father's heir and replacement, as though the country were the Mubarak family's own personal estate. How can we convince the world that we are building a democratic state when the poet Omar Hazek has been sentenced to two whole years in prison just because he dared to ask an officer why he was beating up activists and arresting them.

I don't address here Hazem el-Biblawy, Hossam Eissa, Mustafa Hegazy, Zyad Bahaa El Din or Sekina Fouad. I know how loyal they are to the revolution and how they have worked diligently to build a lawful state, but it is clear that there are certain decisions that have been imposed on them to which they cannot object. It's more sensible to address whoever appointed this government and chose its members. General Abdel Fattah el-Sisi is the main person in charge of what happens in Egypt until an elected president and an elected government come to power. Dear general, is it fair to persecute the young revolutionaries who faced death for the sake of making Egypt a better place? Is it acceptable to slander people and ruin their reputations without an investigation or a fair trial? Is this the reward for those who responded to your call and took to the streets in order to delegate to you the authority to combat terror? We Egyptians took to the streets on 30 June and we toppled the Muslim Brotherhood for the sake of building the democratic state for which the revolution erupted in the first place. We definitely didn't do it to retain the despotic regime of the Mubarak era. General el-Sisi, please read Omar Hazek's poem and remember that its author is now imprisoned with criminals and killers simply because he dared to ask an officer a question.

In 1968 student demonstrations took place in France against President Charles de Gaulle. The great French writer Jean-Paul Sartre distributed leaflets and incited students against the regime. The French minister of interior suggested to de Gaulle that Sartre should be detained for a short time until things were under control. De Gaulle replied angrily: "It's impossible to detain a writer for his ideas. France will never detain Voltaire." Does General el-Sisi like poetry? If he does, he will definitely take the side of freedom and defend it. He will realise that Egyptians made a revolution in order to be treated with respect, not for an officer to violate their rights, make false accusations against them or oppress them. If General el-Sisi likes poetry, he will never allow the corrupt associates of the old Mubarak regime to retain power. He will not allow the innocent to be oppressed or a single Egyptian to be humiliated. He will work hard to build a state that has its basis in the law, and in which Egyptians enjoy all their human rights. Does General el-Sisi like poetry? We shall know the answer in the coming days.

Democracy is the answer.

Some Remarks on a "Yes" Vote

13 January 2014

Today we are going to vote in the referendum on the new constitution, which is, in my opinion, a very good constitution, except for one clause which allows for civilians to be tried in military courts. This provision is in contradiction with the principles of democracy and I hope that the coming parliament will reject its implementation. Yet, in this referendum, we aren't really voting on the constitution so much as on the ouster of Mohamed Morsi. The millions of Egyptians who revolted against the rule of the Muslim Brotherhood should approve the constitution in order to demonstrate to the whole world that what happened on 30 June was not a military coup, as the Muslim Brothers claim, but rather, a great revolution that reflected a real popular will that the Egyptian armed forces recognised and carried out. My own approval of the constitution is not without reservation, however; it is conditional upon that constitution being respected and implemented. Egypt has known good constitutions before, but they were considered worthless because they were ignored by the authorities. Before 30 June I had met General el-Sisi twice and I got the impression that he is respectable and patriotic person. I admired how he was open to criticism no matter how harsh it was, provided it was for the sake of the public good. But now, however, we need to remind General el-Sisi of certain disturbing practices taking place which go against democracy. These can be summarised as follows:

First: In democratic countries when someone wants to be nominated for the presidency, they have to persuade the voters that they are worthy of the position. In dictatorial systems, on the other hand, the leader wears a sacred halo and the people have to beg them to take the presidency – as if it weren't the leader that needed the presidency, but that the presidency needed them. When Hosni Mubarak took power in 1981, he vowed to all Egyptians that he wouldn't rule for more than two terms. When the two terms were up, Mubarak found himself in an awkward position, so he declared that he would step down as he promised. Then something shameful took place: led by certain members of the People's Assembly and the Shura Council of the time (most of whose members who had won their constituencies through fraud), an agreement was made with Mubarak that they would go to his mansion and start begging him to remain in power. They even presented him a pledge of their allegiance which they claimed had been written in their own blood (though it was later discovered that they had used a bag of blood taken from the blood bank). This silly piece of theatre was even broadcast on television: Mubarak could be seen holding in his hand the pledge written in blood as he looked at the play-acting members of the delegation, and said: "I had decided to step down but you have come to me with this document that you have written in your own blood. I cannot ignore the will of the people so I will remain in power."

In a democracy, the people of the nation are the masters that everybody must serve and please. By contrast, the culture of dictatorships is characterised by the glorification of the leader above the level of mere mortals. In democratic countries, the president is a public servant; they serve the people who have a right to hold them accountable, and to overthrow them if they want. In a despotic regime, the beloved leader is more important than the presidency and nobody is allowed to hold them accountable as it is they who know what is best for the people better than the people themselves. How can we hold a president accountable if we beg and implore them to take the presidency? I was hoping that General el-Sisi would declare his nomination and present his electoral program as candidates normally do in democratic systems. What happened, however, is that hypocrites and sycophants have started beseeching General el-Sisi to accept the nomination for the presidency. Some of them have gone as far as to say that el-Sisi must accept the presidency even if it's against his will; this is truly an astonishing notion that reveals only the stupidity and extreme hypocrisy of whoever hold it.

Sadly, we in Egypt excel in inventing creative methods of flattery that rarely exist in democratic countries. The sycophantic campaigns for General el-Sisi remind us of those that were orchestrated for Mubarak and his cronies; at one time an important figure in the Nationalist Party stated that: "Even the foetus in its mother's womb supports Mubarak." General el-Sisi doesn't need all this flattery; he already enjoys great popularity as a result of the courageous stand he took to protect Egypt against the terrorism of the Muslim Brotherhood. If he wants to be a candidate in a democratic way, he should quietly retire from the armed forces, announce his nomination and present a political programme which can then be compared with those of other candidates so that people can decide which is better.

Second: It's now being said by some media channels that an acceptance of the constitution represents an endorsement for General el-Sisi's candidacy for the presidency. In fact, however, these two issues are completely separate. Did millions of Egyptians demonstrate on 30 June to show they had no confidence in Morsi's presidency after he had suspended the constitution, or did they do so in order to show support for the nomination of el-Sisi? Did the members of the Committee of 50 exert all this effort to draft a constitution that is worthy of Egypt, or was it their aim to pave the way for General el-Sisi to take the presidency? Making a link between the constitution and the nomination of el-Sisi is both strange and suspicious, and throws the revolution off course. Every Egyptian citizen has the right to approve the constitution but reject General el-Sisi's potential bid for the presidency if they wish.

Third: General el-Sisi has asked the army to authorise his nomination for the presidency and they have granted his request. This means that the army now has a presidential candidate whom it prefers to the others, which will definitely lead the army to interfere in politics and all that this entails, including the potential for serious harm to the nation. The law prohibits members of the armed forces from voting in elections in order to guarantee their impartiality and their non-involvement in politics. But how does this sit with the army's authorisation of el-Sisi's nomination? And can anybody imagine that the army's nominee could possibly lose the elections to any other candidate? How can the armed forces be impartial while supervising presidential elections if they are fielding one of their own? How can we convince the world that we are building a democratic state, which is not governed by military institutions, if the army is involved in the nomination of a candidate who will oppose the other candidates?

Fourth: It is our duty to support the Egyptian state in its war against the Brotherhood. We will never forget the martyrs of the army and the police who have died for our protection. Nevertheless, it is also our duty to warn the interim government against the return of the despotic practices that are rarely directed at the Muslim Brothers, but which are often adopted against the revolutionaries who played an important role in toppling the Brotherhood. Why did the government not employ emergency law against the terrorism of the Brotherhood, yet issued an anti-protest law by which it imprisons the revolutionary activists only? Is it reasonable that young activists should be arrested, tried summarily and be thrown in prison for years just for protesting without a permit? Do demonstrations held in support of el-Sisi need permits? The followers of the Brotherhood who killed Copts, burned down churches, threw innocent people from the top of roofs and slaughtered the officers in Kerdasa are given long, drawn out trials after having committed such crimes. This desire on the part of some officials in the Ministry of the Interior to tarnish the January 25 Revolution and take revenge on its supporters, is not in the country's best interests. Instead, it plays into the hands of the Muslim Brothers who claim day and night that 30 June is a return to the old regime.

Fifth: If General el-Sisi is going to be a candidate for presidency then we have a right to ask him to clearly declare his position with regard to the Mubarak regime. The corrupt institutions of the Mubarak regime remain as they were and the interest groups that plundered the Egyptian people are back on the scene. The performance of the police – apart from the great role it plays now in combating terrorism – has been, for decades, blighted by serious violations that led directly to the eruption of the 2011 revolution. If he wins the presidency, does el-Sisi intend to reform the police by rewarding the competent officers and penalising the officers who violated the human rights of Egyptians, tortured and killed them? Will el-Sisi adopt a programme for transitional justice that reveals the truth and punishes the killers of Egyptians in all the massacres that took place since 28 January 2011 till now? What will be the attitude of el-Sisi towards the businessmen who benefited from being close to Mubarak and who made huge fortunes at the expense of the people? Those thieves are back. Can General el-Sisi enforce the law against them? Can he get back the money that Mubarak and his family took from the people, since due to the unwillingness of the military council and the Muslim Brotherhood no attempts to do so have been made? Egyptians have a right to know the answers to these questions before they decide whether they would elect el-Sisi for the presidency or whether they would prefer another candidate.

Finally, if the love of millions of Egyptians for General el-Sisi leads them to nominate him as a president, regardless of the democratic system, that would create a new dictatorship. We have to remember that the first victim of a dictatorship is the dictator himself; despotism blinds him to the honest and sincere criticism necessary for informing his vision and his decisions. Egypt's defeat in the Six-Day War[1] against Israel in 1967 would never have happened if the great leader Gamal Abdel Nasser had presided in a democratic Egypt. The catastrophes that have befallen us are due to the rule of an individual who relied on the false theories that are unfortunately being reiterated anew about the "inspired ruler", the "indispensable president", the leader who is a "gift from God" and other such clichés that are mocked by citizens in democratic states. General el-Sisi, the leader of the Egyptian army, has all our respect and appreciation but as a presidential candidate he has to present his programme and explain to us how he would rule our nation if he wins the presidency. We will then have the right to decide whether we will accept or reject him. Regardless of how great General el-Sisi is and how capable a president he might prove to be, if he takes power without real democratic elections, Egypt would go back to the year 1954 and we would be embracing the rule of the individual anew. Any dictator, no matter how popular and loyal he is to the people, will definitely lead the country to a disaster as long as he's despotic; that's what history teaches us if we learn the lesson. Democratic elections mean equal opportunities between the candidates, revealing the truth about their wealth and the sources of their funding, applying the law to them if they exceed the limit of spending on their election campaigns, and cancelling the result of any

1 The Six-Day War (1967), also known as the June War, was fought between 5–10 June 1967 by Israel and the neighboring states of Egypt, Jordan, and Syria. The war began when Israel launched a surprise series of airstrikes against Egyptian airfields following the mobilisation of Egyptian forces along the Israeli border in the Sinai Peninsula. Within six days, Israel had won a decisive land war and had taken control of the Gaza Strip and the Sinai Peninsula from Egypt, the West Bank and East Jerusalem from Jordan, and the Golan Heights from Syria.

constituency where it has been proved that election rigging has taken place. Who would apply these rules to General el-Sisi?

All Egyptians are required to approve the constitution to ensure the legitimacy of the change that took place on 30 June. Yet, a difficult and inevitable battle lies ahead for us after the constitution is approved; this battle will be to establish the rules of democracy and to avoid a new dictatorship under any name.

Democracy is the answer.

What Do You Know about Chairophilia?

20 January 2014

The word *kursi* in Arabic can be used to mean a chair, a bed or a throne. Chairophilia is a well-known disease: when someone catches it, their main goal in life becomes obtaining a higher post. When they get a high post, their thinking then focuses upon holding onto it by any means.

So how common is it? Chairophilia is widespread in Arab, African and many Latin American countries. It has been observed that the disease is most virulent in dictatorial regimes, is rare in democratic countries, and reaches its lowest rates in Sweden and Denmark. Its incidence in Egypt is the highest in the world. Statistics prove that one of every three Egyptians has chairophilia. A study proved that 60 per cent of guests on television talk shows in Egypt are plagued with this disease, while the percentage amongst ministers reaches 95 per cent. It has been noted that amongst the thousands of persons who have occupied ministerial posts in Egypt since 1952, only ten or so have ever resigned; this confirms just how wide-spread the disease has become amongst Egyptian authorities over the last decades. Some studies have also observed that resigning does not necessarily indicate that a minister does not, in fact, have chairophilia, since in Egypt, a minister who resigns their post may not have done so of their own free will. In democratic states, a minister resigns and leaves office, whereas Egyptian ministers don't dare to present their resignation in person. Instead they place it on the desk of the president. If the president refuses it, they feel extremely pleased as they are reassured that they are still needed by the president. At this point they withdraw their resignation and continue their work as if nothing has happened.

What are the causes of the disease? Genetic caues of the diseases have not been proven but it has been observed that there is a direct correlation between the prevalence of chairophilia and despotism. The sufferer is often a highly educated and intelligent person who feels it is their right to occupy higher positions, but is aware that reaching a high position under a despotic government has less to do with competence and more to do with loyalty. The sufferer is sure that whatever their gifts, they wouldn't get a political promotion unless they were able to please the president and prove their unconditional loyalty. Many scientists confirm that the widespread presence of corruption and injustice, the loss of faith in the application of justice, as well as ambition and the desire to distinguish oneself are all factors that can lead to the contraction of chairophilia.

What are the signs and symptoms? There are two types of chairophilia: the first type is contracted before one has achieved power and the second types strikes after one has done so. Those with type 1 will flatter the president in order to obtain a higher post. Once they have achieved this they will get type 2; they will continue to flatter him in order to hold onto their post. There are also many, however, who skip type 1 and go straight to type 2. These people tend to live normally and respectably, but as soon as they become ministers, the symptoms of chairophilia appear. They turn into pandering lapdogs that justify whatever the president says, does or even thinks. The symptoms of the first type of chairophilia appear when one tries by all means to reach the decision maker, flatter him and draw his attention to one's talents. The sufferer in this case shows a rare ability to know the inclinations of the president and always manages to indulge them.

One of the most famous cases of type 1 chairophilia was after the 2011 revolution in Tunisia. Sensing that the Mubarak regime feared that revolution would spread to Egypt, a number of political consultants (all infected with chairophilia) appeared on Egyptian television channels claiming that Egypt is totally different from Tunisia and that such a revolution could never occur in Egypt. They even used fake studies and diagrams to demonstrate that the nature of Egyptian society is different from that of Tunisian society, and that this makes it scientifically impossible for any revolution to break out in Egypt. When the revolution in Egypt did take place, these same political experts suddenly altered their positions; they started applauding the Egyptian revolution and asserting that they had all along predicted that it was inevitable.

In a separate study – which has not yet been published – the prevalence of chairophilia amongst those who call upon General el-Sisi to stand for presidential elections is discussed in detail. Those who are carried out this study state that el-Sisi does enjoy real popularity; however, they also note the much of the praise being directed at him has come from those infected with type 1 chairophilia and, therefore, constitutes a highly exaggerated form of flattery. One such person claimed that General el-Sisi is a gift from heaven, the kind that Egypt is only blessed with once every hundred years.

A television presenter confirmed that what el-Sisi has accomplished is much more important than what Nasser achieved. A famous journalist declared that the general doesn't want or need the presidency of Egypt, but that it is the people who are appealing for him to accept the position. The second type of chairophilia can be observed in the behavior of many ministers. Here it takes the form of paranoia at the prospect of losing their posts, leading them to justify all the decisions made by their president even if they contradict long-held principles. The minister who used to be a socialist will become an ardent defender of a market economy and the minister who spent his whole life defending human rights will now justify unlawful detentions as a temporary necessity in the interests of the country.

What are the stages of the disease? The consequences of chairophilia are very serious; the condition of the sufferer deteriorates as he goes from flattery to justifying crimes, to complicity in the crimes committed by the authorities, and ultimately, he will commit the crimes himself. It has been proven that the consequences of an individual's chairophilia have a wider impact on the whole of society: those around the ruler are infected by chairophilia and so they applaud all of their decisions, which deprives the president of honest opinions and advice, and thus, it results in autocratic decisions that lead the country to disaster. Two of the best examples of the consequences of chairophilia are Egypt's defeat in the Six-Day War of 1967 and Iraq's invasion of Kuwait in 1990. In both cases the ruler surrounded himself with ministers who had chairophilia and so none of them dared to warn him of the dangers in his decisions; in both cases this led to catastrophe.

What is the treatment? Chairophilia is often incurable. Several scientists have tried implementing various methods of treatment including psychotherapy and the use of medication; however so far, no treatment has proven successful. Studies maintain that the second type of the disease might respond to treatment involving "shock". This can be described as follows: an infected minister is confronted by an acquaintance, who accuses them of hypocrisy and moral deterioration because they decided to justify the crimes committed by the regime. Then they remind the minister of their honourable personal history and the principles they have betrayed. This method has been useful in treating a few cases but it has more frequently put the patient into a state of denial, causing them to defend their behavior even though it contradicts their earlier principles. The patient will insist that they are still loyal to their principles and will accuse their critics of being childish revolutionaries, of being stupid and ignorant, of never having read anything about history, or other insults by which they try to hide the ugliness of their own behaviour. Here we remember what the socialist leader, Lenin, wrote: "Intellectuals are the ones who most betray the revolution because they are the most capable of justifying betrayal."

How do you prevent chairophilia? Chairophilia cannot be prevented by medical precautions as the disease is related to the nature of the political system and so the disease will only worsen while the state is subject to despotism. It has been noted that the relationship between despotism and chairophilia is one of mutual interest. A sufferer seeks power by all means and a despotic ruler prefers people with chairophilia because they will work in his service, justify all his decrees and never compete with him for fame or leadership. Accordingly, combating chairophilia necessitates combating despotism and the establishment of a real democracy.

How do you diagnose the disease? Several studies have been conducted to find a scientific way to diagnose chairophilia at an early stage. The German social scientist Birnbach devised a test to measure chairophilia. He recommended applying the test to ministers and people in power at least once a year. The test comprises two parts. For the first part, doctors register the personal and political history of the minister, and in the second part they ask the minister the following questions:

1. Do you feel overwhelmed with happiness when the president looks at you and smiles?

2. If the president insults you in front of your fellow ministers, do you feel pleased and proud because the president has honored you with this familiarity?

3. Do you consider it a duty to show admiration and support for any decision made by the president even if it's against your beliefs?

4. During a cabinet meeting, if the president asked you to bring an ashtray instead of asking the office assistant, would you be glad to do so?

5. If the president met you with a sulky face, would you be scared and fear that one of your colleagues had turned him against you and, therefore, try to work hard to make him happy with you by flattering him till he regains his absent smile?

6. If the president is talking about something in the field of your specialisation and he says something that you know to be inaccurate, would you keep silent because it's inappropriate to say that the president is mistaken?

7. Do you consider your being dismissed from the ministry to be the worst thing that can happen to you?

8. What makes you feel happier: being addressed as "Your Excellency" or by your academic title?

9. Do you consider those who oppose the president's policies as traitors, agents in the pay of foreign states, terrorist sleeper cells, fifth columnists, or stupid adolescents?

10. If the president's decisions led to the detention or killing of innocent citizens or to violations of human rights, would you consider this to be an individual transgression that shouldn't be objected to in the present critical situation of the country, and would you lie to cover up the crimes of the president?

If the minister replies "yes" less than three times, then he doesn't have the disease. If he replies "yes" three to five times, then he's on the verge of contracting the disease, but if he answers "yes" six to ten times then he has chairophilia. The disease will turn him from a respectable man to a humble follower of the president, leading him to abandon all notions honour and dignity.

Democracy is the answer.

Are Egyptians Looking for a Father?

27 January 2014

Imagine that you were late for work and your boss got angry and insulted you. You would certainly condemn such behavior because the relationship you have with your boss is governed by laws which do not allow your superiors to insult you. They have the right to sanction you in certain ways determined by the law, but it's not within their rights to insult you; humiliating employees is an offense for which they should be held to account.

Suppose the same thing happened with your father: you were a bit late when you went to meet him and he insulted you. In this situation, you couldn't hold him accountable because both religion and tradition compel you to take your father's insults on the chin. There are things you will take from your father that you would not take from others; it's your father who helped bring you into this world, provided for you, brought you up and educated you. As a result, you are forever obliged to him and you should forgive his transgressions no matter how unpleasant they are.

The difference between your relationship with your boss and that with your father is that the former relationship is a professional one which is governed by legal rules. The latter, however, is a familial relationship wherein the father has greater rights with regard to his children. The difference between a boss and a father is the same as the difference between an elected president and a dictator.

An elected president is a civil servant who works for the good of the people; they observe the president's performance and hold them accountable through the parliament, which can remove them from power if necessary. A dictator, on the other hand, is a father in the eyes of the people; obeying them is a duty and humbling oneself before them is a virtue. They know what's best for us and we have to put up with them no matter how ruthless they are, because their ruthlessness stems from their love and concern for us. Reprimanding the president in a democratic system is perfectly normal and even the humblest of citizens can do it. They can criticise the president, accuse them of lying or of being incompetent – as happens in Western countries – and feel no fear of punishment. Opposing a dictator, on the other hand, is considered an offence; anyone who does this is denounced as a traitor, a fifth columnist or somebody who's funded by the nation's enemies to cause disorder at home.

History teaches us that dictatorship is fulfilled on two conditions: the despotism of the ruler and the compliance of the people. Free peoples, on the other hand, are those who are capable of esteeming their leaders without bestowing a sacred halo on them or putting them above the level of human beings. Winston Churchill, the former prime minister of Britain, led his country and its allies to victory in the Second World War, but he lost his position in the first elections after the war in 1945. Had Churchill led any Arab people to victory in a war, he would have continued in power until his death and he might have even have installed his children in power after him. The people would have granted him a mythical position above the law, criticism or accountability. But Britain is an established democracy and the British people know where the rights of each citizen start and end. Despite their great appreciation of Churchill as a national hero, they refused to let him continue in his position as a prime minister after the war because they saw that while someone might be a great leader in times of war, this does not necessarily make him a great prime minister in peacetime.

Consider the huge campaign in Egypt to persuade General el-Sisi to stand in the presidential elections. General Abdel Fattah el-Sisi performed a great patriotic task when he took the side of the people's revolution against the Muslim Brotherhood terrorist group, and this gained him great popularity amongst Egyptians. But does his being a successful leader of the army necessarily mean that he can lead the country? Is it enough to have courage and military experience to be able to successfully govern the state, which requires proficiency in the fields of politics, economics, planning and development? What will the policies of el-Sisi be if he becomes president? What is his political programme and how will he implement it? What is el-Sisi's opinion on the January 25 Revolution? Does he view it to have been a conspiracy carried out by the Americans and the Brotherhood, as those with ties to the old Mubarak regime portray it? Does he approve of the detention of revolutionary activists at the hands of the security services that fabricate charges against them? The latest victims of such campaigns have been the most high-minded and honourable revolutionaries, including Nagi Kamel, Nazly Hussein and Khaled al-Sayed.[1] Does el-Sisi approve of the cheap slandering of revolutionaries meted out by state security through its agents in the media? Does he intend to punish the businessmen who exploited their connections with Mubarak and robbed the Egyptian people of their money? Does he intend to conduct independent investigations into the massacres that took place during the rule of the military council in which hundreds of Egyptians were killed and thousands were injured, even if this were to lead to the condemnation of General Tantawi, whom el-Sisi thinks of as his mentor? Will el-Sisi continue the policies of Mubarak, such as privatisation and the sale of public assets, or does he believe that the state has a role in supporting the poor and providing them with a good standard of living?

All of these questions remain unanswered. Apart from a vague statement about not returning to the past, el-Sisi has not revealed his political stance and inclinations. That millions of Egyptians would ask a man to be the president despite knowing nothing about his political orientation is strange to say the least. There are several types of Egyptians amongst the supporters of el-Sisi. There are those with links to the old Mubarak regime who are trying to force their way back onto the scene, as though the revolution against them had never happened. They support el-Sisi fervently, as they consider him to be relatively close to the Mubarak regime and so, according to their logic, if el-Sisi were to take power they believe that he would act kindly towards them, whereas an outsider who takes the presidency might open their old files and ask them to return the land and the money that they plundered from the people – if not have them prosecuted and imprisoned.

The second group of el-Sisi's supporters are professional hypocrites who blow horns and beat drums for every president. They support el-Sisi today in order to reap rewards tomorrow. They believe in a return to despotism and, therefore, they assist in the making a dictator, so as to be rewarded later with positions and privileges. The third type of el-Sisi supporter is the Nasserite whose love for the great leader Nasser has reached such levels that they wish to revisit the old days of his rule in whatever way possible. This type of supporter yearns for a historic leader who will side with the poor, defy imperialism and restore our national dignity. In the past, this Nasserite dream has caused many

1 Nagi Kamel, Nazly Hussein and Khaled al-Sayed were activists arrested on the third anniversary of the 25 January uprising while taking part in demonstrations in downtown Cairo. Al-Sayed was a member of the Youth of the Revolution Coalition which was a main organising front for the revolution during its first 18 days.

idealists, whose intentions were good, to get involved in supporting tyrannical killers such as Gaddafi, Saddam and Hafez al-Assad. This type searches for a new Nasser everywhere. They are well-intentioned, like Don Quixote in the novel by the great Spanish writer Cervantes who wanted to be a heroic knight but ended up fighting windmills that he mistook for giants.

In their fervent enthusiasm to view General el-Sisi as a successor of Nasser, however, the Nasserites miss two important issues: firstly, in spite of Nasser's greatness, courage and loyalty, he replaced the democratic system with an autocracy; this led to Egypt's disastrous defeat in the Six-Day War in 1967 – the consequences of which we are still suffering from today. Similarly, Nasser's system collapsed with his death because he didn't take steps to preserve its achievements. Secondly, Nasser's socialist tendency of siding with the poor was clear from the beginning, but the same cannot be said of General el-Sisi. Even now we don't know whether his views are socialist or capitalist in nature and we don't know where he stands with regard to the corrupt and despotic Mubarak regime.

In any event, those with links to the old Mubarak regime – the hypocrites, and the dreamy Nasserites don't account for el-Sisi's popularity, which relies mostly on the support of the simple citizens who see in the general their only saviour. These simple people were glad when Mubarak was ousted and they had high expectations for positive change. However, for three years they have suffered from unemployment, economic inflation and the lawlessness caused by the neglect of duty on the part of the police. They also suffered because of the massacres that took place under the rule of the military council and the slanderous media campaigns intended to tarnish the revolution, which led them to hate it or at least doubt its sincerity. The Brotherhood then took power and things got worse. People felt that the country had fallen to the rule of a criminal gang and that taking it back would be impossible, until millions took to the streets to get rid of the Brotherhood and el-Sisi took their side, respecting their will, and responding to it. This role played by el-Sisi cemented his popularity and made many Egyptians want him to be a president regardless of his competence or political views.

Egyptians who carry placards of el-Sisi in the streets are not actually looking for a president; they are looking for a father who will embrace them and provide them with security after their long suffering. They want el-Sisi even if he continues Mubarak's policies, even if he oppresses them, rules by emergency law or sanctions the practices of detention and torture. They would accept all of these things from el-Sisi in the same way that we accept all wrongdoings of a father. All that they want is for el-Sisi to provide them with security and to defeat terrorism. Even if things went back to how they were during Mubarak's time, they would accept it. They don't care how el-Sisi takes power or whether the elections are fair or not; the important thing is to feel that they have a new father who can protect and control them and provide them with the safety they need.

Obviously we can't blame frightened citizens because they look for a protective father. The counter-revolutionary forces led by the former military council, the Brotherhood and its supporters who carry out terrorist acts and kill innocent people every day, have all put Egypt in a worse place than it was when Egyptians revolted against Mubarak's rule. A large sector of el-Sisi supporters aren't, therefore, looking for a president but for a father to protect them from evil, and they are so keen for this to happen immediately that they will say on television: "We want el-Sisi to be president at once. There's no need for the expenses of elections, publicity and such things."

Here we have a dilemma. The Egyptian revolution broke out in order to abolish the idea of the father-president and to establish a democratic state where the president is the servant of the people. Twenty million Egyptians who had a certain awareness, as well as dignity and courage, revolted in January 2011 against one of the worst and most oppressive regimes in the whole world, forcing Mubarak to step down and then making the military council put him on trial.

If el-Sisi does stand in the elections he will, most probably, be the next president of Egypt, but the way he reaches power will determine the form of the Egyptian state for decades to come. If General el-Sisi understands that a democratic system is more important than the power of an autocrat, and allows for fair presidential elections, he will gain real legitimacy both in Egypt and abroad. Egypt will then turn from a despotic backward state into a respectable democratic one. But if General el-Sisi becomes president through fake elections, like those through which Mubarak ruled for 30 years, this would be an offence against the people and the revolution; it would push Egypt towards a new dictatorship and we will all pay the price, as we have done so many times before.

Democracy is the answer.

Let's Listen to Them This Time

3 February 2014

On every metro train in Cairo there's a carriage reserved for women, in which men are not permitted. Some men, however, ignore this rule and enter the carriage regardless. One day, a young woman objected when some men boarded the women's carriage and insisted that they get off immediately. The men tried to shut her up but she made for the door of the carriage and used her hand to prevent it from closing. This meant that the train could not depart the station because it cannot move unless all the doors are safely closed. The men tried to pull the woman away from the door but she held on to it. One of them tried to hit her, but some other young women of her age came to her defence and asked the men to leave the carriage. Finally, the conductor of the metro appeared; he took the side of the men and tried to persuade the women to let the matter go. They all refused, however, and eventually he was forced to make the men leave the carriage. The train finally started moving after the women had successfully stood up for themselves. Immediately after, however, some older women in the carriage started complaining, making comments such as: "What's the point of this? It's just a headache that is delaying us" and, "Does the whole world have to follow your whims?"

When the conductor realised that opinion amongst the other women was against what the young women had done, he let men enter the car at the next station and things returned to how they were before.

This incident, which took place a few days ago, offers important insights. There are men who don't respect the law, except when they fear punishment and who, in addition to their selfishness and lack of civility, harbour a deep contempt for women; they will lash out at them verbally and physically when they ask that their rights be respected. We seem to have this institutional idiocy in Egypt, inherited from the time of Mubarak, and represented by the negligent metro conductor whose backward beliefs made him side with the men against the women, even though the women were in the right. Most importantly, there's the incongruity between the behaviour of the young women and that of the older women. The young women decided to courageously battle for their rights, and they won. The older women, on the other hand, were more preoccupied with their own affairs and had no will for such a dispute; they didn't support the young women in their stand and the result was that everything went back to the way it had been before.

These young women belong to the generation of the revolution and the older women to the previous one – the gap between them is considerable. I know that generalising is dangerous and that many amongst the older generation enjoy the same enthusiasm as the youth. Furthermore, I don't wish to antagonise the older generation – I myself belong to it. The reality in Egypt, however, is that we do have two generations that are totally different from each other in vision, culture, sentiments and behaviour. The older generation has lived, gotten married and had children under the corrupt and despotic regime of Mubarak. They never thought of revolting against it; they learned to cope with the regime in order to get on with their lives. They were faced with three options: they could either surrender to their suffering, become corrupt or emigrate to the Gulf countries in order to find work where they had to endure the arrogance of their bosses' and their rights being violated just so that they could get out of poverty and one day return to Egypt with some money.

The older generation never rebelled or protested. For them, political activism was the worst of all follies; their advice to their children was to avoid politics, avoid conflict, study hard, graduate and get a job contract in the Gulf that would secure them wealth. The older generation were rarely interested in public affairs; they have always been model self-centred citizens who care only about their homes and their families; who never vote in elections, but who take a day off to be with their daughter during her prep school exams; who are fastidious about cleaning their apartments but who throw their rubbish down into the alley because they don't care about anywhere beyond the confines of their own apartments

The older generation was deprived of political awareness and incapable of working collectively; they were ignorant of any type of struggle except that of struggling to earn a living. It was normal for this generation to raise children like themselves. At first, all the signs indicated that the younger generation would be much worse than their parents; they were all raised in an unpleasant and chaotic reality with no national project to unite them, no role models, no respectable media, and lacking a good education. Then the January 25 Revolution erupted and a new generation of youth emerged. It was like a biological mutation, a generation of beings unexpectedly obtaining new characteristics not enjoyed by previous generations. These young people refused to put up with corruption, rejected emigration as a solution, and decided to change the country with their own hands. The youth embraced a culture different from that of their parents. Their social circles are much wider than the family unit, they're interested in politics, they believe that reform must start by changing the regime and that a democratic state is the path to progress. They do not consider submission to be wise, nor cowardice to be sensible. Their parents, who feared entering a police station, somehow raised children who stood against trucks that were shooting bullets at them during the revolution without trembling or retreating. Their fathers who spent their lives longing for the approval and friendship of their superiors raised the children who forced Hosni Mubarak to step down and then forced the military council to have him tried and sentenced to prison.

Today, 60 per cent of Egyptians are under 29 years old, which means that even though young people comprise the majority of the population, it is, nevertheless, largely their elders that occupy the positions of power. It is the youth who protest, it is they who are shot, killed or blinded by bullets, while their elders are the ones who enjoy the fruits of these sacrifices; they take power having done nothing to deserve it. When they get into power they betray their principles and turn into mere servants of the president. For the past three years, Egypt's young people have been warning us of the dangers we face. Their elders have mocked them for this, but then we discover that the young had been right all along. They have a vision and they refuse to compromise, whereas the old are trained to accept compromises for the sake of continuity. The young people have committed mistakes too, of course, but they have always understood what was happening, while their elders have spent time theorising, and their ambition to get governmental posts has taken precedence over speaking the truth. The youth refuse to compromise any of the principles of the revolution while the old always bargain and accept half of their initial demands; the result, however, is that they achieve nothing. The older generation were willing to allow Mubarak to stay in power for a further six months, but the youth insisted that he step down immediately; without their insistence he wouldn't have left. The youth called for a presidential council instead of the military council but their elders accepted the military council's rule and the whole of Egypt paid for this mistake. The youth warned that the military council was leading a counter-revolution but their parents didn't believe them. The youth suffered several massacres in which they bravely defended the revolution against failure, while their elders started blaming the victims and denying crimes that they witnessed with their own eyes because they couldn't bear the thought that they might lose the privileges bestowed upon them by the military council.

Then, the Muslim Brothers took power and their true character was revealed. The older generation started to curse the revolution and admitted that they yearned for the time of Mubarak. They felt that even though he had robbed, humiliated and impoverished them, he had at least provided them with security and stability. The youth, on the other hand, toppled Morsi in the same way they had toppled Mubarak. They started the Tamarod petition which succeeded in collecting millions of signatures. The people protested on 30 June and the army, taking the side of the people, removed the Brotherhood from power. Those with ties to the old Mubarak regime then re-emerged and began a campaign to oppress, arrest and imprison the young revolutionary activists. The older generation ignored these oppressive measures as they had been raised on the motto: "No voice is louder than the sound of battle." The state is fighting a war against terror and so it has a right, according to them, to do whatever it wants to citizens. The young, however, reject this logic, arguing that the battle against terrorism doesn't justify the oppression of innocent people.

It then became clear that General el-Sisi would be the next president of Egypt, so the older generation began to create a new pharaoh, just as they have done with other Egyptian rulers before. The youth, however, while not denying that el-Sisi is a brave, military man, refused to sign a blank check for anyone and demanded democratic elections be held in which all candidates, including el-Sisi, have the same rights and opportunities. They called for el-Sisi to declare the sources of his funding for any campaign just like the rest of the candidates. The result of this, however, was that a media campaign was launched against those who were calling for fair elections in which el-Sisi would receive no special privileges. As a consequence, anyone who was considering standing in the elections against el-Sisi has been slandered, humiliated and ridiculed on television. Some media channels are owned by figures from the Mubarak regime who insist upon el-Sisi's nomination because they believe that he won't hold them accountable for their crimes and that he will let them hold onto the fortunes they accrued by stealing from the people. Furthermore, the state media know only how to glorify the president and praise his wisdom and genius.

On top of this, there is a campaign led by people in the media who are known to have close relationships with state security officers. This campaign has sought to ruin people's reputations by airing private calls of dubious origin on television. The purpose here is to slander the youth who have changed the whole of Egypt with their courage. The campaign violates morality and the law and has been condemned by the interim prime minister, Hazem el-Beblawi, but it continues nonetheless, indicating that whoever is behind the campaign is much stronger than el-Beblawi.

The youth are now rejecting what is happening in Egypt. Signs that can no longer be ignored demonstrate that the security services have reverted to their old practices of oppressing the innocent and forging charges against them. The lawmakers have returned to their work; they produced the anti-protest law by which the authorities can now have anyone who dares to express dissent thrown in prison. Some cosmetic work is being carried out to beautify the military courts, which will then resume their activities of punishing opponents very soon. There is also to be a new law on terror – a new stick with which the authorities will beat those they don't like. Those associated with the old Mubarak regime are heading meetings and delegations while the crackdown on freedom of speech is getting fiercer: journalists have been arrested and defamed, an article by Belal Fadl in *Al-Shorouk* has been censored because he dared criticise General el-Sisi. The youth are angry and suspicious about the intentions of the current government. They ask for real guarantees to protect the democratic system if el-Sisi does become president. They reject the establishment of a new dictatorship no matter who creates it. Let's listen to the youth this time. They have always been right.

Democracy is the answer.

When Will Hajj Saleh Respond?

10 February 2014

I had always dreamed of buying a flat overlooking the sea in Alexandria. When I had enough money saved, I started looking at flats with an eye to buying one. After a few days of searching I found a small, beautiful apartment for a good price. The building was old, but it was sturdy, elegant and it overlooked the sea. Its gate opened onto a side street that was said to have witnessed exciting events. I asked about the owner of the apartment and I was told that his name was Hajj Saleh (the name in Arabic means "pious") which is appropriate as he is indeed a pious man. He has performed several pilgrimages in addition to other religious visits to Mecca, and established charity projects in different areas of Alexandria to help the poor. Added to this were his constant efforts to protect the people of this neighbourhood against attacks from thugs.

The most dangerous of these attacks was one that took place last year when a thug named Al Sunni (for he was bearded and pretended to be a religious man, despite being far from religion and morality) controlled the whole area. Al Sunni imposed compulsory fares on all the shop owners and subjugated the inhabitants, making their lives a living hell. The followers of Al Sunni bullied whoever objected to their tyranny. Al Sunni went as far as declaring more than once that he could burn down the whole district and its inhabitants if he so desired. For a whole year the residents were dominated by Al Sunni until they eventually got fed up. One day they all took to the street to ask him to leave their district. While Al Sunni's followers were preparing their arms to crack down on the residents, Hajj Saleh emerged to defend them. A fierce battle took place between the two parties, which lasted for a whole day. Finally, Hajj Saleh managed to defeat Al Sunni and his followers, and he handed them to the police who put them on trial. For his role in all this, the residents considered Hajj Saleh to be a real hero because he put his life at risk in order to protect them. All the residents of the district with whom I talked mentioned Hajj Saleh with love and gratitude, but I felt that there was something about him that they were hiding and didn't want to reveal.

I negotiated the price of the apartment with the followers of Hajj Saleh and we agreed on a certain price. I then went to meet him in his office and he welcomed me warmly. I immediately noticed that Hajj Saleh left the whole thing to his followers while he sat at his desk smiling and watching what was happening. The followers of Hajj Saleh were young men, all wearing T-shirts with the picture of their leader printed on them, and led by a muscular hulk who looked rather stern. After greetings and compliments, I gave them a small briefcase with the money inside. The hulk, together with his men, started carefully counting the money and then one of them took the briefcase and rushed outside. The hulk smiled and gave me a key ring with some keys, saying: "These are the keys to your flat. Congratulations."

I took the keys and looked at him saying: "Did you prepare the contract for me to read?"

The hulk stared nastily at me and said: "What contract?"

"The contract of the flat I've just bought."

He barked at me: "Are you crazy? How dare you ask for a contract from Hajj Saleh?"

I ignored the insult and said: "It's normal that people sign contracts when they buy and sell."

Another follower shouted: "Damn anybody who asks for a contract from Hajj Saleh. Hajj Saleh is not like the rest of the people. He's the hero who risked his life and saved us from the gang of Al Sunni. He's our role model, our leader and the saviour sent to us by God."

"I admire the courage of Hajj Saleh just like you but I bought an apartment and it's my right to get a contract signed by the owner," I said.

"Hajj Saleh's word is more important than a contract. You're lucky that Hajj Saleh agreed to accept your money. We begged him to accept. And you do have the keys, don't you? What else do you want?"

I said: "You offered your apartment for sale, so don't begrudge me this. I paid the required price and I have the keys but I need a document to prove my ownership. Nobody sells a flat without signing a contract. Our lives are in God's hands, Hajj Saleh or I might die, God forbid, and so there must be a written document to confirm the rights of both parties."

The follower shook his head and rudely replied: "Whoever asks for evidence of the honesty of Hajj Saleh deserves a good beating."

Starting to feel in danger, I answered him: "Please watch your language. How can you ask me to pay that much money and not get a contract to guarantee my rights and the rights of my children after me?"

"Shut up," shouted yet another of the followers.

I decided not to get involved in a fight. I ignored them and started talking to Hajj Saleh: "Speak up, Hajj Saleh. Did I ask for something that I shouldn't ask for? I just need a contract to prove that I bought the apartment."

Hajj Saleh kept his smile and said calmly: "I love you all."

I said angrily: "I like you too, Hajj, but does it harm you to write a contract to record the sale of the apartment?"

The Hajj kept smiling and said calmly: "God knows, you're all dearer to me than the apple of my eye."

I realised that Hajj Saleh doesn't like to declare his opinion so I got furious and yelled at his follower: "Listen, either Hajj Saleh signs the contract in front of me or I change my mind about buying the apartment."

He gave me a vicious look and said: "What do you mean?"

"Take your keys and give me back my money."

They looked at me as if I had committed the most terrible of all crimes. All the followers came closer to me, surrounded me, and with malice in their eyes they began to level accusations against me, saying: "You're an agent."

"You're a fifth columnist."

"You're a sleeping cell of Al Sunni's gang."

"They sent you here to cause chaos, so that their gang can regain control over the district. You're evil."

I shouted at them: "What are these insults? I don't know Al Sunni and I am not a fifth or sixth columnist. I just want my rights. Either you write me a contract or I take back my money."

The hulking follower came closer to me and yelled: "Don't ever think that you're going to fool us. We know everything about you. You'll suffer hell at our hands. We have recordings of you talking dirty on the phone with your mistress. Her name is Loubna, right? We'll blacken your name everywhere."

I felt as if I was in a nightmare and started to lose my concentration. The hulking follower said: "If you don't leave now we'll call the police."

"I didn't commit a crime!" I answered.

"You'll be punished for whatever crimes we say you have committed," he said.

"Who are you to charge me with crimes while I'm innocent?"

"We are the ones who defended this district and it's our right to do what we want."

"Protecting people once doesn't justify being unfair to them afterwards."

The hulking follower laughed and said: "We're in a war with Al Sunni's group and in war everything is permitted."

I said: "A war against thugs doesn't justify injustice against the innocent."

His reply was melodramatic: "You and Al Sunni's thugs can never defeat us. We'll sacrifice our lives for Hajj Saleh. His name is engraved in our hearts. He's our leader and we're his soldiers and children. We kiss the floor where he treads. Allahu Akbar."

The others repeated the cheers after him, looking scornfully at me. It occurred to me that they might be really mad. I remembered the sum I paid and decided to calm things down. I said in a soft voice: "Gentlemen, I swear to God I like Hajj Saleh the same way you do and I think of him as a real hero but it's my right to get a contract for the apartment I bought. Anyway, no problem. If the contract issue offends you, we can cancel the deal at once.

Take the keys and give me back my money so we will remain friends."

But they attacked me again as if I'd committed a grave sin; they held me down to make sure I was incapable of moving. The hulking man dealt a severe blow to my stomach and I almost lost consciousness.

I screamed: "Hajj Saleh, all this beating and humiliation because I ask for my rights? Do you approve of this tyranny?"

Hajj Saleh kept watching us with a gentle smile on his face as if what was happening was none of his business and then said in a serene voice: "You should know that I love you all and I would sacrifice my own life to defend you."

I tried to approach him but the followers stopped me in my tracks. "Hajj Saleh, you're a brave man and I do respect you but what's happening is a farce," I said. "You saved the district from Al Sunni's thugs but those who surround you are no less criminal. I ask for my rights and they harm me in front of your eyes, and you just reiterate statements about love. Do you believe in doing the right thing, Hajj Saleh, or are you pleased by the injustice your followers are committing? If you don't take a stand then you saved people from Al Sunni's thugs just to hand them over to thugs of another kind."

Hajj Saleh nodded and his smile grew wider but he kept silent. I shouted once more, saying: "Hajj Saleh, asking for my rights by no means diminishes my love for you and my appreciation for your courage. These hypocrites who surround you do you a lot of harm. Don't ever believe that they like you. They flatter you for their own interests. You should keep them away from you. Your silence about what they do makes me believe that you like it. If you reject their deeds then you need to kick them out. Give people their rights and don't surrender to this corrupt company that will turn you from a hero into a tyrant. Until when are you going to keep your smile and silence, Hajj Saleh?"

The followers became crazed and started kicking, slapping and beating me. I tried to fight back by raising my hand to return the blows and I kicked them, but they gathered around me and subdued me. I had no choice but to give in to them, and they pulled me outside the room. Before going out of the door, I shouted: "Hajj Saleh, your followers are tyrants, why do you let them slander people and tarnish their reputations and arrest the innocent and put them in jail? Are you happy with their transgressions or are you incapable of stopping them?"

I'm still waiting for a response.

Democracy is the answer.

The Revolution is Going Backwards

24 February 2014

Hamdi Qandil was, and still is, a loyal Nasserite who emerged during Nasser's time and deservedly became a pioneer in television journalism, as well as one of the most important and effective figures in the Egyptian media. In 1961, Hamdi Qandil presented his famous programme *From the Newspapers* on Egyptian television – a programme which achieved growing success with every episode, until the fifth episode when, to Qandil's surprise, the new boss of the station called him into his office and said: "Mr. Qandil, the minister asks you to take some time off."

At the time, this kind of statement was usually directed at those who were not liked by the authorities. Qandil's programme was taken off the air and he took some time off in Ras El Bar. However, he also made some calls to find out why his show had been cancelled. It seems that his great sin had been to broadcast a piece of news about the president at the end of the programme instead of at the beginning, as was the custom whenever there was a news item concerning the president. Qandil didn't stop here however, he got an appointment with Sami Sharaf, then minister of presidential affairs. He told him what had happened to him and said: "I would like to know from the president himself whether he personally objects to airing a piece of news about him at the end of the programme."

Sami Sharaf carried the message to the president and came back with the following response: "Mr Qandil, President Nasser requests that you continue your programme and not discuss this incident with anyone."

Qandil then returned to his program as if nothing had happened.

In 1967, with the threat of war against Israel growing, Qandil, like all Egyptians, was convinced that the Egyptian armed forces would be victorious. He presented a daily news broadcast from the war front and on 5 June he went to Fayid Air Base. He was having breakfast there with the air force pilots when, suddenly, he heard the sound of loud explosions; these were caused by an Israeli aircraft attacking the base. He sped off to the pilot's clubhouse where he found some 20 pilots shouting hysterically – one of them even banged his head against the wall until it bled. Their planes had been destroyed by the bombs while they were still on the ground; only three of their fellow pilots had managed to take off in theirs but nobody knew anything of their fate. Qandil left the base in a state of distress. He later ran into Hussein el-Shafei, a member of the Revolutionary Command Council, who asked him whether he had details about what had taken place. Qandil told him what he knew. El-Shafei then asked him what the best road for getting back to Cairo was and

Qandil advised him to take the desert road as it was safer.

Hamdi Qandil talks about both of these incidents in his marvellous autobiography *I Lived Twice*. Although he mentions these two incidents separately, I believe there is a connection. In the first incident a talented and successful television presenter, who was loyal to the regime and to the revolution, reads a piece of news at the end of his programme. His act was considered a crime and so he was sidelined without an investigation or even a chance to defend himself. He had to complain to the president himself in order to be forgiven. This is a perfect example of what happens under a despotic regime where the leader transcends criticism and is considered more than human – every decision they take demonstrates their wisdom and genius. The media under such a regime does not tell the truth but, rather, it disseminates propaganda and acts a machine for misinformation that brainwashes people and shapes their minds in ways that are decided by the ruling regime. Furthermore, laws are annulled and enacted at will according to the needs and aims of such a regime, and the arms of its police state extend to control everything and oppress the citizens without anybody objecting for fear of an unknown fate. The ruler is no mere political leader, but becomes the father of the people and the essence of the nation, so nobody dares oppose him or even discuss his decisions. The inevitable result, however, is that the leader becomes divorced from reality because he is surrounded by those who tell him what he likes to hear – whether out of fear or self-interest – until the moment comes when the leader takes a decision that leads to disaster.

This is exactly what happened in the second incident. Under a despotic regime, the Egyptian army was unjustly exposed to a shameful defeat. The brave pilots experienced feelings of shame because they were incapable of performing their duty of defending the country as a result of carelessness and misjudgement on the part of the military leadership. The tragedy became a farce when Hussein el-Shafei, a high-ranking military figure, had to ask Hamdi Qandil about the safest road back to Cairo. It is true that the Egyptian army eventually overcame the defeat and managed to regain its position in a very short time, retaliating for its defeat in 1967 and achieving a victory of which we Egyptians will always be proud. Nevertheless, the lesson here is that despotism will definitely lead to defeat no matter how patriotic and well-loved the leader is, and no matter how legitimate his battles may be.

Today we have a great need to learn this lesson. Millions of Egyptians took to the streets on 30 June to get rid of the Muslim Brotherhood; the army took the side of the people and saved Egypt from the danger of a civil war. The name of General el-Sisi came to the fore and he gained the love and respect of the Egyptian people who now think of him as a brave hero. This love, however, has now bestowed a halo on el-Sisi, just like the one worn by Nasser. The media now describes el-Sisi as the saviour from heaven, by whom we are blessed only once every 100 years. A few days ago, a well-known writer appearing on television went so far as to say that Egyptians have loved the name "el-Sisi" for 6,000 years ago because the ancient Egyptians called their sacred river *Sisi Ra*. El-Sisi has now been raised above the level of a mere human being and nobody is allowed to criticise him or even compete with him in elections. He knows what we don't know and takes decisions that are always in for our benefit even if we don't believe that they are. The leader has been hesitant for months concerning the question of his standing for president in the elections and we, the citizens, are supposed to organise daily marches to exert pressure on him so that he will agree to be the president of Egypt.

General el-Sisi leads the people in a real battle against terrorism in the same way that Nasser was leading the people in a real battle against colonialism. Unfortunately, though, the battle was used in both cases to justify oppression: innocent people have been detained, tortured, had false charges made against them and been humiliated in various ways. According to the regime, objecting to such practices is not permissible, as no voice should be louder than the sound of the battle, as the saying goes. On 12 February, 16 human rights organisations convened to issue a joint statement denouncing the documented incidents of oppression and torture in which Egyptians' human rights have been violated and neglected by the present judicial authorities headed by a senior judge whose role it is to defend the rights of the people. In response, the media attacked these human rights activists for denouncing torture and accused them of treason.

With every passing day it becomes more obvious that the constitution, which that the Egyptians were engaged in discussing for a very long time, item by item, and which was approved by a great majority, is more or less worthless, insofar as it has not been implemented. In fact, most of authorities' actions are unconstitutional. The constitution states that parliamentary elections should occur before the presidential elections, but the authorities have decided to do the opposite. The constitution protects the private life of the citizens and prohibits tapping their phone calls without a warrant, but private television channels have broadcast the most intimate content of people's private conversations through criminal and unverified recordings. The purpose behind this has been to slander the revolutionaries, and accuse them of being undercover agents and traitors. The constitution prohibits torture, but detainees are subjected to it every day at the hands of officers who know they won't be punished. The constitution allows demonstrations, but the young activists of the revolution are handed long prison sentences simply because they dare to demonstrate against what the authorities are doing. The constitution allows for strikes, but railway workers have been imprisoned on charges of going on a strike.

After the revolution, we expected the media to be honest and respectable, but they have continued to act as an organ of propaganda for the regime, whether it be the state television, which does nothing but deceive and fabricate, or the private channels owned by businessmen, several of whom made their fortunes through their links to the Mubarak family. They push for the return of the Mubarak regime in the hope that they won't be held accountable for the land they seized or the wealth they accumulated. The constitution calls for transitional justice; this should bring justice to victims but the Ministry of Transitional Justice has not done anything, and so, with all due respect to our great legal system, nobody has been held accountable for the killing of thousands of demonstrators.

The state has undertaken a war against terrorism and it's our duty to support it. The martyrs of the army and the police are great heroes who were killed while defending the people, but the war against terrorism does not justify the return of the police state. Indeed, we cannot win victory over terrorism by acting above law. History teaches us that human rights and dignity are more important than any battle and that it's impossible for an authority that oppresses its people to win victory no matter how legitimate and patriotic its projects are. A humiliated citizen who is tortured and violated won't make a good soldier in any battle even if he's convinced that the battle is just. It is very worrying to see that Egypt is now heading towards a police state; this is far from the goals of the revolution. Thousands of martyrs fell while dreaming of a modern democratic state that respects its citizens and applies the law to everybody without discrimination. If General el-Sisi wants to put the country back on the right path, he must follow these five steps:

1. He has to retire from the army and stand for presidential elections as a common citizen who has nothing to do with the armed forces and does not get any support from the state apparatus. He must then run in fair elections that uphold the principle of equal opportunity for all candidates, that are transparent with regard to funding, that abide by the rules concerning campaign spending, and that demonstrate equal application of laws regarding all candidates.

2. He has to suspend the law against protest; it is unconstitutional. He must stop the trumping-up of charges against people, prevent torture, and prosecute any officers involved in torture.

3. He must activate the Ministry of Transitional Justice and form independent committees to investigate the killing of thousands of Egyptians that took place from the beginning of the revolution up to the present time.

4. He must ensure that the media act responsibly and stop tarnishing the reputations of citizens with accusations of treason for the mere reason that they have a different opinion than that of the people in power.

5. He must initiate real dialogue with the young revolutionary activists, most of whom have already lost confidence in the present authorities after seeing their peers detained, betrayed and accused of being treasonous agents working for foreign powers.

The above steps are, in my opinion, likely to rectify the situation. Otherwise, we'll be heading towards a new despotism, and despotism, as history teaches us, is doomed to end in disaster – a fate which Egypt will hopefully avoid.

Democracy is the answer.

In Defence of Adversaries

3 March 2014

I used to work as a resident dentist at the Faculty of Dentistry at Cairo University where I was in charge of the dental extraction clinic, a large hall with dozens of dental chairs. Poor patients used to visit the clinic every day, buy a five piaster ticket and sit on the chairs where senior students took out their teeth. One day, I noticed that some patients were crying particularly loudly while their teeth were being extracted and I suspected that the anaesthetic might not be effective. I administered the anaesthetic myself to two patients with the same result: the anaesthetic was very weak. I then asked the students to stop extracting teeth and went up to the office of the head of the department. I reported the situation to him and he seemed to be more upset by the fact that I had stopped the work in the clinic than by my complaint that the anaesthetic was ineffective. He asked me to resume work immediately. I apologised saying that extracting teeth without effective anaesthetic was inhumane. In response, he yelled at me: "Your job here is to listen and obey!"

I decided I would not take part in tormenting the patients no matter what the consequences might be.

The head of the department called in one of the assistant lecturers in the department and asked him to resume work in the extraction clinic, which had turned into a torture ward filled with the cries of the poor patients growing louder and louder from pain. Many teeth were broken during the extraction process by the students who were nervous because of all the crying. At the end of the day, the head of the department called me in and said to me, in a paternal tone: "Son, you're still young. Whatever happens we can't stop work in the extraction clinic because that will cause havoc and expose us to gossip. We don't need that. And don't forget that we have bitter adversaries who shouldn't be given the chance to harm us."

I didn't answer the head of the department but I wondered about who these bitter opponents of the dental extraction clinic were. Years later, I was in the United States studying for my M.Sc. at the University of Illinois under one of the most important scientists of histology in the world, Professor Denis Weber, who supervised five students, amongst which I was the only Egyptian. Two weeks after the start of term, Professor Weber gathered us together and asked us to share our criticisms and opinions of his course. He said: "If you have negative comments, please don't hesitate to voice them."

The situation was beyond my comprehension. I, who came from Cairo University where the professor is a demi-god, was being invited to critique this great scientist – the mere thought of criticising him was unimaginable to me! And what was my scientific status to assess his performance anyway? I kept silent while my American colleagues started to criticise Professor Weber. One of them said that his explanation of the steps of research was not sufficient and another colleague asked him to devote more time to explaining the apparatus being used. Professor Weber carefully noted their comments and then he smiled, saying: "Thank you very much for your comments. I now know what I need to work on in future." We left feeling proud that we had been listened to by this eminent scientist and that we had shared the responsibility for the research we were conducting.

I always remember those two incidents in relation to each other as they constitute two opposing ways of thinking. The former incident is common in a despotic society because form is more important than content; the young cannot criticise their elders under any circumstances. What was important was for the clinic to continue working even if the patients were being tormented and their teeth were being taken out with bad anaesthetic. The director didn't care about the performance as much as he cared about his image in the eyes of his superiors. He was too busy thinking about the bitter adversaries waiting for the slightest mistake to kick him out. The reason for this insecurity might be that perhaps he didn't deserve his position. In despotic states, loyalty comes before competence as a criterion for granting positions.

The second incident, on the other hand, is typical of the democratic culture where the professor or the director is the first one to admit that he or she is just a human being who can be right or wrong, and doesn't feel at all embarrassed to respond to students' observations in order to improve his or her performance. We Egyptians have been raised amidst despotism, and know nothing but the former way of thinking. People in power in our country never accept criticism and the most important thing for them is to convince the public and their superiors that everything is alright. Whoever has taken power in Egypt has always lived in a fantasy world in which they have performed the greatest deeds and taken the wisest decisions, and whoever opposes them is a jealous enemy or an undercover traitor.

For 30 years the Mubarak regime plundered Egypt, brought utter decline in all fields, and oppressed and humiliated Egyptians. Yet Mubarak has still not owned up to his failures and crimes; he still considers himself a great ruler and a national hero, accusing the opposition of being a group of conspirators funded by foreign organisations. The revolution toppled Mubarak and the military council took power. The military council mismanaged the country to the extent that some Egyptians came to regret the revolution. During the rule of the military council a series of massacres took place and hundreds of innocent people were killed. Yet, the former military council still hasn't taken responsibility for the massacres. On the contrary, one of its members keeps reiterating a vague statement about a huge international conspiracy against Egypt that has considerable reach and cells operating in Egypt. Then the Muslim Brothers came to power and we discovered that they were dangerously deluded, considering themselves to have the exclusive right to speak in the name of religion as its true defenders. In light of this, anyone who opposed their politics or rejected their opportunism and hypocrisy was considered to be an enemy of Islam. This conviction blinded the Brotherhood and, eventually, millions of Egyptians revolted and ended its rule. Yet, the Brothers are still lost in their fantasy world; they view the second wave of the great revolution on 30 June as a conspiracy against Islam orchestrated by the military, the Copts and the secularists.

I recently met a university student who belonged to the Brotherhood and I found her totally convinced that those who took to the streets on 30 June were a just handful of Egyptians, and that the film director Khaled Youssef photographed them and then photoshopped the image to make it appear as though there were millions demonstrating. I told her that I myself participated in the protests and saw millions of people. She smiled sarcastically and looked at me meaningfully as if to say: "Well you would say that because you're a secular enemy of Islam."

We got rid of the Brotherhood but unfortunately we didn't get rid of their lies. Those with links to the old Mubarak regime have spent millions on starting up satellite channels, and now we discover their aim: to carry out the collective brainwashing of Egyptians. The process includes defaming the revolutionaries, tarnishing their reputations with false charges and persuading the public that the revolution was simply an American/Serbian/Qatari/Turkish/Israeli plot. It's absurd, of course, to discuss such nonsense. It's no use reminding the supporters of the old regime that Mubarak was himself the main servant of American–Israeli policies, with the acknowledgment of the authorities in both countries. It's no use reminding them that the Egyptian revolution laid its seeds ten years before it broke out. There's no use arguing with them because the world inhabited by these pro-Mubarak media people is built upon lies and delusions, and whoever goes against their line of thinking is considered a jealous enemy. Whoever objects or expresses a different opinion is immediately accused of being a sleeper cell of the Brotherhood, a fifth columnist or an American agent.

This miserable way of thinking can be seen most clearly in the recent incident in which the Egyptian armed forces announced the invention of a piece of equipment that can diagnose and cure AIDS. The Egyptian army, like all armies, undertakes research to improve its warfare capabilities. Their research is usually confidential; nobody knows about it except when it's used on the battlefield. During the October War (1973), the Engineering Corps developed a kind of cement that dried faster than others and helped to combat fire. It was used to seal pipes, which had been filled with explosives by the Israelis in an attempt to turn the waters of the Suez Canal into a river of fire. Similarly, General Baki Zaki used powerful water hoses that made a hole in the Bar Lev Line and caused it to collapse.[1] Clearly, innovations in the army are nothing new and there are thousands of military doctors and engineers who enjoy a prominent standing in the scientific community.

All this makes us proud of the Egyptian army. However, when an invention is announced to the public, it is no longer a military secret; it is a piece of research that has to be tested scientifically before it can be accepted internationally. In this case, however, it was surprising to see a press conference in which a person, who does not speak for the Egyptian army, was talking about a device that he had invented which is capable of diagnosing and curing AIDS. Instead of explaining the mechanics of the device in a scientific manner, he startled us by claiming that that the device removes the virus, and then feeds it to the patient like a skewer of Kofta to nourish them. When interviewed by the press, the inventor then declared that international organisations tried to buy this device for two billion dollars and that all international intelligence agencies put him under observation to seize an opportunity to kill him and deprive us, Egyptians, of his genius.

Everybody who is familiar with proper methods of conducting scientific research objected to presenting the findings in this inappropriate manner. The reason for the objection is our love and esteem for the army – but the media channels, owned by the supporters of the Mubarak regime, attacked anyone who objected. Acting on the instructions of the security forces and

1 The Bar Lev Line was a chain of fortifications built by Israel along the eastern coast of the Suez Canal. During the October War, the Egyptian army overran the Bar Lev Line in less than two hours using water cannons fashioned from hoses attached to dredging pumps in the canal.

according to the interests of the owners of their channels, these hypocritical media professionals began banging their drums and dancing to the tune of their masters. They accused anyone who objected to the unprofessional and unscientific way in which this miracle device was presented as being enemies of the army or agents working for the West. They even went as far as to hold up the scientific degrees that some of these objectors had obtained from American universities as evidence of their accusations. By this they seem to imply that ignorance is a prerequisite for patriotism.

It's true that Egypt has great potential and that there are regional and international forces that don't want Egypt to fulfil this potential, but we defeat ourselves with despotism and backward thinking. We will never take one step forward unless we respect everyone's opinions and consider those of the opposition before those of our supporters. Egypt will not progress unless we get rid of the false notions that prevent us from realising our errors and our weaknesses. We have to see the reality as is, not as we wish it to be. When we respect whoever criticises our behaviour, listen to them and work hard to correct our mistakes, only then will our renaissance take place.

Democracy is the answer.

Down with the Virtual Republic

10 March 2014

The president stands in a large hall, elegant as always, with a formal, serious expression on his face. The minister of the interior stands in front of him like a soldier standing in front of his leader. Dozens of cameras take the minister's picture as he reads the official results of the referendum. He starts with the number of those who are registered as having the right to vote, then the number of those who actually voted, followed by those who voted "yes" and those who voted "no". Finally, the minister of the interior congratulates the president on his victory in the referendum with more than 90 per cent of the votes.

That scene was nothing new; it is the same scene that we Egyptians have seen time and again for decades, except in 2005 when Hosni Mubarak changed the title of the farce from a referendum to presidential elections. I used to ask myself: why didn't Mubarak save the millions of pounds he used to spend from the state's budget on those referendums by just declaring to the people that he would stay in power by force, as nobody could make him leave anyway? But a dictator needs a script in which he plays the main role with a group of minor actors around him. A dictator needs elections, constitutional reforms, observers, journalists and an elections committee. The aim is to create a favourable image of despotism, both at home and abroad. This scam begins with the president and spreads like a disease through the state's institutions and then to society as a whole. After years of despotism, society begins to accept the lies and deceit propogated by the despot as truths. We see the president thanking those who elected him, so it seems as if the president were an elected president when in fact he's a dictator. We see heated discussions in the parliament, and so the speakers look as if they were real representatives of the will of the people when, in fact, they are lying hypocrites who don't utter a word without the consent of the president and the security institutions. We see serious media people on television who appear to be neutral when actually they're following the instructions of a state security officer who's in charge of them.

An official language of the regime emerges within the virtual state. It is a collection of lies delivered in a sombre tone – a language that the people learn not to believe as it means the exact opposite of what it says. If the government claims that it won't raise the prices of oil, the people realise that the cheap oil will disappear so that they have to buy the expensive type anyway. If the Ministry of Health states that there are no signs of summer diseases, people understand that cholera is now a widespread epidemic. If the Minister of Interior assures everyone that a citizen committed suicide while under arrest, everybody realises that he was tortured to death.

Soon, the contagion of the virtual republic is transmitted from the regime to society as a whole: form is separated from content, religion is separated from behaviour and people care more about their image in the eyes of others than about maintaining coherence between their manners and moral standards. This virtual reality has made Egyptians – according to statistics – one of the best peoples in practicing religious rituals and one of the worst when it comes to involvement in corruption, bribery and sexual harassment. A political regime constitutes the spine of society: if it's fair and straightforward, the citizens' sense of justice will provide them with a motive for work. They will know that the way to promotion in their work is competence, not loyalty to the regime. But if the regime is unjust and corrupt, the citizens become frustrated. They lose faith in justice, and so selfishness, negativity, hypocrisy and opportunism become predominant characteristics, because these are the ones that guarantee them advancement in life. In the virtual republic, relations between the people and the regime seem to be real, but in reality they're false. The state pays teachers a small sum of money as if it were a salary, the teachers pretend to accept it, but then go to school to find clients to whom they can give private lessons. The state pays doctors a few pounds as if it were a salary and they pretend to accept it; they go to the government hospital to sign for attendance, but then play truant and work in private hospitals that give them real salaries. The governor makes inspections that the civil servants know about in advance, so that the governor looks active and the civil servants can give the impression that they are extremely competent.

Despotism always leads to the destruction of society, as positive values such as honesty, courage, and integrity are replaced by hypocrisy and opportunism. That's how Egypt was under the rule of Mubarak and so it declined in all fields. Egyptians then revolted and toppled the tyrant, and for a while it seemed that they were cured from the disease of the virtual state. The Egyptian who takes good care when cleaning their apartment but throws their rubbish down onto the street or onto the outer stairs doesn't have a sense of belonging beyond the confines of their apartment. After the revolution, we saw this destructive, insulated citizen go out with their family to clean and decorate the streets. After the revolution, we saw the Egyptian who had never voted in elections before go out and spend hours standing in the long queues in front of the election committees in order to vote. The Egyptian, who used to fear entering a police station, started to demonstrate and face bullets without fear. Thanks to the revolution, the sense of belonging and self-worth that Egyptians lost under the rule of Mubarak was regained.

Then, however, instead of drafting a new constitution, the former military council collaborated with the Muslim Brotherhood in order to push through a reform of the old one and, thereby, maintain the foundations of the Mubarak regime. The members of the military council were nervous about change and its consequences, and the Muslim Brothers betrayed the revolution, abandoning its aims for the sake of consolidating their own power in Egypt.

The former military council is responsible for the decline of living conditions in Egypt, the deterioration of security, and for several massacres in which hundreds of demonstrators were killed, and for which nobody has been held accountable. The rule of the Brotherhood was the other side of this corrupt coin and an extension of Mubarak's rule. The Brothers tried to restore the virtual republic because they're divorced from reality and incapable of grasping the truth; they live in a world where they consider themselves the only defenders of religion, which allows them to commit the most horrible of crimes while thinking that they are protecting Islam. On 30 June millions of Egyptians took to the streets to get rid of a liar, a failure and a despotic president who had abolished democracy and placed his personal decisions above the law. This moment was a great opportunity for establishing real democracy. Egyptians of all political orientations participated in overthrowing the Brotherhood and formed the 30 June Front,[1] which included the whole spectrum of society without any exception. The army then listened to the demands of the people and a political road map was drawn up, about which everybody was enthusiastic. Later, the Committee of 50[2] was established, and it made strong efforts to draft a democratic constitution that would lay the basis for a lawful state and the Egyptian people approved it by a great majority. Yet, we now discover that the present authority still lives in the virtual republic and that Mubarak's policies continue to prevail in Egypt. There may be some in power who are comitted to establishing a true democracy, but it's clear that there are powerful elements that are hostile to the revolution because they want to maintain their privileged positions. They have a great desire to take revenge on the revolutionaries and they are carrying out a plan intended to restore the Mubarak regime in its entirety.

The Egyptian state is engaged in a war against terrorism and it's our duty to support it, but there are elements in positions of power whose main war is against the revolution. They use the war against terrorism as a pretext to end the revolution and to take revenge on the revolutionaries who ousted their former leader, Mubarak, and had him thrown into prison. What is the connection between a war against terrorism and rounding up the revolutionaries and imprisoning them for years on trumped-up charges? What is the connection between war against terrorism and tarnishing the reputations of the revolutionaries and slandering them on television? Why doesn't the attorney general take action against the hired slanderers who defame the revolutionaries on television channels mostly owned by those with links to the Mubarak regime? In whose interests is it to see the brave youth of the revolution thrown into prison for years simply because they demonstrated peacefully? What's the value of the constitution – which was approved by a referendum that cost Egypt millions of pounds – if whoever rules Egypt now thinks of it as a mere trifle and violates it every day? The elections law that was issued a few days ago violates the constitution in more than one place. It was tailored in favour of a certain candidate and this is the best evidence that there are people in powers who want to return Egyptians to the times of Mubarak. Which democracy are they talking about if the interim president ignores the opinion of the Council of State – the authority in this matter – by filling the Supreme Electoral Committee with his own

1 The Tamarod campaign launched a front to administer the 30 June demonstrations and the transitional period likely to follow it. The campaign was the first to call for nationwide demonstrations demanding the overthrow of the current government and the holding of early presidential elections.

2 The Committee of 50 were charged with revising a draft proposed by a 10-member committee. Both groups were appointed by interim President Adly Mansour. Headed by former Arab League chief and Mubarak-era Foreign Minister Amr Moussa, the Committee of 50 comprises an impressively diverse cross section of Egyptian political and societal interests – save the conspicuous absence of political Islamists.

followers? Didn't the same thing lead to the declaration of Morsi's victory in the presidential elections before investigating the claims of misconduct that were levelled against him? Didn't that committee bury the appeals presented by Sabahi against Shafik in the first round of elections? Who will implement the terms of the elections law where General el-Sisi is concerned? Which is the institution that can reveal the sources of funding for el-Sisi's campaign and ensure that he stays within the lawful spending limit? How can we talk about equal opportunities while state and private media channels have no occupation except to flatter el-Sisi day and night, and the streets of Cairo swarm with propagandists carrying banners of him? Who dares remove the pictures of el-Sisi from the streets, and who dares ask about the budget of his campaign? What's the difference between the lawmakers who tailored the recent elections law and those who made the constitutional reforms to pave the way for Gamal Mubarak to inherit the country of Egypt from his father?

General el-Sisi has played a heroic role in protecting Egyptians from terrorism and it's his right to stand in the presidential elections according to the law, but Egypt is now going back to square one, as if a revolution had never happened. It's another attempt at fabricating a despotic state that merely looks as though it is a democracy. They want to restore the virtual republic, but they won't succeed because Egyptians are not willing to return to living under the grip of fear. The millions of Egyptians who faced bullets and tanks and carried the dead and the injured on their shoulders will not give up their dream of freedom. Whoever drafted the elections law still lives in the era of Mubarak, but they should know that the old system can no longer be applied in our country. The enemies of the revolution, who remain in power, think that they can do whatever they want to Egyptians and that the security forces will discipline anyone who objects. They worked hard to defame the revolution through their agents in the media, they put the heroes of the revolution in prison thinking that it would end the revolution, and now they want to retrieve the whole regime in its entirety. Their calculations are stupid and hollow because Alaa Abd el-Fattah, Ahmad Douma, Omar Hazek and their fellow activists may have participated in the revolution but they're not its owners. The revolution belongs to the Egyptian people as a whole, and they will never rest until all the its goals are acheived. There is a wave of strikes taking place over the whole of Egypt. Those on strike are the real makers of the revolution and they now demand the rights for which they revolted. The revolution shall continue and it shall prevail because the future belongs to it while its enemies live in the past. And who can stop the future?

Democracy is the answer.

Reviewing the Lessons of History

17 March 2014

The Mustrod incident constitutes an important event in modern Egyptian history. On 15 March 2014 a terrorist group killed six Egyptian soldiers at an army checkpoint in the area of Mustrod. Investigations proved that the martyred soldiers were asleep and no rounds were fired in defence. The incident highlighted a number of deficiencies on the part of the armed forces. The terrorists, who supported the Muslim Brotherhood, also declared that they aimed to bring down the Egyptian army, which has always been the backbone of the nation. Although General el-Sisi was the acting minister of defence at the time, he has been, in effect, the real ruler of the country since the Brotherhood was ousted. Historians agree that, after the Mustrod incident, el-Sisi understood that he had two options: either to continue the fight against terrorism according to the policies he adopted following the fall of the Brotherhood, or to introduce the following reforms to combat it:

First: The abolition of the anti-protest law and the release of all the detainees. Although the constitution made provision for the right to demonstrate, the interim government issued an unconstitutional law against protesting; this was exploited by the security forces to randomly arrest demonstrators, beat and torture them, and then fabricate charges against them such as causing disorder, disturbing the peace amongst others. This led to the detention of thousands of citizens, most of whom had nothing to do with the Muslim Brothers. In fact, some of them were revolutionary activists who had played a significant role in overthrowing the Brotherhood. Some in the security authorities were motivated by a desire to retaliate against those who had ousted Mubarak in January 2011. All these oppressive measures tarnished the image of the Egyptian authorities in countries abroad, some of which had supported the rule of the Muslim Brothers. Furthermore, the Brotherhood had been trying to persuade the world that the events that began on 30 June constituted a coup, not a revolution. The prevailing despotism caused many young people to withdraw their support for the interim government because they had seen how their friends and fellow activists had been detained and then handed long prison sentences simply for taking part in demonstrations. Historians believe that had General el-Sisi suspended the unconstitutional anti-protest law, released detainees and respected the constitution and human rights then he would have improved the image of the Egyptian government and restored the trust of all citizens – things which would have aided the fight against terrorism.

Second: The introduction of special courts for hastening verdicts in cases involving terrorist crimes. While young revolutionary activists had been given speedy trials before being thrown into prison simply for taking part in demonstrations, the real terrorists who used bombs and killed innocent people had been given slow trials. It was, therefore, necessary to designate special courts where terrorists could be quickly tried and sentenced in order to better combat terrorism.

Third: The introduction of measures to improve social equality. Some Egyptians possessed great fortunes that put them amongst the wealthiest in the world. Meanwhile, at least half of the Egyptian population was living below the poverty line and spending less than one dollar a day on their families. It is worth noting that 60 per cent of Egyptians lived without a proper sewage system and that one in every three of Cairo's inhabitants lived in a slum. That wide gap between the rich and the poor was one of the causes behind the revolution, but the issue was not properly dealt with by the successive governments after the revolution took place. Historians believe that el-Sisi should have immediately implemented steps to promote social justice, such as implementing higher taxation to the rich; ending the subsidies for the gas, electricity and water used by factories that sell their products at international prices; and linking the minimum wages to the maximum in the governmental sector. In addition, steps should have been taken to get rid of thousands of consultants in the different ministries, whose salaries amount to millions of pounds without them having to do any real work, and abolishing the special funds which people in power use to steal public money without the judiciary knowing about it. These procedures would have been likely to secure new income for the state through which it could have provided a more dignified life for millions of the poor. Such steps would have helped to end social tensions that were given expression in a series of strikes that involved a broad section of society. The achievement of social justice represented a fundamental factor in winning the war against terrorism.

Fourth: Putting in place a code for good conduct in the media. After the revolution, some of the wealthiest amongst the remnants of the Mubarak regime founded wide-reaching and succesful media channels. After the fall of the Brotherhood, the television channels belonging to Mubarak's old guard waged a bitter war against the revolution because they considered it a conspiracy. They accused the revolutionary youth of treason, and state security agents became media stars who obtained millions of pounds and presented television programmes devoted to defaming the revolutionaries. The smear campaign against the revolution exceeded all limits of morality and law; the agents amongst those working in the media started to broadcast private calls of some of the young activists, revealing details about their personal lives. This represented a violation of the constitution which asserted that a person's privacy could not be infringed upon without authorisation from the attorney general. The smear campaign was condemned by the authorities, but the state itself didn't do anything to stop it, which gave the impression that it was pleased with it; either that, or those with links to the old Mubarak regime were stronger than the state itself. Giving the revolution a bad name was an important step for the these people so that they could maintain their privileged positions and regain their power. Accordingly, the revolutionary youth – the noblest and the most courageous of all Egyptians, who faced death, and tens of thousands of whom were killed and injured for the sake of freedom and justice for all Egyptians – were then accused of treason by some sycophants who had been followers of Gamal Mubarak and obedient servants to his mother, Suzanne. With the continuation of the slandering and detention campaigns, it was natural for the revolutionaries to take a stand against the interim government which they accused of being counter-revolutionary. Therefore, implementing a code of good conduct in the media and stopping these unjust campaigns against the revolution was a necessary step for the revolutionary youth to regain their trust and to support the state in its war against terrorism.

Fifth: The application of transitional justice. Since the start of the revolution, thousands of Egyptians have been killed. These deaths took place during the last days of Mubarak's rule, under the rule of the military council and then under the Brotherhood. After each massacre various narratives emerged and accusations were thrown around. During the massacres, Egyptians witnessed security officers killing demonstrators and running them over with their trucks; yet, not a single person was held accountable for these crimes. All of the police officers who were accused of killing demonstrators pleaded their innocence and many were even promoted to higher ranks, which caused anger and bitterness amongst the families of those who had been killed and injured. Implementing a system of transitional justice was a necessary step through which legal committees, independent from the regular legal system, should have been formed to investigate all the massacres that Egyptians suffered and, thereby, expose the identity of those who killed peaceful demonstrators. In this case, the relatives of the victims could have forgiven the killers in return for damages, or the killers could have been put on trial depending on the evidence. Historians surmise that General el-Sisi would have known that the society would never heal until justice for those who had been killed had been achieved. Thus, transitional justice would have aided the battle to eliminate terrorism.

Sixth: Ensuring free and fair elections. When the nomination of General el-Sisi for the presidency approached, the lawmakers, who for so long had tailored laws according to Mubarak's desires and those of his son, burst into action and reinforced the decisions of the Supreme Electoral Committee (SPEC). Those who ran in the presidential elections could not appeal the decisions made by the SPEC except directly through the committee itself. This made the committee both judge and jury in matters pertaining to itself, something that contradicted the most basic rules of justice. The State Council rejected the new authority of the committee, insofar as it constituted a clear violation of the constitution. Yet, the government insisted on its autonomy and passed an elections law that was impossible to enforce fairly on all candidates. This meant that the presidential elections, in which el-Sisi was the victor, were reminiscent of the rigging that took place under Mubarak which allowed him to rule the country for 30 years. Historians noticed that el-Sisi's publicity campaign used the same methods that Mubarak had used. They noticed that the remnants of the Mubarak regime put all their support behind his nomination; they spent millions on his publicity, believing that el-Sisi would be a continuation of Mubarak's rule and that they would get to keep the money and the lands they plundered from the country. Making the SPEC an accountable body, and that holding the presidential elections in accordance with democratic standards and under international supervision would have given the new president legitimacy and would have filled Egyptians with trust after having revolted for the sake of real democracy.

All historians agree that taking these measures would have led to victory in the battle against terrorism and they confirmed that General el-Sisi could have entered the history books as the founder of the first real democracy since the revolution in 1952. Did el-Sisi realise the seriousness of the situation after the Mustrod incident and introduce the necessary reforms or did he continue without altering his ineffective policies? Did General el-Sisi support the revolution or oppose it? Did he try to accomplish the aims of the revolution or did he consider it a conspiracy, like his former boss, General Tantawi, did? These are the questions that we shall explore in more detail during our next lesson.

Lesson exercises

Give a brief answer to the following questions:

1. What is the real significance of the Mustrod incident?
2. Why did the young revolutionary activists stop supporting the interim authority even though they were the main participants in toppling the Muslim Brotherhood?
3. What were special funds and what was their effect on the national economy?
4. Who were the lawmakers and what did they offer General el-Sisi?

5. Why did the television channels belonging to those with links to the Mubarak regime attack the revolutionaries?

Fill in the blanks using the appropriate word:

1. For General el-Sisi to maintain the trust of Egyptians, he should have supported _____ against the Mubarak regime.
2. Society will not begin to heal until there is _____ for the martyrs.
3. In the light of the inequality of opportunity between the presidential candidates, the bias of the state apparatus being behind General el-Sisi, the continuation of oppression and the strengthening of the Supreme Electoral Committee, the presidential elections would turn into a _____ that has only one protagonist.
4. We can never convince the world that the regime in Egypt is democratic when people are randomly _____ and tortured.

This ends the fifth lesson in the second unit of the third-grade history book of the academic year 2070–71

Democracy is the answer.

From Albert Einstein to General el-Sisi

31 March 2014

Just before midnight, a taxi driver stopped on Qasr al-Nil Street to pick up a client who asked that she be taken to Giza Square. The taxi made a stop at the end of the street when it hit a police checkpoint. A young policeman approached and said to the driver: "The license number is not clearly visible. You can't drive this car."

The driver said imploringly: "I'm very sorry, officer. I'll repaint it first thing tomorrow so that the number will be clear."

The officer got angry and swore at the driver, even insulting his mother. The driver, however, stayed silent.

Then, the woman in the car piped up, saying: "Shame on you, officer, for insulting a man of your father's age."

The officer looked at her angrily and said: "It's none of your business."

The woman replied: "I'm a lawyer and your job is to execute the law, not to insult people."

He smiled through gritted teeth and answered: "Do you want to execute the law? Fine."

The officer took the driver's driving license and gave him a receipt signed in his name allowing him to drive his car for one week. When they had driven away from the checkpoint the lawyer cheerfully told the driver: "You see? You have to stand up for your rights. That officer had no right to insult you. If every citizen whose rights had been violated did what we just did, then that officer would learn how to respect the law."

Before getting out of the taxi the lawyer gave the driver her business card which contained her phone number and the address of her office. She suggested that he call her so that they could go to the Traffic Department together and get his license back. He thanked her but went on his own the following day without her. He didn't get his license, however. He returned everyday that week, but to no avail. When the signed permit expired he was forced to stop driving his taxi. Even though he went to the Traffic Department several times after his permit had expired the licence was not to be found. One of the civil servants who worked in in the administration of the department asked him: "Did you make trouble with an officer?"

The driver told him about what had happened. The civil servant then said that the officer had probably held onto the license as a form of punishment. So the driver went to find the police officer. At first he denied that he had the license, but the driver persisted and begged until the officer forgave him and gave him back his license.

Later, the driver told me this story and when I asked him why he hadn't asked the lawyer to help him. I was surprised by his response. He said: "Damn the lawyer. She's the one who caused all this trouble."

I said to him: "The lawyer meant to defend your rights."

To which he replied: "I didn't ask her to defend my rights. I was about to reach an agreement with the policeman. She interfered and what did I gain from it? My license was taken, I had to work hard to get it back and I couldn't earn my living."

I asked him: "Do you think it's acceptable for an officer, who is the same age as your son, to insult you like that?"

The driver smiled, saying: "I did violate the law; the license number was more or less erased. The officer meant to give me a piece of his mind and reprimand me with a couple of words before letting me go. He's a young officer who's proud of the uniform; he wanted to show off and to use strong language. It's fine. Do insults stick to me? I'd rather he insulted me than prevented from earning my living."

This incident took place a few years ago and, in my opinion, is indicative of the situation in Egypt prior to the revolution. The driver – like millions of citizens – simply became accustomed to being humiliated. He despaired in his attempts to get justice and, so, he accepted injustice. On the other hand, there was a despotic authority, represented here by the police officer, which got used to doing whatever it wanted to citizens without any controls or accountability. It used to selectively implement the law, applying it or suspending it, according to its whims – not with the purpose of achieving justice, but as a means of punishing whoever dared rebel against it. With the tyranny of the authorities and the submission of the people, calls for liberty used to arise from time to time, but they fell on deaf ears. That was the case with Egyptians, until they suddenly rose up in a revolution that astonished the whole world. Submission, fear and surrendering to the will of the authorities was ended forever.

On 25 January 2011, millions of Egyptians revolted; they bravely confronted one of the most oppressive regimes in the world and forced Mubarak to step down. Egyptians who used to think being humiliated at the hands of those in power was an inevitable evil had a change of heart; they stood in front of police tanks and faced bullets with their bare chests, without fear and without any attempt to escape. It was as if Egyptians suddenly ran out of patience and rebelled. Quite simply, what happened was a miracle. Egypt lost thousands of martyrs and then faced several massacres for which the former military council was responsible. Egyptians weren't defeated, nor did they forget their dream of justice and freedom. Then the Muslim Brotherhood took power and it soon became clear that it was no different to the Mubarak regime. Egyptians took to the streets in millions and managed to oust President Morsi, who had lost his legitimacy when he staged a presidential coup and issued a constitutional decree that suspended the democratic system and put his presidential decrees above the law.

What happened in Egypt has happened before in all revolutions. Suddenly, Egyptians became transformed: they found their courage, claimed ownership of their country and decided to change it with their own hands. The real achievement of the Egyptian revolution is this human change that occurred in Egyptians; it altered their vision, thinking and behaviour. This change was not understood by any of those who reached power after the revolution, be it the military council, the Muslim Brotherhood or even the present authority – they have all dealt with the people as if a revolution had never taken place. Everything that the present authority does is taken verbatim from the Mubarak textbook. Several satellite channels and newspapers have taken it upon themselves to flatter the regime and slander the opposition using media people who are puppets in the hands of state security. The elections law stands in contradiction with the constitution and defies the verdicts of the State Council; it makes the Supreme Electoral Committee unaccountable, so that it can do whatever it likes with the results, just as it did during Mubarak times. The guarantees regarding the fairness of the elections are false and have, in fact, been tailored to serve General el-Sisi.

Added to this is the anti-protest law. It doesn't conform to the constitution and is used by the authorities to take revenge on the young revolutionary activists by throwing them in prison for years simply because they dared to protest or raised banners that said: "No to the constitution". Members of the opposition have been defamed on television with alleged recordings of their telephone conversations being aired; this is a violation of their privacy. When they complain to the attorney general, their complaints gather dust in drawers for months and no attempt is made to investigate them. On the other hand, a judge speedily sentences 529 defendants to death after only two sessions in court. Random detentions, torture and selective implementation of the law continue to be prevalent.

What's really saddening is that, unlike the Mubarak regime, the present authority doesn't have to resort to despotism; it came to power with the legitimacy it was granted by the millions of Egyptians who demonstrated on 30 June to end the rule of the Brotherhood. Is it necessary for the interim government to commit all these violations of human rights? The Muslim Brothers committed crimes that would lead to their sentencing under any fair legal system, so why do the authorities get involved in show trials, random detentions and torture? The present authority violates human rights and when the world denounces these violations, the people in power talk about a universal conspiracy of the whole world against Egypt. If there were such a conspiracy against our nation, the policies of the present authorities would help it succeed. The present government deals with us the same way Mubarak did, as if we were its subjects and as if it is at liberty to grant us our rights or deprive us of them at will. This is the same old reasoning that lost its validity in the wake of the revolution and that led to the fall, and subsequent imprisonment, of Mubarak. Yet, the interim government still tries to re-impose it on Egyptians. Despite our respect for General el-Sisi, who heroically sided with the people against terrorism, what is happening now in Egypt will not lead to democracy. El-Sisi is surrounded by several types of people: dervishes who sing his praises and who are always ready to drown out whoever criticises him in a torrent of insults; those who flatter him today so that they can benefit from him tomorrow, the same way they have done with every ruler before him; and the remnants of the old Mubarak regime that robbed Egyptians for 30 years and now want to safeguard their interests by any means.

El-Sisi will not benefit except from those who advise him and alert him to his errors. He still has a great opportunity to change Egypt, to accomplish the goals of the revolution and to establish a real democracy, but what is happening now is leading him away from the right path. It's el-Sisi's right to stand for elections and it's the right of the Egyptian people to have free and fair elections after a revolution in which they lost thousands of martyrs.

El-Sisi enjoys such popularity that he would most probably win the presidency, so why not ensure that the elections have fair and transparent rules? In this way, were he to win, his victory would be well-deserved and respected by everybody. The state combats terrorism that targets our police and army soldiers but history teaches us that despotism doesn't end terrorism; on the contrary, it provides a pretext for its continuation. Only justice can end terrorism, because justice combats the root causes of terrorism. If General el-Sisi wants to establish a democratic state, he has to follow the following steps:

1. Abolish the unconstitutional anti-protest law and release all those detained under this law.

2. Revoke the Supreme Electoral Committee's immunity and keep the state apparatus neutral during elections. Furthermore, elections must be conducted under the eye of international observers and guarantees must be put in place to ensure that all candidates are given the same opportunities.

3. Implement transitional justice by forming independent legal committees that will reinvestigate all the massacres that Egyptians have suffered in recent years, so that the victims are compensated and the killers are put to trial.

4. Take measures to address the issue of social justice, such as a progressive tax on individuals and companies, and putting the minimum and maximum wages into action. Furthermore, "special funds" involving billions of Egyptian pounds taken from the people must be taken by the state and used for the public good.

5. Enforce the constitution and respect human rights, prohibit torture and random detentions.

The above are the steps that General el-Sisi should follow immediately if he wants to put Egypt on the right path. Yet, if the present authority continues to imitate the Mubarak regime, it will come to the same end. Albert Einstein once reportedly said: "I can't understand how a person repeats the same behaviour in the same manner of thinking and the same circumstances and expects different results."

I hope el-Sisi understands the meaning of Einstein's words.

Democracy is the answer.

How Can We Stop the Conspiracy?

7 May 2014

When I was a student at the University of Illinois in the United States, graduate students had to pay the secretary of the department a few dollars a week towards the "coffee fund". The money was used for buying coffee, tea and snacks that the secretary put in a separate room for us all to partake of. There was an Egyptian colleague who was the head of the Egyptian Students Union and he used to drink more of the coffee and eat more of the snacks than everybody else. Yet, he only paid his share of the coffee fund once or twice before he stopped paying it altogether. The secretary asked him to contribute his share to the fund but he avoided paying her time and again, so she decided to confront him. He got very angry and said: "Do you know who I am? I'm the head of the Egyptian Students Union in the United States; I'm a representative of Egypt. It's wrong of you to ask me to pay a share for coffee and things like these. I won't tolerate it."

The secretary didn't understand the link between representing Egypt in the students union and making a contribution to the coffee fund, so she quarrelled with him and said that he had one of two options: either to pay his share or to stop having coffee and snacks. Thus, the colleague had to reluctantly pay his share. We met once after this incident and he tried to persuade me that the secretary hated Arabs and Muslims, quoting things that she had said before in an attempt to prove that she was racist. I told him: "The secretary may or may not be a racist but your quarrel doesn't have anything to do with Egypt or with Islam. She fought with you because you made the mistake of thinking that you can eat and drink at your colleagues' expense. Therefore, if there's anybody who brings shame on Arabs and Muslims, it is you and no one else."

He wasn't convinced of course, because, like many others, he found it difficult to admit when he was wrong. Instead he found it much easier to blame others for his own mistakes.

I recall this incident because we often act like this in Egypt. We blame others for our failures and mistakes as if we are not responsible for our own actions. The media keeps trying to convince Egyptians that all the nations of the world conspire against us. No one asks themselves if the problems we suffer from are purely the result of our mismanagement and our own failure to handle the crises.

What the media refers to as a "grand conspiracy against Egypt" is not a new discovery; it has been the nature of international relations throughout history. Super-powers are not charity associations directed by the feeling of mercy, but political entities that don't care for anything except following their own interests, including conspiring or even waging wars. It's by no means new for a nation to conspire against another in order to further its own interests. The United States claims to defend democracy, yet it has supported the worst dictatorial regimes – it supported the oppressive and corrupt Mubarak regime for 30 years because this served its own interests. When the revolution erupted, the United States tried its utmost to save Hosni Mubarak until it realised this was futile, so it gave him up. It then turned to the Brotherhood as a substitute for Mubarak, and so it supported it while turning a blind eye to all of Morsi's crimes. Morsi issued his infamous constitutional declaration, annulled the democratic system, ordered thousands of demonstrators to be detained, ordered the killing of demonstrators in front of Heliopolis Palace, and then demanded the killing of 45 citizens in Port Said. We didn't hear the American administration speak up against any of these crimes because it considered Morsi an ally whose crimes should be condoned. When Egyptians revolted against the Brotherhood on 30 June and toppled it, the US showed very little enthusiasm for the new regime in Egypt.

The interim government could have taken genuine steps to guarantee a democratic transition. It could have publicly endorsed freedom of expression and enforced the law on everybody equally. It could have shown respect for the new constitution which Egyptians voted for. These steps would have forced the international community to acknowledge that Egypt was a functioning democracy. However, the authorities did the opposite of what they should have done: they carried out arbitrary arrests, detentions and other despotic measures on a large scale. They issued an anti-protest law that goes against the constitution and violates human rights. The law was used to hand out long prison sentences to hundreds of citizens just for demonstrating. Some youths are even spending years in prison for the mere reason that they carried a banner asking other citizens to say no to the constitution. A judge – with all due respect to him – sentenced 528 defendants to death after only two sessions in court. Given all this, do we also now consider the criticisms of the these despotic measures levelled by human rights organisations to also be part of the grand conspiracy against us or, rather, should we instead blame the interim government, which came to power through the revolution but then turned against it and continued Mubarak's despotic policies and the practice of tailoring of laws to suit itself? A government that commits human rights violations doesn't want anybody to criticise it and it thinks of its opponents as undercover agents and traitors simply because they stand up for justice and their rights.

The conspiracy theory propagated by the media day and night has always been an defining part of all dictatorial regimes throughout history. No dictator can dispose of the conspiracy theories because they provide them with several benefits, the most important of which are discussed below:

First: They help with covering up crimes. Mubarak ruled Egypt for 30 years and let it decline in every field. A small, fortunate elite enjoy most of the wealth while half of the population live below the poverty line. Millions of Egyptians live in slums without proper sewage systems, clean water or electricity. They suffer from poverty, illness and a lack of education. Egyptians revolted against Mubarak and ousted him but the Mubarak regime remains intact in the form of its institutions and interest groups; it was maintained by the former military council and then later by the Muslim Brotherhood. The people revolted and toppled the Brotherhood on 30 June and the Mubarak regime is now trying to regain power, and in doing so, it adopts conspiracy theories to wash its hands of the crimes it committed against Egyptians. The remnants of the Mubarak regime have spent millions on new satellite television channels so that they can brainwash the masses of Egyptians and convince them that the Egyptian revolution was nothing more than an American/Serbian/Israeli/Turkish/Qatari plot. They would have us believe that the millions of Egyptians who revolted for the sake of freedom on 25 January 2011, and who lost their lives as a result, were a group of foreign-hired agents. This nonsense doesn't even deserve a response. Hosni Mubarak wasn't a fighter against Western imperialism; he was an obedient servant of American policies, to the extent that the leaders of Israel described him as a strategic asset for the Jewish state. In any case, there were signs that revolution was on the cards ten whole years before it finally erupted. Those who were aware of the vigorous political activism for change already knew that the revolution was inevitably on its way. The United States' shock at the eruption of the revolution in Egypt is well documented, and we all saw America's attempts at rescuing the Mubarak regime. Nevertheless, despite this, the conspiracy theory is continually rolled out by the Mubarak gang as a means to get their power back.

Second: They can be employed to justify oppression. A dictator usually uses a conspiracy theory to delay demands for greater rights. If countries conspire against our nation, nobody is allowed to ask for minimum wages that can guarantee decent living standards for the poor. Nobody is allowed to ask for a limit on high wages that those in power receive, or for the implementation of progressive taxation for the rich, because we're too busy fighting against an international plot against the country. A tyrannical regime also uses conspiracy theories to justify the repression of its opponents. If the whole world is conspiring against the adored leader, then he should have the right to throw citizens in prison. Horrific torture could even be considered a necessary evil when the country is facing an international conspiracy. Psychological studies maintain that the officer who practices torture has constructed a negative image of his victims in order to override his conscience. The officer is a human being after all; in his daily life he plays the role of a father, a husband and maybe even a good neighbour who helps out in his local community. He's often a highly religious person and so he needs the conspiracy theory to justify to himself the crime of torturing others and violating their human dignity. He needs to be convinced that all the opponents of the regime are traitors who want to destroy the nation; only then can he see himself, not as a torturer, but as a hero who is acting to protect the people and the nation.

Third: They are useful for crushing opponents. When the conspiracy theory takes root there's no space for differing opinions; there's only one opinion that takes the interest of the country into consideration. That is naturally the opinion of the leader, and whoever deviates from it or disagrees with it is either a fifth columnist or part of a terrorist sleeper cell. What is happening in the Egyptian media at present has no equal in the entire world; some television programmes have turned into investigation agencies and courts of law that issue verdicts on air. Some presenters have turned into political preachers who spend hours teaching audiences the official line and slander whoever expresses a different opinion from their own. The use of smear campaigns by channels belonging to those with links to the old Mubarak regime against anyone who doesn't support the present authorities violate all moral and professional standards. It has become normal for a presenter to curse opponents, to use incidents occurring in people's private lives against them and to accuse them of being undercover agents on programmes watched by millions of people. These character assassinations are completely unsubstantiated by any evidence. Instead they are backed up by the idea that the people they are attacking are working on behalf of some mysterious international plot.

There's no international conspiracy against us and it isn't logical to believe that foreign countries always want to harm us; those countries simply have interests that they are going to protect even if this leads to us being deprived of our rights. Instead of spreading the fear of conspiracy, we need to ask ourselves: if these plots really do exist, how can we put a stop to them? We need to work hard and competently to further the interests of our nation. But when the authorities propagate a conspiracy theory so that they blame it for their own failures, they are guilty of even greater failure. Egypt faces a wave of criminal terrorism that has led to the cowardly murders of police officers and soldiers. Furthermore, our country is going through a serious crisis because of corruption, neglect, poverty, disease, and ignorance – the inheritance left to us by Mubarak, the military council and then the Brotherhood. We can't combat terrorism by using oppression; we can only triumph over it through justice. We can't go forward until we get closure on the past.

A transitional justice system should be implemented to get justice for those who were killed and so that their families are given compensation for their losses. Thanks to the revolution, Egyptians have changed and they will never again accept despotism under any name. Our only way forward is to take real steps towards establishing democracy and the rule of law. Only then will all conspiracies be rendered void.

Democracy is the answer.

On the Evils of Brainwashing

14 April 2014

A friend of mine used to dream of becoming a journalist, so he enrolled in Cairo University's Faculty of Mass Communication. After he graduated he worked as an intern at a national newspaper. During one of the referendums held by Mubarak to renew the term of his presidency, my friend said to me: "I have a problem. My boss asked me to cover the referendum in the Qasr al-Nil district. I stayed at the polling station all day long but very few people actually came to vote. I'm supposed to submit the coverage this evening and I don't know what to write."

I said to him: "What's the problem? Write what happened."

"Experienced colleagues at the paper gave me a warning. They said that if I write that the polling stations were empty, the piece won't be published and I will lose my place at the newspaper. But if I write the opposite, my boss will recommend that I be given a job at the paper."

I told him many things about the conscience of a journalist and the ethics of writing and warned him against lying to the readers. He listened to me in silence and then he shook hands with me and left. When I read what he wrote in the newspaper I was shocked; he elaborated on the long lines of voters queuing in front of ballot boxes and confirmed that the percentage of participation was unprecedented. He attributed this to the great popularity enjoyed by Hosni Mubarak. My friend was appointed and quickly promoted. He is now the head of a media institution where hundreds of journalists work. I recall him now when I watch how some television presenters shower General el-Sisi with praise while denouncing and insulting anyone who criticises him, no matter how objective the criticism may be. There's no doubt that those announcers are like my friend; they faced the same dilemma: either to stick to the truth and satisfy your conscience and lose everything, or, do whatever is asked of you, no matter how immoral, and be rewarded with wealth and fame. We shouldn't tar everyone with the same brush, of course. There are still many people working in the media who strictly adhere to their principles and perform their work with integrity and professionalism. Yet, there are others who continue to serve the security apparatus and the regime. To abandon one's principles in return for personal gain is a human phenomenon that flourishes in societies governed by despotic authorities. Most people are not heroes, they're just ordinary people who want to earn their living and raise their children even if the price is a bad conscience.

An honest media is an advanced tool for knowledge that provides people with accurate information and shows all points of view for people to be able to form an opinion. In the Egyptian media, however, you will find that many outlets have adopted the following tactics:

First: Many outlets employ insinuation and smear tactics, as demonstrated in the following statement: "The security forces managed to arrest a member of the April 6 Youth Movement; he was in the company of a foreigner in a downtown hotel, and on inspection, a laptop and foreign currency were found in his possession."

This piece of news, which is by no means unique, identifies the defendant through his membership to the April 6 Youth Movement; this represents an attempt to tarnish the wider group. Moreover, mentioning that the defendant was in the company of a foreigner, that he had a laptop and foreign currency all hint at his being an agent who gets his funding from abroad. None of these things are crimes, of course; he may simply have a friend who happens to be a foreigner, while the foreign currency could have been obtained through a wire from his father in the gulf, for instance. And finally, "finding" a laptop requires no inspection; it's a big appliance that cannot easily be hidden.

Such poisonous news doesn't exist in democratic countries, but it's always used in Egypt to smear anyone who opposes the regime. Another tactic used by the authorities is to publish articles in an unknown newspaper accusing their opponents of horrible crimes, such as forging their university degrees, for example. You would think of this as a trivial matter that doesn't deserve a response, but were it to happen to you, you might be shocked the next day when you get a call from a journalist in one of the national newspapers asking you to comment on the accusation. Then you would fall into the trap: if you refused to comment, the journalist would say that you refused to talk about your forged degree, and if you denied the accusation, they would simply write that you refused to admit that your degree was forged. Finally, after endless media exposure, your name would inevitably be connected to your supposedly forged degree in the minds of many people. The third way that they ruin the reputations of their opponents is by having them interviewed on television; they get people to call into the show and angrily accuse the interviewee of being an agent who wants to destroy the nation. The television presenter will then smile and might even object to the insults, yet still allow them. There are also those who specialise in slander; they are like guard dogs that tear apart anybody who dares to take a stand in opposition to the regime. These people usually enjoy protection from the state, so there's no hope in taking them to court. These slanderers take out indecipherable pieces of paper from their pockets and explain that they're reports from security agencies. Then they start cursing their opponents, accusing them of being anything from Israeli agents to the clients of prostitutes or homosexuals. Thus, some media institutions in our country act in the most unethical ways possible.

Second: Many media outlets seek to incite the people. In November 2009, a football match between Egypt and Algeria was held in the city of Omdurman, in Sudan. Some trouble broke out between Algerian and Egyptian fans, and the media in Egypt subsequently waged a massive campaign in which they insulted the whole of the Algerian people and claimed that the Egyptian fans had been exposed to what amounted to a slaughter. Alaa Mubarak called in to a talk show and started insulting the Algerians. The campaign soon achieved its goal: thousands of angry Egyptians surrounded the Algerian Embassy asking for the expulsion of the ambassador. The Algerian media returned even worse insults. Algerians demonstrated and burned down buildings that belonged to Egyptian companies. Recently, Ahmad Abou al-Ghiet, the minister of foreign affairs during the rule of Mubarak, declared in a television interview that that problem had been caused by the Egyptian media, that it had started the media war and accused Algerian fans without any proof. Nobody apologised to the Algerian people and none of those in the media who were responsible for the slander were held accountable, because they had been performing a task that they had been asked to perform. Another instance of incitement took place during the Maspero Square massacre in October 2011 when an anchor from the state media declared that Copts were assaulting the army and called upon the citizens to protect their armed forces; this led to hundreds of Islamic extremists attacking Copts some of whom were killed. Inciting violence is considered a crime in any democratic country, but in Egypt it seems to be one of the tasks performed by the media and so whoever dutifully performs this task is rewarded and promoted.

Third: They adopt binary thinking and distort the idea of criticism. After the revolutionary wave that ended the rule of the Brotherhood on 30 June, the Egyptian media started to follow George W. Bush's maxim of: "You're either with us or against us." If you think of 30 June as a revolutionary wave then you have to support what the police do without any reservations even if you use the anti-protest law to put innocent people in prison for years or randomly detain citizens and torture them. If you reject these oppressive measures the guard dogs will be let loose and you will be branded a traitor and a foreign agent. Egyptian media no longer allows for the idea that criticism can stem from caring about the interests of the nation or as a means to defend what is right. Criticism in the eyes of the media has become evidence that whoever utters it is a conspirator in a grand plot against the nation. Here the media establishes a hysterical binary type of thinking. If you object to the oppression of the innocent, then you don't care about the policemen who have fallen victims in the fight against terrorism. If you scientifically object to the piece of equipment that was invented by somebody affiliated with the army who claimed that it was a cure for AIDS and hepatitis C, then you hate your country's army, and you want to bring down the state, and perhaps you might even be funded by huge pharmaceutical companies seeking to undermine the value of this extraordinary invention.

Right now there is no space in the media for a balanced standpoint – one that strongly supports the security forces in their war against terrorism while denouncing torture and arbitrary detentions. No voice is given to those who are proud of the armed forces, but who are also critical of this absurd story about the device that can cure AIDS – a story which is damaging the army's reputation. You now have to choose between accepting everything the armed forces and the police do, or risk being branded a traitor to your country. The end result of this media hysteria is the collective brainwashing of Egyptians, totally blurring their vision in preparation for the return of the Mubarak regime to power. What is meant by "regime" here are the institutions of the Mubarak state which remain present and intact, and the huge interest groups represented by business people who made unimaginable fortunes thanks to their relationship with Mubarak, and who fear any change lest they should lose the wealth and the lands that they robbed from the Egyptian people.

The message of the media revolves around the notion that the January 25 Revolution was nothing but an American/Brotherhood/Qatari/Turkish/Serbian/Iranian/Israeli conspiracy and that the revolutionary activists are all traitors and undercover agents who get paid by their American handlers to bring anarchy to Egypt. On the other hand, the bloody hands of the Mubarak regime have been washed clean and all the crimes are now attributed to the Brotherhood while Mubarak is presented as a nationalist leader who stepped down to save the lives of Egyptians. The Muslim Brothers committed horrible crimes but let's not forget that the Battle of the Camel was executed by prominent figures of the Mubarak regime; we saw them with our own eyes while they were gathering thugs to attack Tahrir Square, just as we saw the police killing demonstrators during the revolution.

The United States and Israel supported their obedient servant, Mubarak, for 30 years until he was forced to step down after killing and injuring thousands of Egyptians. The young revolutionary activists are the noblest and the most honourable of all Egyptians and there isn't a shred of evidence that they received any foreign funding of any kind.

Several media channels have turned from being windows to the truth into huge machines that fabricate lies in order to erase the collective memory of Egyptians with the aim of ending the revolution and reinstating the old regime. If this miserable attitude doesn't change, we will all pay the price: first, because it creates an atmosphere of mistrust and suspicion amongst the members of society that prevents them from accomplishing any nationalist task, and secondly, because the exaggerated praise that is constantly being directed at General el-Sisi obscures the truth and prevents him from making right decisions. In democratic countries, there are popular standards that the media must adhere to. If a media person violates professional and moral codes, then audiences boycott their programme, which causes great losses to the producer, thereby forcing them to respect the public's opinion. Media channels should be institutions that report in the interests of the people and not just a few businessmen. In all cases history teaches us that the effect of dishonest media, no matter how it manages to influence public opinion, will be transient because nobody can fool all of the people all of the time. No matter how successful media campaigns are in deluding and slandering, they won't persuade millions of poor Egyptians to give up their right to live a dignified life. The revolution will continue, God willing, until all of its goals have been achieved.

Democracy is the answer.

Our Way to Good Morals

21 April 2014

There's no doubt that if you're a father of a young woman, you fear for her and worry about her being seduced by an unscrupulous young man. You might even imagine him hugging and kissing her, or worse. What can you do to protect your daughter? There are two methods: the first is to watch your daughter closely, not letting any hint or gesture pass unnoticed. You need to check her mobile phone while she's asleep and read her messages. You must ask the driver and the maid to tell you what she does minute by minute. You cannot allow her to go out except in the company of her brother or her mother, so as to guarantee that she doesn't get involved in any immoral act. This way you will enjoy peace of mind regarding your daughter. This is an illusory feeling, however, as she can always escape your surveillance and do whatever she wishes to do. There's another method which is to bring her up well and work on developing her conscience and then put your trust in her so that instead of feeling your oppression, she'll fear losing your trust. In this situation, you can allow your daughter to mix with society and trust that she will avoid being seduced because her virtue comes from inside; it's not imposed on her from the outside.

The relationship between a ruler and the people is similar to the relationship between a father and a daughter.

A democratic president considers their citizens capable of taking the right decision; they respect their will and don't impose anything on them. A dictator, on the other hand, never trusts the citizens to distinguish between what's right and what's wrong, no matter how educated or experienced they may be. A dictator believes that they know what is best for the citizens and will make decisions without consulting them. A few days ago, Egyptians were surprised by Prime Minister Ibrahim Mahlab's strange order to stop screenings of the movie *Halawet Rooh*, starring Haifa Wahbi, despite the movie having been approved by the censors. The issue here has nothing to do with the artistic value of the movie; the issue here is that the prime minister is interfering, for whatever reason, to stop the viewing of a movie. Ibrahim Mahlab is a politician who graduated from the Mubarak school. He is a member of the Shura Council and of the Policies Committee which was founded with the aim of helping Gamal Mubarak inherit the rule of Egypt from his father. Mahlab doesn't hide his links with the Mubarak regime, to the extent that during the Easter celebrations he congratulated Pope Tawadros II by presenting two notables of the old Mubarak regime to him: Ali Moseilhi, the minister of social solidarity, and Hamdy Zakzok, the minister of religious endowments during the rule of Mubarak. Mahlab's order to stop the viewing of the film *Halawet Rooh* resembles Mubarak's decrees in the following aspects:

First: Arbitrariness. Mahlab decided to stop the movie despite not having seen it; he simply responded to a complaint made by someone who pleaded for a ban on the film because the hero is a child who spies on a naked woman in one of the scenes – as if stopping the viewing would provide millions of street children with housing and a dignified life. The prime minister has no right to stop or release a film or even to evaluate it from an artistic point of view; he's not a film critic, a director or a script writer. His arbitrary decision is reminiscent of another arbitrary decision that was taken by Mubarak at one time when he ordered all of the pigs in Egypt to be killed, thinking that by this act he was combating swine flu. Mubarak was neither a specialist in viral diseases nor a veterinarian, and had no grounds to suggest a cure for swine flu but, like Mahlab, he thought he had the right to take final decisions regarding all issues and to impose them on specialists regardless of their soundness.

Mubarak's decree caused a farcical situation as hypocrites in positions of power competed over who could kill the largest number of pigs to the extent that one of the governors tried to show his loyalty to Mubarak by burying dozens of poor pigs in a pit full of burned lime. Mahlab's decree caused a similar farce as many citizens quickly presented pleas to him that he ban a certain television series and another film, although these two productions had also been approved by the official censors. It seems that from now on, any writer or film maker will need to ask for a meeting with the prime minister so that they can present their novel or film in order to avoid the possibility of him banning them at any moment.

Second: Paternalism. Mahlab said: "My conscience and my patriotism were what motivated me to ban the film." The meaning here is that Mahlab is more patriotic and conscientious than the film makers and all those who work as official censors. If Mahlab is so much more watchful of good values, why doesn't he intervene to stop the random detentions and torture that have been documented in several reports? Why doesn't he intervene to stop the slander and the accusations in official media channels against anyone who opposes the present regime? Why doesn't he stop programmes that broadcast private conversations of political opponents with the aim of smearing them? What did Mahlab do to combat the epidemic of sexual harassment against Egyptian women that far outweighs the effects of the *Halawet Rooh* film? Will banning the film put an end to sexual harassment, media misconduct and torture? If we don't object to the banning of *Halawet Rooh*, regardless of our opinion of it, then it will set a precedent for Mahlab to ban future books, films or plays; decisions he will justify by saying that he was motivated to uphold the good morals of Egyptians by conscientiousness and patriotism.

Third: In distracting the public. Sixty per cent of Egyptians live without a proper sewage system, one third of the inhabitants of Cairo live in slums, while more than half of the population of Egypt live below the poverty line, each of them spending less than ten Egyptian pounds a day on their family. This means that at least 40 million Egyptians live in dire poverty and inhumane conditions. What does Mahlab do for them? Added to this is the fierce war that the state wages against the terrorist groups where police and army officers are being killed daily. I thought that the prime minister would be more preoccupied with this imminent threat than a simple film. The economy is in a bad state, tourism is drawing its last breath and there is a huge shortage of electrical power because of Mubarak's decision to export gas to Israel because he wanted to win its support for his continued rule of Egypt. Instead of trying to find solutions to these huge problems, Mahlab brings up the subject of an allegedly immoral film in order to distract public attention away from our real problems. The decision to ban *Halawet Rooh* has divided people into supporters and opponents of the film's star actress, Haifa, and they have now become involved in this useless controversy, forgetting the misery in which they live. This is one of the hallmarks of Mubarak-style politics. We all remember how the Mubarak regime used to address people before football matches against foreign teams; media channels used to air patriotic songs and passionate speeches about having a love for Egypt; they would make it look like we were about to wage a war, not just to play a football match.

The question is this: does the prime minister really believe that his ban will stop people watching the movie? If he checks the internet, he will discover that the ban has actually made people want to see the film; initially it achieved little success in the cinemas but it is now watched by hundreds of thousands online. Since the internet revolution, it has become impossible to effectively ban a movie. Meanwhile, the Censorship Bureau is a despotic institution that pretends to safeguard religion and morality when its real goal is to prevent artists and intellectuals from criticising the regime – all of which helps to stabilise the rule of the dictator. Censorship of cinema is a fascist idea that considers the censor to be like the father of young children, as somebody who knows better than the people which films are suitable for them. The censors are ordinary civil servants who are trained to cut whatever is forbidden from films (and the most offensive material is, of course, political criticism) and they're often not even qualified to assess films from an artistic point of view. In democratic countries there's no censorship of cinema.

Many people will object, asking the eternal question: what can we do about pornography and how can we protect adolescents from viewing it? Firstly, let's remember that we're in the age of the internet, in which any adolescent can watch pornography for free. Secondly, I hope that we follow the steps of civilised countries that establish bodies like arts councils, which comprise artists and writers. They read the proposals for films and plays, evaluate them according to artistic merit and label them for general viewing or for adults only. By so doing, they protect the public taste and protect young people from being exposed to material that is not suitable for them. After a film is released, nobody has the right to ban it including the president but any citizen still has the right to resort to a court of law if they find that a film includes anything that contravenes any law. Establishing an arts council that can take up the task of evaluating films will help to protect freedom of expression and at the same time sideline tasteless films.

Why don't we apply this system in Egypt? The answer is that it would totally liberate the cinema from political restrictions and open a door for criticism of the president – which is exactly what the dictatorial authority does not want. Instead, it wishes to keep censorship in the hands of civil servants who are controlled by the minister of culture, who is an obedient employee under the prime minister, while the prime minister, in turn, enthusiastically supports any decision the president takes.

In democratic countries there's no one opinion or one taste. They have what is called "the culture of the remote control" which presumes that people's tastes are varied; even if you don't like a given film, others certainly will, and they have a right to watch it. You can easily use the remote control to change the movie that you don't like and to search for one that appeals to your taste. This is what takes place in countries that respect their citizens and treat them as mature adults, not as children who need the ruthless censorship imposed by a father. If Mahlab wants to uphold good morals, he should ban torture and arbitrary detentions, he should impose progressive taxation on the rich, minimum to maximum wages should be linked proportionately and he should do away with the ministers' councillors who earn millions of pounds. He has to abolish special funds and have the billions of pounds that they amount to be taken for the public purse. He should stop the subsidies for factories that sell their products at international prices while they get gas and electricity at prices subsidised by the people's money. Only then will the state have the resources to take it out of debt and to provide the poor with a decent and humane standard of living. This is how the prime minister should protect the values of Egyptians, instead of worrying about banning Haifa Wahbi from appearing on the screen.

Democracy is the answer.

What Happened to General el-Sisi?

28 April 2014

General Abdel Fattah el-Sisi woke up at five in the morning as usual. He took a shower, did his ablutions and put on his clothes. He felt a bit tired because of several meetings he had had the day before. He performed his prayers and started reciting the Qur'an while still sitting on the prayer mat. The general felt calm as he contemplated the meanings of the holy verses. Suddenly, however, he heard the loud bang of something heavy smashing to the floor. The general put the holy book down, jumped to his feet with his gun in his hand and cautiously walked towards the source of the sound. His room was large and separated from the rest of the house by a short corridor. He inspected this carefully, but found nothing out of the ordinary. "It must be exhaustion that made me imagine there was a banging sound," the general muttered to himself as he sat back down. He put the gun beside him and went back reading the Qur'an. He soon heard another sound, but this time the sound was like a hiss of steam. The general stood up quickly and looked towards the corridor; he could not fathom what he was seeing before him. The corridor was completely filled with a cloud of thick white steam, and soon after a figure emerged and started to walk towards him. Bit by bit, the general was able to make out the figure of a young man in a white sharkskin suit and a thin, blue tie in the style of the sixties. The general thought the figure looked vaguely familiar, but he was unable to place him. "I am Gamal Abdel Nasser," said the man.

The general was dumbstruck and stared at Nasser in disbelief: "I know that my visit from the other world will be a mystery to you, as you, people of the Earth, are imprisoned by your senses. I'm a young man now, although I died at the age of 50. I have come here today to talk to you about an important issue."

The general, trying to hold himself together, whispered: "Sir, I'm a pious man. God almighty said that the spirit is by command of my Lord, and there's nothing that's beyond the power of the Supreme Creator. Welcome, sir, I'm very pleased to see you. I have long admired you and considered you my idol."

Nasser sat on the couch next to the window and said: "How would you like me to address you? Shall I call you 'general'?"

The general replied excitedly: "Excuse me, sir. Firstly, I have retired from the army and I don't have a military rank anymore. In any case, I consider myself your student, sir. Please call me by my name."

"Very well Abdel Fattah, I have come down to say a few of words to you, but I must be brief because I don't have much time. Please sit down."

The general sat down and Nasser began: "I, together with some other former leaders of Egypt – Mohammad Farid, Mustafa Kamal, Saad Zaghloul and Mustafa el-Nahhas – have been watching you from the other world, Abdel Fattah. We all admired you when you took the side of the Egyptian people and helped to topple the Brotherhood. History will remember this, Abdel Fattah, that you rid Egypt of religious fascism and protected it from a civil war."

"Thank you, sir. I merely did my duty, no more, no less."

"Performing your duty at a time of danger is heroic. I also admire your diplomatic moves towards Russia. This is the best way to exercise pressure on America in order to force it take a just stand that would work for the benefit of Egypt."

"Hearing your words makes me feel proud, sir."

Nasser smiled as though he was thinking carefully about how to proceed, then he continued: "You know, I didn't take the trouble of descending from the other world just to praise you. Although I admire your courage and loyalty, my real purpose in coming was to alert you to your errors."

"Please do, sir, so as I can rectify them."

Nasser looked at the general and said: "The January 25 Revolution was a great moment in the history of our people; it proved to the whole world that we are civilised nation and that, whatever happens, we will never give up our dream of freedom and social justice. Then the Brotherhood came to power, suspended democracy and tried to hold the state to ransom. Millions of Egyptians took to the streets on 30 June to defend Egypt against the fascism of the Muslim Brothers."

The general nodded in agreement, and Nasser's voice got louder: "Abdel Fattah, with all due respect to your loyalty to the revolution, you now take decisions that serve the interests of the revolution's enemies."

The general's face showed signs of anxiety, so Nasser now spoke in an apologetic tone: "Forgive me for these harsh words. You know that we military men are known for being straightforward in word and action. I want you to know that I think of you as a son. If you really believe that the January 25 Revolution was a great thing, why do you allow it to be smeared by the liars in the media? Why do you allow those in the media, whom you know to be agents of the security forces, to appear on television every day claiming that the revolutionaries are unpatriotic and that they are foreign agents. Why do you allow the satellite channels owned by Mubarak's old guard to deceive the public by presenting the revolution as an American conspiracy? You know very well, Abdel Fattah, that this is a lie because you were the head of the military intelligence; you know that the revolution was a slap in the face for America and Israel. Why don't you declare this to the people?"

The general didn't answer, so Nasser continued: "I can understand that you chase killers and terrorists and present them to court, but why do you put the revolutionary activists in prison for the mere reason that they demonstrated? These youth are the finest of all Egyptians; without their courage and sacrifices, Egypt would never have brought down the Brotherhood."

Then the general spoke: "Allow me to explain, sir. I was only the minister of defence; I had nothing to do with the media or the law."

Nasser's smile grew wider, then he said: "Abdel Fattah, I told you that I don't have much time."

The general replied: "We had to issue the anti-protest law so that the country could settle down."

"This is a huge mistake. The protest law has been used to suppress the revolutionary activists while the terrorist attacks have not stopped. This way you're losing the revolutionaries. If the media accuses them of treason and the police detains, tortures and puts them in prison for years, do you expect them to support you after all this?"

"Sir, do you approve of the daily demonstrations and sit-ins?" asked the general.

"Demonstrations and sit-ins are the people's means of claiming their rights. Give them their rights or promise to provide them after a while. Then they will stop demonstrating."

"But they don't realise the complexity of the situation."

"On the contrary, you asked for a mandate from the Egyptian people to fight terrorism and millions of them granted you what you asked for; they put up with curfews for months without complaining. I don't understand how you can support the revolution but put those who started it in prison."

"I do support the revolution but I want stability."

"Stability will never be achieved unless there's justice. The stability that's based on the despotism of the Ministry of the Interior was what led to Mubarak ending up in prison. You have to take clear decisions, Abdel Fattah, as you are going to be the next president."

The general hastily said: "I still have an elections battle to go through."

Nasser laughed and said: "I told you, I don't have much time. I heard that you helped bring about a reconciliation between two sportsmen who had had a disagreement. Wouldn't it have been more worthwhile to bring one about between the government and the revolutionary activists?"

"Sir, don't forget that we're waging a war against terrorism. Not a single day passes without members of the army and police being killed in terrorist attacks."

Nasser answered: "War against terrorism is one more reason to put your house in order by cancelling the anti-protest law and releasing the activists that have been unjustly imprisoned. You also need to give guarantees to the poor."

"The poor of Egypt are the apple of my eye," answered the general.

"Wonderful words. Yet, social discrimination in Egypt cannot continue and you won't be able to stay on the fence. You have to declare your stand clearly; are you going to stand for the presidency in order to protect the rights of the poor or to serve the interests of the rich?"

The general smiled and said: "Sir, I wish there was no poverty in Egypt but the resources of the country are very limited ..."

"Please don't repeat Mubarak's words," Nasser interrupted. "Egypt is affluent but it is being plundered. Have you considered abolishing the system of special funds and using the billions they amount to for the public good? Have you thought of implementing minimum and maximum wages? Is it logical that some civil servants earn a million pounds a month while thousands of others earn less than a thousand pounds? Have you considered applying progressive taxation that can then go towards building schools and hospitals, as happens elsewhere in the world? Haven't you asked yourself why those with links to the old Mubarak regime spend millions on your election campaign?"

"I'll never protect anybody who has gone against the law."

"If you really believe in what you're saying," said Nasser, "then you need to get rid of the remnants of the Mubarak regime who are now trying to hijack the 30 June Revolution, the same way the Brotherhood hijacked the January 25 Revolution."

The general nodded without commenting, so Nasser reiterated: "Listen to me, Abdel Fattah. Protect the rights of the people and don't protect the interests of the rich the same way Mubarak did. I visited Mubarak from the other world more than once to warn him but he didn't listen and now he's in prison. You are now at a crossroads and you must put your trust in this great people; if you defend their rights, they will protect you against those who want to take the country backward."

The general said: "All of your remarks are useful and constructive. God willing, I promise to follow them."

Nasser looked hard at him as if to reassure himself that the general's promise was sincere, then he said: "I have done my duty and told you my opinion frankly. Now my conscience is at ease. I must ascend quickly."

The two men shook hands and embraced warmly. Nasser then turned his back and walked into the white cloud. He swiftly disappeared and the smoke dissipated little by little. The corridor then returned to its normal state. As for General el-Sisi, the smile with which he had bid Nasser farewell lingered on his face. He paced around his room and sat down in deep contemplation.

Democracy is the answer.

How to Become a Strategic Expert?

5 May 2014

In Egypt a strategic expert can be someone of any background. There are no defined criteria for being an expert. It is a label applied by the media. A doctor graduates from a medical school and an engineer from a college of engineering, but a strategic expert graduates in television studios, gains celebrity and people's respect and closed doors open for him and he is most often given a senior position in the civil service. If you are a retired officer, a university professor in any subject or a veteran journalist in your fifties, you are a prime candidate to become a strategic expert if you take the following steps:

First: Start immediately and take care of the details. Straight away seek out a friend or a relative who works in television and convince them to invite you to take part in a programme, even if for only ten minutes. Appearing on television is the moment of launch for you. When the host of the programme asks you how you would like to be described, tell him confidently: "as a strategic expert." Once that title is flashed along with your name beneath your image on the screen you will be embarking on a new stage of your life. Take care of the small details because they are crucial. Do not wear shirt and trousers or a light summer suit. You have to appear in a lounge suit with a tie in order to look elegant and dignified. You need to be aware that the anchorwoman interviewing you will know little about the subject and is being directed by the producer through an earpiece you cannot see because her long smooth hair, usually not her own, is obscuring it from view. Whether you are on a state of private television channel, you should know that the opinion they want you to express is theirs, not your own. There is always a red line which you should not cross which is defined by the station management in coordination with the security establishment and your task as a strategic expert is to convince the audience of it using innovative and persuasive argument. If you cross the red line the media will boycott and blacklist you and you will never become a strategic expert.

Second: Speak in a complex and specialised manner. Do not speak in a clear and direct way or from the heart like the generality of people. You are different. You are a strategic expert. You must appear to be weighed down by knowledge. The viewers must feel that you are expending a great intellectual effort to simplify all the complex political theories. Every three or four sentences in Arabic you should utter an English phrase and then splutter out its Arabic translation so that your viewers will feel that you simply cannot help using English words because of your encyclopaedic knowledge of foreign culture. Use as many foreign sources as you wish. Refer for example to articles in the *New York Times* or the *Guardian* without specifying the dates. That means you can say whatever you wish and no one will check the references. Mention the names of foreign authors to inspire awe among your listeners. Say, for example: "Personally, in this matter I am in complete agreement with the views of the great American intellectual George Campbell." Then you can attribute anything you want to George Campbell, as the anchorwoman nods in confirmation with a look of admiration on her beautiful face. No one will ever ask you if there is actually an intellectual of that name. At the end of your first television interview, the studio staff must be left with the impression that you are a great intellectual and a top-drawer strategic expert. They must be left feeling indeed fortunate that you agreed to accord them some of your valuable time.

Third: Attack the January 25 Revolution aggressively. The media, both state-run and private, are against the revolution. The staff in the state-run television are still in thrall to Mubarak and the owners of the private channels resent the revolution because it constitutes a tangible danger to their interests. You have to say what they want to hear but in a professional and suave manner. First speak about the theory of creative chaos which the United States wishes to see destroy our country. Concentrate on the revolutionary activists who are all funded from abroad and who have received military training in Serbia, Turkey and Qatar. No one will ask you for any evidence of your accusation. Don't forget to slip in a message of greeting to President Mubarak. Say, for example, that history will be the judge, and that even if he might have committed a few mistakes, he is still a nationalist personality, proof of which being that he stepped down from power in order to prevent Egyptian blood being spilt, and that he refused to leave Egypt, preferring to die there. With regard to the 3,000 people killed and the 18,000 wounded before Mubarak stepped down, say that you have verifiable information that those who killed the demonstrators were Iranian revolutionary guards and Hamas militias and that the police had no hand in it. If the TV anchorwoman is smart, and that is a rare occurrence, she will grab the opportunity to ask your opinion about the principle of political isolation for the remnants of the Mubarak regime which some people are calling for. Then you should say enthusiastically: "The phrase 'remnants of the Mubarak regime' is specious, because we are all Egyptian and time has proved that the people termed 'remnants' love the soil of Egypt and are more nationalist than the whole bunch of activists who are traitors and foreign agents.

The anchorwoman may have reservations about your accusations, but don't worry because her reservations are for show and the channel management will be completely delighted with your words. Accuse the revolutionaries of being traitors. Give their names and don't be afraid, for as long as you toe the correct political line you will receive complete legal protection. Before you the interview is over, don't forget to lay responsibility for the breakdown in security, the economic recession, the drop in tourism and the hike in unemployment, squarely at the feet of the Revolution. The anchorwoman will smile and ask you your opinion about the anti-protest law and the imprisonment of activists who have participated in unlicensed demonstrations. You must become angry and start shouting:

"Forgive me, Miss. I am a straight-speaking person. If it's a question of the country's national seucirty, then I don't care who goes to hell. I am directing my words to those who call themselves 'revolutionaries' but who are all traitors and agents of foreign powers. Have mercy on Mother Egypt. Don't sell the country for dollars, euros or yen. Shame on you!"

If you can manage to get tears into your eyes, the camera will focus on you and your victory will be crushing. If you cannot manage to cry, don't worry. Just make sure that your facial expressions convey your distress.

Fourth: Expose the conspiracies and debunk the conspirators. The fundamental role of a strategic expert is to expose conspiracies. In every interview you should uncover yet another conspiracy and you find the anchorwomen and programme team responding with enormous encouragement. Say whatever you want and don't worry for no one will ask you for your sources. Speak about intelligence reports which have uncovered suspicious meetings between groups of activities and foreign intelligence agents. Speak of a secret meetings having taken place in Cyprus, giving any old date for it, where American, Israeli, Turkish, Iranian, Serbian and Qatari intelligence agents got together to fund local activists with the aim of destroying the Egyptian state. No one will ask you how you got to know all the fine details. Then you will be able to segue into a defence of the government against Western criticism. If Western governments have criticised torture in prisons or mass execution sentences, you should just praise our robust legal system and state forcefully that you reject interference in our internal affairs. Then go on to affirm that all Westerners have joined in a conspiracy to bring Egypt down but that Egypt will never be humbled.

Fifth: It's the poor what gets the blame; It's the rich what gets the pleasure. The anchorwoman will feel constrained to ask you, as a strategic expert, about your ideas for solving the economic crisis. At this point you must blame the poor. Tell the anchorwoman that the solution to the crisis lies in hard work. The anchorwoman will be delighted and ask you for further clarification, so you must state forthrightly: "There's too much talking. We just need to get to work. For three years we have been talking and demonstrating. Surely that's enough. We just need to shut up and get back to work."

Then state that you call upon the government to remove the red tape surrounding investors and not to listen to the communists or Nasserites. The anchorwoman will get your drift and ask you about the issue of minimum and maximum wages. Dismiss the notion and say that the minimum wage teaches people how to be lazy and a maximum wage limit would simply deprive the state of much needed expertise. Tell her that these are all outdated communist notions and that the government should remove all subsidies immediately. State that the state is not our mother and we are not clinging children begging to be fed. Then express your deep appreciation for the noble businessmen who speculate with their own money out of a deep-seated sense of nationalism and that they love every last speck of our beloved Egyptian soil. The anchorwoman will then ask you for your opinion about the law promulgated by the interim president to protect contracts signed by the state from being challenged. Defend the law and say that this is what happens in any democratic state. You will not be asked to provide any proof. Then wonder aloud disapprovingly: "So what if some investor who loves Egypt and puts his money into investments which are of great benefit the working population. Should any Tom, Dick or Harry be allowed to challenge a contract he signs with the state? I appeal to the President not to respond to this provocation by communists and immature activists."

Six: Go all out in praising General el-Sisi. General el-Sisi, our next president, enjoys grassroot popularity because he responded to the will of the people and challenged the Brotherhood. However there is now fierce competition to praise al-Sisi from position-seekers. Be innovative and use a different sort of praise. Say that until now we have not properly understood el-Sisi's way of thinking. Rattle out the general's words like some sort of holy text. Then describe the meanings hidden in every word he has spoken. State that General el-Sisi had no desire to be president but the people were so insistent that in the end he had to concede. Describe how sympathetic you feel for General el-Sisi over the enormous responsibility now thrown onto him and that are worried about how he looks ten years older than his actual age because he is shouldering the burden of the state. The anchorwoman will then ask you if you have seen in him any characteristics which make him capable of leading the country. This is your chance. Reel off el-Sisi's fantastic attributes such as courage, wisdom, patience, expertise, strength of character, nationalism and feelings for the poor. Then conclude your response by adding: "I detest hypocrisy but General el-Sisi is the commander we need who has been appointed by God to steer Egypt back to security."

This is how you will become a recognised strategic expert. The satellite TV channels will all be clamouring to invite you onto their programmes and hey presto the government will invite you to participate in a community dialogue. First be clear as to what the president wants, give him your enthusiastic support and refute the arguments of any and every opponent of his. In the end the day you have been waiting for will arrive and you will be given a high government position. Well done!

Democracy is the answer.

RH

A Conversation Between a Revolutionary and a Law-abiding Citizen

12 May 2014

The following happened at Cafe Strand in Bab al-Louq at five o'clock in the afternoon. The cafe was fairly empty and near the glass window sat a young man writing on his iPad. At the next table, there was a grey-haired man in his fifties cheerfully smoking a water pipe. The young man stopped writing, stretched his arms in the air and gazed through the window. The older man sitting at the table next to him struck up a conversation, saying in a friendly tone: "Are you studying? May God help you, son."

Revolutionary: "Not at all, I graduated from university a long time ago but I look much younger than my years; I'm actually 30."

Citizen: "Thirty years old! I envy you. I'm 58, so only two years away from retirement."

Revolutionary: "Where do you work?"

Citizen: "My name is Abdel-Hameed Shetta and I'm the head of the Revision Department in the Ministry of Supply and Internal Trade."

(The young man shook his hand.)

Revolutionary: "How do you do? I'm Nagy al-Bassiouny, a communications engineer. I have a small office in Giza Square."

Citizen: "Tell me, Mr engineer, do you think General el-Sisi is going to appear on television again tonight?"

Revolutionary: "I really don't know."

Citizen: "I enjoy watching him a great deal. That man is the hero that our country needs. I'm afraid the Egyptian people have fear but no shame. Only mercilessness works for us. We need a strong man like el-Sisi to keep us under control."

Revolutionary: "Do you not think, sir, that the Egyptian people are deserving of kinder words? Had we been cowards, as you claim, we wouldn't have been able to rise up in revolution and imprison two presidents in the space of three years. The job of a president is to serve the people and enforce the law. It's not his job to control the people as if we were chickens or rabbits."

Citizen (looking at him suspiciously): "Are you one of the activists of the revolution?"

Revolutionary: "Actually, the term 'activist' is being used by the media to make fun of the revolutionaries. I'm an engineer. I took part in the revolution and I am proud of that. The revolution was one of the greatest times of my life."

Citizen: "And why don't you like el-Sisi?"

Revolutionary: "Who told you that I don't like him? General el-Sisi played an important role when he supported the people in getting rid of the Muslim Brotherhood but this doesn't mean that we should write him a blank check, or that he deserves to automatically become our president."

(Abdel-Hameed looked puzzled.)

Revolutionary: "Sir, suppose that you're going home when you are attacked by criminals who have knives and they try to steal your money. Suddenly, a police officer appears and arrests the criminals, saving you from them."

Citizen: "Then he should be thanked; he's a hero."

Revolutionary: "He really is a hero but does this mean that he should now be given the position of minister of supplies?"

Citizen: "Of course not. They're two separate things."

Revolutionary: "God bless you. Likewise, however, the same is true of el-Sisi. Just because he is a great military leader who played a patriotic role doesn't automatically make him qualified to be a president."

Citizen: "Forgive me, Nagy. You're my son's age, but your way of thinking will lead the country to a disaster. We are lucky to have found a man we can trust and who can pull the country out of the abyss it has fallen into. Enough of the revolution! What did we gain from the strikes and sit-ins except troubles and economic recession?"

Revolutionary: "The revolution cannot be held responsible for the economic recession, the revolutionaries have never been in government. Any decline must be attributed to the policies of the military council which ruled after Mubarak and of which el-Sisi was a member. They share responsibility, however, with the Muslim Brotherhood, whom the military council helped into a position of power."

Abdel-Hameed (angrily): "No, those who gave us the Brotherhood were the corrupt elite who supported Morsi and signed an agreement with him at the Fairmont Hotel."

Young man (smiling wryly): "That is not true. I too objected to the Fairmont agreement,[1] but it was signed after ballot boxes were closed. The political figures who met at the Fairmont Hotel made Morsi take a pledge to protect the revolution but they didn't support him in the elections, as they were already over. But the satellite channels owned by the remnants of the Mubarak regime are brainwashing the public in order to incite hated against the revolution and those who made it. Do you remember who changed the Constituent Assembly to bring the Brothers into it? Who allowed religious parties to be founded although they were prohibited in the constitutional declaration? Who turned a blind eye to the Brothers' transgressions during the parliamentary elections? Who surrendered power to Morsi through elections that – we have now discovered – were rigged? The answer is that it was always the military council who deliberately gave power to the Brotherhood. Added to this are the massacres in which many young people were killed

1 In June 2012, a coalition of opposition parties and movements pledged support for Egypt's new president at the Fairmont Hotel. Disillusioned 12 months later, they joined 30 June protests against Morsi

and for which the former military council must be held responsible."

Citizen: "General el-Sisi may have been a member of the military council but the one in charge was Field Marshal Tantawi. He was the leader and all of the members had to obey him."

Revolutionary: "The personal responsibility of General el-Sisi aside, there should be justice for every Egyptian who was killed during the past three years. There should be a system of transitional justice put in place. The state's institutions are still the same and they will never see themselves as guilty. Notice how el-Sisi never makes any mention of transitional justice or the rights of those who have been killed. He has never talked about combating corruption or returning the money smuggled out of the country by Mubarak and his gang. Moreover, half of the members of el-Sisi's campaign are notables from the old Mubarak regime."

Citizen: "Do you want el-Sisi to get rid of those who support him?"

Revolutionary: "He must. It's not a personal issue. If el-Sisi really supports the revolution, he shouldn't allow those with links to the Mubarak regime to return. They flatter him because they want him to allow them to keep the fortunes that they plundered from the Egyptian people. If el-Sisi supports the revolution, how can he allow the young revolutionaries to be put in prison simply for demonstrating?"

Citizen: "There is an anti-protest law in all democratic countries."

Revolutionary: These are the claims of the hypocritical media. There's no democratic country in the whole world in which a citizen is imprisoned for five years for marching in a demonstration."

Citizen: "Alright, but what does el-Sisi have to do with the anti-protest law anyway?"

Revolutionary: "El-Sisi himself said on television that he called for such a law; this means that he approves of people being unfairly imprisoned. I have many friends who are in jail with the criminals because they carried a banner or marched in a demonstration and sometimes just because they were just passing by."

Citizen: "So you want protests happening every day until they bring the country to collapse?"

Revolutionary: "I agree that demonstrations must be happen in moderation, but a peaceful demonstrator should not have to spend five years in prison, while the policeman who shot and blinded countless demonstrators with his gun is imprisoned for three years only. Demonstrations reflect a social crisis. Most ministries hold special funds with billions of pounds in them. A few hundred Egyptians earn a million pounds every month while millions of Egyptians can't find enough to eat. The wealthy in Egypt pay the lowest taxes in the world, if they pay anything at all. Only justice can stop people from protesting, not oppression."

Citizen: "There's been enough idle talk. We need security first, at any price. I have a daughter who's a university student. By God I spend the whole day in fear till she comes back home."

Revolutionary: "What I say is not idle talk. Suppose you have a furnished apartment and I find you a tenant, can you make him stay in it without a contract?"

Citizen: "No, it doesn't work without a contract."

Revolutionary: "Even if I tell you that he's a kind and pious man?"

Citizen: "Even so, he will still have to sign a contract."

Revolutionary: "Does your insistence on his signing a contract mean that you don't trust the man?"

Citizen: "Of course not, the tenant can be the best man on earth but he has must still sign a contract."

Revolutionary: "Great. Similarly, I don't object to el-Sisi as a person; I object to his being a president without signing a contract with the people. The contract is a democratic system that enables us to remove him from power after four years through ballot boxes, should we wish to do so."

Citizen: "So you consider the elections results false before they even start?"

Revolutionary: "Democratic elections have prerequisites and one of them is funding transparency. This means that we should know the financial resources of each candidate, and its origins. Not only do we not have this, but also, the elections law goes against the constitution; it indemnifies the decisions of the Supreme Electoral Committee, even though, in the past, this led to the elections being manipulated in favour of Morsi. Moreover, the elections law counts only financial funds but not in-kind ones. If you make banners or set up tents for millions of pounds for a specific candidate, it won't be counted as part of the assigned sum. These elections are undemocratic even if they aren't rigged. General el-Sisi himself said that democracy won't be feasible in Egypt for another 20 years. So he knows that there's no democracy for the time being."

Citizen: "No matter what you say, I love el-Sisi."

Young man (laughing in a friendly manner): "It's your right, Mr Shetta. You just need to remember that when Egyptians loved Nasser and did away with democracy, the Six-Day War took place. We have to learn from history."

Citizen: "I still love el-Sisi and I'll vote for him."

Revolutionary: "I wish I could carry on with the discussion but I have an appointment at the office. It was very nice meeting you."

Abdel-Hameed stood up and warmly shook hands with Nagy, then they exchanged phone numbers. Nagy picked up his iPad and turned to leave when Abdel-Hameed called out to him once more.

Citizen: "I forgot to ask you about who you're going to vote for. It sounds as though you're going to boycott elections."

Revolutionary: Frankly, I intended to boycott it but I've changed my mind. I'll vote for Hamdeen Sabahi. Do you know why? He's going to sign a contract with the people, release my unjustly imprisoned friends, and prevent the Mubarak regime from ever ruling over us again."

Abdel-Hameed smiled and followed him with his eyes till he left the cafe. He then turned his attentions back to his water pipe; he asked for fresh coals to be brought and resumed smoking, contemplating what Nagy had just told him.

Democracy is the answer.

Who Dares Speak?

2 June 2014

Like millions of Egyptians, I experienced the atmosphere that prevailed before the Six-Day War in 1967. I can still remember the banners in the streets with slogans such as "We're going to drink tea in Tel Aviv" and "Israel into the sea". At that time, I was a young boy living with my family in Cairo's Garden City district. In the building next door lived an Italian family consisting of the husband and wife, three children and the grandmother, who over time became a friend to me and we would chat daily in French from our balconies. The war broke out on 5 June, and the Egyptian media started broadcasting patriotic songs and military communiqués, and started vaunting our crushing superiority over the Israeli army. I would stand on the balcony translating the communiqués to my old Italian friend. I told her that we had shot down 23 Israeli airplanes, and then the number went up to 45. When a communiqué stated that we had downed 100 Israeli planes, I was surprised to see the Italian woman dismiss this with a hand gesture.

"Listen," she said, "I lived through the Second World War. It is impossible for this number of Israeli planes to have been shot down. Your government is lying."

The conversation left me angry, and when an uncle of mine dropped in I told him what had happened. "Foreigners don't wish us well," he told me. "They support Israel and are angry at the crushing defeats we have inflicted."

I was not convinced by his logic because I knew that the Italian woman was kind-hearted and that she loved Egypt and Egyptians. The following day I learnt that the old Italian woman was right, when it became evident that we had suffered a defeat greater than any in all the history of Egypt, and that the military communiqués had been a pack of lies. The men who concocted them have not been made accountable to this day. We got over this defeat, after the War of Attrition and the October War in 1973, but for a long time I used to ask myself: Gamal Abdel Nasser was a great leader and military man, so how could he have led Egypt to such a crushing defeat? The answer is that what defeated us was authoritarianism. We were defeated because we worshipped him as a leader with no flaws; we were defeated because no one dared to speak up. Anyone who opposed the policies of Abdel Nasser was accused of being a traitor and a foreign agent. As repression and constraints upon freedoms intensified, what happens to all autocrats happened to Abdel Nasser. He lost his ability to see his own mistakes. He made misjudgements and we were defeated. My Nasserite friends claim that the United States was plotting against the regime of Abdel Nasser. It was the case, but did the US make Abdel Nasser keep Abdel Hakim Amer on as his chief of staff when he was aware of the shortcomings in his military capability? Did the US turn Field Marshal Amer into a womaniser who paid more attention to his trysts than to leading the army? Was it the US who kept Egyptian fighter planes exposed on the ground so that the Israeli Air Force could bomb them more easily? No matter what achievements an authoritarian regime may have made, authoritarian rule always ends in a catastrophe, as happened in 1967.

History teaches us that when an authority has a monopoly on the truth and on nationalism, it will accuse anyone who opposes it of treachery and of being a foreign agent, but it inevitably leads the country into catastrophe. We are experiencing the same atmosphere again now. Through my articles, I urged Egyptians to take to the streets on 30 June and I consider that the army's intervention to disperse the Brotherhood gangs represented a great deed for the country. I thought, and still do, that General el-Sisi did a heroic job in carrying out the will of the people, but I did not agree with the way Egypt has been managed since 30 June. The oppressive state has come back into existence and arrested tens of thousands of people, many of whom are innocent of the trumped-up charges levelled against them. The torture of the Mubarak days, or perhaps even worse, has made a come-back. The unconstitutional anti-protest law, which, unlike in any other country in the world, imposes long prison sentences on demonstrators. Then the Council of State passed an election law, which breaks the constitution and would make even un-rigged presidential elections inconsistent with any democratic criteria.

I wrote that el-Sisi's election campaign was being managed by army people, which thus makes him the army candidate and the elections undemocratic. That was my opinion and I waited for someone to discuss it with me, but I was surprised to find a group of loudmouths on satellite television accusing me of being a foreign agent and a traitor merely because I expressed an opinion which General el-Sisi did not like. The only thing allowed in Egypt now is to sing the general's praises and to make remarks which underpin his genius.

If you should dare to criticise el-Sisi, the loudmouths on the satellite channels will all start attacking and slandering you, accusing you of being a fifth columnist, a traitor and an agent of a foreign power. The climate of repression and the clamping down on freedoms is getting worse every day. After all the accusations of godlessness the Brotherhood have levelled against anyone who opposes them, we are now having to put up with accusations of treason from el-Sisi's followers for having directed any criticism at him. Having got rid of the Brotherhood's theocratic fascism, el-Sisi's men are now trying to impose a new fascism which has a monopoly on truth and nationalism.

A few days ago, el-Sisi's men went on television to declare that anyone boycotting the elections was a traitor and a foreign agent seeking the destruction of the country. All citizens have the right to boycott elections without being accused of treason or of being a foreign agent. All citizens have the right to criticise el-Sisi without having their nationalism doubted. Some of el-Sisi's men are trying to turn him into a new pharaoh, and if they succeed Egypt will pay the same crushing price it has paid under every autocratic ruler. A few days ago, some officials complained to a newspaper owner at what a young journalist had written. The newspaper owner wanted to dispense with the young journalist to keep in favour with the authorities. The editor-in-chief, however, refused to do so, and defended the young journalist but he felt unnerved and handed in his resignation. Previously, the journalist Bilal Fadl had left *Al-Shorouk* newspaper because of articles he had written which were critical of el-Sisi. He was out of work for months because no newspaper would touch him even though he is one of Egypt's most talented writers, as they are all terrified of irking el-Sisi's men. Bassem Yousuf's political satire programme was taken off air more than once, and they managed to get it moved from MBC by a decree from the king of Saudi Arabia. Democratic countries respect and listen to the views of their opponents. They know that it is the duty of an intellectual to express their view, even if it offends the public, in order to alert them to any dangers or risks they can foresee. In 1906 an argument broke out between British officers and some peasants in the village of Denshawai. The court unjustly sentenced four of the peasants to be hanged, and dozens to prison sentences. At the time, the British playwright George Bernard Shaw wrote:

> "If her [England's] empire means ruling the world as Denshawai has been ruled in 1906 – and that, I am afraid, is what the Empire does mean to the main body of our aristocratic-military caste and to our Jingo plutocrats – then there can be no more sacred and urgent political duty on earth than the disruption, defeat, and suppression of the Empire ..."

No one accused Shaw of being a traitor or hostile to his own country's army. On the contrary, the British government responded to the harsh criticism, and Lord Cromer, the British consul-general in Egypt, was removed. In the sixties, the French writer and philosopher, Jean-Paul Sartre, went against public opinion in France by demanding that the Algerians be given the right of self-determination and no one accused him of plotting against his country. When George W. Bush launched the war on Iraq, the American filmmaker Michael Moore stood up and told the whole world: "We live in a time where we have a man sending us to war for fictitious reasons. Whether it's the fiction of duct tape or fiction of orange alerts we are against this war, Mr. Bush. Shame on you, Mr. Bush, shame on you."

No one accused Michael Moore of being a traitor. Democratic countries respect people who have a different opinion, whereas under authoritarianism the opposition is discredited and maltreated. That is why the Western countries keep making progress while we are gradually sliding towards the abyss. The climate of repression now in Egypt has also seeped into our relationship with the world. There are tens of thousands of detainees in Egypt, and should a foreign journalist raise this subject, the official media will accuse them of being an Israeli agent or in the pay of the Brotherhood. The Egyptian government requested the European Union to send a mission to monitor the presidential elections. It had hoped that they would confirm that everything was tickety-boo. Egyptian officials might have been expecting the European mission members to sing everywhere of good tidings, but the Europeans followed their conscience and wrote a balanced report, which recorded the positives and negatives, but salso tated that the election law was unconstitutional and that there was an atmosphere of repression in

Egypt because of the anti-protest law which threatens demonstrators with long prison terms.

All hell broke loose. There were accusations that the mission members were pro-Brotherhood and anti-Egypt, that they were carrying out a foul American plan, and most ridiculously of all, there was the pathetic scene when Mirvat al-Talawi made the head of the mission leave a conference on women to the applause of the attendees who sat shouting "Allahu Akbar" as if they were taking part in a holy war against a foreign woman who, all said and done, was a guest in Egypt and someone who should not be treated in this manner. Should we invite members of international delegations to come and monitor the elections, and then, if we are not thrilled by their report, should we call them all sorts of names and expel them from conferences? Is this sort of behaviour going to improve Egypt's image abroad? In the middle of all this repression, acting president Adly Mansour passed a law punishing anyone who does not respect the flag or upsets the peace with a fine and imprisonment. Do Egyptians need a law to tell them how to love their own country, and does a citizen only love their country because they risk being fined otherwise? Having due regard for the flag is one thing, but surely having respect for the individual citizen is more important. The acting president may have fines issued against people who do not stand up for the flag, but he does nothing against the people who arrest Egyptians and then torture and degrade them in custody as documented in scores of reports. General Abdel Fattah el-Sisi is now formally taking over the presidency of Egypt. Notwithstanding our differences of opinion over what took place during the transitional period, it is our duty now to put those differences to one side and help the president to make a success of his position. The best way we can help President el-Sisi is by meting out fair and honest criticism, harsh as it may sound. President el-Sisi must get rid of the bunch of "yes-men" around him: the drummers and the pipers, the security agents with their fingers in every pie and the thieving Mubarak henchmen. He must annul the anti-protest law and immediately release the detainees who have not committed any crime, because his success as a president is contingent on him creating a climate conducive to freedom and giving due respect to people whose views are not his own. Only then will the future begin in Egypt.

Democracy is the answer.

RH

Egyptians Who Missed the Celebration

9 June 2014

1.

> The burden will be lessened when you realise that you won't be burned to death in one of the trucks that the Egyptian police use to carry prisoners to where they're going to be jailed. But watching a rape attempt will reveal the truth about the situation you live in. After one day of detention and torture, and just before they were about to kill me, I was released, thanks to the intervention of the German Embassy, but the fate of the rest of the detainees is unknown to me as they are not German citizens.

From the testimony of the German journalist, Sebastian Bacchus, who was randomly detained in Cairo and only released following intervention by the German Embassy.

2.

> If I love Egyptians then I don't want anybody to cause them harm or hurt their feelings. We want to regain security with the support of the police without violating human rights.

General Abdel Fattah el-Sisi in a television interview.

3.

Dr Ibrahim Abdel Razzek was arrested on Faggala Street and arbitrarily detained while he was buying books for the fellowship exam he was preparing for. He said:

> Whenever I said to them, "Have mercy, I'm a doctor," they would hit even harder. They beat me in Azbakeya police station and in Abu Za'bal prison. Myself and the other detainees were forced to take off our clothes, then they poured cold water on us and left us in that state until the following day without anything to cover us on a floor that was soaked with water. Every day, during inspection time, they made us stand up facing the wall and they beat us. They prohibited visits and I couldn't contact any of my relatives.

4.
Torture takes place in every prison, but Abu Za'bal surpasses all the others in the savagery that occurs there. The testimonies of the detainees in Abu Za'bal about the torture they experienced are horrifying. The office of the attorney general made a point of not documenting the violations. The attorney general decided to allow only six out of 40 people to be medically examined in light of their claims about being tortured. This decision wasn't implemented until nine days after the victims had made their claims, after which time any traces of torture had largely disappeared. The public prosecutors then came out and cheerfully announced that torture does not occur in the prisons.

Yasmine Hossam, the attorney of a number of the detainees in the Abu Za'bal prison.

5.
The organisations signing this statement call for a speedy and independent investigation into the horrid claims of savage torture and sexual abuse that detainees, both male and female, suffered in prisons and police stations in Egypt, after being arrested during the demonstrations of the third anniversary of the January 25 Revolution. Khaled Al-Sayed recounted the details of the torture suffered by large group of detainees who were randomly arrested and taken to the Azbakeya police station. He said that the policemen in the station put the well-known political activists in a room where they were blindfolded and tortured. The policemen forced them to hear the screams of the detainees who were beaten up and given electric shocks. They said things like: "You revolutionaries, you're responsible for what's happening to those kids. Had it not been for you, we would have released them and let them go home." More than one person, amongst those who were returned to the common detainment room after their torture, said that they were sexually assaulted and that they were exposed to electric shocks on different parts of their bodies. The organisations that have signed this statement want to express their deep concern at some of the testimonies they documented of women who were detained in Kanatter prison and forced to endure vaginal examinations. Furthermore, women who have been detained in several police stations have reported that they were sexually assaulted by policemen.

From a joint report issued by 16 Egyptian human rights organisations on 12 February 2014.

6.

Egyptians are a calm and patient people by nature; they just want to live in peace and safety. The most important thing is to live in dignity.

General el-Sisi in his interview with Al-Masry Al-Youm.

7.

Dozens of civilians have been subjected to enforced disappearance, being held for months during which time they have been exposed to torture and other sorts of ill treatment in order to force them to confess that they have committed certain crimes or to implicate others in crimes. Some of the detainees who agreed to confess to crimes when presented to the public prosecutors were allowed to leave prison without being tortured. Lawyers told Amnesty International that they were not allowed to attend the preliminary investigation sessions and they weren't told of the date of the investigation. The number of reports on torture in Egypt is constantly increasing. It seems that fierce oppression is hidden behind the elegant discourse of the authorities about the road map that will lead the country to democracy.

A statement by Amnesty International dated 22 May 2014.

8.

I look upon all Egyptians with love, appreciation and respect, and, God willing, I hope that they can see all the good I do.

From an interview with General el-Sisi.

9.

Ahmad Mohammad Idris is a high school student who was arrested while he was returning from a private lesson, during a campaign of random detentions. He was standing on the platform of the Shubra el-Kheima metro station. His belongings were inspected and there was a photo of a demonstration on his mobile phone. He was transferred to Shubra el-Kheima police station and then he was handed over to state security, and then transferred to the central security facility in Benha, where he was accused of demonstrating without a permit, attempting to overthrow the regime, delaying the metro and belonging to an outlawed group. The prosecutor has continued to renew Ahmad's imprisonment for the last three months, during which time he's been exposed to the most terrible kinds of torture in Benha. His family is not allowed to visit him.

10.

They make them lie on their stomachs with their hands tied behind their backs and their eyes covered while police dogs bite them. The cells and the prisoners were covered with water. They burned their clothes and their belongings including exam books. Mahmoud Farahat is a student in the first year of the Faculty of Engineering, Al-Azhar University. He has a permit that allows him to keep books and to attend exams. On his way to and from exams, they used to beat him with a whip or a stick. He told his family: "I don't want to sit my exams; I don't want to leave my cell." His attackers were members of the riot police. Mahmoud told his family in the five minute visit: "I don't want to see you again. I don't want anybody to come except my father. I don't want you to see me like this."

A testimony on the torture of Mahmoud Farahat who is detained in the Wadi El Natroun prison 430.

11.

On Saturday there were calls for a hunger strike in objection to the inhuman treatment meted out by the guards. We awoke to find ourselves surrounded by large men wearing masks, dressed all in black with dogs. It was like being in Guantanamo. The prisoners with criminal charges were scared and sat apart from the group and we started to shout: "Open the cells and let us out." They made us take off our clothes and then they collected all our belongings, poured kerosene over them and set them on fire. They burned everything: the books, the clothes and all of the food. We were barefooted and with only our underwear on. They gathered around us and started beating and insulting us. They tied our necks with ropes like dogs and dragged us across the floor on our stomachs. They forced us to sing for el-Sisi and repeat: "El-Sisi is my president", and whoever refused was exposed to severe beating. We were subjected to electric shocks, beaten with wooden sticks and tear gas till our colleague Mohamad Abdullah died; he couldn't take it because of his old age. The elderly amongst the detainees were injured in many parts of their bodies. The soldiers were competing to steal our watches. We were transported to Al Fayoum prison in our underwear.

From the testimony of the detainee Karim Taha during his transportation from Wadi El Natroun prison to Al Fayuom prison.

Dear President Abdel Fattah el-Sisi,

Despite my disagreement with the way that the interim authority ran the country after 30 June, I still wish you every success as president of Egypt. It is the duty of all Egyptian people to support you so that you can accomplish your task and bring stability to Egypt. The prosperity of the nation depends upon your success. There are thousands of Egyptians who were not able to celebrate your election as they are detained in prisons and are being tortured in horrific ways. The testimonies and the reports cited above are only a few examples of systematic torture and humiliation now taking place across Egypt. The constitution that was supported by the Egyptian people states: "Whoever is arrested, imprisoned or detained must be treated in a way that maintains their dignity. They should not be tortured, terrorised, forced or harmed physically or mentally. They should not be detained or imprisoned except in places designated for this purpose that are suitable from human and hygienic perspectives. The state is obliged to provide assistance for the handicapped. Violating any of the above is a crime whose perpetrator will be punished according to the law and the defendant has the right to anonymity. Anything that is proven to be said by a detained person under any of the above or the threat of it is void and will not be taken into account."

President el-Sisi, you took an oath to respect the constitution and, as head of state, it is your duty to stop torture at once and to punish those responsible in the court of law. The sacrifices made by the army and police force in the fight against terrorism are greatly appreciated and the names of those martyrs will be in our hearts and in the memory of the nation for ever. However, war against terror shouldn't be used as a pretext for the random detention of innocent people, for torture or humiliation. A defendant is innocent till they are proven guilty and torture is a crime and not a punishment; torture shouldn't be used against even the worst of criminals. Instead, defendants should be given a fair trial that results in appropriate sentencing. The only way to combat terrorism is to establish justice; torturing people and degrading their humanity will not end terrorism but will further its causes. Thousands of Egyptians with no links to terrorism have been detained on trumped-up charges. Some of them were unlucky passersby that happened upon a demonstration by mistake. Others are young revolutionaries whose heroic stand on 30 June forced Morsi to step down. The authorities have rewarded them by throwing them in jail on charges of unlawful demonstrations, of which there is no equivalent in democratic countries. It's natural to have a law to organise the right of protest but there's no country in the whole world that penalises peaceful protest with five years in jail. We call upon you, Mr President, to review this law and to stop detentions and torture. You took an oath, Mr President, to protect the constitution and you promised to defend the dignity of Egyptians and we're waiting for you to keep your oath and to fulfil your promise.

Democracy is the answer.

A Message from an Undercover Agent

16 June 2014

Dear Sir,

Forgive me for not mentioning my name. I'm one of the revolutionaries who the media ridicules day and night, and accuses of incompetence and failure. I wear low-waisted jeans and I have long pony-tailed hair, but I am not a failure or a trivial person. A backward and trivial person is one who judges people for what they are wearing and how low they wear their jeans. I graduated from the Faculty of Economics with distinction in 2010. I belong to an affluent family and live in a villa in Sheikh Zayed City. My father is a successful architect; he has an architectural office in the Gulf and one in London. After I got my high school diploma in the Gulf, I entered Cairo University and discovered Egypt for the first time. Thus, I was saddened by the corruption I encountered and the difficult economic and social problems now facing the country. I decided not to be indifferent and I felt that it was my duty to do something to alleviate the suffering of millions of Egyptians. I joined the Kefaya movement and then the National Association for Change. I participated in all of its activities and demonstrations. I was arrested and spent some days in jail during which I became aware that Egyptians were practically without rights and that the most minor officer in the state security service could do whatever they liked to the people of Egypt; even if they killed you they would not be held to account. This made me more determined to continue my political activism.

In spite of my mother's objections and my father's worry, I kept on participating in the meetings and demonstrations until the revolution erupted. I lived in Tahrir Square for 18 days and they were the best and the happiest days of my life. I faced death and saw with my own eyes officers of the Mubarak police killing my comrades. I witnessed the horrific events that led to the Battle of the Camel and I defended the revolution with my all power. I saw thugs hired by the National Democratic Party as they passed between the army lines unobstructed by anybody. I didn't leave the revolution for even one day. I saw death with my own eyes at Mohamed Mahmoud Street, Abbasiya, and the Council of Ministers. Many martyrs were suffocated by tear gas, cartridges and bullets, and I was a friend of Mina Danial who was killed in the Maspero Massacre. Many of my friends lost their eyesight and I personally threw myself across women and girls to protect them from the soldiers. I still have bruises and scars from these incidents. In the presidential elections, I gave my vote to Khaled Ali[1] in the first round and I boycotted the second one, as I was unable to support either Mohamed Morsi or Ahmed Shafik. Then the Brotherhood reached power and I participated in the demonstrations against them. There was no difference; the people in power killed us whether in the name of the Brotherhood or in the name of the military council. I then participated in the demonstrations on 30 June and I disagreed with my friends who refused to protest alongside the remnants of the Mubarak regime. I believed that nothing should get in the way of ridding Egypt of the rule of the Brotherhood. I managed to persuade many people to join in the demonstrations in front of the Ittihadiya presidential palace in Heliopolis. When the army decided to support the people in toppling the Brotherhood, I went to Tahrir Square to show my support. Putting aside the massacres carried out by the military council while in power, the Egyptian army was still a national institution whose duty it was to protect Egyptians against terrorism. After the fall of the Brotherhood, I noticed that the state media, headed by the remnants of the Mubarak regime, was waging a fierce campaign against the revolution in an attempt to discredit it. I suspected that the Mubarak regime used the revolutionaries to get rid of the Brotherhood and now it renewed its efforts to abort the revolution and to defame the individuals involved. These suspicions were confirmed when the Protest Law was issued and the media moved to defend this flagrant attack on human rights. There is no other democratic country in the world that wilfully imprisons demonstrators for up to 15 years if they do not have the necessary permit. On 25 January of this year, I organised a silent protest and we held banners on which we wrote: "The revolution continues". We

1 Khaled Ali is a prominent Egyptian lawyer and activist. He is known for advocating for the reform of government and private sector corruption and for promoting social justice and labour rights.

were arrested and quickly put on trial, which resulted in two years jailtime as well as a fine of 50,000 Egyptian pounds. I won't tell you about the beating, the insults and the torture; you just need to review the reports of the Egyptian and international human rights organisations to know that the oppression is worse now than under Mubarak. Please do not trust the reports of the National Council for Human Rights for the simple reason that its members need the permission of the Ministry of the Interior before inspecting prisons. Have you ever heard of an inspector asking permission from the very institution they plan to inspect? Doesn't this give the administration of the prison an opportunity to hide the traces of torture?

I'm now in one of those prisons (I won't mention its name). As soon as I leave prison, I plan to emigrate, even though I love Egypt dearly. I will leave my homeland forever, visiting only during the holidays. Don't ever think that prison broke me. I swear to God that even if I spent twenty years in jail and the torture was twice as severe, it wouldn't shake my faith in the revolution even for a moment. Why would I emigrate then? Because I have come to realise that the revolution was a lie. From the outset, the people did not want us to defend them or to demand equality on their behalf. It is perhaps true that Egyptians want and need a strong ruler to control them.

I'm convinced that el-Sisi has been the real ruler after the 30 June demonstrations and that the Protest Law was issued by an order from him. I don't blame el-Sisi for he's a military man and it's natural for him to get offended by opposition as he's used to issuing orders and executing them. The American writer Noam Chomsky says: "All military men have the same culture based on imposing a status quo and terminating the opponents." I'm not resentful towards el-Sisi but angry that people, for whom the revolution presented thousands of martyrs for it to gain its freedom, now believe that the revolutionaries are traitors and that they're funded from abroad. Please don't tell me that it was the media that misled ordinary Egyptians; the people are not stupid and they are able to decide for themselves. Did you ever hear about the undercover agents who were blinded and killed for the sake of freedom? Was that their reward from the people they defended with their own blood? When I was arrested on 25 January, I was brutally beaten up by the police to within an inch of my life. I did not scream, but tried to bear the beating as bravely as I could. Yet a few men seated in a café opposite stood up and started shouting at us: "You traitors, you foreign agents, how much did you sell Egypt for?" This exchange broke my spirit and I wept until the soldiers stopped beating me. I joined the revolution so that those citizens, who accused me of treason, could lead a dignified life in their own country. The revolutionaries have been labouring under a false apprehension. The revolution called for real change in Egypt; it called for a free and just society. It seems that the people of Egypt neither wanted nor asked for this and they allowed the counter-revolutionary forces to break the law and impede progress. They turned a blind eye when the government violated the new constitution time and again. They were silent when the government issued the Protest Law, and when they gave immunity to the decisions of the Supreme Elections Committee. So where are the people that danced in the street to celebrate the new constitution and why did they not object to its violation? Do they yearn for a powerful ruler to control them?

These submissive Egyptians were also silent when President el-Sisi urged them to use bicycles instead of cars, because the constant use of motor vehicles is very costly to the state.[1] If he really wished to lower consumption, why did no one question el-Sisi and demand that he get rid of the huge number of Mercedes cars owned by the presidency? If he wants to boost the Egyptian economy, why doesn't he sell off some of the presidential palaces – surely this would raise millions of pounds for the Egyptian state? Why didn't anybody ask President el-Sisi to revisit the reports submitted by the Central Auditing Organisation regarding the state's budget? Is it not obvious that the economy would be much improved if the budget included the money accrued by special funds? Why doesn't the president save money by doing away with the fraudulent consultants who earn millions of pounds every month?

The revolutionaries have long understood this and have risen up against state corruption. The ordinary Egyptians however seem to be happy as long as the ruler is "a macho man" and he's powerful enough to control Egypt. It was for these people that I put my life at risk; the very same people who have accused me of treason. As soon as I am out of prison, I will leave this godforsaken country where people accuse martyrs of treason. My father managed to register my name as a Masters student at the London School of Economics. I'll leave Egypt to a country that respects my humanity, a country ruled by the law where I'll never be jailed for two years because I carried a banner in a peaceful stand on the street, a country that doesn't accuse those who died for it of being thugs and agents.

Egyptians, I apologise for misunderstanding you; you didn't need

1 President Abdel-Fattah el-Sisi took part in a bicycle marathon together with artists, media figures and students in Cairo to encourage low consumption of fuel which is costing the government billions of dollars every year.

a revolution, you didn't understand it and you don't deserve it. I'll leave you this stagnant water that we tried to clean for your sake and for which you accused us of being foreign agents and traitors. I will try to make a better name for myself elsewhere. I hope that you enjoy the stability that's mixed with oppression and humiliation. Enjoy corruption, favoritism, crippled justice and the media that have its programs prepared in the corridors of the State Security. I wrote you, Alaa, this message to explain my position and whether you agree with me or not, my respect for you will never change.

Regards,

[...]

I received this letter from a young revolutionary currently serving a prison sentence in Egypt. Dear readers, if you have a response to what this young man wrote, kindly send them to me and I will endeavor to reply to him next week.

Democracy is the answer.

Afterword

In June 2014, Alaa Al Aswany decided to take a brief pause from writing his weekly articles about Egypt's years of revolution. This decision was the result of unwelcome external pressures, but also because the mood in Egypt had changed considerably and he found that popular support for the revolution had deteriorated. The author believed that it was his responsibility, as a writer, to go back out and listen to the Egyptian people in order to better understand the deep malaise that has taken hold of Egypt and stifled progress and democratic change.

Glossary

El-Adly, Habib (born 1938) is a former Egyptian politician, who served as interior minister from 1997 to 2011, the longest serving under Hosni Mubarak. Following the 2011 revolution, he was charged with ordering the killing of demonstrators, money-laundering, profiteering and corruption. In May 2011 he was sentenced to 12 years for money-laundering and profiteering and was later sentenced to life imprisonment for contributing to the killing of demonstrators. In June 2014, the conviction for money-laundering and profiteering was overturned.

The April 6 Youth Movement is an Egyptian activist group established in 2008 by Ahmed Maher and Ahmed Salah in order to mobilise support for the workers in El-Mahalla El-Kubra, who were planning to strike on 6 April. It was the first youth movement in Egypt to use internet-based modes of communication like Facebook and Twitter, and it aimed to promote democracy by encouraging public involvement in the political process. The group was heavily involved in the 2011 revolution and organised a number of marches and sit-ins. An Egyptian court banned the movement on 28 April 2014, a ruling that was later condemned by Mohamed ElBaradei and various human rights organisations as a violation of free expression.

The Al-Nour Party, the second-largest Islamist party, was created after the 2011 revolution. It supported Morsi and the Muslim Brotherhood but has pushed for the implementation of Sharia law. However, it took a neutral stance during the 30 June 2013 protests that called for Morsi's ouster and supported the political roadmap agreed upon by anti-Morsi forces on 3 July. Al-Nour were criticised by other Islamist movements for supporting General Abdel Fattah el-Sisi in the presidential elections and not responding to the calls for a boycott. Al-Nour is currently facing a legal charge to have it dissolved for violating the constitution, which bans the license of any party that has a religious base.

Al-Banna, Hassan (1906–49) was an Egyptian political and religious leader who founded the Muslim Brotherhood. Al-Banna was disillusioned with the British cultural colonisation and worried that attempts to rapidly modernise Egypt were harming Islam. For a while al-Banna tried to maintain a tactical alliance with the government, but he and his followers had become a threat to the central authorities. In the turmoil of the post-war years, he lost control of many elements within the organisation and members were implicated in a number of assassinations, notably that of Prime Minister Mahmoud an-Nukrashi Pasha in December 1948. With the connivance of the government, Hassan al-Banna himself was assassinated the following year.

The Egyptian Revolution (1919) was a countrywide revolution against the British occupation of Egypt and Sudan. It was led by Saad Zaghloul, a former education minister and founder of the Wafd Party, who was later arrested by British forces because the nationalist movement was gaining too much power. After much unrest,

Britain finally declared limited independence for Egypt on 28 February 1922. A new Egyptian constitution was created in 1923, and in the 1924 election the Wafdists won a significant majority of seats in parliament. Zaghloul later became prime minister and his party was prominent politically until the early 1950s.

The Egyptian Revolution (1952) was led by Muhammad Naguib and Gamal Abdel Nasser of the Free Officers Movement. Its initial aim was the overthrow of King Farouk, but it also aimed to abolish the constitutional monarchy and aristocracy of Egypt and Sudan, establish a republic, end the British occupation and secure the independence of Sudan. The revolutionary government adopted a staunchly nationalist, anti-imperialist agenda, which came to be expressed chiefly through Arab nationalism, and international non-alignment. The Free Officers staged a military coup on 23 July and forced King Farouk to abdicate his throne. On 28 July 1953, Muhammad Naguib became the first president of Egypt, which marked the beginning of modern Egyptian governance. Egypt was ruled autocratically by three presidents over the following six decades, by Nasser from 1954 until his death in 1970, by Anwar Sadat from 1971 until his assassination in 1981, and by Hosni Mubarak from 1981 until his resignation in the face of the 2011 Egyptian revolution.

ElBaradei, Mohamed (born 1942) was vice president of Egypt from July 2013 to August 2013. He was the former director general of the International Atomic Energy Agency, an intergovernmental organisation under the auspices of the UN, and, jointly with the IAEA, was awarded the Nobel Peace Prize in 2005. He returned to Egypt two days after the January 25 Revolution to take part in the demonstrations and declared himself ready to lead a transitional government, if that was the nation's will. In 2012, he had been set to stand as a liberal, secular candidate in the presidential elections, but withdrew his bid citing concerns about the undemocratic way the military was governing Egypt. As co-ordinator of the main alliance of liberal and left-wing parties and youth groups, the National Salvation Front, he was seen as a potential leader of the transitional government after Morsi was ousted but was instead named interim vice president in July 2013. He resigned from that position on 14 August 2013 after Egyptian security forces led a bloody crackdown on supporters of Mohamed Morsi.

Enan, Sami Hafez (born 1948) was chief of staff of the Egyptian armed forces from 2001 to 2005. After the revolution, he became second-in-command of the army, behind Field Marshal Tantawi. He appeared in front of demonstrators in Tahrir Square in February 2011 and promised to safeguard the interests of the people. Morsi forcibly retired General Enan on 12 August 2012, awarding him the Order of the Nile and appointing him as an advisor. On 2 October 2012, the attorney general announced that Anan would be investigated for corruption, the first such investigation against a military figure.

El-Essawy, Mansour (born 1937) is an Egyptian politician and the former minister of the interior. He is the former head of security for Giza, which is in greater Cairo, and is a former governor of Minya in Upper Egypt. He was appointed interior minister to the interim government led by Essam Sharaf on 5 March 2011, in a sign that ousted president Hosni Mubarak's old guard were being removed from the cabinet. He resigned as interior minister in November 2011.

The Free Egyptians Party is an Egyptian liberal party founded after the 2011 Egyptian revolution by business tycoon Naguib Sawiris. The party calls for freedom and democracy, and a civil state that is based on citizenship. Its economic programme is a free market economy and social justice, to be achieved through giving loans and lands to young people to set up their own small projects.

El-Sisi, Abdel Fattah (born 1954) is the sixth, and current, president of Egypt. He graduated from the Egyptian Military Academy and US Army War College. He was the youngest member of the military council during the Egyptian revolution of 2011, serving as director of the military intelligence and reconnaissance department. He was chosen to replace Field Marshal Tantawi and serve as the commander-in-chief and minister of defence on 12 August 2012. He played the leading role in ousting Morsi after an uprising against him in 2013. He installed an interim government, remaining as minister of defence and first deputy prime minister. On 26 March 2014, after calls for him to run for president, he resigned from the military to stand as a candidate for the 2014 presidential election. He won a resounding victory in the poll, held between 26 and 28 May 2014.

El-Ganzouri, Kamal (born 1933) is a US-trained economist with decades of experience in Egyptian politics. Following Hosni Mubarak's rise to power in 1981, el-Ganzouri was appointed minister of planning in 1982 and then minister of international co-operation in 1984. He served as deputy prime minister from 1986 to 1996, and then prime minister from 1996 to 1999. On 25 November 2011, el-Ganzouri was asked by Field Marshal Tantawi, head of Egypt's military council, to accept the position of prime minister and form a new cabinet. Protesters, however, rejected el-Ganzouri's appointment, arguing that he was far too old and entrenched in Mubarak-era institutions to successfully lead a post-revolution Egypt. His government resigned after the election of Morsi as president on 26 June 2012 to make way for the new government.

The Kefaya Movement is an indigenous movement for political reform organised in late 2004 in opposition to the regime of President Hosni Mubarak, and the likelihood of his son Gamal succeeding him as president. Its profile grew during the 2005 constitutional referendum and presidential election campaigns as the group organised a series of protests pressuring the regime to make concessions. It participated in the 2011 revolution, with Magdy Ahmed Hussein as its general coordinator.

Morsi, Mohamed (born 1951) was the fifth president of Egypt from June 2012 to July 2013, when he was removed by General el-Sisi following mass protests. He was a member of parliament in the People's Assembly of Egypt from 2000 to 2005 and a leading member in the Muslim Brotherhood. He became chairman of the Freedom and Justice Party when it was founded by the Brotherhood after the 2011 revolution and won the run-off election against Ahmed Shafik in the 2012 election, making him the first democratically elected head of state in Egyptian history. On 30 June 2013 protests against Morsi erupted, calling for his resignation. The next day the military gave him 48 hours to meet their demands and solve political differences. Three days later he was declared unseated and was later accused by the attorney general of committing an array of offences, including escaping from a high-security prison, defaming the judiciary, murder and collaborating with foreign entities to harm national security.

Mubarak, Hosni (born 1928) was appointed vice president by Anwar Sadat in 1975. He became president eight days later when Sadat was assassinated. He ruled in a semi-military style throughout his presidency, never lifting martial law. He won three elections unopposed between 1981 and 2005 when, after pressure from the United States, he changed the electoral system to allow rival candidates. The 2005 election was criticised for being weighted in his and his party's favour, and Mubarak won 88 per cent of the vote. He appointed his first vice president, Omar Suleiman, on the 29 January 2011 after protests. This was seen as an attempt to bolster his support in the military. Protests against Mubarak started in earnest in January 2011, with an 18 day uprising that saw him removed from power in February 2011. In May 2011, he was put on trial, along with his two sons, for the deaths of anti-government demonstrators. He was found guilty in June 2012 of being complicit in the murder of some of the demonstrators who took part in the January 2011 protests and was sentenced to life imprisonment. In January 2013, there was an appeal against the convictions, leading to a retrial. This trial began in May 2013, but was adjourned several times. On 19 August 2013, he was acquitted of one corruption charge and, two days later, he was released from prison and placed under house arrest.

The Muslim Brotherhood, founded by Hassan al-Banna in 1928, is Egypt's oldest and largest Islamist organisation. By the end of the Second World War, the group was estimated to have 500,000 members in Egypt, and its ideas had spread across the Arab world. It supported the 1952 revolution, but was implicated in the attempted assassination of Egypt's president and dissolved. It was legalised in 2011 after Mubarak's regime ended. It then won the 2012 presidential election, through the Freedom and Justice party, with Morsi as its candidate, although he was ousted a year later. In August 2014, a court ruling banned the Freedom and Justice party from participation in electoral politics in wake of General el-Sisi's crackdown on the movement.

Nasser, Gamal Abdel (1918–70) was the second president of Egypt, serving from 1956 until his death in 1970. He was involved in the 1952 revolution, and became a controversial leader of the Arab world, creating the short-lived United Arab Republic (1958–61), twice fighting wars with Israel (1956, 1967), and engaging in such inter-Arab policies as mediating the Jordanian civil war (1970). Nasser's neutralist policies during the Cold War led to tense relations with Western powers, who withdrew funding from the planned Aswan Dam, leading to Nasser nationalising the Suez Canal Company. This was acclaimed within Egypt and the Arab world. Nasser's popularity subsequently grew due to his calls for pan-Arab unity, culminating in the formation of the United Arab Republic with Syria. He began his second presidential term in March 1965 after political opponents were legally forbidden from running. After the defeat to Israel in the 1967 War Nasser resigned, only to retake office after popular demonstrations called for his reinstatement. After the conclusion of the 1970 Arab League summit, Nasser suffered a heart attack and died. He was succeeded by Anwar Sadat.

The National Democratic Party (NDP) was an Egyptian political party founded by Anwar Sadat in 1978. It wielded uncontested power in state politics, in what was de facto a single party system inside an officially multi-party system until Mubarak's resignation. It was dissolved on 16 April 2011 by court order and its assets transferred to the state. The electoral system in which the NDP operated did not meet internationally recognised standards of electoral democracies.

The National Salvation Front is an opposition coalition formed of political parties who opposed Mohamed Morsi and the Muslim Brotherhood. The front includes the Constitution party, the Egyptian Popular Current, the Social Democratic Party and the

Socialist Popular Alliance party. One of the group's leaders, Hamdeen Sabahi, is a leading voice against Morsi and came third in 2012 presidential elections.

Sadat, Anwar (1918–81) was the third president of Egypt, from 10 October 1970 until his assassination by fundamentalist army officers on 6 October 1981. He was a member of the Free Officers who overthrew King Farouk in the 1952 Revolution. Sadat succeeded Nasser in 1970, and would later purge major establishments of Nasserists, especially the hated secret police, as well as encourage the emergence of Islamist movements. That, and the initial victories in the October War, hugely increased Sadat's popularity. The peace process with Israel also led to the regaining and reopening of the Suez Canal. In 1977, Sadat became the first Arab leader to visit Israel officially. An Egyptian-Israeli peace treaty was finally signed in March 1979, a year after the Camp David Accords. The end of his presidency was marked by internal uprising. On 6 October 1981 Sadat was assassinated during the annual victory parade in Cairo to celebrate Egypt crossing the Suez Canal.

Shafik, Ahmed (born 1941) was appointed prime minister of Egypt by Hosni Mubarak on 31 January 2011. After Mubarak resigned, Shafik remained in office, despite pressure from protesters and the opposition. On 3 March 2011, Shafik resigned as prime minister following a widely criticised appearance on a popular talkshow, in which he defended the state security service and sought to distance himself from Mubarak, a long-time friend. He ran for president against Mohamed Morsi, winning 48.27 per cent of the vote to Morsi's 51.73 per cent. In September 2012, Morsi issued an arrest warrant for Shafik on suspicion of corruption.

Sharaf, Essam Abdel-Aziz (born 1952) was the prime minister of Egypt from 3 March 2011 to 21 November 2011, under acting president, Field Marshal Tantawi, and was preceded by Ahmed Shafik. He was a member of the National Democratic Party and Egyptian minister of transportation from 2004 to 2005, resigning amid an uproar over a series of deadly train accidents blamed on government negligence. He was active and present in Tahrir Square during the 2011 revolution and was asked by the military council to form a government after Shafik's resignation. Although the crowds in Tahrir Square supported his appointment, his term was viewed as anti-revolutionary towards the end. His initial cabinet reshuffles involved the removal of several Mubarak-era ministers. However, without the support of the military council he was not able to remove more ministers and was subsequently accused of being reactionary. He eventually resigned, just six days before the 2011 parliamentary election, due to public pressure.

Suleiman, Omar (1936–2012) was an Egyptian army general, politician, diplomat and intelligence officer. He was appointed vice president by Mubarak four days into the 2011 revolution in a desperate attempt to save his presidency. On 11 February, Suleiman announced Mubarak's resignation, and ceased to be vice president as power was transferred to the military council. On 6 April 2012, he announced that he would run for president. On 19 July 2012, while undergoing medical testing in Cleveland Ohio, he died from a heart attack. He was given a military funeral, attended by Field Marshal Tantawi.

Tamarod Campaign is an Egyptian grassroots movement which was founded to register opposition to Morsi and force him to call early presidential elections. It was founded by five activists, including spokesman Mahmoud Badr, on 28 April 2013 with an aim to collect 15 million signatures by 30 June 2013. It announced that it had collected 22,134,460 signatures on 29 June 2013 and thus demanded that Morsi step down. The movement was supported by several political forces, including the Kefaya Movement, the National Salvation Front and the April 6 Youth Movement. Members of the Muslim Brotherhood and other Islamist organisations opposed the campaign. On 8 October 2013 it announced that it would run in the 2014 parliamentary election.

Tantawi, Mohamed Hussein (born 1935) was the commander-in-chief of the Egyptian armed forces and chairman of the military council, and so was de facto head of state from 11 February 2011 to Morsi's election on 30 June 2012. After Mubarak stepped down, Tantawi transferred authority to the military council, which he was the head of. The military council dissolved the Egyptian parliament, oversaw the constitutional referendum and the trial of many Mubarak-era officials. Amidst protests in November 2011, he pledged to speed up presidential elections and promised that the armed forces were completely prepared to relinquish power. Morsi ordered his resignation a month after he was elected, although he decorated Tantawi with the Order of the Nile (Egypt's highest state honour) and appointed him as an advisor.

The Wafd Party was a nationalist, liberal political party founded in 1919. It was instrumental in the development of the 1923 constitution, and supported moving Egypt from dynastic rule to a constitutional monarchy where the nationally-elected parliament wielded power. It was generally Egypt's most popular party from its founding until the 1930s. Between 1923 and 1952 there were ten general elections; the Wafd Party won seven of these, with six clear majorities, including five where they won over three quarters of the vote. It was dissolved in 1952 after the revolution.

Index